SUCCESSFUL DIRECT MARKETING METHODS

Eighth Edition

SUCCESSFUL DIRECT MARKETING METHODS

Interactive, Database, and Customer-Based Marketing for Digital Age

BOB STONE AND RON JACOBS

McGraw Hill

New York   Chicago   San Francisco   Lisbon   London   Madrid
Mexico City   Milan   New Delhi   San Juan   Seoul
Singapore   Sydney   Toronto

ISBN 13: 978-0-07-145829-0
MHID : 0-07-145829-8

McGraw-Hill books are available at special quantity discounts to use as premiums and sales promotions, or for use in corporate training programs. For more information, please write to the Director of Special Sales, McGraw-Hill Professional, Two Penn Plaza, New York, NY 10121-2298. Or contact your local bookstore.

This book is printed on acid-free paper.

CONTENTS

CHAPTER 6
Building Customer Relationships   115

CHAPTER 7
Implementing Global Direct Marketing Campaigns   145

SECTION TWO
Media of Direct Marketing

SECTION THREE
Internet Direct Marketing   335

ABOUT THE AUTHORS

Bob Stone 1919–2007

On February 26, 2007, while the editing of the eighth edition of *Successful Direct Marketing Methods* was being completed, Bob Stone passed away. Bob was 88.

With Bob's passing, an era ends for direct marketing. Bob was an author, teacher, business leader, and had a great family. Yet, he freely gave his time to mentor generations of direct marketers, sharing his knowledge and his passion for direct marketing.

Bob Stone was an evangelist for direct marketing around the world. His books, articles, presentations, and business career spanned seven decades and six continents. He forever changed the way that marketers think about direct marketing, its tools, and techniques.

Bob's journey began in 1932, during the Depression. He paid his way through Northwestern University, taking all the marketing and writing courses offered. In 1937, he began selling used cars for his father. Bob would say that he was the only member of the Direct Marketing Hall of Fame who started out as a used car salesman.

Bob started his direct marketing career in 1945 with the National Research Bureau, a business services company. He stayed with NRB for 15 years, developing the "Businessmen's Record Club," which sold recorded speeches. The club's success convinced Bob to share his time between the record club and freelance direct marketing assignments.

Bob met Aaron Adler on a freelance assignment. They talked about starting a direct marketing agency in Chicago. In 1966, Stone & Adler opened its doors. Bob was the outside face of Stone & Adler and Aaron worked on the inside, running the agency day to day. They cracked the code to work with clients such as Amoco Oil Company, Allstate Insurance, AT&T, Hewlett-Packard, Sears, SBC, and United Airlines.

Rather than open a New York City office, they found two like-minded people in Stan Rapp and Tom Collins, who had their own direct marketing agency. In 1971, they formed Rapp Collins, Stone & Adler. This lasted until Doyle Dane Bernbach (DDB) offered to buy out Rapp Collins, which unlike Stone & Adler had no competitive accounts to DDB. In 1975, Stone & Adler became an independent agency again.

In 1978, Bob Stone learned from Les Wunderman that Young & Rubicam (Y&R), one of the largest ad networks at that time, wanted to expand its direct marketing agency holdings. Wunderman had sold his agency to Y&R, and he convinced Aaron and Bob to sell Stone & Adler to Y&R as well. Aaron stayed on for two years after that. Bob was named to the Y&R Board of Directors, and he stayed with Y&R until his "retirement" in 1983.

Retirement? Bob Stone never wanted to retire. He kept an office at Stone & Adler, returning to run the agency in the 1990s before Stone & Adler was consolidated into Wunderman.

However, Bob had an avocation–education. He taught classes at the University of Missouri–Kansas City and in the Integrated Marketing Communications program at Northwestern University in Evanston.

Bob Stone published his first book, *Profitable Direct Mail Methods*, in 1947. After that, Bob Stone became a columnist for *Ad Age*. In 12 years, he wrote over 200 articles. Some of those articles became the foundation for *Successful Direct Marketing Methods*.

The first edition of *Successful Direct Marketing Methods* (SDMM) was published in 1975. In addition to English, there are editions in Japanese, French, German, Italian, Spanish, Portuguese, Romanian, Russian, and Swedish. More than 250,000 copies of SDMM have been sold worldwide. And Bob's legacy will continue with the release of the eighth edition of the book in 2007, some 32 years after the first edition. Not a bad run!

In 1992, Bob co-authored *Successful Telemarketing* with John Wyman, a former vice president at AT&T. In 1995, Bob published *Direct Marketing Success Stories*, a book of case studies from organizations such as Helzberg Diamonds, Spiegel, and Quill Corporation.

Bob's commitment to direct marketing education was unambiguous, and he didn't worry about the profits from writing. From 1975 to 1985 he contributed the royalties—over $95,000—from *Successful Direct Marketing Methods* to the Direct Marketing Educational Foundation.

Accolades and Honors

Bob Stone was a past president of the Associated Third Class Mail Users Association; a Charter Senior Fellow of the International Society for Strategic Marketing; Director of the Direct Marketing Association; a member of the Direct Marketing Association Hall of Fame; a founding trustee of the Direct Marketing Educational Foundation; a recipient of the DMEF Edward N. Mayer Award for contributions to direct marketing education; an eight-time winner of the Direct Marketing Association's Best of Industry Award; winner of two DMA Gold Echo Awards—one for an 8-page fund-raising letter for the DMEF; and the winner of a John Caples Award for copy excellence.

Bob Stone made his mark in business, academia, and on the whole of the direct marketing community. He was a leader, teacher, mentor, and writer. While his name and picture hang proudly in the Direct Marketing Hall of Fame, his influence is felt by everyone who uses the tools and techniques of direct marketing. And that influence will continue to be felt for years to come.

Ron Jacobs

Ron Jacobs is president of Jacobs & Clevenger, a multichannel direct marketing communications' agency that provides direct, database, and digital marketing solutions. Founded in 1982, J&C's clients have included Allstate Insurance, the American Marketing Association, Cars.com, HSBC, IBM, International Trucks, Microsoft, National Restaurant Association Educational Foundation, Orbitz, Ulta, and the U.S. Federal Reserve Bank. Ron has served as an expert witness in court cases in the United States and Canada. Ron is both a practitioner and teacher. He is Senior Lecturer in the Medill/Integrated Marketing Communications Program, Northwestern University. He was Program Coordinator for the Certificate of Direct Marketing Program at DePaul University from 1991 to 1995. Ron is a 1994 recipient of the Direct Marketing Educational Foundation's Outstanding Direct Marketing Educator Award.

In addition, Ron works with governments, global post offices, and stakeholders to clear obstacles to market development and implement best practices for sustainable growth. His consulting work and seminars take him to Asia, Europe, Latin America, and across the United States, where he shares his passion—to evangelize the tools and techniques of multichannel direct marketing.

A past president of the Chicago Association of Direct Marketing, Ron has served as a Trustee of the Chicago Association of Direct Marketing Educational Foundation and is Past General Chairman of CADM's Educational Foundation Campaign Committee. He was CADM's 1998 Direct Marketer of the Year. He is on the Advisory Board for the DMA Political Action Committee.

FOREWORD

When the late Bob Stone first wrote this book over three decades ago, he was well ahead of his time in recognizing what today we recognize as "the Power of Direct." In those days, direct marketing was still seen as a kind of advertising specialty at the margin of sales and promotion.

Over the years, propelled by all the developments in communications and computing, direct marketing has evolved into a broad, multifaceted strategic process with a common denominator: the customer always calls the shots. Generations of marketers have sharpened their customer strategies by studying *Successful Direct Marketing Methods* and putting its insights and wisdom to work for them.

With every major update, this book has ascended to the level of a marketing classic. Bob Stone and co-author Ron Jacobs lead readers on a journey of discovery, helping them recognize and understand the underpinnings of what is basically a new and constantly evolving way to sell. Countless marketing professionals have benefited over the years from their guidance and advice. The authors draw on a multichannel smorgasbord of response-driven advertising that includes mail, telephone, newspapers and magazines, broadcasting, inserts, out-of-home, e-mail, and the Internet.

Marketers realize that in order to create value, they must represent the common needs of both the producers of goods and services and the consumers who buy or use them. Today, in a world transformed by digital technology, creating that value gets more and more challenging with each passing day. Multichannel marketing has become a key strategic concept for marketers of the 21st century, and multichannel direct marketing has evolved as an essential conduit for the information dialogue that takes place between consumers and producers, or buyers and sellers.

In today's digital, multichannel universe, this information dialogue takes place 24/7 and is carried on in virtually any location. The options for conducting this exchange have multiplied in availability, diversity, and speed. Along the way, the consumer has seized complete control of the media consumption process and redefined the channels.

As marketing adapts to these changes, traditional day-to-day thinking still tends to separate key functions into silos—image and product, branding and selling, direct and indirect. But business, with its emphasis on serving customers and solving problems, does not really recognize these boundaries. As a result, the lines between brand management, direct marketing, and general sales are increasingly blurred. These disciplines are fusing together into a new set of customer-focused actions and processes, with the capability and muscle of today's nearly miraculous information systems and data networks.

This trend represents a significant opportunity for those who are well versed in using multichannel direct marketing to reach customers, with information that is relevant and delivered responsibly. The disciplined scientific approach that forms the basis of multichannel direct marketing is what many people working in many different kinds of organizations are beginning to realize they need to move ahead and to get these new customer-focused actions and processes built.

Successful direct marketers have the opportunity to take real leadership of these changes. Competence in using the tools and techniques of direct marketing across an array of multichannel options will be a key professional skill in the new era we have entered, and allowing consumers to call the shots has never been more critical to productively executing strategic goals.

Business and nonprofit organizations of every size and across every industry are tapping into the power of direct marketing. It is efficient, effective, and accountable for results. Direct marketing now drives sales that make up more than 10 percent of the entire U.S. gross domestic product, and provides over 10.5 million jobs. U.S. direct-marketing-driven sales are growing faster than total U.S. sales, actually accelerating overall national economic growth.

Successful Direct Marketing Methods, in its latest update by Ron Jacobs, serves as a comprehensive and important resource for students who want to learn about applying this essential discipline across today's multiple marketing channels. In addition, experienced marketers will find an abundance of proven strategies and success stories that can spark ideas about the many challenges they face with today's increasingly multichannel marketing strategies.

Students and practitioners alike will appreciate the easy-to-read style and detailed exhibits that accompany each chapter. The work contained herein has been years in the making. Yet, it is current and up to date thanks to a diligent effort by Ron Jacobs to address emerging issues, including the need for a consensual approach to public policy issues, new technologies and techniques in customer relationship management, and the latest in e-mail, Web, and search marketing.

You are about to embark on a wonderful journey of discovery. Bon voyage!

John A. Greco, Jr.
President & CEO
Direct Marketing Association
New York City
Washington, D.C.

PREFACE

Welcome to the eighth edition of *Successful Direct Marketing Methods* (SDMM). This marks the 32nd anniversary of the first edition, published in 1975. It is also the last edition to which Bob Stone contributed his wisdom, wit, and vast knowledge of direct marketing.

I first met Bob Stone through the pages of SDMM. The first edition was the text for a direct marketing class that I took in graduate school. Bob Stone's prose was easy to read and understand. SDMM was as useful for academic study as it was for professional development.

Back then, SDMM was called the "Bible of Direct Marketing." It was an essential book that marketers kept close at hand, referring to it whenever they needed to know about direct marketing channels, copy, design, offers, testing, timing, etc. Bob Stone helped make direct marketing a field of study and research, a career choice for the best and brightest students.

When it was released, the first edition of SDMM was the only book on direct marketing. Today, a search on Amazon.com yields 9,407 books with relevant references to direct marketing. Search on subjects that direct marketing has directly influenced, such as database marketing, digital marketing, or CRM, and you'll return two to three times that many titles. Searching the term "direct marketing" on Google brings up 14,800,000 references. Much has changed over three decades.

Bob Stone was as proud of this eighth edition as he was of the previous books. Published four to five years apart, each edition of *Successful Direct Marketing Methods* was a historic snapshot, capturing direct marketing's maturity. With each new edition, a reader could see a further blurring of the lines between general advertising and direct marketing. With the growth of online media channels, this blurring of the lines is starting to become complete. This evolution of marketing communications, and how it has been influenced by the tools and techniques of direct marketing, is reflected in the pages of the eighth edition as it has never been before.

What was unique to direct marketing 30 years ago is mainstream knowledge today. Communications need to be targeted, relevant, measurable, and accountable. For marketers to get messages read, watched, or listened, they must routinely segment markets by demographics, psychographics, and category usage. Even for traditional communications there are expected goals for a specific return on investment.

The eighth edition is fully updated, with new chapters on customer marketing and global marketing. There are new case studies to help the reader learn how the latest tools and techniques are applied.

The eighth edition recognizes the impact and growth of the Internet for marketing communications, which has been enabled by direct marketing. E-mail marketing is similar to direct mail, targeting messages that can be personalized for each individual, with messaging that incorporates benefit-oriented copy, calls to action, offers, and other elements that drive behaviors direct marketing has capitalized on for years.

Search, banner ads, personalized URLs, and landing pages allow for testing and measurement of response, identifying unique customers, viewing what gets read, how long consumers spend with it, and identifying what triggers a response. Using new testing techniques, marketers are able to complete dozens, hundreds, or even thousands of tests, learning what works and what doesn't. Direct marketers of yesterday could only dream about the increased level of measurement and knowledge and customers and marketing programs.

Today, the velocity of change is much greater than it was in 1975, when the first edition of *Successful Direct Marketing Methods* was published. New channels and media such as social networking, second life, and mobile marketing are changing the way both B2B and B2C organizations go to market. Additional channels seem to be created every week. Many of yesterday's "new media" have morphed into the mainstream media of today. And there is no end in sight to the unprecedented period of change and innovation that marketing communications are going through.

What should not escape attention, however, is that these new channels are engaging, targeted, include offers and calls to action, and their success is measurable. Results are real-time and digital, so processes can be analyzed, quantified, and compared much more easily than with traditional media. It is clear, however, that many of these new channels are built on a foundation using the tools and techniques of direct marketing. Like other direct marketing channels, they put customers at the center of everything. How they do it, and the extent to which customers are at the center of marketing, is what is different today.

The collective voices of consumers, focused by online tools, now rival the voices of both private and public organizations. Using virtually free Web 2.0 technologies such as blogs, wikis, podcasts, vlogs, and social networking software, consumers and business users can write, produce, and create audio and visual content that streams across the globe.

Intermediaries such as Technorati, Wikipedia, YouTube, MySpace, Linkned, and iTunes provide globally spaces in which users can collaboratively produce, edit, package, and critique knowledge on nearly any subject. Organizations, accustomed to controlling information about their brand's benefits, offerings, performances, and reputations, find that consumers have wrestled such control away. The range of unedited, unembellished, and often raw online information is expanding.

To grow and flourish in this new environment, organizations are learning a new awareness of prospects' and customers' needs, and developing new processes to interact with them. Organizations are communicating and collaborating with customers about a wider range of topics than ever before, gathering reactions from customer communities before the design stage of product development.

In this new landscape, the tools and techniques of direct marketing are adapting to change. Marketers are less interested in saturating unknown prospects with communications, reserving their critical investments in personalization, dynamic content, and cool new technologies for their high-value, highly engaged, responsive customers. When marketers don't hear from customers over time, they stop sending direct mail, e-mail, or other communications, even from the brands and Web sites consumers have opted-in to. Successful marketers are focusing energy on their best and most growable customer segments, while the more costly infrequent or nonresponders are left to opt-in again or get fewer communications.

Prospecting, lead generation, and customer acquisition are becoming more complex. Marketers are doing more testing, sharpening their targeting skills, and negotiating deals on a contingency basis (pay to perform) whenever possible. With increased postage, list, and communication costs, marketers are searching for new methods of acquisition, nurturing prospects rather than sending large numbers of messages out, hoping to catch customers just at the right time.

The pages of the eighth edition explore the growing richness of interaction, and overall effect on the customer experience for every brand, product, and service. Pervasive information sharing makes differentiation a key to success. While marketers are made smarter by it, competitors have access to the same information. It is no longer about who can communicate the longest or loudest. Today, it is about who can communicate the quickest and the smartest and provide the greatest value in the eyes of their customers.

The eighth edition also adds a chapter on global direct marketing. Over the last few years, I have spent a lot of time traveling around the world, presenting on the tools and techniques of direct marketing. There is great hunger for this knowledge in Asia/Pacific, Eastern Europe, South America, and in other emerging markets around the world.

For years, marketers have heard about the "global" economy. Online media give an organization international reach, but this does not make them a global marketer. While the world has become a marketplace beyond anyone's wildest dreams, each market is local.

Markets have to be evaluated individually, taking into consideration culture, religion, demographics, and marketing infrastructure. Marketers have to gauge each country's level of sophistication, evaluating logistics, credit usage, and per capita mail as well as consumer and business decision processes. Mailing lists are not uniformly available around the world, and many countries have no accurate census data. Landline phones are not uniformly distributed. Credit cards have low penetration and usage outside of the United States, and their data is often not shared with marketers. And many local consumer marketing companies are advertising-centric and are not familiar with the tools and techniques of direct marketing.

In many countries, the greatest opportunity may be at the bottom of the economic pyramid. However, lower-income consumers can't be sold in the same ways as higher-income consumers. Distribution networks may need to be rethought. Products may have to be re-engineered, often into small unit packages, with low margins per unit, but with the potential of selling in high volumes. Customers may need to be educated on benefits, taught how to consume products, and given reasons why they need the product.

India, with 1.2 billion people, looks tantalizing. The average age in India is 24.66 years. Average household income is 34,551 rupees (U.S. $735). India's middle class, which likely numbers around 300 million people, has an annual income of U.S. $1,000–$4,800.

However, India is the world's most culturally, linguistically, and ethnically diverse country. India's people come from a variety of Asian and Indo-European backgrounds. There are hundreds of different religions and beliefs. Each of the 14 major regions of India has its own language. The majority of these languages are related to European languages such as Greek, German, or English. Others are related to Dravidian, whose people were most likely creators of the great Indus River civilizations. Indians in the northern mountains speak languages related to Chinese, Tibetan, or Mongolian.

Consumer goods shopping is just starting to expand in India. Major American, European, and Japanese automobile and track brands have only expanded into the Indian market in the last few years. In India, 30 percent of personal care products and consumables such as shampoo, tea, aspirin, and over-the-counter medicines are sold in single-serve packages, priced at one (1) rupee (44 rupees = U.S. $1). While India has tremendous potential, clearly marketers must overcome serious barriers to use the tools and techniques of direct marketing. There are many more examples of how these international barriers are being approached throughout this book.

In the previous paragraphs, I have tried to give you a peek at what awaits inside the eighth edition of *Successful Direct Marketing Methods*. Direct marketing practice has changed greatly since the first edition. Each edition has reflected those changes, and this edition is no different. It is truly a journey through the breadth of contemporary direct marketing, and a fitting legacy for Bob Stone, its founding author.

Ron Jacobs

ACKNOWLEDGMENTS

As with all editions of *Successful Direct Marketing Methods*, this, the eighth edition, reflects the thinking and influence of many outstanding authorities throughout the world. Academia has embraced direct marketing as an integral part of the total marketing curriculum, especially in the last decade. And we received both help and encouragement from many of the world's leading direct marketing practitioners.

Particular thanks go to John Greco, President & CEO of the Direct Marketing Association (DMA), for writing the Foreword to the eighth edition of *Successful Direct Marketing Methods*.

Charlie Prescott, VP Global Knowledge Network Services of the DMA, deserves thanks for his help with the chapter on International Direct Marketing.

Thanks to Vic Hunter, Hunter Business Direct, for his contribution of the chapter on business-to-business direct marketing. Vic, an author himself, is a widely sought-after lecturer. In the B-to-B chapter, he clearly spells out the specific differences between consumer direct marketing and business-to-business direct marketing.

For the chapter titled "Mathematics of Direct Marketing," special thanks go to Pamela Ames, vice president of Kestnbaum and Company for 22 years. The Kestnbaum organization, now consolidated with Knowledgebase Marketing, served all the major mail-order houses, major airlines, telephone companies, banks, and insurance companies as well as automotive manufacturers.

This new edition benefits from nearly all new direct marketing case studies from around the globe. Special thanks go to Steve Kelly, director of the Institute for Interactive and Direct Marketing at DePaul University, and Debra Zahay, the Acxiom Corporation Professor of Interactive Marketing at Northern Illinois University. We also appreciate case study contributions from: Gordon Bell, LucidView; Sy Dordick and Joe Kallick, Web Direct Marketing; Marisa Furtado, Fabrica Comunicação Dirigida, São Paulo, Brazil; Carolyn Goodman, Goodman

Marketing Partners; Dan Hill and Andrew Langdell, Sensory Logic; Susan Kryl, Kryl & Company; and Atsuko Morimoto, AM Associates, Tokyo, Japan.

Not to be overlooked in our acknowledgments are Roberto Amaya, Meg Ciccantelli, and Diana Lopez Negrete for their research and editing expertise, Randy Mitchell for his creative and case study rewrites, and Kim Redlin and the creative staff at Jacobs & Clevenger.

Thanks also to our McGraw-Hill editor, Ed Chupak.

Ron Jacobs

SUCCESSFUL DIRECT MARKETING METHODS

DIRECT MARKETING
ESSENTIALS

THE SCOPE OF DIRECT
MARKETING

In little more than a century, direct marketing has grown beyond its roots in traditional mail order to embrace a host of new technologies, customer relationship-building techniques, and performance measures that set the bar for the future of marketing communications. According to *Ad Age*, direct marketing, once the "unsexy stepchild" to general advertising, now garners 25 percent of the U.S. marketer's budget, surpassing newspapers and broadcast TV.

This is far removed from direct marketing's beginning, when early Americans could order seeds and a host of products not available across the 13 colonies. By the end of the 19th century, many companies selling direct to consumers were serving the needs of a rapidly growing rural America. They brought convenience, breadth of style, and value to a rapidly expanding consumer population. Mail-order companies offered ready-to-wear clothing, in the latest fashion, at a time when many Americans still wore clothing tailored from fabric purchased at a local dry goods store. Early direct marketers sold a breadth of products for home or farm use—even prefabricated homes and barns.

A hundred years later, direct marketing is at the center of a communications revolution. It is a revolution that has witnessed a sea change in media consumption habits. A revolution where the Internet has become an essential element in consumers' and business peoples' lives. It is a revolution where marketers demand that their budgets are used for targeted, customer-centric communications. And, it is a revolution where communications must provide measurable results and a reliable return on investment.

Direct marketing now provides the ever more complex selection of tools and techniques that engage customers and prospects in marketing dialogues, allows them to respond to their preferred channel, and gives marketers the accountability to accurately measure the results of each program.

Much of direct marketing's recent growth has been in nontraditional business categories. Credit card companies, banks, investment companies, and insurance all are heavy users of direct marketing. Telecom, cable, and utility companies are users. Airlines, associations, and automobile manufacturers all use direct marketing. From computers to electronics, hardly a category is missed. Even retailers and shopping centers use direct marketing to drive traffic into stores.

Businesses selling to other businesses are also heavy users of direct marketing. Business-to-business marketing is growing faster than business-to-consumer selling in dollar volume and number of employees. It may surpass consumer direct marketing in total revenues in the near future.

Today, it is hard to imagine an organization that doesn't use direct marketing in one form or another. Long trumpeted as a stand-alone discipline, direct marketing has matured to become the foundation of multichannel communications that provide measurable, targeted, one-to-one relationships between marketers and customers.

Economic Impact of Direct Marketing

The size and economic impact of direct marketing in the United States has been debated for decades. The Direct Marketing Association (DMA) commissioned the first study in 1992 to analyze the extent of direct marketing in the United States and to develop an economic model for forecasting purposes.

According to the DMA study "The Power of Direct Marketing (2006 & 2007)," in 2006 companies spent an estimated $166.5 billion on direct marketing in the United States. Measured against total U.S. sales, these advertising expenditures generated an estimated $1.94 trillion in increased sales in 2006, or 7 percent of the $28 trillion in total sales in the U.S. economy (which includes intermediate sales). Altogether, direct marketing accounted for 10.3 percent of the total U.S. Gross Domestic Product in 2006.

In that same study, the DMA states that most DM advertising expenditures continue to be spent in business-to-consumer marketing (52 percent, or $86.8 billion), as compared with the business-to-business market (48 percent, or $79.7 billion) for 2006. However, expenditures in the B-to-B market are growing faster than in the B-to-C market, with growth projected to be 5.3 percent and 5.1 percent respectively for the compound annual growth over 2006–2011. Both forecast growth figures represent significant improvements on growth rates logged for 2006–2011 (5.1 percent for B-to-C and 5.3 percent for B-to-B).

Direct Marketing Defined

Continuing growth and development in the field makes it more difficult to reach consensus on a standard definition of direct marketing. Such terms as *targeted marketing*, *relationship marketing*, *database marketing*, *one-to-one marketing*, or *integrated marketing* often are substituted. Indeed, these terms seem to share a number of common elements, such as the ability to reach a specific audience, create or enhance customer bonding, create dialogue, or combine various media and disciplines.

While the definition of direct marketing has evolved over time, the authors believe that the term *direct marketing* is still the best description for the tools and techniques used in these various endeavors.

The definition that we have chosen is:

Direct Marketing is the interactive use of advertising media to stimulate an (immediate) behavior modification in such a way that this behavior can be tracked, recorded, analyzed, and stored on a database for future retrieval and use.

While what direct marketing is called may be the source of some debate, the uniqueness of direct marketing is not. Let us elaborate on the chosen definition.

Interactive. One-on-one communications between marketer and prospect/customer is communication that initiates a dialogue. Two-way interaction is a fundamental building block of direct marketing.

Use of Advertising Media. Direct marketing is not restricted to any one medium. Indeed, direct marketers have discovered there is synergy among media. Using a combination of media is often more productive than using a single medium.

The variety of media available for direct marketing is ever expanding. Direct mail is just one medium. Magazines, newspapers, short-form TV, infomercials, radio, transit advertising, and the telephone are all used. Much of the promotion on the Internet, from banner ads to e-mail, can be considered direct marketing.

Track, Record, and Analyze. Measurability is a hallmark of direct marketing. Every form of direct marketing activity, with rare exceptions, is measurable. Direct marketing programs become part of a history to learn from, with a variety of metrics that track spending, response, and return on investment. Internet marketing using e-mail or the Web is measurable, just like print advertising, telemarketing, direct mail, and broadcasting.

Stored in a Database for Future Retrieval and Use. Databases are used to store compilations of known data about a prospect or customer, including their history of purchases, sources of response, credit rating, and so on. It is one thing to create history. A database stores this information in a way that it can be accessed—customer groups aggregated, segmented, identified—and used to make future programs more efficient. The use of a database is another fundamental building block of direct marketing.

The Basics of Direct Marketing

The basic purpose of any direct marketing program is to get a measurable response that will produce an immediate or ultimate profit. To create a measurable response, there must be an offer—a call to action. An offer to sell a product or service direct to a consumer or a business is but one way to create a measurable response. Offers that create leads for sales representatives, get people to inquire for information, build traffic in retail stores, and impel people to give to causes can also be measured.

EXHIBIT 1–1

Elements of Promotion

This chart shows the weight given the elements of promotion in a direct marketing program.

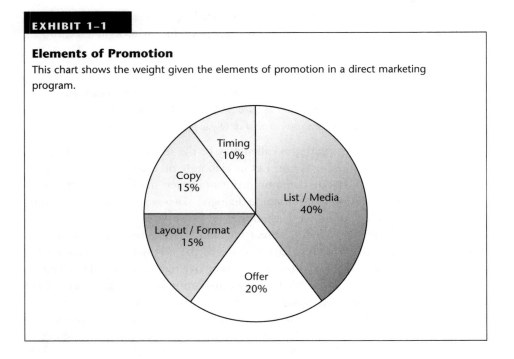

Traditionally, direct marketers have identified lists/media, creative, and the offer as the key components to producing response. These decision variables can be divided into four parts, which we call the Elements of Promotion (see Exhibit 1–1), and ranked by importance: media/lists (40 percent), offer (20 percent), copy (15 percent), layout (15 percent), and timing (10 percent).

Choosing the best media/lists is the key to reaching the right target group. This is true whether you are mailing to prospects or trying to reach them with a television, radio, newspaper, or magazine campaign. Even on the Internet, it is key to bringing together the right buyers and the right sellers.

The best creative or offer may not generate any response if the target group doesn't find the product or service relevant to its needs. Conversely, badly executed creative or a poorly formulated offer will depress response to the right target group, but not completely eliminate it.

Marketers continue to enhance their ability to reach the best target groups using direct mail. Lists that contain only names of individuals or business firms are being supplanted by enhanced databases that help profile prospects and customers and make it possible to target specific market segments. Profiling allows users to target prospects more effectively, identify and build relationships with their best customers, increase the relevancy of their offers, and improve their return on investment.

Many media forms can be selected geographically, demographically, or psychographically (by lifestyle). Newspapers can be selected by day of week or section to reach a target group (e.g., food day, business section, classifieds, Sunday magazine, etc.). Television can be selected by program type, day part, or network. Cable, local stations, and even major networks program against different demographics, targeting broad or narrow niches such as young adults, sports enthusiasts, women, families, or ethnic groups. The choices among consumer and business publications are incredibly broad and include thousands of titles.

The use of the Web as a communications and buying channel has grown steadily. And, multichannel communications, using both online and offline media, are the norm for many users of direct marketing. The largest marketers now say that they moved too cautiously and slowly into online marketing and Web 2.0.

Budgets for various forms of online direct marketing may have grown slowly, but they do so now at the expense of traditional advertising budgets. Consumers and business people spend time online in activities that serve different interests and niches, from social networking sites to eBay. Web advertising, search marketing, and e-mail are communications media that provide marketers with more options that can be measured and tracked.

The offer, also known as the proposition, is another key to success. It is the terms under which a specific product, service, or brand is promoted, i.e., the promise of the transaction. It includes a mix of factors that motivate individuals within the target group to respond—the product or service, price, payment terms, guarantee, and incentives. Creative execution is used to package the offer in the most flattering way. If the offer doesn't convey perceived value, response suffers.

Creative execution is broken into the two elements of copy, and layout or design. While creative execution is not ranked as high as media or the offer, it is a mistake to assume that different degrees of creative make little or no difference. To the contrary, given the right lists and the right offers, superlative creative often increases response by 50 percent or more. Results like this are no accident. They start with customer insights that help the creative team to get into the head of the reader. Creative must always address how the customer's life will be better, how the product or service solves their problems or will make them more successful at some endeavor. And it should involve the reader, stimulating emotions that can evoke response.

Brilliant direct marketing creative often starts with copy. Copy needs to compel readers to respond by giving them rationales on why they should believe the offer, convincing them that they can trust the organization making the offer, and assuring them that they won't make a mistake by responding.

Most direct response copy falls into four categories: benefits, description, support copy, and sweeteners and facilitators.

Benefits are the most important kind of copy, showing how the product or service will improve the potential responder's life. Descriptive copy replaces personal examination (i.e., the ability to touch, feel, or try out a product or service) before purchase. Support copy validates the claimed benefits (e.g., data, statistics, research, case studies, testimonials, etc.). Sweeteners and facilitators "sweeten" the offer. Sandra J. Blum, in *Designing Direct Mail That Sells*, declares that sweeteners give the reader more reasons to take the offer by using incentives, offering choices, reducing anxiety, and making it easier to respond or pay.

Direct marketing design builds on the copy. It should enhance the copy and graphics by making the most of the natural eye flow and eye path of the reader. Design should make it easier for the reader to continue reading rather than put it down and stop reading. Speaking of the elements within a direct mail package or in a complete campaign, Heiki Ratalahti, one of the foremost direct marketing designers, said, " . . . they should bear a family resemblance, or at least interconnectedness." He continued, "To be successful, they should more or less tell the same story in more or less the same way. They should also more or less look like they've met before."

Finally, timing is important. The best creative and most compelling offer will not work unless you reach the right target group at the right time. Response to mailings is affected by holidays, events, the environment, climatic seasons, and category response seasons. Consumer behavior is not easy to change and most marketers simply work within mailing and response periods established by observation.

Reaching consumers when they are in the market is also important. Marketers need to respond to requests in hours, not days, or risk losing opportunities. Trying to resell lost cell phone subscribers, just after they have signed a two-year agreement with a competitor, is equally difficult. Nevertheless, contacting them again in 18 months, when they are back in the market, will likely provide better results. Today, timing plays a greater role than ever before.

Measuring Customer Value

The ultimate objective of a successful direct marketing program is to build the long-term or lifetime value of a customer. This objective applies whether direct marketing methods are applied solely to a mail-order business or to other channels of distribution. Either way, the customer database is available to cultivate customers.

As later chapters will reveal, direct marketers often avail themselves of rather sophisticated calculations. However, four terms—long-term or lifetime value (LTV), recency, frequency, monetary (RFM)—summarize the financial dimensions of direct marketing. Brief definitions will be sufficient at this point.

Lifetime value (LTV) (also called long-term value): The total of financial
    transactions with a customer over the life of a relationship
Recency: The amount of time since a person or firm last purchased
Frequency: The number of times a customer buys within a season, or a year
Monetary: The amount of money a customer spends within a season or a year

Knowing the lifetime value of a customer reveals how much time and resources a marketer can afford to invest in a customer and still realize a satisfactory profit. A typical customer database includes information on recency (date of last purchase), frequency (number of purchases within a given period), and monetary (amount spent). Applying these criteria and looking at the results in different ways enables the marketer to identify segments of the customer base that offer the greatest profit potential. Practitioners of direct marketing have always pointed to measurability as a key reason for direct marketing's continued growth. As marketers have demanded more accountability from their advertising expenditures, direct marketing has benefited.

Marketers began to seek greater efficiency in their communications programs as the consumer marketplace became more segmented. In a *Wall Street Journal* article in July 2006, Gary Conway, VP of corporate marketing for Sprint Nextel Inc, described the shift this way: "There is more and more clutter than ever before, and more and more channels to talk to our customers through than ever before, so . . . there is more science associated with it."

Instead of seeking to capture as large a share of market as possible, marketers now seek to capture the greatest share of a particular customer segment. In many companies, promoting to prospects and customers is seen as an investment. And, like other investments, advertising dollars are held accountable for creating specific results.

Marketers are asking tough questions about their promotional programs. How do they make them measurable? How do they reach markets splintered into hundreds or thousands of subsegments? How do they use media fragmented to reach fewer and fewer people? And, how do they reach segments of one? For a growing number the answer is applying the tools and techniques of direct marketing.

Building Customer Loyalty

Another of direct marketing's use is in growing and maintaining customer loyalty. In many markets such as long-distance and wireless telephones, Internet service providers, and credit cards, churn (the rate of customer defection) is very high. Customers are often attracted by the use of low, short-term, promotional rates. Once these rates expire, customers exposed to similar rates from competitors often move to a competitor to take advantage of savings. In these cases, customer loyalty spells the difference between keeping and losing a customer.

Maintaining customer loyalty is important for all companies. It can cost five to ten times more to create a customer than it does to keep one. Ongoing customers are an important source of referrals and continued sales; they will pay increased prices if they believe they are getting value for the goods or services. As a result, reducing customer defections as little as 5 percent may increase profits by 25–85 percent. If a company could turn 5 percent more of its customers into loyalists, profits would increase 25–100 percent a customer.

A focus on profits or return on investment is important. Pareto's Law, which states that 80 percent of customers provide 20 percent of sales income, was refined by Ogilvy & Mather executive Garth Hallberg. In Hallberg's book, *All Consumers Are Not Created Equal*, David Ogilvy put it this way: 90 percent of customers provide 10 percent of profits. The implication is that a small percentage of customers (10 percent) provide the largest percentage of profit (90 percent).

The tools and techniques of direct marketing are useful at maintaining and maximizing the relationships with such groups.

One-to-One and Customer Relationship Marketing

The tools and techniques of direct marketing also facilitate personalized customer communications. Using information in customer databases about customer behavior or demographics, companies can target the wants and needs of individual customers, thus building stronger customer loyalty and individualizing the total customer experience. This kind of marketing has become known as one-to-one marketing.

Many people use the terms one-to-one marketing and direct marketing interchangeably because many of the same tools and techniques are used for both. One-to-one marketing often involves direct interaction with an individual customer and then some form of mass customized treatment of that customer. The difference between direct marketing and one-to-one marketing is mainly in how solutions are approached.

Don Peppers, a chief proponent of one-to-one marketing, believes that a diligent application of one-to-one marketing principles will prompt a business to find products and services for the customers it knows rather than finding customers for the products it has on hand. "The one-to-one marketer looks at the entire marketing proposition from the other end of the binoculars . . . from the customer's perspective," he says.

Pepper's point, that the one-to-one marketer finds or creates product(s) for the customer rather than finding customers for the product(s), is valid. This is how traditional direct marketers built their businesses. Gaining customer insight through research that identifies the wants and needs of customers is key to the success of direct marketing. Mining the data that organizations already have about their customers is another.

Much information about customers has been locked up in databases created for purposes other than marketing. In the past, these large mainframe "legacy systems" remained difficult if not impossible for marketers to gain access to. Marketing, sales, and customer service staffs were also often separated by hierarchies and silos that kept them from sharing information and ideas. This changed as top management in corporations began to adapt a concept known as Customer Relationship Marketing (CRM).

CRM practitioners use many of the same data technologies used in direct and database marketing. But they use this technology to seamlessly integrate every area of a business that affects customers, including marketing, sales, and customer service. CRM strives to make information a driving force within the organization, not just within the marketing department. Recovering, managing, and using information from legacy or from new systems becomes a goal of CRM. This is a fundamental shift in control of the demand side of business.

The success of CRM is based on many of the ideas explored in this book. CRM uses contact strategies based on defining customer needs; identifying the value of a relationship; investing in customers according to their worth; integrating all contact channels in the plan (advertising, direct mail, promotion, sales, call centers, e-mail, Internet, etc.); supporting this with sophisticated information systems, hiring capable staff, and quantifying and measuring results.

These systems allow organizations that might not consider using "direct marketing" to market directly to consumers with ease. Pharmaceutical makers, tobacco companies, automobile manufacturers, as well as firms marketing directly to businesses, have all adapted CRM. CRM communications programs use the tools and techniques of direct marketing to efficiently use the information that they have mined from their vast databases.

These concepts have gained rapid acceptance on the Internet. Popular Web sites have millions of click-throughs (CTRs) a day. The ability to capture new pieces of data about each user creates an astounding opportunity for marketers.

Successful CRM programs are a convergence of traditional direct marketing techniques, database marketing decision support tools, and digital marketing capabilities. This convergence is creating new genres of direct marketing which approach the individual communications promised by customer relationship marketing.

Behavior, Context, and Observation

Traditional direct marketers are behaviorists. Catalog marketers rent each others' lists based on the premise that mail-order buyers are likely to purchase again via mail order. Knowing what they purchased and how they purchased puts these purchases into context. So, buyers of outdoor equipment soon find their mailboxes full of offers for outdoor products and services. Traditional direct marketers, observing the results of test after test, proved that this hypothesis rings true.

While traditional direct marketers learned their customers' behaviors, they generally didn't unlock the secrets of their customer's motivations. Marketing in a multichannel world is much more complex. Yet new schools, such as Behavioral Marketing and Contextual Marketing, seem to be built on these same sets of ideas. So, how do marketers work through the staggering number of choices for reaching prospects and customers?

There is the traditional DRTV, radio, newspaper, magazines, and direct mail. Web marketing, e-mail and search have all become ubiquitous. Add to that word of mouth, blogs, RSS feeds, text messages (SMS), podcasts and tomorrow's next big thing.

Just observing behavior is no longer enough for marketers. Marketers have to see through these ideas, and get to the trends that are actually driving them. In an article titled "New Technology, New Media and New Paradigm" in *BtoB* magazine's print edition, Paul Gillin summed this up very succinctly:

> *We hear a lot about blogs, but blogs aren't important. What's important is personal publishing, or the ability to communicate a message to a global audience almost instantaneously. Personal publishing will permeate*

electronic media, providing counterpoint to mainstream sources and adding depth and color to the conversation.

We hear a lot about podcasts, but podcasts aren't important. What's important is time-shifted media. The phenomenon that started with TiVo has spread to digital audio and will soon capture portable video. Information consumers will no longer be beholden to program schedules or even their living rooms. Our TV shows will travel with us.

We hear a lot about RSS, but RSS isn't important. What's important is the ability to subscribe to information that really interests us . . . in the future, (we) will use it to subscribe to ideas.

Added David C. Baker, in his *MediaPost Email Insider Electronic Newsletter,*

. . . We hear a lot about e-mail, but e-mail isn't important. What's important is our ability to communicate in a synchronous and asynchronous fashion in a mixed-media world. E-mail will be our notification agent, alarm clock, Post-it® Note, pager, cell phone, fax machine, instant messenger, and document management system all combined.

While behavior, context, and observation remain important concepts, marketers need to do a better job of understanding the trends, learning why prospects and customers are moving in these new directions, and not just observing the outcomes. Knowing this will help marketers make better decisions, in a world where disciplines, media, and selling channels are converging.

Integrated Communications

The tools and techniques of direct marketing work well for many kinds of offers. Mail order, financial services, insurance, lead generation, and traffic building are just some of the ways that direct marketing can be used successfully. Direct marketing is particularly powerful when used with customer segments where past behavior can be used to predict future behavior. More and more, direct marketing methods are being used as part of an overall marketing communications campaign by traditional advertisers.

The move away from the mass marketing message, where one message means the same to the target market, is a great shift for consumer goods marketers. The 21st-century consumer is more diverse than ever. Customers have gained the upper hand, and, newly empowered, they demand communications that reach them when, where, and how they want. At the same time, marketers demand measurable, accountable communications strategies which directly link budgets to customer outcomes. Marketers are taking a more holistic approach to their customers by using Integrated Marketing Communications (IMC) campaigns. IMC is the integrated management of all communications to build positive and lasting relationships with customers and other stakeholders. It is a customer-centric, data-driven approach to marketing and branding that stresses communicating to consumers through multiple forms of media and technology.

Much research on IMC has been done at the Medill School of Northwestern University (NU). NU's Integrated Marketing Communications Graduate Program has been a leader in demystifying the challenges of the changing communications landscape. NU's IMC Triad shows the building blocks of IMC (See Exhibit 1–2).

IMC begins with customer insights, an understanding of customer motivations, desires, and interests, which provide the foundation of strategic communications. The centerpiece of IMC is strategic brand communications, in which all aspects of the customer experience are managed around a core brand strategy. Lastly, IMC utilizes databases to identify target markets for a communications strategy and to measure and evaluate customer purchase behavior.

IMC has developed from an idea to a kind of holistic marketing that is beginning to dominate the thinking of marketing communications. IMC emphasizes the building of relationships with customers in narrowly defined targeted market segments, rather than trying to reach mass markets with mass media. IMC recognizes that technologies such as databases, the Web, and wireless communications have created opportunities for unique, targeted communication methods. And IMC answers to the demand from marketers for measurable, accountable communications strategies—strategies that directly link budgets to customer outcomes.

EXHIBIT 1–2

The IMC Triad

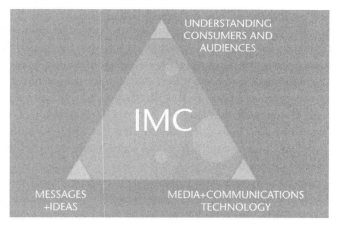

Source: IMC Graduate Program, Medill School of Journalism, Northwestern University.

It is only a short leap from IMC to what is quickly evolving into what we call Brand Direct, the merging of brand and response marketing. Brand Response is a trend well on its way. The once metaphorical line separating the philosophies of traditional advertising (above the line) from direct, digital, and other promotional tools (below the line) has, in the words of Merrill Lynch, nearly reached "neutral status." They complement and depend upon each other, with new strategies that combine brand building and response techniques.

While dotcom marketers use awareness-building ads to drive prospects to their Web sites, Procter & Gamble is using direct response TV ads to help build relationships with customers of their consumer package goods brands. And, consumers no longer consider themselves catalog buyers, online shoppers, or retail customers. Such single-channel categorizations are now, according to Winterberry Group, relegated "to the business archive."

Too Much of a Good Thing

While the use of direct marketing continues to grow, there are some issues that must be addressed. The media of direct marketing are obtrusive and uninvited, something that no one asks for in their home or office. Too often, consumers complain about the very things that marketers like about direct mail, e-mail, and tele-marketing. It has caused issues with privacy, which is not in any marketer's best interest. As we move toward a more multichannel view of customers, can the debate over opt-in versus opt-out continue?

Direct marketing users must navigate a maze of legislation meant to reduce the amount of promotion that prospects and customers receive. In some cases this has been very effective. The national Do Not Call registry, with over 100 million numbers registered, has reduced the volume of calls to consumers, while exempting businesses . . . for now.

Do Not Fax legislation, which requires marketers to have prior consent before sending faxes, has significantly reduced unsolicited faxes. Can Spam did not noticeably reduce unsolicited commercial e-mail; however, anti-spam software has begun to filter and control e-mail volumes. And, Direct to Consumer (DTC) promotions from pharmaceutical companies, marketing to children, and the use of personal data, all face serious regulation.

While legislation and consumer pressure has not changed the trend of marketers moving budgets away from fragmented mass media to more targeted direct media, it can have a chilling effect.

Is it too much of a good thing? Marketers must see these trends for what they are. Relevant communications never go out of style. In a time of unprecedented consumer choice and control, marketers need to learn what the optimal weighting of communications is. When they do, it will promise a good future for us all.

CASE STUDY: **M&M's® Valentine's Day Campaign**

Adapted from the Direct Marketing Association International Echo Awards 2006.

BACKGROUND

MY M&M's® is a customized version of the well-known M&M's chocolate candies that allows for personalized messages in a variety of special colors. This product is only sold to consumers through its Web site.

CHALLENGE

The main marketing challenge: add enough value to a well-known brand to justify a 10× mark-up price. The campaign goal was to raise awareness of the option to create personalized M&M's, in colors of your choice, but only when you buy online. Other obstacles were the high price point (upwards of $45.00) and the need to purchase the product two weeks in advance to receive it in time for Valentine's Day. This is a departure from the impulse/low-cost mentality of the traditional M&M's candy buyer at the store, and from the last-minute Valentine's Day male shopper.

TARGET AUDIENCE

The target audience consists of affluent working-age adults, both men and women, who like to give that "perfect gift." Gift giving is a chance to express their individuality and create special connections.

CHALLENGE

Because each order is custom-made, there is a limit to the number of orders that can be manufactured each day. The challenge was to drive as many Valentine's Day orders as possible without exceeding the daily capacity limitations. Anything under 100 percent of the goal would not pay out; anything over 125 percent would impede timely delivery. The margins for error were slim.

The objective was to successfully sell customized M&M's as a Valentine's Day gift—in a volume that would fill, but not overload, production capacity. Free shipping and a free Valentine's Day gift box were included to boost value and impact.

MEDIA AND STRATEGY

Printed free-standing inserts (FSIs) and online media were used for their flexibility and ability to control response volume. Results could be monitored daily and adjustments could be made to circulation and exposures to narrow in on the target order volume. The marketing media for the Valentine's Day campaign included:

- Full-page FSIs in regional advertising supplements to local newspapers ran from January 5–31 with the free shipping and free gift box offer (See Exhibit 1–3).
- Banner ads ran on various Web sites from January 5–19 featuring the free shipping offer.
- Corporate "house" e-mails (to past purchasers and nonpurchasers): a message promoting the free shipping and free gift box offer dropped on January 5.
- Callouts on mms.com: link was active from January 15–19; this did not include an incentive offer.
- Homepage spotlights: three separate Valentine's Day messages were used in rotation from January 5–19 without an incentive offer (See Exhibit 1–4).
- All advertising stopped January 31, 2006, to account for the 14-day lead time necessary to fulfill custom orders before Valentine's Day.

CREATIVE

The creative elements encouraged the target audience to say "Be My Valentine" their own way. Visuals of M&M's® in pink and red with personalized Valentine's Day messages helped bring this proposition to life and inspired people to think of what their own custom Valentine's Day message might be.

RESULTS

January 2006 Web site sales increased 373 percent versus January 2005 performance. Web site conversion rates doubled during the duration of the promotion. 50 percent of the customers were males, which indicated it was possible to inspire men to think about Valentine's Day two weeks prior to the holiday. Sales were 22 percent above projections, achieving revenue goals without exceeding daily capacity limitations.

EXHIBIT 1-3

M&M's FSI

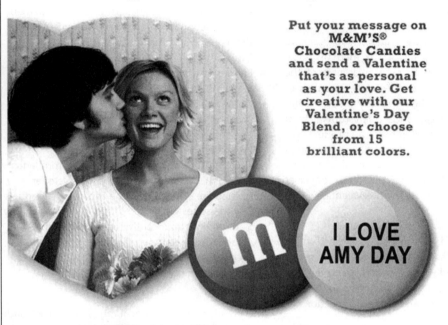

Say
Be my Valentine
your way.

Put your message on
M&M'S®
Chocolate Candies
and send a Valentine
that's as personal
as your love. Get
creative with our
Valentine's Day
Blend, or choose
from 15
brilliant colors.

I LOVE AMY DAY

Receive Free Shipping when you order
Custom Printed M&M'S® today!
Enter promo code MYMM07 at shop.mms.com

Put your own message
on your favorite colored
M&M'S®. It's loads of fun.
Visit **shop.mms.com**
to get started now.

OFFER EXPIRES 1/31/06

Free Shipping!

FREE GIFT BOX
When ordered by 1/31/06

Give someone you love Custom Printed
M&M'S®. Order today and receive Free
Shipping and a Free Valentine's Gift Box.

Enter the promo code below at
shop.mms.com

PROMO CODE **MYMM07**

®/TM Trademarks © Mars, Incorporated 2006

CASE STUDY: **M&M's® Valentine's Day Campaign** *(continued)*

EXHIBIT 1–4

M&M's Website

The M&M's Valentine's Day case study shows how a common consumer good (candy) can be turned into a high-value product using multichannel direct marketing communications and selling only through e-commerce on the Web. The entire direct marketing elements of promotion were called into play: media/lists; creative (copy and layout); offer; and timing.

PILOT PROJECT

Using these same elements, describe how this product could be offered as a product in the business-to-business marketplace. You will need to make some assumptions about how businesses would use personalized M&M's.

A. What kinds of businesses might you target for personalized M&M's?

B. What media/lists might you use to reach these business prospects?

C. Describe what your copy and layout emphasize differently to business prospects than to consumers.

D. Develop an offer that would include an incentive for business buyers to purchase.

E. Develop some alternative timings for this promotion appropriate for the business market.

Key Points

▶ The tools and techniques of direct marketing can be translated across business categories, media, and marketing objectives. Testing allows marketers to discover the most appropriate technique for each objective, campaign, category, or client.

▶ While tools and techniques are evolving, direct marketing programs must engage consumers in relevant dialogues, empower them to interact, and provide measurable response that will produce a quantifiable return on investment. The ultimate objective is to build the long-term or lifetime value of a customer. These characteristics make direct marketing techniques attractive to traditional marketers.

▶ Multichannel direct marketing is an excellent tool for developing one-on-one customer relationships and for growing and maintaining customer loyalty—a critical factor in markets that experience high "churn" or customer turnover. It costs five to ten times more to acquire a new customer than it does to retain an existing one.

▶ More and more, communications campaigns are planned and executed using holistic *integrated marketing communications* strategies. The line separating the philosophies of traditional advertising (above the line) from direct, digital, and other promotional tools (below the line) may finally be an idea of the past.

BUSINESS, STRATEGIC, AND DIRECT MARKETING PLANNING

Direct marketing is, by nature, an action-oriented discipline. However, marketers have to decide what the right actions are in order to achieve efficient, effective, and expected outcomes. Deciding upon the right actions is complicated by the choice of tools, techniques, channels, media, and even combining of branding and response communications. This is sorted out through a process of strategy and planning.

Strategy and planning give organizations a framework for choosing the right tools and techniques to take advantage of direct marketing's immense versatility. Strategy and planning go hand in hand. Without a formal plan, even the best strategy may be doomed to failure. Plans are blueprints for taking an organization, business unit, or brand into the future. They plot a course to reach a set of stated objectives.

A plan will typically lay out a set of long-term objectives and provide guidelines for establishing short-term goals that need to be achieved along the way. Short-term goals act as benchmarks that allow for measuring how far the plan has come toward achieving its overall objectives. Benchmarks help managers to recognize when a plan needs adjustment or when a more complete change in direction may be necessary. Finally, plans provide a baseline managers can use to focus resources on the highest priority issues that they face to run a business effectively and achieve the best results.

The goal of planning is to make certain that an organization remains on track, stays up to date with emerging technologies, and optimizes its unique resources. Businesses once planned strategies three, five, or even ten years out based on assumptions about long-term growth prospects. Today, organizations review their plans annually, even quarterly, and make revisions based on a host of internal and external factors.

Businesses use many different types of planning tools. In a start-up organization, knowledge of business planning techniques is important. An established business will mobilize managers from different areas to develop a strategic plan to help shape the organization's long-term future. The marketing planning process is the mechanism by which many organizations analyze their markets, assess the impact of trends, and design a strategy to meet current and near-term needs of their customers.

Plans should use simple uncomplicated language. Major headings should be clear and followed by paragraphs that highlight the key points of the section. It should be easy for a reader to scan the document and decide which sections to devote more attention to. The plan writer should give particular attention to grammar, spelling, structure, and punctuation—elements that have great impact on the overall impression of the document.

Plans need to be tested and proved on a continuous basis. They need to be reality checked to gain support within an organization, and they need to be performance tested in the marketplace. In evolving, emerging, or new marketplaces, several strategies or hypotheses are frequently tested at once. Through this process, organizations learn which strategies work and which don't. Successful organizations create an environment where experimentation and learning is approved of and rewarded.

There are many different schools of thought on business strategy. Some argue that businesses are too complex for deliberative and rational processes to have great impact. It is true that there is no simple prescription that works for every business. And, the best strategies sometimes wear out over time. In the real world, individuals within an organization make decisions about which corporate initiatives to emphasize, which customers to give the greatest attention to, and which companies to partner with. What's more, changes in the marketplace can render some strategies ineffective overnight.

This chapter looks at three kinds of plans: the business plan, the strategic plan, and the multichannel direct marketing plan. All three are critical to the organization using the tools and techniques of direct marketing.

Three Key Strategic Questions

Strategists often start a review by asking the three questions detailed in a white paper from the Harvard Business School, "Corporate Strategy: A Manager's Guide."

1. *First, Where should we focus the greatest effort and why?*

   This question goes to the root of how a company generates its revenue and profit. Often a company's profit center is not clear. Answering this question helps companies focus on strategies that garner the greatest reward. Today, theorists believe that companies must identify and make the most of their strengths while continuing to search for new profit opportunities from their existing value chain.

2. *Second, What do we bring to the table?*

   This question puts the focus on the internal capabilities and strengths of an organization. The white paper points out that successful organizations like

Federal Express have bundles of skills and technologies that affect and shape their strategies. In addition to core competencies, organizations have distinct capabilities that can't be easily duplicated by competitors—perhaps a recognized market position, strong brand, and a reputation over time.

3. *Third, Do our core capabilities suit our position?*

Exploring this question helps organizations focus on capabilities that provide long-term opportunities. Companies shouldn't put effort into a marketing position that they can't sustain over time. Nor should they put resources into developing competencies from which they don't gain an advantage over their competitors.

Michael Porter, author of *Competitive Strategy*, believes that competitive advantage lies not in a single competency but in a whole system of activities. Amazon.com is a good example.

Amazon.com's strategy is to spread its resources over new business categories. Amazon is able to use the same systems to develop, promote, and fulfill products in these new categories while maximizing the customer base it has cultivated.

To outsiders, it may appear that Amazon.com's chief competitive advantage is its large customer base. Not so. Amazon.com has developed a sophisticated business and technology infrastructure. Its merchandising skills and product offerings are important, and so is its large customer base. But what sets it apart from competition is the combination of its efficient Web development process, ordering system, distribution capabilities, and customer service. Amazon.com maximizes the use of customer information while building a business on systems that together give customers the real advantage in shopping with them.

It is hard for other companies to challenge Amazon's strategy. Few competitors have the resources to try to duplicate Amazon's mix of capabilities, which gives Amazon.com a unique advantage to capitalize on.

Amazon continues to expand globally using its competitive advantage. It has set up Web sites in Britain, France, Germany, and Austria, where the company believes that denser populations and shorter delivery distances create an ideal market for Internet sales. By contrast, the sprawling geography of the United States means that delivery times using standard ground methods (e.g., UPS, USPS, etc.) can be several days, compared to overnight in much of Europe.

The Strategic Business Plan

A business plan is written to help attract outside investors and financing. It can help crystallize a fledgling organization's business model, market niche, organizational structure, and cash needs. It can also help reduce the risks associated with starting a business by including alternatives, a series of "what ifs" for the company's future.

A business plan answers questions that an investor not familiar with the business might ask. Investors, who are the "customers" for the plan, want the plan to:

- Describe the key concepts of the business

- Establish that there is a market for the products and services the company sells

- Outline the organizational structure of the business

- include financial projections that show the company's expected sales growth over a three-year period

The job of the business plan is to sell readers on the idea that a business plan is worth investing in. One key to accomplishing this task is comprehensive research. Without it, a business plan will seem vague, shallow, or incomplete—causing the reader to doubt how much the writers know about their business, market, or customers. When doubts occur, the plan has not done its job.

The length of the finished business plan can vary. In some plans, the marketing or product/service section may be detailed and complex, while in others it can be short and concise. The rule of thumb is that the plan must be long enough to communicate main ideas. It must contain enough information so that anyone who reads it will understand it, especially those unfamiliar with the concept.

There is no single "right" way to approach a business plan. Much depends on the kind of business or product/service that you plan to market. A plan for an Internet service business will surely be different from that of a manufacturing company selling mass customizing products created on an assembly line.

Elements of the Business Plan

The following elements, summarized in Exhibit 2–1, are included in most business plans.

Introduction. This short section describes in no more than a page why the plan is being written, its intended audience, and sets out the plan's business objectives and purpose as well as the business concept.

Executive Summary. To give the reader a clear picture of what the business is all about, this section includes the mission statement; the start date of the business; founders' names and functions; number of employees; location of headquarters and any branch offices; description/size of facilities; the products/services category; current investors; bank name(s); growth summary and plan; financial highlights; market potential; and a summary of management's plan.

Mission and Vision Statements. These statements set forth the central purpose of the business and its planned activities, as well as its major objectives, key strategies, and primary goals.

EXHIBIT 2–1

Elements of the Strategic Business Plan

Introduction
What is the purpose of the plan? Who is the audience?

Executive Summary
Summarizes the key elements of the plan (e.g., the mission statement; the products/services category; current investors; founder's names, financial and growth plans).

Mission and Vision Statements
What are the major objectives, key strategies, and primary goals of the business?

Market Analysis
Includes SWOT analysis, competitive analysis, likely target groups, research, and market share projections.

Customer Analysis
Who buys this product/service; are there multiple buyers, decision makers, or buying authorities; what is the size of the market, demographic or geographic dispersion, pricing analysis; what media or sales channels reach them?

Business Description
Describes the business, industry, developing trends, growth potential, emerging technologies, unique patents, trademarks, or names. What sets it apart from competitors?

Organization and Management
Outlines the organizational chart, staffing needs, job descriptions of top management, and biographies of founders and board of directors.

Integrated Marketing and Sales Plan
Includes detailed marketing plan, integrated marketing communications plans, methods of selling, distribution channels, pricing guidelines, expected competitive responses, budgets and timing, and rationales.

Funding Request
Details of the funding requirements, sources of funds, likely terms, and the projected return on investment (ROI)

Financial Projections
Three- to five-year forward-looking profit and loss statements, balance sheets, detailed cash flow projections, and the path to profitability.

Appendix
Additional support materials, including research reports, specific product plans, samples of promotion materials, Web site, etc.

Market Analysis. The market analysis details the company's strengths, weakness, opportunities, and threats, describes its competitive environment, and defines the target group most likely to purchase the products/services offered and how the target group was determined. It also describes the share of the market the company hopes to gain and the share of market held by competitors.

Customer Analysis. Explains who buys this product/service, how many potential buyers there are, how much they typically spend for this product/service, and where buyers can be found. It also identifies whether multiple buyers, decision makers, and buying authorities are involved and what brand contacts can be used to reach them.

Business Description. Describes what business the organization is in and includes information about trends in its industry. It also describes the products/services offered and explains what sets them apart from competitors, including any patents, trademarks, or names that the organization holds.

Organization and Management. Details the anticipated organizational structure, staffing needs, and job descriptions of top management of the organization as well as triggers for adding additional staff and management. It includes an organizational chart, details of compensation, incentives, benefit plans, and biographies of top managers as well as biographies and qualifications of the founders and board of directors.

Integrated Marketing and Sales Plan. This detailed summary of the marketing plan explains the methods of selling and channels of distribution, along with the rationale for the proposed mix of advertising, direct marketing, Internet, promotion, public relations, and events.

Its plans for selling and communications are compared with competitors. Other topics covered include credit and terms of receivables, credit approval procedures, pricing guidelines and markups, competitive response analysis, budgets and timing, and responsibilities and duties of involved staff. This section also explains what will be revised if anticipated growth is not met.

Funding Request. Details the funding requirements, potential sources of funds, likely terms, and the projected return on investment (ROI). This section needs to be realistic, as investors are unlikely to put money into something that doesn't make sense.

Financial Projections. A detailed accounting of how much money is needed, when it is needed, and when investors can expect a return on investment, usually in the form of a balance sheet and income statement (P&L) for the current period as well as for the future. Carefully developed financials show a firm grasp of the costs involved in operating the business. This section also includes a detailed cash-flow projection showing:

- Cash in (with all sources of cash identified)

- Cash out (with all uses of cash identified)

- Timing (when will each of the above occur?)

The financial projections should show an organization's path to profitability—an enduring key to success that is even more important in the post-Internet boom period.

Appendix. Appendices contain information referred to in the text of the business plan, such as research reports, tables, detailed market or sales projections, analyses, and exhibits.

What Investors Look for in a Business Plan

Investors want to know one thing: Will I recoup my investment?

To answer that question, they examine a number of areas closely. They want to know that the potential market for the product and services is sufficient. They look closely at the research and rationales for market size, expect to see growth options, and want to know what factors could impede success. And they look to see that the organization's value proposition is in alignment with the customers.

Investors want to see evidence that management is accomplished and dedicated. Besides business experience, they are looking for vision, diversity, competency, capabilities, and teamwork and networking skills. Networking ability is significant because business partnering is so important. Investors want to know if the company's partner offers it a competitive advantage. Investors also want to know the company's path to profitability. They peruse the financials to see if the revenue model is real. They test it to see if it makes sense, if growth projections are achievable, profit projections can be reached, and if the overall financial plan is credible.

Lastly, investors look for plans that are truly unique. Recently, too many business plans have emphasized the uniqueness of the Internet rather than the uniqueness of the business proposition. In fact, it is more important to be different than to be digital.

Mohanbir Sawhney of the Kellogg Graduate School of Management has an interesting test for uniqueness. He asks entrepreneurs, "*What would happen if your business plan were published in the Sunday paper?*" If publication would be a disaster, Sawhney gives them only a slim chance for success. His rationale is that a business plan should be so unique that only the organization developing the plan should be able to execute it. This reinforces the importance to be in a business that is difficult, if not impossible, to replicate.

The Strategic Plan

A strategic plan is a blueprint of short- and long-term activities, strategies, and work plans, developed after considering external market forces and an organization's internal competencies and capabilities. One of the most useful tools for all organizations, strategic planning is an ongoing business process that enables an organization to make decisions about its vision and mission and develop the necessary procedures and operations to achieve that future, as well as determine how success is to be measured (See Exhibit 2–2).

EXHIBIT 2–2

Elements of the Strategic Plan

Introduction
- Describes the purpose of the plan and whether its scope is for the full organization, division, brand, or one product/service.
- Quantify how forward-looking it is (e.g., three years).

Executive Summary
- Summarizes the key elements of the plan (e.g., the scope, objectives, SWOT, mission, vision, the products/services category, current investors, founders names, financial and growth plans).

Goals and Objectives
- Highlights achievements to be realized over the next one to three years.
- Relates these to the business, customers, and other stakeholders.

Situation Analysis
- Competitive analysis—looks as far inside competitors as possible.
- Market analysis—includes market size and in-depth customer analysis.
- Environmental analysis—identifies key events and trends in the industry.

SWOT Analysis
- What are the key strengths and weaknesses of the organization?
- What are the key opportunities and threats in the marketplace?

Mission Statement
- What does this business really do and what does it hope to do?
- What makes this business, organization, or brand unique?

Vision Statement
- What will the business look like in one to three years? (This section can be aspirational).
- This needs to be translatable into behavior within the organization.

Business Values
- What are the principles governing the business and its relationship with customers, partners, the community, and other stakeholders?
- This section is often included with the mission or vision statement.

EXHIBIT 2–2

Elements of the Strategic Plan *(continued)*

Key Strategies
- Identifies what success looks like.
  Will the company build on strengths, resolve weaknesses, capitalize on opportunities, or avoid threats?
- Strategies can be organizational (e.g., diversification, organic growth, or acquisition) or functional (e.g., management, marketing, sales, operations, R&D, etc.).

Action Plans
- Outlines the major action programs in order of importance. Specifies what, who, where, how, and when for each.
- Prioritizes plans.

Financial Plans
- Identifies financial goals and creates P&Ls.
- Matches revenue and spending to period of the strategic plans.

Performance Measures
- Establishes measures to meet goals, complete strategies, improve or change direction.
- Identifies benchmarks, dates to know that plans are on track.

A strategic plan can bring together an organization's management, employees, stakeholders, and customers by communicating a common understanding of where the organization is going, how everyone involved can work to that common purpose, and how to identify the benchmarks for progress and success. However, this plan must be shared and reviewed with everyone constantly if it is to be a truly integrated strategic plan. A plan that molders neglected in a drawer is no plan at all.

Increasingly, the voice of the customer drives the operations and charts the course for the future. Customer-driven organizations create plans while actively examining their products, services, and processes through the eyes of the customer. As part of the planning process, customer-driven organizations learn their customers' preferences and requirements, as well as their standards for performance, timeliness, and cost. And they not only listen to the expressed needs and expectations of the customers, but also gather independent information about the preferences of customers and categories they hope to serve in the future.

Customer-driven does not mean blindly taking action based upon the results of customer input. It means looking at what customers do—not just what they say—in determining their needs. For example, in new and emerging markets where customers are not familiar with a product or service, customers may not know what their needs really are. With new product introductions, customers may not know what kind of improvements to expect. It is important to match customer behavior to customer expectations when looking at results.

Two important elements of the strategic plan are the mission statement and the vision statement. The terms are often used interchangeably. However, in each type of statement there are differences worth noting.

Mission Statement

A mission statement should describe why an organization exists and what it hopes to achieve going forward. It should articulate the essence of an organization's nature, its values, and its business. To be effective, it must resonate with an organization's staff, as well as with prospects, clients, business partners, and others that the organization hopes to affect. It must express the organization's purpose in a way that inspires commitment, innovation, and teamwork and gains the broadest consensus.

An organization's mission statement should answer three key questions:

1. What is the purpose of the organization and what are the opportunities or needs that we exist to address?

2. What business are we in and what are we doing to address these needs?

3. What are the values, principles, and beliefs that guide the organization's work?

These questions should be answered in one or two brief paragraphs that are free of jargon and misleading business terms. A reader unfamiliar with a business should be able to decipher its mission statement without the need for additional learning. Without knowing that the following mission statement is for a company that provides E-commerce infrastructure support services, would you be able to identify its business?

We leverage eBusiness technology, innovative business processes, and new economy channel partners, to create the next generation Value Chain for the IT industry. As a result, everyone in the IT channel ecosystem wins.

Compare this to the mission statement for Hanna Andersson, a catalog and E-tail marketer of European clothes for children and their families:

We market clothes to enhance the lives of our customers through quality, functionality, durability, and design. We celebrate our beliefs with integrity. Our culture bears witness to our values. Our participation confirms our responsibility to the larger community.

Vision Statement

A vision statement is a fundamental tool for helping a company see into its future.

Visions are big pictures. They paint a picture of an organization's future through the eyes of that organization's leader or senior management team.

They are often written by the CEO. At the very least, the effective leader will contribute ideas, concepts, and ways of thinking, staying at the center of development until the vision statement crystallizes. It is up to the CEO to translate the vision for employees and motivate them to embrace the vision.

A vision statement must be consistent with an organization's mission, goals, strategy, and philosophy. Its key objective is to guide an organization's behavior. A good vision statement is clear, concise, easily understandable, and memorable. It excites, inspires, and challenges an organization.

For a vision statement to be effective, it must be perceived as strategically sound. It must gain widespread support within an organization to become real and translate into behavior. Individuals within an organization must embody the vision by their actions, words, and deeds. In this way the vision is reinforced and becomes part of an organization's culture.

The importance of a powerful vision statement can't always be measured. However, consumer goods company Johnson & Johnson can attest to its value. It spent time and money building credibility with constituencies through its "Credo," a one-page vision statement outlining the company's value system. The credo reads in part:

> *We believe our first responsibility is to the doctors, nurses and patients, to mothers and fathers and all others who use our products and services. In meeting their needs everything we do must be of the highest quality. . . . We are responsible to the communities in which we live and work and to the world community as well. We must be good citizens—support good works and charities and bear our fair share of taxes.*

In the 1980s, packages of the company's Tylenol® brand were adulterated with cyanide, causing the deaths of some customers. With Johnson & Johnson's name and reputation at stake, company managers and employees made countless decisions inspired by the philosophy in the Credo. As a result, customers were willing to give the company the benefit of the doubt in the Tylenol-tampering crisis and the brand was able to survive and even thrive.

SWOT Analysis

A strategic plan includes an analysis of an organization's internal strengths and weaknesses and external threats and opportunities. An effective process for identifying these elements is SWOT analysis—Strengths, Weaknesses, Opportunities, and Threats. Research and analysis of the situation is often completed first. SWOT puts the information into a framework that reveals changes that can often be implemented without further analysis.

SWOT doesn't create answers; it allows the key issues to be identified, classified, and prioritized, which helps shed light on alternative solutions. When all elements have been identified, it is easy to establish points that balance strengths and weaknesses and opportunities and threats. These can then be plotted together, so that decision makers can see how best to build on strengths and take opportunities while eliminating weaknesses and threats (See Exhibit 2–3).

A SWOT analysis is usually completed in groups of no more than 10 people, to keep the discussion moving. Each of the four elements of the analysis is given its own section. Questions related to each section are written within the framework of that section. Questions should be considered from the organization's point of view as well as that of customers. Answers should be honest and realistic. Questions to address include:

Strengths:
What are the organization's real advantages?
What are the organization's core competencies? What does it do well?

EXHIBIT 2–3

SWOT Analysis Template

This template allows for up to six items under each heading, but a business or brand can have many more. Limit the items to focus on the biggest issues, not smaller ones.

Instructions: Briefly list major *existing* Strengths, Weaknesses, Opportunities, and Threats. Strengths and Weaknesses are **internal** to the business. Opportunities and Threats are **external**.

Strengths	Weaknesses

Opportunities	Threats

What are the organization's core capabilities?

Are we better financed than competitors, better able to retain key staff, or have a better reputation?

Weaknesses:

What needs to be improved in products, services, processes, etc.?

What is it that we don't do very well?

Are there areas that should be avoided?

Do competitors have better market share, deeper market penetration, and is there one competitor than can't be unseated?

Opportunities:

Where are the bright spots in the organization's market?

Are there technologies or trends that favor the organization?

Do changes in population profiles, lifestyles, etc., offer an advantage?

Do changes in government policy, taxation, etc., benefit the organization?

Threats:

What obstacles does the organization face?

What is the competition doing to offset our gains?

What impact is the Internet, E-commerce, or other technology having on our industry?

Are changing marketing practices (e.g., the use of CRM, Sales Force Automation, etc.) threatening our position?

Do we have high bad debt, cash-flow problems, or an uncontrolled burn rate?

Completing a SWOT analysis can be illuminating. It can point out what needs to be done to improve an organization's performance. It is a way to take complex business issues, sort them out in an orderly manner, and keep problems in perspective. It is a tool that can be used in developing situation analyses for strategic planning, business planning, even marketing plans.

The Multichannel Direct Marketing Plan

Although the growth of the Internet as a marketing, distribution, and media channel has added many new twists to the traditional marketing planning process, this chapter presents the elements of the direct marketing plan in a familiar way. The direct marketing plan remains part of a common language that traditional marketers, direct marketers, and Internet marketers can identify.

Like other kinds of plans, the multichannel direct marketing plan is a road map to be followed. Its content requires research, organization, and patience in its development and execution. However, it is not a static document. It needs to be constantly reviewed, updated, and revised as an organization's goals evolve with its marketplaces.

The direct marketing plan by its nature includes a strategic as well as a tactical side. The strategic side must be developed before an organization commits resources to its exceptional elements. Inadequate or poorly thought-out strategic market planning means a company may invest in areas that are unlikely to ensure financial success. This is as true for Internet companies as it is for catalog businesses.

Developing the Multichannel Direct Marketing Plan

When you take planning in context, it is easy to see the relationship among different kinds of plans. For example, the financial projections contained in a business plan are based on the assumptions contained in the marketing plan. The marketing plan sets out where, how, and when promotional expenditures will be made, based on the expected level of sales. Together, these are key elements of the financial projections.

Some elements in the direct marketing plan are simply reframed from the strategic or business plan. There is a synergy among plans that increases when members of an organization ask the same questions over and over again, and arrive at the same answers.

The multichannel direct marketing plan begins with a customer-centric approach to planning. The goal is to invest in the prospects, customers, and customer segments that the organization believes will help it reach the projected income flow goals. To accomplish this, the organization begins by calculating or estimating the value of the prospects, customers, and segments to determine the right investment strategies for each group.

Elements of the Multichannel Direct Marketing Plan

The elements of a typical direct marketing plan include:

Introduction. A short section describing the plan's purpose and its intended audience. It also sets out the business objectives and purpose of the plan, and often of the business concept.

Executive Summary. A short summary that gives the reader a clear idea of the plan's contents. It includes the objectives of the plan, the marketing strategies, key target groups and market segments, elements of the tactical plan, a budget summary and rationales.

Situation Analysis. This section describes the marketing environment in which the organization operates and competes as well as the results of any customer or market research. Its subsections include:

- *The macroenvironment of the marketplace*, which describes demographic trends, economic indicators, relevant technologies, political, social, and cultural events, supply, and other forces that can impact the company.

- *The competitive situation*, which includes information on major competitors with size, sales, goals, market share, product quality comparisons, marketing strategies, marketing spending, etc. Mapping out key competitors' marketing and business strengths, as illustrated in Exhibit 2–4, will help illustrate where the best marketing positioning opportunity lies.

- *Target group analysis*, which identifies demographic, psychographic, and behaviors of target buyers, decision makers, and end-users. It identifies the needs and wants of these groups and categorizes the most lucrative segments for marketing efforts.

- *Distribution channels*, which provides information on size, trends, and importance of online, offline, retail, or direct distribution channels for the company's products/services. It can include product/service or category demand analysis.

- *Product situation*, which includes key aspects of the product including sales, prices, and contribution margins as well as the net profits of each product line addressed in the marketing plan.

- *Research*, which includes results of any primary or secondary research, prospect or customer surveys, or information gleaned from previous market tests conducted.

Opportunity and Issue Analysis. This section includes the elements of the SWOT analysis germane to the marketing plan, using techniques similar to those discussed in the strategic planning section. Analyzing the internal strengths and weaknesses and external opportunities and threats to the organization in a competitive context is the first step. Once the key issues are described, the organization needs to address decisions to be made based on the SWOT analysis. This helps to determine objectives, strategies, and tactics for the direct marketing plan.

Goals and Objectives. This section outlines major company goals as well as marketing and financial objectives. A marketing objective must be quantified in terms of results and an achievable time or date. Results can be expressed in terms of results, sales, retention, etc. A quantified objective gives a benchmark on which

EXHIBIT 2–4

Competitive Analysis

To visualize the relative strengths of competitors, map key consumer decision variables into quadrants. This example plots competitors for high net worth financial planning services. Note the proposed positioning in a quadrant where there is little competition.

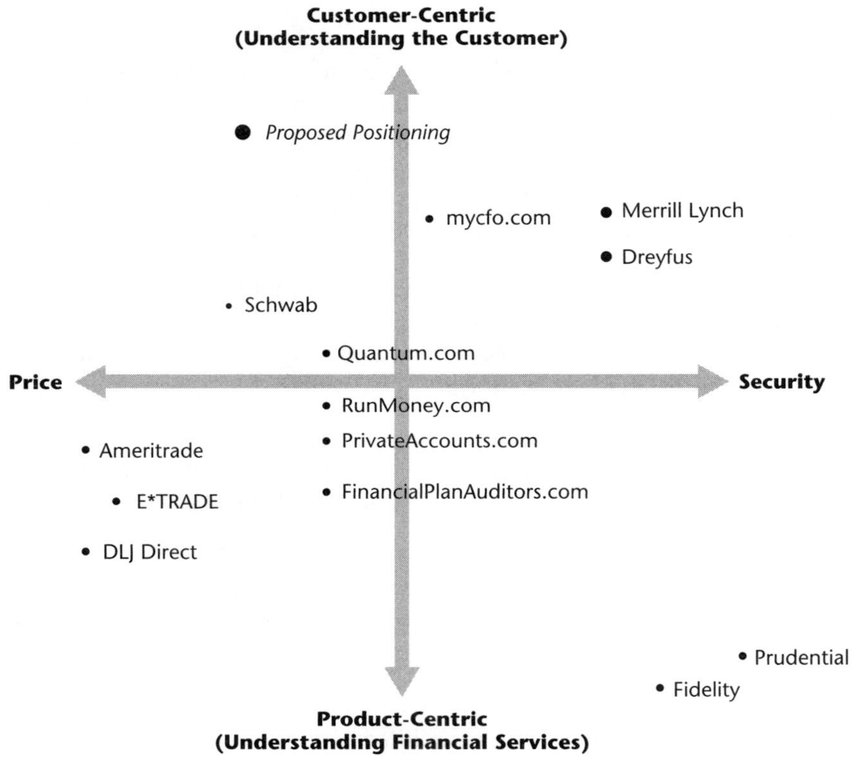

Customer-Centric
(Understanding the Customer)

● *Proposed Positioning*

● mycfo.com   ● Merrill Lynch

● Dreyfus

● Schwab

● Quantum.com

Price   **Security**

● RunMoney.com

● PrivateAccounts.com

● Ameritrade

● E*TRADE   ● FinancialPlanAuditors.com

● DLJ Direct

● Prudential

● Fidelity

Product-Centric
(Understanding Financial Services)

to measure the success of the marketing plan. Examples of quantified objectives are "To get 30,000 click-throughs during the first month of operation," "To create 5,000 new customers during the second quarter," or "To generate 2,000 leads per week for next eight weeks."

The Marketing Strategy. This section orchestrates the elements of the marketing program. It includes a marketing strategy statement that summarizes the key target buyer description, explains how the organization plans to sell and market to those customers, and how the company wants prospects and customers to perceive it.

This can include the competitive market segments the company will compete in, the unique positioning of the company, brand, or product/service, targeting strategies, benefit strategies, competitive price strategy, marketing and promotional spending strategy, and any possible R&D and market research expenditure.

Rationales for the marketing strategy may include an analysis and appraisal of the brand, category, multi-line, product, price, and promotion strategies and the rationale for why it is unique or compelling to buyers. This may include an analysis of competitive strategies as well.

A marketing strategy is successful when it is in alignment with the needs and wants of customers. This means that the organization must have a clear understanding of its prospect, customer, and end-user's behavior. When possible, this should be gleaned from information on the database, past results, or current performance.

Tactics. This section details each specific marketing event and action planned, including media and mailing list plans, communication plans for direct mail, DRTV, response advertising, e-mail, and banner ad programs. It may include a summary of quarterly promotion and marketing communication plans, with spending, timing, share, sales, or product shipment goals for each program and medium. It may also detail sponsorship, affiliate, event, or other kinds of programs planned.

It will include a description of each vehicle to be used in each program, with detail across media, disciplines, prospects, customers, the trade, etc. It will include separate tactics for acquisition, retention, activation, up-sell, cross-sell, or other kinds of programs planned.

Tactical marketing communication plans are the most detailed elements of the direct marketing plan. However, the whole of the plan should build into the communication plans. The communication tactics should simply flow from all that was written in support of them in the plan. This makes it a real working document, with a great chance of it translating into program success.

Budgets. There is no magic bullet for developing budgets. Budgeting usually starts with identifying the current or potential value of prospects, customers, and segments in order to estimate how much can be invested to achieve each goal. Competitive spending, changes in the market, and other uncontrollable forces impact budgets.

Budgets generally cover a calendar year, broken down by month or by quarter. They should contain a financial summary of quarterly promotion and marketing communication plans, broken down by program. They include spending, timing, sales, and share/shipment goals for each program.

Budgets are not static. They need to be updated quarterly and managed constantly against results. Budgets are often adjusted down or up as is necessary during the course of business. The impact of budget changes must be included in forecasts.

The Message Strategy Plan

Not all plans are book-length manifestos rivaling the works of the greatest authors. Marketers often use a shorter type of plan, often termed a marketing brief. A form of marketing brief used as an input document for creatives at agency Jacobs & Clevenger is called the Message Strategy Brief.

This form, shown in Exhibit 2–5, fits on one side of an 8¼ × 14 inch sheet of paper. It is meant to communicate in just a few lines the key elements necessary to begin the creative process. No section of the plan has room for more than two or three lines of explanation.

There are two sections to the brief. The marketing strategy section asks three questions that pinpoint the objectives of the creative assignment. The creative strategy section includes information on the target market as well as on what is to be communicated to prospects.

Elements of the Message Strategy Brief

Key Fact. This is the single most important fact related to preparing this communication. In other words, why are you doing a promotion? The answer to this could be to increase sales by X percent, to support other efforts, or to introduce a new product, service, brand, or line extension.

Consumer Problem This Creative Must Solve. The second question is related to the key fact. Its answer must be stated in consumer terms. It is not what the brand/product/service needs . . . it is what the customer needs! The answer might be: "High net-worth consumers now have a Web site where they can access sophisticated financial tools previously only available through specialized financial planners," or "Now you can refinance your mortgage at 1 percent over prime rate with no points or closing costs."

Communication Objective. This explains how this creative proposes to solve the problem stated above. An example might be: "Develop a multi-channel direct mail, e-mail and search marketing campaign to drive savvy, high net-worth prospects to the Fidelity.com website," or "Create a personalized direct mail with telephone follow-up campaign targeted at prospective home buyers."

Creative Strategy. This section asks for information on seven points that help to focus the creative strategy.

- *Prospect profile*. This requires a few words about the demographics, psychographics, etc., of prospects or customers. The more we know about them, the more targeted the promotion.

EXHIBIT 2–5

Message Strategy Brief

JACOBS & CLEVENGER

Client
- Company, division, brand

Product
- Description of the product or category

Project
- Use a descriptive name

Key fact
- The single most important fact related to preparing this advertising

Consumer problem this creative must solve
- Related to the key fact. State in consumer terms. Not what the brand/product/service needs... What the customer needs! (i.e. The value proposition)

Communication objective
- How this creative proposes to solve the problem stated above

Creative strategy
- Prospect profile
- Competition
- What is the current perception of the brand, and what perception of the brand do we want after this contact?
- What is the prospect's current behavior and what behavior do we desire after they receive our message?
- What action do we want the prospect to take now and how?
    o What is the call to action?
- Proposition
    o What do prospects/customers get, and what's the incentive for them to respond?
- Reason why
- Secondary support
- Legal & policy considerations / Mandatory factors

- *Competition*. In thinking about the competition, consider what needs to be replaced to get people to purchase your product or service. Don't think of the competition too narrowly. Think of substitutes for your product/service.

  What is the current perception of the brand, and what perception do you desire? In order to know where you are going, you need to know what consumers think and know. Is what you are proposing credible, or does it require a leap of logic that would not be credible? For example, it is easy for Amazon.com to make a customer service claim, but harder for a start-up company. A delivery guarantee might help overcome this.

- *What is the prospect's current behavior and what behavior do we desire?* Are consumers buying a competitor's product or are you breaking ground for a new category that will require change? Think of getting a prospect to go from buying VCRs to DVDs to Tivo to on-demand cable. Where it is a short leap, the messaging is easy. When the communications require a trip into uncharted territory, the messaging requires more explanation and additional benefits.

- *What action do we want the prospect to take now and how?* Are you trying to generate a lead, gain trial of new product, get someone to purchase, respond by mail, phone, or the Web, etc.? What is the specific *call to action*? Make it verbatim, the specific action you are asking prospects or customers to take. This call to action defines the response the marketer desires. It is an element that defines the communications as direct response.

- *Proposition*. The proposition is the main element of the offer, including the product/service as well as incentives. Prospects and customers are moved by benefits, not the tangible product or features of a service. It is important to describe the benefits prospects get when they respond. Also, describe and explain the offer that will be used to generate the response. Identify if a strong incentive is necessary to get people to respond. This is deeply related to the call to action and the objectives of the communication. The offer must be synchronized with both, or the communications are not likely to be successful.

- *Reason why?* This is the rationale, the main reason that someone can believe the claims in communications. It should be a clear explanation, supporting the proposition and benefits.

- *Secondary support*. Often there are research studies and other support materials that are helpful in making claims believable. This section may reference them and the location of where the information is available. It may be an attachment to the brief or at a Web address online.

Legal and Policy Considerations/Mandatory Factors. In many categories there are legal and policy issues to be considered. Some companies prefer not to do sweepstakes for fear of blemishing their image. Insurance companies must create different forms for residents of different states. Interest rate ceilings vary from state to state. These are the kinds of issues dealt with here.

The creative strategy is an easy-to-use creative brief. It is a tool used by most agencies in the development of creative. It is one that you should try if you are responsible for giving input to creative staff.

CASE STUDY: Ameritrade Last Market Hour

Adapted from the Direct Marketing Association International Echo Awards 2005.

BACKGROUND

Ameritrade (TD Ameritrade) develops financial products and services for individual investors. The self-directed active trader, usually males aged 25–55, was the target audience for this campaign. This target, already customers of competing online brokers, tends to place a large number of trades, and therefore provides the greatest opportunity for Ameritrade to profit. The active trader is less deterred by the state of the economy and more likely to trade even when there is a downturn in the market. Further, active traders are optimistic and willing to take risks; they have the confidence to find opportunity in the market on their own. Often pressed for time, the active trader values the tools that can give them an edge in spotting trading opportunities and executing trades.

CHALLENGE

Deliver hard-hitting customer acquisition goals in a marketplace transitioning from bearish to bullish. Corporate earnings were on the rise, the unemployment level was dropping, and trading volume reached near-peak levels. Also, the online discount brokerage category was growing, as most brokerages were offering a similar set of product and services, so differentiation was key.

This environment often led to price and offer wars. In addition, there was the ongoing challenge to lay a foundation for building customer loyalty with an audience that tends to have multiple accounts with other brokerages. Given all this, Ameritrade needed to revitalize its own offerings, positioning themselves to the active trader as the category leader, while emphasizing value and integrity.

MARKETING STRATEGY

The final hour of the trading day is characterized by sudden changes in markets and can create big opportunities for traders. This is when a trader needs real-time tools and accurate information to keep pace. Ameritrade positioned itself as the "owner of the last hour" by offering tools traders need to make fast, informed decisions.

MARKETING TACTICS

This campaign provided the platform to create the awareness and buzz to take Ameritrade to the next level. Each channel (Online, DRTV, OOH, and PR) performed a different role in order to assist account generation and increase awareness. The media strategy capitalized on the unique behavior and media consumption of the active trader during the last market hour of the trading day. The integrated plan provided ownership of iconic financial media properties both online and in television from 3 to 4 p.m. (EST), allowing Ameritrade to convey the campaign

EXHIBIT 2-6

Ameritrade Last Market Hour Campaign Elements

CASE STUDY: **Ameritrade Last Market Hour** *(continued)*

---

message at a time when it was most relevant. The majority (95 percent) of media weight was allocated to Online and TV—the two media outlets that traders look to most during the waning hours of the market for real-time information.

Within the Online space, partnerships with both Yahoo! Finance and CBS Marketwatch created integrated and innovative online creative, resulting in branded clocks that appeared on these respective Web sites with a countdown to market close.

The campaign promoted a special offer during the final trading hour. In addition to 25 free trades, customers who signed up for an Ameritrade account received a free PalmOne Tungsten T3 ($399 value) with the alarm set to 3 p.m. to mark the start of the final trading hour of the day.

CREATIVE STRATEGY

The creative strategy was an integrated effort across various channels. The message challenged active traders to think about what they could accomplish in the last hour of a trading day. It was communicated in the context the active trader would consult during the last market hour. In addition, a strong incentive offer (free PalmOne Tungsten T3 plus 25 free Internet equity trades) was packaged with this program (Exhibit 2–6).

RESULTS

A brand-tracking study, URLs, and 800 numbers were used to measure results. The campaign generated over 50 percent more account openings than originally projected. These accounts were the higher-value accounts. The delivered cost-per-account was 35 percent lower than projections. Cost-per-response for the Television program was 97 percent lower than historic results for that channel. Per the communication objective, brand-tracking results for the integrated campaign showed that Ameritrade became more relevant and top-of-mind in the life of the active trader. Unaided awareness of Ameritrade improved by 54 percent against its core target, those who execute 10 or more transactions. Ameritrade also experienced a significant lift in brand favorability of 30 percent

---

PILOT PROJECT The Message Strategy Brief is one of the most heavily used tools at Jacobs & Clevenger. No creative work is ever started without the elements of the brief being completed and thoroughly discussed by the account and creative teams.

Using the Ameritrade case study, see if you can fill out each element of the Message Strategy Brief to better understand how Ameritrade arrived at their decisions.

Once you have filled out the form, see if there are other paths that could be taken. Describe one such path, and explain how you believe it improves upon what was described in the case study.

Key Points

▶ Planning helps an organization remain on track, stay up-to-date with emerging technologies, and optimize its unique resources. All plans need to be reviewed annually, even quarterly, and revisions should be made as external and internal factors change.

▶ To attract outside investors or financing, the business plan describes the key concepts of the business, establishes that there is a market for its products and services, outlines the organizational structure, and includes financial projections for three years. Its job is to persuade investors that they will recoup their investment.

▶ The strategic plan provides a blueprint of short- and long-term activities, strategies, and work plans developed after considering external threats and opportunities and internal strengths and weaknesses.

▶ The multichannel direct marketing plan is strategic and tactical. It estimates the value of prospects, customers, and segments to determine the right investment strategies for each group, outlines measurable goals and objectives, and tells how the organization will compete.

▶ The elements of all three types of plans are linked. The financial projections contained in a business plan are based on the assumptions made in the marketing plan. The marketing plan sets out where, how, and when promotional expenditures will be made, based on the expected level of sales. Some elements in the direct marketing plan are simply reframed from the strategic or business plan. The synergy between the plans increases when members of an organization ask the same questions over and over again, and arrive at the same answers.

THE IMPACT OF
DATABASES

In the 19th century, shopkeepers pursued a highly personal, "customer-centric" approach. Small shopkeepers memorized the preferences of their best customers. As their customer base grew, they kept written records of the size, color, and merchandise that their customers purchased. They maintained historical records of when customers bought, how often they bought, and how much they spent.

Today's successful companies still apply a "customer-centric" approach, maintaining information on transactions, behaviors, and individual information on their customers. This is driven by technology that allows organizations to identify and differentiate, interact with, and create customized communications for millions of customers.

Skillfully used, technology creates the impression that goods or services are offered specifically for a specific customer's consideration. The truth is that customers are rarely individually identified. They are aggregated, then broken down into increasingly smaller groups that share similar behaviors, attitudes, demographics, and/or lifestyles. These elements are analyzed individually or combined to identify propensities for product demand, purchase, or defection. Once analyzed or combined, these elements can help organizations identify customer segments that can have remarkably different results. Customers that have the greatest value to an organization can be differentiated from those with a lesser value or potential. Customers with different needs can be identified so that promotions, offers, even products can be tailored to their specific needs. And customers who make major purchases can be acknowledged with thank-you letters, special offers, incentives, and other communications designed to increase customer loyalty.

The knowledge that enables an organization to accomplish these goals is contained in a database—the heart of customer-centric strategies.

Organizations use databases for a variety of operational purposes. This includes order entry, billing, inventory management, and customer service. This chapter will focus on marketing databases—databases created to support marketing business processes.

Marketing databases are essential to 21st century marketing. The terms *direct marketing* and *database marketing* have often been used synonymously. Many companies have marketing databases but don't consider themselves users of direct marketing. Consumer goods companies use their databases for promotion programs. Stockbrokers use marketing databases for prospecting, cross-selling, and up-selling. Semantics aren't important. Marketing databases enable the use of the tools and techniques of direct marketing. So long as these tools are carefully and profitably applied, companies can be successful.

Marketing databases are important to organizations that can no longer personally know their customers. They provide organizations with the customer information necessary to support decisions that can help reduce the inherent risk in marketing programs. Marketing databases allow organizations to serve customers as individuals, creating ongoing dialogues to customize the relationships between marketer and customer.

There is no standard or "right" procedure for developing a marketing database. A marketing database is a customized application. Its development must take many variables into consideration. It requires a complex group of inputs from promotions, external data, and internal systems (See Exhibit 3–1).

These databases can be created using off-the-shelf solutions, but they must be configured and integrated into the systems of users. Many vendors offer marketing database systems that run on mainframe computers, client server networks, or on PCs. Some are meant to stand alone, some to extract data from legacy systems (large computer systems that remain from a previous generation and time), or run with Internet applications.

Which system to select depends on a business's organizational structure, culture, and way of doing business. The number of records to be stored will impact the choice of a database. The kinds of marketing programs (e.g., brand building, promotion, direct mail, Internet) will impact database needs. The size, capabilities, and empowerment of the marketing staff are drivers for the choice of a marketing database. Most importantly, the sources of data will shape an organization's database needs.

The Internet has created a virtual ocean of data for marketers to collect and try to make sense of. Activity on Web sites, e-mail programs, search, and inquiries left many marketers unprepared and unable to take advantage of this rich new data source. Add that to contact center, sales force activity, customer service, and information still stored in a host of operational systems (e.g., billing systems, fulfillment, etc.), and it is easy to see why marketers often have trouble synchronizing the information on databases within their firms. For many organizations, the goal of a "360-degree view of customers" or a "single customer view" remains elusive.

Every organization has its own needs that shape its unique marketing database. We will look at some of those factors in this chapter. Most important, we will look at how to *use* the information stored in a database.

EXHIBIT 3–1

A Marketing Database System

A marketing database helps build customer relationships by capturing historical and behavioral data from an organization's marketing activities. Increasingly, information is a strategic resource, and databases are used to integrate the breadth of an organization's activities. Information can be used to drive product, channel, and marketing communications programs.

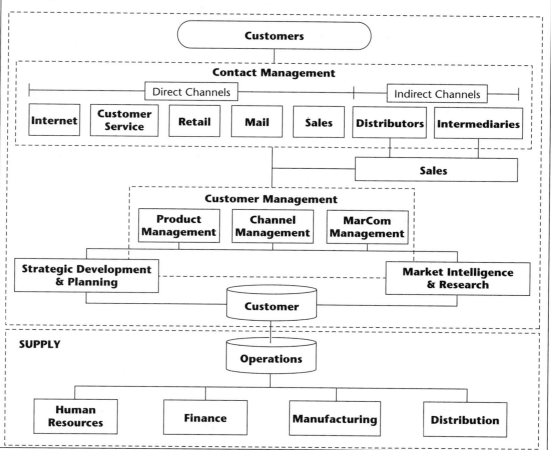

What Is a Database?

In its simplest form, a database is a list. A card catalog could be considered a simple database sorted in alphabetical order, indexed by last name, and randomly accessed. At the other end of the spectrum, a database is an engine that can link a virtually unlimited assortment of characteristics or variables together in a dynamic array.

The most common kinds of databases are "flat file" and "relational."

Flat-File Database

A flat-file database is a simple list that is sorted in one sequential order, most likely in customer number sequence. Each customer record must be kept in the same format. It would probably include a customer number, last name, ZIP code, and phone number indexes.

Because information is retrieved sequentially, as a flat-file database grows, it takes longer to run through the entire sequence in order to retrieve information. A flat-file database is useful for storing information that does not need to be accessed quickly in order for customers to place an order by phone or to check its status on the Internet. It also can be used to store information on promotional events for later analysis, modeling, or future promotions.

The flat-file approach becomes cumbersome when customer characteristics in addition to name, address, city, state, ZIP, etc., are added. Marketers often add dozens—even hundreds—of customer variables related to behavior, demographics, and lifestyles. These variables, used mainly for marketing or financial analysis, are often maintained in secondary files called tables. The order processing system doesn't have to wade through this data as a customer attempts to place an order.

Relational Database

Secondary files are linked by a duplicate variable in each table (e.g., a customer ID number). Each table can have its own format. When these files are put into linked tables (a table is data put into rows and columns, like a spreadsheet), and placed within a larger database structure, it is called a "relational" database (See Exhibit 3–2 for further details).

The practice of Customer Relationship Management (CRM) requires sophisticated database systems that help marketers to gain insight into customer behaviors, drive multichannel campaigns based on customer preferences, and track customer interactions across traditional and E-business initiates. A system designed to support quarterly mailings for a small business won't need the same level of sophistication, but may result in a significant return on investment for the organization. A rudimentary knowledge of computers and information processing is helpful in assessing an organization's needs.

Sources of Information

Most of the information needed to begin a customer database is readily available within an organization. Accounting records, shipping and fulfillment records, service reports, inquiries, warranty cards, and survey research results can all yield valuable marketing information (See Exhibit 3–3).

But just because the information is there does not automatically qualify it for entry into a marketing database. Some information is unnecessary; other information is too expensive to acquire. A guideline to follow is this: collect the relevant data

EXHIBIT 3–2

Relational Database

A relational database structure reduces processing time by having a single element in a table relate to a single element in another table. While information in the tables can be extensive, only the information that "relates" is used in processing. This example shows a business-to-business database.

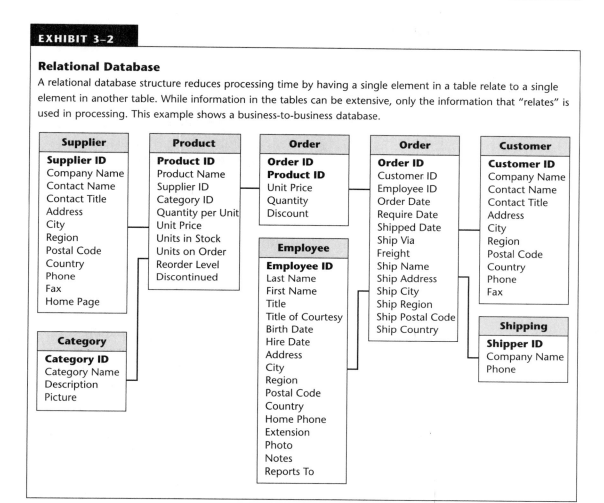

you think you'll need to know . . . and no more. Usually this will be information necessary to better understand a prospect's or customer's individual needs, better assess their possible value, or identify their propensity for future response. A good tool for this, shown in Exhibit 3–4, is Google's search engine, which contains large, diverse searchable databases that are either proprietary or contractual.

Many kinds of data are stored on a marketing database. For companies selling direct, the most useful information is historical purchase data: the first date and all following date(s) of activity; the dollar amounts of each purchase; and products purchased (recency, frequency, monetary, and type of product purchased).

Promotion history adds information on customer behavior that can also be used to improve future programs. Maintaining a record of the campaigns, offers, or types of promotions that a customer has responded to adds information that can be used to segment customer groups.

EXHIBIT 3–3

Types of Data

Both consumer and business databases usually combine internal and external data, but the sources and types of data vary.

Internal Data (Customer)	External Data
• Purchases	• Address (street, telephone, e-mail)
• Customer transactions	• Household
• Amount spent	• Demographics
• Transaction dates	• Socioeconomic data
• Promotion history	• Lifestyle psychographics
• Customer services	• Firmographics technographics
• Profitability	(Business data)
• Lifetime value	• Geo-demographics

Customer data is often limited to name, address, city, state, and ZIP code. To give a clearer picture of customers, demographic and lifestyle data can be appended to a database: age, income, gender, marital status, home value, presence of children, education, hobbies, interests, and other kinds of information. Demographic and lifestyle data often close the loop on customer knowledge.

A large credit card company was designing a marketing database. Its records contained only the merchant number, date, and amount of a purchase, not what was purchased with their card. The records indicated if the customer bought from a major vendor like an airline or from a chain store like Kmart or Pizza Hut. Instead of trying to discover more about customer buying behavior, it appended data to each record, adding more than 250 individual-level variables like type of car, age, income, etc. While appending data was an important element for identifying the heaviest users and for developing programs for the future, it would have been far better for the company to take what it did know about customer behavior (even if it took some creativity to decipher).

Attitudinal data—data on brands, category usage, purchase motivators, purchases barriers, customer satisfaction, etc.—can help an organization leverage the equity they have built with customers and determine new segmentation strategies. When gleaned from surveys or other research and added to demographic data, it can be a powerful tool for identifying loyal customers, swing users, or potential changers.

Business and industrial databases require unique data. Customers are often not the end-user, but rather a buying authority. It is important to capture multiple names within a company so that decision makers, decision influencers, and buying authorities can be tracked. In addition, relevant data for databases include North American Industry Classification System (NAICS), headquarters or branch office, revenues,

EXHIBIT 3–4

Google Databases, Features, and Shortcuts and Equivalents in Other Major Search Engines

Searchable Databases (Proprietary or Contractual)

	Google	Yahoo!	Teoma/Ask Jeeves
Where to find	www.google.com	search.yahoo.com	static.wc.ask.com/docs/announcements/searchsmarter.html
Web pages	• 4.2+ billion (1 billion not indexed)	• 3+ billion	• About 1 billion (in Teoma)
Directory	• 1.5+ million	• 2 million	• No equivalent
Images	• 800+ million	• Unspecified "millions"	• "Pictures" from PicSearch.com
News	• 4,500 sources	• 7,000 sources	• From Moreover.com
Shopping and products	• **Froogle:** Web pages + merchant-supplied catalogs and info	• **Products:** Search, browse, compare, set price limits	• **Products:** from PriceGrabber.com
	• **Catalogs:** scanned and uploaded catalogs		
Local businesses and services	• **Local search:** Web pages + yellow pages; with maps, proximity choices Type product and U.S. city or Zip code: **cameras berkeley**	• **Yellow pages** closest equivalent	• No equivalent
	• **bphonebook: name city**		
Groups	• **Groups:** Usenet newsgroups since 1981 plus new content	• **groups.yahoo.com:** Create or join existing groups	• No equivalent
	• **Groups2:** Create new groups		

Source: UC Berkeley Teaching Library.

number of employees, length of time in business, socioeconomic information about the organization's location, and even data about the personality of individual buyers.

Today's technology encourages the collection of vast quantities of data—but what data a database should include depends entirely on its future value in use. "Nice to know" or "We may need that somewhere down the line" are not valid reasons for accumulating data. Information costs money and that cost must return a value.

Information is a perishable commodity. Not only does the degree of customer activity (or inactivity) fluctuate, but the people and organizations comprising a database are far from static. Customers' demographics change as they go through various life stages or raise families. Business buyers change jobs, within as well as between organizations. Customers' attitudes and preferences change. They move. They no longer have the need for a category (e.g. baby products). In 12 months, 20 percent of an average customer list could change addresses.

Such volatility demonstrates the importance of adequate mailing list maintenance. It demonstrates, too, that customer lists that are mailed to and maintained religiously have greater deliverability value to the direct marketer than do lists compiled without data qualification, from directories or rosters.

Data about customers and their transactions must be kept up to date. While monthly, then weekly updates were once the norm, many of today's databases are updated many times a day. Marketers need to be constantly vigilant, and be concerned with maintenance as well as with ongoing updating of transactions and other data contained within each customer record. Data hygiene, address standardization, and National Change of Address information helps to reduce duplications, ensure that addresses are deliverable, and helps marketers keep track of their customers.

Marketers must often choose between a simple database and simple analysis. Experience shows that the greatest success comes from continuously expanding the variables in a database. Adding appended and census variables does not mean that recency won't be the most powerful and predictive variable. But if the variables are not added in, a marketer may never know.

Database Marketing and Customer Relationships

The first sale to a newly acquired customer is but a forerunner of additional sales to that customer in the future. Additional sales are key to the customer relationship marketing process. Because it costs far less to keep a customer than to acquire a new one, increasing numbers of companies are focusing extensive resources on customer loyalty, seeking to retain customers through programs and incentives driven by their marketing database.

From the outset, customers are not homogeneous. Their one common characteristic is the relationship or affinity they form with companies they favor with their business—and often their continued loyalty. When customers perpetuate such relationships, they expect in return to receive quality, value, and service. Organizations, in turn, seek customer loyalty in the hope of cementing the relationship and keep customers coming back.

Relationships or affinities with customers can be developed to such a degree that loyal customers trust and buy the company's brands above all competitive offerings. Affinity and good customer relationships extend their value, too, well beyond the first sale . . . to cross-selling of unrelated products/services, even from unrelated organizations. The power of the marketing database makes all of this, and more, possible.

Defining an organization's best customers is often not easy. Many organizations identify the customers that purchase the most as the most valuable. Other organizations identify their most profitable customers as their best customers. As few as 10 percent of an organization's customers contribute 90 percent of its profits. For a start-up business, it may be the most growable customers that are most valuable. It is different and unique for each business.

A second group of core customers, with average profitability, make up the largest group of customers. A final group of marginal buyers, often infrequent or high-maintenance customers, often provide little or no profit (See Exhibit 3–5).

Yet many organizations strive to retain money-losing clients. These "marquee clients" may give the organization credibility even as they drain profitability. Some large advertising agencies, for example, keep their largest and least profitable clients because they are household names or long-time clients who provide high visibility in local markets, assignments in a prestigious category, or unique opportunities for creativity.

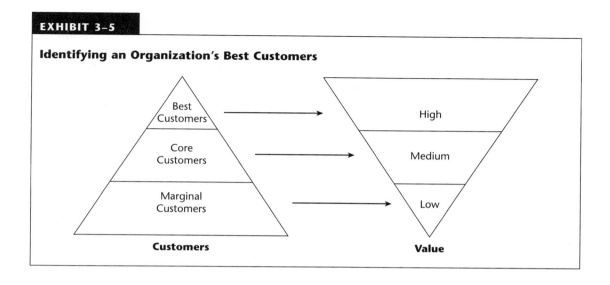

EXHIBIT 3–5

Identifying an Organization's Best Customers

Such behavior may seem illogical, but it isn't uncommon. What often seems illogical is that few organizations develop retention programs that distinguish their most profitable customers from their least profitable customers.

The first step in leveraging an organization's core group of loyal and profitable customers is to understand their motivations. Some customers are easily predictable, preferring long-term, stable relationships. Other customers may spend more, pay their bills more promptly, or require less maintenance. Others may value the organization's products or services over all others. These different groups make up an organization's best customers, and the more of them an organization can acquire and keep, the more profitable they will be.

There are various kinds of databases; among them are object databases, object-relational databases, spatial databases, OLAP databases, and XML databases.

Customer Relationships and Lifetime Value (LTV)

In the past, it was difficult to evaluate how well a company nurtured its customer relationships. Though businesses knew that the number of customers increased or decreased, that advertising attracted some new customers, or that competitors took away others, there were few ways of knowing which customers came or went, or why.

But database technology has changed that. An organization can at last identify its loyal customers, its repeat purchasers, and its one-time-only "triers," especially within well-defined market segments. Moreover, marketers can now trace each customer's actions and transactions. This ability makes customers a significant—and measurable—asset like buildings, equipment, inventory, and accounts receivable.

Customers are a source of future revenues and future profits which can go well beyond recovering the initial costs of acquiring these customers through selling, advertising, and other sales promotions. However, generally accepted accounting principles actually hide the value of customers on a line on balance sheets called "goodwill." The investments in programs to reduce customer defections and improve customer loyalty are written off as an expense rather than an investment that can have a long-term impact on profits. When the high costs of creating a marketing database are simply seen as an expense, they easily fall victim to marketing budget cuts. When seen as part of a customer loyalty effort, the impact of marketing databases is no longer hidden.

The concept of lifetime value of a customer (LTV), adopted long ago by mail-order firms to guide marketing decision making, also applies to the value of the database. More companies began adopting the LTV concept after the Supreme Court ruled in favor of a New Jersey newspaper that claimed depreciation deduction for its acquisition of a paid-subscriber customer list as part of a sale transaction. In reaching its decision, the Court rejected the IRS argument that customer lists are a form of goodwill and therefore never depreciable.

Direct marketers truly appreciate LTV when they engage in both continuity selling and cross-selling, and when they develop a database of customers. The LTV approach, too, is ideally suited to determining the market value of an enterprise in cases where an acquisition or a sale is contemplated. Since such an asset valuation of a database reflects anticipated future performance, it can be a better gauge of value than the commonly used multiples of sales or profits. The arithmetic involved in determining LTV is calculated in Chapter 22, "Mathematics of Direct Marketing."

Accessing Data Through Data Warehouses and Data Marts

All database systems have trade-offs. One of those trade-offs is in ease of access to data. Marketers usually ask for such access to get closer to answers about customers, segments, and program results. This usually requires significant time and expense, including vendor evaluation, hardware, and software implementation. Often marketers are able to get slick point-and-click query tools that require days or weeks of staff training, only to find that this is not what they were looking for.

Most databases maintain data as rows and columns of numbers and words. Queries to the database return data in the same way. In addition, queries must be constructed carefully to return the information that marketers are really looking for. What marketers would prefer is to ask questions and get answers in the form of charts, graphs, and maps.

Decision Support Systems and Executive Information Systems (EIS) provide access that is quick and easy to use, but the trade-off here is that charts and graphs must often be pre-programmed to some degree. Quick count engines are another technology for doing data analysis and extraction. These tools often feed into an EIS system but reduce the limits on ad-hoc queries and reports or questions of the database that allow for unlimited exploration.

Many large organizations have data helpful to marketing locked up in systems designed for such operational purposes as order entry, purchasing, logistics, or transaction processing. These so-called *legacy systems* are often added at different times, created on different hardware platforms, and run software optimized for the purpose of that system.

Legacy systems offer a challenge to marketers. While they contain information that may be important for marketing, this information is not easily accessible. Information from multiple systems simply multiplies the problem.

One solution to this problem is the *data warehouse*—a storage facility that takes data from a number of transaction systems and brings it together into a central repository. The job of the data warehouse is to create a set of standardized fields for all of the different data elements in the various legacy systems.

A data warehouse is often designed for a whole host of corporate needs and departments. A separate system can house all the customer and transaction data along with accounting, manufacturing, and any number of other data. Data warehouses can make it easier to query and report data from multiple transaction processing systems and external data sources.

The data warehouse is a good data storage and reporting system, but it is not easy or flexible to use for heavy data processing or modeling. A better solution is to extract information from the data warehouse and put it into a *data mart*, a database system designed for a smaller number of users with more specialized data uses. The warehouse feeds relatively raw data into the mart—leaving out accounting data, perhaps, but including those data fields that marketing is genuinely interested in. Inside a data mart, marketing can use the analysis tools best suited to specialized tasks. Data can be summarized to suit need and new variables can be created or appended (bought from outside data providers and added to the customer records).

Although marketing databases have come a long way, there is no simple way to gain access to all the data necessary to make decisions. There is a great demand to call upon specialists who are trained in database design, execution, and analysis and can work hand-in-glove with marketing departments. The explosion of data created by the growth of the Internet has added even more demand for such individuals. Anyone embarking on a database project would be wise to work with specialists either inside or outside of their firms.

Using Data Mining to Make Decisions

Many marketers busy themselves looking at their data in an almost endless process of discovery. Data is infinite; that is, there are an infinite number of variables that can be gathered about any particular item or event. Data is also historical. It is a collection of facts about events that have already transpired. At the same time, decisions are finite and must be made in time.

When tracking history, there is always a gap between yesterday and tomorrow. There is always something else that can be taken into consideration. This means that no matter how much data you have, there is never enough data to make a decision. But, marketers must make decisions in order to move their businesses forward.

The growth of the Internet has exacerbated this quandary. Organizations with busy Web sites can capture millions of pieces of data about users each day. So can retail marketers, consumer goods companies, and many other users. Kraft Foods, for example, has captured information on more than 30 million respondents to promotional offers. Large data sets such as these are difficult to maintain but even more difficult to gain knowledge from. That's why marketers who are swimming in data need tools that let them use the right data to make decisions that impact the bottom line.

Data mining is a process for discovering patterns and trends in large database sets to find useful decision-making information. There are a number of data mining tools and techniques. Some are used to identify significant relationships that exist among variables. Such tools are useful when there are many possible relationships. For instance, a packaged goods company may track up to 200 variables about each customer on its file. There are many possible ways of combining 200 variables. A data mining application can quickly help recognize which patterns of relationships among the variables are significant. Once these relationships are identified, other types of tools are then used to understand the nature of the relationships.

There is no one best data mining technique; different techniques work better with different types of data. The most common are Cluster Analysis, Market Basket Analysis, and Neural Networks.

Cluster Analysis

Cluster analysis is a data reduction technique that groups variables based on similar data characteristics. It is useful for segmenting customer groups based on demographic, financial, or purchase behavior characteristics. A bank used cluster analysis to identify three groups of customers based on the types of accounts they had opened. The first group, labeled "General Customers," opened equal percentages of accounts of all types. The second group, "Long-term Customers," opened more mortgages, investment accounts, home improvement loans, and CDs and had a higher lifetime value and a longer customer lifecycle. The third group, "Short-term Customers," opened more checking and savings accounts and personal loans. They had a lower lifetime value and were more likely to switch accounts or institutions. Once data from the cluster analysis helped the bank identify differences in behavior, especially attrition, between the groups, it was able to treat each segment differently, creating specific offers and promotions for each group and adjusting the promotional budget for each group.

Market Basket Analysis

Market basket analysis is one of the most common data mining techniques. Named for the cart that customers use while shopping, its purpose is to determine what products or services customers purchase together.

Instead of making marketers guess what customers should logically buy together, market basket analysis lets customer sales data speak for itself. Developed as a means for retail marketers to interpret checkout scanner data, market basket analysis can be used to help stores place products that are frequently purchased together in the same area. A mail-order company, cataloger, or E-commerce company can use market basket analysis to determine the layout of a catalog, Web site, or order form. Direct marketers can use the results to determine what new products to offer their prior customers or which products to offer as an add-on when customers call or complete an online transaction.

Some related products are obvious. It's hard to imagine a fast-food restaurant failing to ask, "Would you like fries with your order?" Other associations are not so obvious. For example, a company that sells wine direct learned that buyers of champagne were likely to add glassware, chocolates, or gift items to their order. Buyers of California wines would often add other California wines to their orders. Red wine buyers were more likely to take advantage of full case discounts. By matching offers to various behaviors, the company was able to substantially increase sales.

Neural Networks

Neural networks are used to discover and predict relationships in the data. Unlike traditional statistical modeling, neural networks can be "trained" to discover relationships that cannot be described with linear algebra and can often compensate for low-quality data. Neural networks are the ultimate black box. They build complex formulas that are nearly impossible to decipher, but seem to work in many cases. They are certainly worth testing where large amounts of data exist.

Neural networks can effectively reveal what elements of a company's total offering affect customer satisfaction. One midwestern utility company used neural networks to analyze customer satisfaction surveys in order to identify the specific service elements that had the greatest impact on overall customer satisfaction and to measure how those elements changed over a period of time. This information was then used to target areas of improvement that could lead to increased customer satisfaction ratings.

Because the utility was going through deregulation, it would face real competition for the first time. Hot summers and an aging power grid had given the utility a dubious reputation with customers. In order to remain competitive, the utility conducted a series of surveys the year before restructuring was to take place.

Neural networks were chosen to analyze the answers because of their ability to measure multiple and complex interactions between variables. A model was created that compared answers about various facets of customer service, perceptions of the company and its concern for the community, and customer demographics over time. Many questions had multiple levels of response. The neural network was able to discern between different overall ratings of satisfaction by customers, and key predictors of satisfaction were extracted from the models.

This analysis revealed key elements of service that customers found most important. It identified demographic segments that were most and least likely to be satisfied by company efforts. And it helped determine the most effective message delivery channels for reaching customers. This important information was used by marketing communication decision makers to develop direct marketing strategies for improving customer satisfaction and retention.

Taking Your Database Global

Creating a database for global use, particularly on the Internet, adds many complications.

A look at Web sites from companies like Cisco Systems, Microsoft, National Semiconductor, and Outpost.com shows the flags of many countries. Often, these large companies accept and ship orders to customers around the globe. Information on these customers is collected and stored in a marketing database.

To accommodate this data, a number of changes must be made. Name fields must be enlarged as it is common in some countries to use a maternal family name as well as a paternal family name. One or more middle names are quite common in some countries, as are longer names than those used in the United States. Character sets must be added to accommodate language differences. Languages that share Roman characters with English often use different accent marks and punctuation. Spelling the name of customers properly is a worldwide courtesy.

Postal and address coding is another issue. According to the Universal Postal Union, a specialized institution of the United Nations that regulates postal conventions in its 190 member countries, only 69 countries, including the United States, have sophisticated postal delivery systems. Of those, only about 30 use street names for identifying addresses.

International mail codes (e.g., in the United States, the five- or nine-digit ZIP code) come in various lengths, can have different placement within an address, and can be numeric, alpha, or alphanumeric. Databases that capture international data must be flexible and designed with the needs of different countries in mind.

Privacy Rules and Regulations

While marketing databases create benefits for both consumers and organizations by reducing wasted promotion, increasing targeted products/services, and personalizing customer service, their use also raises privacy concerns. These concerns collide when consumers' expectations of privacy conflict with what organizations believe are fair commercial uses of personal information.

Marketers in the United States prefer to apply self-regulation to balance the scales. Nevertheless, marketers must be aware and comply with a myriad of legislation regarding the use of specific kinds of personal data, including financial data (Gramm-Leach-Bliley Act), health data (Health Insurance Portability and Accountability Act or HIPAA), telephone (Federal Do Not Call); e-mail (Can Spam), etc. Government has moved from a regulatory to an enforcement posture. The number of laws, their breadth, and the velocity of their implementation means that marketers must be ever vigilant to monitor their compliance.

The security of data is a growing issue. Marketers do all they can to maintain personal data as securely as possible. Recent high-profile data security breaches have given privacy advocates ammunition to demand that data aggregators that benefit by collecting and selling personal data, be forced to shoulder a greater share of the risks.

This is continuing to fuel concerns among consumers. In a consumer study titled "Securing the Trust in Your Brand," by the CMO Council, a group representing 2,200 chief marketing officers worldwide, consumer security ranked fourth behind product quality, customer service, and company ethics in terms of driving sales.

The study found that 43 percent of American consumers have abandoned a transaction because of a security concern, usually when a marketer asked for information they don't want to reveal. Fifty-nine percent of respondents answered that after they became aware of a security breach they would "strongly consider" or "definitely" stop doing business with an organization.

The study, conducted in June 2006, was done in both the United States and Europe. The results indicated that U.S. consumers were more worried about identity theft and fraud than terrorism and personal safety. European consumers ranked family safety higher.

This could be because European Union (EU) data rules are very stringent. The EU Data Protection Directive requires that member states protect the "right to privacy with respect to the processing of personal data." It requires that EU member countries enact legislation requiring that online and offline data is:

- Processed fairly and lawfully

- Collected and possessed for specified, explicit, legitimate purposes

- Accurate and kept current

- Kept no longer than deemed necessary to fulfill the stated purpose

Users are given the explicit right to access information, correct or block inaccuracies, and object to the information's use. An individual's consent is required to collect sensitive information (e.g., race, religion, etc.), and these rules forbid the transfer of personal data to any country outside the EU that does not guarantee similar safeguards are in place. This view of privacy is different than in the United States.

U.S. companies that do business within the EU are subject to these rules for data collected within the EU, according to Peter Swire, a law professor at Ohio State University. Swire notes that an airline reservations system was prohibited in one European country from transferring personal data to the United States, such as a passenger's preference for a kosher meal because that might infer that he or she is Jewish.

CASE STUDY: China Post: Building a National Database

Contributed by Ron Jacobs.

BACKGROUND

For decades, China was veiled in mystery to the outside world. But that image has shifted dramatically in recent years. China is now a land in transition, and as this nation looks to the West, Chinese consumer values have changed with the times.

Today's Chinese consumer is still struggling with new issues. The state no longer provides daily sustenance, which leads to savings anxiety. Wealth is unprotected, and there are few property rights protections. This means the Chinese consumer needs to project status, but keep a low profile. Aspirations must seem attainable.

In the midst of this turbulent emerging marketplace, China Post sought to create the "Name and Address Database," the most comprehensive in China. This was certainly no small undertaking, when one considers China's population numbers over 1.3 billion people.

CHALLENGE

In order to have an effective and actionable database, China Post needed to:
- Be able to ensure delivery
- Reach the full market
- Have appropriate detail about the target to ensure the right profile
- Have fresh enough data to be able to clearly identify when someone is interested

These challenges become infinitely more complex when we dive down to the street level. This is where China reveals unique characteristics that could confound any data provider. In fact, the street profile in China varies by each dwelling.

The Chinese Street Profile reveals:
- Different characteristics
- Houses and offices mixed
- Migrants, families, workers
- Income range: $1K to $150K
- Car to bike to public transport
- Mixed by province origin
- Mixed education levels

By contrast, Western geographic lists offer similar customers living in similar areas, grouped by hundreds of households. These tallies can often be obtained from surveys and census data.

China needed to pinpoint similar customers by dwelling type, making the detail of the Chinese residence itself of the utmost importance. With data capture this complex and diversified, only China Post could truly deliver this database.

SOLUTION

In order to get accurate data, China Post collected survey data through each postman. The database covers (June 2005) 43 percent of all cities in China and 31 provinces. The focus of the data is on economically developed areas. As a result, the China Post Name and Address Database now contains 100 million records.

The addresses in the database have descriptions that allow marketers to target unique groups of people. China Post has 135 unique types of housing data that can be used to select customers. Each one

CASE STUDY: China Post: Building a National Database *(continued)*

affords a different profile that could be of interest to marketers. These characteristics can:

- Be used by themselves for mailings
- Be used in conjunction with the other national data
- Add value to local data for mailings today

Valuable address detail provides an even richer level of targeting. Attached to the address detail is a growing pool of accurate demographic and lifestyle data. This data can be used in conjunction with the address detail to further improve the targeting (Exhibits 3–6, 3–7).

The name and address data can be appended to marketer's customer data. This allows marketers to match records between all lists to provide a uniform data set, which is essential in de-duplicating lists, matching lists, and scoring.

APPLICATION

The China Post database was put to the test when it was utilized to develop a campaign for Bank of China Credit Cards. The target market was a high-income, inner-city professional. The China Post database allowed Bank of China to:

- Choose high-quality buildings and communities for income
- Choose only large communities for high-income professionals
- Choose residential to target individuals
- Use postcodes, county, and city to target the most affluent geographies

---

EXHIBIT 3–6

The Value of Address Detail

Building Type		Property of Building	Community Quality	Building Character	Remittance	Subscriptions	Organization	Your Attributes
High Rise	Mid Rise	High Quality	High Quality	Residential	Value	Hobby	Type	1
Low Rise	Town House	Medium Quality	Medium Quality	Office	Demographics	Sex	Employees	2
Country House		Low Quality	Low Quality	Mixed	ID	Interest	Capital & Profit	3

EXHIBIT 3–7

Using Residential Detail for a National Campaign
Developing a Campaign for Bank Of China Credit Cards

Building Type		Property of Building	Community Quality	Building Character	County	City	Postcode
High Rise	Maid Rise	High Quality	High Quality	Residential	Type 1	Rural	Emerging
Low Rise	Town House	Medium Quality	Medium Quality	Office	Type 2	Town	Developing
Country house		Low Quality	Low Quality	Mixed	Type 3	Major	Tier 1

CASE STUDY: China Post: Building a National Database *(continued)*

RESULTS

The Name and Address Database is spurring growth of the Chinese direct mail marketplace.

It is important to note that China is certainly not in a unique situation among developing markets. Databases and mailing lists are key to growth of any consumer and business direct marketing.

Where no private players exist, an organization such as China Post must take the lead. The China Post example shows that private and public partnerships can be created to help a new marketplace grow.

Most businesses market either to businesses or to consumers. This changes the kind of data each kind of organization will need to maintain. Multichannel marketers add the need to include street addresses as well as e-mail or other electronic addresses.

Define the main differences in building a marketing database for consumers versus businesses. Think in terms of the sources of this data, the differences in data fields, and the kinds of information that are specific to maintaining information about consumers versus businesses. Are the kinds of marketing programs done for consumers different from those for businesses? If so, what are the implications of that for a marketing database? And what of the need to include online addresses? How is this different for consumer versus business marketers?

Key Points

▶ Databases aggregate customers and break them down into increasingly smaller groups that share similar behaviors, attitudes, demographics, or lifestyles. Analyzing or combining these elements helps identify customer segments with similar needs so that promotions, offers, even products and services can be tailored to their needs.

▶ Look for customer database information in your organization's accounting records, shipping and fulfillment records, service reports, inquiries, warranty cards, and survey research results. Add historical purchase and promotion history, attitudinal data, and demographic information to segment customer groups. Steer away from data that is merely "nice to know" and seek information that returns a value.

▶ By combining data from a number of transaction systems, a data warehouse can make it easier to query and report data from multiple transactions processing systems and external data sources. For heavy data processing or modeling, extract information from the data warehouse and put it into a data mart that can summarize and analyze data and create or append new variables.

▶ Three data mining techniques—Cluster Analysis, Market Basket Analysis, and Neural Networks—can help marketers discover patterns and trends in large database sets to find useful decision-making information.

▶ Building a global database involves a host of considerations: larger name fields, additional character sets, address coding variations, international mail codes, and privacy laws that vary from country to country.

CONSUMER AND BUSINESS MAILING LISTS

Should we invest more in creating new customers or in building better relationships with our existing clientele?

This question is nearly impossible to answer.

If the program is mature, if there are a large number of customers, and if profit is the key focus, the common wisdom would argue for building better customer relationships. The tools and techniques of direct marketing are well used when targeting consumers or businesses where there is an established relationship. Results will be significantly greater and profits higher when customers are targeted. Even former buyers will respond better than individuals who have no previous experience with an organization.

But creating new customers is also essential.

To promote a new product or service or a new venture, or to thrive in the growth stage of a business, an organization needs to prospect for new customers. Even established organizations need new prospects to replenish their customer base. Successful customer retention programs don't keep 100 percent of customers. Maintaining a balance between customer and prospect marketing efforts is one of the keys to business success.

Many organizations rely upon direct mail for their main medium or as a support medium for their prospecting efforts. Mailing lists can help them target businesses or consumers, sell a product or service direct, generate a lead, drive traffic into an online or offline store, sell subscriptions, or persuade contributors. They may also use television, radio, print advertising, co-ops, the Internet, or other media to create new customers. They may even supplement with trade shows or events. However, if organizations use direct mail, they will likely need to use mailing lists. A thorough understanding of traditional list practices is a building block of direct marketing, and the goal of this chapter.

Mailing List Basics

Mailing lists are not sold but rented, typically for a one-time use. If after testing a portion of a list, the renting organization wants to re-mail or roll out the list (e.g., in continuation), it must pay an additional rental fee.

The list provider *seeds* the list with names that come back to it in order to monitor list usage. Companies that repeatedly violate the rental agreement soon find they are unable to rent lists from any organization. Seeding is a significant deterrent to abuse. Many organizations rent their lists. According to the Direct Marketing Association (DMA), the practice of making lists available for rental or exchange has remained consistent over the past few years. The number of names rented by companies has increased. Companies find it a significant additional revenue source. According to Worldata, Inc., the average lists rents for $120.92 per thousand but may cost $140 or more per thousand depending upon the number of names rented and the selection criteria (see Exhibit 4–1 for further information). The more responsive the names on the list, the more it costs and the more likely that the list will be rented frequently.

Specialty lists of hard-to-get names such as buyers of airplanes, sailboats, and exotic cars, small and large cap investors, and foreign lists may rent for a three to four times premium! The quality of the names and difficulty in acquiring them is always a major factor in list rental costs.

Hotline names also are rented at premium price. These are names with the most recent activity on file, typically defined as added within the last 90 days. It can be up to six months or a year depending upon how the list owner defines it. Hotline names remain a very popular category of names to rent.

An organization with a list of one million names may be able to rent every name on the list seven or more times a year. The average cost list is $120.92 per thousand,

---

EXHIBIT 4–1

Worldata's Average List Price for Mail and E-mail List in Cost per Thousands

Data list category	Average price July 2005	E-mail list category	Average price July 2005
Attendees / Members	$109.00	Business-to-Business	$281.00
Books & CD's	$123.00	Consumers	$175.00
Bus. Mags/Controlled	$141.00		
Bus. Mags/Paid Circ.	$139.00		
Bus. Merch. Buyers	$118.00		
Consumers Book Buyers	$ 95.00		
Consumer Magazines	$104.00		
Consumer Merch. Byrs	$ 99.00		
Databases/Masterfiles	$131.00		
Donor	$ 77.00		
Newsletters	$175.00		
Public Sector	$140.00		

Source: Worldata, Inc., 2006.

so turning the list seven times annually would generate gross revenue of $846,440. While the list owner might have to pay fees, commissions, and some processing costs, this list becomes incremental income to their business. It is easy to understand why organizations are involved in the practice of renting their list of customers or members. According to the DMA's 2006 annual report, revenue from list rentals increased 42 percent, to $73,790 from $51,981. This indicates that companies are still using lists to increase business.

Some organizations choose not to rent their lists. But even they will often exchange lists with other companies that have noncompetitive offers. Organizations usually exchange an even number of names. Some organizations won't exchange their hotline names or will only exchange names of former buyers. This dilutes the value of the exchange, but it still may be worth testing in categories where new names are difficult to acquire.

Types of Mailing Lists

There are three kinds of mailing lists: house lists, response lists, and compiled lists. Each type offers advantages but may have drawbacks. However, all lists must be maintained, kept up to date, to provide value or offer competitive advantage.

House Lists

House lists are simply the databases of an organization. Considered the key asset of any organization, they include current customers, former customers, and inquiries (i.e., prospects). Because the house list is so important, it must be maintained and updated constantly.

Each organization builds its house list to fit its unique needs. Records may be gleaned from a variety of internal sources, such as direct mail, phone, retail, or Internet transactions. A company may have more than one business unit and maintain purchase records separately or aggregate them. Even the definition of a customer varies from company to company.

The word "customer" usually refers to an "active" buyer. In mail-order companies this usually means someone who has purchased within the last 12 months. It is the same for contributors to causes. Subscribers to publications have finite expiration dates. They may be considered "active" and sent copies of the publication for as long as three months after the expiration date. Purchasers of long-life high-ticket items, such as computers or automobiles, may be considered active for the years that they own the product.

Although it also varies, former customers fall outside of an organization's definition of active. Former customers are valuable because they are more likely to purchase, subscribe, or contribute than prospects. The longer it has been since a transaction, the less likely it is that a former customer will purchase again. This is true in both the consumer and business markets. Recency of purchase, frequency of purchase, type of product purchased, and monetary value of transactions are clues to a customer's propensity to purchase again.

According to the USPS, about 14 percent of the nation's population moves every year, generating more than 45 million address changes. Frequent job changes are commonplace, house lists can age quickly. Publications will re-mail lapsed subscribers within six months of expiration. Most organizations continue to mail former customers for up to three years. It is different for every organization and/or industry.

Not all organizations maintain lists of inquiries or prospects. The benefit of prospect files is that they have indicated some interest in the products or services offered by the organization. It is more common to maintain prospect files in the business marketplace, where qualified leads are often promoted for up to a year after first being identified.

Response Lists

Response lists are the house lists of other organizations. They are made up of individuals with an identifiable product interest and a proven willingness to buy, subscribe, join, contribute, inquire, or otherwise respond to specific offers. Response lists are most often used in the consumer marketplace where customer files are larger than in the business market.

Response lists are made up of individuals who have exhibited a particular kind of behavior. They may have responded to a direct mail offer, a print ad, a broadcast commercial, via telephone, or on the Internet. Marketers have learned that previous behavior is the greatest predictor of future behavior. Someone who has responded by mail once is likely to do it again. Someone who has responded to an outbound telephone call is more likely to duplicate this action. And someone who has purchased a product from a certain category is more likely to purchase from that category again.

Response lists are popular because marketers can select lists where specific behaviors have been exhibited. While this is not a perfect science, it is clear that someone who has responded to a certain medium, a certain kind of offer (e.g., sweepstakes), or a particular product category is more likely to respond to similar future promotions than is someone where the knowledge of such behavior is absent.

Marketers try to match up previous behaviors with the kinds of behaviors they are trying to duplicate. Broad categories reflect this behavior. Response lists can be broken into a number of further categories. Among them are: Buyer, Attendee/Membership/Seminar, Donor, Credit Card Holder, and Merged Database lists.

Buyer Lists. These are lists of individuals who have purchased something direct, through a solo direct mail offer, a catalog, a print ad, a Web site, a short-form television commercial (30, 60, or 120 seconds in length), or an infomercial (10, 15, or 30 minutes in length).

Attendee/Membership/Seminar Lists. These are lists of individuals who have attended a conference, trade show, or industry event. The individuals on these lists are often extremely valuable. They often spend hundreds, even thousands, of dollars to increase their knowledge about specific subjects. Individuals on these lists are likely to respond to offers that closely match their identified fields of interest.

Subscription Lists. These are individuals who have subscribed to business or consumer publications or newsletters. There are two kinds of subscription lists: controlled circulation and paid circulation.

Controlled circulation publications, common in business, are free to qualified readers. To qualify, subscribers must fall into a certain professional or managerial category and certify that they are decision makers or influencers for products offered by advertisers in the publications. Proof is accomplished by completing and signing a subscription request form or "qualification card." Subscribers are asked to give their name, address, phone, job title, job function, size of company, and the types of products that they purchase. Typically, controlled circulation lists are selectable by all of these characteristics.

With paid circulation publications, subscribers pay a fee and are not required to provide information in addition to their name and address. Both business and consumer publications use this model. Paid publication titles often reach individuals with very specific interests. These lists can be highly responsive if the interests of subscribers are a good match for a product or service offered.

Donor Lists. Fund-raisers use donor lists because they contain the names of people who have contributed money to charities and nonprofit organizations. Political parties, special interest groups, religious assemblies, and cause-related organizations all use these lists. Knowing the source of names (direct mail, television, telephone, etc.) is important. When sending a request for contributions by mail, use direct-mail-solicited names.

Credit Card Holder Lists. These names are useful because most credit card solicitations are sent and responded to by mail and most direct offers require a credit card. Although credit cards seem ubiquitous, they are not. Active credit card users often fit a profile similar to direct mail buyers.

Merged Database Lists. This type of list includes the merged lists of companies that often won't rent their lists individually. Using the merged list simplifies the selection process because duplicate names are eliminated. Therefore, the list owner can offer the remaining names as a single, unduplicated list at a higher rental fee.

Reed Business Information, a publisher of qualified trade publications, aggregates its various lists. These databases allow users to reach a large portion of a specific market segment without having to track down many hard-to-find lists.

Reviewing your merge/purge report can help you determine how well or poorly a list will do. The process of elimination can:

• Help you in future list selections

• Determine if the list you received was what you ordered and is usable

Compiled Lists

Compiled lists are made up of individuals or companies without any previous indication of willingness to respond, but with some defined and identifiable characteristic(s) known as "segments or selects." These include demographics, psychographics, ZIP code, etc.

Compiled lists offer broad national coverage. Some pieces of demographic information are available on nearly every consumer, household, and business in the United States. Compiled lists are useful for retail, consumer goods, and business offers where reaching the right target group is more critical than knowing that they have previously responded to a direct-response offer. They can also be used to enhance or profile house files or are combined with response lists to add missing consumer demographic or business firmographic (e.g., business demographic) data.

There are three kinds of compiled lists: consumer compiled lists, consumer lifestyle enhanced lists, and business compiled lists.

Consumer Compiled Lists. Many consumer product marketers have developed clear pictures of their best customers. This picture may include demographics and psychographics, and may be limited to specific geographic areas. For example, an automobile manufacturer may have a clear demographic picture of the buyers of its brand. There may be differences among purchasers of different models of the brand (e.g., convertibles, family sedans, and sport utility vehicles). There might be differences in the popularity of each model in different geographical regions of the country. It is imperative for this marketer to reach the right target groups. Compiled lists are the only rented lists that would yield broad national or geographic penetration and pinpoint targeting (see Exhibit 4–2).

Consumer compiled lists are created from a number of different public and private sources. Name, address, and phone numbers are gleaned from telephone directories and credit bureau records. [Note: Credit bureau data may be used for name and address, but the Federal Trade Commission (FTC) forbids the use of private financial data on these files for marketing purposes.]

Additional information comes from other sources. Homeowner data (e.g., home value) is compiled from county property records. Driver's license and auto registration data is available from many states and added to the mix. Income and demographic information is derived from the U.S. Census Bureau's data and local

---

EXHIBIT 4–2

Consumer Compiled List Segments

Demographic data is compiled from public sources, while lifestyle information is usually compiled from surveys and other self-reported sources. Not all segments are available for every prospect. Choosing more segments gets you closer to your primary target market, but it also reduces the available universe.

Demographic

- Age
- Household Income
- Gender
- Marital Status
- Family Composition (e.g., presence of children, 0-1 people per Household, etc.)
- Dwelling Unit Type
  - Single Family Dwelling Unit (SFDU)
  - Multiple Unit Dwelling (MUD)

- Home Value
- Credit & Savings
- Occupation
- Education
- Mail/Phone Responsive
- Telephone Number
- Automobile Type

Lifestyle Interests

- Brand/Category Usage
- Ailments
- Financial/Stocks
- Household Income/Home Ownership
- Presence of Children
- Pet Ownership
- Mail Order Shopping
  - i.e., has responded to direct mail in the past

- Travel (domestic, international, ecotourism)
- Sports (e.g., golf, skiing, cycling, etc.)
- Books
- Wine
- Gourmet Food/Cooking
- Fine Dining

Chambers of Commerce. Compilers create elaborate algorithms to combine these various data (census, property owner records, and automobile registrations) to create even more accurate household profiles. Children's age data is collected from different sources and included on some list databases. One of the best pages on the bureau's Web site is the State and County Quick Facts page and the FedStats. Both are government agencies that produce statistics of interest to the public.

Consumer Lifestyle Enhanced Lists. Sometimes knowing customer demographics isn't enough. Many of the large compilers use syndicated surveys or warranty cards to capture a broad range of consumer information, including hobbies, personal interests, pet ownership, category and brand usage, and additional demographic information. This information is usually rented at the household level.

Often, this compiled list is a terrific way to identify households that have specific sports interests such as golf, fishing, or biking, or are pet owners (e.g., dogs, birds), or are mail-order buyers. Consumers will identify themselves as being health-conscious, having a diet interest, or as users of a particular product category.

Self-reported data may not be totally accurate. It reflects an individual's perception of self. Individuals who say that they are avid readers may not be, but they may be heavy buyers of books. Income may be overstated, but individuals may live a lifestyle that meets this exaggeration. While such lists may cover only 18–20 million U.S. households (less than 10 percent), these households tend to be some of the most promotionally responsive names available.

Business Compiled Lists. Business lists, compiled from a number of sources, contain address and phone numbers and key firmographics that describe the size of a company and the type of business that it is in. Typical firmographics include:

- North American Industry Classification System

- Annual sales

- Number of employees

- Headquarters or branch office

- Geography

- Business structure (e.g., corporation, subsidiary)

- Recent relocation

Where business compiled lists often fall short is in reaching an individual decision maker. Typically, the names of only a few top officers of a company appear, forcing users to mail to "premium buyer," "office manager," "CMO," "Vice-President," or "President"—which greatly reduces response. Combining compiled lists with lists that provide specific executive names (e.g., house files, trade publications, other response lists) may help to better target promotions. This is often done through profiling.

Profiling

Profiling is a first step in understanding an organization's customers by identifying demographics, firmographics, or lifestyle attributes of each customer. Appending this information to the customer file adds valuable information for targeting future promotions, understanding customer defections, and identifying cross-selling and other new business opportunities.

Business-to-business house files can be matched against a national database of businesses such as AccuData America, USADATA, or InfoUSA. This profiling process will result in a more thorough knowledge of the current client base—a well-defined target market for future prospecting. With this knowledge comes

EXHIBIT 4–3

Customer Profiling

Customer Profiling is completed by overlaying additional data to a customer or prospect database. The "best" customer segments can be identified and segmented with the appended data added to the known customer information.

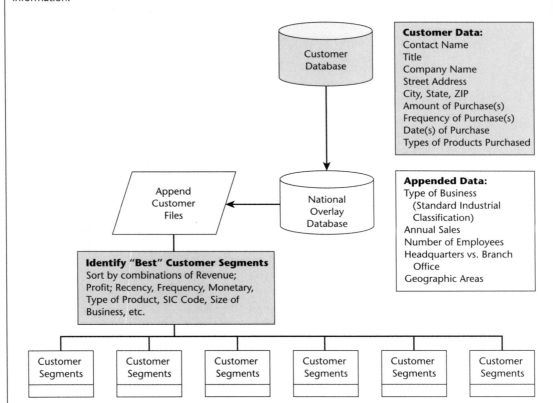

Customer Data:
Contact Name
Title
Company Name
Street Address
City, State, ZIP
Amount of Purchase(s)
Frequency of Purchase(s)
Date(s) of Purchase
Types of Products Purchased

Appended Data:
Type of Business
   (Standard Industrial
   Classification)
Annual Sales
Number of Employees
Headquarters vs. Branch
   Office
Geographic Areas

a better understanding of the marketing and communications programs necessary to more effectively penetrate the desired segments (See Exhibit 4–3).

The information and insights obtained through profiling can help the business-to-business marketer accomplish a number of objectives and is usually developed in three phases:

Phase I: Account identification and matching, consists of linking the national database operations files to the business-to-business house file.

Phase II: Appending data from the national database to the business-to-business house file, utilizes the existing compiled business establishment data (e.g., geographic, type of business, size of business, and type of location) from the national database.

Phase III: Development of market segmentation profiles, consists of analyzing the business-to-business customer file on the basis of the distribution and concentration of customers within specific market segments (e.g., the extent to which the current best customers are concentrated within certain areas such as NAICS codes, geographic areas, company size, and revenue contribution groups).

Another way of analyzing the activities of current customers and assessing their potential value is by drawing maps or creating matrixes of current purchasing activities, as shown in Exhibit 4–4. Based on the purchase activity quadrant in which the customer falls, customer files can be segmented and specific messages and offers can be targeted to best leverage the different opportunities.

Quadrant 1 represents the best customers, those who spend the most dollars and purchase the most frequently. Clearly, the emphasis in this segment is on maintaining loyalty and providing rewards for continuity.

Quadrant 2 represents customers who spend a lot of dollars but spend infrequently. Large average-order sizes combined with low levels of purchase frequency indicate that the customer might be using this vendor for a few specialized purchases.

EXHIBIT 4–4

Purchase Activity Matrix

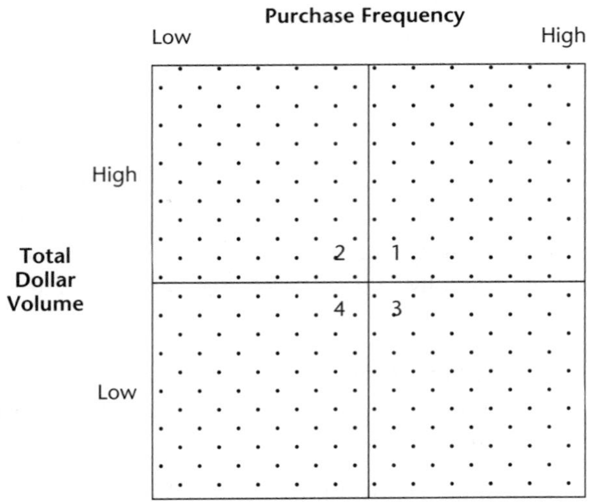

Supplementary research, such as in-depth personal interviews among a sample of customers in this quadrant, can help uncover the reasons they buy on an infrequent, specialized basis. These issues can then be addressed in both the creative and the offer to move customers into Quadrant 1.

Quadrant 3 represents customers who spend just a few dollars but make purchases relatively frequently. Small average-order sizes combined with high levels of purchase frequency indicate that these customers are "cherry picking," concentrating on the lowest-cost sales items. Again, supplementary research, such as in-depth personal interviews among a sample of customers in this quadrant, can help uncover problems to be addressed with both creative and offers to stimulate purchases of a wider range of merchandise, particularly higher-ticket items.

Quadrant 4 represents the worst of all worlds, the customer who doesn't spend very much or very often. The potential payoff in identifying these customers is in saving money by targeting a higher proportion of spending toward customers in the first three quadrants.

The potential of these customers can be further assessed by observing the degree to which companies with certain characteristics, such as SIC code, size, and geographic location, tend to be concentrated in certain quadrants. For example, if customers from four SIC codes are predominant within Quadrant 1 (highest sales volume, greatest purchase frequency), then the share of market or degree of penetration in each of the four SIC codes can be analyzed. By comparing the customers in the house file against the total number of businesses within each SIC code on the national database, a profile of market penetration can be drawn, as shown in Exhibit 4–5.

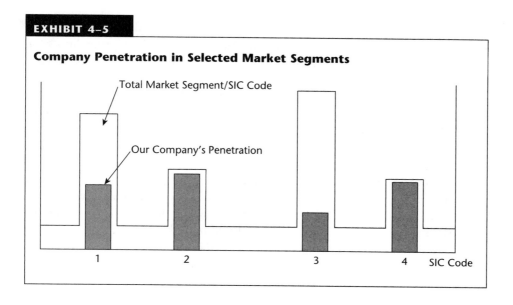

EXHIBIT 4–5

Company Penetration in Selected Market Segments

Total Market Segment/SIC Code

Our Company's Penetration

1   2   3   4   SIC Code

List Selection Guidelines

Evaluating list selections is not easy. There are many categories of lists, types of lists, and ways of creating lists. There is no perfect way to select information from lists, but some guidelines based on experience are helpful.

Description. Who is on the list? There may be mail-order buyers, former buyers, subscribers, expires, donors, former donors, inquiries, coupon redeemers, etc. It is important to match the offer and target group as closely as possible to the description of those on lists that are mailed.

Affinity. A close relationship with the target group that the marketer is trying to reach. It is not possible to rent competitive response lists. It is not likely that a perfect match exists. Marketers try to rent relevant list choices that approximate their target group as closely as possible. A marketer of holiday fruit baskets might test lists of other food products sold at holiday time. Opera season ticket holders might be targeted for a subscription to the symphony. A marketer of waterproof sport boots might mail readers of outdoor and sporting magazines, buyers of outdoor clothing, or those who have purchased shoes direct.

List Source. The origin of the names on the list. Knowing the source of a list is important. Individuals who purchased via direct mail or a catalog are more likely to respond to direct mail than a buyer who responded to a print ad, television, etc. It is also a clue to the accuracy of the information.

Renting Mailing Lists

Mailing lists may be rented from list owners, list managers, and list brokers. Each source has its strengths and weaknesses.

List owners make the final decisions on any list rental and determine the appropriateness or competitiveness of a prospective renter's request. They generally ask for, or require, a sample mail piece before agreeing to rent their lists. If there is any concern that an offer might offend the list owner's customers, they will reject the request.

Some response list owners rent their own lists but most use intermediaries and will only negotiate large, multi-use deals. Compiled list owners are the exception. Organizations such as Donnelly Marketing, Experian, R.L. Polk, InfoUSA, and others rent their own lists. Their sales forces tend to focus on large customers. Compiled lists are available from other sources as well.

List managers administer the lists for list owners. They generally manage a number of lists and handle fulfillment, billing, and list hygiene. Typically, list managers get monthly updates of the list from the list owner. Because they maintain the list outside of the list owner's system, they benefit both the owner and renter of the list by speeding up the processing of list orders. Many list managers rent lists other than their own as well. However, list managers have a vested interest in renting the lists that they manage and should not be considered impartial list sources.

List brokers are the key link in the list rental process. A list broker provides timely and informed recommendations about which lists should be tested and why and will provide a detailed report on each list recommended. Brokers also handle the administrative aspects of list rental and fulfillment. Most brokers are paid a commission by the list owner or manager and do not charge list renters. Brokers may require a minimum order of 5,000 names per list (not per order). For large orders, volume discounts ranging from 10 to 60 percent are available.

Some brokers ask to be compensated for the consulting service they provide, not just for net names rented. This fee is usually credited toward list rental as an incentive to rent from the broker. This method assures that the broker's consulting time is compensated whether a list order is placed or not.

The best way to find a good list broker is through referral. Ask colleagues or associates for their recommendations. Many brokers specialize. Finding one with experience in a particular category is important.

Evaluating Mailing Lists

A good starting point for list evaluation is SRDS Media Solutions, a provider of advertising research and marketing lists. Subscribers receive a printed volume and have access to the same information online. Although it is comprehensive, SRDS information is timely only immediately after publication. Rates and other information still need to be confirmed through a list professional. Because SRDS organizes all the information for every list in exactly the same way, it is very easy to compare lists. SRDS updates its lists monthly. Exhibit 4–6 is a sample page from SRDS.

List information can also be found on "data cards" provided by list owners and brokers (A sample data card from Edith Roman Associates is shown in Exhibit 4–7). Because information is not presented in a standard format, comparisons can be difficult. Stevan Roberts, president of list brokerage Edith Roman Associates, Inc., notes that the following information, included in most data cards, should be evaluated when deciding upon a list rental:

- *List size*. Lists range in size from less than 2,000 names to 1 million names or more. The traditional approach to direct mail is to test a small portion of the list, then mail to a larger portion if the test is successful. For this reason, some mailers avoid small lists because the opportunity to expand after a successful test is limited by the total number of names available. On the other hand, to the mailer seeking unusual or hard-to-find prospects, such small specialized lists may be the only means of reaching certain markets.

- *Cost per thousand*. Depending on the list, prices typically range from $75.00 to $120.92 per thousand names, with specialized lists going for

EXHIBIT 4-6

Sample Entry from Standard Rate and Data Services (SRDS)

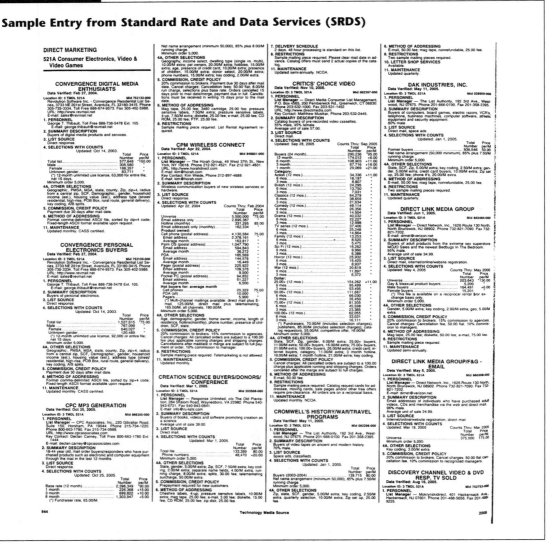

$139 to $175 per thousand or more. Be wary of firms offering so-called "bargain lists." Often, these are absolutely worthless.

- *List description.* Each data card contains a paragraph or two about the background of the list: its source, history, a profile of the type of buyers it represents, and a description of the product they bought, the publication they subscribe to, or the seminar they attended. Read the description to get a feel for the market represented by the list.

EXHIBIT 4-7

Sample Data Card

This data card for Catalog Success subscribers includes a description of the list, the different categories of the list and what they consist of, available list quantities, selections available, minimum order size, and other information.

CATALOG SUCCESS MAGAZINE

18,287	Active Subscribers	. . . . $140/M
16,788	Subscribers W/Phones	. . . . +$60/M
13,093	Email addresses	. . . . $250/M*
	Advertiser Rates	. . . . $112/M

Published by North American Publishing Company (NAPCO).

CATALOG SUCCESS, reaches corporate, general, marketing, database, sales, operations, fulfillment, production, design, and creative management involved in the business-to-business and consumer catalog industry arenas.

The catalog market is extremely competitive. The subscribers to Catalog Success are continuously searching for products and services that can increase their organization's efficiency and bottom line. They have the purchasing power to make any campaign a success.

Job Function:
Corporate/General Management............................10,793
Marketing/Database Management 4,957
Production/Prepress Management..............................558
Operations/Fulfillment/Call Center Management 944
Creative Services- Copy/Design 1,061

Firm's Primary Business:
Catalogers 17,239
List Professionals 1,138
Creative Services 3,735

Job Involvement Areas:
Marketing...10,188
Production/Prepress.......................................7,248
Operations/Fulfillment/Call Center 5,174
Internet/Electronic Retailing 5,486
Lists- Broker, Manager, Compiler...........................3,849
Creative Services- Copy/Design 5,307
Merchandise...3,751
Database/Circulation 3,461

Marketing Activities in Addition to Catalogs:
Direct Mail 8,250
Telemarketing 3,592
Electronic Media/Internet.................................1,416

Additional Information

---Date----
6/06

---Gender---
Male 10,432
Female 5,349

---Media---
CD $50/F
4-Up Cheshire ....NC
E-mail $65/F
Diskette $50/F
PSL $10/M

---Selections---
Phone Number $60/M
One Name Per Site $15/M
Job Function...................$20/M
Bus/Industry Type...........$20/M
SCF $10/M
State $10/M
Zip.................................$10/M
Gender $20/M
Job Involvement Areas $20/M
Marketing Activities in
  Addition to Catalogs $20/M

---Key Code---
$5/M

---Minimum Order---
5,000 Names

---Source---
100% Qualified
Subscribers

Sample Mailing Piece Required

***Transmission:**
$95/M - Text
$115/M - HTML

--Cancellation--
$10/M + $50 Flat Fee
Cancellation After Mail Date
Requires Payment in Full

Contact

For Postal List Info Contact:
Kevin Collopy at 845-731-2684
mailto:kevin.collopy@edithroman.com

For Email List Info Contact:
Michael Spohn at 845-731-3860
mailto:michael.spohn@epostdirect.c

Edith Roman Associates, Inc. • One Blue Hill Plaza • 16th floor • PO Box 1556 • Pearl River, NY 10965-8556
Voice: 845-620-9000 • 800-223-2194 • Fax: 845-620-9035
www.edithroman.com • mailto:kevin.collopy@edithroman.com

- *Average order size.* Given as a dollar amount, this represents the average size of the mail-order purchase made by the buyers on the list. Average order size is a good indication of how much individuals on a list might be willing to spend via direct mail. It is unlikely that individuals who have spent 25 dollars will respond to offers for 100 dollars.

- *Percentage of the list that is direct mail-generated.* Data cards often contain the phrase "95 percent direct mail-generated" or "100 percent direct mail-generated." This indicates the percentage of the names on the list obtained through response to direct mail. Higher percentages are better because direct-mail-generated prospects and customers are more likely to respond to direct mail than people who became prospects or customers through other avenues.

- *Hot lead.* The segment of the list containing customers who made a mail-order purchase within the last 30 to 90 days (the more recent, the better). Hot leads typically rent for $15 to $35 more per thousand than the rest of the list.

- *Active versus inactive, buyer versus prospect.* Customer lists almost always pull better than prospect lists. When testing a list of newsletter subscribers, first select the current (active) subscribers rather than the former (inactive) subscribers. When renting a list from a mail-order catalog company, obtain the names of people who actually bought from the catalog, not those who merely requested a free catalog but did not buy. The rule of thumb is to test the most likely group first and then test the others after the best names have been exhausted.

- *List usage report.* Try to get the list supplier to tell you how well the list pulled for others who rented it—especially those with similar offers. This information probably won't appear on the data card but it may be contained in a separate List Usage Report available from the broker. These reports usually show rental activity by tests (initial mailings) and continuations (rental of additional names following a successful test). If a high percentage of the mailers who tested are also listed under continuations, they are getting test results profitable enough to warrant continued use of the list—a good sign.

- *Selections available.* The data card indicates the selection criteria by which the list can be segmented. In general, the more selections the better, because selectability allows you to mail only to those names closest to a marketer's target profile.

- *Frequency of updating.* Are the names current and is the list frequently updated? Some list suppliers may guarantee their lists to be clean and will refund postage costs on pieces returned as "undeliverable" (called NIXIEs) in excess of some certain small percentage. The fewer NIXIEs per list, the cleaner the list. The USPS considers returns of 2 percent or lower of the mailing as very good, in other words, a clean list.

As 14 percent of Americans move every year, compiled and prospect lists get outdated quickly. As a rule, a list should be updated (meaning that names no longer current are removed) at least twice a year, if not quarterly. The National Change of Address File (NCOA) for example, is updated weekly. Updating frequently lowers the cost for address corrections.

Output Media Formats

In the past, the most common format for receiving rented lists was pressure-sensitive or paper Cheshire mailing labels, the format preferred by letter shops that used automated equipment to cut the paper into single labels and affix these labels to envelopes.

Today, lists are likely to be delivered electronically via CD, DVD, cartridges, magnetic tape, and even by e-mail. Traditional analog methods, such as mailing labels, pressure-sensitive, and 3 × 5 sales lead cards are also available. When names are ordered, each mailing record may include a key code provided by the marketer, to identify the list source (essential for determining response when testing several mailing pieces or lists).

For most mailing programs, a number of lists may be ordered. If the lists are similar, names may be duplicated from one list to another. This is to be expected when trying to reach a specific target group. Sometimes unexpected duplication occurs. Several brokers may release data cards for the same list under different titles with varying descriptions. Or, a list owner will market different parts of a single file as separate lists. Mailers protect themselves in two ways.

Net name arrangements can be negotiated with brokers so that only unduplicated names are paid for. These agreements may be negotiated at a flat rate (e.g., a marketer may only pay for 80 percent of names ordered) or as a discount based on all of the duplicate names where the list owner controls the de-duping of the lists. Whether a net name arrangement is negotiated or not, some duplication is likely to exist. To reduce duplication, multiple lists go through a process known as merge/purge. According to all the major mailing list providers, the merge and purge data coincide in the idea that as your in-house database file ages, it becomes less effective because of incorrect and old records, duplicate files, and undeliverable addresses. Having this in mind, these companies can provide a service where they would perform a number of procedures to help you eliminate useless records on your list. Merge/purge is part of a broader area known as list hygiene.

List Hygiene

According to the Direct Marketing Association, "The most important step every mailer can and should take is to improve list hygiene." Standardizing formats, merging multiple files, eliminating duplicates (merge/purge process), and updating and verifying address elements are all critical steps that are essential to maximizing deliverability.

The USPS also offers discounts to mailers for helping to automate mail distribution by presorting and bundling mail. There are discounts for presorting by three-digit ZIP code (SCF), five-digit ZIP, ZIP+4 (nine-digit ZIP), and carrier route. Carrier route and ZIP+4 coding offer the lowest postal rates in all classes. Mail rates are based on First Class, Periodicals (the former Second Class), or Standard Class, which includes Nonprofit (formerly Third and Fourth Classes) service. Postal regulations are very stringent. Check with a letter shop or the USPS Web site (www.usps.com) to determine which discounts a mail piece qualifies for.

Proper care in the creation and maintenance of prospect and customer files has become more important than ever. Taking steps to ensure the maximum USPS discount rates can result in savings of thousands of dollars, not to mention a better return on investment.

A typical list cleaning exercise, for example, is shown in Exhibit 4–8, "The Economics of Merge/Purge." On a 1 million piece mailing with a $1 per-piece cost, a 2 percent response rate, and a $55 average-order value, the combination of cost avoidance and additional revenue generated through proper list hygiene provides a return on investment of $64,250 on the first mailing. Subsequent mailings increase these returns.

Applying List Hygiene

There are a number of steps that can be taken to clean lists before mailing. Planning these steps carefully can help a marketer derive more marketing information from the hygiene process. For example, if a marketer is doing site planning, media selections, or risk assessment, longitude and latitude data can be appended onto each household record to allow for geographic analysis. Finding ways to combine steps can save considerable time and money.

List Standardization. Standardization is the process of normalizing data records from multiple sources to ensure completeness and standard formatting for each data element. The outcome of this process should be to flag affected records to be fixed or eliminated. This data consolidation and standardization ensures that these particular addresses are standardized to meet the United States Postal Service requirements. As the company Accudata, this process includes:

- Validation and correction of street, city, and state

- Standardized street prefix, suffix, and secondary address components

---

EXHIBIT 4–8

The Economics of Merge/Purge

Removing duplicate names can greatly improve marketing efficiency. In this example, the savings from running the merge/purge are far greater than the cost of analysis.

	With Merge/Purge	Without Merge/Purge
Quantity to mail	128,426.00	180,269,00
Cost to Print & Mail at 65¢ each	$83,476,90	$117,174.85
Cost to run Merge/Purge	$350.00	Not Applicable
Total Costs	$83,826.90	$117,174.85
Cost Savings	$33,347.95	

Please note that prior to Merge/Purge all lists have been run through National Change of Address Postal Software and standardized for addressing. It is important to start with the cleanest names and addresses to ensure the best deliverability.

- ZIP+4 codes are enhanced, added if missing, and corrected
- United States Postal Service carrier Route Codes are added
- United States Postal Service Line-of-Travel data is added
- Delivery Point Bar Code data is added
- Undeliverable addresses are identified and tagged

Editing and Reformatting. This process involves editing and reformatting records so that every field is handled uniformly. To do that, the standardization routine must first parse out every element in the name and address. Additional fields can be appended to the records during the editing and formatting procedure.

Merge/Purge. Duplicate identification is particularly important for Periodicals and Standard Class mailers. Good merge/purge systems eliminate duplicates, improve targeting, and increase response rates. The system must be flexible and customizable to accommodate unique situations based on marketing objectives. Multi-family dwellings, rural addresses, prestige addresses, cohabitants, married versus maiden names, misspellings, previous versus current occupants, and other common address problems must be considered. Merge/purge flags dupes and permits intelligent marketing decisions (See Exhibit 4–9).

EXHIBIT 4–9

Merge/Purge Report

There is always duplication among lists targeting individuals with similiar demographics, psychographics, or affinities. In this example, there is duplication within and among the lists in a 150,000-piece mailing.

List Name	List Quantity	Interdupes*	Intradupes**	Total Dupes (Inter and Intra)	Total Unique Records
House File	61,782	0	0	0	61,782
List 1	12,685	125	5,640	5,765	6,920
List 2	13,076	336	7,533	7,869	5,207
List 3	12,989	414	2,027	2,441	10,548
List 4	12,954	223	5,672	5,895	7,059
List 5	13,305	19	3,405	3,424	9,881
List 6	12,955	26	5,671	5,697	7,258
List 7	14,723	17	4,299	4,316	10,407
List 8	13,798	235	7,988	8,223	5,575
List 9	12,002	2	8,211	8,213	3,789
Totals	180,269	1,397	50,446	51,843	128,426

* Interdupes are duplicates found within a single file.
** Intradupes are duplicates found from multiple files during Merge/Purge.

Merge/Purge Criteria: One mailing piece should deliver to a single household.
Address, city, state, and zip code will determine each household location.

List Criteria: Houe File has the highest priority. All additional lists should be purged against the House File.

Verification and Correction. To identify and correct bad addresses, use USPS-certified address-matching services offered by commercial vendors or service bureaus.

Coding Accuracy Support System (CASS) software identifies and corrects bad addresses to the carrier route and ZIP+4 level. It is used for all classes of mail and is updated every three months. Mailers use CASS ZIP code corrections in updating lists to receive an automatic discount or lower rate. However, the updates must have been made less than 90 days prior to mailing for the discount or lower rate to apply. For mailings with "old" CASS updating (more than six months), there is no discount or lower rate.

Delivery Sequence File (DSF) contains every deliverable address in the country (at the mailbox level). It has more than 135 million addresses on file, offering nearly 100 percent of all city-style, rural route, highway contract, P.O. Box, and standardized business addresses. It is the most complete address database available and will fix between 1 and 3 percent of the bad records in a file.

Locatable Address Conversion System (LACS) converts rural routes with box numbers and other addresses the USPS considers "nonstandard" into city-style or standard address delivery points. This USPS database currently includes more than 5 million records, covering mostly southern and midwestern regions.

The National Change of Address is a crucial component of data hygiene. It contains more than 160 million address changes (all of the address changes occurring in the past three years) and is updated weekly. Matching files against NCOA improves address hygiene by reducing undeliverables (NIXIEs). Many mailers routinely find about 7 to 10 percent of their file comprised of NIXIEs each year if they do not update. Typically 1 to 3 percent of addresses in a list will change every six months. NCOA is required for First Class mailing discounts.

Prospect Databases

When targeting new customers, marketers have followed a tried and tested process for renting prospect lists since the earliest days. Each part of the process is treated as a separate event. In a simplified form, the process works as follows:

1. Identify the target market.

2. Review available lists with the greatest affinity for the product, category, and offer.

3. Rent lists and run a merge/purge to de-dupe the lists (i.e. ensure that duplicate mailings are not sent to the same prospect).

4. Complete a solo mailing to prospects.

5. Complete an analysis of those who have responded.

6. Based on who has responded, start the process over.

This process assumes that lists of perfect prospects are available, that one effort is all that is necessary to reach prospects, and that no other channels are used to reach prospects. This may be true for some consumer mailings. It is almost never true for B-to-B mailings, where prospecting for complex sales require much more effort and is a lengthy process.

While it is often possible to rent the names of companies that fit a prospect profile, and include job titles it is harder to obtain the names of decision makers and influencers. Often, one mailing is not enough. A series of efforts are mailed over weeks or months to prospects. And, while a marketer is mailing, a salesperson may be trying to contact the prospect, and the prospect may be going to the marketer's Web site.

A prospect database may be one solution. A prospect database often starts with the rental of few mailing lists, which are "bought out" so that they may be re-mailed. After merging and de-duping the lists, this list is passed along to telephone representatives, who outbound call companies on the list to identify the names and titles of decision makers. Additional information, such as the prospect's e-mail address, may be added at this time. Transactional history and behavioral data can be appended as well.

Once created, the marketer does not have to pay for subsequent usage, although they must add to and maintain the hygiene of the prospect database regularly, so that it is always ready to be mailed. In addition, the marketer can maintain contact data, promotional data (what offers were mailed to the prospect?), channel preference data (how and when do they respond?), and other types of historical data.

Prospect databases are a useful tool when a rented mailing list can't provide all of the information necessary to reach a target group. The use of prospect databases in consumer mailings is just beginning to grow. No doubt, in the future, prospect databases will be an even more useful tool.

Privacy

Questions of data compilation and usage are sensitive. Many consumers and businesses alike view them as privacy issues. When carelessly asked questions about age, marital status, or children are included as part of a general direct marketing program, they seem out of context and may reduce response. A consumer may ask, "Why do they need to know the value of my home to complete an order for a pair of jeans?"

Such questions can't be taken lightly. Information privacy is a significant issue for marketers. Most consumers want some control of the terms under which their personal information is acquired by others and used. At the very least, research shows that most individuals prefer marketers to disclose how their information will be used. Mary J. Culnan, a professor at Georgetown University, has done extensive research into consumer privacy. Culnan points out that information privacy concerns can arise in different contexts.

Consumers understand that there are times when they need to disclose personal information. Financial information may be necessary to qualify for automobile insurance, a mortgage, a credit card, or to open a bank or a brokerage account. Medical information may be necessary when applying for health or life insurance, a new job, or before being exposed to physically stressful situations (e.g., a ride in a fighter plane). Surveys show that people do not object to this. It is secondary use of the information provided that raises privacy concerns.

Secondary use refers to collecting information for one purpose and subsequently using the information for other purposes. It also includes unrelated use by the organization that collected the information, e.g., for the creation of rented mailing lists, as well as sharing the information with third parties—especially personal information contained in public records, credit reports, and other databases used for credit or hiring decisions. Privacy concerns arise when this reuse is unrelated to or incompatible with the purpose for which the information was originally collected, and the mailer or list renter does not offer consumers the opportunity to object to this reuse.

Culnan notes that public opinion surveys and her own research have shown that firms can balance these privacy concerns with their legitimate business need for the information by observing fair information practices. When consumers are offered notice and choice (e.g., opt-out), privacy concerns are no longer significant and a majority of consumers do not object to secondary use of personal information.

Another concern for consumers is the unauthorized access to their personal information. This can come through a security breach or because the custodian of the information has not implemented appropriate internal controls (e.g., pretext calling, identity theft, or having one's credit card number stolen online by hackers).

Observing information practices which consumers view as fair is a win-win solution for consumers and businesses. Disclosure and options such as opt-out reduce the perceived risk to consumers, while allowing an individual to control the use of his or her personal information.

Most marketers allow consumers and businesses to opt out of promotions. To do so, an individual must ask to be excluded from future promotions from the organization, cross-sell opportunities from the organization, and/or the renting of his or her name to other organizations. This is good for the marketers as they don't spend money to send promotions to individuals who would prefer not to receive them.

The DMA's "Privacy Promise" requires all of its members that market to consumers to give notice and choice if personal information is shared with third parties and to respect consumer requests not to receive solicitations from the company or its affiliates.

Opt-out is not without controversy. In the online realm, opt-in is the standard, and individuals must give their permission in order to receive promotional offers of any kind. This proactive approach reduces the number of people on such lists. Informed consent (i.e., opt-in) is required in certain regulated markets such as telecom. Considering list rental revenue, the number of lists available, and the history of opt-out in traditional direct marketing, it is unlikely opt-in will ever be adopted.

The Last Word on Lists

Mailing lists remain one of the most important tools for marketers. They are important to the continued growth of direct mail and e-mail marketing. Data security and privacy issues must continue to be addressed by marketers. In the meantime, it is likely that marketers will continue practices that are virtually unchanged over the last 100 years.

CASE STUDY: International Truck List Procurement "All Family" Promotion

Written by Jacobs & Clevenger with approval of its client, International Truck and Engine Corporation.

BACKGROUND

International Truck and Engine Corporation is the operating company of Navistar International Corporation. The company produces International® brand commercial trucks, mid-range diesel engines, and is a private label designer and manufacturer of diesel engines for the pickup truck, van, and SUV markets. A wholly owned affiliate produces school buses. With the broadest distribution network in North America, a wholly owned affiliate provides financing for customers and dealers.

International produces different classes of trucks, each class representing a different size and weight. The different classes of trucks represent different types of trucking needs and vocational applications. For instance, medium-duty trucks are used for services such as local moving and delivery, heavy-duty trucks are used for long-haul transport, and other classes are used for services such as construction and building. The different International trucks are sold through a network of dealerships.

CHALLENGES

Once a year, International invested in a campaign called "All Family," which promoted all classes of vehicles. The "All Family" Promotion was a multi-channel integrated campaign, featuring print advertising, telemarketing, and direct mail. The objective of the promotion was to generate leads and drive interested prospects to the dealerships for a test drive and purchase.

Effective Targeting Tops the List

Because of the wide variety of trucking classes, trucking needs, and vocations addressed in this campaign, International needed an equal and corresponding variety of target lists for the telemarketing and direct mail.

To achieve this end, International worked to:

- Research various list sources, including selection criteria, pricing, available quantity and usage agreements.

- Compile a mix of lists that would provide an equal distribution across vehicle classes and all International dealer territories.
- Procure the best lists from various sources, and process data to provide one final output ready for mail and telemarketing.
- Ensure that the performance of lists could be measured and tested, so that better performing lists could be renewed and used for future campaigns. Key measurements were the number of test drives generated and the number of trucks purchased.

SOLUTION

International started by defining the targeting strategy for the campaign. This meant looking at the market on two different levels, first at the company level (for example, identifying the best-fit vocations and fleet sizes, such as "local moving companies with a 25-truck fleet"), and second at the contact level (identifying the roles and titles of a potential decision maker, such as "Fleet Manager" or "Procurement"). Carefully defining both levels of the strategy was important to ensure that the communications reached the right decision makers at the right companies.

With the target market in mind, a collection of 50 potential lists were compiled from a variety of sources. See exhibit 4–10 for a sample of International Truck Direct Mail Kit.

Transforming Potential into the Perfect Fit

Each list was reviewed and qualified for potential fit with the specific campaign targets. This first pass was done by reviewing:

- Type of list (such as response, directory or compiled lists, and including both horizontal—i.e. reaching a specific function such as fleet management that occurs in a range of vocations—and vertical lists—i.e. reaching a specific vocation such as construction that covers a range of functions).
- Description of the list (to learn how the data was collected, how often the data was updated, and who owned each list).

EXHIBIT 4–10

International Truck Direct Mail Package

- Selection criteria or "selects" available on each list (a list of preferred selects that best defined the campaign targets, but knew different lists would offer different combinations of selects).
- Quantities available (a combination of selects would be applied to focus the list, and each select reduced the pool of contacts; thus, lists needed to be large enough to accommodate the winnowing process and still net enough contacts to meet a typical minimum purchase quantity of 5,000 contacts).

Through this more thorough review the original 50 potential lists were pared down to 12 lists for further consideration. At this stage, the 12 lists included a mix of response, compiled, and directory lists. The response lists were built from publications that targeted the right audience, the directories were qualified, and the compiled lists were from known sources within the trucking industry. Each of these lists also offered the range of selects needed to target the specific types of companies and decision makers outlined in the campaign strategy.

Those 12 lists were prioritized and sorted based on that selection criteria. This was a critical and complicated step because each list afforded a different set of criteria. Because no single list would be a complete solution many combinations were considered, including:

- Vehicle class
- Vocations such as Moving, Manufacturing, Retail Delivery and Construction
- Fleet size, targeting those specific sizes outlined in the marketing strategy
- Purchasing authority, either listed as its own variable or determined based on titles
- Geography, in order to make sure each dealer received enough marketing support
- Availability of telephone information for telemarketing

Counts on the various selection criteria were run to estimate how many records would net out of the process for each list. Cost per thousand were also factored in, knowing that the more qualified the list and the more selects applied, the more expensive the information usually was. The last thing considered was usage rights, knowing that a buy-out of a list (rather than a fixed-use rental), while initially more expensive, could also provide contacts for other campaigns, have its costs amortized, and ultimately prove more efficient.

Practicing the art and science of list evaluation, the 12 lists were ranked and sorted. Ultimately four lists were selected.

RESULTS

The following four lists were chosen:

- **List 1** was a response list from a leading industry magazine geared toward owners, administrators, and maintenance managers of vehicle fleets. Often presidents of their own companies, subscribers were prime decision makers in the purchase of vehicles, components, parts, equipment, and more. This list had a base quantity of over 100,000 contacts, and offered selects within fleet size,

class, fleet type, purchasing authority, and job function.

- **List 2** was also a response list from another leading industry magazine, geared toward owner-operators. These were independent businessmen who personally managed their own trucking concerns and purchases. This list had a base of almost 100,000 contacts, and offered selects within job function, number of trucks in fleet, age of trucks owned, plan to buy another truck, and business type.
- **List 3** was a compiled list based on records of trucking companies licensed by the Department of Transportation. This list had a base of over 600,000 contacts, and offered selects within cargo classification (business type) and number of trucks in fleets. The contact was the name on the trucking company license and no specific titles were offered.
- **List 4** was a compiled list, supplied by a publishing company, based on a compilation of government records and publication lists. All records were qualified via telemarketing before being compiled. The list had a base of over 500,000 records, and list parameters were built to fit specific marketing needs, offering a range of selects and business information based on SIC codes (business type), fleet sizes, fleet make-up, purchasing cycles, and more.

These four lists provided the right combination of quantity and quality to drive the telemarketing and direct mail. In the end, the extensive research, filtering, and segmentation paid dividends. The lists enabled the diverse "All Family" Promotion to pinpoint a complex group of target audiences. The campaign generated test drives and sales for International dealers across North America.

And testing also paid off, with results showing certain lists performed better than others. List 1 and List 4 surpassed objectives for truck sales and test drives, illustrating that those lists had better qualified prospects. List 2 performed just

---

| CASE STUDY: | **International Truck List Procurement "All Family" Promotion** *(continued)* |

below average on test drives and the lowest in truck purchases. Lists 3 drove a significant amount of test drives but performed below objectives for truck purchases, suggesting a less qualified group of less serious purchasers. An ROI analysis was performed on each list to confirm that Lists 1 and 4 should be renewed and expanded in the next campaign.

PILOT PROJECT You are the marketing director of a multichannel retailer selling clothes for children up to age 13. These are high-end products, with an average order of $100 plus. You sell through retail, catalogs, and a Web site. And, although you have a lot of transactional information about your customers (products purchased, amount of purchase, purchase date, and historical customer/order data), you don't know very much about the demographics of your customers.

Up to now, the catalog has only been mailed using response lists of direct mail buyers of similar products. You have exhausted the list choices, and must make some decisions about going beyond response lists and test compiled lists for your summer mailing.

How would you learn about the demographics of your customers? What other kinds of lists would you test? How many list segments would you test in the summer mailing? Can you find lists that include postal address as well as e-mail address to execute a multichannel marketing campaign?

Key Points

▶ There are three kinds of lists: house lists, which are the customer databases of organizations; response lists, or house lists of other organizations; and compiled lists of individuals or companies without any previous indication of willingness to respond, but with some defined and identifiable characteristic(s) such as demographics, psychographics, or ZIP code.

▶ Profiling is the process of understanding customers by identifying their demographics, firmographics, or lifestyle attributes. Appending this information to the customer file adds valuable information for targeting future promotions, understanding customer defections, and identifying cross-selling and other new business opportunities.

▶ Mailing lists are rented, typically for a one-time use. If after testing a portion of a list, the renting organization wants to re-mail or roll out the list (e.g., in continuation), it must pay an additional rental fee. List owners make the final decisions on any list rental and may reject rental requests that are inappropriate or competitive.

▶ Data cards provide details on the list size, cost per thousand, its source and history, the average size of the mail-order purchase made by the buyers, and the percentage of the list that is direct-mail generated. Data cards also indicate the presence of hot lead names—customers who made a mail-order purchase within the last 30 to 90 days—and the selection by which the list can be segmented.

▶ Lists age quickly and should be updated frequently (meaning that names no longer current are removed). Routine updating lowers the cost for address corrections. Service bureaus can also prevent address corrections by standardizing names, editing and reformatting records, purging lists of duplications, and verifying and correcting addresses.

▶ Privacy concerns often arise when information collected for one purpose is subsequently used for other purposes. Concerns abate when mailers and list renters offer consumers the opportunity to object to this reuse. The National Do Not Call Registry enables consumers to remove their names from contact lists.

THE OFFER

Since the earliest days, the offer has been one of the key elements of direct marketing. The offer remains at the center of much marketing communications. It cuts through the clutter and noise of marketing communications to implore prospects and customers to respond, often when they would prefer to eat dinner, watch television, or simply relax after a long day.

What is the offer? The offer is *the terms under which a specific product or service is promoted, i.e., the promise of the transaction.* It tells the consumer what they will get when they inquire, answer, go to a landing page, purchase, or otherwise respond. An effective offer will capture a consumer's attention, stimulate their imagination, and hook into their most basic impulses. It creates an urgent desire to reply now. A good offer hits that uncontrollable switch, emotion, or trigger that stops the readers, in their tracks, and makes them do something that they may not have been intending to do . . . Respond!

Objectives Guide the Offer

Direct marketing has many response objectives. They include selling a product or service, creating new members or subscribers, generating leads for follow-up, responding for product/service information, fund-raising, or driving traffic to a retail store or Web site. Different objectives require different offer strategies. The incentives necessary to get someone to purchase direct are more robust than those employed to persuade a prospect to look at a landing page or a Web site.

Product categories, legal restrictions, context, and business considerations also impact the offer. For instance, banks and insurance companies don't use highly promotional offers such as sweepstakes. Pharmaceutical companies don't offer random product samples. Circumstances may dictate that some offers are simply off limits.

While offers are meant to stimulate response, some may do their job too well. A marketer using a free-gift offer for sales leads may learn that the offer brings in unqualified respondents, or those that only want the gift and are not interested in meeting with the salesperson. Sales staff, in turn, will learn quickly and may resist following up leads from that promotion. Marketers need to strike a balance, usually through careful testing, of which offers provide the most cost-efficient response.

Product/Service Is Key Element of the Offer

The heart of any proposition, the most important element of any offer, is the product or service. Great communications cannot overcome a bad product.

Direct marketing is built upon the idea of loyalty and repeat purchases. Other aspects of the offer may stimulate response, and gain trial. But customers won't buy again if they are not delighted by a product or service. This is why a free trial offer is so powerful. It tells the prospect that the marketer is so certain that they will like its product or service that they are willing to let them take it for a test drive and learn for themselves.

The product or service is the star of any communications. Well-known and successful direct marketing copywriter Gary Bencivenga puts it this way: *"A gifted product is mightier than a gifted pen."* Bencivenga attributes these nine words to advertising luminary Rosser Reaves, who also created the concept of the Unique Selling Proposition in communications.

Bencivenga notes that copy simply conveys the advantages of a product, it doesn't invent advantages that don't already exist. To learn about a product or service, marketers and writers should begin their assignments like an investigative reporter, submerging themselves in the product or service and asking a flood of questions.

Below, we have adopted ten questions Bencivenga says must be answered before the offer can be developed and the creative started:

1. Why is this product made the way it is?

2. What consumer problems, desires, and needs is it designed for?

3. What's special about it—why does it fulfill a consumer's needs better than the competition?

4. Who says so besides you?

5. What are your strongest proof elements to make your case believable?

6. What are all the product's best features and how does each translate into a consumer benefit?

7. If you had unlimited funds, how would you improve this product?

8. Who are its heavy users—the 10 percent who generate 90 percent of profit?

9. What irresistible offers might trigger an explosion in sales?

10. What premiums or incentives can be used to press the prospects' or customers' hot buttons?

Regardless of the kind of response expected, successful offers focus on the product or service offered.

Incentives

Incentives are the sweeteners that help motivate prospects or customers to respond. They are promised with a purchase, a trial, or in lead generation, where they are brought with a salesperson to the meeting. Incentives include free gifts or premiums, free trials, free information, discounts, special interest rates, sweepstakes, etc.

Incentives need to be carefully matched to their audience. Knowing what will trigger response in specific segments is important. Even when carefully thought out, incentives must be tested front-end and back-end. Are people "buying" the free gift or sweeps? Will they be as good repeat customers as those who bought in the first instance without incentive? It is possible to make the incentives too good. Marketers need to strike the balance where the incentive helps get the response, but where customers are still responding to the product or service offered.

Guarantees

The guarantee provides an additional level of comfort for responding. They have been an important part of direct marketing since its earliest days. Guarantees are useful in all manner of direct marketing efforts, even when the objective is not to generate a direct sale.

The guarantee may promise that a consumer's personal information won't be shared with others. It may promise that no salesperson will call. It may even be a guarantee of response: "We will confirm your request within 24 hours." Marketers have learned that to delight customers and prospects they must exceed their guarantees. So, while the guarantee may be the promise of a response within hours, the reality should be a response with minutes.

For more than 90 years, L.L. Bean has guaranteed satisfaction for every article offered (Exhibit 5–1).

The importance of the guarantee is perhaps best understood by recognizing a fact of life: people are hesitant to send for merchandise unless they know that the product may be returned for full credit if it does not meet their expectations. Guaranteed satisfaction should be a part of any offer soliciting a direct sale.

Selling Direct

When a direct sale is the objective, there are other factors to consider when creating an offer.

EXHIBIT 5-1

Bean Guarantee

Guaranteed
You Have Our Word™

> Our products are guaranteed to give 100% satisfaction in every way. Return anything purchased from us at any time if it proves otherwise. We do not want you to have anything from L.L.Bean that is not completely satisfactory.

From kayaks to slippers, fly rods to sweaters, everything we sell at L.L.Bean is backed by the same rock-solid guarantee of satisfaction. It's been that way since our founder sold his very first pair of Bean Boots in 1912. Today we're proud to continue the tradition – by offering quality products and standing behind them.

Of course, we want you to be the final judge of quality. If you're not satisfied with your purchase, we'll replace it or give you your money back. It's that simple.

L.L. Bean placed this notice on the wall of our Freeport store.

- *Price*. Nothing is more crucial than setting an appropriate price. Does the price allow for a sufficient markup? Is the price competitive? Is the price perceived by the consumer to be the right price for the value received? If you want to sell your item for $7.95 each, how about two for $15.90 (same price, but you get twice the average sale)? How about selling the first for $11.95 and the second for $3.95 (same total dollars if you sell two units—and if you don't sell two units, you get a higher price for a single unit)? Testing to determine the best price is vital to maximizing long-term payoff.

- *Shipping and Handling*. Where applicable (usually not for a publication or service), shipping and handling charges can be an important factor in pricing. It is important to know how much you can add to a base without adversely affecting sales. Many merchandisers follow a rule of thumb that shipping and handling charges should not exceed 10 percent of the basic selling price.

Free shipping, is a powerful incentive, but one that may be too costly to offer on a regular basis. Consumers love it, but free shipping has been the downfall of many traditional and E-commerce organizations, as shipping costs have risen. Some firms offer free shipping after a certain dollar level is achieved. Testing and careful back-end analysis is advisable to learn if free shipping meets your allowable cost per response.

- *Unit of Sale.* Will your product or service be offered "each"? "Two for"? "Set of X?" Obviously, the more units you can move per sale, the better off you are likely to be. But if your prime objective is to build a large customer list fast, would you be better off to offer single units if you got twice the response over a "two for" offer?

- *Optional Features.* Optional features include such things as special colors, odd sizes, special binding for books, personalization, and the like. Optional features often increase the dollar amount of the average order. For example, when the publisher of a dictionary offered thumb indexing at $2 extra, 25 percent of total purchasers opted for this added feature.

- *Future Obligation.* Common offers are book, tape, cell phone, and others that commit the purchaser to future obligation ("Take ten tapes for $1 and agree to buy six more in the coming 12 months." "Two-year contract required"). A continuity program offer might state: "Get Volume 1 free—others will be sent at regular intervals." Future obligation offers, when successful, enable the marketer to "pay" a substantial price for the first order, knowing there will be a long-term payout.

- *Credit Options.* In addition to credit cards (American Express, Diners Club, Visa, Master Card, Discover), many marketers offer PayPal or "It pays." The average charged order is usually at least 15 percent larger than a cash order. Some major direct marketers offer credit for 30 days, others offer installment credit with interest added (oil companies are a good example).

Alternative online payment processing options, such as Google Checkout or PayPal (owned by eBay), are growing. With these services, offered by Web merchants, consumers type credit card and/or bank information, plus billing information one time. Once the account is open, consumers pay for purchases by clicking onto the online payment processor much like they would select Visa or American Express as a payment option. These methods not only speed up checkout but offer the consumer theft protection because the Web merchant does not have access to the user's credit or banking information.

Merchants prefer these as they reduce their exposure to credit card fraud, have lower transaction fees than those charged by credit card companies, and pay quickly. They are very useful for international orders, as they handle the currency conversations, notifying the consumer of the amount that will be charged to their account in their currency, while the merchant receives payment in its local currency.

- *Time Limits.* Time limits add urgency to an offer. In fields like insurance, such deadlines may relate to mandated enrollment periods. For most marketers, deadlines are arbitrary, and simply a well-known way of producing quicker response. The use of such deadlines is a common tool in direct marketing. One word of caution: if you establish a time limit, stick to it.

- *Quantity Limits.* One of the major proponents of quantity limits is the collectibles field ("Only 5,000 will be minted. Then the molds will be destroyed"). There is something in the human psyche that says: "If it's in short supply, I want it." Even "Limit __ per customer" often outperforms no limit. But if you set a limit, stick to it.

Nothing should happen in the creative process until you have structured an offer, or offers, that will make the creative process work. But remember this: what you offer is what you live with.

Selecting Response Channels

Today, marketers may give prospects and customers a wide variety of media to respond to an offer. The four primary channels are mail, phone, fax, and the Web.

By mail, the marketer can provide a postage-free card or envelope, or the marketer can specify that the responder provide the postage. We're talking about pennies here, but surprisingly the postage-free card or envelope usually pulls better.

Order forms are another mail-response vehicle. The number one rule in creating an order form is that the order form must look too important to throw away. Close to that rule is: you should make it easy for the prospect to respond. Challenging the second rule are order forms that seem quite complicated. Publishers Clearing House comes to mind. Its order forms certainly look too important to throw away, plus they are loaded with *involvement devices*—various stamps that must be affixed to the order form prior to returning it.

Offers with a toll-free number appeal to prospects who have an urgent need for a particular product or service. On the other hand, those who have more of a curiosity than an urgent need would prefer to respond by mail. This group might be of a mindset that says, "Why should I voluntarily submit myself to a phone sales pitch?"

Currently, consumer and business respondents demand that marketers offer them choices for response. So, while mail and telephone are offered, so is

Internet response. Here again it is imperative for marketers to respond quickly. Companies that conduct business online should confirm orders by e-mail just a few minutes after they have been placed. Companies that still batch Internet orders and enter them offline—and there are a few—should confirm as soon as possible via e-mail.

An In-Depth Look at Unique Offers

Before going over the following offers, review each with the basic question: "How can I adapt this offer to my line of business?"

Exhibit 5–2 is a USPS offer of a free kit to general advertising agencies and direct marketing agencies. Answering research questions becomes a condition of receiving the free kit.

Exhibit 5–3 is taken from a Boston University political fund-raising effort. Note that there are suggested amounts ($25 and $30), but the opportunity to give a different amount, either more or less, is also given. Experienced fund-raisers know the average donation is larger if one or more amounts are suggested.

Exhibit 5–4, the Multi-CD offer, reflects common knowledge among music clubs that the number of new members acquired from a given ad is positively or negatively affected by the number of CDs offered. The choice of titles is enhanced even more by encouraging the prospect to consider additional titles on its Web site.

Exhibit 5–5 is a survey/win a free gift card offer. This survey solicits user feedback on the Web site www.ubahealth.org and obtains user contact information in exchange for a chance to win a $100 Wal-Mart gift card.

Exhibit 5–6 shows a direct mail offer from OfficeMax. Customers can save a total of $50 by using the enclosed coupons and savings card to purchase items on the Web, in store, or by phone. Each of the savings devices contains a personal tracking number, which can be used to collect information about the customer.

Merchandising the Offer

Each of the offers reviewed has wide application. As a matter of fact, many of the offers can be used successfully in combination. However, as powerful as many of these offers are, one must keep in mind that to maximize success the offers must be merchandised properly to target markets.

Free-Gift Offers

Exhibit 5–7 is an offer from the *Economist* magazine that gives readers four free trial issues. If you subscribe, you receive two free gifts.

Giving free gifts for inquiring, for trying, and for buying is as old an incentive as trading stamps. It is not at all unusual for the right gift to increase response by

EXHIBIT 5-2

USPS Free Kit Offers

It's about time someone was on your side!
Order your FREE **Outsmart the Office** kit.

☑ YES! Rush me the kit, jammed with smart marketing ideas and concepts, plus collectable character magnets designed to help me take on those insensitive Direct Mail bullies.

Name

Company Name   Title

Address   Dept./Mail Stop

City   State   ZIP™ Code

E-Mail Address

Are you involved in direct marketing at your company? (Choose one.)

☐ Yes   ☐ No

On an annual basis, how much does your company spend on its own direct marketing initiatives? (Choose one.)

☐ $250,000 or less
☐ $250,001 – $500,000
☐ $500,001 – $1 million
☐ more than $1 million

In a Direct Mail campaign, which best describes your company? (Choose one.)

☐ Client
☐ Mail House/Letter Shop
☐ Printer
☐ List Broker/Vendor
☐ Direct Marketing Agency
☐ General Marketing Agency
☐ Direct Marketing Consultant
☐ Other Marketing Supplier

Mr. Big Idea

The DM Veteran

ROI Guy

Collect characters including "Mr. Big Idea," "The DM Veteran," and more. (Hurry! "ROI Guy" has limited supply.)

AD5793

Send for your FREE Inspiration Kit!

☐ **YES, floor me! Send my FREE Inspiration Kit right away, and show me how to make my Direct Mail stand out.** (Please print clearly.)

Name

Company Name   Title

Address   Dept./Mail Stop

City   State   ZIP™ Code

E-Mail Address

FREE Inspiration Kit

We'd like to know more about you!

What is your role in your company/department? (Choose one.)

☐ Advertising
☐ Strategic Planning
☐ Creative
☐ Sales
☐ Public Relations
☐ Direct Marketing
☐ Brand/Corporate Marketing
☐ Product Marketing
☐ Production/Operations

What is your role in determining marketing resources for your company/department? (Choose one.)

☐ Sole decision maker
☐ Decision influencer
☐ Joint decision maker
☐ No role in decision

What role does Direct Mail play in your marketing mix? (Choose one.)

☐ Major role
☐ Complementary role
☐ No role

What is your company's primary advertising objective? (Choose one.)

☐ Increase sales
☐ Build brand awareness
☐ Improve customer loyalty
☐ Generate leads

Your information is protected by our privacy policies. See usps.com for details. ©2006 United States Postal Service. Eagle symbol and logotype are registered trademarks of the United States Postal Service.

AD5763

25 percent or more. On the other hand, a free-gift offer can actually reduce response or have no favorable effect on the basic offer. This is particularly true in cases where the unit of sale or amount of sale overshadows the appeal of the free gift.

What's more, there is a tremendous variance in the appeal of free gifts. Testing for the most appealing gifts is essential because of the great differences in pull. In selecting gifts for testing purposes, follow this rule of thumb: gifts that are suited to personal use tend to have considerably more appeal.

EXHIBIT 5–3

Boston University Fund-raising Response Card

Boston University

One Sherborn Street, Seventh Floor • Boston, MA 02215 • Phone 800-447-2849

Annual Fund Leadership Giving Societies

Honoring the distinguished group of contributors who, year after year, help the University to prepare young people for success. For membership in an Annual Fund Leadership Giving Society, gifts must be received by June 30, 2006.

Bronze Annual Giving Society (*$500*)   President's Associates (*$10,000*)
Silver Annual Giving Society (*$2,500*)   President's Circle (*$25,000*)
Gold Annual Giving Society (*$5,000*)

I am pleased to support the SMG Fund with a gift of:

☐ $25
☐ $50
☐ $100
☐ Other $_____

☐ Enclosed is my check, payable to Boston University.
For credit card information, please see reverse.

U324712010 SMG2003   6ASMGN 35933   24-000198548

Please correct any errors in your personal information.

Please note that for membership in an Annual Fund Leadership Giving Society, all gifts must be received before June 30, 2006.

Please charge my gift of $_____ to my credit card as specified below:
☐ Single payment of $_____.
☐ Monthly payment of $_____beginning in the month of_____ for_____months.

☐ MasterCard   Card Number
☐ Visa
☐ AMEX
☐ Discover

Expiration date

_____   _____
Signature   Today's date

How can I increase the value of my gift?

Matching gifts are a corporation's way of multiplying the benefits of their employees' charitable gifts. If you or your spouse works for a company that offers a matching gift program, your gift to Boston University could be doubled or even tripled. Find out if your company matches gifts by visiting the Web site www.bu.edu/alumni/giving/matching or by contacting your human resources or benefits office, or call us at 800-447-2849.

☐ I have included the Annual Fund in my will or estate plans.

There is yet another consideration about free gifts: is it more effective to offer a selection of free gifts of comparable value than to offer only one gift? The answer is that offering a selection of gifts of comparable value usually reduces response. This is perhaps explained by the inability of many people to make a choice.

Adopting the one-gift method (after testing for the one with the most appeal) should not be confused with offering gifts of varying value for orders of varying amounts. This is quite a different situation. A multiple-gift proposition might be a free travel clock for orders up to $40, a free miniature sports radio for orders from $40 to $75, and a free camera for orders over $75. Offering gifts of varying value for orders of varying amounts is logical to the consumer. The advertiser can afford a more expensive gift in conjunction with a larger order. The prime objective is accomplished by increasing the average order above what it would be if there were no extra incentives.

The multiple-gift plan works for many, but it can also boomerang. This usually happens when the top gift calls for a purchase above what most people

EXHIBIT 5–4

Multi-CD Offer

EXHIBIT 5–5

Survey/Free Gift Card

REUSABLE SHOPPING CARD

WAL·MART

YOU COULD WIN ONE OF THREE $100 WAL-MART GIFT CARDS!
FILL OUT OUR SURVEY HERE

Complete and send in this survey by October 1 and you'll be entered to win one of three $100 gift cards from Wal-Mart.

1. After reading *ehealth* magazine, is your likelihood of visiting a UAB specialist:
   - ○ Greater than before
   - ○ Less than before
   - ○ About the same as before

2. Which health topics are of interest to you?
   - ☐ Allergies
   - ☐ Alzheimer's disease
   - ☐ Arthritis
   - ☐ Blood pressure
   - ☐ Cancer
   - ☐ Diabetes
   - ☐ Headaches
   - ☐ Heart disease
   - ☐ Incontinence
   - ☐ Menopause
   - ☐ Men's health
   - ☐ Osteoporosis
   - ☐ Stroke
   - ☐ Weight management/nutrition
   - ☐ Women's services
   - ☐ Other

3. Are you currently a patient of the UAB Health System?
   - ○ Yes
   - ○ No

4. Have you visited the new UAB Health System Web site at uabhealth.org?
   - ○ Yes
   - ○ No
   (If no, skip to the end of the survey.)

5. What do you like most about the new UAB Health System Web site? (check all that apply)
   - ☐ physician directory
   - ☐ articles and publications
   - ☐ health library
   - ☐ medical services
   - ☐ videos
   - ☐ Other

6. How would you recommend we improve the Web site?

7. Would you recommend this site to a family member or friend?
   - ○ Yes
   - ○ No
   - ○ Maybe
   If no, why?

Name
Address
City
State
ZIP
Birthday
*e-mail address (to receive e-newsletters)

* This information is voluntary. Please provide an e-mail address if you would like to receive UAB e-newsletters on health topics of interest.

Submit my answers

---

can use or afford. The effect can also be negative if the gift offered for the price most people can afford is of little value or consequence. The multiple-gift plan tied to order value has good potential advantages, but careful tests must be conducted. An adaptation of the multiple-gift plan is a gift, often called a "keeper," for trying (free trial), plus a gift for keeping (paying for the purchase). Under this plan the prospect is told he or she can keep the gift offered for trying even if the product being offered for sale is returned. However, if the product being offered is retained, the prospect also keeps a second gift of greater value than the first.

Still another possibility with gift offers is giving more than one gift for either trying or buying. If the budget for the incentive is $1, for example, the advertiser can offer one gift costing $1, two gifts combined, costing $1, or even three gifts totaling $1. From a sales strategy standpoint, some advertisers spell out what one or two of the gifts

EXHIBIT 5–6

OfficeMax Direct Mail Offer

are and offer an additional "mystery gift" for prompt response. Fingerhut Corporation of Minneapolis is a strong proponent of multiple gifts and "mystery gifts."

Free gifts are a tricky business, to be sure. Gift selection and gift tie-ins to offers require careful testing for best results. The $64,000 question is always: "How much can I afford to spend for a gift?" Aaron Adler, cofounder of Stone & Adler, maintains that most marketers make an erroneous arbitrary decision in advance, such as "I can afford to spend 5 percent of selling price." He maintains

EXHIBIT 5-7

Economist **Free Trial Subscription and Free Gifts**

that a far more logical approach is to select the most appealing gift possible, without being restricted by an arbitrary cost figure, rather than being guided by the net profit figures resulting from tests. For example, Exhibit 5–8 shows a comparison of net profits for two promotions on a $29.95 offer: one with a gift costing $1 and the other with a gift costing $2, given a 50 percent better pull with the $2 premium.

It is interesting to note that, in this example, when the $1 gift was offered the mailing just about broke even. But when the cost of the gift was doubled, the

EXHIBIT 5–8

Comparison of Profits from Promotions with Free Gifts of Different Costs

Item	$1 Gift	$2 Gift
Net pull of promotion	1%	1.5%
Sales per thousand pieces	$299.50	$449.25
Less		
Mailing cost	120.00	120.00
Merchandise cost (45%)	134.98	202.16
Administrative cost (10%)	30.00	44.93
Premium cost	10.00	30.00
Total costs	$294.98	$397.09
Profit per thousand pieces	$4.52	$52.16

profit jumped from $4.52 to $52.16 per thousand mailed. Another advantage of offering more attractive gifts (which naturally cost more) is to offer gifts of substantial value tied to cumulative purchases. This plan can prove particularly effective when the products or services being offered produce consistent repeat orders. A typical offer under a cumulative purchase plan might be, "When your total purchases of our custom-made cigars reach $150, you receive a crystal decanter absolutely free."

Get-a-Friend Offers

One overlooked and profitable offer is the get-a-friend offer. If you have a list of satisfied customers, it is quite natural for them to want to let their friends in on a good thing. The basic technique for get-a-friend offers is to offer an incentive in appreciation for a favor. Nominal gifts are often given to a customer for the simple act of providing friends' names, with more substantial gifts awarded to the customer for friends who become customers.

Based on experience, here is what you can expect in using the get-a-friend approach: You will get a larger number of friends' names if the customers are guaranteed that their names will not be used in soliciting their friends. Response from friends, however, will be consistently better if you are allowed to refer to the party who supplied their names. To get the best of two worlds, therefore, you should allow customers to indicate whether their names may be used in soliciting their friends. For example: "You may use my name when writing my friends" or "Do not use my name when writing my friends."

Response from friends decreases in proportion to the number of names provided by a customer. One can expect the response from three names provided by one person to be greater than the total response from six names provided by another person. The reason is that it is natural to list the names in order of likelihood of interest.

Two safeguards should be applied to get the maximum response from friends' names: (1) limit the number of names to be provided, for example, to three or four, and (2) promote names provided in order of listing, such as all names provided first as one group, all names provided second as another group, and so forth. Those who have mastered the technique of getting friends' names from satisfied customers have found that, with very few exceptions, such lists are more responsive than most lists they can rent or buy.

Short- and Long-Term Effects of Offers

A major consideration in structuring offers is the effect a given offer will have on your objective.

1. To get a maximum number of new customers for a given product or service as quickly as possible.

2. To determine the repeat business factor as quickly as possible.

3. To break even or make a profit in the shortest time.

So, the key question to ask when designing an offer is: "How will this offer help to accomplish my objective?" Say you are introducing a new hobby magazine. You have the choice of making a short-term offer (three months) or a long-term offer (12 months). Because your objective is to determine acceptance as quickly as possible, you would decide on a short-term offer. Under the short-term offer, after three months you will be getting a picture of renewal percentages. If you have made an initial offer of 12-month subscriptions, you would have to wait a year to determine the publication renewal rate. In the interim, you would be missing vital information important to your magazine's success.

If the three-month trial subscriptions are renewed at a satisfactory rate, you can then safely proceed to develop offers designed to get initial long-term subscriptions. It is axiomatic in the publishing field that the longer the initial term of subscription, the higher the renewal rate is likely to be. Circulation professionals know from experience that if they are getting, say, a 35 percent conversion on a three-month trial, they can expect a conversion of 50 percent or more on 12-month initial subscriptions. This knowledge, therefore, can be extrapolated from the short-term objective to the long-term objective.

Terms of Payment

Where a direct sale is involved, the terms of payment you require can hype or depress response. A given product or service can have tremendous appeal, but if payment terms are too stringent—beyond the means of a potential buyer—the offer will surely be a failure. Five general categories of payment terms may be offered: (1) cash with order, (2) cash on delivery (COD), (3) open account, (4) installment terms, and (5) revolving credit.

If a five-way split test were made among these categories, it is almost certain that response would be in inverse ratio to the listing of the five categories. Revolving credit would be the most attractive and cash with order the least attractive terms. With each loosening of terms, the appeal of the offer is hyped.

In a four-way split test on a merchandise offer, here's how four terms actually ranked (the least appealing terms have a 100 percent ranking): cash with order, 100 percent; cash with order—free gift for trying, 144 percent; bill-me offer (open account), 177 percent; and bill-me offer (open account) and free gift, 233 percent. As the figures disclose, the most attractive terms (bill-me offer and free gift) were almost two and a half times more appealing than the least attractive terms (cash with order).

When merchandise or services are offered on open account, payment is customarily requested in 15 or 30 days. Open-account terms are customary when selling to business firms. When used in selling to the consumer, however, such terms, while appealing, can result in a high percentage of bad debts, unless carefully selected credit-checked lists are used.

The best appeals lie in installment terms and revolving credit terms. Both mechanisms require substantial financing facilities and a sophisticated credit collection system. Installment selling in the consumer field is virtually essential for the successful sale of "big ticket" merchandise—items selling for $69.95 and up.

Sweepstakes

Sweepstakes offers were once standard for mass mailers like *Reader's Digest* and Publishers Clearing House. The prize structures for those firms and their ilk have promised and delivered grand prizes that fulfill the giddy dream of becoming an instant multi-millionaire. Direct mail sweepstakes reached their peak at the end of the 20th century, when they became the target of federal government legislation.

The hype of the basic offers is the sweepstakes. It is generally known by the general public that "you need not purchase to win." However, consumer behavior being what it is, there is an uncalculated percentage of the general public that do buy because they think that will increase their opportunity to win.

While sweepstakes are no longer used in direct mail as they once were, they continue to be an important part of many marketers' arsenals. Rumors of the death of sweepstakes as a purchase incentive are highly exaggerated. You can find them online with a simple search (See Exhibit 5–9).

EXHIBIT 5-9

Sweepstakes E-mail from Publishers Clearing House

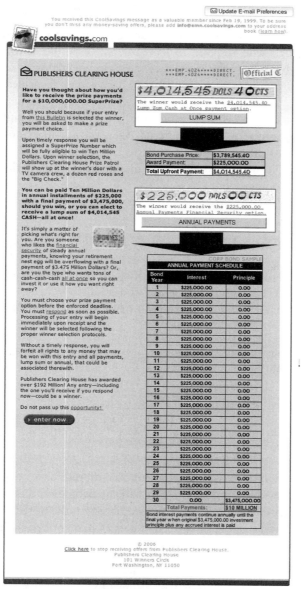

Hard Offers vs. Soft Offers

Free offers and sweepstakes are sometimes called soft offers. Offers that give less away, asking for payment with order, for example, are called hard offers.

Respondents to soft offers are more loyal to the offer of winning than they are to the product or service offered, and don't convert into paid customers as well as those individuals who respond to hard offers. Respondents to soft offers have significantly higher recession rates (i.e., they decline delivery and/or payment) and product return rates than respondents to hard offers, regardless of the product category.

Respondents to hard offers are generally more qualified and have a greater interest in the product or service offered. Generally, a marketer will get fewer responses to a hard offer. The ultimate hard offer is *"Cash with order."* While we don't recommend it, we recommend that marketers test offers that provide some balance between too hard and too soft.

Danger of Overkill

The power of an offer cannot be overestimated. But there's such a thing as too much of a good thing—offers that sound too good to be true, or that produce a great front-end response but make for poor pay-ups or few repeat customers. Here are two thought-provoking examples.

1. A comprehensive test was structured for a fund-raising organization to determine whether response would best be maximized by (a) offering a free gift as an incentive for an order, (b) offering a combination of free gift plus a cash bonus for completing a sale, or (c) offering a cash bonus only. The combination of free gift plus cash bonus pulled the lowest response by far; the free-gift proposition far outpulled the cash-bonus proposition.

2. A $200-piece of electronic equipment was offered for a 15-day free trial. This was the basic proposition. But half the people on the list also were invited to enter a sweepstakes contest. Those on the portion of the list not invited to enter a sweepstakes responded 25 percent better than those on the portion invited to enter.

In both these examples, the more generous offer proved to be "too much." One must be most careful not to make the incentive so overwhelming that it over-shadows the product or service being offered. Another important consideration in structuring offers is the axiom: "As you make your bed, so shall you lie in it." Here's what we mean: if you obtain thousands of new customers by offering free gifts as incentives, don't expect a maximum degree of repeat business unless you continue to offer free gifts. Similarly, if you build a big list of installment credit buyers, don't expect these buyers to respond well to cash-basis offers, and vice versa.

The offer—it is the carburetor with just the right mix that powers the driving machine.

Terms and Conditions

It is important to include terms and conditions when completing offers for purchases of products or services, sweepstakes offers, and terms of use for Web sites. Terms and conditions are a form of legal agreement that become binding when a buyer or user signs a response device or checks a click box on the Web site. Terms and conditions provide important safeguards that limit a marketer's risk of doing business.

Terms and conditions generally include language that waives the buyer's legal warranties, which are implied in the purchase of products and services. They provide contractual remedies for the seller if a buyer or user does not pay or provides false information when making a purchase. And, terms and conditions help protect intellectual property when it is involved.

While a marketer may have an "express warranty" such as a 30-day product warranty, unless the buyer has agreed to the terms and conditions, they would still be covered by the implied "Warranty of Merchantability," which applies when a product doesn't do what it was intended to do. There are additional implied warranties (e.g., Warranty of Non-infringement, Warranty of Title, and the Warranty of Fitness for Purpose) that still apply unless the buyer waives those rights in a written agreement such as the terms and conditions.

Terms and conditions usually cover several areas including product or service scope, when pricing is binding, retention of title, payment conditions, liability for defects, compensation of damage or loss, property rights, jurisdiction of agreement and remedies, and election for dispute resolution. Where intellectual property is involved, these agreements help protect it.

Typically, terms and conditions are written by an attorney and are not part of the promotional copy. In a direct mail package, the terms and conditions are usually included on the back of the response device or in some other conspicuous area. Signing or checking a box on the response device is an indication that the buyer has read and agrees with the terms and conditions. In e-mails and on landing or Web pages, the terms and conditions are usually in a text area with their own check box.

For financial service mailings they may be many pages long and included as a separate insert. Interest rates and financial rules are usually governed by states, so this requires versions for each state.

Online, a "clickwrap" agreement is used. They are used for user agreements as well as for terms and conditions. The term "clickwrap" was taken from the term used for offline software terms and conditions, which are generally placed within view and readable inside the "shrinkwrap" used around software packaging.

For online "clickwrap" terms and conditions to be binding, the marketer must make it compulsory for users to "view" the agreement and the user must agree to it by use of a check box or other device. In addition, the user may not be permitted to advance within the Web site or landing page without agreeing, and the user must have the option to end use at that point without further obligation.

Research shows that most users click the agreement box within a second or two, in less time than it would take to read or review the terms and conditions. It is likely that the same behavior occurs in direct mail. So long as they are properly written and properly provided, terms and conditions are often found to be enforceable agreements by courts and provide important protection for marketers. Most marketers are not attorneys. Marketers and their agencies rely on the use of lawyers to review and provide opinions on their promotions and the elements of their offers. Often lawyers will revise copy, layout, offers, and other elements to bring them into compliance with the law.

Where an experienced lawyer has been involved, it is important to get a written opinion. A written opinion provides advice and guidance for business conduct. It is something that marketers' rely upon to demonstrate that they have done their due diligence to assure that their promotions meet compliance standards. And, in the event of litigation or other challenges, a written opinion is an important protection.

Special Categories

When creating offers, the category of the marketer plays an important role. Not every offer is appropriate for every category, and some categories are greatly restricted in what can be offered, what information can be used, etc.

Campaigns for pharmaceuticals, insurance, financial services, children's products, sweepstakes, contests, and other categories of direct mail, e-mail, and Web sites require an additional level of screening. There are specific laws such as HIPAA (Health Information Portability and Accountability Act) designed to protect consumers' personal health information. Marketing to children is protected under COPPA (the Children's Online Privacy Protection Act). Sweepstakes are covered under the Deceptive Mail Prevention and Enforcement Act. Financial services and insurance are covered under a myriad of local and national rules and regulations, so that mailing typically will be versions by each geographic jurisdiction.

CASE STUDY:	**American Marketing Association Tests Membership Offers**

Written by Jacobs & Clevenger with approval of its client, American Marketing Association.

BACKGROUND

The American Marketing Association (AMA) is one of the largest professional associations for marketers, with 38,000 members worldwide in every area of marketing. Membership cuts across corporate marketing, research, and service companies, and includes individuals in marketing agencies, research firms, and database companies. Membership also depends upon a strong membership base within the academic community.

For over six decades the AMA has been an essential resource providing relevant marketing information that experienced marketers turn to every day.

Membership benefits include resources for professional development, including connections with their local AMA chapters and online Special Interest Groups, along with reduced pricing for more than 70 AMA events and conferences every year. AMA members also have access to a wealth of information since they receive a subscription to *Marketing News* and another AMA publication, along with unrestricted access to the members-only resources on the AMA Web site, including case studies and articles. The AMA also provides their membership with a variety of networking opportunities via the *M-Guide*, a marketing services directory, and the AMA member roster.

In order to recruit new members, the AMA conducts semi-annual acquisition campaigns. The main component of the acquisition campaigns is direct mail. The campaigns are spearheaded by the International Headquarters Marketing Team and coordinated with the regional AMA chapters.

It is important to note that the AMA offers memberships on an individual basis, although membership is sometimes paid by companies/employers.

CHALLENGE

While AMA name recognition tends to be high, research has demonstrated that nonmembers are not always familiar with all of the membership benefits. Since the acquisition campaigns are the main driver to gaining new membership, the key challenge lay in identifying ways to maximize these campaigns. Refining offers became a priority, given that offers tend to be one of the largest drivers in driving campaign response.

Price/value relationship is typically the biggest hurdle in generating AMA membership. Offers have been utilized to help encourage response, add to immediacy, and work effectively against fence sitters, but in this category they generally won't convince someone who is not yet interested into responding.

During acquisition campaign periods, the AMA generally offers a two part incentive:
1. Waive the membership application fee
2. Provide an incentive

In the end, the primary challenge was finding incentives that could work as effectively as possible to convert prospects to members.

SOLUTION

The AMA decided to conduct an online survey to provide insights and direction for new member acquisition offers. The online survey was distributed to over 33,000 contacts via e-mail. The survey was designed to measure the relative impact of various incentives versus a baseline offer; for example a waived application fee plus a travel alarm clock valued at $25. These types of surveys are typically helpful for gauging relative performance but should not be utilized for specific response forecasting, as intent to purchase and actual response are typically not an accurate representation.

The survey tested several offers across three distinct categories:

1. Monetary discount off an AMA product such as AMA conference discount.
2. Business related studies such as a proprietary research on *Marketing Expenditures* with comparative marketing expenditure to sales data by industry or a *Corporate Salary*

Survey with salary data on marketing employees nationwide.

3. Personally related premiums such as a micro cassette recorder or pro-style binoculars.

The proprietary research and conference discount demonstrated the greatest likelihood of increasing AMA membership. In a research environment these offers generated significantly more interest (almost double) than premium offers.

Premiums were not viewed as motivating to joining the AMA or having an element of usefulness. In addition, many respondents implied that premium-based offers "cheapened" the AMA's efforts. Since many premiums had been used historically in campaigns, it was decided that these offers should be tested against alternatives in an in-market situation to gauge impact.

Putting Offers to the Ultimate Test

After conducting the offer research, the AMA was eager to put these learnings to use in a live test market setting. Like many business-to-business efforts, quantities were limited. Quantities usually totaled about 60,000 people per campaign, so testing multiple offers during one campaign period proved to be rather difficult (See Exhibits 5–10 and 5–11).

Generally, one offer was tested per campaign period. If a specific offer outperformed the control, it was then used as the control in the following campaign period. If results were close between test cells, then a re-test would usually be conducted.

As often is the case, attitudes in research and behavior in actual decisions can prove to be different. Even though the proprietary research and conference discount generated the greatest interest in research,

EXHIBIT 5–10

American Marketing Association Buckslip

the premiums outperformed other options in in-market testing.

In research, respondents indicated that they wanted something that could be used for *business* and their career. But in reality, respondents chose something that could be used *personally*, during their leisure time.

Through additional probing, it became clear that different segments might find different offers appealing. However, profile characteristics did not exist up-front to direct tailored messaging. Given that more and more prospects were responding via the Web, it was decided that one offer would be promoted in the mail and several offer choices would be given at the time of sign-up via the Web. While it is important to only provide one choice in direct mail to simplify response, the Web provides an appropriate medium to provide choices.

RESULTS

Personally related premiums such as binoculars continued to be the control for the first three campaigns following the research. These types of premiums continued to outperform business-related premiums, including AMA conference coupons and USB flash memory sticks.

In spring 2006, personally related premiums were defeated for the first time by a Prepaid MasterCard, generating almost twice the response. In fact, the Prepaid MasterCard helped the AMA have their most successful acquisition campaign to date. The campaign delivered a 64 percent membership increase from the fall 2005 campaign.

The popularity of prepaid cards has been significant in the consumer marketplace, but their interest is universal and has great applications in many facets of direct marketing.

EXHIBIT 5-11

American Marketing Association Buckslip

PILOT PROJECT The American Marketing Association (AMA) sent out a survey to test the appeal of several different membership offers. The offers included discounted products, proprietary research, and personal items. Keep in mind this is a business-to-business case and the AMA's membership objectives. Develop four additional offers. Explain the rationales for why they are appropriate.

Key Points

▶ A dynamic offer can succeed even if selling copy is fair to poor—but dynamic copy cannot make a poor offer succeed. The ultimate, of course, is a dynamic offer supported by dynamic copy.

▶ Use testing to find the offer that best matches your target audience and accomplishes your objective: getting a maximum number of new customers for a given product or service as quickly as possible, determining the repeat business factor as quickly as possible, or breaking even or making a profit in the shortest time.

▶ Consider the long-term effects of your offer. If you obtain thousands of new customers by offering free gifts as incentives, you will need to continue to offer free gifts to get repeat business. Similarly, installment credit buyers will continue to respond to installment terms, not cash-basis offers.

▶ The focus of the offer should always be the product or service. Keep it at the center of your strategy, and make sure that incentives, and other offer elements, remain consistent with it.

▶ When creating offers, the category of the marketer plays an important role. Not every offer is appropriate for every category, and some categories are greatly restricted in what can be offered, what information can be used, etc.

▶ It is important to include terms and conditions when completing offers for purchases of products or services, sweepstakes offers, and terms of use for Web sites. Terms and conditions provide important safeguards that limit a marketer's risk of doing business.

CHAPTER 6

BUILDING CUSTOMER
RELATIONSHIPS

It has been called the decade of the customer, the customer millennium, and virtually every name that can incorporate "customer" within. There's nothing new about businesses focusing on customers or wanting to be customer-centered. However, in today's marketplace just saying an enterprise is "customer-centric" is not enough. It is a promise that organizations must keep. The problem is that most organizations still fall short of this goal.

This chapter will address customer management and the variety of techniques used in customer relationship building, nurturing, loyalty, retention, and reactivation. These include Customer Relationship Management (CRM), Customer Performance Management (CPM), Customer Experience Management (CEM), and customer win-back. The objective of these techniques is to help organizations coax the greatest value from their customers. While the strategies are different, all of these methods use the tools and techniques of direct marketing in their execution.

What is "Customer-Centric"?

There is a clear definition of "customer-centric." To be customer-centric, an organization must have customers at the center of its business. Many organizations are sales-focused and not marketing-oriented. Many enterprises that have a marketing focus are brand- or product-centric. Being a customer-centered organization is much more complex than it appears.

Enterprises can't just decide to organize around customers. Today, it is often customers who dictate how an enterprise should be organized to better serve their needs. Customers want their needs met, to be cared for, and to be delighted. Customers don't want enterprises to put up barriers. Customers are not concerned with the organization's policies or processes, business rules, mission, positioning, the software they use, or their infrastructure. And, customers are not concerned with an organization's profits. But, organizations can't put customers ahead of profits, can they?

Customers *are* the source of an organization's profits. A firm's existing customers are its surest and most reliable source of future revenue. And, customers are the one key asset that can separate one organization from another. So, in successful organizations, corporate strategies are customer strategies, where customers have become the mission of the business.

Focus on Customer Equity

In their book, *Driving Customer Equity: How Customer Lifetime Value is Reshaping Corporate Strategy*, Roland Rust, Valarie Zeithaml, and Katherine Lemon write about a conceptual framework that realigns an organization's strategies to make it more customer-centered and to help it build "Customer Equity." They define a firm's customer equity as the total discounted lifetime value of all of its customers.

The concept of Customer Lifetime Value is well known to traditional mail-order and direct marketing firms (see Chapters 21 and 22). What makes the concept of customer equity so important is that Rust, Zeithaml, and Lemon contend that while a firm's physical assets, competencies, and intellectual value are also important, customer equity is the most important component of a firm's value. Intuitive and actionable strategies for driving customer equity must be central to a firm's core activities.

For Rust, Zeithaml, and Lemon, there are three drivers of customer equity and organizations should focus on those that most influence the organization:

- Value equity

- Brand equity

- Retention equity

Value equity is primarily formed by the perceptions of an organization's quality, price, and convenience. These perceptions are cognitive, objective, and rational. Value equity may be as simple as picking up milk at the corner store to save time. Or, it may be as complex as bidding on designer products on eBay to save money.

Brand equity is made up of perceptions that are not explained by a product or a firm's objective attributes. These are perceptions that are emotional, subjective, and sometimes irrational. Customers of nearly every great brand exhibit this behavior, as they remain loyal to the brand, pay more for it, and will often do without something in a category rather than purchase a different brand. Driving a $50,000-plus BMW SUV while living in the city and fuel approaches $4 a gallon is an example. As researcher Clotaire Rapaille notes, we don't drive cars, we wear them like a piece of clothing.

Retention equity comes from customers who have chosen the firm in their most recent purchase for any reason. These customers are most likely to be positively affected by retention and relationship-building activities. These most recent customers are often the most likely to purchase again, often before they have a need. However, they must be nurtured; loyalty cannot be assumed.

Profitability, Retention Measures of Customer Equity

Central to this idea is that organizations must balance growth with profitability. Growth requires acquisition, which is expensive and a significant expense to an organization. Retention yields profitability but must be balanced to maximize value. When an organization spends too much on growing its customer base, it may never be profitable. When an organization stops adding customers to its database, the database shrinks through attrition and changes in customer lifecycles. It is a balance that must be achieved.

To maintain the balance, enterprises must be able to measure the customer performance. And, customers must become an element in the organization's summary of key performance indicators. Cost targets and headcounts may be where they need to be, but the organization must know how it is doing with customer value. It needs to be able to have a way to improve customer value or react quickly if the value of a key customer segment begins to erode. One way is to track profit goals for various customer segments, and to clearly differentiate customer groups based on value. This helps organizations to invest in customers where it will do the most good.

Organizations need to identify and manage their *Most Valuable Customers* (MVCs). Who are the most valuable customers? It depends on how the organization defines it. It may be customers that have the greatest propensity to buy. It may be the profitable customers. In many organizations, as few as 10 percent of the customers provide 90 percent of the profit. It is different for every organization.

Organizations need to identify and manage their *Most Growable Customers* (MGCs). These may not be the most profitable customers, but they may represent the future for the enterprise. MGCs include segments that may represent lower purchase amounts but have higher potential, such as second-time buyers. For a children's clothing marketer, it might be buyers of younger sizes.

Another group that needs to be addressed is the *Most Costly Customers* (MCCs). This group, while still customers, often cost more to service than the revenue that they bring in. Often, this includes segments that have high return rates, high bad-debt rates, or only purchase items on deal. The most costly customer segments need to be identified so that they may be removed from further promotional activities.

The Nature of Loyalty and Satisfaction

While satisfaction and loyalty are related, they are different attributes of marketing effectiveness. Satisfaction reflects how well an organization fulfills customer expectations of quality, service, and other material elements of a brand's value proposition. Both logic and emotion affect satisfaction.

Loyalty is a behavioral system of repetition that helps to build value over time. It is transactional in nature and becomes habitual (e.g., stopping at a Starbucks on the way to the office). While it may seem counter-intuitive, organizations don't always need to satisfy customers to generate loyalty.

Contractual, emotional, or functional loyalty are types of loyalty that are less dependent upon satisfaction to affect purchase events or trigger defections. Service gaffs, the kinds reported in satisfaction surveys, are often ignored or forgiven. This is common where there is a long-term emotional bond to a brand, where loyalty is based on vendor agreements (e.g., where a purchase threshold must be met to qualify for a discount), or where loyalty is based on convenience (e.g., the only air carrier with nonstop flights to a destination). While service lapses may be forgiven, they are not overlooked. It may simply take longer for them to have a negative effect.

What's more, an organization can reach high satisfaction levels but not generate customer loyalty. There is more than one example of this. In the automotive field, J.D. Power is well known for measuring satisfaction. Routinely, they report satisfaction levels for auto brands in the 80th percentile. However, repurchase rates for auto brands are in the range of 30–40 percent. And, only 20 percent of customers return to the same dealer to purchase their next car. It is clear that there is a disconnect, one not explained by statistical variations, which is why marketers must work to improve both satisfaction and loyalty. It is misleading to assume that if one improves, so will the other.

This complexity makes it difficult to measure effects of a single program. The short-term transactional gains of CRM tactics don't always turn into long-term profits. Nonetheless, loyalty is a behavior that marketers can focus on as a way of growing and building their businesses.

Segmenting for Loyalty

Segmenting customers is one key to building customer loyalty. The idea of value segmentation as a tool for building customer loyalty is not new. In the 1920s, Alfred P. Sloan, president of General Motors (GM), developed a system for GM brands in which they were differentiated by style, quality, and performance. Each brand (Chevrolet, Pontiac, Buick, Oldsmobile, and Cadillac) was a step up from the last. The concept was based on the idea that upwardly mobile consumers were willing to pay progressively more for the added features and status of owning a more prestigious brand, while remaining within the GM family.

This idea was in sharp contrast to the positioning and thinking of Ford Motor Company. At the same time, Ford's president, Henry Ford, remained fixed on a lowest delivered cost strategy. Ford's quest was focused on keeping a low unit

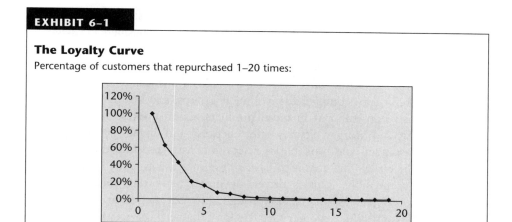

EXHIBIT 6–1

The Loyalty Curve
Percentage of customers that repurchased 1–20 times:

cost for the manufacturing of their cars. They did this by only offering one model of automobile, the Model T.

Loyalty remains complex. Exhibit 6–1, "The Loyalty Curve," demonstrates one aspect of this. Loyalty curves almost always have the same hook shape. More people are loyal at the start than after a number of purchases. In this example, the group or segment is tracked over 20 purchases. Of those who made the first purchase, only a few remain. It is the goal of loyalty programs to identify those most likely to continue to purchase, and find ways to keep them loyal.

Today, marketers routinely use analytics to predict which customers are likely to buy more, be profitable, defect, or cost an organization money. They do this by segmenting age, income, geography, purchase history, and other recognizable patterns. Each segment can be targeted with different kinds of offers, such as savings, different levels of service, offers to repurchase, retain, etc. These offers can easily be driven by database marketing programs. CRM programs help to automate this process. So, small shifts in customer demand for products or services can be monitored in real time and trigger changes in communications, channels, offers, and messaging to produce the desired customer behavior.

For example, credit card marketer Capital One conducts over 30,000 tests, matching different customer segments and offers annually. Such testing would be unmanageable without a CRM system that automates and bridges customer-facing and back-end analysis.

Managing Customer Lifecycles

One of the goals of CRM is to help gain a greater share of a customer's wallet. One way to earn a greater share is to extend relationships with customers through the customer lifecycle. The customer lifecycle summarizes different stages in a customer's relationship with an organization. It is based on consumer or business life stages or events where needs change. Enterprises have different brands, product, and service offerings, so the customer lifecycle is different for each. This concept benefits organizations with broader product offerings, such as banks or financial institutions.

Banks, credit card companies, investment groups, and insurance companies offer an extensive portfolio of financial products. Companies such as Citibank, HSBC, Fidelity, and Morgan Stanley offer checking and savings accounts, loans, credit cards, insurance, and brokerage services to consumers at different points in the customer lifecycle. The goal is to have a customer use as many of their product offerings as possible. This is driven by direct marketing communications targeted to consumers as they pass through different stages in the lifecycle. Exhibit 6–2 illustrates the customer lifecycle for a financial services firm.

A financial services firm may start by giving a teenager a *student loan* for college. The consumer will get direct mail and e-mail offers for a *checking account* and a *credit card* during college years. When the student graduates from college, they will be offered *auto loans* and *car insurance* for the purchase of a new car. Then, they will receive communications for a *savings account* as they plan for marriage, the purchase of a home, and college for their children. They will receive offers for *mortgages* and *homeowners' insurance*. As they grow older, consumers will receive offers for *life insurance*, *investment*, and *retirement accounts*.

EXHIBIT 6–2

Customer Lifecycle

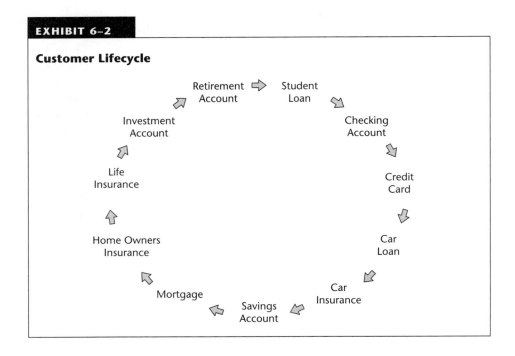

Often, a customer lifecycle is made up of a number of shorter lifecycles. BMW expects to maintain customers by offering a variety of models, each appealing to different demographics. Each purchase is an entry point into a longer customer lifecycle. BMW tracks customers through lifecycles and knows that someone purchasing a 3 Series sedan may be a good candidate for a Sport Utility Vehicle or 5 Series sedan as their needs change with their family size.

The purchase of each new vehicle becomes a smaller customer lifecycle in itself, as the buyer compares models online, goes to the BMW Web site for product information, test drives at the dealer, decides upon the model and accessories, decides on financing, takes delivery of the car, and returns to a dealer for service. Then, after a few years, the cycle begins again. The longer-term lifecycle is made up of a group of shorter-term lifecycles viewed repeatedly.

Customer lifecycles are an important tool for marketers. While decisions as to what to communicate and when are complex, understanding a customer's lifecycle is a starting point for managing customer relationships.

The Role of Customer Relationship Management

Customer Relationship Management (CRM) is a ubiquitous acronym that has no single definition. The accepted definition of CRM is often different for each organization and for different groups within the organization. Marketing may have its definition of CRM, sales its definition, customer service its definition, and information technology (IT) its definition.

The authors prefer a definition of CRM from research company The Gartner Group: "A business strategy that maximizes profitability, revenue and customer satisfaction by organizing around customer segments, fostering behavior that satisfies customers, and implementing customer-centric processes."

In *CRM Unplugged*, authors Philip Bligh and Douglas Turk add to this idea by proposing that CRM investments should be aimed at providing sustainable competitive advantage for an organization, not just operational efficiency. Bligh and Turk note that high failure rates associated with CRM are often the result of a focus on short-term improvements versus long-term profit goals. Long-term advantage comes from a business strategy that is driven by improving the effectiveness of overall customer outcomes. This includes improved return on investment for customer acquisition, retention, win-back, up-sell, and cross-sell of products, services, and solutions.

Failure has long plagued the concept of CRM. Many experts have predicted the death of CRM or have already decreed its end. Yet, many important customer marketing analytical tools, such as customer scorecards and dashboards, have come out of CRM. While the goals of CRM are laudable, unfortunately the results do not match up.

It is estimated that organizations have spent $80 billion on CRM software over the last decade trying to create the elusive 360-degree view of their customers. Yet, according to Gartner, 41.9 percent of CRM software "licenses" bought by respondents were never deployed. A study by AMR Research concluded that more than half of CRM implementations had, at best, difficulty with end-user adoption and, at worst, created chaos among end-users.

Too often CRM was thought of as a software technology that could be implemented across an enterprise. It was likened to database marketing, and it was argued that much of CRM can simply be duplicated with databases. While CRM is supported by technology, it is not driven by software. While CRM technology can centralize customer data, making it useful requires a much more complex approach. Corporate management has discovered that CRM's real challenge is improving staff skills and commitment, unifying intelligence from many internal data sources, and implementing ways to apply the data across multiple touchpoints to enable relevant customer interactions.

There are three factors that influence the success of CRM programs:

- People

- Process

- Technology

The People Factor

People are the most important factor in the success of CRM. No other business strategy cuts across so many organizational lines or requires so much interdepartmental cooperation. This is not something that can be implemented with an e-mail asking everyone to just get along. It requires that top management make clear that the goals of CRM are one of their priorities. Management must invest resources and let staffers know that they expect a return on the investment for CRM.

Employees need to understand where they are going and why. This may require rethinking organizational structures, compensation, and training to help staffers learn how to integrate new processes and applications into their daily work flow. It is not just *customer-facing* staff that must change the way that they think and act. Everyone within the organization must be trained to understand the goals of CRM and be enlisted to help make it work.

In this lies the paradox of CRM. When asked why they want to implement CRM, the number one goal of most CRM programs is to integrate data captured by sales, marketing, and customer service. Yet, according to The Gartner Group, the number one reason CRM programs are unsuccessful is the failure of sales, marketing, and customer service to cooperate. Bain & Co. ranks CRM as the fastest growing management "tool," with the third-lowest satisfaction score. For CRM to be successful, this must change.

While successful CRM requires top management's commitment, implementation requires the cooperation of employees and staff. Those that will be using new systems need to be involved from the beginning to help manage their own change. Organizations should let users test drive systems and have input on specifications, to find strengths and weaknesses and gain valuable buy-in. And, enterprises should have good internal communications through every stage to keep staff up to date on the CRM initiative, its timeline and benefits, and how it will impact the day-to-day work environment.

From a people perspective, CRM is a two-way street. While it offers many benefits, it requires many changes in the ways that business is done. It will require a new level of participation from employees, a new level of cooperation among departments, and a new way of implementing dialogue with customers. These are not simple changes; however, they are right for these times.

The Process Factor

One of the outcomes of CRM is that the many business processes are automated. Most CRM systems come with their own built-in business processes. They are usually generic and don't correspond to the way that an organization's processes work. Trying to make these processes work can be a difficult and frustrating task.

Some organizations simply take their old processes and try to implement them within their new CRM system. Generally, these processes need a complete review to learn which can be implemented, which need updating, and which need to be replaced.

For CRM to be successful, an enterprise must carefully review internal and external customer-facing business processes to make the greatest use of technology. The organization needs to decide what the objectives of the processes are, how it measures success, and who owns and maintains the business process.

A process as simple as communicating information about products and services requires significant thought. Will the firm have a FAQ (Frequently Asked Questions) on its Web site? If so, who will keep it updated? If a prospect or customer wants additional information, can they get it via phone? By e-mail? Will someone be available 24/7 to respond? If not, how quickly will contacts be responded to? Will a confirmation e-mail be sent immediately when an information request is received? Will someone respond with the information requested the next business day, and what is the measurement standard for response time? Who will respond? The contact center, customer service, or sales? Are inquiries viewed as prospects and qualified for follow-up by the sales force? Will inquiry e-mail addresses be added to the contact database? Will other contact information (name, company, address, phone number, etc.) be asked for at the time of inquiry or in a later communication?

Now, imagine the hundreds or thousands of an enterprise's daily business processes going through the same analysis! Businesses processes must have documented procedures and the capability to be implemented, no matter what department or channel is responsible.

Cross-departmental processes must have buy-in from all sides, clear rules and interfaces for customer information flows across departments. Organizations can't make the mistake of expecting bad processes to work better once they are automated. CRM will simply allow the issues with bad processes to be seen more quickly, but only addressing process improvement can help repair processes that don't work.

The Technology Factor

Technology is the most difficult factor, given the number of CRM alternatives now available. Organizations need to know what capabilities they are looking for, which of their current systems they must integrate with CRM, and have some idea of their budget. There are endless CRM vendors and applications from which to choose, and the number continues to grow.

There is Enterprise cRM (e.g., PeopleSoft) as well as applications for various functions of CRM (sales force automation, campaign management, call center management, etc.). There are installed software solutions (e.g. Oracle) as well as hosted services (Salesforce.com). The choices of solutions and vendors are endless. However, enterprises must do their due diligence. They shouldn't believe what vendors tell them without doing a thorough review. They should have real-time examples of the software in action, not just PowerPoint presentations or sample reports.

Integration with existing systems is always an issue with software. Fixes can almost always be found, but they may require expensive middleware or other software not part of the CRM suite. This should be discussed thoroughly with IT included in discussions. It is important to confer with references who have implemented the same applications, not just with any organization that has implemented a vendor's CRM suite.

While it is not possible for organizations to be aware of the CRM technology trend, organizations do need to track technologies that are likely to impact their efforts. This may include a variety of future capabilities, such as building their own permission e-mail list, computer telephony integration, interactive voice response, Web-support services, workforce optimization, etc. Organizations should consider the future and what their ideal CRM system will look like in a few years. Doing so may change their decisions about CRM implementation and so avoid a costly and avoidable investment in a system that won't scale as their business does.

Loyalty and Frequency Programs

Too often, CRM initiatives become nothing more than a loyalty or frequency program. Airlines, credit cards, and supermarkets all have extensive loyalty marketing programs. There is nothing wrong with clubs, bonus, or points programs. However, the problem is that most consumers belong to a number of frequent flier, frequent shopper, and other frequent buyer programs and don't see any differentiation among them. Strictly speaking, frequency and loyalty programs are not CRM.

Frequency programs reward customers for purchases. The more a customer purchases, the more points are earned and the greater is the reward. Loyalty programs capture vast amounts of customer data. The promise of these programs is that captured data will be used for additional programs and processes, which will lead to greater customer loyalty. Too often, loyalty programs are nothing more than a series of tactics such as e-mails, direct mail, etc. Consumers simply don't see the value, even as their wallets are filled with loyalty cards.

The goals and emphasis of CRM are different. CRM is focused on effectively and efficiently using information to segment customers based on profit, value, events, etc. A loyalty program can be part of an enterprise's CRM initiatives. However, as this chapter has described, CRM is much more.

Often, loyalty programs send out monthly communications. Too often, every member receives the same newsletter. Compare that to Amazon.com's approach. Amazon's analytical CRM system uses past-purchase behavior to trigger targeted e-mails to customers.

Exhibit 6–3, "Amazon's Customer E-mail," is an example which was triggered by a past book purchase. The copy explains that Amazon.com noticed that buyers of books by author Sam Hill have also "purchased books by author David Apgar." The e-mail describes a new book available by David Apgar and includes links so that the recipient can go to the Amazon.com Web site and review and purchase the book.

Customer Experience Management

While there can be a debate on whether customers can be "managed," there can be no doubt that marketers can manage the customer experience. And, they can do it without the large investments, robust technology, and organizational process improvements required of CRM. At a time when the velocity of change is increasing, Customer Experience Management (CEM), with its emphasis just at the point of a customer's interactions and experience with a brand's product, channels, and communications, has great appeal.

The customer experience is the set of connections between a customer and a brand that delivers benefits through touchpoints. Each connection is an event between the brand and the customer. Connections are defined by:

- The mode of the connection (how the connection occurs)
- The benefits delivered through the connection
- The touchpoint where the connection takes place

EXHIBIT 6-3

Amazon's Customer E-mail

To be successful, a customer experience must go beyond personalized and customized connections. It must become a collaborative process where there is a fair exchange of value for both the customer and the brand at all touchpoints. Organizations that focus on the customer experience provide a broad portfolio of solutions and benefits adapted to each customer preference, especially the customers considered the most valuable to the enterprise. They are empowering and provide access to customers that allow them to define their own experience as much as possible.

The quality of these interactions must be very high. The dialogue must be transparent. There can't be a hard sell or hidden agenda. Organizations must ask questions but leave ample time to hear the answers. This is an iterative process, where touchpoints become interactive to provide immediately accessible and tangible benefits/value to customers.

Two keys to providing a great customer experience are consistency and relevancy. Each touchpoint should be used for what it is best at to deliver an optimal experience. And, there can be no gulf between what communication promises and the experience the enterprise delivers.

The focus on customer experience has gained great interest since the development of the Internet, where the customer experience can be observed, altered, and measured in real time. Marketers have learned that very small changes in the customer experience can have a great impact on results. While this parallels what direct marketers have learned through testing, the Internet's ability to change so many variables and measure them has caused customer experience to become a center of attention itself.

Today, organizations must manage the customer experience across all touchpoints. This includes: communications (advertising, DM, promotion, PR, online, etc.); visual/verbal identities (product names, logos, packaging, signage, etc.); brand environments (retail spaces, offices, trade shows, Web sites, etc.); people (sales, service, etc.); co-branding (event marketing, sponsorships, partnerships, alliances, product placement, etc.); and all other controllable brand contacts.

CRM, loyalty, and Customer Experience Management are all interwoven. They are focused on helping organizations market to customers based on their differences, not their similarities. On an objective basis, this requires the enterprise to direct a complex combination of results, benefits, paths, and touchpoints, making it different from customer to customer. On a subjective basis, it varies based on the customer's personal mindset, making it personal and unique, even as a result of the same inducements.

Customer Performance Management

At a time when organizations have never been more concerned with measurement and accountability, customer marketing tools have gained a new focus based on how well they work. Customer Performance Management (CPM) is the next generation, the evolution of CRM and CEM, evolving into a way of not just communicating and delighting customers, but enabling better financial and business performance monitoring (See Exhibit 6–4).

The importance of developing customer performance metrics should be on every marketer's mind as they look for ways to ensure their seat at the table. Too many CRM and customer marketing investments fail on this count. Marketers shouldn't enjoy reaching their customer's marketing goals unless those metrics can be related to their own organization's financial and profit goals.

To track performance, top management needs a more granular approach, one where success metrics are related to the thousands of financial variables locked up in the organization's data. The data needs to be linked to profitability metrics such as profit per promotion, percentage increase customer, employee, quarter, etc. Some additional metrics might be:

- Overall customer acquisition versus the acquisition goal per segment

- Adoption rates of new product/service adoption versus segment goals

- Percentage change in revenue by period, segment, and/or customer

- Change in profit percent by period, segment, and/or customer

- Customer service performance (e.g., turn-around time, delivery time, defects, service calls on time, etc.) by segment or customer versus goals

Lastly, these financial and profitability metrics need to be published in a way that top managers, line managers, and anyone else that needs them can have access to.

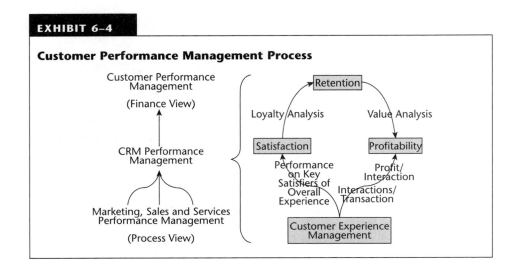

EXHIBIT 6–4

Customer Performance Management Process

For example, a franchise organization knew that point of sale at its stores was an important touchpoint for customers. Its CPM system shared customer data from their loyalty program with store managers to help them develop programs to bring more customers into stores. A credit card company consolidated the view of their customers so that phone reps would have the information on one customer screen to instantly make decisions on waving the annual fee, forgiving a missed payment, or reversing an interest fee or service charge.

Customer Performance Management seems a method of the future. By including the best of CRM and CEM, but adding performance metrics and monitoring, CPM provides a set of tools that marketers need. One tool that has come out of CPM and been adopted by many marketers is the marketing dashboard.

Marketing Dashboard

A marketing dashboard is a graphical representation of the most important performance indicators of an enterprise. Marketing dashboards can be customized to provide the relevant information that a marketing group may need and be adapted to share essential marketing metrics to other groups within the organization. Information can be displayed online in HTML, within PowerPoint files, or distributed as printed files within a work group or more globally. Some marketing dashboards provide information in real time, others as a morning e-mail, and yet others as part of the monthly reports circulated throughout the organization.

The amount of information included in the marketing dashboard is different in each organization. It may show just a few of the most critical marketing metrics or as many as 25 different metrics depending upon the company. It may show leads to sales conversions; the number of new customers per day, week, or month; revenue by customer segment versus costs; or the latest results from a win-back program.

Marketing dashboards allow marketers to monitor what's working and what's not. The use of charts and graphs helps to simplify complex marketing metrics, which are a constantly moving target in most organizations. Organizations can tailor the dashboard to monitor customer segments, program results, systems, and processes through the marketing organization. It is a tool that improves efficiency and effectiveness while helping to communicate each organization's key data.

Exhibit 6–5 is a marketing dashboard for a global lead generation program. It includes a U.S. domestic and international lead pipeline report (where the lead is in the sales funnel), closing percentages, and lead flow by source. In this, the lead program can be adjusted quickly to ensure that it meets the organization's lead generation goals.

EXHIBIT 6–5

Marketing Dashboard

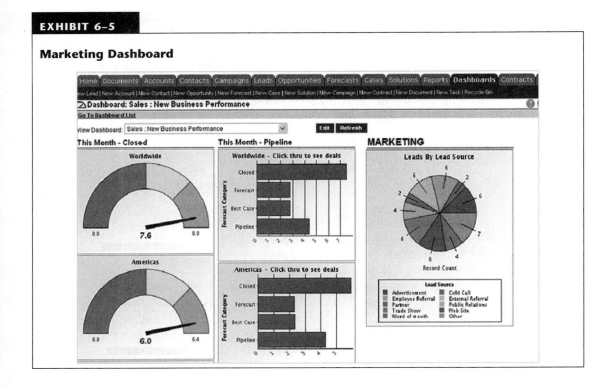

Customer Scorecards

To make customer insights valuable, they must be a product of two or more data or information elements. True customer insights can be gained by looking at the points where various data elements cross. Marketers can segment groups and see their similarities and differences by viewing various data intersection points (e.g., customer needs, behaviors, demographics, etc.). By looking at the various segments from different perspectives, marketers get closer to the more extensive view of customers that is a goal of customer marketing.

One way to monitor this is to create a customer scorecard. The customer scorecard helps to communicate to every department within an enterprise how various initiatives are doing. In many organizations, multiple versions of the scorecard are maintained for various uses (e.g., financial, marketing, management, etc.) to provide the most information in the most relevant way.

A customer scorecard graphically displays important marketing metrics. It tells a story about the health of a marketer's customers, providing knowledge, not just data points. The customer scorecard generally shows changes in the metrics over time, for example on a quarterly basis. This provides a way to gauge how well the enterprise is doing, what its strengths are, and where weaknesses start to show up.

This allows marketers a way to make positive changes before issues become a problem for the firm.

The first step in developing the customer scorecard is to identify marketing metrics that will be tracked. One view of the metrics may be for all customers. However, it is best to display metrics for various customer segments. For example, new customers will likely have different trends than mature customers. High-value customers will have a different trend than low-value customers. For an example of a customer scorecard, see Exhibit 6–6.

The first step in creating a customer scorecard is to define the marketing metrics that will be tracked. These may include:

- *Existing Customers.* Identify current customers vs. former customers.

- *New Customers.* Evaluate this against customer acquisition goals.

- *Retention or Defection.* Are you keeping or losing profitable customers?

- *Market Penetration.* What is the opportunity for growth in a segment?

- *Category, Product, or Brand Penetration.* Displays the percent of customers that have purchased, own, or use.

- *Cross-Sell.* The ratio of additional products, services, or categories purchased.

- *Up-Sell.* This can be average order, market basket of products, frequency of purchase, monthly revenue, or average balance in financial accounts.

- *Profitability.* Current margins or other drivers of fees such as warranties, etc.

- *Customer Lifetime Value.* This gives an idea of the long-term potential and shows if the trend is increasing or declining.

- *Channel Penetration.* This has become important as different channels have different revenues, costs, and other metrics. It can be retail vs. online, ATM vs. branch visit, or auction vs. "buy now."

EXHIBIT 6–6

The Customer Scorecard

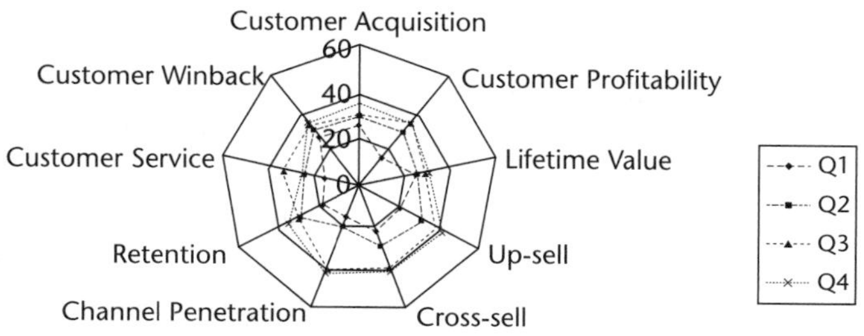

- *Customer Service*. Displays the number of service calls and/or results satisfaction surveys.

Like other areas of business, customer scorecards are dynamic. Scorecards should be updated when there are changes in business drivers, strategies, customer segments, and when you simply need another view. Surveying customers may help learn what is important to them and should, therefore, be important to the organization. The goal of the customer scorecard is to improve and refine the metrics of a business. It is an important and valuable tool.

The Net Promoter Score

Times have changed for marketers. While many organizations are focused on turning their best and most loyal customers into advocates, they find that a small, vocal minority are in the marketplace doing harm to their brands. In the past, this unhappy group would be satisfied to simply not purchase from an enterprise again. Today, they actively communicate their unhappiness, with e-mails, Web sites, and damaging word of mouth. While marketers do what they can to improve satisfaction levels, they must come to grips with the role that is played by both their most loyal customers and those that actively disparage their organization.

Marketers focus on advocates, as they should. More time needs to be spent on detractors. Detractors are no longer benign. They can build their own Web sites to express their anger, or find comfort in many Web sites all too willing to bash corporate behavior. One such site is Consumerist.com, one of Gawker Media's titles. Consumerist.com works, in the words of some, as a "brand killer." The site acts as a channel for getting consumers "through the delinquencies of retail and service organizations." The site skewers the customer service shortcomings of cable companies, computer makers, phone companies, ISPs, and organizations in the travel and entertainment category (e.g., airlines, hotels, and fast-food chains).

An article in *BusinessWeek* magazine pointed out that major brands worry about blogs and sites like Consumerist.com as much for their misinformation as their truths. These Web sites allow posts by readers, which are only later checked for their veracity.

BusinessWeek reported an event where Consumerist.com was quick to post a damaging audiotape of a phone call to America Online (AOL) in which a member found it difficult to near impossible to simply cancel their membership with a live agent. The poster, whose voice was heard on the tape placing the call to AOL, became an instant celebrity.

This post was picked up by many other Web sites, including news sites, and spread throughout the Web. The poster and the tape were featured on cable and radio talk shows and news programs, although there were rumors that the poster had made a number of calls to organizations "fishing" for just such a result to tape and post. When Consumerist.com was able to post a copy of AOL's Customer Retention Manual, AOL found itself in a very defensive posture, as their detractors found an "I told you so" rallying point.

Contrast this to Dell Computer's experience reported by *BusinessWeek*. In July 2006, while Dell Computers was undergoing criticism for overheating batteries, which it later recalled, Consumerist.com posted a claim by a reader that Dell's computers "contained equipment that secretly recorded a user's every keystroke." The Web site referenced national security, privacy, and the Freedom of Information Acts. They added a minor note at the bottom of the post as follows: "Edit: D'oh! This is much ado about nothing. Snopes debunks." It seems that a Web site called "Snopes," which focuses on finding the truth regarding urban legends, had already debunked this rumor as false. Yet, the message was posted and the damage was done.

Detractors have many avenues for their complaints. These complaints can quickly spread throughout the Web and even to traditional media channels. While arguments about responsibility can be made, the truth is that such errant posts by detractors can severely wound an otherwise strong brand. Organizations do well to mollify and placate detractors or at least move them to the neutral range.

In his book *The Loyalty Effect*, Fred Reichheld of Bain & Co. forced marketers to take a new look at customer loyalty by pointing out that a 5 percent improvement in customer retention can boost profits by up to 100 percent. This observation has had great influence on customer marketing. In his book *The Ultimate Question*, Reichheld provides a measurable bridge between word of mouth communications and customer loyalty. Reichheld calls it the Net Promoter Score (NPS).

The NPS is based on the answer to a simple question, *"Would you recommend us to a friend?"* This question may be asked as part of a user or customer satisfaction survey, personal contacts with customers, at the end of every phone contact and e-mail, or on Web site visits. NPS has been used by organizations as diverse as General Electric, Enterprise Rent-a-Car, Amazon.com, and Intuit (Turbo Tax).

The concept is simple: the answer to this question provides feedback to help an organization identify customers that have potential to help or hurt their profitability. NPS divides an organization's customers into categories based on their answer to the Ultimate Question. Their response puts them into one of three categories:

- Promoters

- Passives

- Detractors

Notes Reichheld: *Promoters* are "loyal enthusiasts who keep buying from a company and urge their friends to do the same." *Passives* are "satisfied but unenthusiastic customers who can be easily wooed by the competition." *Detractors* are "unhappy customers trapped in a bad relationship." The goal for an organization is to create more "promoters" than "detractors."

To measure how well a company is doing, Reichheld recommends that promoters be thought of as assets and detractors as liabilities. Passives are neutral, and often the greatest percentage of customers. They can be swayed one way or the other, so they cannot be ignored.

To calculate an enterprise's Net Promoter Score, the percent of customers that are detractors is subtracted from the percent of customers that are promoters. This can be expressed as a simple formula: Promoters – Detractors = Net Promoter Score. Based on this formula, customers that score nines and tens are "promoters," customers that make up over 80 percent of an enterprise's positive word of mouth. This segment accounts for a business's organic growth, growth that comes from existing customers. "Passives" fall in the range of sevens and eights and are satisfied for now. An organization may have a share of their wallet, but "passives" are switchers who shop with whoever has the best deal. "Detractors," those scoring one to six, give the enterprise a failing grade. They are vocal, they complain, their average purchase is smaller, and they have a high propensity for defecting.

The importance of this is in Reichheld's experience. According to Reichheld, in more than 24 industry segments analyzed by Bain, the enterprise that had the highest net promoter score was the leader, with growth at two and a half times that of their competitors.

It is human nature to look for silver bullets or an easy way to achieve a difficult goal. When it comes to customers, businesses know that they need to acquire, maintain, grow, nurture, and turn their customers into advocates. They have learned that it is much more profitable to market to customers than to prospects. And, they have learned that customer loyalty is key to long-term growth. How to accomplish that is still a mystery for most.

Win-Back: Too Little, Too Late

Most organizations don't have strong win-back policies, programs, or monitoring systems. Research shows that less than 50 percent of organizations monitor defection rates. This is potentially troublesome for organizations. When asked, most think defections are in the 7–8 percent range. However, on average it is a minimum of 20 percent for most B-to-C organizations.

There is too much apathy toward customers that defect. When asked, half of the organizations don't know how many customer they could win back. Most consider "churned" customers lost, with no chance of revival. Many don't interview lost customers. However, many lapsed customers are "dormant" and awaiting resuscitation. There is a 60–70 percent probability of selling again to "active" customers. And, there is a 20–40 percent probability of successfully selling to lapsed customers. Compare this to the 5–20 percent chance of making a successful sale to a new prospect and it is clear why focusing on churned customers is so important.

On average, firms lose 20 percent of their customers annually. They believe that an 80 percent customer retention rate is good enough. However, retaining 80 percent of customers means that the enterprise is losing 20 percent of the customer base per year. Over just four years that is like losing half of the customer base. In five years, just 40 percent is left. Exhibit 6–7 shows how that progression works.

Here is where this becomes important: If a company has 10,000 customers and wants to grow its customer base by 25 percent annually, its goal would be to add 2,500 customers annually (10,000 × 25 percent = 2,500). However, if it loses 20 percent of its existing customers annually (10,000 × 20 percent = 2,000), it must replace those 2,000 customers in addition to the 2,500 it wants to add for growth. So, the company would need to add 4,500 customers annually. Each year, it would have to account for defections in its overall growth plans.

While marketers can't stop defections, it can detect a customer's reasons for defecting. This usually starts with an analysis of account histories. The focus should be on order, re-order, and return patterns. Reviewing customer-service records adds another dimension. This often helps to distinguish differences in product, service, and customer issues.

Marketers need to get both sides of the story. They should conduct in-depth exit interviews with customers. These can be done by phone, mail, e-mail, via the Web, etc. Marketers must be prepared to learn the unexpected. Sometimes product, delivery, or service problems are identified. Or, it may be that the terms and conditions of the offers become an issue once customers become aware. Or, it could simply be that competitors are making offers that are just too good for customers to turn down.

Once a customer has defected, don't try to get too much information right away. Timing can be an important consideration in the response. Wait 30–60 days before asking too many questions. This makes it easier to separate reasons such as emotion or logic. Emotional defectors may churn regularly, drifting from one

EXHIBIT 6–7

Example of Defections at a 20 percent Annual Rate over 5 Years

YEAR	NUMBER OF CUSTOMERS
1	100
2	80
3	64
4	51
5	41

vendor to another. Sometimes emotional defections are easy to repair, once the reason for the defection is identified.

Another tool for this is a "Lost Customer Report." Produced monthly, the goal of the Lost Customer Report is to anticipate reasons and help to prevent future lost customers. This report highlights sales histories and fluctuations as well as the top reasons for customer defections. It may include overall satisfaction and a range of the highest and lowest-rated satisfaction attributes. Plus, it should include verbatim customer comments. A sample of a Lost Customer Report is included as Exhibit 6–8.

Ultimately, some customers always defect. There are many reasons for defections. And, before any efforts to win back lost customers begin, lost customers need to be segmented into groups so that future actions can be properly targeted. Segments are usually based on the reason for the customer defection. Organizations need to distinguish between avoidable and unavoidable defections.

Some customers are *intentionally pushed away* because they are unprofitable to serve, poor credit risks, etc. No win-back action should be taken with this segment in the future.

Another segment of customers are *unintentionally pushed away*. This group finds that brand, product, or service doesn't meet their expectations. The reasons for this can be identified in research. It is likely that this group is a candidate for win-back.

EXHIBIT 6–8

Elements of a Lost Customer Report

- Products/Services
- History
  - First contact
  - Last contact
- Sales
  - Trend
- Profitability
- Source
- Channel(s)
- Demographics/Firmographics
- Customer service contacts
  - Resolutions

Another group of defections are customers that are *pulled away*. They may have found a competitor with a better offer, left for better service, higher quality, etc. Sometimes they leave paying a higher price but perceive that the overall value proposition is simply better. This is another group worth targeting for win-back efforts.

Another segment is customers who are simply *bought away*. For this segment it is all about the lowest price. They are attracted to low ball or introductory price offers. Likely, that's how they became one of your customers as well. However, this group has loyalty that can be bought. They are likely to churn for the next best offer. This is a group to suppress from win-back offers.

The last group of customers is those who have *moved away*. While this is often used in the geographical sense, some customers have moved into different lifecycles and life stages. Disposable baby diapers can only be sold as long as babies need them. Sears was able to predict that they could keep young families until their middle years, when teenagers and adults became status-conscious, and were attracted to higher-end brands. Sears would attract the same customers as the adults became empty-nesters and focused more on capital conservation than status, and as their children started young families of their own. Changes in demographics also affect loyalty, as needs and wants change through swings in age, income, and personal status. The reasons for *moved away* defections need to be addressed individually to determine if they should be targeted for win-back.

EXHIBIT 6–9

The Win-Back Decision Map

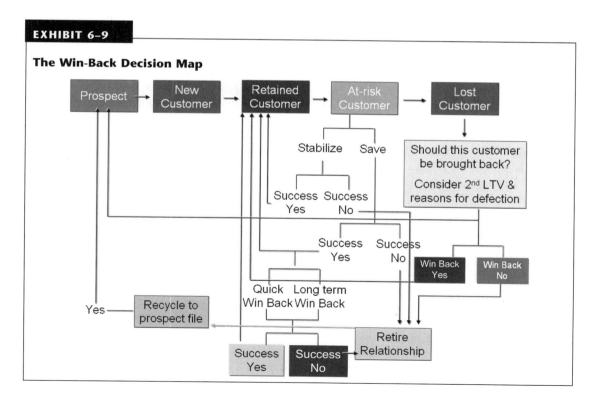

Once groups have been identified, their win-back potential needs to be scored. Often, this is done by calculating a second lifetime value for the segment. This is different from the first lifetime value. Win-back customers are already familiar with the organization's products/services. There is more data about customer likes/dislikes. And, there is a shorter prospect and new customer phase where performance is often increased by recognizing these segments as former buyers, not as prospects. This is all factored into the win-back lifetime value.

Because this group is so important, the win-back process must be ongoing. There are decisions that need to be made about groups, and specific win-back programs need to be developed. The win-back process includes decision points and creative efforts targeted at lost customers. Exhibit 6–9 shows how such a process might work. Note that the process takes into consideration the fact that marketers won't win back all of their customers. It identifies specific decision points where there will be a hard-stop of efforts. Decisions are based on the segments that we described above, as well as exhausting the win-back lifetime value.

CASE STUDY: Guinness Relationship Marketing

Adapted from the Direct Marketing Association International Echo Awards 2005.

BACKGROUND

Trends in the Irish alcohol market were threatening Guinness's market position. The price of drinks in pubs had increased, as a result more consumers were drinking at home, switching brands when doing so. Consumers become less loyal in a market with more and more product choice. In recent years, a smoking ban was enacted, prohibiting smoking in all workplaces including pubs. Because the majority of Guinness is sold in pubs rather than for at-home drinking, these events posed a major challenge for Guinness.

With 90 percent of Guinness consumed by 10 percent of drinkers, the first goal was to secure this volume against such threats by acquiring 100,000 new drinkers to the existing Relationship Marketing program. The idea was to communicate with these drinkers to maintain and deepen their brand commitment (by one pint per week) and to cross-sell products to them from within the Guinness portfolio. The key at-home product offering from Guinness is cans of Guinness Draught. This product suffers from a lack of perceived quality among those consumers who drink Guinness in pubs, resulting in only 5 percent of Guinness in-pub drinkers drinking it at home. This was a big issue in a rapidly changing market, where the future of the brand could depend on converting pub drinkers to at-home drinkers.

TARGET AUDIENCE

For many loyal male Guinness drinkers, aged 21–60. Guinness is the number one brand they choose when having a pint in their local pub. The Guinness drinker has a unique and emotional attachment to Guinness. The quality of the pint influences their preference for the "local" pub and, very often, the quality of the actual night out. For Guinness drinkers, there is an "unspoken" drinking ritual which begins with the way the pint is poured, served, and consumed. Loyal Guinness drinkers can identify with this ritual.

MARKETING STRATEGY

The strategy was to maximize the value of the relationship between consumers and their pubs, leveraging that relationship to build further brand loyalty, and cross-selling cans of Guinness Draught to consumers who change brands when drinking at home.

CASE STUDY: Guinness Relationship Marketing *(continued)*

Objectives were: acquire 100,000 Guinness drinkers to the database; significantly increase sales (by 1 or more Guinness pints per week) while retaining loyalty among consumers by the end of the first year; and convert 20 percent of loyal Guinness consumers to drink cans of Guinness Draught at home (as well as drinking it in the pub), from a base of 0 percent currently drinking it at home.

SOLUTION

For acquisition the program was sold to pubs via sales representatives who provided pubs with "The Big Black Book." The Black Book gave owners and managers the information needed to train staff and recruit consumers, including sign-up forms and point-of-sale material for their pub. Pubs were eager to participate due to a decrease in the numbers in their pubs and the guarantee of consumers being sent back to their pub with a pint voucher on a regular basis. The point-of-sale posters allowed consumers to see themselves as "One of Guinness' most wanted" and encouraged them to register. The pubs were allocated a unique code (on all sign-up forms) so that consumers could be mailed personalized vouchers for their local pub (See Exhibit 6–10). Consumers completed a simple form, which clearly explained the benefits of the program, gathered the essential date of birth and signature information (essential for responsible marketing of alcohol brands), together with their affinity to the brand and all contact information (See Exhibit 6–10). Consumers received a Welcome Pack within six weeks of signing up, followed by maintenance communications to sustain their increased consumption over the course of the year. These maintenance communications prompted consumers to feel like they were being "called" when that black envelope came through the letterbox. The mailings worked to create anticipation of a great night out, while also providing subtle reassurance of the quality of the pint waiting for them. Competition incentives in each mailing ranged from sports tickets to holiday prize draws (incentives shown by research to be of most interest to these consumers).

For cross-sell communications, extensive analysis of the database was undertaken to extract consumers who were loyal to Guinness in the pub, drank at home, but did not drink cans of Guinness Draught. These consumers (hosts) were targeted with an invitation to sign-up friends to watch matches of their favorite sport on three consecutive occasions, facilitated by Guinness who provided them with product vouchers and drinking glasses. The initial communication invited the consumer to sign-up three friends who would then receive invitations to the host's house the week before a big soccer match. All parties received reminder communications on the week and day before the match. The kit box was delivered the week before the match and included vouchers for product, glasses, and a welcome mat which hosts were invited to put outside the door to prompt the guys to "let themselves in, the match is on."

Measurement for acquisition was tracked through the database itself, maintenance mailings were tracked through voucher redemption and pre-post/test and control telephone research. Cross-sell activity was tracked through response rates, telephone research, and voucher redemption rates.

RESULTS

This campaign was a winner. The goal was to hit the acquisition target within 12 months by signing up 5,000 pubs—approximately 70 percent of the pubs targeted—and 98,000 consumers. Acquisition rollout started in October, and after just three months pub sign-ups had increased 8 percent and 70,000 consumers were acquired.

Based on telephone research on the first two mailings, consumption levels were on track to increase by one pint per week over the course of a year. Voucher redemption rates of 35–55 percent indicate that pub owners/managers are happy with the program. The campaign achieved a participation rate of 73 percent from hosts; the brand conversion rate was 42 percent—well above the 20 percent target rate.

CASE STUDY: Guinness Relationship Marketing *(continued)*

Guinness Reply Form

MOISTEN AND SEAL   MOISTEN AND SEAL

⇒ SIGN UP THE LADS ⇐

If you have a friend who is over 18 and regards GUINNESS stout as their drink of choice, hand
out the FREEPOST form below for them to fill in and return. Then we'll be in touch with them soon.

Your details Enter your contact details here if you would
like to receive news about GUINNESS and special offers by
post. Please complete in BLOCK CAPITALS

Title   Male   Female

Name

Surname

Address

Phone   Date

Would you be happy to have a quick conversation with us
about **Guinness** sometime? Yes   No

Enter your email address here if you would like to receive
news about **Guinness** and special offers by email

Enter your mobile phone number here if you would like to
receive news about **Guinness** and special offers by SMS

0 8

You & GUINNESS Thinking about all beer/cider brands,
which statement applies to you most? (please choose one)

I drink mostly/only **Guinness**

Guinness is one of the drinks I drink

I rarely drink **Guinness** and actually prefer

I never drink **Guinness**

Sign here IF THE FOLLOWING ARE NOT COMPLETED WE
WILL NOT BE ABLE TO COMMUNICATE WITH YOU

X Signature

X Date of Birth   dd/mm/yy

At Guinness & Co. we promote sensible drinking, so if we don't know that
you are over 18 we won't be able to send you any mailings or offers.

I do not want to receive special offers and news about
Diageo's other alcohol brands through the post

We will only use your data in accordance with our privacy statement which
you can view online at www.guinness.com

G WR 06   G1004MW0033AB / 123456

MOISTEN AND SEAL   MOISTEN AND SEAL

MOISTEN AND SEAL   MOISTEN AND SEAL

⇒ SIGN UP THE LADS ⇐

If you have a friend who is over 18 and regards GUINNESS stout as their drink of choice, hand
out the FREEPOST form below for them to fill in and return. Then we'll be in touch with them soon.

Your details Enter your contact details here if you would
like to receive news about GUINNESS and special offers by
post. Please complete in BLOCK CAPITALS

Title   Male   Female

Name

Surname

Address

Phone   Date

Would you be happy to have a quick conversation with us
about **Guinness** sometime? Yes   No

Enter your email address here if you would like to receive
news about **Guinness** and special offers by email

Enter your mobile phone number here if you would like to
receive news about **Guinness** and special offers by SMS

0 8

You & GUINNESS Thinking about all beer/cider brands,
which statement applies to you most? (please choose one)

I drink mostly/only **Guinness**

Guinness is one of the drinks I drink

I rarely drink **Guinness** and actually prefer

I never drink **Guinness**

Sign here IF THE FOLLOWING ARE NOT COMPLETED WE
WILL NOT BE ABLE TO COMMUNICATE WITH YOU

X Signature

X Date of Birth   dd/mm/yy

At Guinness & Co. we promote sensible drinking, so if we don't know that
you are over 18 we won't be able to send you any mailings or offers.

I do not want to receive special offers and news about
Diageo's other alcohol brands through the post

We will only use your data in accordance with our privacy statement which
you can view online at www.guinness.com

G WR 06   G1004MW0033AB / 123456

MOISTEN AND SEAL   MOISTEN AND SEAL

EXHIBIT 6–11

Guinness Direct Mail Personalized Voucher

IT'S THE RESULT THAT COUNTS

For every team, before any match comes hours and hours of training, clever thinking and attention to every detail. But after they've left the field and played their best, all that anyone remembers is the result. The GUINNESS Team put the same energy and commitment into developing cans of GUINNESS Draught stout. Now with over 800 million cans sold in over 70 countries since its launch, we think the result speaks for itself.

THE GRAND FINALE

MIDDLESBROUGH
VS
LIVERPOOL
AT
FRANK'S

Hi Frank,

Will it be the best of three? Get round to Frank's on Saturday 20th of November and find out for yourself. The afternoon promises top action, quick play, sharp banter and the great taste of cans of GUINNESS Draught.

It's the last match of three, so don't miss out. Get your two free cans of GUINNESS Draught and get round to Frank's for some quality craic.

Sláinte,

The Guinness Team

The **GUINNESS®** Team

P.S. Keep an eye out for the black envelope, GUINNESS will be in touch again soon!

TWO
COMPLIMENTARY
500ml CANS
OF GUINNESS.
DRAUGHT

Guinness & Co. is a trading name of Diageo Ireland. The GUINNESS word, the HARP device and ARTHUR GUINNESS signature are trade marks. © Guinness & Co. 2004.

00801000012345667063

Voucher Terms & Conditions

1. This voucher entitles the bearer to two complimentary 500ml cans of GUINNESS Draught.
2. The Promoter reserves the right to refuse to redeem torn or defaced vouchers. Photocopies will not be accepted.
3. This voucher can only be redeemed by persons aged 18 or over.
4. No cash will be given in lieu of this voucher.
5. This voucher has no monetary value.
6. The Promoter is Diageo Ireland, St James's Gate, Dublin 8.
7. This voucher is only valid from 15/11/04 to 17/01/05.

To the Retailer:
This voucher will be redeemed by Diageo Ireland for the recommended retail price of two individual cans of GUINNESS Draught (up to a maximum of €1.99 per 500ml can). This cannot be redeemed against any multi-pack or tray. This voucher is invalid if redeemed against any product other than GUINNESS Draught 500ml.

For reimbursement: Please return vouchers by 19/02/05 to: GUINNESS Complimentary Vouchers, Coupon Redemption, Section Number 2120, PO Box 5149, Freepost, Crumlin, Dublin 12.

RETAILER

9 822558 130005

PILOT PROJECT

Adapted from "The Case of North State" by Dr. Debra Zahay, Northern Illinois University.

You have been assigned to design a customer relationship management program for the alumni association of the undergraduate programs of North State University. The university currently graduates 1,000 engineering students each year, 100 veterinarians, 700 business students, and about 300 students in various other disciplines. North State U.'s unique positioning among the university system is as a technically oriented school. It is listed among the top engineering programs in the United States.

Currently, the alumni association classifies its alumni into four categories: Named-Building-Candidates, Big Donors, Small Fry, and Off-the-Map. Named-Building-Candidates are those who potentially could give a lot of money to the university in the form of a building or other major gifts, the $10 million-plus range. These alums typically graduated 30-plus years ago. There are several schools whose buildings are waiting for a named donor.

Big Donors give smaller amounts and usually fund scholarships or make gifts to the general fund of $100,000 to $1 million in range. These alumni have been out typically 20-plus years. Students looking for financial aid find these scholarships helpful. Small Fry typically give $50 to $100 a year and have been out for five to ten years. Off-the-Map graduates are those who do not give at all and in many cases cannot be located. In many cases, the university has lost touch with its Off-the-Map graduates. They were recently embarrassed when the local CEO of Big Cap, a dot-com start-up, announced he was giving a building to arch-rival Downstate University, even though he was a North State University graduate. He was not on the current list of alumni as he frequently moved during his rise to the top of the corporate ladder. Total annual fund giving across all categories is $50 million.

Develop a multichannel Customer Relationship Management Program for North State University's undergraduate alumni that makes use of online media. You will want to consider the overall business strategy, and set a reasonable annual fund goal for North State University. Provide a rationale for your goal.

A. Identify: What are the four segments North State University has identified? What are the segment needs and the individual needs? Would you change these segments in any way?

B. Differentiate: Think about how these customers can differentiate themselves. By their value to the university? By their needs by segment? By individual needs?

C. Interact: How would you interact with each segment/each customer within the segment? What interaction mechanism would you use and with what frequency? Would you use the Web? Develop a matrix that explains the strategy for each customer.

D. Personalize/Customize: How would you personalize your feedback and customize your products (services) based on feedback from that interaction?

E. What tactics would you use to reach and nurture the potential donors?

Key Points

▸ Success comes from finding the right mix of customer equity drivers, and focusing efforts on them.

▸ Don't forget to ask the "Ultimate Question," *Would you recommend us to a friend?* Then, be ready to act upon its results.

▸ Organizations need to find a more balanced approach to customer marketing, unlocking data.

▸ Technology doesn't make an organization customer-centric.

▸ Align people, processes, and technology to be successful.

▸ As few as 20 percent defections can reduce a customer base by half in four years.

▸ Win-back processes can be as complex or simple as needed, but an organization must learn the real reasons that customers defect.

▸ Segment, segment, segment.

IMPLEMENTING GLOBAL DIRECT MARKETING CAMPAIGNS

Over 90 percent of the world's population lives outside the United States. Political and economic policy liberalization is making it easier for companies to enter markets outside of the United States. In the emerging markets of Eastern Europe, Latin America, the Middle East, and Asia Pacific, economic growth rates are up to 10 times those of the United States.

Direct marketing is benefiting from the growth of emerging markets. Response rates from direct mail campaigns are often two to five times higher in emerging markets than in the United States, simply because there is less of it in consumers' mail boxes to compete with. This can yield a significantly higher ROI (return on investment).

In recent years, editions of this book have been translated into Spanish, Romanian, and Russian, highlighting the international interest in direct marketing. The tools and techniques of multichannel direct marketing are well known in some countries (e.g., Australia, Canada, Germany, the United Kingdom, etc.). To benchmark top global countries in direct marketing use outside of the United States, review Exhibits 7–1 and 7–2.

Direct marketing remains embryonic in many emerging markets. There are about 100 such markets, including Brazil, Russia, India, China, and their Latin American, Eastern European, and Asian neighbors. Most of these markets do not have high levels of direct marketing development (See Exhibit 7–3).

Emerging markets are characterized by a growing middle class, defined as having disposable income to purchase homes, cars, and a variety of consumer goods. Younger consumers, who account for 50–60 percent of the population, are entering the workplace and starting families. Marketing communications efforts are largely dominated by traditional advertising such as television. Direct marketing is only now starting to make inroads. While budgets are much lower in these markets, marketers are starting to focus on the efficiency of their marketing spending. What is true for economic growth around the world is the need for marketing communications that are precise, accountable, and more measurable. That can only be a good thing for direct marketing.

EXHIBIT 7-1

Direct Marketing in the United Kingdom

- 5,418 million items were mailed in 2004. This was split between 78 percent (4,221 million items) consumer mailings and 22 percent (1,197 million items) business mailings.
- £2,468.63 million was spent on direct mail advertising in 2004.
- The overall volume of direct mail has increased by 87 percent in the last 10 years while expenditure on direct mail has increased by 118 percent over the same period.
- For every £1 spent on consumer direct mail £14 is generated.
- It is estimated that consumer direct mail generates nearly £27 billion worth of business every year.
- The average British household receives 13.9 items of direct mail every four weeks and spends approximately £590 through direct mail per annum.
- Business managers open 66 percent of their direct mail, 9 percent is re-directed to a colleague, and 20 percent is filed or responded to.
- An average of 60 percent of consumer direct mail is opened and 40 percent is read.

Source: Direct Mail Information Service (DMIS) Letterbox Factfile 2005.

In this chapter we will look at the nature of multichannel direct marketing growth and its adoption around the world. We will explore the opportunities for direct marketing and some of its obstacles, from culture, language, and law, to the lack of the basic infrastructure needed to execute direct marketing programs.

We will identify some of the early adapters, such as multinational organizations, and look at the models they use for implementation. We will identify some regions with great potential for direct marketing, and look at how direct marketing is growing within some specific markets. We will also examine some examples of how organizations have overcome marketing obstacles and begun to implement direct marketing programs around the world. This chapter focuses mainly on elements in global direct marketing unique to direct mail. Individual chapters within this book address other issues that are just as applicable to international direct mail campaigns.

The Growth of International Markets

International markets are dominated by broadcast, print, and out-of-home advertising. Marketers often lack both the knowledge and reference to use some of the basic tools and techniques of direct marketing. It is not just the stakeholders that need education. Newly minted middle-class consumers also don't understand direct marketing. In countries such as India and China, many consumers get fewer

EXHIBIT 7–2

Direct Marketing in Australia

- Direct marketers and their suppliers employ over 660,000 Australians (Source: CEASA).
- Direct marketing now represents over 32 percent of all media spending with direct marketers currently spending over $9.4 billion on advertising media (Source: CEASA).
- The telemarketing industry is currently growing at a rate of 17 percent per year (Source: ADMA).
- Over 113,000 Australians have registered for the ADMA Do Not Mail/Call service (Source: ADMA).
- In 2003, there were 485,000 Australian business sites on the Internet (Source: ADMA).
- In a 12-month period (Jan–Dec. 2001) over 13,800 individual direct mail campaigns aimed at Australian consumers were recorded by AC/Neilsen MailTrack (Source: ADMA).
- The volume of domestic letters was 4.97 billion items in 2004–2005 (Source: *Australia Post*).
- Promotional letters comprised 15 percent of all letters (promotional letters involve marketing communications, i.e., direct mail) (Source: *Australia Post*).
- 45 percent of counsumers who receive addressed promotional mail will read it compared to the 13 percent who will read unaddressed promotional mail (The Letterbox Diary—*Australia Post*).
- 18 percent of consumers will respond to addressed promotional mail versus the 8 percent who will respond to unaddressed promotional mail (The Letterbox Diary—*Australia Post*).

EXHIBIT 7–3

Levels of Direct Mail Market Development

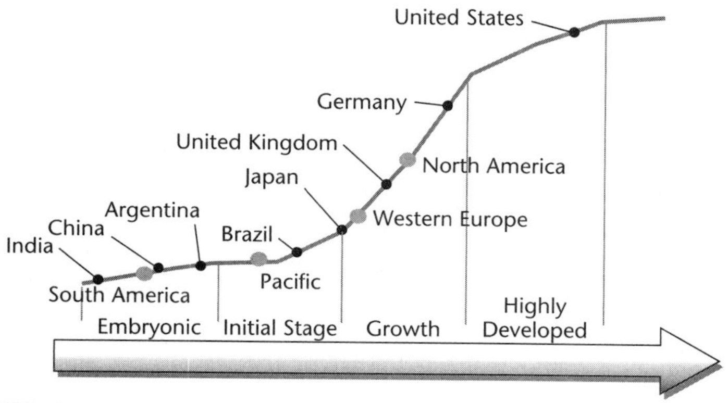

pieces of promotional mail per year than U.S. consumers get in a single day. Like their counterparts in more developed parts of the world, these new middle-class consumers are facing the same stresses as they struggle with work/life demands and are looking for solutions to the demands of modern living. Identifying the underlying drivers of response behavior in individual marketplaces is one of the challenges, albeit a necessary one, to help these markets grow.

Many international marketers are global companies that count on the broad reach of such media to build awareness of their brands. The visual aspects of advertising help to overcome the barriers that language and literacy play in many countries. The impact of local campaigns is often reinforced by the use of global media—CNN, MTV, Star TV—or print media such as the *International Herald Tribune*, the *Economist*, and others that target worldwide audiences.

According to global ad agency network WPP, the United States accounts for nearly half of global spending on advertising and marketing services. With nearly 300 million people, and a relatively large middle and upper class, the United States has created a strong economy based on consumption. The growth of the U.S. economy in this century has been driven by innovation in marketing, media, and technology. This has revolutionized advertising—and direct marketing.

More than half of the global brands are headquartered in the United States. Many top-20 global brands are household names in the United States. They include Disney, GE, Google, IBM, McDonalds, Microsoft, UPS, and Wal-Mart. The implication of the U.S. market's strength is that firms need to be well established in North America in order to build a global brand (See Exhibit 7–4).

Nearly half of the global brands are headquartered outside of the United States, although their names may be familiar, e.g., BMW, Nokia, Vodaphone, and Toyota. Populations of the world are growing at a rate much greater than that of the United States. It is difficult to overlook the signs of change in global demographics.

Marketers build their plans upon growth. The largest non-U.S. markets have included Japan, Germany, the UK, France, Italy, and Spain. Yet, populations in the United States, Japan, and Western Europe continue to age. As populations both age and shrink in the more developed global markets, multinational corporations are looking toward markets with greater opportunities for expansion.

The new battlegrounds, according to WPP, include the emerging markets of Asia Pacific, Latin America, Africa, the Middle East, plus Central and Eastern Europe. For example, in the emerging markets of these regions, the average age of the population is just 25, vs. 36.5 in the United States. These younger and growing markets have caught the eye of global business leaders.

Economists at Goldman Sachs coined the term "BRIC" for the emerging markets of Brazil, Russia, India, and China. In a research paper, Goldman Sachs predicted that given current rates of growth, by 2025 the BRIC countries' combined economies could reach half that of the six largest global economies. Further, they projected that with some luck and good policies, by 2050 the BRIC

EXHIBIT 7–4

Top 20 Global Brands

		(000.000)
1. Microsoft	Microsoft Corp.	$62,039
2. GE	General Electric Co.	$55,834
3. Coca-Cola	Coca-Cola Co.	$41,406
4. China Mobile	China Mobile (HK) Ltd.	$39,168
5. Marlboro	Altria Group, Inc.	$38,510
6. Wal-Mart	Wal-Mart	$37,567
7. Google	Google Inc.	$37,445
8. IBM	IBM Corporation	$36,084
9. Citi	Citigroup Inc.	$31,028
10. Toyota	Toyota Motor Corp.	$30,201
11. McDonald's	McDonald's Corp.	$28,985
12. Bank of America	Bank of America Corp.	$28,155
13. Home Depot	The Home Depot, Inc.	$27,312
14. Nokia	Nokia Corporation	$26,538
15. Intel	Intel Corporation	$25,156
16. Vodafone	VodafoneGroup Plc	$24,072
17. BMW	BMW AG	$23,820
18. Disney	The Walt Disney Company	$22,232
19. UPS	Unitied Parcel Service, Inc.	$21,830
20. Cisco	Cisco Systems, Inc.	$20,922

Source: Millward Brown Optimor.

countries' combined economies could surpass that of today's six largest economies, potentially creating a new world economic order.

It is hard to argue with the numbers. China's population is estimated at 1.2 billion people. India is slightly ahead at 1.3 billion people. Brazil, with 180 million people, is the fifth most populated country in the world. Russia, with 143 million people, while undergoing sharp economic growth, is the only emerging market with negative population growth.

To enter these markets, however, great care must be taken. For example, it is easy to see similarities between China and India. But a quick look can be deceptive. At 1.2 and 1.3 billion people respectively, they are two of the world's largest populations and cover the world's largest geographical areas. However, they have greater linguistic and cultural diversity than other countries as well as the greatest income disparity in the world.

There is no "average" Chinese or Indian customer. Each country's "middle class" consists of more than 300 million people, with considerable diversity in income, geography, climate, culture, habits, language, and religion. Success requires a strategy tailored to local markets or market segments. While these countries are still mainly advertising-driven, marketers around the world are demanding the efficiency, engagement, measurement, and accountability offered by the tools and techniques of direct marketing. Direct marketing allows for a strong marketing position to be established in one segment, then tested and adapted to additional segments.

As markets outside of the United States become more significant, multinational corporations are looking to these large markets to build their businesses. Non-U.S. markets are increasingly important and tremendous growth areas for direct marketing, as well as other forms of marketing communications. Direct marketing's growth has initially been among large multinational companies.

Multinational Direct Marketing Models

There are a number of challenges and barriers to the growth of direct marketing around the world. The process of communicating in global markets is more complex because communication takes place across diverse contexts of language, literacy, and other cultural factors. Target audiences in each market vary in their perceptions and reactions to marketing stimuli, in their response to humor, and how they respond to utilitarian, rational, or emotional appeals.

Mailing lists and other elements of the direct mail value chain often don't exist outside a few major countries. Because of the lack of accurate mailing lists and data hygiene products, direct marketing has been used more for customer marketing than for acquisition. In many of these markets, business-to-business (B2B) marketing is more established and leads business-to-consumer (B2C) direct marketing's growth. Large multinational corporations have been the early adapters in both B2B and B2C marketing, although local companies are starting to jump into the fray.

Year after year, some of the best creative direct marketing on the globe comes from outside the United States. Work from countries such as Spain, Australia, and Argentina wins the top direct marketing creative awards. Although the use of direct marketing is growing domestically in international markets, multinational organizations have been the early adapters of direct marketing. Most local agency personnel are multinational agency alums.

As the reach of multinational organizations grows, it can be difficult to engage resources to coordinate communications in local markets. Unaffiliated and country- or city-based advertising and marketing services agencies often cannot offer the breadth or depth of services multinational companies need, particularly when the client has needs that cross borders. Many multinational clients have led their advertising agencies to open direct marketing arms in international markets to service their businesses (e.g., OgilvyOne, JWTConnect, Wunderman, etc.).

There are many different models among different markets for how organizations implement direct marketing campaigns. Some generalizations about their activity can be made. In nearly all cases, marketing communications end with local implementation. How they get there is different among agencies, clients, and markets.

Reimer Thedens, former Chairman/CEO of OgilvyOne Worldwide, explained that there are three principal service models for managing multinational clients, although there are many variations in between. These models reflect the way clients are organized. Many global advertisers—especially those with more than one product or division—use more than one of these models at the same time. The three models are illustrated in Exhibit 7–5.

In the centralism model, the strategy and creative are provided by a central "brand administration" directly from the client or through its communications agency. It may be in the form of creative templates, where sizes, offers, brand imagery, and graphics are supplied. Communications may be simply translated for the local market. Or, in some cases, production materials are provided and local implementation simply means media placement or putting promotions into the mail.

Centralism is more common in the B2B environment than in the B2C arena. B2B organizations are likely to have established customer databases that are rich sources of the data necessary to drive direct marketing programs. These can be managed or maintained easily from central locations, either through local implementations or across international borders.

The bigger the budgets, the bigger the desire to centralize. The motivating factor is control and brand consistency. The justification is savings and efficiencies. There is a natural resistance to centralism in the markets. Direct marketing and marketing services are often the last bastion of local control. This is where the locals decide. Naturally, they want to protect this ground.

Recommendations, suggestions, etc., don't help. Taking the local money into the marketing center does. Matching funds, i.e., "for every dollar you spend you receive one from me if you use what we developed centrally," is another often used, but less effective method.

EXHIBIT 7–5

Multinational Communications Models

	I. Centralism	II. Adoption	III. Localism
	Central coord.	Central coord.	Central coord.
	Central devp.	Central devp.	Local devp.
	Central exec.	Local exec.	Local exec.
	Local implm.	Local implm.	Local implm.

Adoption is another popular model. In the adoption model, image-consistent templates are provided, but the local market has the ability to write copy rather than just translate. They may also adopt offers as well as graphics for the local market.

The adoption model allows latitude at the local level, while allowing the overall creative and positioning to remain consistent with the global campaign positioning. For example, while a "no preset spending limit" offer for a credit card may work in many markets, the adoption model allows the local agency to suggest offers, benefits, message strategies, even channels, where they believe the wisdom gained from other markets may backfire. Being on the ground means that the local agency staff may better understand the cultural and societal aspects, not just communications issues.

The localism model is the most loved locally, but the riskiest from a multinational brand perspective. It allows the local market to create as well as execute. For the localism model to be successful, it requires that there is sharing of best practices from around the globe to maintain brand and messaging integrity. Internal communications such as Intranets help, but being pragmatic and having clear financial incentives and agreed-upon objectives is even better.

Often, big ideas and major breakthroughs work in nearly every market unless they are in conflict with social and cultural norms. But it takes an effort to get the local market to test and prove it to themselves. The idea that it was "not invented here" is always in the background for multinational communications.

Challenges of Global Direct Marketing

Marketers cannot simply overlay onto international markets the strategies and tactics that are common in the United States. What may seem like best practices in the United States may be unknown, disapproved of, or even illegal in some countries. Marketers implementing global direct marketing programs face many issues that are unique. These issues include:

- Business and consumer familiarity with direct marketing tools and techniques

- Lack of direct marketing and direct mail infrastructure

- Specific data and privacy legislation

- Lack of address standardization, address updates, and data hygiene products

- The post office's roles in advertising and promotional mail

Over the following pages we address these issues, illustrating how they apply to direct marketing. Often the issues are related and don't fall into the organization that neat bullet points allow.

Culture and Society

Culture has implications for businesses that go beyond the differences in how each country's culture has developed. It also has implications for work and business cultures, which are impacted by the values of people in different countries.

Culture and society are driving forces in our lives. People of different cultures behave and act distinctly. Yet understanding what is behind decisions based on culture is complex. Religion, money, sex, relationships, and health are some of the things that shape the values that guide consumer behavior and consumption of products and services. Business customs and ethics equally affect how marketing can be approached within different countries. Understanding these differences is imperative to successfully market across borders.

In his book *The Culture Code*, Clotaire Rapaille, a cultural anthropologist and marketing expert, points out that understanding each country's culture code is imperative for marketers. This code, imprinted at an early age, is reinforced as we grow up within our culture. It unconsciously shapes our motivations, and makes us act in a way that is distinctively American, Argentinian, Chinese, French, Japanese, etc.

As consumers, we may be unaware of our motives for acting as we do. As marketers, we need to unlock each culture's unique code for work, shopping, buying, money, health, beauty, or other behaviors. By understanding the attributes unique to a culture, marketers can construct the right messages, offers, and communications. Attempting to position brands or include messages that work against the established code of a culture can only lead to failure.

One way to look broadly at cultures is as collectivist or individualistic. Collectivist cultures generally put a high priority on the welfare of the group rather than that of the individual. Family ties, history, and deeds are more important than any one family member's accomplishments. Individuals within collectivist cultures work for the good of the family and group and are dependent upon each other. They have strong social networks with long-standing relationships and unquestioned loyalty to their group. Asian, Middle Eastern, and Latin Americans are often collectivist cultures. They value skills, education, and health.

Within individualistic cultures, emphasis is on the objectives and accomplishments of the individual, not their groups. Individuals must be independent of others and not look to their group for help. When accomplishing goals, consideration of others is often limited to include only oneself and one's immediate family. Western cultures such as the United States, Australia, Canada, and Europe are individualistic cultures. They value time, freedom, and personal challenges.

In collectivist cultures such as those in Japan, China, and other Asian countries, the context in which communications' messages are surrounded is important (Hall & Hall, *Understanding Cultural Differences* 1990). These are called high-context cultures. Consumers in high-context cultures are often more effectively reached by image or mood appeals, and rely on personal networks for information and content (Craig & Douglas, *International Marketing Research* 2005). Direct mail and Web sites in these cultures make significant use of symbols that local consumers understand.

For example, in Japan a direct mail package may include an element die-cut into the shape of chrysanthemum blossom with 16 petals or a crane (*tsuru*), a symbol of luck and happiness. In a high-context culture like Japan, such an element might be critical to a mailing's success. However, the use of graphical elements has its downsides in many cultures. Any graphics that resemble religious symbols should be avoided. This is especially true in the Middle East and Asia Pacific region of the world.

The United States and most other Western cultures are considered low-context cultures. In these societies, words are the key providing information. Communications copy would include enough words to provide adequate information regarding the product or service to satisfy the need for content (de Mooij, *Consumer Behavior and Culture*, 2004). Unlike in Japan, the cost of the die-cutting would be considered prohibitive in the United States, and the same message would be delivered in an efficient folded-paper document or words on a Web page.

Each culture has specific issues, where words, colors, envelopes, and even channels chosen can have an impact on the success of a program. Color is a powerful symbol within cultures. Each color has meaning, but depending on the culture, it will invoke something different. Its symbolism must be considered when using color in direct mail packages, print ads, Web sites, or TV commercials.

For example, the color white is used for funerals in Eastern cultures and for weddings in Western cultures. The color red is a symbol of good luck and celebration in China, purity in India, and mourning in South Africa. Yellow represents courage in Japan, mourning in Egypt, and nourishment in China. Green is the symbol of criminality in France and cleanliness in Mexico. In the Middle East, green would be avoided for commercial use, as it has a special meaning within Islam.

Marketers developing global direct marketing campaigns must be aware of their cultural bias. Through careful research and planning and even more careful execution, marketers aware of the issues can overcome them and be successful.

Religion

Elements of culture are often complex. However, religious belief adds a level of complexity to marketing communications that must be handled even more carefully.

The following estimates are most useful for putting world religions in order, rather than for certainty. Christianity, including Catholic, Protestant, Orthodox, and other variations, is the widest held belief in the world, with 2.1 billion people. Islam is at 1.3 billion people. At its current growth rate, Islam will surpass Christianity sometime during the 21st century. Hinduism has about 900 million adherents. There are about 386 million followers of Chinese religions. Buddhism has 376 million followers, while African religions have 100 million adherents. Sikhism has 23 million followers and there are 14 million believers of Judaism worldwide.

Religion is an important element of culture that affects marketing communications. The Middle East is made up of 31 countries, 53 languages, and 2 billion consumers. Within this region there are 1.5 billion Muslims and 500 million people of other religions.

Within the Middle East there is a region known as the Gulf Coordination Countries, or GCC. The GCC is made up of the Kingdom of Saudi Arabia (KSA), Kuwait, Bahrain, Qatar, the Sultanate of Oman, and the United Arab Emirates (UAE). In these countries, the Islamic faith impacts marketing communications. In the KSA and many other Islamic countries, it is forbidden to show skin or a woman's face in marketing communications. In Kuwait, Oman, and Qatar, most of the direct marketing is done by financial institutions such as banks and credit card companies. In the UAE, much of the marketing communications are bilingual—English for the expatriate audience (most multinationals have their regional headquarters in the UAE) and Arabic for the local audience.

What is true of marketing communications for Kingdom of Saudi Arabia may be different in the UAE, or other Middle Eastern countries. This region is a good example of the importance of religion in marketing communications.

Language and Literacy

Language is a major gap for marketing communications. Translations are often spotty and made more difficult by the idiosyncrasies of language and dialects. Speakers of one language must trust that writers of another language have not only caught the meaning of what they were trying to communicate in copy, but also the energy and spirit of it. The same words often mean different things in different countries or in different parts of the same country. Direct translations never capture the meanings, nuances, or tone of language.

Much has been written about marketing *faux pas* in foreign countries. There are numerous incidents in which a company's tag line, eight-word billboard, 25-word print ad, or TV spot did not translate correctly and wound up causing the company embarrassment. For direct marketing, this is an even greater issue. Imagine the care that must be taken in writing, translating, and proofreading the thousands of words in a direct mail package, Web site, or e-mail/landing page.

It is frequently a matter of faith that concepts, strategies, offers, and calls to action have been properly explained in another language. This is especially true for U.S. organizations, where American managers are less likely to be fluent in multiple languages than their European, Asian, African, Latin American, or Middle Eastern counterparts.

Too often central or offshore translations are the issue. It is always best to have local copywriters do this work, even when they are limited to translating creative executions that have been provided. This is a way to ensure that messaging is culture-specific and on target. However, marketers can't simply assume that such translations are perfect. Copy for direct mail packages, e-mails, newsletters, and Web pages should be back-translated and reviewed in the event that the message has become intentionally or unintentionally altered due to a cultural or linguistic misunderstanding.

Mistakes don't only occur when communicating with customers or prospects. Even marketing concepts don't always translate the way that we expect. You can imagine how that may shade marketers' understanding of the tools and techniques necessary to execute marketing communications campaigns.

For example, in Chinese there is no direct translation for the concept of direct marketing. The words used for direct marketing in Chinese roughly translate into "sales operations." This is not exactly how the authors think of direct marketing.

This had a nearly devastating effect on direct marketing a few years ago when the Chinese government promulgated a set of strict regulations to control direct sales companies such as Amway and Avon. These restrictions were the result of the rapid growth of commission-based direct selling, without the training necessary to adapt it to the Chinese culture. Inevitably, some sellers were unsuccessful, which caused direct selling companies to run foul of China's strict labor and compensation laws.

In the United States, direct sales is door-to-door or party-plan marketing like that championed by Herbalife, Mary Kay, and Tupperware. It isn't "the interactive use of advertising media, etc.," although it is arguably targeted. Because of the translations, direct marketing was lumped in with direct sales. It took marketers some time and some effort to have bureaucrats not schooled in marketing concepts understand the differences in the two ideas. Eventually, direct marketing was separated from the rules binding direct sales, but some damage was done to China's nascent direct marketing marketplace.

Although China has an official language (Putonghua, also known as Standard Mandarin Chinese, written using standard Chinese characters), there are more than 55 different languages and dialects spoken or read in China. Chinese leaders routinely employ translators when traveling to some of the 30 provinces, autonomous regions, and municipalities that are controlled by China's central government. Chinese literacy rates are estimated to be about 75 percent.

In India, there are nearly 700 dialects spoken. While English is widely understood, Indians don't always understand each other. With a literacy rate of 65 percent, about 400 million of India's people are illiterate. Developing countries with large numbers of people that are illiterate greatly reduce the opportunities for direct marketing.

Yet India has a growing direct mail marketplace focused on its expanding middle class, mostly in major urban areas of the country. Acquisition and loyalty program communications are mainly sent out in English, which this group understands and responds to.

We think of languages as universally understood across regions. It isn't true. For example, Spanish is spoken in over 22 countries across Central and South America. Residents of Argentina, Uruguay, and a few other countries speak a colloquial dialect of Spanish, known as Castellano and pronounced "Ka sta zha no." This dialect of Spanish borrows some elements of its pronunciation from Portuguese and Italian. In most Spanish dialects, the consonant "ll" is pronounced like the consonant "y," a sound merger known as yeísmo. In Castellano, "ll" is pronounced "zh."

It would be an error to send a Brazilian a communication in Spanish. In Brazil, the largest country in South America by size and population, they speak Portuguese. Although Portuguese and Spanish are related, there are significant differences. Spanish has words of Arabic origin, while Portuguese use words with Latin roots for the same meanings. Portuguese also has some words of French origin which are not shared with Spanish.

Spanish and Portuguese share many words that are spelled the same but pronounced differently. Or, the spellings are different but the pronunciation is identical. Brazilian Portuguese is similar but differs from that written or spoken in Portugal. Portuguese names can be up to 50 characters in length, but it would be a mistake to abbreviate Portuguese names in direct marketing communications.

While it seems to make sense that mailings should be sent in a country's native language, it is not that simple. The European Union has more than 20 national languages. In Belgium, for example, people identify themselves as speakers of French, Flemish (Dutch), or German. They expect that direct promotions will address them in their native language. This can be done through targeting geographically or asking prospects or customers their preference. In Canada, the law requires that all promotions be sent in English and French. Letters, brochures, and response devices may be produced bilingually, or a direct mail package may have two letters, two brochures, etc.

Language remains one of the most critical issues for marketing communications. Because it varies within each country, it must be studied individually to learn the best approach.

Legal Structure

One significant issue for international marketers is the variety of laws that they must deal with. These include trade tariffs, foreign business ownership, tax laws, privacy laws, and a variety of rules that govern marketing communications and the use of consumer and business data.

There are no tricks to avoiding the regulations within a country without breaking other laws, particularly for U.S. companies. European Union privacy laws are among the strictest in the world. Countries as diverse as Argentina, Sweden, and New Zealand have laws governing aspects of consumer privacy that affect the creation of mailing lists. A full understanding of these laws must be part of the due diligence of any marketer. Marketers planning programs in those countries must conform and work within those regulations.

We often read about the strict laws in countries such as China. However, before passing quick judgment, consider what a Chinese company doing multichannel direct marketing in the United States might face. They would have to follow U.S. privacy rules, do-not-call regulations, Can-Spam, and conform to a host of other regulations depending upon their business category (e.g., financial services).

The Multichannel Direct Marketing Value Chain

One way to look at additional issues related to the creation of direct marketing communications globally is to review them against the multichannel direct marketing value chain. It is derived from the direct mail value chain used by the Direct Mail Advisory Board of the Universal Postal Union (www.upu.int) to help postal operators see the categories of value-adding activities needed to create direct mail. Here, it incorporates all of the planning and executional elements that marketers must have in place to develop direct marketing campaigns within global markets (See Exhibit 7–6, which illustrates some of the greatest barriers and enablers of direct marketing growth).

Many of the most important elements in the creation of multichannel direct marketing are lacking in global markets. They need help in developing planning skills, as clients and agencies alike are not well versed in the tools and techniques of direct marketing. In most global markets, only a few universities offer classes in direct marketing. Local direct marketing associations may offer courses, using texts such as this one. Postal administrations, which see direct mail as a way of adding necessary revenue, may also have forums, seminars, or direct mail centers where stakeholders can learn more about using direct marketing as a tool for their marketing communications programs.

This chapter will not cover all of the points in the multichannel direct marketing value chain. However, it highlights the key points as it relates to a healthy and growing direct marketing marketplace.

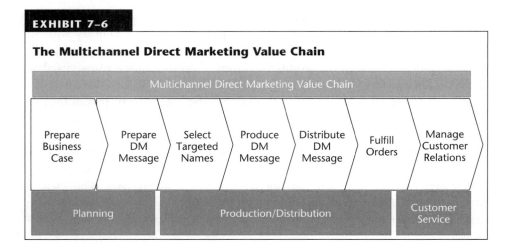

EXHIBIT 7–6

The Multichannel Direct Marketing Value Chain

Multichannel Direct Marketing Value Chain

| Prepare Business Case | Prepare DM Message | Select Targeted Names | Produce DM Message | Distribute DM Message | Fulfill Orders | Manage Customer Relations |

| Planning | Production/Distribution | Customer Service |

Creating the Business Case

A key element in creating a business case is research and market knowledge. Such information is not so readily available for other countries as it is in the United States due to privacy laws and different socio-cultural perspectives. In Korea, although they do an extensive census of their population, they don't ask a household income question. This information, which is routinely used in the United States, would likely impact the results of the Korean census negatively. Despite an American executive's perceived need of such information, it is unlikely that question will be included on the next Korean census.

It is much easier to get to general market information. The *New York Times*, The *Economist*, The *Wall Street Journal*, *Business Week*, and other publications provide information on international business.

One source of general market and economic information on countries is the *CIA World Factbook* (www.cia.gov/cia/publications/factbook/). Published annually by the United States Central Intelligence Agency, the Web information on world countries is updated every two weeks. The *CIA World Factbook* provides two- to three-page summaries of 268 countries recognized by the United States. It includes information on each country's demographics, geography, economy, communications, etc. Primarily written for U.S. Government officials, it is a great resource for businesses, the press, and research. Information from The *CIA World Factbook* can be accessed without cost, although a printed version of it is available for purchase.

Euromonitor International (www.euromonitor.com) offers international market intelligence on industries, countries, and consumers. Euromonitor publishes market reports, business reference books, and online information systems and can be hired to do specific research projects. Most of their materials must be purchased; however, they provide summaries of some reports and research online.

Euromonitor offers reports on a country-by-country basis of credit and financial card usage. Their reports look at credit card issuers and operators in each market, the number of cards in circulation, the number of transactions and value of transactions, etc. In addition, they offer forecasts and trends.

Credit card issuance, penetration, and usage is one way to look at the growth of consumer markets. Credit cards remain largely an untapped market, since many emerging markets are mainly cash societies. For example, in 2005, Mexican consumers still used cash for 86 percent of their transactions. Banks required that applicants have at least a monthly minimum wage of 5,000 pesos (U.S. $446) to obtain a card (Per capita income in Mexico is the equivalent of U.S. $6,770).

Low-income consumers find that they have trouble paying the high interest rates offered by bank cards. An article in the Mexico City daily newspaper *La Jornada* reported that annual interest rates for credit cards ranged from 34.9 percent (Bital Clasica Mastercard) to 39.6 percent (Citibank Classic Card). Even the American Express Bankcard carried a 38 percent annual interest charge.

While this is a great opportunity for credit card marketers in emerging markets, very little consumer direct marketing can be accomplished without credit cards. Small business direct marketing is often dependent upon credit cards. So credit card penetration becomes another issue that marketers need to be aware of as they look at global markets.

Preparing the Direct Marketing Message

Global markets are developing a host of choices for creating great direct marketing efforts. There are great specialist direct marketing agencies residing within the large multinational agency networks, as well as many local direct marketing and creative agencies to provide professional help in developing global direct marketing campaigns.

Wunderman, OgilvyOne, Draft/FCB, and other affiliated direct marketing groups have offices around the world. There are also terrific stand-alone specialist consultants and agencies such as AM Associates, Japan; Dakoo Marketing Group, China (www.dmg-china.com); di Paola & Asociados, Argentina (www.dipaola.com.ar); Fabrica Comunicação Dirigida, Brazil (www.fabricad.com.br); and Grupo Shackleton, Spain (www.shackletongroup.com).

To find these resources, marketers need only seek them out online or through their country's direct marketing association. National DMAs are one of the greatest resources for direct marketers.

The Role of the Post Office

Postal services play an important role in the growth of direct marketing internationally. However, our understanding of what a post office is, and what it does, depends on where in the world we are from.

All posts have as their key mission the Universal Service Obligation. This obligation is to ensure that all residents receive the letter mail, remittances (bills and invoices), and payments that are sent to those within their country. Most post offices also include parcels as one of their growth areas.

Post offices around the world have come to recognize that direct mail is an effective and powerful way to counter the substitution of traditional letter mail and remittance mail volume with a host of different kinds of electronic communication.

The latest Universal Postal Union (UPU) statistics show that in 2005, global domestic letter mail volumes rose by 0.4 percent, while international letter mail volumes decreased by 2.5 percent. In contrast, direct mail has been experiencing significant and continual growth. More than 60% of UPU member countries now offer an advertising mail service. In 2005, advertising items accounted for

37 percent of all domestic letter post items and 11 percent of international letter post. Evidence shows that growth has reached double digits in some developing countries. Industry statistics correspond with these figures and indicate growth, even in mature markets.

The concept of "post office" is very different in these markets. China Post is one of the largest banks in the world. While its customers have one of the highest savings rates globally (40 percent savings rate), they physically go to their China Post branch to make remittances for utility bills, to subscribe to magazines, and for other banking services.

Postal coverage in cities is often unreliable, and it simply doesn't exist in the countryside. In some countries there are no addresses for mail to be delivered to. Basic postal services that we take for granted, such as address standardization, bulk mailing rates, and national coverage, simply aren't available. Home mail boxes often don't exist, and where they do they are not the sole province of the postal service (USPS has a monopoly on the mail box. Legally, no other entity can put anything into it).

Unaddressed mail, illegal in the United States under current USPS regulations, is popular with retailers and early-stage direct mailers across the globe. It is a lower-cost alternative to addressed direct mail and therefore can produce a lower cost per response for the advertiser. Depending upon the country, items may be placed upon, supported by, attached to, hung from, or inserted into a mail box.

Similar to saturation mail, unaddressed mail are items bearing no destination address, but of a uniform weight, format, contents, and layout for distribution to a given category of recipients. These categories include detached homes, multistory homes, vacation homes, offices, retail stores, farms, etc. Unaddressed mail is targeted by postal code or other regional designations.

The benefit of unaddressed mail is that the marketer needs no mailing lists or databases to send the mail to. This is a significant issue in countries where mailing lists are hard to acquire due to privacy regulations, cultural barriers, or the maturity of the direct marketing industry within the market. The cost of unaddressed mail is often significantly less than postage rates for addressed mail available to direct mailers. Many post offices around the world don't offer special bulk direct mail postage rates, but allow marketers to negotiate lower rates based on quantities and the number of mailings a marketer agrees to. And, because unaddressed mail does not flow through the traditional postal system, the size and shape of pieces do not have to conform to the requirements for high-speed, automatic postal sorting equipment. This allows more creative freedom, as seen in the sample of an unaddressed mail piece from Japan offering insurance in Exhibit 7–7.

Couriers in countries often compete with the national post office for even basic mail delivery services. Stakeholders argue that couriers offer greater value than national post offices. They are often cheaper, offer greater delivery flexibility, higher rates of deliverability, and better service (e.g., pick-up at client locations). While many post offices are going through liberalization (privatization), siphoning off their energy and attention, others are in the early stages of working with their stakeholders to develop a basket of products necessary for a healthy direct mail marketplace.

This includes bulk postage rates with incentive discounts, data hygiene and address standardization products, change of address data, marketing databases, parcel post products, and other products that can help the post office to offer something that no other competitor in a marketplace can offer.

Post offices play an important role in the multichannel direct marketing value chain. Many, such as China Post, Japan Post, Correos (Brazil), and Royal Mail (UK), offer a variety of direct mail education, marketing, and other services to support the growth of direct mail in their markets.

EXHIBIT 7–7

Unaddressed Mail Sample

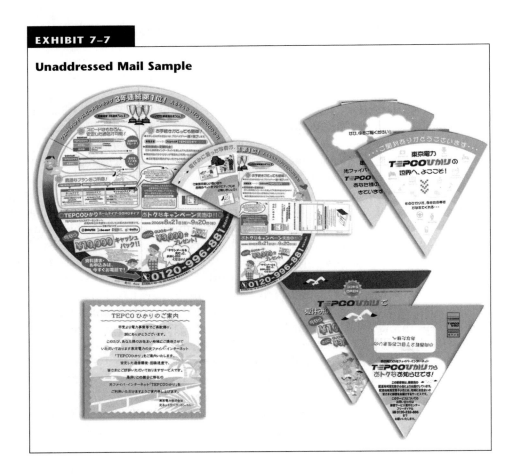

International Database, Name and Address Issues

There are many elements in building global databases. Many of these elements are addressed in Chapter 3, "The Impact of Databases." One property of international databases that is unique is that of proper names and address conventions. These are different in each country, even countries that use the same language. It is often different for business use than for consumer use.

While there are no universal guidelines, most marketers don't include more than six lines (*including* country name) in their international address databases. The length of each field must be assessed on a country-by-country basis. In France, no more than 38 characters per line are allowed by postal authorities. Mailings that don't adhere to these guidelines may be rejected by automatic sorting machines, slowing down delivery. However, in some cultures names can easily be longer than 38 characters, and truncating names (i.e., shortening or abbreviating them) is generally not recommended.

The use of salutations (e.g. Mr., Ms., Mrs., Sr., Sra., etc.) is specific to each country. In some countries they are used, while in other countries they are to be avoided. The use of Ms., common in the United States, is often not acceptable in other countries. Honorifics, which may come before or after an individual's name (e.g., Dr., Professor, Ph.D., Coach, etc.) are used in some countries and not in others.

The proper use of names is one of the most difficult issues for global direct marketing, according to Graham Rhind, of GRC Database Information in Amsterdam, The Netherlands. Names follow different conventions in various countries. Making sure that they are correct in a marketer's database can make a difference in the response rate.

In Hungary, the given name follows the family name, for example Matura Andras (where Andras is the given name). Married females may take a modified form of their husband's family name: Pósciné Munkcási Gabriella (Gabriella Pósci, married to Munkcási).

In Iceland, family names are formed from the father's given name with the suffix –son (for males) or -dottír (for females). For example, if Magnus Magnusson marries Bjork Jandottír, their daughter might be called Sally Magnusdottír.

Among Islamic cultures, most people do not have family names but take a series of names which might indicate family, occupation, or religious or tribal affiliations: for example, Abu Jafar Mohammed ibn Musa al-Khwarizmi (meaning "Mohammed, the father of Jafar and the son of Musa, from Kwarizmi").

In Portugal, people have two given names and two family names, one from each parent, for example: Sergio Hercules Ulhôa Lisboa. If he marries Maria Rosa Soares Magellen, their child's name might be José Hercules Soares Ulhôa. Managing addresses is equally hard. In the United States, addresses are printed out with the individual's name at the top, proceeding to the most general, the country name, at the bottom. This order is not necessarily used in every country (e.g., Iran, Russia). In some countries it is common to include neighborhood names or numbers (e.g., *chome* in Japan). This may come before or after the city line.

Although a global mailing may be in English, municipal names must be in the official language of the country, as the postal system of most countries will deliver mail in that country's language. The use of postal codes (the U.S. version is called the ZIP code) is now generally universal around the world. While their use is universal, their format is not. In some countries, postal codes are numeric (e.g., the United States). They may contain spaces or a hyphen. European postal codes generally have an alphabetic prefix, denoting the country, separated by a hyphen (such as DK-1234 in Denmark). Canada, the UK, and a number of other countries have alphanumeric postal codes, containing both numbers and letters.

Depending upon the country, postal codes may be on the city line (to the left or right of the city), above it, or below it. In many countries where the postal code is to the right, it is separated by two spaces. The exception is where it is a zone (e.g., Dublin 5) and not actually a postal code.

Exhibit 7–8 is a sample of international mailing address formats. This illustrates the diversity among countries as well as within a country. In Belgium, individuals expect mail to be addressed and written in their language of choice, either French or Flemish.

One source of information on proper country addressing is the Universal Postal Union. However, to be certain, marketers should refer to each country's postal authority. Having the correct addressing information is not only the difference in having mail opened by consumers; it can also be the difference in having direct mail delivered by that country's post office.

Evaluating Global Mailing Lists

Mailing lists are one of the most important tools in global direct marketing. With the exception of Canada, the UK, Australia, and New Zealand, the mailing list business is far less developed than in the United States. List sharing among mail-order companies is often unheard of. Response list choices are often limited to a few magazine subscription lists. Compiled lists provide only a fraction of the available universe within many countries, although this is changing as major compilers such as Experian, Acxiom, and others enter the international list marketplace. Postal authorities, such as China Post (see case study at the end of Chapter 3), have also developed compiled lists. Nonetheless, mailing globally takes a different perspective than mailing in more data-rich countries.

James Thornton, of MLA Global List Specialists, recommends a careful strategy when testing global lists. Thornton recommends testing multicountry "global" response lists first. Global response mailings cut across many countries.

EXHIBIT 7–8

Sample International Mailing Address Formats

Country	Postal Address	Address Elements
Argentina	Sr. Juan Pérez Editorial International S.A. Av. Sarmiento 1337, 8° P. C. C1035AAB BUENOS AIRES-CF	S.A. = Sociedad Anónima (corporation) Av. Sarmiento = name of street 1337 = building number 8° = 8th. P = Piso (floor) C = room or suite C1035AAB = postcode + city CF = Capital Federal

Salutation: Sr.=Señor (Mr.); Sra. = Señora (Mrs.); Srta = Señorita (Miss). Don't use given names except with people you know well.

Belgium **(French speaking)**	Monsieur L. Bogaerts Éditions Internationales S.A. Rue P. J. Delcoche 19 4020 LIÉGE	S.A. = a corporation Rue = street 19 = building number 4020 = postcode + city (City must be a capitalized)

Salutation: Monsieur = Mr.; Southern Belgium speaks French. Use Mr./Mrs. or Monsieur/Madame.

Belgium **(Flemish/Dutch speaking)**	Dhr. W. Sterckx Internationale Uitgeversmaatschappij N.V. Pelikaanstraat 104 2018 ANTWERPEN	N.V. = a corporation Pelikaanstraat = street name 104 = building number 2018 = postcode + city (Brussels is bi-lingual.)

Salutation: Dhr. = De heer (Mr.); North Belgium speaks Flemish/Dutch. Use Mr. and Mrs. Flemish/Dutch equivalents are generally not used.

Germany	Herrn Gerhardt Schneider International Verlag GmbH Schillerstraße 159 44147 DORTMUND	Herrn = To Herr... GmbH = Inc. (incorporated) -straße = street ('ß' often written 'ss') 159 = building number 44147 = postcode + city

Salutation: Herr = Mr. Frau = Mrs. Fräulein obsolete in business. Business is formal. Do not use given names unless invited. Use academic titles in the address, but not in the salutation unless title is accepted as part of the name, e.g., Dr. and Prof.

Japan	Mr. Taro Tanaka Kokusai Shuppan K.K. 10-23, 5-chome, Minamiazabu Minato-ku TOKYO 106-1234	K.K. = Kabushiki Kaisha (corporation) 10 = Lot number 23 = building number 5-chome = area #5 Minamiazabu = neighborhood name Minato-ku = city district City + postcode

Salutation: Given names not used in business. Family name + job title are used. Or use family name + -san. (Tanka-san). More respectfully, add -sama or -dono.

Source: Merriam Webster's Guide to International Business Communications.

They consist of individuals and businesspeople in various countries who have previously responded to an international offer mailed from offshore. Names on these lists have demonstrated their ability to charge their orders to an international credit card or remit a bank draft in U.S. dollars. Such lists often provide the best prospects internationally, and can often be tested first, before mailing local lists in any one country.

International addresses from the United States and other cataloger lists are another category to consider. They often work well, especially from high-ticket mail-order buyer files and magazine and newsletter subscriber lists. Quantities are usually small, but responsiveness is typically very high. As with other responder lists, recency of purchase is an important selection. The amount of purchase from rented lists needs to be carefully matched when mailing these lists. Such lists need to be tested cautiously. While lists are not readily available in many markets, testing new lists and new countries helps you build the universe of good lists and good countries that work for you.

According to James Thornton, one of the most important elements to consider when selecting lists for an international mailing is the list/country combination. Response by country within the same list can vary consistently by 1000 percent and more. When using regional or global lists, it is absolutely essential to monitor comparative response by country within lists, across all the lists that are tested.

Thornton also notes that marketers should get to know and trust international list owners over time. When a list works well, the list broker should be asked what other lists are held by the same list owner. While many list owners are honest, some dilute their lists with old names or compiled names which can reduce response. Others show the source of the list as direct mail, when it is actually print ads or TV. As discussed in other chapters of this book, matching list sources is key when using response mailing lists. Lists must be continually refreshed with new names, properly labeled and carefully maintained.

There are relatively few mail-order buyer files that are multinational. Most are local files generated locally using local lists or using off-the-page print advertising in local media. Businessmen and professionals on business newsletter and magazine subscriber files, merchandiser buyers, or seminar attendee lists are multinational and they often generate good response to consumer offers, as businesspeople are also "consumers." Their most important attribute is to have responded previously to an international offer from offshore, regardless of the nature of the offer to which they have responded.

Another good source of international mailing lists are magazine subscription files, where specific target groups or interests can be matched to a marketer's offers. In many countries, this is a key source of lists. *Business Week*, The *Economist*, and other publications have offshore lists available to marketers around the world. However, many countries have local publishing companies where lists are available.

In Brazil, for example, Abril (www.abril.com.br) publishes Portuguese-language editions of some of America's best-known magazines (e.g., *Disney*, *Elle*, *Men's Health*, *National Geographic*, and *Playboy*), while also publishing a number of Brazilian titles as well. Abril publishes over 300 different magazines annually, with a circulation of 164 million.

Subscriber files, which are ABC or BPA audited, tend to be cleaned and updated regularly by the magazine publishers. Publishers keep files clean because it is expensive to mail to expired or unqualified subscribers. Paid subscriber files are often more accurate than controlled circulation files, because subscribers must be renewed annually, keeping these files continually refreshed. Unaudited local magazine subscriber lists should be looked at very carefully. Often list datasheets for these publications seem okay, but in truth exaggerate quantities. It is truly a "buyer beware" marketplace.

In some smaller countries, all that are available are names and addresses compiled from trade directories and telephone books. These may be the only alternative where no other local lists are available. In larger markets, such lists work for up to six months after they are first compiled. Business-to-business mailers often improve their results by adding relevant job titles to the company names and addresses on compiled lists. Known as mailing "Title/Address," this directs the mailing to the appropriate decision maker within targeted firms.

Because the global list universe is not large, marketers can only reach larger volumes after careful testing. James Thornton recommends that marketers begin to roll out to local lists on a local basis after careful testing of a range of potential local markets from offshore, then multinational/regional lists. This should be done before taking greater risks in any one onshore market. Thornton recommends that marketers continue to mail smaller countries from offshore, especially where there is no local direct marketing infrastructure and no local lists. But collectively, all such countries represent a sizable and growing universe of names that can only be reached using this "offshore strategy."

In the past, international mailers would have no more available lists after mailing *Fortune* and *Business Week* subscribers, Alexander Hamilton, Collin Street Bakery, *Harvard Business Review*, and a few other multinational lists. This situation has improved. There are many new regional, multinational, and local mailing lists available to the market. The ratio of consistently successful lists to marginal and poor lists is not particularly good, but then it never has been either in international or domestic markets.

One of the most exciting developments is that many more countries are responding well to international offers from offshore than ever before, which is gradually increasing the universe of names available to international mailers pursuing an "offshore strategy." The Internet is also generating new lists with both postal and e-mail addresses, the next big thing in multichannel global direct marketing.

Producing Direct Marketing

The production infrastructure necessary for direct mail marketing is not as readily available around the world as it is in the United States. Most countries have robust printing industries, although not all printers are well suited to the quality, sizes, and personalization necessary for direct marketing. Lettershops, who insert elements into envelopes, sort, bag, and put mail into the postal mail stream, are also not well known in many countries. Printers with experience in direct mail tend to be one-stop shops, trying to do the full range of production for their clients. Some direct marketing agencies also do some production. Both printers and agencies offer database marketing services, further blurring the lines.

In Japan, Nishikawa Communications (www.nishikawa.jp) is one such company. They offer turnkey services including creative development, database management, printing, and lettershop. In China, China Post (www.chinapost.com.cn) also offers turnkey services. In fact, their excellent compiled database is only available to customers who allow them to do creative development, production, and lettershop.

In working through global markets it is imperative to find partners that have experience with direct mail. It is different in quality and tolerances. In many developed countries there are excellent sources available. In less developed countries it is not so easy to find the skills necessary for direct marketing. The best way to locate experienced local production facilities is to get referrals from people within the countries or work through the local direct marketing association.

Conclusion

The growth of direct marketing is impacting international markets. There are robust direct marketing communities on nearly every continent. While the early adapters were business-to-business marketers and those doing customer marketing, this is quickly changing. And, while international markets have been advertising-driven, the ability to target, plus the accountability and measurability of direct marketing, is very appealing. There is no doubt that international direct marketing will continue to grow at a rate well above that of more established countries. With careful research, the right products, the right offers, and a clear understanding of the cultural, societal, and language differences, the global market beckons and the tools and techniques of direct marketing are right for it.

CASE STUDY: **Saishunkan Pharmaceutical Company: An Asian Direct Marketing Success**

Contributed by Atsuko Morimoto, AM Associates, Tokyo, Japan. ©2005 World Marketing Group.

BACKGROUND

Saishunkan Pharmaceutical Company is a direct merchant of anti-aging skincare products and Chinese medicine. The company was established in 1932, and is located in Kumamoto City, Japan.

What sets the Saishunkan Pharmaceutical Company apart is a clear corporate philosophy. The company provides a unique blend of natural and herbal ingredients working in harmony to rejuvenate the inherent power of the human being.

This combination of Chinese medicine and Western science has certainly proved effective in generating high awareness among the target.

CASE STUDY:	**Saishunkan Pharmaceutical Company: An Asian Direct Marketing Success**

(continued)

Most Japanese women answer, "Yes, I am aware of the brand name, Domohorn Wrinkle" (which is the anti-aging skincare).

CHALLENGE

Saishunkan made a mistake in their early years of direct marketing. They employed a hard-sell approach via an outbound auto-call system, coupled with a performance-oriented remuneration scheme. Initially, this approach seemed effective. It resulted in record sales in 1993. However, Saishunkan later suffered from an extremely high return rate. Clearly, this provided a lesson in the pivotal role that Customer Relationship Management (CRM) must play in effective, long-term integrated direct marketing.

SOLUTION

Saishunkan made the significant shift from "push" to "pull." In other words, they shifted from outbound calling to encouraging inbound calls. Print ads announced this critical change in approach. Saishunkan also established a Customer Satisfaction Division to handle inquiries, comments, and claims. Customers proactively proposed improvements in products, packages, and services. The feedback of these customers created a voice for the new product development.

At today's Saishunkan, customer retention and cross-selling take center stage. The company uses direct marketing and supports these efforts with Web site, community, and e-marketing (See Exhibits 7–9, 7–10). They have also established a point system that rewards frequent buyers. Saishunkan is also a good corporate citizen, with sponsorships of a women's golf tournament, children's soccer, and musicals. They even send out birthday cards with flower seeds enclosed.

RESULTS

Today, Saishunkan Pharmaceutical Company continues to grow its annual sales with an emphasis on CRM. Customers with three or more purchases account for 90 percent of the company's profit. The push to pull efforts have also paid dividends. Currently 78 percent of the calls are inbound rather than outbound. The bottom line is also healthy. One-to-one customer relationships have made Saishunkan a very successful direct marketer with annual sales of U.S. $110 million.

EXHIBIT 7–9

Saishunkan Holiday Card and E-card

森本 篤子 様   07825706-1

日頃よりドモホルンリンクルをご愛顧いただきまして誠にありがとうございます。
街中がクリスマスのイルミネーションで賑わい、お出かけの機会も多いのではないでしょうか。
心弾む季節だからこそ健やかなお肌でお過ごしいただきたいと願っております。暖房や冷たい風に負けない肌づくりを応援いたします。
再春館コミュニティ【つむぎの村】の「お肌の相談室」には、冬のお手当てのヒントがいっぱいです。

「つむぎの村」にも雪が降り、冬がやってきました。村の景色を2種類のeカードにしました。
お友達にeカードを送りませんか？

CASE STUDY: **Saishunkan Pharmaceutical Company: An Asian Direct Marketing Success**
(continued)

EXHIBIT 7–10

Saishunkan Pharmaceutical Company Web site

PILOT PROJECT   Your client, a multichannel direct marketer of expensive (U.S. $200–300) bathing suits for women 21–30 years old, has asked you to develop a plan to expand its business globally. Initially, they would like to look at three countries with large sea coasts: Brazil, the United Arab Emirates, and Spain. They would like to use direct mail initially.

1. What tools can you use to assess these three markets?

2. What cultural or societal issues are there in creating marketing communication for these three markets?

3. Are there any language considerations?

4. Are there mailing lists available in the three markets? From whom?

5. Which of the three markets would you choose as the best for this expansion? Why?

Key Points

▶ International markets require a different kind of research and planning.

▶ Marketers need to be aware of social, cultural, language, and legal issues in preparing global marketing communications.

▶ While creative work can be adopted over markets, the most successful communications take into consideration elements of each individual market.

▶ Post offices can play a pivotal role, from consulting to mailing lists, in the development of global direct marketing campaigns.

▶ Mailing lists remain one of the main issues in growing globally, but they are becoming more readily available.

BUSINESS–TO–
BUSINESS DIRECT
MARKETING

*Vic Hunter, founder and president of Hunter Business Direct, Inc.,
Milwaukee, Wisconsin, has developed an approach to business-to-business
direct marketing that has proved highly successful for many Fortune
500 companies. This chapter is based on his ideas.*

The opportunities in business-to-business direct marketing are great: to get
qualified leads, to screen leads, to sell by telephone, to create catalogs and sales support material, and to conduct E-commerce. Business-to-business direct marketing
uses the same tools as consumer direct marketing, but significant differences separate the two (see Exhibit 8–1). The major difference is an economic one.

The average order size of business-to-business direct marketing offers is large
and the lifetime value of a single customer can be enormous. For example, IBM
sells $50,000 equipment using direct marketing techniques. With order sizes of this
type, the lifetime value of a business-to-business customer can be extremely high.
It is not uncommon for a single business-to-business customer to represent millions of dollars in lifetime value.

Although economic value is high, target market universes can be small.
In some cases, this involves fewer than 100 companies. Therefore, the mass marketing techniques that work so well in consumer direct marketing are often not
applicable in business-to-business.

This means that businesses must invest far more in building and supporting
a relationship with the customer—the loss of one customer can have a great economic impact on the business. As a result, direct marketing takes on new dimensions when used in business-to-business applications. No longer are its goals the
capturing of an order or the acquisition of a new customer. Rather, the goals
become increasing sales productivity while sustaining relationships with existing
business customers. Instead of emphasizing new-customer acquisition, we "cultivate" existing customers and use that information to broaden our customer base.

Through this we begin to build a spirit of community among our customers.
We want to leverage our relationship with the customer to build a bond that

---

EXHIBIT 8–1

Consumer versus Business-to-Business Direct Marketing

Consumer Direct Marketing	Business-to-Business Direct Marketing
Individuals frequently buy for themselves	Individuals buy on behalf of an organization
Buying decision involves relatively few others	Decisions frequently involve multiple individuals
Single buyer groups	Multiple buyer groups
Informal buying process	Formal and informal buying process
Transaction-based	Relationship-based
Average order size is relatively low	Average order size tends to be large
Lifetime value is relatively low	Lifetime value can be very large
Easy to reach individuals	Difficult to reach individuals
Large target market universe	Small target market universes
Transaction-focused	Relationship process-focused

Source: Hunter Business Group, LLC

---

translates into a lasting relationship based on mutual interests, mutual trust, and healthy interdependence. We make the customer community economically desirable and stable through lowering selling costs for the seller and delivering higher product/service value to the customer.

Of course, this means that direct marketing processes look quite different in business-to-business marketing. For example, the functions or uses for direct marketing change. In business-to-business applications, direct marketing is used for such functions as reducing the number of face-to-face contacts with the customer, reaching marginal accounts that might not be profitable to contact through a face-to-face sales call, and building sustainable relationships with the customer at lower costs.

Also, the measurements or metrics used to evaluate results change. Rather than focusing on transaction- or campaign-based measurements, such as cost per thousand, number of calls per hour, response rates, etc., business-to-business direct marketing uses such qualitative measures as customer satisfaction, product penetration, account penetration, referrals, and loyalty.

Another difference is that we are dealing with individuals who represent economic value beyond themselves. They are the buyers, procurement officers, approvers, etc., who influence or direct purchases for companies, institutions, or other organizations. As such, they are not spending their money but someone else's. As a result, this is a more complex buying process. Typically, more than one person is involved in a single buying decision; or there might be multiple buying groups within the same organization, buying the same type of product. With this complexity, it is difficult to find key buying influences and the purchasing patterns within an organization.

Value-Added Direct Marketing

In the early 1980s, Hunter Business Group, LLC, began using and refining a highly effective business-to-business direct marketing technique called value-added marketing. The differences between traditional and value-added marketing are shown in Exhibit 8–2.

In value-added marketing, Hunter starts with the premise that it is dealing with a market size of a single individual. This is the key—marketing to individuals, not to accounts or organizations. Individualized messages go to target markets. Each has a size of one.

Make that paradigm shift, from selling to accounts to selling to individuals who buy on behalf of others, and the rest of the elements fall into place. For example, if you're selling to individuals, you can ask what their needs are and store them in a database. You don't have to guess. You can then look for product or service applications that meet their specific business needs.

In this approach, businesses manage contacts with the customer through a centralized operation called the customer center (CC) or market center. This gives them the ability to integrate direct marketing tools with field sales to provide the

---

EXHIBIT 8–2

Traditional versus Value-Added Direct Marketing

Traditional Marketing		Value-Added Marketing
Mass Marketing	–	n = 1
Projected needs	–	Actual needs
Product driven	–	Customer driven
Account focus	–	Individual focus
Activity based	–	Application based
Acquisition focus	–	Retention focus
Events and activities	–	Systems and procedures
Project results	–	Actual results
Independent contacts	–	Integrated contacts
Impersonal communication	–	Personal communication
Support traditional sales channels	–	Support all sales channels

Source: Hunter Business Group, LLC

customer with a seamless flow of value-added information. That is, they ensure that every contact with the customer delivers value, as perceived by the customer.

A key concept here is to focus on retaining customers and building customer loyalties. Studies have shown that retaining existing customers is significantly less expensive and more profitable than acquiring new customers. So, direct marketing tools must focus on retaining customers, not simply getting them to place an order. This requires another paradigm shift, away from the transaction-based traditional approach to one that is focused on building long-term relationships.

A strategy of retention can build customer loyalty. This has distinct advantages: loyal customers are less likely to defect and more likely to become your "champions" within their organization and industry. Once we understand who our loyal customers are, it is only then that we can look at acquiring new customers. The reason is simple: we want new customers that look like and act like our best loyal customers; we can't do that until we see who our best loyal customers are. If we blindly pursue an acquisition strategy designed to replace lost customers, we are likely to get some new customers that look like the customers we just lost. That's not smart marketing.

The principles and techniques of value-added marketing produce three major benefits:

1. Improved sales force productivity and reduced sales costs to revenue of up to 15 percent.

2. Increased customer loyalty, which leads to customer retention.

3. Sales revenue growth and increased profitability.

These are dramatic benefits in today's highly competitive business-to-business world. They can be accomplished through a four-stage process. The major phases of this process include: (1) understanding the customer, (2) developing a value-added communication strategy, (3) using cultivation to build retention and loyalty, and (4) acquiring new customers based on existing customer experience.

Listening to the Customer's Voice

Value-added marketing is built around the premise that all contacts with the customer deliver value. It is through this value-based approach that businesses can build long-lasting and sustainable relationships with customers. The first step in this process is understanding what the customer values in the relationship. As Stephen Covey noted in *The Seven Habits of Highly Effective People*, we must "seek first to understand." To accomplish this, first listen to the voice of the customer. Try to understand why customers buy from you, what needs your products or services fulfill, how you stack up against the competition, and how you can use this information for competitive advantage. Exhibit 8–3 summarizes the steps to take.

EXHIBIT 8-3

Understanding the Customer

Task	Description	Implemented by	Information Source
Customer needs assessment	Identify basic, unfulfilled, future, and at-risk needs	Marketing	Customer surveys
Attribute/feature analysis	Identify all attributes or features of your product or service	Marketing	Marketing
Competitive analysis	Compare attributes/features with competitors	Marketing	Competitive intelligence
External service values	Determine why customer buys product/service from you	Marketing	Attribute/feature and competitive analyses
Segment target markets	Group customers with common set of needs into target segements	Marketing	Database

Source: Hunter Business Group, LLC

One of the most difficult aspects is identifying customer needs. Needs fall into three categories: basic, unfulfilled, and future needs. Basic needs are those you need to satisfy in order to be considered by the customer. These are needs that every entrant into the market must meet or they become barriers to entry. If all competitors only satisfied basic needs, we would be dealing with a commodity-type product or service.

Unfulfilled needs are the path to competitive dominance. If you can uncover and meet needs that the competition is not meeting, that gives you a distinct advantage. At the same time, if you are not meeting unfulfilled needs, and the competition is, these become at-risk needs and can cause customer defections. By listening to the customer's voice, you can anticipate a customer's future needs. This requires a means of continuously monitoring a customer's changing needs.

Businesses identify customer needs by determining external service values—the reasons that customers buy a product or service, and buy from them.

Determining External Service Values or Brand Promise

The step-by-step process used to uncover external service values starts with an understanding of the products and services. First, identify all of the product's features or attributes. In some cases, this can involve more than 100 attributes. Next, compare these attributes with those of competitive products or services. The result is a competitive analysis that helps to distinguish your product from competitive offerings and leads to defined external service values. Exhibit 8–4 shows a portion of a competitive attribute/feature analysis.

This type of analysis provides a clear picture of the competitive position. It shows a unique set of features or attributes that distinguishes your product from the competition. However, this is strictly an internal analysis and must be tested against market realities by asking customers what is important. This can be accomplished in several ways. The simplest is to call customers following receipt of the order and ask why they purchased. Then match that answer to the unique feature list.

A more systematic approach is to conduct periodic customer surveys. These surveys identify the key attributes/features and ask the customers to rate your unique value for that attribute compared to the competition's. Then ask them to rate each in importance in the buying decision. By multiplying the unique value by the level of importance in the purchasing decision, you have a quantitative measure of external service values. It's always good to go back and verify that this is why customers buy from you.

Another technique is to interview customers who defected or are no longer buying from you. By asking them why they are no longer buying, you can determine what external service values were not satisfied. This not only gives you valuable information about unfulfilled customer needs, but also can be an early warning system to help prevent additional defections.

EXHIBIT 8–4

Competitive Attribute/Feature Analysis

Feature	Our Company	Competitors A	B	C
Time to ship	Same day	2 days	5 days	Same day
Guarantee	Unlimited	60	120	90
Handling charge	No	No	Yes	No
Quote turnaround	8 hours	2 days	24 hours	N/A
Volume pricing	Yes	Yes	Yes	Yes
Accuracy of order fulfillment	100%	98%	95%	100%
Recycled packaging	No	No	No	No
Price guarantee	90 days	No	30 days	No
Toll-free number	Yes	Yes	Yes	Yes
Customizing	5–10 days	6 weeks	5 weeks	No

Source: Hunter Business Group, LLC

A New Segmentation Tool

The external service value analysis enables you to group customers with like needs and reasons for buying. For example, when customers rank-order the attribute/feature list, they are building a basis for target market segmentation. If no-cost shipping and handling, order turnaround time, and volume discounts are important to a select group of customers, these customers represent an identifiable target segment. Segmentation is a critical early step in grouping your customers to allow for creation and execution of far more effective communications.

Contact Channels and Communication Strategies

Successful businesses manage communications with their internal and external customers at every possible point of contact and use the knowledge gained from those contacts to create value in the relationship. Contact points are information pathways. Whoever owns these vital pathways owns the relationship with the customer.

    There are two main objectives in developing specific communication strategies and plans. First, direct marketing enables you to leverage the high cost of field sales. For example, the cost of a typical business-to-business sales call averages more than $400. Therefore, direct marketing techniques should and can, be used to support and leverage the field sales process. Second, studies have shown that frequency of valued contacts is more important than contact media. Therefore, focus on the use of low-cost contact media if the same value-based communication can be made. Exhibit 8–5 summarizes the steps used in developing an effective contact plan and communication strategy.

EXHIBIT 8–5

Contact Plan and Communication Strategies

Task	Description	Implemented by	Information Source
Contact analysis	Identify all contact points with customer by type and content	Marketing	Internal observation
Communication workshop	Identify customer contact preferences	Marketing	Customer
Grade customers	Determine which are most valuable customers (AA, A, B, C, D)	Marketing	Database
Customer contact matrix	Match customer contact preferences with contact media cost with economic value	Marketing	Database
Communication plan	Determine specific communication elements for contact matrix	Marketing	Marketing and sales
Develop offer	Base offer on external service values	Marketing	Database
Customer contact	Implement the communication plan	CIC	Database

Source: Hunter Business Group, LLC

First you need to know how, when, and about what customers contact you and you contact them. To do this, start by analyzing current contact practices. Identify every customer contact point within the organization, no matter how infrequent or at what location. Over a predetermined period, record all contacts with the customer. This is typically done using a contact log like the one shown in Exhibit 8–6. The contact log not only records the contact, but it also identifies the information content, the source of the contact (inbound or outbound), the contact owner, and the frequency of contact. You can then prepare a cumulative analysis that covers all contact points.

If you understand how customers want to receive certain types of information, and then proceed to deliver it to them in that manner, this adds value to the relationship with the customer. This forms the base for the next step and helps in building the infrastructure for the customer center.

EXHIBIT 8–6

Sample Contact Log

Department (Group)	Key Contact:		Approvals	
	Time Period			
Activity	Phone		Mail		Electronic	
	In	Out	In	Out	In	Out
A. Sales/revenue generation						
1. Orders/applications						
2. Contracts/confirmations/modifications						
B. Requests/exchange of information						
1. Product information						
2. Pricing/bid requests						
3. Literature/material						
4. Account related						
5. Special programs						
6. Other: _____						
C. Problems/customer service						
1. Shipment/completion status						
2. Problems/complaints						
3. Account corrections/adjustments						
4. Service related						
D. Messages/transfers						
E. Prospect/lead identification (solicited)						
F. Invoices/payments/claims/purchase orders						
G. Misdirected contacts/referrals						
H. Other: _____						

Source: Hunter Business Group, LLC

Customer Contact Preferences

After you understand current contact practices, and what the customer values, you need to ask customers about their contact preferences.

- What types of information does the customer consider important or value-based?

- How does the customer want to be contacted on each occasion?

- When does the customer want contact?

- How frequently does the customer want to be contacted?

One way to gather this customer-specific information is to ask customers during the normal course of business. That is, during a phone call with the customer, the representative is prompted to ask specific questions related to communication preferences. A second way is to use a mail survey. Another technique is the customer communication workshop. Here, groups of customers, sales representatives, and product marketing representatives meet to:

- Review the cumulative contact log

- Have each group identify the top 10–12 contact items

- Have each group present their selections and state reasons for selecting the item

- Resolve differences between groups

This process has the customer, together with the business, define what contacts and what content are important, what contact medium the customer prefers, and how frequently the customer wants the information. From this process a contact model can be developed for communication planning. Exhibit 8–7 shows a sample contact model. For example, it shows that the customer is willing to have 12 notifications for program specials. They prefer to have this notification through e-mail, but consider mail, phone, and face-to-face notification acceptable.

Grading Customers

One mistake some companies make is to consider that all customers are equal for the purposes of direct marketing programs. This is highly ineffective—customers are not equal. They have different needs (market segment) and have different economic potential/value (grade). Some require more contact than others; frequent contact is not economically justified for other customers. To avoid such mistakes, it is wise to grade customers on an economic basis and develop direct marketing programs that specifically address the needs of each economic grade of customers.

Most marketers are familiar with the 20/80 form of grading customers: 20 percent of your customers account for 80 percent of your sales volume.

EXHIBIT 8–7

Value-Based Contact Model

Contacts	Frequency	E-mail	Phone	Field	Mail
1. New-product announcements	4	P	A		A
2. Product application information	4	P	A	A	A
3. Product updates/new releases	4	P	A	A	
4. Case studies 　　a. Product application 　　b. Results	4	P			A
5. Industry research	1	P			A
6. Article reprints	6	P			A
7. Program specials	12	P	A	A	A
8. Industry trends	2	P			A
9. Product uses/performance assessment	4		A	P	

P = Preferred medium　A = Acceptable medium

Source: Hunter Business Group, LLC

Taking this a step further, you can grade customers into five categories—AA, A, B, C, D—to allow for a closer match of economic value to contact mix and frequency. The criteria used can include past sales history, profitability, potential, or any other measure of customer value. Typically, active customers can then be divided as follows:

AA	=	Top 5 percent
A	=	15 percent
B	=	25 percent
C	=	25 percent
D	=	30 percent

Creating a Customer Contact Plan

Once you have the customer contact preferences and have graded customers, you can build a contact plan that economically leverages sales contact costs in a highly effective manner. In essence, the plan delivers value, as defined by the customer, with every contact. Because the financial aspect is essential, you first need to set a budget. This includes setting a total budget and a budget for each customer grade. Next, establish costs for each type of media. Then generate a mix of media that satisfies the objectives of leveraging higher-cost media and being effective. After these steps, a customer contact plan is developed. Media costs can vary dramatically from one medium to another. Exhibit 8–8 shows the range of typical media costs.

The next step is to develop a mix of contact media that best fits your objectives and meets your budgets. Be advised that as you build a contact plan you need to repeatedly adjust the mix until you reach the optimum plan.

EXHIBIT 8–8

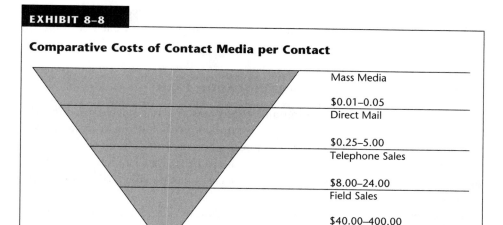

Comparative Costs of Contact Media per Contact

Mass Media
$0.01–0.05

Direct Mail
$0.25–5.00

Telephone Sales
$8.00–24.00

Field Sales
$40.00–400.00

Source: Hunter Business Group, LLC

Exhibit 8–9 shows a completed customer plan. This sample is derived from a base of 1,000 buyer groups. To illustrate what each item represents, let us use Grade B customers. First, this group represents customers with $20,000–40,000 in annual sales revenue. There are 250 customers in this category. According to the contact plan, this group is expected to generate about $7.5 million in sales revenue during the year. The plan is to invest approximately 13 percent of sales revenues, or $988,000, into communication and contact with customers. This translates to

EXHIBIT 8–9

Customer Contact Plan Sample

Grade/Sales ($000)	1,000 = Buyer Groups	Mail	Count	Phone	Count	Field	Count	Sales Cost ($000)	Percentages of Revenue
AA $60+	50	75	3,750	50	2,500	20	1,000	$ 469	13.4%
A $40–60	150	75	11,250	40	6,000	15	2,250	1,076	14.4
B $20–40	250	50	12,500	25	6,250	8	2,000	988	13.2
C $10–20	250	25	6,250	12	3,000	4	1,000	491	13.1
D>$10	300	25	7,500	10	3,000	1	300	218	14.5
Total	1,000		41,250		20,750		6,550	$3,242	13.6%

Source: Hunter Business Group, LLC

50 mailings (about one per week), 25 phone calls (about one every two weeks), and eight face-to-face sales contacts (about one every six weeks) for each customer in this buyer group.

Marketing and Sales Communication Plan

Specific marketing communication and sales plans are now developed. First the 50 direct mail pieces must be developed: what each piece will consist of, its format, its content, and which external service values will be stressed. The customer's external service values are known so they are the basis for message content. Remember, these contacts are defined by the customer to have value if mailed to them with this frequency.

To show how this works in practice, let us assume you have a monthly newsletter that you send to customers. You plan the newsletter so that each issue includes information related to your core external service values. Then you use the cover letter to call attention to specific pieces of information within the newsletter that meet the individual customer's external service values. This adds value to your communication with the customer and delivers 12 mail contacts throughout the year.

Building the Customer Center

Because value-added direct marketing uses the full range of direct marketing and sales tools, you need a means to manage and monitor the process: the customer center (CC). All activities are coordinated and flow through the CC. Exhibit 8–10 shows the CC model. The CC's role involves acquiring customer information and then using that information for marketing activities. It is the central contact point for customers and the place from which all outgoing contacts with the customer are initiated.

Database is the Heart of the CC

In direct marketing, the database is the heart of the process. It serves as the collective memory of all customer transactions and is the depository for customer attribute information. Because all customer information is contained in the database, it must be accessible to anyone who has contact with the customer. Through this the business can achieve seamless, synchronized interaction with the customer.

For example, a salesperson could access the customer's file before making a sales call. Then the salesperson could review all contacts since the last sales call, review all actions taken on behalf of the customer, and access any specific interest areas the customer has identified. Equipped with this information, the salesperson has a more productive sales call and adds value to the relationship. The database plays a critical role in many aspects of business-to-business direct marketing.

EXHIBIT 8–10

Customer Information Center

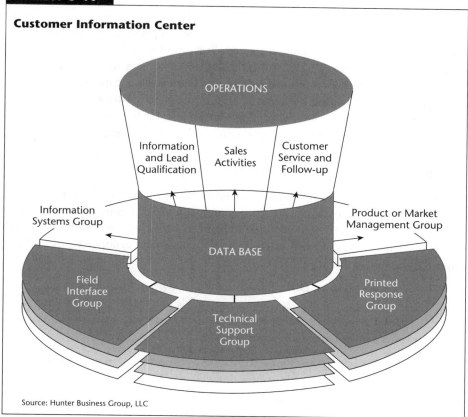

Source: Hunter Business Group, LLC

- *Target Market Segmentation.* Use the customer attribute information for segmenting target markets.

- *Single Source for Customer Inquiries.* Access to the database enables fast answers to customer inquiries and eliminates unnecessary transferring of customer calls.

- *Product Development.* Record customers' changing needs to detect new product opportunities.

- *Analysis.* Information stored in the database can be used for analysis such as expense to revenue ratios to determine customer profitability.

- *Metrics.* Database information facilitates a number of measurements such as the effectiveness of lead-generation sources or loyalty of a customer.

Operations for Customer Interface

The operations portions of the CC are shown at the center of the model in Exhibit 8–10. This is the core set of functions that include information and lead qualification, sales activities, customer service, and follow-up. Typically a centralized group of telemarketers are the primary contact point for customers and field sales reps.

The CC phone reps input and extract data from the CC database during their dialogue with customers and sales reps. This high-frequency, two-way dialogue continually validates and refreshes the database at low cost. Each group of telemarketers performs a function defined by the marketing and sales communication plans.

Communication Management Group

This group plans and executes direct marketing campaigns. It controls the message being delivered to the customer. It designs campaigns and contact plans. A primary responsibility is to ensure that all communications with customers and prospective customers deliver value. The communications management group performs several important functions.

- *Design and Develop Direct Mail Pieces and Electronic Communications.* Communications managers are responsible for creating and producing direct mail items, generating and acquiring lists, and mailing. They also produce all electronic communications.

- *Define Telemarketing Guides.* In business-to-business direct marketing, scripts are rarely used for outbound calling. The length of a call becomes a minor issue in building dialogue with the customer because obtaining certain types of information requires lengthy conversations. The guides remind the telemarketing representative of the information needed.

- *Determine Measures.* Develop methods to measure customer satisfaction, customer loyalty, profitability, lead sources, etc.

- *Develop Lead-Generation Programs.* Create and execute electronic, advertising, direct mail, and telemarketing lead-generation programs. Define lead-qualification criteria.

- *Coordinate Program Training and Instruction.* Provide training and instruction to keep telemarketing representatives current on product/service features and applications.

Print and Electronic Response Group

This group performs all mail room functions for printed material or personalized letters and responses. The group stocks, mails, and reorders literature supplies and other fulfillment material. They also manage electronic communications.

Technical Support Group

This group answers technically specific questions from customers, end-users, or channel distributors that cannot be answered by the telemarketing representative.

Field Interface Group

This group provides a central, personal contact for dealers, jobbers, franchisees, national accounts, sales reps, wholesalers, and retailers to interface with the CC. It supports sales and channel management functions to coordinate account planning activities among the customer, field sales reps, and telephone contacts.

Information Systems Group

This group interfaces with electronic communication networks and the centralized database. It maintains the internal network linking together all functional groups with the database (e.g., inventory, order processing status, accounting). Obviously, the CC involves a highly integrated process. To be effective, the processes leading up to the CC must be completed. Completion of these processes enables businesses to better plan, design, and staff the CC. Too often companies make the mistake of starting with the CC and ignoring the other processes. This leads to under-utilizing the inherent power of the CC and results in disappointment.

Cultivating Customers and Acquiring New Customers

The two major goals of direct marketing in a business-to-business environment are: (1) to increase sales productivity (while reducing sales costs), and (2) to build customer relationships. The CC is the tool used to accomplish these goals. The specific applications that lead to satisfying these goals are labeled cultivation and acquisition.

The cultivation process is designed to build the customer relationship. Businesses must build a bond with the customer that leads to a long-term relationship that benefits both parties. Exhibit 8–11 summarizes the steps in this process.

An adage in business-to-business marketing is that your best source for new business is your current customers. Existing customers represent growth opportunities. The cultivation process takes advantage of this by actively searching out sales opportunities and by closely monitoring the relationship.

Increasing Sales Opportunities

After gaining a customer, businesses can use the CC and direct marketing to pursue penetration strategies. They should penetrate the account to search out additional sales opportunities and strengthen relationships. They pursue this at

EXHIBIT 8–11

Cultivation Process

Task	Description	Implemented by	Information Source
Product penetration	Determine which other products customer has application for	CIC	Database
Account penetration	Obtain customer referrals for others within buying group	CIC	Database
Location penetration	Obtain customer referrals for others within location and/or organization	CIC	Database
Complaint handling	Procedures for handling customer complaints	CIC	Marketing and database
Customer-at-risk	Determine which customers or target segments are at risk	CIC and marketing	Customer surveys and database
Measurements	Continuously monitor and measure the customer relationship	CIC and marketing	Database

Source: Hunter Business Group, LLC

several levels: the individual, the buyer group, the location, and the organization. Exhibit 8–12 illustrates an account model and the penetration strategy.

1. At the individual level is the product penetration strategy. Businesses must ask customers what additional needs they have and what solutions might meet those needs.

2. At the buyer group level, they ask the customer to refer them to other people within the same department or function, at the same location. The idea is to find additional applications for the businesses' products or services.

3. At the functional level, they find out whether the customer can lead them to other buyer groups within the customer's location. Here, the area sales manager introduces his company to people in finance, manufacturing, and engineering located in the same area.

4. Finally, they move to the account level and determine whether there are other locations or operations within the organization with similar applications. The same area sales manager now introduces them to other area sales managers within the company or with affiliates.

Combined, these efforts enable businesses to build a stronger bond with the customer. By referring them to others within the organization, the customer takes

EXHIBIT 8–12

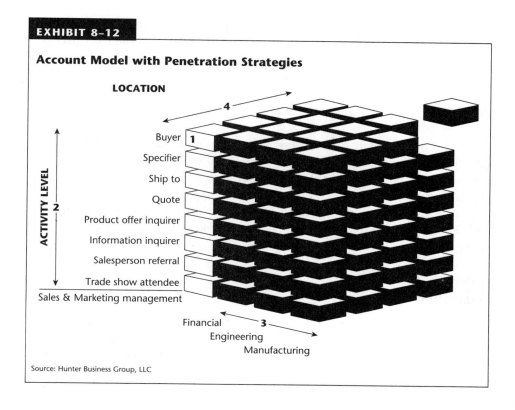

Account Model with Penetration Strategies

Source: Hunter Business Group, LLC

a proactive role in the relationship. By focusing on delighting the sales manager, an apostle is created, more loyal to the company and helpful in growing the business profitably.

Protecting Your Customer Base

Although expanding your customer base is important, so is protecting this base. This involves customer-at-risk detection. Detecting customers at risk requires an ongoing program of monitoring the state of your customer relationships. This is an early warning system that detects changing customer needs, etc., and permits corrective actions before customers defect.

Acquiring New Customers

Acquiring stable, long-term customers is only possible if you know and retain your current customers. The most profitable new or prospective customers will look like your best current customers. The customer information gathered by the CC will help you to acquire new customers. Using the information in the CC's database, you can identify attributes among current customers that will help you identify potential customers. From these attributes you can build a target segment, identify the unfulfilled needs or external service values of that segment, and determine how to position the product or service in respect to competitive products or services.

The next step in this process is lead qualification. The CC is used to qualify leads before sending them to the sales force or other channel members. A communications plan is developed, similar to that used with current customers, for those qualified leads that express a current interest and have a customer buyer profile. This becomes the qualified prospect list and is managed through the CC. The goal here is to advance the sales process so that the prospect is converted into a buyer.

Assimilation

Finally, new customers need to be assimilated into the customer community. Assimilation is the process of absorbing customers into the culture of the company—an initial "bonding" with the customer by acquiring and sharing valuable information. Think of it as welcoming a new employee into a company. It is the building of a "community of customers."

Meeting the Challenges of Our Decade

Nothing has had greater impact on the B2B marketplace than electronic media. Web sites, search, and e-mail have impacted lead generation, procurement, logistics, and customer service processes. B2B marketers have become multi-channel marketers more easily than B2C marketers.

Technology has made available a phone button on the terminal screen and even in search results. When clicked, a phone operator with the same screen in front of him or her is connected to the prospective customer through the Internet. This can be available 24/7.

Phone-assisted E-commerce will grow just as phone-assisted catalogs have proven successful in the business community. The addition of real-time, personal video-to-audio customer contact will continue to grow the importance of electronic media. International Data Corp. estimates that the worldwide B2B E-commerce market will grow to $6.4 trillion in sales in 2007.

The temptation is to revisit the marketing mania of the first Sears Roebuck catalogs, the advent of ZIP codes, and computer-managed mailing lists. These were times when the cost to get a customer contact significantly dropped.

The result was an ever-increasing volume of contacts with less concern for relevance than for cost per contact. Those times are gone.

Marketing to Small Businesses

Small business is a category that is easy to describe, but hard to define. The United States Small Business Administration defines small businesses as companies with up to 500 employees. Others define it as companies with 200, 100, or even 20 employees. All agree that small businesses act differently than large corporations, and that this group is growing. In total, small businesses account for an estimated $4 trillion in revenue annually.

According to Pitney Bowes, one segment of this market—those with fewer than 20 employees—account for 23 million small businesses. Although small, these businesses perform like large businesses in their purchase behavior. They purchase products on need, not on impulse. They have multiple decision influencers, not decisions made by a "head of household." Each decision influencer—the buying authority, the paying authority, the end-user, and the business owner—must all be delighted by the purchase.

But, like consumers, small businesses go through various life stages as they evolve from start-up, to growth, to profitability and maturity. Small business purchase habits will be different at each of these life stages. Consumer attributes, such as convenience, anxiety reduction, reliability, and trust, are also important to small business managers.

For marketing purposes, this category must be approached like any other business, but with the attitude of a consumer. Collateral such as references, case studies, and other ways of demonstrating how your business can help them improve their business is necessary to resonate with the small business executives.

The small business/home office segment continues to grow in the marketplace. It is a unique market, one in which multichannel communications make a world of difference.

Businesses Buyers Are Still Buyers

Knowing a prospect's name and sending out communication is not enough in the B2B market. Too much untargeted communication can hurt as much as help. Business prospects can screen their calls, put in multiple gatekeepers, and click away undesired e-mails.

Unwanted contacts with a business-to-business customer are not only a waste of money but a "vaccination" for the customer. Those ongoing pricks of valueless faxes, e-mails, mailings, and phone calls build up immunity, which leads to unreturned phone calls and broken sales appointments. The result is customer and prospect alienation and poor economic results. That is no way to get noticed or to build loyalty. And, it is not a best practice in direct marketing.

CASE STUDY:	National Restaurant Association Educational Foundation (NRAEF) ServSafe Third Edition Launch

Written by Jacobs & Clevenger with approval of its client, the National Restaurant Association Educational Foundation.

BACKGROUND

The National Restaurant Association Educational Foundation (NRAEF) is the educational arm of the National Restaurant Association. Together, these organizations serve the 925,000 restaurant and foodservice operations in the United States. The restaurant and foodservice industry is enormous. With over 12 million workers, the industry is the largest employer outside of government, and with over $500 billion in annual sales, it is one of the largest sectors of the economy, contributing 4 percent of the U.S. Gross Domestic Product.

The NRAEF's role is to develop and educate the industry's workforce. The Foundation's activities focus on recruiting new workers, helping retain those that enter the industry, and helping operators minimize the risks inherent to serving food and beverages. To this last end, the flagship product of the NRAEF is ServSafe®, the industry's leading food safety training and certification program.

Many restaurant and foodservice operators are required to have a manager trained and certified in proper food safety practices, to avoid the risk of foodborne illness among customers. For over 10 years, ServSafe has been the dominant player in this category, certifying more than 2 million people. ServSafe is important to the industry and its customers, but also to the NRAEF, as it is the leading source of revenue for many of the Foundation's scholarship and educational initiatives.

New Edition Merits a Fresh Approach

The NRAEF faced a critical juncture with ServSafe. It was ready to launch the new third edition of the program, which was much improved in content, tools, and materials. But the market environment had grown considerably tougher. Two competitors were more aggressively marketing their programs, and beginning to bite into ServSafe's market share.

And over the years, the brand image had grown out-of-date and was no longer reflective of the quality and leadership of the program.

Additionally, ServSafe was affected by a complicated distribution model, which allowed many customers to purchase materials from foodservice distributors, state organizations, and independent contractors. While some of the larger restaurant chains maintained a relationship with the NRAEF Sales Department, many others were not in contact and many smaller operators had no contact with the Foundation at all, relying solely on the network of local distributors for their needs. The result was that it was difficult for the NRAEF to deliver a consistent message, communicate the benefits of the new edition, and build the relationships that would increase customer value over time.

The NRAEF Marketing Department was ready to launch the new edition, but needed new positioning and a fresh direct marketing strategy. The NRAEF Sales Department was ready to talk to customers, but they needed ammunition and a pipeline of new leads. There was no marketing database, lead generation, or customer relationship activity. They knew what they wanted, but lacked the infrastructure and plan to make it happen.

CHALLENGE

The challenge was to develop and execute a plan to launch the new edition of ServSafe, and build a business-to-business marketing platform that would continue to serve the NRAEF going forward. The objectives were:

- Reposition the brand to better reflect the competitive advantages of ServSafe and the leadership and authority of the NRAEF.
- Develop a strategy to more efficiently market direct to customers, including lead generation among the higher-value segments.
- Drive sales of the new product to achieve a 2:1 ratio of revenue to marketing expense.
- Develop an infrastructure for marketing data that could become an information asset and

CASE STUDY:	**National Restaurant Association Educational Foundation (NRAEF)** **ServSafe Third Edition Launch** (continued)

better inform strategies and targeted communications over time.

SOLUTION

Customer and prospect information was reviewed. The NRAEF did not have a customer marketing database but did have a transactional database containing records of exam scores, class information, and past purchases for a select group of customers. Customer data was extracted from the transactional database, while other information came through the knowledge of the frontline sales team. Firmagraphics were appended to the file from outside data sources and some segments of the file were tele-verified.

For prospects (not existing customers), industry research and outside data sources were used in order to paint as complete a picture as possible. The available information was enough to segment the market based on potential customer value.

The market was segmented into these groups:

- **Large national restaurant and foodservice chains** with approximately 100 or more locations and product sales potential of $25,000 and up.
- **Regional and local chains** with approximately 5 to 100 locations and product sales potential of $1,000 to $25,000.
- **Independent restaurant owners** with approximately 1 to 5 locations and product sales potential of less than $1,000.

A contact plan was devised to deliver a stream of communications to each segment commensurate with the return the NRAEF could expect from that segment. *The highest-value segment,* large chains, represented a relatively small number of contacts, each worth considerable value. They would be put through a complete lead-generation program and receive the richest stream of communications, including personalized sales calls from their NRAEF sales representative, telling them about the new edition and the changes happening for ServSafe. Sales reps would also ask research questions of their customers, helping to fill any gaps in the data that would be important for future marketing and sales efforts. Members of this segment also received a specialized, dimensional direct mailer with a premium designed to break through the clutter of a busy corporate manager.

The middle-value segment, with significantly more prospects but lower revenue per customer, would also be put through the lead-generation program. This segment would receive a more modest stream, including centralized telequalification and a more modest direct mail package. As part of the telequalfication, prospects were asked a series of questions about their company's needs and food safety training resources. A grade was assigned from A through D, indicating the quality of the lead and the urgency with which the contact should be re-contacted. The direct mail sent was a 6 × 9-inch package with letter and brochure.

The lowest-value segment was the largest in terms of total numbers. For that reason it was extremely important. But the revenue per customer could not warrant the same investment in marketing, lead generation, and sales support. This group would receive a simple, cost-efficient direct mail piece. This value-based contact strategy ensured an allocation of marketing budget that would deliver the targeted revenue to expense ratio.

Lead-Generation Process

A phased-campaign approach was implemented to migrate prospects through the customer acquisition cycle. This process guided the timing and sequence of the multichannel, multisegment campaign.

The first phase, Awareness, introduced the brand and built awareness. This was achieved through targeted ads in trade publications, containing tip-in cards for response measurement. This phase also included online advertising and search engine marketing, which led to campaign-themed and targeted Web site landing pages. This phase ensured the market would have a basic comprehension of the program and its changes.

National Restaurant Association Educational Foundation (NRAEF) ServSafe Third Edition Launch *(continued)*

The second phase of the campaign was Lead Generation and Qualification, in which prospects were targeted with their value-based phone and mail contacts and qualified for their decision-making authority and intent to purchase. *A third phase*, for Conversion and Sales, consisted of follow-up calls and the taking of product orders, turning the investments in marketing into revenue.

Finally, *a fourth phase* for Cultivation and Cross Selling continued the dialogue through e-mails, sales calls, and direct mail. This alerted customers to new products and new promotions and helped strengthen the relationship with NRAEF and ServSafe, maximizing the lifetime value of each customer.

Success Goes by the Book

For the product repositioning and creative strategy, the logo and brand identity needed an update.

The logo appeared out of date and was no longer the asset it should be for such a leading program. Through an iterative process of creative development and research, a new logo was unveiled that communicated the right attributes for the program: authority, trustworthiness, and forward thinking. A number of advertising and direct mail concepts for the new ServSafe program were considered.

The idea that resonated best across all media and delivered upon customer insight was a campaign titled "Go by the book." This campaign leveraged the strength and heritage of ServSafe while asserting its value to the customer—in essence, telling restaurant owners and managers that if they want to protect themselves and their customers, they need to go by the book. This theme clearly referenced a recognizable and iconic element of ServSafe, the textbook used by students of the program. The "Go by

	PHASE 1: AWARENESS	PHASE 2: LEAD GENERATION AND QUALIFICATION	PHASE 3: CONVERSION AND SALES	PHASE 4: CULTIVATION AND CROSS-SELLING
Large chains (*highest individual value*)	Print ads with tip-in cards and online ads and search engine marketing drive to Web landing page	Sales calls from NRAEF account reps and dimensional mail with premium + follow-up postcard	Sales calls and field visits and distribution of collateral	E-mail (tailored for audiences) and subsequent campaign direct mail
Medium chains (*moderate individual value*)	Print with tip-in cards and online ads and search engine marketing drive to Web landing page	Telemarketing from outside vendor and 6 × 9 direct mail + follow-up postcard	Targeted sales calls to those who qualify	E-mail (tailored for audiences) and subsequent campaign direct mail
Independent operators (*lower individual value*)	Print with tip-in cards and online ads and search engine marketing drive to Web landing page	Direct mail self-mailer	Handled by state distributors	Subsequent campaign direct mail

CASE STUDY: **National Restaurant Association Educational Foundation (NRAEF)**
ServSafe Third Edition Launch *(continued)*

the book" theme was carried through all forms of media, with a distinctive brand identity and clear, focused, and integrated message. See NRAEF's ServSafe Direct Mail kit in Exhibit 8-13.

But what about all of the information that was captured on prospects and customers? This included hundreds of contacts among the top two segments,

with newly developed profiles from telequalification and sales rep interviews, and hundreds of thousands more sample names and addresses from the independent segment.

A new data infrastructure was implemented that automated many of the processes and organized the information for future use. One part of this was a new

EXHIBIT 8-13

ServSafe Direct Mail Kit

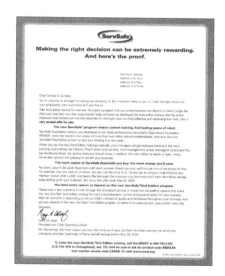
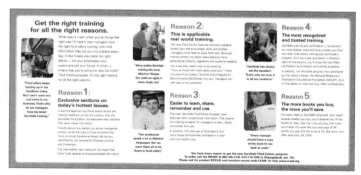

prospect file, which consolidated all of the various data sources into a single, integrated source for mailing, telemarketing, and e-mail communications. The other part was a new salesforce automation system that tracked key leads and accounts, sorting by grade and territory to the Sales Department for follow-up and maintenance, creating a pipeline of opportunity.

RESULTS

The launch of the new edition of ServSafe was a success on every level. Economically, the program had its best year ever and the campaign itself exceeded objectives with a 2.5 revenue-to-expense ratio. Thousands of new sales were driven and over 500 high-value leads were qualified and generated for the Sales Department.

The new brand was unanimously well received across the industry and continued to anchor the look and feel of ServSafe communications for years to come. Print advertising consistently scored in the highest ranks for recall and awareness within its target. And the seamless integration from product packaging to Web to direct mail to sales collateral ensured that every customer received the clear and consistent message about ServSafe. The next year, based on the success of this initial campaign, marketing investment in ServSafe increased and the program continues to thrive on a new trajectory of success.

PILOT PROJECT The National Restaurant Association Education Foundation (NRAEF) segmented their customer base using potential customer value as the criteria. There are many other ways that they could segment prospects. However, no matter what segmentation scheme they use, it must be reachable using mailing lists.

A.   Identify three other segmentation schemes NRAEF could use.

B.   Choose one of those segmentation schemes and describe how it might be executed by NRAEF.

C.   Explain your rationale for choosing that scheme.

D.   Describe a type of list that could be used to reach that segment

Key Points

▶ Large average order sizes, enormous lifetime values, and small target market universes dictate that the goal of business-to-business direct marketing is to increase sales productivity while "cultivating" relationships with existing business customers—the buyers, specifiers, approvers, etc., who influence or make direct purchases for companies, institutions, or other organizations.

▶ To uncover and meet needs that the competition is not meeting, seek to understand why customers buy from you, what needs your products or services fulfill, and how your products' features or attributes compare with those of competitive products or services. Ask customers to rank-order this attribute/feature list to find new opportunities and to begin to segment customers.

▶ Identify how and when customers want to receive certain types of information, and develop an effective contact plan and communication strategy that delivers it in that manner.

▶ Establish a contact center to manage all contacts with customers—ingoing and outgoing. It can acquire customer information for marketing activities and coordinate those activities.

▶ Develop strategies to penetrate existing accounts to search out additional sales opportunities and strengthen relationships.

▶ Use database information to identify attributes among current customers that will help you identify potential customers. From these attributes you can build a target segment, identify the unfulfilled needs or external service values of that segment, and determine how to position the product or service in respect to competitive products or services.

▶ Qualify leads before sending them to the sales force or other channel members. The goal is to advance the sales process so that the prospect is converted into a buyer.

MARKETING TO BUSINESS WITH LEAD GENERATION

The traditional role of personal selling is changing. Not long ago, the sales force was the "face" of a company. The sales force answered questions, demonstrated the product, offered solutions to problems, and established loyal relationships. Salespeople *were* the company.

The sales force is still an important function of marketing and sales, but its job is difficult. The face of competition has changed and includes alternative solutions that require more inventive product and service offerings. Prospects often obtain information from a variety of channels and sources. The sales cycle is often disconnected from the buying process. Prospects don't want to see a salesperson. Technology has made it easier for customers to make purchase decisions on their own without a salesperson's visit.

Today, office supplies or office equipment can be purchased online. eBay has become a busy marketplace for high-end business purchases. Businesses can even negotiate complicated telephone service agreements over the phone. Once, it was inconceivable that high-tech or high-ticket items could be sold via traditional direct marketing channels. A sales force was needed to explain complicated products or stay with the prospect while he or she considered a high-ticket purchase. This took considerable time. Today, you can buy an interest in a private jet from a direct mail package.

However, many sales still require a salesperson. They are usually those with a complex selling proposition. Nevertheless, the constantly increasing costs of a sales visit make them prohibitive for many companies. While some estimates peg this cost at $400 per call, it is not unusual for the complex sales call to cost three or four times that much, when all of the support for the sales call is included. And, according to the Sales and Marketing Institute, the number of sales calls to close a complex sale is up from 5 in 1990 to 8–10 today.

The sales force needs a careful process to move customers through the sales funnel. It is a system where prospects are identified so they can focus on closing sales, not on cold calling. This process is known as lead generation (See Exhibit 9–1).

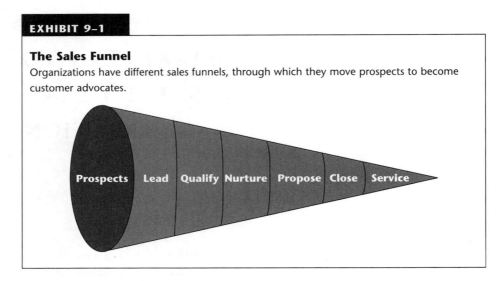

EXHIBIT 9–1

The Sales Funnel
Organizations have different sales funnels, through which they move prospects to become customer advocates.

Prospects · Lead · Qualify · Nurture · Propose · Close · Service

Lead-generation programs are a method devised to flow qualified leads into the sales force and classify those leads so that the sales force knows how to prioritize their efforts and focus on closing more sales, more often.

Today's Sales Force: People or Process

A sales organization can be a group of specially trained salespeople or, alternatively, a communications process driven by technology. Many industries today utilize a human sales force or people organized into territories and sales districts with clearly articulated sales quotas. For industries that don't have the manpower or the budget to keep a sales force in operation, communications must fill the void, and alternative channels of distribution must be created. The Internet is a terrific example of communications creating alternative methods to distribute product literature, demonstrate benefits, and close the sale.

Communications can never replace the sales force completely. There is no substitute for personal relationships between buyer and seller. However, communications such as print ads, direct mail, e-mail, search, Web sites, etc., can augment, enrich, and support the traditional sales organization.

Sales Coverage Models

Today, where a sales force is involved, it is often for a complex sale. This type of sale can't be completed without the help of a salesperson. Transactions require the involvement of many decision makers, influencers, and buying authorities. These individuals come with many perspectives, from many disciplines, often crossing silos, cultural, and even national borders. The sales cycle can run for weeks, months, even years.

Developing the right sales coverage model is important. The sales coverage models must provide economic value across segments, channels, and media. It includes integration between sales and marketing. Marketing is charged with inquiry generation, lead qualification, and sales opportunity development.

This new model is charged with increasing sales productivity. It uses low-tech techniques such as inside sales, yet it takes full advantage of technology such as databases, contact management, sales force automation, and CRM systems to supplement sales force contact and cultivate leads. Even communications are included in the sales coverage model (See Exhibit 9–2).

At the heart of most successful sales coverage models is a well-planned and well-executed lead-generation program.

Planning Successful Lead-Generation Programs

To develop a successful marketing program, you have to know what you're up against. Here are some facts from the Advertising Research Foundation:

- Up to 60 percent of all inquiries are made with a view to purchase within one year.

- Up to 25 percent of those with a purchase in view will have an "immediate need," and will purchase the product or service advertised from the company of which they inquired, or from a competitor.

EXHIBIT 9–2

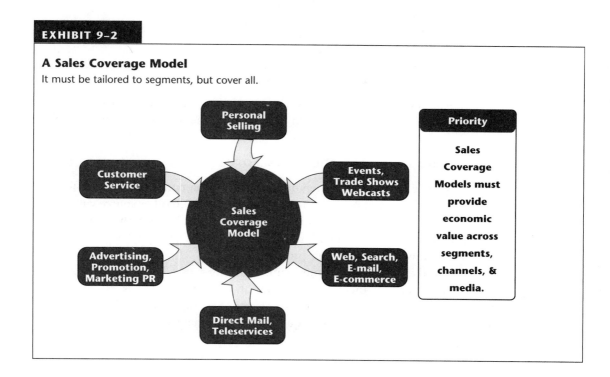

A Sales Coverage Model
It must be tailored to segments, but cover all.

- Up to 10 percent of those with a purchase in view will be "hot" leads.

- Up to 60 percent of the inquirers who contact you also contact your competitor.

- In 20 percent of all prospects' requests for information, the respondents never received any material.

- In 43 percent of those inquiries, the material was received too late to be of any use.

- 59 percent stated that they threw away one or more pieces of the response material because it provided no value.

This data suggests that there is a substantial waste of communications expenditures, which results in a feeling of disenchantment by large numbers of people because of unresponsive companies. So how does one overcome these hurdles?

Successful implementation involves consideration of eight key steps:

1. Involving the sales force

2. Determining objectives

3. Developing the promotion strategy

4. Developing the creative strategy

5. Developing the media strategy

6. Planning capacity and lead flow

7. Developing the follow-up strategy

8. Measuring results after the promotion has begun.

Each step creates a feedback loop so that actual results can be measured against objectives, modifications can be made, and the process can begin again.

Step One: Involving the Sales Force

If a company utilizes a lead-generation program to support a human sales force, it should involve the sales force in the planning process. No other source will be able to relate as well to the marketplace. The sales force is on the "firing line." Salespeople know the competition, the specific needs of their territory, and the spheres of influence among their prospect base.

Even the message in your communications can be influenced in both tone and content by the sales force. Front-end involvement is essential. And, don't discount their ability to judge the effectiveness of the promotion. A feedback loop should be established for a qualitative assessment of positive and negative results.

Step Two: Determining Objectives

The need for objectives in a lead-generation program relates to the quality and quantity of leads, and the cost of generating them. An abundance of leads can be meaningless if an insufficient number convert to sales. Key questions are:

- What ratio of leads to sales (often called conversion percentage) is needed to make this program profitable?

- What is the maximum allowable expenditure for every qualified lead generated?

It is important to set these benchmarks at the beginning of the planning process and to use them as guideposts for the development of the program. It is extremely inefficient—and sometimes impossible—to change objectives mid-stream.

Step Three: Developing the Promotion Strategy

Strategies should identify the steps required for accomplishing the program's objectives. They are the road map for getting from where you are to where you want to be. In addition, they should mesh with the strategies being applied by the sales force and other distribution channels. For example, if a computer manufacturer has identified the legal profession as a prime opportunity segment, the promotion strategy may be to develop a lead generation program directed to the same target audience timed in conjunction with personal sales force contact. Qualified leads generated from the program will augment efforts of the sales force and result in a greater sales closing percentage than if the sales force had no support.

Step Four: Developing the Creative Strategy

The creative strategy for any lead generation program *must* reflect the brand promise. The look and feel of all brand communications should be consistent with the overall image of the company in order to leverage the full benefits of an integrated campaign. This is not to say that all communications should slavishly adhere to precise elements of the current general advertising campaign. The intent is to represent the brand consistently, so that universal brand attributes and emotions are reinforced with every contact the consumer has with the brand.

Step Five: Developing the Channel Strategy

The key question is: given the target market and the product offering, what channels will most effectively accomplish the task? Whether it be direct mail, e-mail, search, banners, print, events, or trade shows, consideration must be given to historical effectiveness, penetration, number of contacts, and so on. Once the channel strategy is developed, it is possible to project lead flow and to begin the capacity planning process.

Step Six: Planning Capacity and Lead Flow

Lead flow is not a faucet that can be turned on or off at will. It must be planned so that leads come in at a rate equal to the sales force's capacity to handle them. Although there will be more on this subject later in this chapter, the key point to remember is that either too few leads or too many leads will work to the detriment of the program.

Step Seven: Developing the Fulfillment Strategy

Immediate response and rapid cycles of contact improve the chances of gaining and maintaining a customer. The sooner information can be delivered or fulfilled, the higher the odds of closing the sale. The smartest marketers will use lead-generation programs to pre-empt a customer inquiry, and send information and/or pertinent offers at the precise moment the customer is ready to receive them. This demonstrates the symbiotic relationship between lead generation and database marketing (See Chapter 3, "The Impact of Databases").

But how does one know what customers want, and when they are ready to buy? The answer: leverage every contact with a customer to learn more about him or her. Asking the appropriate questions leads to highly profitable answers.

And, as simple as it sounds, one must know exactly what will happen to a lead once it is received. If there is to be a brochure, for example, ample quantities must be in stock before the initial communication occurs. Measurement systems must be in place for scheduling sales calls, referring leads to the field, re-contact programs, and so forth. Failure to be ready to fulfill promptly can kill the best of promotions.

Step Eight: Measuring Results

It is imperative that the program be measurable and accountable. Success and failure factors need to be identified before the program is developed to ensure that results tracking and analysis are conducted properly once the program is in place.

So, how will your program be measured? Gross sales? Revenue? Cost per lead? Cost per order? Beyond these traditional measures, you'll need to ask yourself some additional questions:

- What constitutes a good/bad lead?

- How many leads are enough?

- Which is worse, no leads, or too many?

- How will we track leads? Who will be responsible for them?

- How will we automate our processes for secure dataflow?

- What is the best way to convert leads into profitable sales?

- How will we report our progress to management?

Other Ingredients of an Effective Lead-Management System

A good inquiry follow-up system should address the interaction problem often associated with the activities of the salespeople, the marketing manager, and the advertising manager.

Sales representatives in general loathe and avoid paperwork. They often resent any intrusion into their territory, and scorn measurement and control. A good lead-management system must be simple to use, easy to work with, and not be looked upon by salespeople as a burden. Also, sales representatives typically do not supply the complete feedback necessary for proper evaluation. A smart system must be able to supply the necessary analysis without total reliance on the sales representative.

The Inquiry System Does Not Exist Without an Offer

Communications objectives should be inquiry-oriented. The creation of advertising that employs known response techniques should be the mission of agency and/or staff copywriters and art directors. The advertising produced should be measured against response-oriented goals.

The offer must be in line with program objectives, and with the company's operational ability to follow-up on responses. If the objective is to generate leads, make an offer that will generate only as many as you can effectively handle. Too many leads can be even more destructive to the program than not enough. Lead quantity is not as important as lead quality.

When testing a less expensive offer against your control offer, don't assume that a lower response rate is less effective. Include the costs for the offer, then review the total direct marketing costs per responder and per order. You might find that the less expensive offer produces a more valuable customer over time, thus producing a more profitable program.

Do Not Be Afraid to Mention the Price

As stated previously, lead-generation programs were initially developed for products and services with high price tags. Even if the price is prohibitive, it will immediately weed out those who cannot afford it. They are unqualified. You should spend the majority of your time talking to prospects that have the money, authority, need, and desire to purchase what you have to sell.

Ask the Prospect Some Leading Questions

The questions you ask will allow you to determine where the prospect falls in the purchase decision process. Use every available opportunity, but don't turn your qualification effort into market research. There's no need to overload a single contact with a customer or prospect by asking them lots of questions—too many questions can actually decrease response. Spread them out; use several contacts. This will not only improve the probability that you'll get answers to all your questions, it will also provide a reason to keep communicating. After all, don't forget the out-of-sight, out-of-mind rule. Stay in your prospect's field of vision at all times. Sample questions and their implications are shown in Exhibit 9–3.

Note that answers to these questions can provide important learning. Use all this data to build a rich database from which to develop ongoing marketing communications. Constantly add new data to the old; refresh worn-out data. If, in your database, you find a prospect who: (1) already has experience with your company, (2) is the decision maker in the buying process, and (3) has an immediate need, make sure you get to him or her quickly. You're about to close a sale!

EXHIBIT 9–3

Questions for Sales Prospects

Authority in the buying decision	How would you describe your involvement in the decision to purchase our product? • You make the decision. • You investigate and recommend. • The decision is made elsewhere in the company *(Make sure to get the name of that person)*.
Monetary resources	How much are you willing the spend?
Potential sales volume	How many people in your company could benefit from our products? How will you put our product to use?
Predisposition to buy from you/customer loyalty	Have you purchased any of our products in the past? Which ones? Would you like to remain on our mailing list?
Immediacy of need/desire	Are you ready to buy now? In 3–6 months? 6–12 months? Over 12 months? Would you like a salesperson to call/visit?

Incorporate a Feedback Loop

Consider adding a device that poses some of the questions above into your fulfillment offering. This could be a bounce-back postcard or fax form, an e-mail (assuming you've already captured the prospect's e-mail address), or even a page within your Web site. A feedback loop will allow you to qualify the lead after the prospect has a chance to review the information requested.

Monitor the time from the shipment date of the fulfillment package. If the feedback device is not returned within a specified time, send another one. After three unsuccessful efforts, you can call it quits. Additional follow-up beyond this point is unproductive. Analyze and compile the data from the feedback device and the original inquiry to classify the lead as qualified or unqualified.

Understanding the Art of Communications

Hierarchy of Effects

Any purchase decision is an evolutionary process. The advertising industry has accepted a model developed by researchers Lavidge and Steiner to explain how advertising works (see Exhibit 9–4). Their model is based on a hierarchy of effects in the communication process that move the prospect from awareness to purchase.

Before purchasing action occurs, an evolution takes place. Mentally, the prospect moves through a series of steps starting with awareness and ending in the purchasing action. Within these stages of involvement, different modes of communication play different roles. Although responsibility overlaps, it is clear to see how direct marketing plays a significant role in the selling process.

General advertising is most effective in generating awareness, knowledge, and interest. Direct marketing's strength lies in encouraging evaluation, preference, conviction, and ultimately purchase. These steps often require more information,

EXHIBIT 9-4

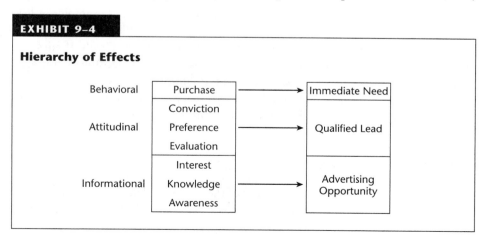

Hierarchy of Effects

Behavioral	Purchase	→	Immediate Need
Attitudinal	Conviction / Preference / Evaluation	→	Qualified Lead
Informational	Interest / Knowledge / Awareness	→	Advertising Opportunity

whether that is delivered in a one-on-one conversation (in person or on the telephone), a product demonstration, an information-rich brochure, or a home page on the Internet.

To increase efficiency and cut costs, marketers should insist that each mode of communication is accountable for what it does best. General advertising should be measured on its ability to generate awareness and consideration; direct marketing should be evaluated on its ability to move the prospect from consideration to purchase and beyond. An effective lead-management system assigns specific roles to both, and leverages the strengths inherent within each. Working seamlessly together, they comprise a communications program that is unbeatable.

Checks and Balances

Multimedia synergy (the combination of two or more forms of communication) can dramatically affect results and productivity. For example, if you are running television advertising in a market and simultaneously mail within that market, you will see lifts in response. But there's another benefit to integrated marketing programs: checks and balances.

Advertising is expensive. You need tools to measure and compare results in order to focus your resources on the most effective channels and activities. The lead-management system should provide reports of inquiries by medium, product, and sales territory. This is a valuable tool, not only for results analysis, but also for advertising planning.

Adjusting Quality and Quantity of Leads

All types of lead-generation programs can produce what are commonly referred to as "soft" or "hard" leads. Soft lead offers can be expected to produce a higher front-end response; hard lead offers can be expected to produce a lower front-end response, but a higher closure percentage. Exhibit 9–5 shows ten examples of lead softeners, and ten lead hardeners.

Experience will dictate whether you want soft leads or hard leads. If salespeople close only one out of ten soft leads, for example, they may become discouraged and abandon the program. On the other hand, if salespeople close three out of ten soft leads versus five out of ten hard leads with twice as many leads to draw from, they (and management too) might opt for the soft lead program.

Capacity Planning

Capacity planning is a critical component of the up-front planning process, and key to managing the program on an ongoing basis. No matter how carefully planned, a program can change because of internal and external variables.

EXHIBIT 9–5

Lead Softeners and Hardeners

Softeners:
1. Tell less about the product.
2. Add convenience for replies.
3. Give away something.
4. Ask for less information.
5. Highlight the offer.
6. Make the ad "scream."
7. Don't ask for the phone number.
8. Increase the offer's value.
9. Offer a contest or sweepstakes.
10. Run in more general media.

Hardeners:
1. Mention a price.
2. Mention a phone or sales call.
3. Tell a lot about the product.
4. Ask for a lot of information.
5. Specify terms for the offer.
6. Ask for postage on the reply.
7. Bury the offer in the copy.
8. Tie the offer to a sales call.
9. Change the offer's value.
10. Ask for money.

For instance, market conditions may change, postal deliveries might be slower or faster than anticipated, a computerized customer file might malfunction, a complex new product could take twice as much time to sell as anticipated. The possibilities are endless, but the point is simple: *Plan your capacity to be flexible to change.* Exhibit 9–6 is a typical capacity planning chart for a direct mail program, indicating optimum lead flow for various sales districts.

Assuming a salesperson can average one cold prospect call a day, Exhibit 9–6 shows how many calls each office can make in a working month of 20 days. This information determines what quantity of mail is required at a 5 percent return to furnish leads for these calls, given that probably 20 percent of them will be qualified, and the rest will be screened out prior to a sales call.

Thus, control can be exercised over mailings so that the two salespeople in Denver, for example, will not be suddenly swamped by scores of sales leads. In their district, 4,000 mailing pieces would be needed to furnish them with 40 qualified leads—as many as the two salespeople can follow-up in one month. ZIP code selectivity helps to target mailings within a district.

To keep a constant flow of leads moving to the field at an average of 3,500 a month would require 70,000 mailing pieces per month. A year's campaign (12 months multiplied by 70,000) requires 840,000 mailing pieces.

Lead-Flow Monitoring and Contingency Planning

As mentioned earlier in this chapter, the more quickly a lead is acted upon, the higher the likelihood of conversion. The theory behind this is that the interest is

EXHIBIT 9–6

Capacity Planning Chart

District Offices	No. of Salespeople in Each	Total qualified Calls Needed Each Month	Total Leads Required (at 20% Qualified)	Mailings Required (at 5% Return)
Indiana	10	200	1,000	20,000
Tennessee	14	280	1,400	28,000
Virginia	10	200	1,000	20,000
Michigan	10	200	1,000	20,000
Illinois	16	320	1,600	32,000
West Virginia	13	260	1,300	26,000
New Jersey	5	100	500	10,000
San Francisco	8	160	800	16,000
Maine	9	180	900	18,000
Seattle	9	180	900	18,000
New York City	10	200	1,000	20,000
Ohio	10	200	1,000	20,000
Texas	7	140	700	14,000
Utah	3	60	300	6,000
Connecticut	6	120	600	12,000
Pittsburgh	9	180	900	18,000
Philadelphia	11	220	1,100	22,000
Miami	3	60	300	6,000
Des Moines	7	140	700	14,000
Los Angeles	2	40	200	4,000
Denver	2	40	200	4,000
Atlanta	3	60	300	6,000
Totals	**177**	**3,540**	**17,700**	**354,000**

highest when a prospect first responds to an offer. The longer a lead sits, the "colder" the prospect becomes.

But as anyone who has worked with a lead-generation program will tell you, sometimes leads come in at a greater rate than anticipated. This will not cause a multitude of cold leads, but it could have impact on sales force morale, overhead costs, and so on. Whether too high or too low, it pays to have contingency systems in place.

Let us look at a typical lead flow planning model to see the normal distribution of leads from a direct mail program (see Exhibit 9–7). It has been proven that responses to direct mail programs will almost always follow this response curve, with 50 percent of total responses in the first four weeks, and the balance over the

EXHIBIT 9-7

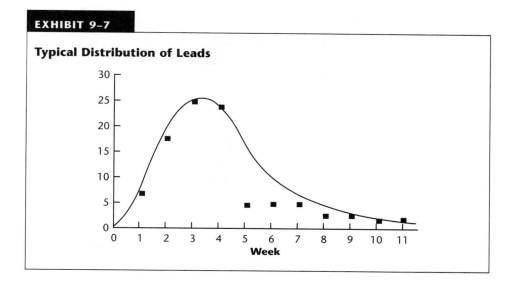

Typical Distribution of Leads

next six weeks. Lead distribution will vary depending on the medium utilized. Although lead generation will always be measured on a bell curve, specific response over time will vary; thus the height and width of the curve will vary.

Exhibit 9–8 is a series of these response waves, each representing mailings. The dotted line represents capacity, the maximum number of leads that can be handled effectively within a predetermined time period. At best, our planning will keep us within 90–110 percent of the dotted line. But what if some of the internal or external events mentioned earlier should change our response curve and create a shortfall? There are two basic systems that can be employed to effectively manage around this: in queue (or lead bank) and shelf contingency systems.

EXHIBIT 9-8

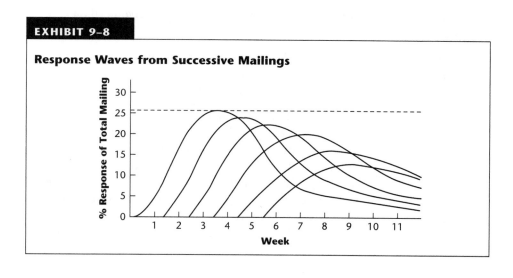

Response Waves from Successive Mailings

In Queue (Lead Bank) System

Many companies create a lead bank system, which is a purposeful manner of always operating above capacity. When a lead enters the sales center, it first enters the lead bank before being dispatched for follow-up. If there is always an extra week's worth of leads, and they are handled first in, first out, no leads are penalized or allowed to get cold. Naturally, the lead bank would be stocked with mail responses. You must handle Internet, e-mail, and telephone responses immediately.

If and when there is an underdelivery of leads, the lead bank is drawn down until additional leads can be driven into the center. Or the bank can be increased temporarily when an overdelivery occurs until the up-front solicitation can be decreased.

Shelf Contingency

It is always wise to have additional up-front communications "on the shelf," produced, and ready to go in the event of an underdelivery of leads. If the lead-generation program utilizes direct mail, for example, two weeks of additional mail packages in reserve will ensure a timely response to an underdelivery problem; after normal capacity resumes, the shelf can be replenished.

Lead Classification and Scoring

It is no secret that in any lead-generation program lead quality varies a great deal. The 80/20 rule can be applied here. Generally speaking, 80 percent of total sales revenue will be driven by about 20 percent of all leads received. Given this, it makes sense to optimize time and effort with a good lead classification system. There are two good reasons for optimizing time and effort:

1. *Time is money*. It simply costs too much to have a salesperson call on unqualified prospects.

2. *Good leads get cold*. If salespeople are spending their time pursuing low-quality leads, high-quality leads will get cold. Each day a lead is not acted upon makes the likelihood of sales conversion less likely.

How can leads be qualified? The best way is to build screening devices into the up-front media selection. Lists in the business field, for example, can be selected by sales volume, number of employees, net worth, etc. It must be recognized, however, that while such selectivity can produce a better-qualified lead, it can also reduce the volume of leads generated, sometimes significantly. If a product or service tends to have more of a mass application, this may not be desirable. Not all leads are created equal. A classification system is needed to prioritize which ones to respond to first, assuming that they have an immediate need and will close most quickly.

ABC Classification

ABC Classification is a one-dimensional approach to lead classification (see Exhibit 9–9). It is based on categorizing leads by likelihood of when that lead is expected to convert to a sale. When a salesperson is requested, or any other clues are given that the prospect is ready to buy, the lead is classified as "A," and sent to the sales force for immediate follow-up. This "A" will be used for forecasting sales potential.

Leads that are analyzed as having a continuing interest are classified as "B." They are qualified leads and need to be developed either through personal contact with a salesperson, or by sending more information.

All other inquiries are classified as "C." They are the emerging market, and a very responsive mailing list for future efforts. It is this group that represents the advertising opportunity. The goal here is to drive the group up the purchasing decision hierarchy through a combination of media. Keep an eye on this group. Too often, companies discard inquiry names if they are not immediately productive. This is a major error and a waste of excellent business potential.

Three-Dimensional Scoring

The previous model assumed that every lead generated by the system, if closed, would become a profitable customer. That is not always the case. Which would you rather have, a sale to a one-time customer, or a sale to a customer who would

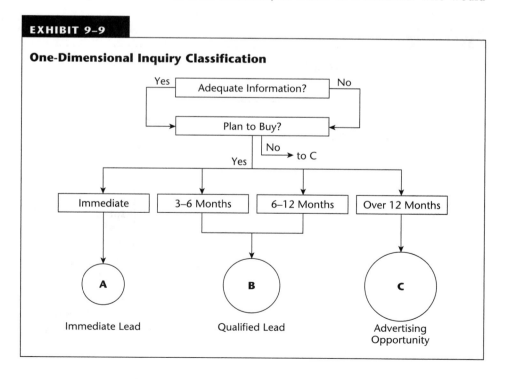

EXHIBIT 9–9

One-Dimensional Inquiry Classification

continue to buy from you over time? Of course, you want to close both sales, but it would be wise to focus your effort on the latter first. In order to factor other elements into the lead classification process, you need to evaluate those factors in three dimensions:

- *Speed of Action.* How quickly will the buying decision be made?

- *Closing Potential.* How well can we satisfy the consumer's need?

- *Account Value.* What is the total anticipated amount of the purchase, or the projected value of the customer to your company?

A three-dimensional model scores the relative value of leads compared to one another and provides learning that will allow you to appropriate the best communications plans (see Exhibit 9–10).

To rank the prospect on three dimensions, you need to assign values that will classify each component. For the purposes of illustration, let us assign the value 3 as "high," 2 as "medium," and 1 as "low." This allows a potential for 27 possible scores, where the best lead is classified as a "333," and the poorest lead as "111." This model will help to determine the best next steps: determination of your allowable spending per lead, when to time the communications, and the basis for evaluation pre- and post-contact.

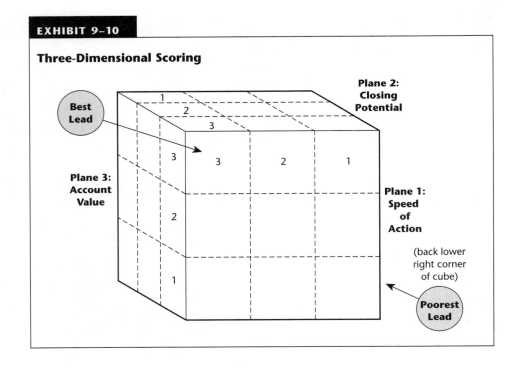

EXHIBIT 9–10

Three-Dimensional Scoring

Inquiry Processing Cost Analysis

We have been looking at inquiry management effectiveness, but it is also very important to consider how much your company is spending to manage inquiries. There isn't any right amount to spend. You can spend too little as well as too much. If your company isn't spending enough to make full use of the inquiries generated, you aren't saving money on inquiry fulfillment, you're wasting money on advertising.

The real questions are what level of service you want to provide and how much should that level cost. Setting levels of service is always difficult, and it is particularly difficult in inquiry management. Wide fluctuations in inquiry volume (see Exhibit 9–11) caused by sudden surges in the number of calls can jeopardize the level of service.

If you are managing inquiries via a traditional sales center, you need to have enough people, machines, and other facilities to handle lead volumes. If you manage these resources to deliver a high level of service, you'll have unused capacity (and high cost) when volumes fall. But lower capacity can lead to poor response times when volumes are high, which, in turn, can waste advertising investment. The trick, of course, is to organize your operation so as to minimize fixed costs, so that costs will vary with volume.

The use of temporary labor and shared facilities can help, but more management time will be required to ensure that service is maintained. Another solution is to obtain inquiry management support from outside sources, which can level the

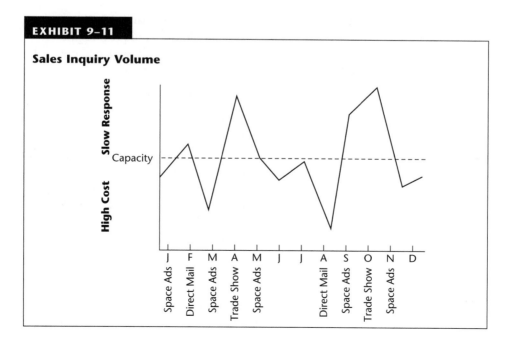

EXHIBIT 9–11

Sales Inquiry Volume

peaks and valleys among many customers, providing universal cost-effectiveness without adversely affecting service levels.

If you are managing inquiries via a Web site or other technologically driven channel, it is always best to have system capacity capable of handling at least three times the projected maximum lead volume. This will ensure consistency of service, even if actual results are much greater than you anticipate.

Tracking and Results Reporting

Tracking and results reporting are as important as management of leads in the sales center. These activities will result in quantification of the actual effort, relating the success of the program to its objectives, and making management aware of the program's return on investment.

Tracking

Which information an advertiser decides to track is largely a function of individual needs. However, the following data will be essential.

Number of Leads by Effort. Whether for a mailing, print ad, Internet banner, or broadcast spot, the number of leads resulting from each effort should be captured. This is usually handled by a specific code for each. For instance, a mailing with a split copy test is actually two mailings. Therefore, each response device should have a specific code so when it is received at the sales center, the proper mailing can be credited.

If telephone response is encouraged, as it should be, a unique phone number or extension should be given for each mailing, thus making it possible to credit the proper promotion effort. Internet banners can be coded by linking to a unique page within the Web site. Quite often, these are "mirror pages" of the home page with a unique URL address, and are completely transparent to the prospect. By capturing information by code, the winning test promotions will emerge.

Quality of Lead/Conversion Information. The marketing effort that pulls the most responses isn't always the most successful, for it is conversion to sales that is the true measure of success. The comparison of two efforts in Exhibit 9–12 illustrates the point. As you can see, effort A would seemingly be more successful if responses were the sole measure. But when conversion is factored in, the greatest number of sales actually came from effort B; this is the more successful marketing tactic.

Results Reporting

There is little question that an efficient lead-generation program will increase the volume of sales and cut sales costs. But it is essential that results be measured and reported.

EXHIBIT 9–12

Comparison of Two Marketing Efforts

	No. Mailed	Percentage Response	No. of Responses	Percentage Conversion	No. of Sales
Package A	20,000	2%	400	6%	24
Package B	20,000	1	200	15	30

Documentation of results is essential for three basic reasons: (1) to measure against original objectives of the lead generation program, (2) to prove value to the sales force, and (3) to prove value to management.

Decision Support Tools

Information generated in any phase of a lead-generation program provides a database from which a wealth of useful information is available. Once the results of marketing efforts are summarized, they can be sorted in countless ways. The resulting information can help provide accountability. It can also prove useful in researching and evaluating new markets. It can evaluate media effectiveness and provide insight into the value of various creative appeals.

Some information can be used to evaluate the effectiveness of sales follow-up activity, and even the equity of sales territory assignments. Once all these variables are understood, the learning can be leveraged into smarter program planning for future efforts.

Sample Reports for Sales Managers

The Purchase Potential Report. When leads are ranked by closing potential, it is possible to track current month activity against previous month activity, and to compare achievements against year-to-date objectives. This report also identifies the volume of potential sales, which is extremely useful for manufacturing planning (See Exhibit 9–13).

The Product Inquiry Report. This report maintains a running record of inquiries by product line. Quite often, there is a correlation between product inquiries and product sales volume. The report can also highlight

EXHIBIT 9-13

The Purchase Potential Report

National Potential for Lead Closing

Date: June
Page: 1

Name	Company	City	State	POT	PROD	TER	REG
R P Sloane	Honeywell	Phoenix	AZ	1	E2	RK	DW
A P Masino	Hansens Lab Inc.	Rochester	NY	1	V0	CD	PC
D Halpern	Easton Corp	Murray Hill	NH	1	U1	JX	PC
C A Chang	Wyeth Labs	Toledo	OH	1	I3	LL	HD
G Larson	A W Lyons	Raritan	NJ	1	L0	LC	PC
C K Kim	Ortho Pharm Corp	Spring House	PA	1	I9	JC	TM
J R Breco	Sherwin Williams	Philadelphia	PA	2	N8	CJ	TM
C T Kitchen	Kitchen Microtech	Morgantown	WV	2	L9	GC	HD
F Randa	Parker Corp	Des Plaines	IL	2	G1	GD	HD
S G Weber	Pennwalt Corp	Aurora	IL	2	V0	DC	TM
D Jung	General Grain	Cranbury	NJ	2	V0	JK	PC
R La Corte	Smith Kline & French	Pittsburgh	PA	2	V0	DC	TM
B Peppe	Univ Pittsburgh	Pittsburgh	PA	2	V0	DC	TM
E N Plosed	S C Johnson Co	Racine	WI	2	I3	GO	HD

those areas where more advertising is needed to increase the number of inquiries (See Exhibit 9–14).

The Regional Inquiry Report. This report compares the effectiveness of one region with another in scoring inquiry potentials. A similar report can compare sales representatives' effectiveness within a region against their record (See Exhibit 9–15).

Sample Reports for Advertising Managers

The Daily Flash Report. This report identifies the daily status of each promotion. A bar chart records total inquiries for each day of the campaign. As time progresses, the bar chart forms a bell-shaped curve that can be used to identify the life of the promotion (See Exhibit 9–16).

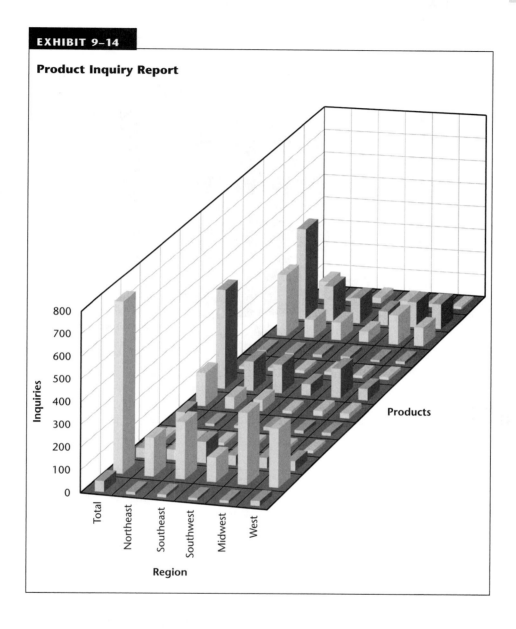

Product Inquiry Report

The Media Effectiveness Report. This report lists the various media employed and identifies the total expenditure of the promotion. This report should also include measures of the percentage of qualified inquiries, the cost per qualified inquiry, and the projected revenue to expense ratio.

EXHIBIT 9-15

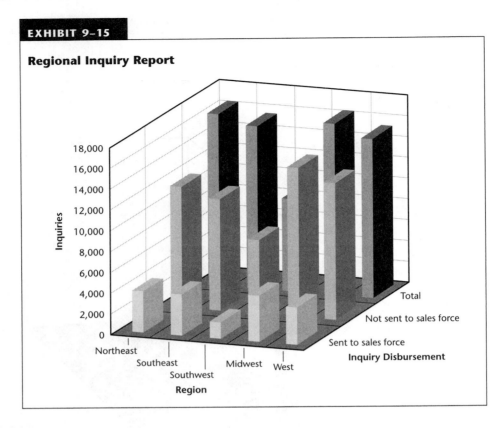

Regional Inquiry Report

EXHIBIT 9-16

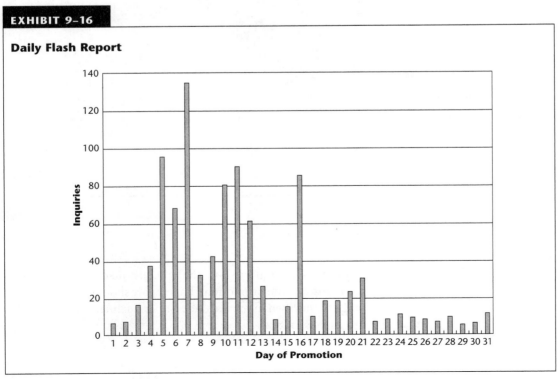

Daily Flash Report

CASE STUDY: Federal Reserve FedACH Information Services

Written by Jacobs & Clevenger with approval of its client, the Federal Reserve.

BACKGROUND

The Federal Reserve is the central bank of the United States. It was founded by Congress in 1913 to provide the nation with a safer, more flexible, and more stable monetary and financial system.

The Federal Reserve's Financial Services Policy Committee (FSPC) is responsible for overall leadership of the 12 Federal Reserve Banks' financial services activities and related support functions.

Making the Transition to Web Access Solutions

In recent years, the Federal Reserve Bank (FRB) announced its strategy to provide access to all Federal Reserve financial services using Web technology. To make this ambitious goal a reality, the FRB developed access solutions that created the "highway" that financial customers used to access Fed products.

One of the primary access solutions is FedLine Web, which was launched to many customers in 2001. Today, the FRB continues to enhance the functionality that FedLine Web provides.

The FRB is also in the process of rolling out other Web-based access solutions, including FedLine Advantage, which has been defined as "the next generation access solution to Federal Reserve Financial Services."

To fully understand the complexities of the transition process, it is important to note that most financial institutions already had FedLine Web while others were being converted to FedLine Advantage. However, most of these institutions were not leveraging the new technologies to their full potential. To remedy this situation, the Federal Reserve was committed to ensuring that customers realized the full benefits that these enhanced services provided.

Keeping Vital Financial Information Flowing

FedACH Information Services is one of the services that can be accessed through FedLine Web and FedLine Advantage. FedACH provides a paperless exchange of debit and credit transactions among business and consumer accounts at financial institutions, establishing an economical and efficient way to process payments.

These information services allow for tracking and research, as well as the enhanced file processing capabilities through FedLine Advantage. As a result, financial institutions can access key information with greatly increased speed, navigate complex data in a single click, and produce reports in less time. The result is greatly increased flexibility and convenience that helps every user in the institution reach new levels of productivity.

Spreading the Word to a Diverse Audience

Financial institutions are remarkably diverse in their size, transaction types, and information requirements. They also differ greatly in the access solutions and current product subscriptions they maintain with the Federal Reserve.

With this vast differentiation in mind, any communications with these institutions must incorporate highly tailored messaging to be both salient and effective to various groups and key stakeholders within the institutions.

CHALLENGES

The primary challenges with these communications were:

- To increase customer awareness and promote the benefits of using FedLine Web or FedLine Advantage to access FedACH Information Services among various targets.
- To create a cost-efficient yet highly customized program.
- To generate leads and acquire new subscriptions for FedACH Information Services.

SOLUTION

Jacobs & Clevenger teamed up with the FRB to develop a multichannel, segment-driven campaign which chaperoned customers through a multistepped

CASE STUDY: Federal Reserve FedACH Information Services *(continued)*

decision-making process. Customers were divided into three distinct groups:

AUDIENCE	GOAL
1. Either cost or technology resistant	• Introduce service benefits • Generate interest • Overcome barriers to conversion
2. Adapted to new technology access solution but not information services	• Promote service benefits • Generate leads and sign-ups • Build on current perspectives
3. Have some information services subscription	• Cross-sell FedACH Information Services • Generate leads and sign-ups • Encourage target to cascade information throughout organization

One of the overriding benefits that stands out with these services is the ability to access critical business shaping information by multiple people within the organization simultaneously. To crystallize this point, the communications focused on promoting the services available via the access technology, not the access technology itself.

The table shown above sharply defined the communications framework. Now the challenge was to develop an overarching creative concept that would clearly illustrate how Federal Reserve services empower each key segment through enhanced information.

Creating Financial Superheroes

The idea that proved to resonate the strongest positioned the target groups in a dramatic, memorable, and highly applicable role. This campaign was titled "Financial Superheroes," because it demonstrated that the target already had impressive financial powers at their fingertips.

Visually, the campaign brought dramatic superhero metaphors into the financial realm. We see fingers wearing a superhero cape. In essence, these are not just fingers anymore. They are hands-on access to remarkable powers, an unmistakable way to connect with a world of impressive services.

The tone of the copy reinforced this vibrant theme throughout the communications. Now these financial superheroes could move mountains (of paperwork), see thousands of miles (and know when a transaction has cleared across the country), and even stop problems before they started (with e-mail notification of errors).

Above all, their super powers were grounded in reality, because they reflected the day-to-day needs of financial institutions (See Exhibit 9–18).

Three Distinct Phases Direct the Decision

The campaign was divided into three distinct phases to address the fact that a deliberate decision-making process would be required for most customers:

- Phase I   Awareness
- Phase II   Drive leads and interest
- Phase III   Close the sales

A three-stepped direct mail program drove customers to an online seminar to learn more. Leads were filtered through to a sales team that was armed with sell sheets to help close the sale. Exhibit 9–17 provides a description of the lead flow.

RESULTS

The multichannel campaign and highly tailored approach proved to be extremely successful at increasing penetration of FedACH Information Services.

Penetration was tripled amongst Target Audience 2. This target had accepted the technology but had not experienced the benefits of an information service from the Federal Reserve Banks.

Target Audience 3 also saw dramatic increases in penetration, with a doubling of penetration. This target included those customers that had another FRB information service.

Additionally, the online seminar was a successful tool at moving customers through the lead funnel, and was viewed by approximately 5 percent of the institutions.

CASE STUDY: **Federal Reserve FedACH Information Services** *(continued)*

EXHIBIT 9–17

Lead Flow Diagram

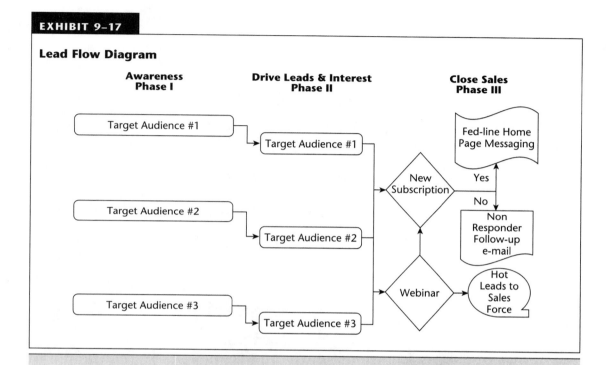

CASE STUDY: **STUDY: Federal Reserve FedACH Information Services** *(continued)*

EXHIBIT 9-18

Federal Reserve FedACH's Direct Mail Kit

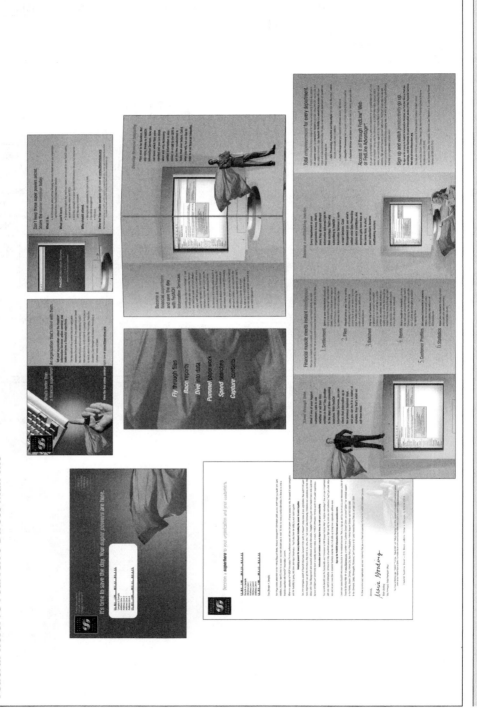

PILOT PROJECT   Selling complex products requires careful planning and a program that not only identifies and reaches prospects, but does so through multiple channels. Once a prospect is identified or identifies themselves by speaking with an inside salesperson, or attending a webinar, it may require additional efforts to nurture that lead over time.

Assume that you have generated a lead for FRB services. Develop a multi-effort program to follow-up those leads. Using material from this chapter, describe:

A. How many efforts you would use.

B. What channels you would use.

C. What frequency of effort you would use.

D. What you would do once a prospect became qualified. What about prospects that indicated they had no further interest?

E. Explain your rationale for answers A–D.

Key Points

▶ The efficient handling and managing of leads is a major problem for many companies. A well-run lead-management system can be a solution and also become a valuable corporate asset.

▶ A single sales call can cost from hundreds to thousands of dollars, and complex sales may require six to eight sales calls.

▶ A well-run lead-management system integrates marketing and selling functions into a unified sales coverage model.

▶ The system can increase sales productivity by the elimination of unproductive follow-up calls; it is an aid in finding prospects ready to buy.

▶ The application of an inquiry system to the advertising and marketing functions can become a valuable management tool, one that is useful in assessing progress toward objectives.

▶ In summary, an inquiry management system works because it measures results—the ingredient most wanted in marketing activity today.

MEDIA OF DIRECT MARKETING

MAGAZINES

The traditional mission of "advertising" is to build awareness and create an image of brands. Direct response ads, on the other hand, had a different mission: to generate a response and often to sell goods and services direct. That purity is beginning to end. More and more, marketers expect that their budgets will do more. Brands need to create customer engagement and build long-term customer relationships. This convergence can be seen on the pages of any magazine, as advertisers adapt to the world of multichannel, brand response communications.

Direct marketers are changing as well. Many are beginning to realize that the days of hard sell are ending. They too need to create customer engagement and build long-term relationships. Brand response means that direct marketers can create awareness of a brand and sell too. Here are two magazine ads, both of which were finalists in the prestigious Magazine Publishers of America Kelly Awards.

Exhibit 10–1 is an ad for Nike, one of the most recognized brand names in the world. The "Go" campaign, created by Wieden + Kennedy, did not just seek to build awareness of the Nike brand, but to grow sales revenue and collect a database of registrants for future direct marketing efforts by driving targeted traffic to the Nike Web site. Each "Go" ad depicted an offbeat outdoor scenario and asked readers to create an ending to the scenario at the Web site. Viewers then read the stories online and voted for their favorites. Over the four-month print media plan, it built traffic of 478,000 visitors to the Nike Web site, accounting for more than 2.7 million page-views.

Wooden boatmaker Mahogany Bay sought to lure high-end prospects to its Web site and increase sales (see Exhibit 10–2). The target audience for this campaign was high-income, over-50 men who understand and appreciate the craftsmanship of wooden boats. The glossy ads, which depict the romance and power of the boats, worked: visits to Mahoganybay.net increased more than 30 percent and phone calls jumped, which led to hundreds of thousands of dollars in incremental sales.

These ads are a far cry from the famous copy-jammed ad: "They Laughed When I Sat Down At the Piano But When I Started to Play!" written by John Caples in the 1920s (see Exhibit 10–3). That ad was legendary for its time. Brand response ads that are created and placed from a marketer's advertising budget, but measured on results, are equally breakthrough today.

EXHIBIT 10–1

Nike "Go" Ad

You are completely naked.
Immobile because you're covered
from head to toe in sap.
A pack of hungry wild dogs approaches.
The river is 4.2 miles away.
You're wearing only a pair of the Air Hydrous by Nike ACG.
You also have a box of baking soda,
a tank of propane,
and a pack of Looby's Sweet-N-Tasty Jerky Bites.

GO.

Tell us how at www.nikeacg.com/go

It wouldn't be fair if we didn't tell you about the Air Hydrous from Nike ACG. It really wouldn't, so we'll tell you. It's going to help you get to the river. How is it going to help you get to the river? Well, pretty much everything about the shoe is designed to get you to the river. The Air Hydrous has built-in shock absorption with a Phylon midsole and a heel Air-Sole unit. And the aggressive lug pattern on the heel of the shoe helps you maneuver through and over steep, slippery sections that you will come across on your way to the river. Oh yeah, the dogs—well, the Air Hydrous is lined with mesh for your comfort when hiking through difficult terrain. So with that, let us know how you handle the situation at nikeacg.com/go. And it will be even more interesting to see what happens with those dogs and all when you get to the water, if you haven't outsmarted them before then.

EXHIBIT 10–2

Mahogany Bay Ad

Handcrafted In 1931 From One Damn Fortunate Mahogany Tree.

There was an era when boats were built with materials and workmanship that will never be surpassed. Those vintage watercraft live on in the hands of our award-winning restorers. Visit mahoganybay.net or call 952-495-3007. We buy, sell and restore the finest vintage watercraft in the world.

MAHOGANY BAY

Magazines are a unique medium. They have many of the targeting benefits of direct mail, as readers often have narrow affinities. How magazines are tested and used depends upon the objectives and success in matching reader profiles with customer profiles.

Consumer publications tend toward larger circulation; business-to-business publications tend toward smaller circulation. Mail-order ads are more likely to appear in consumer publications; lead-generation ads are more likely to appear in business-to-business publications.

The Internet has had a large effect upon editorial content of magazines in that it is commonplace for magazines to have one or more Web sites through which they offer more information about given articles, additional news and features, and

EXHIBIT 10-3

Classic Direct Response Ad

"Can he really play?" a girl whispered.
"Heavens no!" Arthur exclaimed. "He
never played a note in his life."

They Laughed When I Sat Down
At the Piano
But When I Started to Play!—

ARTHUR had just played "The Rosary." The room rang with applause. I decided that this would be a dramatic moment for me to make my debut. To the amazement of all my friends, I strode confidently over to the piano and sat down.

"Jack is up to his old tricks," somebody chuckled. The crowd laughed. They were all certain that I couldn't play a single note.

"Can he really play?" I heard a girl whisper to Arthur.

"Heavens, no!" Arthur exclaimed. "He never played a note in all his life. . . But just you watch him. This is going to be good."

I decided to make the most of the situation. With mock dignity I drew out a silk handkerchief and lightly dusted off the piano keys. Then I rose and gave the revolving piano stool a quarter of a turn, just as I had seen an imitator of Paderewski do in a vaudeville sketch.

"What do you think of his execution?" called a voice from the rear.

"We're in favor of it!" came back the answer, and the crowd rocked with laughter.

Then I Started to Play

Instantly a tense silence fell on the guests. The laughter died on their lips as if by magic. I played through the first few bars of Beethoven's immortal Moonlight Sonata. I heard gasps of amazement. My friends sat breathless—spellbound!

I played on and as I played I forgot the people around me. I forgot the hour, the place, the breathless listeners. The little world I lived in seemed to fade—seemed to grow dim—unreal. Only the music was real. Only the music and visions it brought me. Visions as beautiful and as changing as the wind blows clouds that drifting moonlight that long ago inspired the master composer. It seemed as if the master

musician himself were speaking to me—speaking through the medium of music—not in words but in chords. Not in sentences but in exquisite melodies!

A Complete Triumph!

As the last notes of the Moonlight Sonata died away, the room resounded with a sudden roar of applause. I found myself surrounded by excited faces. How my friends carried on! Men shook my hand—wildly congratulated me—pounded me on the back in their enthusiasm! Everybody was exclaiming with delight—plying me with rapid questions. . . . "Jack! Why didn't you tell us you could play like that?". . . "Where did you learn?"—"How long have you studied?"—"Who was your teacher?"

"I have never even seen my teacher," I replied. "And just a short while ago I couldn't play a note."

"Quit your kidding," laughed Arthur, himself an accomplished pianist. "You've been studying for years. I can tell."

"I have been studying only a short while," I insisted. "I decided to keep it a secret so that I could surprise all you folks."

Then I told them the whole story.

"Have you ever heard of the U. S. School of Music?" I asked.

A few of my friends nodded. "That's a correspondence school, isn't it?" they exclaimed.

"Exactly," I replied. "They have a new simplified method that can teach you to play any instrument by mail in just a few months."

How I Learned to Play Without a Teacher

And then I explained how for years I had longed to play the piano.

"A few months ago," I continued, "I saw an interesting ad for the U. S. School of Music—a new method of learning to play which only cost a few cents a day! The ad told how a woman had mastered the piano in her spare time at home—and without a teacher! Best of all, the wonderful new method she used, required no laborious scales—no heartless exercises—no tiresome practicing. It sounded so convincing that I filled out the coupon requesting the Free Demonstration Lesson.

"The free book arrived promptly and I started in that very night to study the Demonstration Lesson. I was amazed to see how easy it was to play this new way. Then I sent for the course.

"When the course arrived I found it was just as the ad said —as easy as A.B.C.! And, as

the lessons continued they got easier and easier. Before I knew it I was playing all the pieces I liked best. Nothing stopped me. I could play ballads or classical numbers or jazz, all with equal ease! And I never did have any special talent for music!

Play Any Instrument

You too, can now teach yourself to be an accomplished musician—right at home—in half the usual time. You can't go wrong with this simple new method which has already shown 350,000 people how to play their favorite instruments. Forget that old-fashioned idea that you need special "talent." Just read the list of instruments in the panel, decide which one you want to play and the U. S. School will do the rest. And bear in mind no matter which instrument you choose, the cost in each case will be the same—just a few cents a day. No matter whether you are a mere beginner or already a good performer, you will be interested in learning about this new and wonderful method.

Send for Our Free Booklet and Demonstration Lesson

Thousands of successful students never dreamed they possessed musical ability until it was revealed to them by a remarkable "Musical Ability Test" which we send entirely without cost with our interesting free booklet.

If you are in earnest about wanting to play your favorite instrument—if you really want to gain happiness and increase your popularity—send at once for the free booklet and Demonstration Lesson. No cost—no obligation. Right now we are making a Special offer for a limited number of new students. Sign and send the convenient coupon now—before it's too late to gain the benefits of this offer. Instruments supplied when needed, cash or credit. U. S. School of Music, 1031 Brunswick Bldg., New York City.

Pick Your Instrument

Piano	'Cello
Organ	Harmony and
Violin	Composition
Drums and	Sight Singing
Traps	Ukulele
Banjo	Guitar
Tenor	Hawaiian
Banjo	Steel Guitar
Mandolin	Harp
Clarinet	Cornet
Flute	Piccolo
Saxophone	Trombone
Voice and Speech Culture	
Automatic Finger Control	
Piano Accordion	

U. S. School of Music,
1031 Brunswick Bldg., New York City.

Please send me your free book, "Music Lessons in Your Own Home," with introduction by Dr. Frank Crane, Demonstration Lesson and particulars of your Special Offer. I am interested in the following course:

....

Have you above instrument? ....

Name ....
            (Please write plainly)

Address ....

City.......................... State..........

links to past articles on a subject. Many of these sites generate additional income through advertising, which is often offered in combination with print advertising.

Testing Regional Editions

For the buyer of space in magazines today, most publications with circulations of more than 1.5 million offer the opportunity to buy a regional portion of the national circulation.

Regional editions offer important opportunities to the mail-order advertiser. Here are a few of the advantages of regional buys:

1. It is not necessary to invest in the full national cost of a publication to get some indication of its effectiveness for your proposition. In magazines such as *Time* or *TV Guide*, running in a single edition allows determination of relative response with an investment at least 20 percent less than what it costs to make a national buy.

2. Some regions traditionally pull better than others for the mail-order advertiser. For many mail-order products or services, nothing does better than the West Coast or worse than the New England region. Select the best response area for a particular proposition.

    Most publications charge a premium for the privilege of buying partial circulation. When testing a publication, put the advertising message in the better-pulling region to offset much of this premium charge.

3. Availability of regional editions makes possible multiple copy testing in a single issue of a publication.

4. Don't make the mistake of testing too small a circulation quantity. It is essential to test a large enough circulation segment to provide readable results that can be projected accurately for still larger circulations.

Warning: Buying regional space is becoming more difficult. There are fewer options and marketers pay for the privilege in a number of ways. As mentioned, regional space costs more.

Another factor to keep in mind is the relatively poor position regional ads receive. The regional sections usually appear far back in the magazine or in a "well" or signature of several consecutive pages of advertising with no editorial matter to catch the reader. Poor location can depress results as much as 50 percent below what the same advertisement would pull if it were in the first few pages of the same publication. When using regional space for testing, be certain to factor this into the evaluation.

Exhibits 10–4A and 10–4B are sample regional media kits from *Redbook Magazine* and *TV Guide*.

EXHIBIT 10–4A

Redbook Magazine Regional Rate Media Kit

direct response rates

EFFECTIVE WITH THE JANUARY 2006 ISSUE

Redbook is published by

Hearst Magazines
(a unit of The Hearst Corporation)
224 West 57th Street
5th Floor
New York, NY 10019
Phone: 212.649.3334
Fax: 212.307.7715

Rate Base

2,350,000 net paid ABC yearly average circulation. A member of Audit Bureau of Circulations. Subscriptions and single copy prices subject to change at REDBOOK's discretion.

On-Sale & Closing Dates

2006 Issue	On-Sale	Closing
January	12.13.05	10.14.05
February	01.17.06	11.15.05
March	02.21.06	12.16.05
April	03.21.06	01.16.06
May	04.18.06	02.16.06
June	05.16.06	03.16.06
July	06.20.06	04.17.06
August	07.18.06	05.16.06
September	08.22.06	06.16.06
October	09.19.06	07.17.06
November	10.17.06	08.16.06
December	11.21.06	09.15.06

N.B.: Closing dates hold for both space and materials. Closing dates for Regional, Test Market, Split Run and Cover advertisers are 10 days prior to the regular closing date for that issue.

Black & White

1 page	$68,300
2/3 page	$49,500
1/2 page	$40,900
1/3 page	$25,400

4-Color

1 page	$90,200
2/3 page	$70,500
1/2 page	$54,200
1/3 page	$45,100

N.B.: There is no additional charge for bleed ads.

Volume Discounts

Advertisers earn discounts based on the use of space within a twelve-month contract year. Regional insertions contribute to volume based on national page equivalency but do not earn national volume discounts. Direct Response discounts are not additive to National Display discounts.

3 national equivalent pages	12%
6 national equivalent pages	14%
12 national equivalent pages	16%
18 national equivalent pages	18%
24 national equivalent pages	20%
30 national equivalent pages	22%
36 national equivalent pages	24%

N.B.: A variety of special inserts are available. For rates, information and and specifications, please contact your REDBOOK Direct Response Account Manager at 212.649.2924.

Split Runs

Geographic, Perfect A/B and random copy splits are available for full-run advertising. Please call your REDBOOK Account Manager for more information, pricing and specifications.

REDBOOK

10.05

EXHIBIT 10–4B

TV Guide Regional Rates

REGIONAL **RATES**

	NEWSSTAND INSERTS	SUBSCRIPTION INSERTS	NEWSSTAND + SUBS ROB	INSERTS
TOP 10 MARKETS	$38,613	$125,733	$75,541	$128,419
CIRCULATION	110,000	970,000	1,080,000	

New York, Los Angeles, Chicago, Philadelphia, Boston, San Francisco, Dallas-Fort Worth, Washington DC, Atlanta, Houston

TOP 20 MARKETS	$57,925	$154,773	$102,580	$174,385
CIRCULATION	165,000	1,301,000	1,466,00	

Detroit, Tampa-St. Pete, Seattle-Tacoma, Phoenix, Minneapolis-St. Paul, Cleveland-Akron, Miami-Ft. Lauderdale, Denver, Sacramento-Stkton-Modesto, Orlando-Daytona Bch-Melbrn

TOP 25 MARKETS	$64,955	$175,947	$104,269	$177,257
CIRCULATION	185,000	1,479,000	1,664,000	

St. Louis, Pittsburgh, Portland, Baltimore, Indianapolis

HALF NATIONAL	$67,599	$167,397	$100,236	$170,402
CIRCULATION	192,000	1,408,000	1,600,000	

Effective Date: 3/6/06

Regional circulation available for full page units or multiples thereof and may require additional lead time. No discount for 2C or B/W creative. 15% charge for bleed ROB creative.

Insert pricing assumes full-size single sheet insert.

Inserts are to be supplied to *TV Guide* in excess of specified circulation. Please contact your local TV Guide Media Sales Representative for details. If *TV Guide* prints the inserts, additional costs apply.

Half National buy incurs an incremental bindery and production fee equivalent to 10% of the gross open space cost.

Competitive separation does not apply to regional units purchased in *TV Guide*. Circulation for regional buys may vary up to 15%.

3/06

Pilot Publications

When planning your direct marketing media schedule, think about the media universe the way you think about the view of the sky in the evening. If you have no familiarity with the stars, the sky appears to be a jumble of blinking lights with no apparent relationship. But as you begin to study the heavens, you are soon able to pick out clusters of stars that have a relationship to one another in constellations.

The magazine universe is no different. There are over 400 consumer magazines with a circulation of 100,000 or more. The first step in approaching this vast list is to sort out the universe of magazines into categories. Although this process is somewhat arbitrary, it is useful to have a mental map of major magazine groupings.

Once you begin to think of magazines as forming logical groupings, you can begin to determine which of the groupings offer the best marketplace for your product or proposition. Exhibit 10–5 is a basic magazine category chart and lists of some of the publications currently available for the direct response advertiser.

Within each category there are usually one or more publications that perform particularly well for the direct response advertiser at a lower cost than other publications in the group. We call those magazines the *pilot publications* for the group. If you use the pilot publications and they produce an acceptable cost per response, you can then proceed to explore the possibility of adding other magazines in the category to the media schedule.

In selecting the pilot publications in a category, keep in mind that you are not dealing with a static situation. A publication's mail-order advertising viability changes from year to year and what is a bellwether publication this season may not be the one to use next year. What is important is that you check your own experience and the experience of others in determining the best places to advertise first in each category, and the next best, and the next best, and so on.

Think of the media-buying program as an ever-widening circle, as illustrated in Exhibit 10–6. At the center is a nucleus of pilot publications. Each successively larger ring includes reruns in all profitable pilot publications plus new test books. In the same way, you can expand from campaign to campaign to cover wider levels of the various media categories until you have reached the widest possible universe.

Bind-In Insert Cards

The reason for the success of the insert card is self-evident. Pick up a magazine, thumb through its pages, and see for yourself how effectively the bound-in cards flag down the reader. Each time someone picks up the publication, there is the insert card pointing to your message. Another reason is the ease with which the reader can respond. The business reply card eliminates the trouble of addressing an envelope, providing a stamp, and so on.

EXHIBIT 10–5

Basic Consumer Magazine Categories

Demographic	Category	Sample Publications
Dual audience	General editorial/ entertainment	Grit, National Enquirer, National Geographic, New York Times Magazine, Parade, People, Reader's Digest, TV Guide
	News	Time, Newsweek, Sports Illustrated, U.S. News & World Report
	Special interest	Architectural Digest, Business Week, Elks, Foreign Affairs, High Fidelity, Modern Photography, Natural History, Ski, Travel & Leisure, Wall Street Journal, Yankee
Women	General/service/ shelter (home service)	Better Homes & Gardens, Cosmopolitan, Ebony, Family Circle, Good Housekeeping, House Beautiful, House & Garden, Ladies' Home Journal, McCall's, Redbook, Sunset, Woman's Day
	Fashion	Glamour, Harper's Bazaar, Mademoiselle, Vogue
	Special interest	Brides, MacFadden Woman's Group, McCalls Needlework & Crafts, Parents, Working Woman
Men	General/entertainment/ fashion	Esquire, Gentlemen's Quarterly, Penthouse, Playboy
	Special interest	Field & Stream, Home Mechanics, Outdoor Life, Popular Mechanics, Popular Science, Road & Track, Sports Afield
Youth	Male	Boy's Life
	Female	Teen, YM
	Dual audience	Scholastic Magazines

EXHIBIT 10–6

Circle Approach to Media Selection

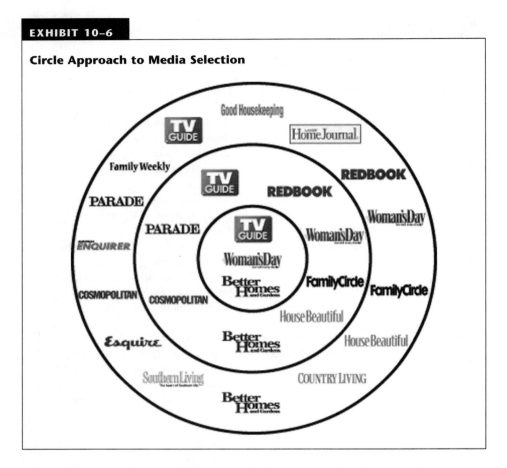

Before the advent of the insert card, the third and fourth covers of a magazine were the prime mail-order positions and were sold at a premium. The bind-in insert card has created a world in which three, four, five, or more direct response advertisers can all have the position impact once reserved for the cover advertisers alone.

When you go to purchase space for a page and an accompanying insert card, you must face the fact that the best things in life are not free. Insert card advertising costs more. You must pay a space charge for the page and the card and sometimes a separate binding charge, and you must then add in the cost of printing the cards. How much you pay, of course, depends on the individual publication, the size of the card, and a number of other factors. There is no rule of thumb to follow in estimating the additional cost for an insert card. Space charges alone for a standard business reply card can be as much as 40 percent of the black-and-white page plus additional binding charges.

When the cost of the insert unit adds up to as much as four times the cost of a black-and-white page, you will have to receive four times the response to justify the added expense.

For most direct response advertisers, the response is likely to be six to eight times as great when pulling for an order and as much as six to eight times as great in pulling for inquiries. As a result, you can expect to cut your cost per response by 50 percent or more with an insert card as opposed to an ordinary on-page coupon ad.

Reader Service Cards

Insert cards have a dramatic effect on response, and so do reader service cards. Often referred to as *bingo cards*, reader service cards were developed by magazine publishers to make it easy for the reader to request more information about products advertised in a magazine. *Bingo card* is really a generic term for any form of reply card, or printed form on a magazine page, on which the publisher prints designated numbers for specified advertisers' literature. The reader simply circles the number designated for the literature desired.

Typically, an advertiser placing a specified unit of space in a magazine is entitled to a bingo card in the back of the publication. Ads reference these bingo cards with statements such as, "For further information, circle Item No. 146." The cards are sent directly to the publisher, which sends compiled lists of inquiries to participating advertisers. The respective advertisers then send fulfillment literature to all who requested it.

Magazine Advertising Response Pattern

There is a remarkable similarity from one insertion to another in the rate of response over time for most magazines. Monthly publications generally have a similar pattern for the rate of response from week to week. However, the pattern of response for publications in different categories can vary. For example, a mass circulation weekly magazine (such as *TV Guide* or *Parade*) will pull a higher percentage of the total response in the first few weeks than a shelter book (such as *House & Garden* or *Better Homes & Gardens*). A shelter book has a slower response curve but keeps pulling for a long time because it is kept much longer than a mass circulation magazine.

Also, subscription circulation will pull faster than newsstand circulation. All subscribers usually receive their copies within a few days, whereas newsstand sales are spread out over an entire month. Consequently, the response pattern is spread out as well.

For an ad calling for direct response from a monthly magazine, here is a general guide to the likely response flow:

After the first week	3 to 7%
After the second week	20 to 25%

After the third week	40 to 45%
After 1 month	50 to 55%
After 2 months	75 to 85%
After 3 months	85 to 92%
After 4 months	92 to 95%

From a weekly publication such as *Time* or *TV Guide*, the curve is entirely different; 50 percent of the response usually comes in the first two weeks.

These expectations, of course, represent the average of many hundreds of response curves for different propositions. You will see variations up or down from the classic curve for any single insertion.

As a general rule for monthlies, you can expect to project the final results within 10 percent accuracy after the third week of counting responses. If you are new to the business, give yourself the experience of entering daily result counts by hand for dozens of ads. Before long you will develop an instinct for projecting how an ad for your particular proposition is doing within the first ten days of measured response.

Timing and Frequency

Once you determine where you want the ad to run, timing and frequency are the two crucial factors in putting together an effective print schedule. Some propositions will do best at one specific time of the year. For example, novelty items are likely to be purchased in October and November, or even as early as late September, for Christmas gifts. But for nonseasonal items there are two major print advertising seasons for direct response.

The first and by far the most productive time for most propositions is the winter season, which begins with the January issue and runs through the February and March issues. The second season begins with the August issue and runs through the November issue. The best winter months for most people are January and February. The best fall months are October and November. For schools and book continuity propositions, September frequently does as well or better.

If you have a nonseasonal item and you want to do your initial test at the best possible time, use a February issue with a January sale date or a January issue with a late December or early January sale date of whatever publication makes the most sense for your proposition.

How much of a factor is the particular month in which an ad appears? It could make a difference of 40 percent or even more. Exhibit 10–7 shows what the direct response advertiser can expect to experience during the year based on the costs per response (CPR).

These hypothetical relative costs are based on the assumption that the insertion is run one time in any one of the 12 issues of a monthly publication.

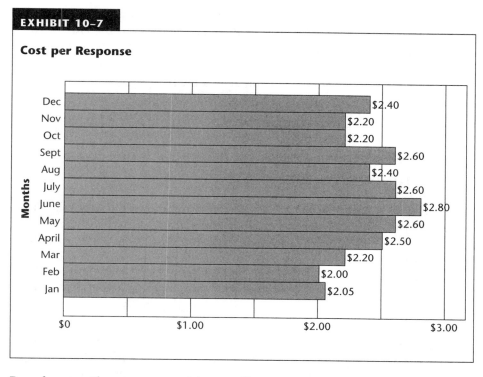

EXHIBIT 10–7

Cost per Response

Month	Cost
Dec	$2.40
Nov	$2.20
Oct	$2.20
Sept	$2.60
Aug	$2.40
July	$2.60
June	$2.80
May	$2.60
April	$2.50
Mar	$2.20
Feb	$2.00
Jan	$2.05

(Horizontal bar chart with x-axis: $0, $1.00, $2.00, $3.00; y-axis labeled Months)

But of course, if you are successful, you will want to run your copy more than once. So now you are faced with the other crucial question: What will various rates of frequency do to your response? Should you run once a year? Twice? Three times? Or every other month?

The frequency factor is more difficult to formulate than the timing factor. Optimum frequency cannot be generalized for print media advertising. Some propositions can be run month after month in a publication and show very little difference in cost per response. At one time, Doubleday & Company had worked out optimum frequency curves for some of its book club ads that required a 24-month hiatus between insertions.

How, then, do you go about determining ideal frequency of insertions? Try this procedure: the first time your copy appears in a publication, run it at the most favorable time of the year for your special appeal. If you have a nonseasonal proposition, use January or February issues.

If the cost per response is in an acceptable range, or up to 20 percent better than expected, wait six months and follow with a second insertion. If that insertion produces results within an acceptable range, you probably are a twice-a-year advertiser. If the first insertion pulls well over 20 percent better than the planned order margin, turn around and repeat within a three- or four-month period. If the response to the test insertion in January or February was marginal, it usually makes sense to wait a full year before returning for another try in that publication.

The best gauge of how quickly you can run the next insertion aimed at the same magazine audience is the strength of the response from the last insertion. What you are reading in the results is a measurement of the saturation factor as it relates to that portion of the circulation that is interested in your selling message.

Of course, like all the other factors that affect response, frequency does not operate in a vacuum. The offer of a particularly advantageous position in a particular month, or a breakthrough to better results with improved copy, can lead you to set aside whatever carefully worked-out frequency you had adopted earlier.

Determining Proper Ad Size

A crucial factor in obtaining an acceptable cost per response is the size of the advertising unit you select. Ordinarily, the bigger the ad, the better job the creative people can do in presenting the selling message. But there is one catch: advertising space costs money. And the more you spend, the greater the response you need to get your money back.

What you want to find is the most efficient size for your particular proposition and for the copy approach you have chosen. Just as with frequency, there is no simple rule of thumb here.

Generally speaking, advertising for leads, or prospects, or to gain inquiries requires less advertising space than copy that is pulling for orders. Many companies seeking inquiries or running a lead item to get names for catalog follow-up will make use of advertising units of less than one column. Only a handful of companies looking for prospects can make effective use of full-page space. Going one step further and using a page and insert card to pull for leads runs the risk of being too effective. This unit can bring in inquiries at very low cost at the possible expense of good quality. Find out at your peril.

For example, if you use a black-and-white page with a tear-off coupon that generates leads at $5 each and that converts at a 10 percent rate, then your advertising cost per sale is $50. Take the same insertion and place it as a page and insert card, and the cost per response could be as low as $3. If the conversion rate held up at 10 percent, the advertising cost per sale would be only $30. But it is more likely that the advertiser would experience a sharp conversion rate drop, to perhaps 5 percent, with a resultant $60 cost per sale plus the cost of processing the additional leads.

When a direct sale or a future commitment to buy is sought, the dynamics usually are different from those when inquiries are sought. As a general rule, the higher the unit of sale or dollar volume commitment, the larger the unit of space that can be afforded, right up to the double-page spread with insert card. However, there are a number of additional factors to be considered:

1. The nature of the product presentation might require a particular space unit. For example, in movie and book club advertising, experience has shown that a maximum number of books and DVDs should be displayed for

best results. As a consequence, many of these clubs run a two-page spread as their standard advertising unit. And in a small-size publication, they might take six or even eight pages to display the proper number of books and tapes.

2. Some propositions, such as Time-Life Books in the continuity bookselling field, require four-color advertising in order to present the beautiful color illustrations that are an important feature of the product being sold.

3. Usually, full-page ads appear at the front of a publication and small-space ads at the back. So going to a full-page unit is often related to the benefits you can expect from a premium, front-of-publication position.

4. If you are successful with a single-page ad with coupon, test using an insert card before you try to add a second page. If the page and insert card work for you, give the spread and card a try.

5. Most mail-order advertising falls into one of three size categories: (a) the spectacular unit—anything from the page and standard card insert to the four-page preprinted insert, (b) the single full-page unit, or (c) the small-space unit, less than one column in size.

The awkward sizes in pulling for an order appear to be the one-column and two-column units. These inserts seldom work better than their big-brother pages or little-sister 56-line, 42-line, and 21-line units, although a "square third" (2 columns by 70 lines) can be a very efficient space unit.

Always remember that space costs money. The objective is to take the minimum amount of space needed to express the proposition effectively and to return a profit. Start by having the creative director at your advertising agency express the proposition in the amount of space needed to convey a powerful selling message. Once you have established the cost per response for this basic unit, you can experiment with other size units.

If you have two publications on your schedule that perform about equally well for the basic unit, try testing the same ad approach expressed in a smaller or larger space size in one of those two publications. At the same time, run the basic control unit in the same month in the other publication.

Four-Color, Two-Color, Black-and-White

All magazines charge extra for adding color to your advertising. And there will be additional production expense if you go this route. Usually the cost of adding a second color to a black-and-white page does not return the added costs charged by the publication for the space and the expense of producing the ad. If the copy is right, the words will do their job without getting an appreciable lift from having headlines set in red or blue or green. An exception might be the use of a second-color tint as background to provide special impact to the page.

It is with the use of four-color advertising that the direct response advertiser has an opportunity to profit on an investment in color. A number of publications (*Woman's Day, Ladies' Home Journal*) allow you to run a split of four-color versus black-and-white, in an alternating copy A/B perfect split-run. Test results indicate an increase of anywhere from 30 percent to almost 60 percent where there is appropriate and dramatic utilization of the four-color process.

Given a striking piece of artwork related to the proposition or an inherently colorful product feature to present, you can expect an increase in response when you use four-color advertising. You will need more than a 20 percent increase in most publications to make the use of color profitable, so it is wise to pretest the value of this factor before scheduling it across the board. Some products, such as insurance, simply do not benefit from color.

The Position Factor

Position in life might not be everything, but in direct response it often means the difference between paying out or sudden death. By *position*, we mean where an advertisement appears in the publication. There are two rules governing position.

First, the closer to the front of the publication an ad is placed, the better the response will be. Second, the more visible the position, the better the response will be.

The first rule defies rational analysis. Yet, it is as certain as the sun rising in the morning. Many magazine publishers have offered elaborate research studies demonstrating to the general advertiser that an ad in the editorial matter far back in a publication gets better readership than an ad placed within the first few pages of the publication. This could well be true for the general or institutional advertiser, but it is not true for the direct response advertiser.

Whatever the explanation is, the fact remains that decades of measured direct response advertising tell the same story over and over again. A position in the first seven pages of the magazine produces a dramatically better response (all other factors being the same) than if the same insert appears farther back in the same issue.

How much better? There are as many answers to this question as there are old pros in the business. However, here is about what you might experience the relative response to be from various page positions as measured against the first right-hand page arbitrarily rated at a pull of 100:

First right-hand page	100
Second right-hand page	95
Third right-hand page	90
Fourth right-hand page	85
Back of front of the publication (preceding editorial matter)	70

Back of the publication	50
(following main body of editorial matter)	
Back cover	100
Inside third cover	90
Page facing third cover	85

The second rule is more easily explained. An ad must be seen before it can be read or acted on. Right-hand pages pull better than left-hand pages, frequently by as much as 15 percent. Insert cards open the magazine to the advertiser's message and thereby create their own "cover" position. Of course, the insert card introduces the additional factor of providing a postage-free response vehicle as well. But the response from insert cards is also subject to the influence of how far back in the magazine the insert appears. Here is what you can expect in most publications (assigning a 100 rating to the first card):

First insert card position	100
Second insert card position	95
Third insert card position	85
Fourth insert card position	75[*]
Fifth insert card position	70[*]

[*]If position follows main editorial matter.

How to Buy Direct Response Space

Because mail-order advertising is always subject to bottom-line analysis, the price you pay for space can mean the difference between profit and loss. Before you place space, ask the publisher or the publisher's agency these basic questions:

1. Is there a special mail-order rate? Mail-order rates are usually 10–30 percent lower than general rates.

2. Is there a special mail-order section, a shopping section where special mail-order ads are grouped? (This section is usually found in the back of the magazine)

3. Does the magazine have remnant space available at substantial discounts? Many publishers offer discounts of up to 50 percent off the regular rate.

4. Is there an insertion frequency discount or a dollar volume discount? Is frequency construed as the number of insertions in a time period or consecutive issues? Many publishers credit more than one insertion in an issue toward frequency.

5. Do corporate discounts apply to mail order? Sometimes the corporate discount is better than the mail-order discount.

6. Are there seasonal discounts? Some publishers have low-volume advertising months during which they offer substantial discounts.

7. Are there spread discounts when running two pages or more in one issue? The discount can run up to 60 percent on the second page.

8. Is there a publisher's rate? Is this in addition to, or in lieu of, the mail-order rate? It can be additive.

9. Are per-inquiry (PI) deals accepted? In PI deals, the advertiser pays the publisher an amount for each inquiry or order, or a minimum flat amount for the space, plus so much per inquiry or order.

10. Are "umbrella contracts" accepted? Some media-buying services and agencies own banks or reserves of space with given publications and can offer discounts even for one-time ads.

11. Is bartering for space allowed? Barter usually involves a combination of cash and merchandise.

CASE STUDY: American Express AeroplanPlus Platinum Card Drive

Adapted from the Direct Marketing Association International Echo Awards 2005.

BACKGROUND

The American Express AeroplanPlus Platinum Card is the ultimate card in the suite of American Express AeroplanPlus Cards. At an annual fee of $399, the Platinum Card not only earns mileage points at a rate of up to 1.6 miles per dollar spent, it also gives card members access to the Air Canada Lounges.

TARGET AUDIENCE

Current Diners Card holders are predominantly male, high-value frequent business travelers who are willing to pay nearly $400 for a financial card. They live full, busy lives and time is often their most valuable currency, as it is what allows them to devote themselves to all their interests and the people that matter to them. They expect access to the lounge and are not worried about paying a fee to receive this perk.

CHALLENGE

The contract between Diners Club and Aeroplan ended on December 31, 2004. This means that Diners Club card members no longer had access to the Air Canada Maple Leaf Lounge, a core benefit of the product offering. American Express sought to capitalize on this news to gain share of these high-value, high-spending consumers from Diners, encouraging current Diners Club card holders to convert to American Express AeroplanPlus Platinum and retain their year-round access to the lounge.

CIBC, a competitor, had also begun to capitalize on this opportunity with further print advertising and activity centered on its Aerogold Visa card's optional Club Privileges Travel program, the only other program that offers access to the lounges.

MARKETING STRATEGY

Diners Club card holders are frequent business travelers who spend a lot of time in the airport—specifically, in the lounge. Therefore, the goal was to promote the card at every touchpoint in their travel journey—booking the flight, walking through the airport, in the lounge, and even in the flight itself.

Business Objective

Acquire new high-value American Express AeroplanPlus Platinum Card members by surrounding the target with a consistent lounge-access message for the two months before and two months after the contract ends.

MARKETING TACTICS

Complemented by overarching ATL media, a strategic mix of advertising and acquisition channels was used for surround messaging along the travelers' route:

- Booking flight: online presence in monthly Air Canada e-newsletter
- Airport: Air Canada boarding pass with Platinum Card image
- Lounge: update Platinum take-ones to highlight lounge access, replace existing Lounge take-ones
- Take-ones: tipped onto complimentary newspapers and placed on tables. Because the lounge was viewed as the most competitive channel, we incorporated an incremental Aeroplan Miles bonus (10,000-mile Welcome Bonus, as opposed to the usual 5,000) to sweeten the deal and solidify AeroplanPlus Platinum as the card of choice.
- In flight: free-standing insert with lounge emphasis in *enRoute* magazine (Air Canada's in-flight publication)
- Take-one tipped onto in-flight newspapers
- Napkins printed with lounge access reinforcement message

Platinum creative was used in channels targeted to Diners Club card holders. In addition, to ensure prospects who would not be interested in the Platinum Card were not missed, existing creative that offered a choice of all three cards was maintained in the broader channels. Offering a choice of products through these channels had historically proven up to 100 percent more efficient than offering one card only, due to a higher response rate (by attracting a range of prospects to all three cards) and generating higher fees (due to Platinum Card acquisitions).

CREATIVE STRATEGY

The creative challenge was to communicate that the AeroplanPlus Platinum Card gives year-round access to the Air Canada Maple Leaf Lounge, while ensuring the overall creative positioning of the product. A significant investment up until this point had been made in this campaign (TV, magazine, newspaper, airport billboards) that focused on the faster earning positioning for all three AeroplanPlus products—"When you earn miles faster, everything gets closer" (See Exhibit 10–8).

A single creative approach was used for-take ones, tip-ons, and ads.

Using the line "The same Card that gets you closer, is the Card that gets you in," we were able to tie the closer message to the specific lounge benefit. This is paid off by the subhead "Unlimited access to all Air Canada Maple Leaf Lounges."

"Getting in" positions lounge access as taking the high ground, and implies that the AeroplanPlus Platinum is the only way to get in.

RESULTS

The surround strategy was successful: Platinum Cards acquired was 347 percent above forecast. Specific response rates by channel were much higher in the four-month period versus previous months:

- Lounge newspaper tip-on response rate was 311 percent higher
- Lounge take-one response rate was 385 percent higher
- In-flight newspaper tip-on response rate was 220 percent higher
- *enRoute* (Air Canada's in-flight magazine) insert response rate was 75 percent higher

CASE STUDY: American Express AeroplanPlus Platinum Card Drive *(continued)*

EXHIBIT 10–8

American Express AeroplanPlus Platinum Magazine Print Piece

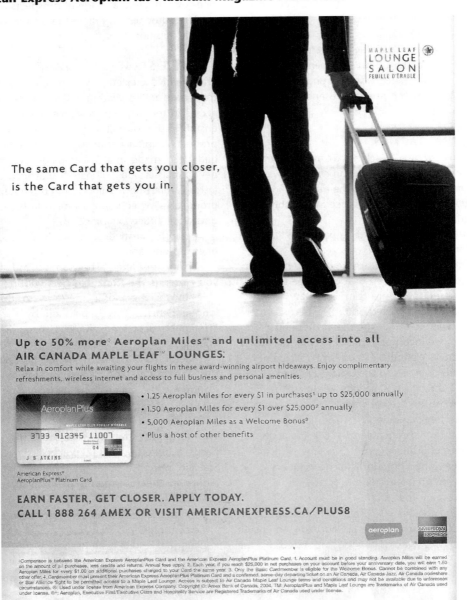

CASE STUDY: **American Express AeroplanPlus Platinum Card Drive** *(continued)*

Over the four-month period the campaign ran, AeroplanPlus Platinum Cards accounted for 39 percent of all AeroplanPlus new cards. This is significant, considering the Platinum Card annual fee is over three times the amount of the AeroplanPlus Gold Card and over six times the amount of the standard AeroplanPlus Card. Also significant: the average AeroplanPlus Platinum Card member's annual income is 126 percent higher than the AeroplanPlus Gold Card member, and 207 percent higher than the AeroplanPlus Card member.

From November 2004 to February 2005 (four months), more Platinum Cards were acquired than in the ten months from launch of the cards (January 2004) to October 2004, during which time TV and print ads had their highest investment. This is clear evidence that the targeted airport surround approach successfully reached the targeted audience (See Exhibit 10–9).

EXHIBIT 10–9

American Express AeroplanPlus Platinum Print Components

PILOT PROJECT

In the next phase of the launch for Delta Airlines AeroplanPlus Gold and Platinum, American Express wants to target prospects that fit the customer profile of male, high-value frequent business travelers who have already shown they are willing to pay nearly $400 for a financial card.

Amex has asked you to develop a print media plan that would use magazines to reach prospects in Delta Airlines' top ten hubs and focus markets: Atlanta, GA; Boston, MA; Chicago, IL; Cincinnati, OH; Fort Lauderdale and Tampa, FL; New York, NY; Los Angeles, CA; Salt Lake City, UT; and Washington, DC.

Using SRDS or other available media planning tools:

A. Identify at least one regional consumer or business publication in each market to reach your target group.

B. Identify at least one national business publication with regional editions available for each market. Note: You may have to run ads in regional editions of more than one publication to cover all ten markets.

C. Determine what size ad (e.g., full page, half page, etc.) you will need to use to meet the requirements for regional publications.

D. Assuming a frequency of four ads over a year, what would the cost of an ad in each publication be?

Key Points

▶ Test the "pilot publications" in magazine categories—publications that perform particularly well for the direct response advertiser at a lower cost than others in the group. If they produce an acceptable cost per response, consider adding other magazines in the category to the media schedule.

▶ Insert cards can increase response six to eight times and cut cost per response by 50 percent as opposed to an ordinary on-page coupon ad. Bingo or information cards can also greatly increase requests for information.

▶ For monthly magazines, 50 percent of the total response comes in the first month after publication; for weekly publications, 50 percent comes in the first two weeks. For monthlies, final results may be projected within 10 percent accuracy after the third week of counting responses.

▶ Advertising for leads, prospects, or inquiries requires less space than advertising for orders. The higher the unit of sale or dollar volume commitment, the larger the unit of space that can be afforded. Take the minimum amount of space needed to express the proposition effectively and to return a profit.

▶ A four-color ad can increase response but requires more than a 20 percent increase in most publications to make color profitable.

▶ The closer to the front of the publication an ad is placed, or the more visible its position, the better the response will be. Right-hand pages pull better than left-hand pages, frequently by as much as 15 percent. Insert cards also pull better because they open the magazine to the advertiser's message, thereby creating their own "cover" position.

▶ When purchasing space, inquire about special mail-order rates and insertion frequency discount or a dollar volume discount. Corporate and seasonal discounts, publisher's rate, per-inquiry deals, and barter are also worth investigating.

NEWSPAPERS

Despite lagging circulation and declining ad revenues, the local newspaper is still an integral part of everyday life. The 1,500-plus daily newspapers in the United States reach an audience of 50 million readers. For a marketer, that's a lot of prospects!

Yet, it's hard to ignore the trend. For many consumers, the Internet has become the main source of news. Its appeal is convenience, diversity of news offerings, and user control.

In June 2006, research from comScore Media Metrix reported that 54 percent of all U.S. Internet users visited sites in the General News category. Yahoo! News topped the list, with 31.2 million visitors, followed by MSNBC with 23.4 million, and AOL News at 20.4 million visitors.

Not surprising, a few newspaper Web sites, such as the *New York Times*, Tribune newspapers, and Knight Ridder digital, were among the top ten sites on the list. Newspapers are still a trusted source of news. For marketers, that means they are a source that can be relied upon where the message delivery goal requires daily frequency and broad local reach to consumers with income for discretionary spending. Newspaper sections allow marketers to place ads within context where readers self-select for interest (e.g., Women's, Sports, Food Day, Automobiles, etc.). And, newspapers can be an important part of any multichannel campaign, especially where the goal is to keep the message localized.

To stem the loss of ad dollars, newspapers are reinventing themselves in ways that benefit the direct response marketer. Most of the large media companies now offer advertisers direct marketing services. This takes advantage of the newspaper's subscriber base, logistics (i.e., daily delivery), and market knowledge. For example, the Tribune company formed Tribune Direct, a national marketing company that offers a full array of targeted marketing services. The Plain Dealer.com, an offshoot of the *Cleveland Plain Dealer* newspaper, offers direct marketing services with consumer geographic, demographic, and lifestyle segmentations.

The pressing question for any newspaper is: how is it differentiating itself among other news outlets? A 2005 study by the National Newspaper Association answered that question this way:

The core advertising advantage of newspapers is in the word engagement. . . . Unlike almost all electronic media, when a person is reading a newspaper that is all they are doing . . . they aren't surfing and the ads don't beep, flash, pop up or interrupt. Newspaper ads don't interrupt the experience, they are part of it.

Reading a newspaper is a highly focused activity. People usually pick up a section of the paper for a specific reason: to peruse the ads, get the sports scores, read a local columnist. Because newspapers are the dominant source for local information, they have access to an already segmented audience. In addition, most papers produce niche publications and special sections geared toward an even more specific readership.

Large national dailies such as the *Wall Street Journal*, *New York Times*, and *USA Today* have the reach, segmentation, frequency, and distribution systems that make them a natural medium for brand response marketing.

According to the 2006 Newspaper Audience Database compiled by the Newspaper Association of America, consumers seek out the newspaper to make product-buying decisions. Consider these findings from a recent shopping study by MORI Research:

- 52 percent of consumers say newspapers are where they go to check out advertisements—5 percent more than any other medium.

- 52 percent see newspaper ads as "valuable" in planning shopping; the Internet and direct mail are second at 13 percent each.

- Advertisers recognize that simple ad impressions are no longer enough to ensure ROI. They want consumers who are engaged and involved with the advertising message.

ROP (run of paper) ads are usually restricted to ads that can be effective without a need for quality four-color printing (See Exhibits 11–1 and 11–2).

Direct marketers have several options when considering newspapers. Newspapers can be thought of as a separate advertising medium, running ads within given sections such as Women's Section, or Business, or Sports, etc. Or newspapers can be thought of as distribution channels carrying their preprints, or ads in syndicated newspaper supplements, or Sunday comics sections, or local TV books, or local magazines.

Online newspaper editions offer breaking news stories and special content on restaurants and entertainment that is highly targeted to local readers. Newspapers generally offer classified ads, their number one revenue and profit center, online as well as offline as they try to stave off competition from job sites, real estate sites,

EXHIBIT 11–1

Direct Response Ad from *Chicago Sun Times*

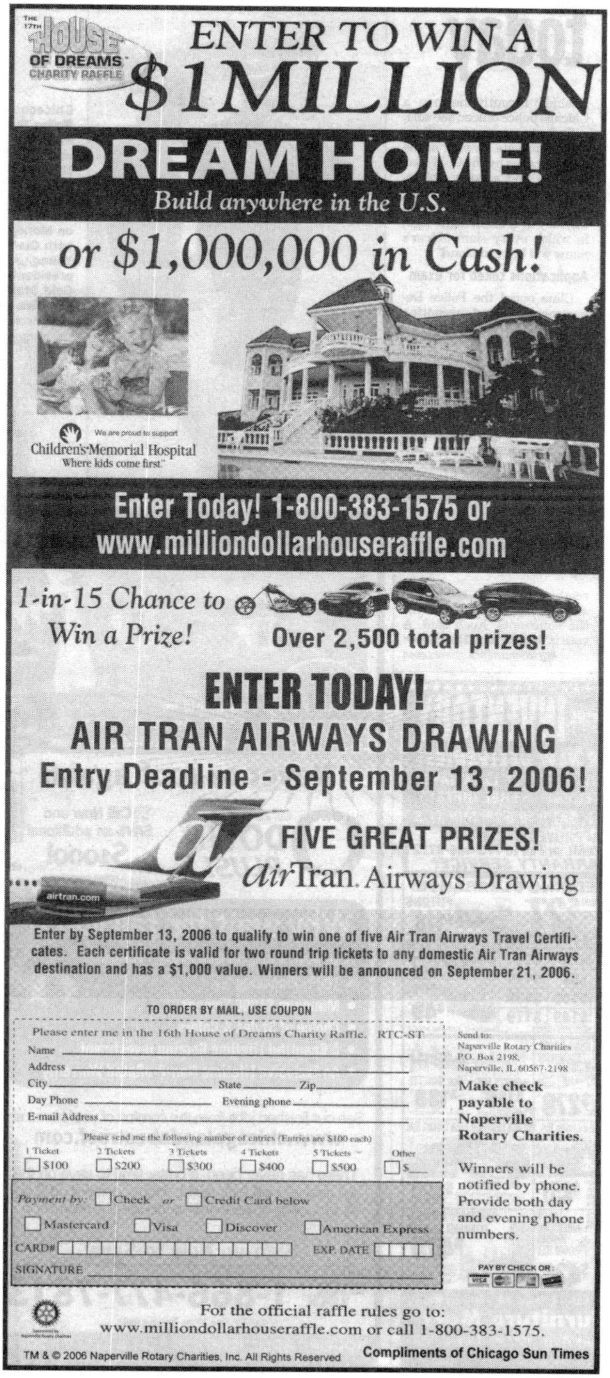

EXHIBIT 11–2

Direct Response Ad from *Chicago Tribune*

auto sites, and auction sites. Some newspapers are even helping loyal advertisers—especially small retailers—develop their own Web sites by providing Web design templates, computer space, and a URL.

Free-Standing Inserts

Free-standing inserts (FSIs), also known as preprints, may be the best-kept secret in direct response media. Often thought of as a sales promotion tool to deliver coupons, FSIs are a proven tool for direct response and mail order as well. Marketers can pick and choose which newspapers to run an FSI in, or find a national network. Companies such as AMG Global have access to a network of over 2,500 newspapers that accept preprinted inserts from clients. Not to be confused with Sunday supplements such as Vallasis, FSIs offer direct marketers an uncluttered environment for offers ranging from collectibles to merchandise, to insurance and financial services—at a fraction of the cost of solo direct mail.

Insert sizes are usually very flexible, from a single sheet to an entire catalog. National newspaper networks can target the single-family homes that you want to reach across a wide range of segmented ZIP codes and demographics that include metro dailies; suburban, community, and Catholic newspapers; specific ethnic groups such as Hispanics, Asian, and African-American populations; or military, teens, and collegiate newspapers.

There are few format restrictions and several advantages to FSIs.

1. Quality of paper and printing is controlled by the marketer.

2. While the "life" of a newspaper is rarely more than a day, FSIs take on a lifetime of their own, depending upon the interest of the reader.

3. Involvement devices, which have proved so successful in direct-mail packages, can be used effectively with FSIs as well.

4. Testing of FSIs is within the control of the marketer since splits can be prearranged at the printing plant.

The cost of printing FSIs is borne by the marketer: the newspaper charges for circulation of the preprint based upon the size and number of pages. The preprint can be as simple as one sheet of board stock or a multi-page brochure (See Exhibits 11–3, 11–4, and 11–5).

Syndicated Newspaper Supplements

Imagine, if you will, placing two space-insertion orders and buying newspaper circulation of 55 million plus! It is possible by buying space in *Parade* and *USA Weekend*. Both publications enjoy a good track record for direct response advertisers. To compare the two publications, here are some figures assuming a four-color, full-page ad has been placed.

Parade is generally distributed among the top 100 metro areas. *USA Weekend* is generally carried by newspapers with smaller locations, basically "C" and "D" counties. The majority of newspapers distributing *USA Weekend* are outside the top 150 metro areas. However, in two newspaper markets, one newspaper will carry *Parade* and the other *USA Weekend*. Both syndicated supplements provide an excellent direct response atmosphere.

EXHIBIT 11–3

Four-Color FSZ Targeted to the Hispanic Segment

EXHIBIT 11–4

Four-Color Sears Insert

EXHIBIT 11–5

Direct Response Mail Order Ad

TABLE 11–1

Comparison of Circulation and Rates for Full-Page Four-Color Ads

		FOUR COLOR	
PUBLICATION	CIRCULATION	FULL PAGE	CPM
Parade	32,700,000	$818,200	$25.02
USA Weekend	22,700,000	$605,800	$26.00

Source: www.Parade.com and www.usaweekend.com, July 2006

While Table 11–1 shows the cost of a four-color page ad going to total circulation of both publications, there is no way this would take place in the real world unless prior testing of the ad and the publications warranted the full runs.

Assuming that both the ad and the publications are unproved, here are some first steps the marketer might take:

1. Negotiate a "direct response rate," usually less costly than general advertising rates.

2. Run the ad as a test in three regions: West, Central, Eastern.

3. Limit the three-region test to either *Parade* or *USA Weekend*, depending upon small market/large market experience.

4. Bargain for remnant space (Remnant space is usually created when package goods advertisers, who do not have total national distribution for a given brand, eliminate certain cities or regions from the schedule. Thus the publishers sell the remnants at bargain rates).

Local Newspaper Magazines

Several steps closer to local markets are newspaper-inserted magazines published by leading newspapers in major markets (see Exhibit 11–6). A case can be made for readership of magazines that cater to local markets from an editorial standpoint.

"Cousins" to local newspaper magazines are the weekly TV books produced by local newspapers containing the local TV and radio schedules. While most of the advertising in these books promotes local TV and radio programming, back cover space for direct response ads is usually available.

Comics as a Direct Marketing Medium

Perhaps the biggest sleeper as a medium for direct marketers is the comic section of weekend newspapers. Comics are not glamorous, nor are they prestigious.

EXHIBIT 11–6

Direct Response Mail from Chicago Tribune Magazine

But their total circulation, readership, and demographics constitute an exciting universe for the direct response advertiser.

The Metro-Puck Comics Network, being the largest, distributes through more than 175 Sunday newspapers. One of the Misconceptions about "the funny pages" readership is that the higher one's education, the less likely one is to read the comic pages. Comic reader research from *The Virginian-Pilot* newspaper advertising department (Table 11–2) shows the opposite. Another interesting finding is that the median age of the adult comics reader is 40 years old. Finally, there is the misconception that the higher one's income, the less likely one is to read comics. Again, the figures from this research refute this.

TABLE 11–2

Demographic Profile of a Comics Reader

	METRO ADULTS	COMICS READERS
Age of Respondents		
18–24	16%	13%
25–34	20%	16%
35–44	22%	22%
45–54	18%	19%
55–64	11%	12%
65+	13%	17%
Median	40.5 yrs	43.5 yrs
Gender		
Male	49%	50%
Female	51%	50%
Annual Household Income		
Under $20,000	10%	10%
$20,000–24,999	6%	5%
$25,000–34,999	13%	11%
$35,000–49,999	20%	22%
$50,000–74,999	18%	20%
$75,000+	21%	20%
Median	$46,320	$47,191
Home Ownership		
Own	65%	70%
Rent	33%	28%

Source: 2003 HROS.

Developing a Newspaper Test Program

When direct response advertisers first consider testing newspapers as a medium, they have a myriad of decisions to make. Should they go ROP, the newspaper preprint route, local Sunday supplements, syndicated supplements, TV program supplements, comics? What papers should they test? Putting ad size and position aside for the moment, there are two initial considerations: the importance of advertising in a mail-order climate, and the demographics of markets selected as they relate to the product or service being offered.

Simple items, which are suited to small-space advertising in mail order or classified sections, greatly simplify the testing procedure. But more often than not, multi-city testing in larger space is required. Prime direct response test markets in the United States include Atlanta, Buffalo, Cleveland, Dallas–Fort Worth, Denver, Des Moines, Indianapolis, Omaha, and Peoria. In the selection of test markets, you should analyze the newspaper to make certain it has advertising reach and coverage and offers demographics that are suitable to your product. If there are two newspapers in a market, it is worthwhile to evaluate both of them. Let us say that because of budget limitations, advertising can be placed in only a limited number of markets. Such criteria as circulation, household penetration, male or female readers, and advertising lineage relating to the product to be advertised should be measured.

A number of sources will provide the data necessary for evaluation. You would begin with SRDS's *Newspaper Rates and Data* for general cost and circulation information. *SRDS Circulation Analysis* would provide information about metro household penetration. *Simmons Total Audience Study* could then be used to isolate male or female readers of a particular age group. Other criteria to be measured are retail lineage in various classifications, and spendable income by metro area.

Demographics are a major consideration whether you are using ROP, preprints, local supplements, syndicated supplements, or TV program supplements. Once an advertiser develops a test program that closely reflects the demographics for the product or service, expansion to like markets makes possible the rapid acceleration of a full-blown program. But selecting newspapers is tedious, because there are hundreds from which to choose as compared with a relative handful of magazines whose demographics can be more closely related to the proposition. As an example, a test newspaper schedule could be placed in the following markets: Atlanta, preprint; Cleveland, Metro comics; Dallas–Fort Worth, ROP; Denver, preprint; Des Moines, ROP; Indianapolis, preprint; Omaha, Metro comics; and Peoria, *Parade* remnant. If there is more than one newspaper in a test market, the paper with the most promising demographics should be selected.

A test schedule like this would be ambitious in terms of total dollars, but it would have the advantage of simultaneously testing markets and formats. Once a reading has been obtained from the markets and formats, the advertiser can rapidly expand to other markets, and will have the advantage of using the most productive formats.

Advertising Seasons

As in direct mail and magazine direct response advertising, there are two major newspaper direct response advertising seasons. The fall mail-order season begins roughly with August, and runs through November (A notable exception is a July insertion, which is often useful especially when using a pretested piece). The winter season begins with January, and runs through March.

Exceptions to the two major direct response seasons occur in the sale of seasonal merchandise. Christmas items are usually promoted from September through the first week of December. A nursery, on the other hand, will start promoting in late December and early January, then again in the early fall. Many nurseries follow the practice of promoting by geographic regions, starting earlier in the South and working up to later promotion in the North.

Timing of Newspaper Insertions

Besides the seasonal factor, timing is important as it relates to days of the week. According to the *E&P Yearbook, Bureau of Advertising Circulation Analysis*, the number of copies of a newspaper sold per day is remarkably constant month after month, despite such events as summer vacations and Christmas holidays. People buy the newspaper to read not only the editorial matter but also the ads. While magazines are often set aside for reading at a convenient time, newspapers are read the day they are delivered or purchased or are not read at all.

Monday through Thursday are favorite choices of many direct response advertisers for their ROP advertising. Many direct response advertisers judiciously avoid the weekday issue containing grocery advertising.

More and more newspapers are accepting preprints for weekday insertions. This can be a major advantage, considering the larger number of preprints appearing in most metro Sunday newspapers.

The Position Factor

Newspapers and magazines have many similarities in respect to the importance of position in direct response advertising. Research has demonstrated high readership of newspaper ads, whatever the position. However, direct response advertisers still prefer right-hand pages. Generally, such advertisers find that ads are more effective if they appear in the front of the newspaper rather than in the back. Placement of coupon ads in the gutter of any newspaper page is almost always avoided.

All newspapers are printed in sections. Special consideration should be given to the reading habits of men and women as they relate to specific sections of a newspaper. Readership habits of men and women are similar, with the exception of four sections: food and cooking, home furnishings, gardening, and sports.

Color versus Black-and-White

The possibilities of using color in newspaper advertising may be regarded as similar to those for magazine advertising, with one major exception. If you plan to use one or more colors other than black in an ROP ad, you simply can't get the quality that you can in a color magazine ad. This does not mean that ROP color shouldn't be tested. A majority of newspapers that offer color will allow A/B splits of color versus black and white.

Studies have used split runs and the recognition method to test the attention-getting power of both two-color and full-color ROP ads. These studies show increases of 58 percent for two-color ads and 78 percent for full-color ads above the level of results for black-and-white versions of the same ads. Comparable cost differences are 21 percent and 25 percent respectively.

EXHIBIT 11-7

"Hold the GERD" Newspaper Ad

ADD CREAM AND SUGAR.
HOLD THE GERD.

IF YOUR FAVORITE FOOD OR DRINK LEAVES YOU BURNING, THERE ARE OPTIONS.

Some people take pills every day to help relieve their GERD symptoms.

But there are *other* treatment options—outpatient procedures that may provide the relief you want.

Learn more about your treatment options

FOR MORE INFORMATION, CALL OR GO ONLINE:

1-866-GOT-GERD
(1-866-468-4373)

www.GotGERD.com

St. Luke Hospitals
Health Alliance

 St. Elizabeth
Medical Center

University Hospital
Health Alliance

"However, there are exceptions in the rules of color vs. black- and- white advertising. Exhibit 11–7, an award-winning black-and-white ad that was part of an integrated media campaign, employs the principles of direct marketing. The message was well-targeted to senior citizens, alternative healthcare seekers and healthcare professionals. It presented several ways to get more information and prompted a good response when it ran."

When Starch "noting score" norms are used to estimate the same attention-getting differential, a different conclusion is reached. The differences are about 10 percent and 30 percent respectively (when size and product category are held constant). Using norms means comparing a black-and-white ad for one product in another city at another time. These variables inevitably blur the significance of comparisons.

For the direct response advertiser, these studies are interesting. However, you should remember that genuine controlled testing is the only way to get true figures.

CASE STUDY: **Estadão Brazilian Newspaper**

Adapted from the Direct Marketing Association International Echo Awards 2005.

CHALLENGE

O Estado de São Paulo is one of Brazil's most established printed newspapers. Affectionately known as "Estadão," the daily faced a sluggish market and difficulty in drawing new subscriptions. To revive the lagging number of subscribers, it sought to attract younger readers, which it was losing to other news media.

SOLUTION

New features and sections were added to rejuvenate Estadão and increase the paper's attractiveness to new readers. A comprehensive communication campaign was launched, including a campaign for new subscriptions with an unconventional approach.

The primary goals were to drive interest in newspaper subscriptions by highlighting Estadão's new graphic project and innovative new sections. The goal was to increase new subscriptions by 50 percent and 20 percent on average in the inbound and outbound channels, respectively.

MARKETING TACTICS

The newspaper was redesigned and offered in an attractive, innovative new graphic project. The campaign story was a competition between telephone operators Paulo and Bia, who "took to the streets" to acquire new subscribers following the paper's new layout launch (See Exhibits 11–8, 11–9).

The media mix included television, radio, newspapers, magazines, hot site, and direct and e-mail marketing, all used in a release customized to different audience profiles. Each of the 60 customized pieces displayed Paulo and Bia's partial score, which was also available in real time on the Web site. Potential subscribers were invited to vote for their favorite operator.

RESULTS

Bia generated more subscriptions than Paulo. Sales grew by over 300 percent in comparison with Estadão's preceding campaign, reaching a 66 percent ROI with 155,000 leads generated and 15,000 new subscriptions in two months.

CASE STUDY: **Estadão Brazilian Newspaper**

EXHIBIT 11–8

O Estado de São Paulo Poster

EXHIBIT 11-9

Newspaper Ad

The challenge between the operators, Paulo and Bia, has come to the end, but you can still make a personalized subscription until April 10th. Go to **www.desafioestadao.com.br**, answer a few questions about yourself and find out more about it. Or call **0800 14 9000** and join the party.

PILOT PROJECT You are the advertising manager of a mail-order operation selling collectibles. You have been successful in magazines offering a series of historic plates. You have never used newspapers, but now you have a $75,000 budget to test the medium.

Outline a newspaper test plan (Note: If you use preprints, your total space budget should cover printing costs).

1. Select your test cities.

2. Will your test run in the Sunday edition or the weekday edition, or both?

3. What formats will you test: preprints, supplements, comics, local TV guides, ROP?

4. What size preprints or ads will you test?

5. At what time of the year will you run your tests?

Note: Remember that if you use preprints, your total space budget should cover printing costs.

Key Points

▸ Newspapers can be relied upon where the message delivery goal requires daily frequency and broad local reach to consumers with income for discretionary spending. Newspaper sections allow marketers to place ads within context where readers self-select for interest.

▸ Newspapers are reinventing themselves in ways that benefit the direct response marketer. Most of the large media companies now offer advertisers direct marketing services. This takes advantage of the newspaper's subscriber base, logistics (i.e., daily delivery), and market knowledge.

▸ To select test markets, analyze the newspaper to make certain it has advertising reach and coverage and offers demographics that are suitable to your product. Measure such criteria as circulation, household penetration, male or female readers, and advertising lineage relating to the product to be advertised.

▸ As in direct mail and magazine direct response advertising, there are two major newspaper direct response advertising seasons. The fall mail-order season begins roughly with August and runs through November (A notable exception is a July insertion, especially useful when using a pretested piece). The winter season begins with January, and runs through March.

▸ While color newspaper ads do draw more attention, it is difficult to get the same quality that you can in a color magazine ad. Two-color ads can cost 21 percent and four-color ads 26 percent more than black-and-white advertising.

TV/RADIO

Direct Response Television

Direct Response Television (DRTV) is the term used to describe goods and services sold directly through television, often avoiding the retail channel. DRTV includes three subgroups: short form (30, 60 or 120 second response TV commercials) long form (also know as infomercials, TV commercials that can last up to 30 minutes) and TV home shopping (live shopping on Home Shopping Network, for example). According to the Electronic Retailing Association, electronic retailing has experienced double-digit annual growth, with sales of over $300 billion in 2005.

Media spending for both short form and long form DRTV has grown significantly, while spending for traditional advertising on network and local spot television has decreased. According to data compiled by TNS Media Intelligence, in 2006 direct response advertisers spent $3.27 billion for short-form media. This represented an increase of 28 percent in just two years. Research compiled by *Response Magazine* found that media spending on long form TV in 2006 exceeded $1.27 billion, a 5.8 percent increase over spending in 2005.

Broadcast Applications

Local and cable television have long been major media for consumer direct response advertisers, producing inquiries, supporting other media, and selling goods and services.

The range of TV direct response offers has greatly expanded in recent years. Although magazines, tapes, CDs, and innovative products certainly continue to be sold direct, many different types of direct response offers have surfaced.

Lead-generation commercials for high-ticket products and services such as home mortgages, insurance, and exercise equipment are now common. In addition, many Fortune 500 companies have started incorporating TV direct response into the marketing mix.

Procter & Gamble began using direct response TV in 2002 for its Dryel brand. Based on that success, it began using DTV for other business units. In an interview with the *DRTV Quarterly* newsletter, Eric Seiberling, a P&G brand manager who pioneered the use of direct response TV at P&G, said that the medium helps find when and where consumers are receptive to the message.

"There is no 'mass' in mass media anymore and we need to work harder to find our consumers," Seiberling said. "Direct Response TV has allowed us to measure the response and move to our most receptive audiences in a way we had great difficulty doing with traditional TV."

A straight application of broadcast TV involves Charles Schwab. Hundreds of thousands of North American and international customers are being practically raised on what Charles Schwab does for its various financial services. Even though each year many of those prospects and current customers moved from one organization to another, Charles Schwab solved the availability problem by initiating a unique TV campaign with the theme, "Rob Wants to Check a Quote" (See Exhibit 12–1).

Outside of the Charles Schwab trading area, this commercial ended with this call to action: "Active Traders CALL NOW 1-800-841-2594. Talk to Chuck."

Cable TV looks like broadcast TV, but it is different in many ways. First, the cable TV audience is highly defined. Cable operators know who is tied into the system. They send them a bill every month. This demographic information and some psychographic information is available to the advertiser. With many more channels available, cable, not unlike the audience selectivity traits of radio and niche magazines, provides more special-interest programming. Thus, the direct response advertiser can tie offers to predefined audiences with a strong interest such as sports, news, history, food, travel, or entertainment.

Home shopping TV has had explosive growth. In some respects, it is the new mail-order catalog, taking advantage of the ability to offer value-oriented products, to demonstrate them, and to reach a broad national audience. The pioneer was HSN (Home Shopping Network). A later entrant, QVC Network, broadcasts its shopping channel live 24 hours a day, seven days a week. QVC built its huge volume by featuring prescheduled programs, offering products from specific product categories such as jewelry, electronics, and apparel.

Customers may order any item presented on QVC at their convenience, provided the item is still in stock. Throughout all TV broadcasts, the QVC toll-free number is flashed constantly. Phone response is almost instantaneous. To promote viewership, QVC mails extensively to cable subscribers, providing them with free membership in the QVC Shoppers Club and notifying them about free prizes awarded each day (See Exhibits 12–2 and 12–3).

Infomercials

The infomercial is no longer the "new kid on the block." The kid, so to speak, is now a grown-up with impressive credentials. There are infomercials running

EXHIBIT 12–1

Charles Schwab's "Rob wants to Check a Quote"

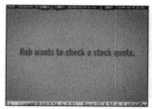

(Fade in)

(Music)

(Music)

VOICE OVER: Introducing StreetSmart.com

Text: for qualified active traders

Schwab's new web based trading with real time streaming data. so you never have to hit the refresh button again

Active traders call now. We're talknig level 2 quotes and streaming watch lists. Plus interactive charts...

that help you stay on top of the market wherever you are.

Conditional alerts that trigger automatically to help you cut losses and lock-in profits...

all in one customizable trading screen for as low as $9.95 a trade

Demo the power today. And if you switch to Schwab now...

Text: (legible)

you ger 50 commission-free traders. So call the number on your screen and get it all. Schwab.com. Online equity trades...

Text: (legible)

for $9.95 each, and 50 commission free trades. Take advantage of this limited time offer. Call 1-800-841-2594.

(Fade out)

EXHIBIT 12–2

Cover Panel of Folder Announcing Free Prizes to Cable Viewers

somewhere on broadcast television or on cable every hour of the day, 24 hours a day, seven days a week, nationally and internationally—between 250 and 300 actively on the air at any one time.

Many spots promise tighter abs, slim waists, enjoyable music, more (or less) hair, or an opportunity to become wealthy. More and more mainstream marketers are using infomercials to target their brand or direct marketing message to increasingly difficult-to-find consumers. Those using DRTV now include Clorox, ESPN, Ford Motor Company, Jenny Craig, Procter & Gamble and Pfizer.

But selling or traffic building with infomercials is no sure thing: a gambling spirit with fairly deep pockets to match is required. Infomercials can cost up to $600,000 to produce, and testing to determine performance will run from $200,000 to $750,000.

To test retail sales impact, an infomercial should run ten times per market per week for a minimum of four weeks so that the before and after impact can be measured. Depending on the size of the market, the media cost can range from $5,000 to $50,000 per market per week. A typical retail sales test runs in two to four markets.

EXHIBIT 12-3

**First Page of Two-Page Letter to Cable Subscribers with Free
Membership Card for QVC Shoppers Club**

MultiVision
QVC Network
Channel 23

1-800-345-1515   1-800-345-1515
QVC MEMBERSHIP NO.   QVC MEMBERSHIP NO.
1449-3828   1449-3828

1-800-345-1515   1-800-345-1515
QVC MEMBERSHIP NO.   QVC MEMBERSHIP NO.
1449-3828   1449-3828

QVC SHOPPERS CLUB

★ MEMBERSHIP CARD ★

MEMBERSHIP
NUMBER   1449-3828

Mr. Don Corley
P.O. Box 641
Cambria, IL 62915

QVC - Cable Channel 23

CAR-RT SORT   **B009   *Place these stickers on your phones so you'll
always have your membership number and
QVC phone number handy!*

Mr. Don Corley
P.O. Box 641
Cambria, IL 62915

Dear Cable Subscriber:

Because you're a MultiVision cable subscriber,
we're pleased to award you a FREE membership in
the QVC Shoppers Club!

Your exclusive membership number is valuable.
It's your key to winning great prizes on QVC. And
you'll have lots of opportunities to win, because
QVC GIVES AWAY HUNDREDS OF PRIZES EVERY DAY!

Hourly $25 prizes. Daily $1000 shopping sprees.
And weekly grand prizes such as new cars and dream
vacations -- all to help introduce cable viewers to
QVC, the new way of shopping, on Cable Channel 23.

QVC stands for Quality, Value and Convenience.
Tune in to channel 23 anytime, day or night,
for a wide variety of high-quality products to
help you look your best, beautify your home and
make your life easier. You can order any item
by phone, with a 30-day money-back guarantee.

However, you don't have to buy anything to win
prizes on QVC. Here's just one way you could win:

Tune in for QVC's hourly Lucky Number drawings.
Every time the number drawn matches either the
first 4 digits or the last 4 digits of your QVC
membership number, YOU'RE A WINNER! Just phone
QVC before the next Lucky Number is drawn and
you'll instantly win $25 credited to your QVC
account. Plus, you'll automatically be entered
in QVC's DAILY $1000 GRAND PRIZE DRAWING!

Your membership number is 1449-3828, which gives
you two opportunities to win during each drawing!
Every time 1449 or 3828 is drawn, YOU'RE A WINNER!

                    Over, please...

TV in the Current Future

In this new technology era, the choices of how to get connected with television and its programming are diverse. It is not necessary to tune into a broadcasting network or be a subscriber to a cable company to have access to it. Just by having a television set, and either a cable modem, router, DSL, or wireless G network, companies can deliver this service. According to companies such as Interactive Television Networks, Inc. (ITVN), they can "deliver the content you want to watch over your existing broadband connection to your TV without the need for a PC."

With programming delivered over television, computers, and cell phones, it seems only a matter of time before marketers test these new channels for advertising. It is unclear if consumers will act upon or even watch ads on their cell phones or computers. Yet, this content will have to be paid for. It is something to watch and test when available.

Other media such as the Internet and companies such as MSNBC, CNN, and all the main broadcast networks are taking individual partnership networks online. Users can click or video on demand (VOD) daily news, sports, weather, and entertainment information 24/7. According to a 2006 study from Nielsen Media Research, "Video on Demand Viewing Update," service was first pegged at 7.1 percent of all U.S. TV homes in September 2003. One year later, accessibility had doubled to 14 percent. The most recent estimate (December 2005) had VOD penetration at nearly 20 percent, or 21.5 million homes, or a 174 percent increase since September 2003 (See Exhibit 12–4).

EXHIBIT 12-4

Video on Demand Penetration

VOD Penetration (%)	2003–04	2004–05	2005–06
Sept.	7.1	14.1	19.4
Oct.	7.4	14.3	19.4
Nov.	7.7	14.3	19.3
Dec.	8.2	15.0	19.5
Jan.	8.5	15.5	
Feb.	10.0	16.5	
Mar.	10.9	17.2	
Apr.	11.4	17.7	
May	12.0	18.0	
June	12.4	18.7	
July	12.8	19.1	
Aug.	13.3	19.4	

Source: Nielsen Media Research, "Video on Demand Viewing Update" research paper, published in April 2006.

What effect this will have on advertisers is still uncertain. If consumers watch the ads, this will have a positive effect. If they skip the ads, this will not be good for advertisers. Consumers are already doing this to a degree with TiVo and other digital or personal video recorders (DVRs/PVRs), which are now in the homes of millions of consumers.

Interactive Television

Digital television is opening up a number of new frontiers for direct marketers. Turner Media, and their Super Station WTBS, have been pioneers in direct response television. Now, Turner has developed eight interactive TV channels. These channels are distributed by Dish Network and are on select regional cable TV systems.

Turner is testing an hour-long program sponsored by the Gander Mountain Company on the Men's Outdoor & Recreation (MOR) channel, one of their interactive channels. The program uses on-screen prompts that will appear across the Dish Network during Gander Mountain Lodge commercials to tune viewers on other channels into the show. Viewers of the program in iTV-enabled households will be able to purchase fishing rods, sleeping bags, archery equipment, and other outdoor products by simply clicking on their remotes. Viewers that don't have the technology can watch the program and then order by phone or through the program's Web site.

Notes Turner Media Group president Marc Krigsman, "This showcases how retailers and media can work together to facilitate a transaction and a sale. TV was created in the beginning to do one thing—market products."

Clearly, this is a test worth watching. Though untested, interactive television has much promise for the future. What will be learned from this test, if successful, will be quickly applied to others in the future.

Radio

Radio has two things going for it over broadcast TV: (1) program formats that are better targeted by advertisers and (2) lower costs for similar time periods.

Targeting the right program format is the key. For example, if an advertiser is soliciting phone-in orders for a rock album, there's no problem running a radio commercial on scores of stations that feature rock music; these listeners are the very audience the advertiser is seeking. Or, if a financial advertiser is soliciting inquiries from potential investors, there are program formats that help the advertiser reach a target audience: "Wall Street Report," for example, or FM stations with a high percentage of upper-income listeners.

This 60-second radio commercial by Merrill Lynch ran in conjunction with program formats with a high percentage of listeners who matched its customer profile:

(Music up and under)

(Music) From Merrill Lynch. A breed apart.
LOCAL ANNOUNCER: *For more complete information and a free prospectus, including sales charges and expenses, call 000–0000. Read it carefully before you invest or send money. That's 000–0000.*

ANNOUNCER: *A word on money management from Merrill Lynch. Today, many banks are trying to copy our revolutionary Cash Management Account financial service. Here's why they can't. Bank money market accounts are simply that: bank accounts. A Merrill Lynch CMA gives you access to the entire range of our investment opportunities. Instead of just an account, you get an Account Executive, backed by the top-ranked research team on Wall Street. Idle cash is automatically invested in your choice of three CMA money market funds. You enjoy check writing, a special Visa card, automatic variable-rate loans up to the full margin loan value of your securities—at rates banks aren't likely to match. So give your money sound management and more to grow on. The all-in-one CMA financial service.*

According to the FCC, the number of licensed broadcast radio stations has increased almost exponentially from the 1990s until today. See Exhibit 12–5 for a look at how this particular trend is moving through the future.

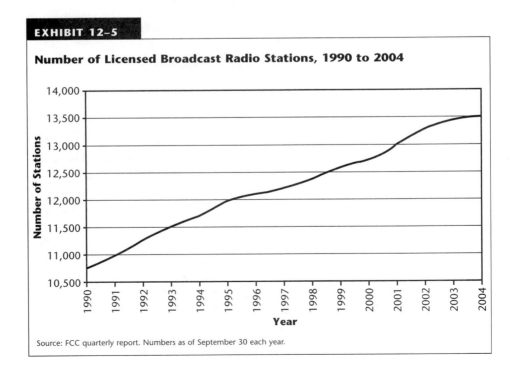

EXHIBIT 12–5

Number of Licensed Broadcast Radio Stations, 1990 to 2004

Source: FCC quarterly report. Numbers as of September 30 each year.

DVDs

The proliferation of DVDs may be bad news for movie theaters and television networks, but not for direct marketers. DVDs are an opportunity rather than a threat, because direct marketers have the opportunity to embed ads.

By incorporating commercial messages in the program, producers can defray the high cost of production. In addition, they might be able to open new distribution outlets. As an example, the hour-long "Mr. Boston Official Video Bartender's Guide," sponsored by Glenmore Distilleries, is available through liquor stores as well as the more usual outlets. Along with the DVD goes an eight-page catalog featuring each Glenmore product.

With such a catalog, or with specific sales and response information incorporated into a taped presentation, a sponsored DVD might prove so productive for an advertiser that it could afford to sell the DVD cheaply, use it as a self-liquidating premium, or distribute it to DVD rental outlets. DVD catalogs also show potential for high-ticket items that benefit from demonstration.

Basic Broadcast Concepts

Buying and scheduling TV and radio time is best left to the experts—direct marketing agencies and some select buying services. But for a direct marketer to recognize the opportunities and pitfalls of advertising in these media, it is imperative that the basics be understood. The following comments about buying and scheduling TV apply equally to radio.

Ratings

It is important to keep in mind that the cost of a commercial time period is based on its rating. This is a measure of its share of the total TV households viewing the show. The more highly rated the show, the higher the cost. One rating point equals 1 percent of the total households in the market. A show with a 20 rating is being watched by 20 percent of TV households.

When the total ratings of all the time periods in a schedule are combined, the result is called gross rating points (GRPs). Simply stated, if a television schedule has 100 GRPs per week, it is reaching the equivalent of 100 percent of TV households in the market in that week. Obviously, this is a statistical reach with varying degrees of duplication. It does not guarantee 100 percent of the individual homes will be reached.

Commercial Lengths

Although 30 seconds is the most common length for general or image advertising, direct marketers seldom find it adequate to tell their selling story in a persuasive way.

One-hundred-twenty-second spots are the standard for a direct sale commercial, although 60-second spots have become the norm. Sixty seconds is usually required for lead-generation commercials. On the other hand, support commercials with sufficient GRPs prove effective with a combination of 10-second and 30-second commercials. But key outlet marketing usually requires longer lengths.

Of course, with the popularity of 30-second announcements and the premium broadcasters can get for them, it is not always possible to clear longer-length commercials, particularly during periods of high demand.

Reach and Frequency

TV advertisers use two terms in measuring the effectiveness of television schedules.

- *Reach* refers to the number of different homes exposed to the message within a given time segment.

- *Frequency* is a measure of how many times the average viewer will see the message over a given number of weeks. Frequency also can be measured against viewer quintiles (e.g., heaviest viewers, lightest viewers).

The combination of reach and frequency will tell you what percentage of the audience you are reaching and how often on average they will see your message. Television schedules often are purchased against reach and frequency goals; actual performance is measured in post-analysis.

For most direct marketers, reach and frequency are not as important as actual response rates, which represent a true return on the media dollar. But knowledge of what reach and frequency are is critical when television is used in a supporting role.

Buying Time

Buying specific time periods is the most expensive way to purchase television time. You pay a higher price to guarantee your message will run at a precise time within a predetermined program environment.

Television time also can be bought less expensively. Stations will sell run-of-station (ROS) time—time available during periods the station has been unable to sell at regular rates. This is particularly true with independent (non-network) stations, which often have sizable inventories of unsold time. If the station, however, subsequently sells the time to a specific buyer, your commercial will be preempted.

Preemptible time can be an excellent buy for direct response advertisers because of the combination of lower cost and quite respectable response rates. When buying preemptible time, it also is possible to specify the dayparts (daytime, early fringe, late fringe, and so on) for slightly more than straight ROS rates. This can be important for direct marketers with a specific target audience for their product. Such spots still may be preempted at any time, however.

Television time also can be purchased on the basis of payment per inquiry (PI) and bonus-to-payout. PI allows the station to run as many commercials as it wishes, whenever it wishes. There is no charge for the time, but the station receives a predetermined sum for every inquiry or sale the advertisement generates for the advertiser. The advertiser is not committed to pay for a spot until it delivers an inquiry or sale, and then only in relation to responses.

But there are disadvantages. It is almost impossible to plan methodically for fulfillment. Such programs cannot be coordinated reliably with other efforts or promotion timetables. And because the station will run the commercials that it thinks will perform best for it, your spot might never run and you will not know it until your entire selling program has been jeopardized.

Bonus-to-payout involves a special arrangement with the station to deliver a certain number of responses. A schedule is negotiated with the station to guarantee a certain minimum schedule. If at the end of the schedule the response goal has not been reached, the station must continue to run the commercial until it is reached. This method provides a better planning base for the direct marketer.

With television time in high demand, such opportunities are not as available as they once were. But if they can be located, they can be a superb vehicle for direct marketers.

TV Schedules

What kind of broadcast TV schedule is most productive and/or efficient for the direct marketer? It depends on the objective. For direct sale or lead-generation commercials, which require the viewer to get up and take some action within minutes, certain criteria apply. For example, the TV viewing day is divided into various dayparts. There are weekday daytime, early evening or fringe, prime time, late night or fringe, and weekend. Each daypart tends to reach one group or combination of viewers better than the others.

It is important to know your primary target group so that you can select the most appropriate daypart. Prime time is so called because it reaches the largest audience with the most exciting shows. It is also the most expensive. The more attentive viewers are to the show, the less likely they are to respond immediately. Therefore, times of lower viewer involvement and attentiveness are better and less expensive for the advertiser who expects a direct response. Reruns, talk shows, old movies, and the like often are the best vehicles for direct response advertising. These tend to run predominantly in daytime, fringe, and late-night time slots.

Similarly, because independent stations tend to run a higher percentage of syndicated reruns and movies, their viewers tend to have a lower level of attentiveness to the programming. But even on independent stations, avoid news shows and other high-interest programming. Check the ratings. They are a good guide.

Seasonality is another factor in direct response TV. The first and third quarters are the best seasons for television response, just as they are for print and mail. Moreover, television time pricing is related to viewing levels, which are seasonal and vary month to month as well as by daypart.

Market Performance

Some geographic locations are good for certain products or offers. Others are simply not receptive. It pays to know ahead of time what a market's propensity is. Previous experience with mail or print can be a reasonably reliable guide.

In any event, it is not necessary to jump in up to your neck. Start with a handful of markets—say, two to five—and test the waters. Try a one- or two-week schedule. As few as ten commercials per week can give you a reading. Monitor your telephone response daily. You'll know within two or three days if it's bust or boom. After a week or so you'll have an even more precise fix on how well your commercial is doing. If it holds up, stay with it until it starts to taper off. Then stop. Don't try to milk a stone.

Meanwhile, move on to other markets in the same methodical and measured way. You always can return to your most successful markets later in the marketing year, after your commercial has had a rest. Or you can come back with a new offer.

Advantages and Disadvantages of Different Types of Stations

Media-buying decisions have become more complex because of the expansion and success of various cable and broadcast stations and programming packages. Let us examine the advantages and disadvantages of the five major options for most TV direct response offers.

Network. The four major networks are ABC (225 affiliated stations), CBS (200 affiliated stations), NBC (230 affiliated stations), and Fox (200 affiliated stations). The advantage of the network option is that network reaches 95 percent of the potential U.S. TV households with each spot. The disadvantages are as follows:

1. There are few, if any, 60–120-second spots available.

2. It is generally cost-prohibitive.

3. Telemarketing blockage problems would occur in most dayparts.

4. Talent payments could present a problem.

Few marketers have been able to make network television pay out.

Spot TV. The use of spot TV is a localized way of making a buy that can be done through independent stations and/or affiliates. Whether you buy one or five stations in a spot market, you are reaching only one TV market. Rates vary greatly, depending on the station's ranking in and the size of the market.

One advantage of spot TV is that it is cost-efficient. Because of competition within a market, reasonable buys generally can be made. Also, you can maximize efficiencies in the better-performing markets and on the better-performing stations. The disadvantage is that for a national campaign, it is more labor-intensive to buy each market individually. Spot TV is the common approach for most direct response television campaigns.

Network Cable. The total cable penetration in the United States is 84 percent. There are 62 advertiser-supported cable networks and 84 regional cable networks. The advantages of network cable are as follows:

1. It is cost-efficient.

2. It enables targeting an offer to a cable network's audience.

3. Back-end tends to be better on cable than on broadcast TV because cable has a more upscale audience.

The disadvantage is that there are limited availabilities, especially if you have a two-minute spot. Network cable is especially appropriate if you have a one-minute spot and an offer perfectly matched to a cable network's audience.

Local Cable. Unlike cable network, local cable enables you to buy on a market basis or, in some instances, on a neighborhood basis. One advantage of local cable is that it allows a very targeted approach that works for products with narrow market segments. Also, it allows securing of additional cable time when networks are tight. The disadvantages include the following:

1. There are no two-minute breaks.

2. Rates aren't particularly cost-efficient.

3. You have to work with five or more cable operators to cover one market.

4. It offers a very fragmented audience.

Local cable is best used for offers that target a narrowly segmented market.

Syndication. Syndication is the sale of a TV program for airing on a market-by-market, station-by-station basis. Though generally associated with reruns and game shows, syndication can include first-run movies and original, first-run TV shows. Some direct marketing agencies have also been able to buy time within a syndicated program, ensuring that the spot will air every time the show runs.

The advantages of syndication are as follows:

1. It is difficult to preempt a syndicated program.

2. It reaches 80–90 percent of the country (similar to network).

3. There are no telemarketing headaches, because each station airs a particular show at a different time of day or on a different day of the week.

4. It allows product-to-program matching—a useful targeting tool.

The disadvantages are that it usually accepts only 60-second spots; therefore, for cost efficiency, buyers often have to wait for "distressed" or unsold time within a syndicated program. Syndication is well suited to one-minute offers that are matched to a specific program and is a good choice for direct marketers having problems with preemptions.

Creating for Direct Response TV

Television is a visual medium and an action medium. And you are using it in a time of great video literacy. Your concept must be sharp and crisp. It must be designed to jar a lethargic and jaded audience to rapt attention. Your concepts, therefore, require the best and most knowledgeable of talent.

When you have arrived at your concept, it is time to write a script and do a storyboard. The script format is two adjacent columns, one for video descriptions and one for copy and audio directions. The two columns track together so that the appropriate words and sounds are shown opposite the pictures they will accompany. Video descriptions should make it possible to understand the general action in any given scene. It is not necessary at this point to spell out every detail.

Some people prefer to work only with storyboards, while others combine scripts and storyboards. The storyboard is a series of artist's drawings of the action and location of each scene. There should be enough individual pictures (called frames) to show the flow of the action and provide important visual information. Most concept storyboards run eight to sixteen frames, depending on the length of the commercial, the complexity of the action, and the need to show specific detail.

Novices make two important errors when preparing TV storyboards. One is failure to synchronize the words and the pictures. At no point should the copy be talking about something different from what the picture is showing, nor should the picture be something that is unrelated to the words.

The second mistake is failure to realize that most people who evaluate a storyboard equate frames with the passage of time. Each frame in an eight-frame storyboard will often be interpreted as one-eighth of commercial time. If some intricate action takes place over five seconds, it could take four or five frames to illustrate. Meanwhile, a simple scene that may run ten seconds can often be illustrated with one or two frames. Imagine the confusion the reviewer of the storyboard faces. Make sure your storyboards show elapsed time. Often an elapsed time indicator next to the picture will do the trick.

Of course, these criteria are guidelines, not rules. Even if they were, the essence of all great advertising, including direct response, is to break the rules to reach people in a way they haven't been reached before. But it is something quite different to violate principles that have been developed over years of observation. Do so only at your own peril.

There is a set of rules that relates to laws. Various industry self-regulatory bodies and instruments of the government watch over the airwaves. They require that advertising be truthful and not misleading. Don't say (or picture) anything in your commercial that you can't substantiate or replicate in person. And don't make promises your product or service can't deliver.

As you design your direct response commercial, there are some important techniques to keep in mind. If at all possible, integrate your offer with the rest of your commercial. It will make it easier for the viewer to comprehend and respond. And it will give your offer and your product or service the opportunity to reinforce each other in value and impression.

Also, if possible, integrate the 800 toll-free number into the commercial. You should plan to have the telephone number on the screen for at least 25 seconds or more, depending on the length of the commercial. Try to find ways to make it "dance" on the screen. Bring it on visually as it is announced on the sound track. Apply similar connection to visual and voice for announcing your Web site.

Once you have developed a television storyboard that you believe is a good representation of what you want to accomplish, it is possible to evaluate it using the following criteria:

1. *Immediacy.* Is there a sense of urgency to "Call this number now"? Does it make viewers feel that an opportunity will be lost if they don't run to the phone?

2. *Clarity.* Is the offer clear? Do people understand exactly what they will receive, or is there room for doubt and ambiguity?

3. *Lack of retail availability.* If the advertised product is not available in any store, make sure that point is communicated to the viewer.

4. *Increased value.* Many tactics can heighten the offer's value, for example, making a "special television offer" and stating "for a limited time only."

5. *Limited options.* If the spot provides viewers with too many choices, they will be confused. Yes-or-no offers usually do better than multiple-choice ones.

6. *Early close.* Ask for the order early and often. If the commercial waits until the final seconds or makes only one request for the viewer to call, it is usually too late.

7. *Less is more.* If you're asking for installment payments, focus the viewer's attention on the installment amount. Do not emphasize the sum total of all the installments.

8. *Show and tell.* If the product does more than one thing, show it. This is the only way viewers will become familiar with the product. Demonstrations work. Make sure the commercial conveys exactly what viewers are getting when they buy the product.

A support television commercial differs from a straight response commercial in significant ways. Because it seeks to reach the largest number of people, it usually runs in time periods when 30 seconds is the prevalent availability. It must have a greatly condensed message, placing a premium on simplicity. As it seeks no immediate response, but directs the viewer elsewhere, such as to a newspaper insert, memorability and a positive attitude about the advertiser become extremely important.

Creating for Radio

In its early days, television was perceived by many copywriters as nothing more than illustrated radio. With the evolution of the medium, we learned how limited that vision was. Now, in this age of video, there is a tendency to think of radio as television without the pictures. That perception is equally wrong.

Radio is the "writer's medium" in its purest sense. Words, sounds, music, and even silence are woven together by the writer to produce a moving tapestry of thought, image, and persuasion. Connection with the listener is direct, personal, emotional, primal.

In writing for radio, it is important to consider a station's format. The country-and-western station has a different listening audience from the all-news station. Different people listen to classical music than talk-back or rock programming. Tailor your message and its style to the format of the station it is running on. That doesn't necessarily mean make it sound exactly like the station's programming. Sometimes it makes sense to break the flow of programming to stand out as a special message, but only within the framework of the format that has attracted the station's listeners.

Remember also that radio is more personal than TV. Radios are carried with the listener—in a car, at the beach, at the office, in the bathroom. Moreover, because the radio listener can supply important elements in the message mosaic, the conclusion drawn from it is likely to be more firmly held than that which the individual has not participated in. Do not fill in all the blanks for your listeners. Let them provide some of the pieces. At the same time, be sure the words you use are clear in their meaning and emotional content. Be sure the sounds are clearly understandable and recognizable. If not, find some way to augment them with narrative or conversation that establishes a setting that is easy to visualize.

Use music whenever you can justify its cost and consumption of commercial time. Music is the emotional common denominator. Its expression of joy, sorrow, excitement, romance, or action is as universally understood as any device available to you. When it comes time to consider music, contact a music production house. There usually are several in every major city. Los Angeles, New York, and Chicago have scores of them. Or consider library music that can be purchased outright at low cost.

Another aspect of radio is its casualness. Whereas television tends to command all of our attention and concentration, radio usually gets only a portion of it. It is important to keep radio commercials simple and intrusive. Devices such as special sounds (or silence) can arrest your listener's attention. To hold it, the idea content must be cohesive and uncomplicated. Better to drive one point home than to flail away at many. If many points must be covered, they all should feed to a strong central premise. This advice is appropriate for all advertising, but for radio it is critical.

The length a radio commercial runs is usually 60 seconds. This not only should be adequate for most commercial messages, but it also is the time length listeners have become accustomed to. Thirty-second commercials are available but are not a good buy for direct response purposes.

One other thing that everyone who listens to radio will appreciate is that radio lends itself to humor. For some reason we have become used to hearing humor on radio and we respond positively to it. The following radio commercial employs humor effectively to address small-business owners while talking to the public at large.

Husband:	How did we get into this anyway?
Wife:	Who knows, we tried to make it work.
Husband:	Well, I guess it's over.
Wife:	We better get on with it.
Husband:	Okay, you get the car.
Wife:	Right.
Husband:	I get the sofa bed. You get the fridge.
Wife:	Right.
Husband:	I get the Bell System Yellow Pages Directory. You get the . . .
Wife:	Hold on—that doesn't mean the Gold Pages Coupon Section, does it?
Husband:	Why, sure it does.
Wife:	I get the Gold Pages Coupons.
Husband:	Well come on—you're getting the bedroom set too.

Wife:	You can have the bedroom set. I want the Gold Pages Coupons good for discounts at local merchants.
Husband:	I'll tell you what.
Wife:	What?
Husband:	I'll throw in the oil painting and the end tables.
Wife:	I want the Gold Pages.
Husband:	Look, you can have everything else. Just let me keep the Gold Pages Coupons.
Wife:	Get off your knees. You really want them that bad?
Husband:	I do absolutely.
Wife:	We could split them.
Husband:	You mean . . . tear them apart?
Wife:	You're right . . . it won't work.
Husband:	No. Neither will this.
Wife:	It won't work.
Husband:	You mean . . .
Wife:	We'll just have to stay together.
Husband:	Dolores—what a mistake we almost made.
Wife:	Lorraine.
Husband:	Lorraine—what a mistake we almost made.
Wife:	Who's Dolores?

TV in the Multimedia Mix

For decades marketers have regarded electronic media as stand-alone media. But astute marketers have joined the trend toward integrated communications. A classic example of this trend was the multimedia campaign for Ryder used trucks, created by Ogilvy & Mather Direct.

Exhibit 12–6 gives a precise description of the campaign, which included direct mail, direct response, TV, print, and radio.

Exhibit 12–7 shows a print ad that appeared in ensuing vertical publications. A vertical publication is one that caters to a specific category of business, such as banking, or a specific interest such as jogging, boating, etc. The headline "Buy a Ryder Road Ready Used Truck and you'll find one problem. The mechanics hate to see them go" carries the campaign theme.

Exhibit 12–8 reveals the 120-second TV commercial. It was tagged as "The Crying Commercial," because it paid off on the theme "The mechanics hate to see them go."

How successful was this multimedia campaign? The combination of direct mail, print, TV, and radio produced a total of 46,046 responses, beating the previous controls by 245 percent.

EXHIBIT 12-6

Description of Ryder Campaign

Product or Service

Used vehicle sales, including vans, gas and diesel straight trucks, refrigerated trucks, tractors, and trailers. Range in price from $7,000 to $35,000.

Target Audience

- Owners/presidents of small service businesses, small wholesalers/retailers, small trucking companies and light manufacturing companies (cabinetry, auto parts, electronic parts, clothing/candy)
- Owner/operators
- Used truck purchasers in large companies with 10+ vehicle fleet size

Medium/Media Used

Direct mail: 300,000 pieces. Lists included previous customers, Dun & Bradstreet selects (targeted industries; less than 100 employees; transportation titles), *Fleet Equipment* subscribers, *Fleet Owner* subscribers, *Allied Truck Publication* subscribers.

DRTV: :60 and :120 local television in spot markets, 3–5 stations/market, 10–15 spots/week/station, for 2–4 week flights

Print: local trade publications *(Truck Trader)*

Radio: local; spot stations

Marketing Strategy

To remain competitive in its primary business–truck rental and leasing, Ryder needs to keep its truck fleet current. Selling its used vehicles helps Ryder fund the purchase of new vehicles while providing an additional source of revenue.

Problem:
- Increasingly depressed market for used vehicle sales
- Aggressive sales objectives within a more competitive category environment
- Inconsistent awareness that Ryder also sells trucks

Solution:
- Leverage Ryders' reputation for quality in truck rental and leasing to sell its vehicles at a premium price.
- Establish "Road Ready" as a symbol of reliability, safety, and value through a lifetime of maintenance.
- Provide a continuous presence in the marketplace to generate awareness that Ryder sells trucks.
- Generate immediate, qualified leads through an offer of a free "How to Buy a Used Truck" booklet.

EXHIBIT 12–7

Print Ad from Ryder Campaign

EXHIBIT 12-8

The Crying Commercial

Ogilvy & Mather Direct

CLIENT: RYDER
PRODUCT: USED TRUCK SALE
TITLE: "CRYING"
COMML No.: RTLR 0111 :120

(SFX-TRUCK HORN) (MUSIC UP-SENTIMENTAL THEME)
MECHANIC #1: There goes my baby.

STEVE: Here we go again. I knew it, every time Ryder sells a used truck this happens.
(SFX-SOBBING, BLOWING NOSE)

STEVE: Alright, there, there.

You didn't know Ryder sells trucks? They do, they sell them. Excuse me.
(SFX-SOBBING)

The same quality trucks they rent and lease to businesses, they also sell to businesses.

Makes these guys fall apart.

MECHANIC #2: We've been caring for them since they were new.

STEVE: See what I mean? They look after these trucks like they were their own.

MECHANIC #3: They've got their whole lives ahead of them.

STEVE: You're going to be okay, don't worry about it. Do you believe these guys?

Ryder sells more kinds of used trucks than anyone. Trucks, vans, tractors, trailers.

Even specialized equipment.

Just call and they'll tell you where to get 'em. They'll even--

MECHANIC #1: (VO) Steve, not the book!
STEVE: Eh. I have to do this.

They'll even give you free advice before you look. It's in here: "How to Buy a Used Truck."

You gotta get this. It's the inside story. What to look for, and avoid. Whether you're buying now or just kicking some tires.

Course, with a Ryder used truck you know what you're getting into.

See this tag. "Road Ready." It means this truck has been maintained at the highest standards since it was new.

Ryder has the records to prove it. And a limited warranty to back it. Impressive stuff.

How ya doin'? (MUSIC UP-SENTIMENTAL THEME)
MECHANIC #4: Great.

EXHIBIT 12-8

The Crying Commercial (*Continued*)

RYDER-"CRYING"   PAGE 2

STEVE: These guys put their hearts into these trucks. They even fix things before they go wrong.

MECHANIC #4: Brakes. Steering. Engine.

STEVE: You'll love your Road Ready truck as much as they do.

MECHANIC #2: Oh please , I don't want to see you go.

STEVE: Only you'll get to keep yours. So call for the Ryder Road Ready Center near you. Ask about financing.

MECHANIC #1: (VO) Steve! STEVE: It's okay, relax.

MECHANIC #1. Don't give him the number, please.

Just call for the free book: "How to Buy a Used Truck."

Even if you're not buying now, you'll be an expert.

But you gotta call.

MECHANIC #4. Please take good care of them.

STEVE: Don't worry. They'll get more trucks. Sorry, I'm out of tissues.

It's a new jacket, get off me I'm not kidding!

(SENTIMENTAL MUSIC UP AND OUT)

CASE STUDY: LendingTree DRTV Campaign

Adapted from the Direct Marketing Association International Echo Awards 2006.

BACKGROUND

Through years of witty, memorable 30-second brand advertising, LendingTree.com became known for giving consumers an alternative to applying for a loan and waiting for an answer: Visit LendingTree.com, turn the tables on banks, and choose from up to four loan offers from a network of qualified lenders who will compete for your business.

Within a few years, online lenders had proliferated and multiple offers were common. The refinance boom had brought in new competitors with cheap, flexible, offer-driven DRTV that did very well. LendingTree needed to try competing in new, aggressive ways, and move people past stubborn sales and online lending barriers.

TARGET AUDIENCE

LendingTree serves a broad audience of male and female homeowners of all ages. The target audience is those looking to buy or sell their home, looking for one of the many loans LendingTree offers, or simply looking to refinance. Within this target are those who are sophisticated and knowledgeable about the market and see their home as a financial tool. These are the cautious computer users who don't trust the Internet for such large transactions, the jaded skeptics who know some rate offers out there are just too good to be true.

CHALLENGE

LendingTree is viewed as a place to get four speculative offers, but not a place specific offers can be responded to. People don't think of LendingTree as a company that can help them leverage their home to solve financial issues. Also, a significant portion of people don't want a transaction of this size online; they want to know what happens after they "visit LendingTree.com."

SOLUTION

Launch a DRTV pilot campaign to test if 60-second DRTV—built around these issues and designed to both entertain in the LendingTree tradition and also teach/sell—can drive better business performance. The goal was to test three spots with different refinance offers and gather fast turnaround learning by the end of 2005, which would affect future call and QF (Qualification Form) volume by maximizing network/daypart efficiencies and creative messaging. Thirty DR cable networks per flight were used, of which each aired a minimum of 6–8 commercial units per daypart across a minimum of 2–4 dayparts.

New direct response creative ran in a mixture of the following network categories:
- Cable news
- Endemic
- Broad reach

CREATIVE APPROACH

"Suiting Up" met the need for a flexible spot that could tout a great offer today and TBD offers in the future. This spot sought to shift the LendingTree brand legacy from "story as hero" to "offer as hero." The 60-second spot took a behind-the-scenes look at LendingTree's signature banker competition.

"Grill" met the need for a spot that sought to educate people about the online process, to make them feel the ease and accessibility of it. The hallmark of the LendingTree brand and their spots is they are fun to watch. And the customer always wins, is always a little smarter than anyone else. "Helping Hands" (see Exhibit 12–9) met the need for a spot that placed LendingTree as a competitor to all those companies who can help leverage your

EXHIBIT 12–9

LendingTree DRTV Campaign "Helping Hands"

Customer: "Honey have you seen my hammer."

(Bankers talking in the background) Narrator: "Want Banks to compete over you. Get the money you need by..."

Narrator: "refinancing with Lending Tree."

Narrator: "Onel simple form gets you up to four cutomized..."

Narrator: "offers which you can compare and act on instantly."

Customer: "So, Who wants to help us with our credit card bills?"

(Bankers talking in the background) Narrator: "Considerate debt, lower monthly payments, pay for college or other big expenses."

Customer: "Ohhh!!! I don't know about the shoes."

(Bankers talking in the background) Narrator: "Lending Tree banks..."

Narrator: "compete to get you the best rates even if you credit is less than perfect."

Customer: "Factoring a quadratic equation." Narrator: "With nine of America's top..."

Narrator: "ten financial institutions in our network. With nine of America's top ten financial institutions in our network..."

Customer: "Percentages" Narrator: "We've already helped over many million peoples."

Narrator: "Refinance now and you can move up to two hundred dollars a month..."

Narrator: "When banks compete you win. At Lending Tree.com."

CASE STUDY: LendingTree DRTV Campaign *(Continued)*

---

home to pay for life events: tuition, big credit card bills, home improvements, and big unexpected personal expenses. Sure, LendingTree can meet that need. But it didn't come top of mind. To counteract this, the spot portrayed bankers in a new way: right there, helping you, fighting to be the one to solve your problem.

RESULTS

All three spots broke copy testing records for a combination of brand likeability and direct response "intent to take immediate action," which was measured by URL and phone-tracked loan requests. All three were part of the LendingTree creative rotation.

"Suiting Up" beat the performance of the control DRTV spot by 56 percent, with a gross cost per response (CPR) of just $78. The "Grill" conversion rate was 27 percent, with a gross CPR of $169. "Helping Hands" converted at 23 percent, with a gross CPR of $204.

PILOT PROJECT Your assignment is to create a 60-second, direct response radio spot (i.e., commercial) for LendingTree. The objective will be to drive prospects to the Web site. Ultimately, its success will be measured on the lowest cost per response and highest conversation rate.

Write the script integrating with one of the creative executions from the TV campaign. Remember that in radio you don't have the benefit of visuals, everything must be communicated through words or sound.

A. After you have written the script, read it aloud to see how it sounds and how much time it takes. Count how many words you used in the script.

B. How many calls to action have you incorporated?

C. How much of the commercial is given to benefits and selling versus the call to action?

D. Is the finished commercial consistent with the theme of the TV commercial that you are mirroring?

Key Points

▶ The cost of a commercial time period is based on its rating, the measure of its share of the total TV households viewing the show. The more highly rated the show, the higher the cost. More important than reach and frequency are actual response rates, which represent a true return on the media dollar.

▶ To buy time economically, ask about preemptible time and payment per inquiry (PI) and bonus-to-payout arrangements. For best response, schedule commercials during fringe dayparts and programs with lower viewer involvement, like reruns, talk shows, and old movies.

▶ The first and third quarters are the best seasons for television response.

▶ Test TV commercials in two to five markets for one or two weeks. As few as ten commercials per week can give you a precise fix on how well the commercial is doing. If it holds up, stay with it until it starts to taper off, and move on to other markets in the same methodical and measured way.

▶ Integrate the offer with the product or service so they reinforce each other in value and impression. Show the 800 toll-free number or the Web address on the screen for at least 25 seconds, depending on the length of the commercial.

▶ Radio costs less than television and offers more targeted program formats. The message and style of a 60-second radio commercial should be tailored to the format of the station it is running on. Keep radio commercials simple and intrusive. Use special sounds to arrest your listener's attention, but keep the main idea uncomplicated. Better to drive one point home than to flail away at many.

INSERT AND CO-OP
MEDIA

Insert and co-op media are growing forms of direct marketing communications. They use preexisting distribution systems, such as advertising co-ops, newspapers, billing statements, and mail order/E-commerce product packages, to deliver inserts, mini-catalogs, or multimedia CDs. Media choices include direct mail co-ops, card decks, newspaper free-standing inserts (FSIs) and coupon inserts, statement stuffers (e.g., credit card), and package inserts. In addition, there are check stub programs, airline ticket jackets, door hangers, and many other inventive formats. We will address the most important of these in this chapter.

There is an implied endorsement with many co-op programs. Offers within co-op mailings and B2B card decks are surrounded by communications from well-known organizations. Inserts, co-ops, and card decks are sponsored or delivered within a package from an organization well known to the recipient. This makes for a very positive message delivery environment. Often, recipients are not available on mailing lists or through other media, which makes the target more appealing to marketers.

Lastly, co-ops and inserts are one of the least obtrusive media. Consumers choose if they want to look through them, although research shows that media such as newspaper FSIs are actually among consumer favorites, and that they look forward to receiving and spending time looking through them. This makes FSIs privacy-friendly, which is another reason for their growing use over the last decade.

Co-ops, in various formats, have been available to marketers for decades. Among the most popular are postcards—$3\frac{1}{2} \times 5\frac{1}{2}$ inch—assembled three to the sheet or loosely. In an effort to make more selling space available, many co-ops accept printed lithographed sheets that measure $8\frac{1}{2} \times 11$ inches, folding down to $5\frac{1}{2} \times 8\frac{1}{2}$ inches. But the ultimate in size is the 24-page mini-catalog with a page size of $5\frac{1}{2} \times 7$ inches.

It is estimated that more than 1,000 B2B and B2C co-ops are available at any one time. The basic appeal of co-ops is that you share the cost with other similar marketers, thus attaining a much lower cost per thousand circulation. Rule of thumb is that participation in a co-op costs about one-fourth as much as a solo mailing. That's the good news.

The bad news is that on average, response rate from a co-op is about one-fourth as much as you would get with a solo mailing. But that's the average. The purpose of this chapter is to beat the averages.

Getting Co-ops Read

Participants in co-ops face fierce readership competition. You can greatly improve your chances for getting your piece read and acted on by knowing the behavior patterns of people who receive co-ops.

In focus group research interview sessions, in which groups of housewives were brought in and handed co-op envelopes filled with discount coupons and other offers, there was an amazingly consistent behavior pattern. The participants, without exception, sorted each envelope's contents into two piles. Later, when they were asked what was the basis for the two piles, they answered: "Interesting—not interesting; like—dislike; value—no value." Your offer must find its way to the right pile during that initial sorting.

The way to get into the first pile is to have a simple message clearly stated with effective graphics. The more alternatives you offer, the less your response might be. In a phrase, don't get sorted out; keep it simple. You only have a few seconds to make an impact. Inserts in direct mail co-ops are more like ads in a magazine than like regular direct mail. If the offer appears to be too much trouble, if it appears that the message is going to take some time and effort to get at, the home shopper goes to the next offer.

Generally, in co-op direct response advertising, the recipient sees little and remembers less. Any purchase is basically made on impulse, and response levels can be seriously impacted if the potential respondent does not act within a short time span. The products and services should fall into the pattern of something wanted or needed now. This is true whether the marketer is seeking an inquiry or a direct sale.

Direct Mail Consumer Co-ops

When direct mail consumer co-ops first came on the scene, the mailing lists they used were for the most part compiled lists. Public information sources constituted a major portion of the compilation.

These were good, clean lists, current for the most part, but little was known about the demographics. If you wanted the names of people who owned a model A Ford, by gosh—they were available. But if you wanted to know the names of Model A Ford owners who were mail-order responders—it wasn't available!

Well, times do change. The large consumer co-ops like ValPack, Valassis, ADVO, Shop Wise, and Money Mailer offer a number of selects within their massive consumer list. For instance, ADVO (now owned by Valassis) offers multiple geographic targeting segments, including:

- National

- Market (retail trade zones)

- ZIP code, SCF, etc.

- Sub ZIP code (ADVO targeting zone)

- Carrier route

- Household

The geographic selections offered by direct mail co-ops include many rural, C and D counties. Category exclusivity is generally not available, and the names are not mail-order buyers. CPMs (costs per thousand) for direct mail co-ops have a great deal of variation. Many offer remnant space in addition to secure positions. Remnant space is unsold inventory from portions of the circulation.

Costs for national direct mail coupon co-op inserts are in the range $12–50 per thousand.

Newspaper Inserts and Free-Standing Inserts

Newspaper coupon co-op inserts are cooperative, full-color, multi-page flyers offering local, regional, and national advertising with coupons, 800 numbers, etc. FSIs such as Valassis and SmartSource Magazine are part of many consumers' Sunday morning rituals. Running an average of 16 pages in four colors, they are loaded with cents-off coupons. Typical among package goods advertisers are Welch's, Oreo cookies, Stouffer's, Wheaties, Cheerios, A&W Root Beer, Healthy Choice soups, Arm & Hammer, and scores more.

However, mixed in with coupons from Procter & Gamble, Unilever, and other large consumer packaged goods companies are on-page, mail-order offers for collectibles, gourmet foods, book and DVD programs, personalized stationery (e.g., labels, checks, etc.), and a variety of response offers. In fact, only half of Valassis revenue is driven by revenue from coupons, indicating the importance of direct response advertising. Available circulation is very high, up to 60 million for national roll-outs. Exhibit 13–1 shows a half-page direct response ad for a collectible from the Hamilton Mint from a coupon co-op. Note the coupon for Oral-B below it.

In addition to newspaper co-ops, free standing inserts (FSIs), also called preprints, are accepted into Sunday or Wednesday local newspapers and local shopping papers (community papers that include ads, local notices, and some editorial

EXHIBIT 13–1

Coupon Co-op for Hamilton Collection and Oral-B

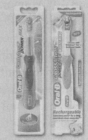

content, published on a weekly basis). Exhibit 13–2 is a direct response FSI for Photo Stamps. Note that there is no order form. Instead, this is drive-to-Web, and there is a simple three-step explanation of how to order. Purchasing requires cropping photos, and order information is taken online.

Costs for national coupon inserts are in the range $4–8 per thousand. Solo inserts can be significantly higher.

EXHIBIT 13–2

FSI for Photo Stamps

Card Decks

Card decks are a group of same-sized cards (e.g., 3 × 5 inch) printed by the sponsoring organization, then enclosed in an envelope, cellophane, or Mylar wrap for shipment to a targeted audience. There are hundreds of such co-ops catering to professionals and manufacturing management. The cards have offers on one side and business reply cards on the second side. In addition, some direct mail insert pieces are folded to fit into the standard of the envelope or mailers. Even more popular are "double" decks that allow for two rows of 3½ × 5½ inch cards that include a mailing label area.

Card decks are often sponsored by business trade publications, which mail them out on a quarterly basis. Their circulation isn't even close to that of consumer co-ops (there are far fewer businesses than there are consumers), but in business-to-business the units of sale can be many, many times a consumer sale. So smaller numbers can be very much worthwhile.

Some are sent out by mail order or other firms that have large customer bases. Card decks are mailed standard rate, like other mailed co-ops. Targeting is based on firmographics and the context of the publication or customer bases. A card deck usually mails via standard mail bulk rate and does not guarantee that the recipients are direct-mail responsive. This is a low-cost medium often chosen by B2B mailers for lead generation. Costs range from $20–25 per thousand, and includes printing of the inserts.

Online Coupon Distribution

Many online companies and consumer brands have tested online coupon distribution, including Home Depot, Walmart, NetFlix, The Sharper Image, Barnes & Noble, PetCo, and many others. The coupon site Coolsavings.com features offers from such prominent direct marketers (See Exhibit 13–3).

Package Insert Programs

Package inserts include ads, offers, brochures, or samples packed along with mail-ordered merchandise. Merchants use this as another revenue source. Targeting by context is available (marketers can choose the merchant), but other selects are typically unavailable. This type of promotion is low-cost, has fewer size and weight restrictions, and provides the marketer with a flexible format. They get high awareness because the package will be opened up. There is an implied endorsement from the sponsoring company, which adds credibility to the insert. However, there is no guarantee of readership.

EXHIBIT 13-3

Online Coupon Distribution

Package inserts arrive at a time when a likely buyer or gift recipient has just received a package. The direct marketing concept of recency has impact here. Exhibit 13–4 is a package insert for the Disney Movie Club that was included with an order for children's products.

Package insert programs have a cost in the range of $40–80 per thousand.

Statement Insert Programs

Billing or statement inserts (often called statement stuffers) are inserts that are included along with monthly statements or bills sent out by credit card companies, banks, gas and electric utilities, cable TV companies, cell phone providers, and other service organizations. Users range from the charity appeals enclosed with a utility bill to the magazine subscription forms and flyers for alarm clocks or stationery included with credit card statements.

EXHIBIT 13–4

Disney Movie Club Package Insert

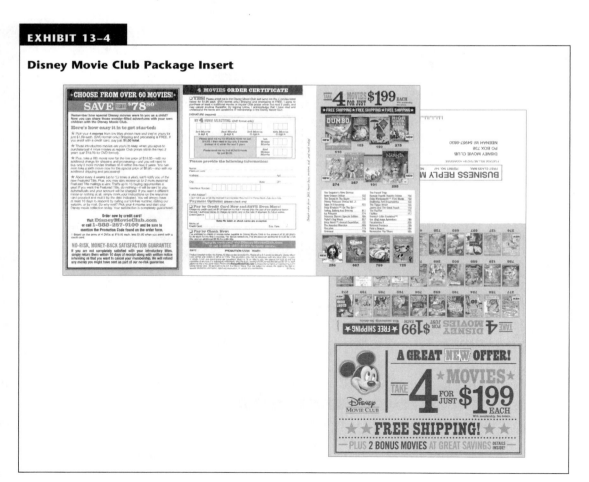

Statements stuffers have an implied endorsement from the billing organization, and they must not detract from the invoice of the host or sponsoring organization. Typically, they arrive in a #10 envelope mailed first class, and there may be up to three inserts in a statement. Some positions may be used by the host company, and not everyone mailed a statement will receive the insert. Sometimes the offer is printed on the reply envelope included with the statement. This uses a special kind of envelope known as a bang tail envelope. Readership may be high, although the insert is not the primary reason that the mail is opened. While the context is known, behavior and demographics are not usually selectable. For example, customers of utilities are not all mail-order buyers. The cost for statement stuffers is from $25–40 per thousand.

Customer Mailing Ride-Alongs

Ride-alongs are closely related to package and statement inserts. They are sent to an existing customer cross-selling additional products and services. Because they are included in mailings or packages already going to customers, they have a low distribution cost. This customer has proven to have purchased via the mail at least once from this company. Amazon.com is a large user of this format, as are other E-commerce and mail-order merchants.

There are three major promotional models for online coupon activity:

1. *In-store redemption*. Users print coupons from a site and redeem the coupons at a retail location.

2. *Online redemption*. When users click on E-commerce coupons placed on coupon sites, the coupons are applied to offers right there on the site.

3. *Continuity/Affinity programs*. These sites provide offers worth a predesignated amount with an offline purchase. Site visitors print these coupons and give them to the offline retailer at checkouts. Like affinity programs, these programs allow Web surfers to earn points toward future purchases of products and services while coincidentally building the lifetime value of customers overall.

Whatever the channels of distribution, the bottom line is that hundreds of millions of coupons are offered and used each year.

Co-ops are a major tool for direct response advertisers when used correctly. They are not suitable for selling a $400 camera, but they are excellent for getting inquiries about a $400 camera or selling a lower-priced product or service. Co-ops are highly preferred for in-store coupon redemptions and for scores of direct response offers requiring a minimum of information for a target audience.

Co-op Testing Rules

Like other forms of direct marketing, inserts and co-ops must be tested. When you test an insert in a co-op, you are doing so with one group of partners; when you "roll out," you are likely to be participating with a different group of partners. So you must live with this variable.

Test quantities need to be commensurate with the program size. Large programs require large test quantities. Tests frequently cost 3–4 times more than larger continuations and roll-outs.

Here are a few simple rules for testing co-ops.

- Because testing is a trial for a subsequent major promotion, it is important to ensure that conditions for the major promotion will be as close to those of the original as possible.

- Know what your break-even point is and test a sample large enough so your result can be acted on.

- Test the co-op first and leave the segments for later unless your product clearly suggests a particular segment. For example, if your product is aimed entirely at a female market, test only the female portion of a co-op mailing.

- Test a cross-section of the complete co-op list. If no "*n*th" sample is available, request distribution in several different markets—all widely dispersed.

- Don't let too much time elapse between your test and your continuation, especially if the item you are testing is of a seasonal nature.

Insert and Co-op Media Buying

Like other media, co-op and insert programs offer flexibility in pricing. Often, the sponsor or media owner has a rate card with a CPM that they expect to receive. This rate is often a negotiable rate based on the quantity discounts, frequency discounts, geographic or demographic/firmographics targeting, timing, availability, insert weight, competitiveness, and the sponsor's distribution costs. Often, there is not category exclusivity, although it can be bought.

Getting rates for insert and co-op programs is not always easy. SRDS offers insert and co-op rates. There are a few specialized insert and co-op agencies that can be found online. Some list brokers also market insert programs. Newspapers and weekly shopping papers must be contacted directly. Magazines, which are the main sponsors of card deck programs, also may be contacted directly. Large coupon co-ops like ADVO, Valassis, and News America (a subsidiary of News Corporation of America) have their own sales forces. Val-Pak and Money Mailer are franchise organizations, and their franchisers can sell their local co-ops as well as their networks. Despite the difficulty, insert and co-op programs can be a worthwhile addition to a direct marketing program. Exhibit 13–5 summarizes the benefits and disadvantages of Co-op direct mail.

EXHIBIT 13–5

The Pros and Cons of Co-op Direct Mail

It enables marketers to share costs. The costs of solo direct mail include preparing or buying a mailing list, buying envelopes, designing and printing the promotional materials, inserting the materials, addressing the envelopes, postage, and redemption. With co-op direct mail, the advertiser shares everything except creation of the insert and redemption of the offer. A co-op mailing typically costs about 10 percent as much as solo mail.

It levels the playing field. A small company looks just as important as the large companies included in the mailing.

It is an effective testing medium. A co-op mailing enables an advertiser to test an offer and decide if the response rate justifies investment in solo mail. Often the sponsor of the co-op mailing can split the mailing list to enable an advertiser to test more than one price or offer simultaneously.

There is one disadvantage of co-op direct mail: the response rate for consumer mailings is lower than that for solo direct mail. However, if the list is well targeted, the respondents are usually of higher quality. Note: Business-to-business co-op direct mail (card packs) usually has a better response rate than solo mail. Why? One possible explanation is pass-along readership.

Source: From the article: "Maximizing Your Co-op Direct Mail Efforts" at www.motivationnetwork.com.

CASE STUDY: **The OfficeMax Mini-Catalog**

Contributed by Sy Dordick and Joe Kallick from WEB Direct Marketing Inc., Wheeling, IL.

BACKGROUND

Even the most astute observers of the catalog industry failed to predict the explosive growth of the Internet and the importance of effective Web sites for catalogers. Paradoxically, while business from the Internet grew to as much as 35 percent for some catalogs, customers continued to place most of their orders offline; hence, the ongoing need for printed catalogs. The catalog now must fill many roles: keep the company's products and promotions in front of qualified buyers, prospect for new customers, and, importantly, drive people to the cataloger's Web site.

CHALLENGE

In the office supply industry, three multi-billion-dollar companies dominate. Each of these is a multichannel marketer, deriving its volume from three distribution avenues: retail outlets, mail-order catalogs, and the Internet. OfficeMax, one of the leaders, sought to increase product orders and to drive prospects to its Web site. It chose to insert a mini-catalog in media targeted toward small and medium-size businesses. The Mini-book is a cost-effective choice (See Exhibit 13–6). It rides along with another carrier—therefore, there is no postage—and each of the primary media offers huge circulations that can be segmented into specific geographic and demographic categories.

The "Big" Mini-book is a 5¼ × 7 inch (a digest-size) 24-page catalog large enough to provide space for OfficeMax to feature a representative offering of its best-selling items. To fulfill its objective of stimulating order response and bringing customers to its Web site, OfficeMax understood the need to make its Big Mini a promotional sales tool with special product pricing throughout and a limited-time offer featured on the cover. The Mini also served to heighten awareness and stimulate store traffic.

CASE STUDY: **The OfficeMax Mini-Catalog** *(continued)*

SOLUTION

OfficeMax focused on card decks reaching the business-to-business and small office/home office (SOHO) marketplace. Initial media research uncovered 52 decks with a total circulation of approximately 7 million, an average of 130,000 per mailing. From this group, OfficeMax selected a test sample of those with circulations that best mirrored its customers' profiles. In addition, a 12-page condensed version of the Mini-book, 3½ × 6½ inches, was prepared to fit into bank and cellular phone statements

RESULTS

With years of customer acquisition experience, OfficeMax was able to set a quantifiable goal for this test program. The program exceeded the objective of delivering new customers at a lower cost than any previous print prospecting efforts. As a result, OfficeMax ordered a continuation program, and followed-up with a third mailing.

OfficeMax was able to learn the performance of each card deck and statement that was mailed, using tracking codes to identify each. This information enabled them to pinpoint the best-performing media and expand into enormous circulations. OfficeMax dropped channels that failed to meet the established goal, and replaced them with new test programs selected from the 50-plus that were originally recommended. See Exhibits 13–7, 13–8 for sample test using the mini-catalog in alternative media and in package inserts.

EXHIBIT 13–6

OfficeMax Mini Catalog

CASE STUDY: The OfficeMax Mini-Catalog *(continued)*

EXHIBIT 13–7

Test Recommendations for Using a Mini-Book in Alternative Media

MEDIUM	CIRCULATION	COST	BUDGET
First-class billing statements	1,000,000	$100/M	$100,000
Package inserts (15 programs)	1,000,000	$110/M	$110,000
Card packs (10 decks)	1,000,000	$90/M	$90,000
Catalog inserts	500,000	$110/M	$55,000

NOTE: The per-thousand prices are based on the combined test circulation of 3.5 million.

EXHIBIT 13–8

Overview for Package Insert Media Recommendation

PROGRAM NAME	ANNUAL CIRCULATION	DISTRIBUTED
1. Blair Women's Catalog	6,125,000	Daily
2. Haband Women's Packages	5,000,000	Daily
3. Bedford Fair Catalog	1,601,000	Daily
4. Seventh Avenue Catalogs	2,290,000	Daily
5. Cosmetique Catalog	1,440,000	Daily
6. Silkies Boutique Catalog	3,500,000	Daily
7. Northern Tool & Equipment Catalog	1,415,000	Daily
8. Harbor Freight Tools Catalog	1,900,000	Daily
9. Barnes and Noble.com	11,000,000	Daily
10. Capper's Magazine	4,680,000	Daily
11. Bookspan General Interest Packages	12,600,000	Daily
12. Rodale Prevention Book Packages	3,454,000	Daily
13. Dr. Leonard's Healthcare Catalog	2,794,000	Daily
14. Better Homes & Gardens Creative Collection Catalog	968,000	Daily
15. Annie's Attic	1,475,000	Daily

Total annual circulation: 60,242,000

You have become promotion director of *Direct Magazine*. Management has decided to develop a co-op postcard program to be mailed four times a year to their 40,000-plus subscribers.

As a prelude to launching, you have been charged with developing a list of products and services that you believe will appeal to the *Direct Magazine* audience.

Break your product and service categories into two groups: primary and secondary. Expand the list for each to 10, using the first three as starting points.

PRIMARY	SECONDARY
1. Direct marketing and database books	**1.** Investment opportunities
2. Premiums and incentives	**2.** Management and leadership
3. Mailing lists	**3.** Office equipment
4. _____	**4.** _____
5. _____	**5.** _____
6. _____	**6.** _____
7. _____	**7.** _____
8. _____	**8.** _____
9. _____	**9.** _____
10. _____	**10.** _____

Key Points

▶ Co-op mailings allow marketers to share costs, thus attaining a much lower cost per thousand circulation. But while participation in a co-op costs about one-fourth as much as a solo mailing, response rate from a co-op is also only one-fourth as much.

▶ To ensure readership, use a simple message clearly stated with effective graphics. More alternatives means less response. If the offer appears to be too much trouble, the home shopper goes to the next offer.

▶ Coupons are an excellent way to generate inquiries for a high-priced item or to sell a lower-priced product or service. They work well for offers requiring a minimum of information for a target audience.

▶ To test co-ops, know what your break-even point is and test a sample large enough so your result can be acted on. Test a cross-section of the complete co-op list. If no "*n*th" sample is available, request distribution in several different markets—all widely dispersed. Don't let too much time elapse between your test and your continuation.

TELEMARKETING/
TELESERVICES

Despite being greatly maligned, telemarketing remains an important medium for direct marketers. It is used for inbound calling, in which it becomes the response mechanism for many promotions. Customer contact centers field customer and prospect calls for product purchases, order tracking, customer service, account maintenance, and many other activities.

Telemarketing is used in outbound calling for business-to-business (B2B), customer marketing, fund-raising, and political marketing. Outbound calling used for consumer marketing has been constrained by state and federal "No Call" rules and regulations. Under these rules, marketers must maintain their own "No Call" lists and ensure that names on the federal and state "Do Not Call" (DNC) registry are purged from the calling lists, with some exceptions. More than 100 million phone numbers have been placed on the DNC registry, which has served to decrease the size of the calling universe for prospecting calls in the consumer market.

While DNC has reduced call volumes to consumers, it has not eliminated consumer outbound calling. There are still tens of millions of phone numbers not registered with the DNC. Nevertheless, the DNC registry has had enormous impact on telemarketing. Robert Coen, who tracks trends and predicts media usage for Universal McCann, notes that restrictions on consumer telemarketing have caused companies to move spending out of telemarketing into other response media. Coen believes that direct mail has been the greatest beneficiary of this budget movement. There is no doubt that Internet media have benefited as well.

The Breadth of Telemarketing

Telemarketing includes everything from broadcasting an 800 number on an infomercial to placing outbound calls to determine the political preference of a household. As call centers transform themselves to meet the needs of consumers who can communicate through a number of media—even simultaneously—telemarketing is stretching to embrace e-mails and Web chats.

There is a growing movement to change the name *telemarketing* to *teleservices*, which better describes its role, for example in customer relationship management. The first identifier for the medium was telephone marketing, which pretty well described it. When AT&T introduced the first centralized telemarketing services 30 years ago, it flourished as a sales medium, particularly in the sale of consumer goods. It became the first line of contact for so many businesses, not just for customer support, but for Internet order processing and other multichannel communications.

The focus of teleservices has changed to include service. In the past, most phone calls were made for the purpose of taking an order or at least attempting to get an order. Now companies have realized that a call to develop a relationship with the customer is just as important as the actual sales call. More and more attention is given to customer relationship management. Hence, the emergence of the term *teleservices*. As the Internet grows the service need of the virtual inbound/outbound industry, its name has been modified to *voicemail telemarketing* and even VOIP (Voice Over Internet Protocol) telemarketing. Why do companies continue to tele-market their products or services? The answer is quite simple . . . because it works!

Teleservice Applications

Although technology has caused a number of changes in the teleservices industry, the applications for the medium have remained quite constant. The Internet has created new opportunities that are still being explored.

Basically there are two disciplines in teleservices: outbound and inbound calling. Outbound is very much proactive while inbound is reactive. Both have applications in consumer and the business-to-business markets. Regardless of the discipline used, the objectives are very similar. The following list demonstrates the basic objectives for using teleservices:

- Sell a product

- Take an order

- Generate leads

- Qualify leads

- Market research

- Up-sell

- Cross-sell

- Political campaigns

- Fund-raising

- Subscriptions and renewals

- Loyalty programs

- Account management

- Customer retention

- Customer relationship management (CRM)

- Customer win-back

This list is not meant to be all-inclusive for teleservices. New applications are being developed on a regular basis. Teleservices was introduced as a way to increase response rates for direct mail; today it survives and thrives on its own, as well as when used with other media. Teleservices continues to be a medium that produces measurable results in a very short period of time, which is what separates it from most other media.

Inbound Teleservices

Inbound teleservices may be the area most profoundly impacted by the Internet. Industry is now gearing up for a world in which customers and businesses communicate through a whole host of media, often simultaneously. In order to serve customers better, companies must seamlessly integrate these contact points. Call centers that once focused on receiving inbound telephone calls are positioning themselves to respond to e-mails, voicemail telemarketing, participate in Web chat requests, and respond to "call me" or "Live Help" buttons now appearing on E-commerce Web sites. These "customer contact centers" are investing heavily in technology that facilitates contacts in many media.

Inbound telephone calls are still the medium of choice for many consumers. Calls are usually generated from a catalog, an infomercial, direct mail, e-mail, blogs, Web sites, or a print ad. Customers like this discipline because they have full control. They decide when to place the call, already have some idea of the product or service offered, and normally do not need to be sold on the product being featured. Ads often use terms such as: "Act Now" . . . "Operators are Standing By" . . . "You Have Ten Minutes to Call" . . . and of course, "Hurry before it's Too Late." All of these phrases convey a sense of urgency because chances are the prospect will not order if the call is not made shortly after reading or viewing the material.

While the customer is on the phone is an excellent time to offer other pieces of equipment. This "add-on" sale is a great way to increase the revenue of the basic sale using low-pressure selling tactics. Most inbound telemarketing centers have the technology to suggest additional products based upon the original order. If a customer is ordering golf clubs, the computer may trigger a question about also ordering golf balls. Another successful add-on technique is to offer a phone special after taking the phoned-in order. This technique, on average, will add one additional sale for every ten people who order by phone.

The consumer who enjoys shopping by catalog expects the convenience of ordering via a toll-free number. Catalogs will normally present their toll-free number on every page as well as on the cover.

Teleservices can be classified into domestic and international, or offshore providers. Some of the better-known agencies that appeared in the *Customer Interactions Solutions* magazine Top 50 Teleservices Agencies Award in 2006 are shown in Exhibit 14–1.

Exhibit 14–2 is an example of how InfoCision Management Corp. advertises its services. What better way for a company in telemarketing to advertise! The representatives for any business who perform telemarketing activities must be prepared to discuss the advantages of their program and attempt to close the sale on the phone.

A very widespread use of inbound teleservices can be found in Exhibit 14–3. Dealer locator programs are very beneficial to the consumer because most of these calls are handled with some type of automatic attendant service. By entering a ZIP code on the touchpad of the phone, the computer identifies the pharmacy closest

---

EXHIBIT 14–1

Customer Interactions Solution Magazine Top 50 Teleservices Agencies Award 2006

CATEGORY A	CATEGORY B — INTERNATIONAL	CATEGORY C — GLOBAL TOP 50 RANKING, AGGREGATE INBOUND & OUTBOUND, DOMESTIC & INTERNATIONAL
3. InfoCision Management Corp. Ph: 330-668-1400; Fx: 330-668-1401 http//www.infocision.com Year began providing teleservices: 1982 Size of projects accepted: Minimum 500 hours Type of calling: B-to-B: 14%; B-to-C: 86% Outbound: 84%; Inbound: 15%; Interactive Inbound: 1% Specialization: political, non-profit and religious fundraising, product/service sales and customer care, volunteer recruitment	1. SR. Teleperformance Ph: +33 155764080; Fx: +33 155764081 http//www.srteleperformance.com Year began providing teleservices: 1978 Size of projects accepted: Minimum varies Type of calling: B-to-B: 20%; B-to-C: 80% Outbound: 31%; Inbound: 64%; Interactive Inbound: 5% Specialization: outsourced CRM services, debt collection, technical support	

Source: Customer Inter@actions Solutions magazine - "Top 50 Teleservices Agencies Award 2006," published in the March 2006 edition.

EXHIBIT 14–2

InfoCision Print Ad

If you value your customers...

...why do you keep them ON HOLD?

With InfoCision, they won't be. We answer your calls quickly and develop a lasting relationship with your customers. A few minutes on the phone with InfoCision means a lifetime of customer loyalty for you.

9 seconds
Average time to answer all inbound calls.

92 percent
Percent of all inbound calls answered in 20 seconds or less.

3 percent
Overall percent of all inbound calls abandoned.

iiC:: InfoCision
THE highest quality call center company in the world!*

877-893-3618
www.infocision.com

*InfoCision is the only teleservice company to win the MVP Quality Award (presented by *Customer Interaction Solutions* magazine) all 12 years since its inception.

Shoe Carnival Newspaper Locator Ad

to the caller's location. For the company, this requires updated technology, but little if any personal interface.

Outbound Teleservices

Outbound business-to-business calling is the fastest growing segment of the teleservices industry. One reason for this is the continued increase in the cost of making face-to-face sales calls. Companies seek new methods of contacting prospects and existing customers in a more cost-effective manner. Outbound is completely controllable in that it usually has a set number of people to contact and a calling window that establishes a definite end date. It can be used alone or in combination with other direct marketing media.

Outbound teleservices is also preparing itself for new technological applications. Already, companies are trying to determine how to stay in touch with customers who forgo "land lines" altogether in favor of cellular telephones. Under what terms and conditions may a company contact cellular customers, who often pay for every incoming call and may answer the phone in places where it is simply not possible to conduct a conversation with a telephone sales representative? How will outbound telemarketers be affected by the emerging Voice Over Internet Protocol (VOIP) technology, or by communications appliances that transfer voice, data, and video? The answers will emerge as new technologies are adapted.

The List is the Most Important Element

A successful outbound program depends upon four basic elements, all of which must be analyzed prior to the implementation of the program. They are:

- List or target audience
- Offer being communicated
- Telephone sales representative
- Script or message to be communicated

Of these four elements, the list is the most important. Says Rich Simms, Development Manager of DialAmerica, "If a list is well targeted, a promotion can still be successful even if the product is less than terrific, the script is weak, the Telephone Sales Representatives (TSRs) are not top-notch, and fulfillment is inefficient." The reverse is also true: a poorly targeted list can doom a great product, script, TSR force, and fulfillment.

A name is not just a name as it once was. Companies using teleservices want to know as much as possible about the names about to be called—both demographics and psychographics. The best list to call is existing customers, because they have already demonstrated that they will buy the product. Now the only question is whether they will buy over the phone.

Companies can no longer succeed with prospect lists that are not a close match to customer list profiles. Modeling programs have to be developed. The result of this sophisticated approach is less calling and better results. Research is now being implemented to determine if the characteristics of a phone buyer are the same as the direct mail customer. Sounds simple, but the industry is very concerned about calling individuals who have little if any likelihood of purchasing the product being marketed.

Most credit card issuers rely heavily on outbound teleservices for ongoing acquisition programs. The typical list is a preapproved audience. The screening process eliminates those individuals with poor credit ratings. Since "list" is one of the most important criteria in a successful program, it is easy to observe that preapproved prospects increase the chances for success.

The offer is usually a short-term, very low interest rate that includes balance transfers from other credit cards as well as current purchases. After the introductory interest rate expires, the interest rate increases to a competitive rate. The goal of the credit card companies is to get the new customer to transfer balances or even cancel other cards, leaving their card as the customer's card of choice. On this type of program, a teleservice representative is able to contact approximately 14–16 decision makers in an hour. In that hour of calling, a normal sales-per-hour rate of 0.75 to 1.0 would be expected. This response rate far exceeds a similar direct mail program with the same offer.

Using Outbound to Qualify Leads

Companies with a field sales force have discovered a unique application for outbound teleservices: generating sales leads. In any given mail response, some responses are very "hot" leads while others are just looking for information. There is a big difference between a generated and a qualified lead. One phone call by a screener gets rid of the "suspects" and identifies the real.

Most salespeople do not like to "prospect" or spend time on the phone because they feel they are more effective when they can see the body language of their prospects. A leading insurance company supplies its sales force with leads on a weekly basis. Over the past two years, each sales representative has received an average of seven to ten leads per week, which produce far more sales than "cold" calls.

The phone is quick and a phone representative is able to make more contacts in a given morning than a sales representative can make face-to-face in a week.

But leads can cool quickly if the lead-generation program outpaces the ability of the sales force to turn leads into business (See Chapter 9 for a discussion of managing lead flow to avoid this problem). In a study of its inbound 800 customer contact centers, which generated leads for its value-added resellers, Xerox discovered that the life of its leads was a mere three hours! To avoid losing sales, Xerox required its VAR sales representatives to place follow-up calls within three hours and notify Xerox that the contact had occurred. If three hours passed without confirmation from the VAR, Xerox retrieved the lead and had an in-house sales rep place the follow-up call.

Using Outbound Teleservices for Market Research

Market research can be as simple as a follow-up to attending a seminar or as complex as a 20-minute telephone survey. Nissan and Subaru, who pride themselves on customer follow-up, send a survey to all new car buyers with a follow-up call if necessary. They are most interested in learning the customer's perceptions about their dealer, and the manner in which the selling process took place. Their data is collected, analyzed, and a Dealer of the Year is identified. Many automobile dealers will call their service customers one week after a car is serviced. These dealers are looking for information that will result in providing better service to the customer.

Outbound Business-to-Business

Outbound business-to-business teleservice opportunities far exceed those of the consumer market. In the business sector, the telephone is an acceptable way to do business. Very often companies decide to use manual dialing as opposed to predictive or power dialing because businesses will answer the phone, thus eliminating the need for costly equipment.

Some companies will use an existing customer list to call, while others may purchase a list of businesses that match their requirements. In either case, it may be more difficult to reach the decision maker.

Business calling tends to be more account management as opposed to direct sales. The typical outbound call to a consumer is a one-time call that results in a decision to buy or not. In business calling, it is more important to develop a rapport with the decision maker and periodically make calls where no sale is attempted. An outbound representative should be able to manage approximately 400 accounts on a monthly basis. It is a more relaxed environment than the consumer-calling unit.

The key to successful customer relationship management is a commitment from the company to continue the program. It should not be done on a short-term test basis, because it will take some time for customers to appreciate regular contacts from the company. A minimum amount of time to test the concept would be one year. In that year, a teleservice representative should be able to contact each account a minimum of four to five times. This will provide the marketing department with ample statistics to make an intelligent business decision. One method of analyzing this activity is to survey your customer base and obtain feedback from them. Perception is reality and if the customer feels the regular contact is beneficial, then it must be considered a positive.

American Hotel Register markets to the hospitality market. Its primary marketing vehicle is a catalog with thousands of products. Initially AHR designed and implemented an inbound order-taking department, which was so successful it was expanded to more than 64 workstations. Although successful, AHR felt it was still missing business opportunities.

AHR acquired a consultant who designed an outbound customer contact program that centered around making "warm and fuzzy" phone calls. The program was designed to introduce the customer contact representative during the first calls and ultimately to feature items on sale. For specific products such as light bulbs, ironing boards, and in-room safes, the department sold more of these products in a month than had been sold in the past year. Today, the department has expanded and the customer contact program is generating record sales.

Hiring: The Lifeblood of the Call Center

Datamonitor research forecasts big growth in the number of Brazil-based contact center agents serving offshore customers. The 2006 report predicts the number of agents will rise from 3,900 in 2005 to 11,500 in 2010. Datamonitor expects demand for service based in Brazil from U.S. companies to grow at a compound annual growth rate (CAGR) of 27 percent between 2005 and 2010, compared to 21 percent from other regions.

When compared to a call center in the domestic market, a center in an offshore location like India saves a U.S. company approximately 25–35 percent per transaction—significant savings. However, a call serviced through speech automation costs approximately 15–25 percent of the cost of a call handled by an agent in India.

The success of a call center, whether it is a vendor or an in-house operation, depends upon the individual on the phone. Companies are spending large amounts of money in developing "training" programs, but few are doing anything about the selection process. Some just accept the fact that there is high turnover, and plan for it. When selecting a location for a service station or restaurant, the secret is: "location, location, location." In teleservice, the secret to longevity of representatives is: "selection, selection, selection."

A phone representative must have three attributes:

- Verbal communication skills

- Ability to read a script or call guide with enthusiasm

- Willingness to overcome objections

While there are a number of other attributes that the rep must possess, if these three are present, then the training job becomes much easier. Instead of investing major amounts in training programs, the bulk of the human resources (HR) budget should be spent on the selection process. If a better method is found for hiring people who will stay longer, then the investment has been more than worth it.

One suggestion to improve the hiring process is to require two phone interviews prior to having a personal interview. During these two interviews, the HR specialist should be able to determine the following:

- Communication skills of the individual—can I understand her or him with little if any difficulty?

- Ability to read a script—this is done by sending out a script that is to be read during the second interview.

- Willingness to follow directions—the HR specialist should ask the candidate to call on a specific day and time.

Each of these steps will go a long way in determining if a candidate is taking your time or if you have a very good candidate. This process also eliminates the initial "first impression" that a candidate normally makes at an in-person interview.

An additional method for improving selection is by administering a written test to candidates who are given a personal interview. Some companies have developed their own test that parallels the skill sets they seek. The more objective steps, the better the rep. Companies should also take the time to check references in writing. Most will not respond to a telephone interview. However, a great deal of information can be gotten in a conversation.

Once the individual has been hired, the real screening process begins. The trainer is responsible for "washing out" inappropriate new hires that happened to get by the recruiter. The trainer may miss a few, because he or she has been told to fill the seats. So the ultimate responsibility falls on the supervisor. If a company pays attention to the selection process and uses the training and coaching periods to eliminate those who should not remain, then a significant improvement in retention should take place.

Research shows that the skill sets for an outbound caller are not the same as the inbound representative. However, with ever-changing technology, the skill sets necessary to do either job will become more advanced. Outbound calling requires individuals who have little if any concern about hearing people say "no" on the phone. The majority of outbound calls, sometimes as high as 95 percent, will result in a "not interested" response. Rather than take it personally, the representative must be ready to take the next call with as much personality and expression as the first call.

Other ways to combat representative turnover are:

1. Develop a career path that is attainable and one that others have followed.

2. Show the new representative that the company really cares whether he or she is successful through the use of coaching, monitoring, and critiquing.

3. Make the call center a fun place to work by implementing games, contests, and other motivational devices.

4. Move representatives from one program to another in order to eliminate staleness or boredom.

5. Develop competition between different call centers or within calling groups.

Call center representatives do want to succeed. They need constant reinforcement that their performance is vital to the success of the company. Implementation of the above ideas should go a long way to reduce turnover.

Scripting

Using a script does not suppress the personality of the representative or place the representative in a straightjacket. In the early '90s, verbatim scripting was the only type of script allowed in the call center. Today, unless the outbound calling is being conducted in a regulated industry, a call guide will generally produce results that exceed the verbatim.

Insurance and investment calling requires a verbatim approach because creative material has to be approved both by the client's legal staff as well as the Commissioner of Insurance's office. In the case of a credit card solicitation, a portion of the verbal authorization must be read verbatim in order to meet the requirements set forth by Truth and Lending regulations.

Call guides are prevalent in the business segment because they are well suited for consultative selling, which requires the representative to discuss various products as well as past purchases with the customer. A genuine rapport must be developed and it can only be done through conversation. The goal is to make the call so pleasant that the customer does not look at it as a sales call.

A conversational, flexible approach works well when services such as credit cards are being promoted. When a prospect indicates that there is no interest in a credit card, it is important to identify the reason why there is no interest. This is done by asking basic questions such as, "Is that because you are already carrying other credit cards?"

Most of the time, the prospect doesn't want another credit card for that reason. At this time, the representative has to find one feature of the credit card that would change the prospect's mind. This has to be done at the option of the representative as opposed to verbatim scripting. Perhaps the question would be, "Are you currently using cards that have an annual interest higher than 10 percent?" Or, "Do you use your cards when you travel?" Each question is directed to create a conversation that will lead to some indication that the credit card may in fact be a good one for the prospect. If there is a second "not interested," then it is in good taste to terminate the conversation.

Most sales in outbound teleservices are made after the prospect has given an initial response of "not interested." This has been researched and the results indicate that it is the same reaction when a salesperson in a retail store asks: "May I help you?" The knee-jerk reaction is "No thank you, I am just looking." On the phone, most people are really not concentrating on what is being said. If they can get off by replying "I'm not interested," they can avoid getting involved in the conversation. After the first "not interested," the representative has approximately 20 seconds to create interest or the possibility of making a sale is very remote.

One final point: keep in mind that scripts can be modified in one day and the entire presentation can be quickly changed if results aren't successful.

The Mathematics of Telemarketing

The power of telemarketing is beyond question. Its place in the totality of direct marketing is firmly established. But the mathematics of telemarketing is not clearly understood by many. For starters, the telephone is the most expensive advertising medium on a per-thousand basis after face-to-face selling. So telemarketing has to be very cost-effective to be successful and for thousands of marketers, it is.

Inbound/Outbound Costs

Two sets of numbers are key to estimating telemarketing costs:

- Cost per call for handling *inbound* calls from business firms and consumers

- Cost per decision-maker contact in making *outbound* calls to business firms and consumers.

Exhibit 14–4 provides the range of costs for each.

The difference in cost range between inbound and outbound calls should be explained. In the case of inbound calls, the initiator is always a prospect or customer; the caller phones at a time of his or her convenience with a view of getting further information or negotiating an order. In the case of outbound calls, the initiator is always the marketer. The call might be made at an inconvenient time for the prospect and the caller might have to generate awareness about a new product or service. Consequently, outbound calls are usually of longer duration, and often require more experienced, higher-paid personnel.

The range of costs, whether for inbound or outbound, depends a great deal on the telemarketing application and the complexity involved for each application.

EXHIBIT 14–4

Per-Call Costs for Inbound and Outbound Calls

Category	Range of Cost
Inbound	
Business	$2.50–7.00
Consumer	1.50–3.00
Outbound	
Business	$6.00–16.00
Consumer	1.15–4.00

EXHIBIT 14–5

Range of Costs by Application

Application	Low Range	Mid Range	High Range
Order processing	×		
Order increase		×	
Customer service		×	
Sales support		×	
Account management			×
Sales			×
Sales promotion	×		

Exhibit 14–5 indicates where ranges of costs are most likely to fall, on average, by application.

Developing Worksheets

Knowing the average range of costs for inbound and outbound calls is key, but it is just a start. The operation of an in-house telemarketing center requires a full range of personnel. Also, it is subject to taxes, fringe benefit costs, incentive costs, equipment costs, and collateral materials costs. To get a true picture of all monthly costs, worksheets are advised.

Two worksheets are provided (Exhibits 14–6 and 14–7): one for inbound and one for outbound. It is important to note that the term *phone hour* means workstation time, *not* connect time.

It is easy to see how worksheets lead to capturing all the numbers. The key numbers to explore are:

1. Cost per phone hour

2. Cost per call

3. Cost per order (or response)

A review of the computations for Exhibit 14–6 (inbound) shows a significant difference in cost, for example, when phone representatives are able to handle 15 incoming calls per phone hour as contrasted to 12 calls per phone hour. The cost per order drops dramatically if the representative is able to close six orders per phone hour, for example, as contrasted to one order per phone hour.

In Exhibit 14–7 (outbound), similar significant differences are to be noted in costs at different levels relating to total dialings per phone hour, total decision-maker contacts per phone hour, and total orders per phone hour. Such computations provide a realistic approach to determine break-even point.

EXHIBIT 14-6

Monthly Expense Statement, Inbound: 9:00 A.M. to 5:00 P.M.

Direct Expenses	Cost	Cost/Phone Hour
Labor		
Manager (⅓ time)[a]	$ 1,250	$ 1.01
Supervisor (full time)[b]	2,750	2.23
Representatives[c] (10 @ 123.5 hours/month)[d]	16,000	12.96
Administrator (full time)[e]	1,213	0.98
Incentives (reps only)	2,000	1.62
Tax and benefits[f]	7,730	6.25
Subtotal	$30,943	$25.05
Phone		
Equipment and service[g]	$ 1,146	$ 0.93
WATS line[h]	7,770	6.29
MTS (Message Toll Service) line	—	—
Subtotal	$ 8,919	$ 7.22
Automation		
Depreciation[i]	$ 2,500	$ 2.02
Maintenance[j]	750	0.61
Subtotal	$ 3,250	$ 2.63
Other		
Lists	—	—
Mail/catalogs (F/S & result of requests)	$ 2,470	$ 2.00
Postage	1,235	1.00
Miscellaneous	1,000	.81
Subtotal	$ 4,705	$ 3.81
Total direct expenses	$47,814	$38,72
G&A (15%)	7,172	5.81
Total	$54,986	$44.53

[a] $45,000/year × ⅓ allocation = $1,250/month
[b] $33,000/year × full allocation = $2,750/month
[c] $9.23/hour × 40 hours/week × 52 weeks ÷ 12 months = $1,600/month
[d] 6.5 phone hours/day × 19 days/month = 123.5 phone hours/month
[e] ($7.00/hour × 40 hours/week × 52 weeks) ÷ 12 months = $1,213/month
[f] 33.3% of wages (including contest incentives)
[g] $50,000 depreciated over 5 years ÷ $3,750 annual maintenance
[h] Average 40 min. (60%) per labor hour. WATS connect time: 40 min. × $0.15/min. avg. cost ÷ access charges for 10 lines
[i] $6,000 per work station for 15 stations (additional for growth) depreciated over three years
[j] 10% of total purchase cost

Note: The average number of calls handled per rep. phone hour is 12 @ 3.1 min. each (as high as 15 per phone hour during peaks).

- 12 calls/hour = $3.71/call
- 15 calls/hour = $2.97/call
- 1 order/rep phone hour = $44.52/order
- 6 orders/rep phone hour = $7.42/order

EXHIBIT 14-7

Monthly Expense Statement, Outbound: 9:00 A.M. to 5:00 P.M.

Direct Expense	Cost	Cost/Phone Hour
Labor		
Manager (1/3 time)[a]	$ 1,500	$ 1.21
Supervisor (full time)[b]	3,000	2.43
Representatives[c] (10 @ 123.5 hours/month)[d]	18,000	14.57
Administrator (2 full time)[e]	2,426	1.96
Commissions[f]	12,529	10.14
Tax and benefits[g]	12,473	10.10
Subtotal	$49,928	$40.41
Phone		
Equipment and service	$ 350	$ 0.28
WATS line[h]	4,991	4.04
MTS (Message Toll Service) line[i]	1,112	0.90
Subtotal	$ 6,103	$ 4.94
Automation		
Depreciation[j]	$ 3,542	$ 2.87
Maintenance[k]	1,063	0.86
Subtotal	$ 4,605	$ 3.73
Other		
Lists	$ 3,088	$ 2.50
Mail/catalogs	617	0.50
Postage	358	0.29
Miscellaneous	1,235	1.00
Subtotal	$ 5,298	$ 4.29
Total expenses	$65,924	$53,39
G&A (15%)	9,890	8.00
Total	$75,824	$61.39

[a] $54,000/year × 1/3 allocation = $1,500/month
[b] $36,000/year × full allocation = $3,000/month
[c] $10.38/hour × 40 hours/week × 52 weeks ÷ 12 months = $1,799/month
[d] 6.5 phone hours/day × 19 days/month = 123.5 phone hours/month
[e] ($7.00/hour × 40 hours/week × 52 weeks) ÷ 12 months = $1,213/month
[f] Reps, 40% of total remuneration; supervisor, 15% of total remuneration
[g] 33.3% of wages
[h] 23 min. per labor hour. WATS connect time: 25 min. × $9.15/min. ÷ access charges for 10 lines
[i] 5 min. per labor hour. Connect time: 5 min. × $0.18/min.
[j] $8,500 per work station for 15 stations (additional for growth) depreciated over three years
[k] 10% of total purchase cost

- 12 (TDs)/hour = $5.12/dial
- 15 (TDs)/hour = $4.09/dial
- 5 (DMCs)/hour = $12.28/DMC
- 6 (DMCs)/hour = $10.23/DMC
- 1 order/rep phone hour = $61.39/order
- 2 orders/rep phone hour = $30.67/order

These two worksheets relate to the sale of products or services, but the same type of arithmetic can help predict likely costs for literature requests, product information, customer service calls, sales support, full account management, or sales promotion. The calls handled or made per phone hour might vary by application, but the principles are the same.

Telephone Sales Rules and the "Do Not Call" Registry

The high volume of calls to consumers has made many people very sensitive to receiving calls at home. Telemarketing is obtrusive, one of the reasons for its success as a medium. Federal and state regulators have passed legislation in an effort to "police" the industry, resulting in a host of state and federal provisions that outbound telemarketers must comply with.

For example, telemarketers and sellers may only call consumers between 8 A.M. and 9 P.M. Telemarketers must promptly identify themselves as a seller and explain that they are making a sales call before pitching a product or service.

Automatic dialing equipment, which is commonly used by telemarketers, spurred rules regarding call abandonment. These rules allow each call to a consumer's telephone to ring for at least 15 seconds or four rings before disconnecting. They require each call to be connected to a sales representative within two seconds of the consumer's greeting, or, if a sales representative is not available, the marketer must play a recorded message stating the name and telephone number of the seller. The message cannot include a sales pitch. Marketers must maintain records that prove their call abandonment rate is 3 percent or less. Automatic dialing equipment may not be used for calling cell phones.

The most important change for telemarketers came in October 2003, when the FTC and FCC revised their telemarketing sales rules under the Telephone Consumer Protection Act (TCPA), and created a federal "Do Not Call" registry. According to the FTC, at the end of fiscal 2005, more than 107 million consumers had registered phone numbers on the "Do Not Call" (DNC) database. The DNC list only covers residential phone numbers.

Consumer numbers remain on the registry for five years until the consumer asks for the number to be removed or changes phone numbers. Consumers must renew their registration every five years. This will create a window of opportunity beginning in 2008, when the earliest numbers on the DNC will "expire," and need to be renewed.

The telemarketing sales rules require significant compliance measures by telemarketers. Telemarketers and sellers are required to register with FTC and certify that their organization is in compliance with all telemarketing laws. In addition, they are required to search the registry at least quarterly and drop from their call lists the phone numbers of consumers who have registered.

There are exceptions to the rules. Marketers can call consumers where they have an existing business relationship, within 18 months of a transaction (i.e., purchase, delivery or payment). They may contact numbers where there has been a consumer inquiry within three months. They may call numbers where they have written permission to call.

Notably, charities, tax-exempt nonprofit organizations, political campaigns, surveys, and polls are also exempt from the DNC requirements; however, callers must identify themselves and the organization that they are working for. Phone companies, airlines, insurance companies, and some financial institutions are also exempt. Calls to businesses, while exempt from DNC, are still covered under the FTC Act, which prohibits unfair and deceptive business practices.

If a consumer asks a company not to call, the company may not call, even if there is an established business relationship. No organization may call a consumer—regardless of whether the consumer's number is on the registry—if the consumer has asked to be put on the company's "do not call" list.

In general, calls made within a state (intrastate) do not fall within the federal DNC, although the calls must follow other rules of the Telephone Consumer Protection Act. According to the DMA, 40 states have passed their own "Do Not Call" laws and list programs. Some are more restrictive than the federal DNC rules governing telemarketing calls between states (interstate). While many states have their own No Call lists, some have merged their list with the national DNC list. Marketers choosing to call within states need to double-check the rules within its local jurisdiction.

Marketers must pay fees to access the DNC for cleaning their lists. As of this writing, the fee is $56 per area code, up to $15,400 for 280 area codes or more. While expecting compliance, the FTC has not overlooked the budget constraints of small, local marketers, retailers, and agents. Under current regulations, the first five area codes requested are free.

Telemarketing sales rules are constantly changing. Exemptions change, state regulations change, fees change, and new rules are added. A recent provision requires telemarketers to transmit their telephone number and, if possible, their name to consumers' caller ID services. There are significant fines and penalties for violations, and there have been a number of enforcement actions. Under regulations at this writing, calling a number that is on the federal DNC register can yield a fine of $11,000 per call. So, it is important for marketers to monitor both federal and state rules for compliance and updates.

Advantages and Disadvantages of Telemarketing/Teleservices

According to the DMA 2006 Response Rate Trends Report, among the highlights and observations about the medium of telephone, it produced the highest response rates for direct marketers whose primary objectives were to generate leads and traffic building. The report stated that telephone and mail continued to serve as the leading response media channels in 2006 as they did in the previous year with an outstanding 31.3 percent and 36.6 percent, respectively.

The DMA compiled a list of the "Top Ten Reasons to Protect and Promote the U.S. Teleservices Industry." Job creation tops the list.

- Provides flexible employment to more than 6 million people.

- Call centers are generally located in small and rural communities—the median population of a town with a call center is 23,000.

- For nonprofit organizations, telephone solicitation is the single most successful solicitation tool.

- Teleservices jobs create opportunities for women, minorities, working mothers, students, part-time workers, and people with disabilities.

- Consumer teleservices professionals can earn more than $12 per hour, on average, with base pay and commissions. Business-to-business representatives can earn more.

- Fifty-one of the 91 urban or rural enterprise zones in the United States have call center businesses.

In his article "Call Centers Are Changing Lives," Rich Tehrani, Group Editor-in-Chief for Technology Marketing Corporation, points out that call centers have been used for admirable activities such as "coordinating life-saving organ transplants, blood drives and fund-raising for virtually all the top charities. More recently, call centers have been responsible for adding jobs to regions of the country and world where jobs were once scarce."

However, outsourcing telemarketing services to foreign countries, while cheaper, is not without controversy. According to the Web site BuyerZone.com and its Telemarketing (Outbound) Buyer's Guide, your choice of provider can affect your corporate image. Choose an offshore provider and some customers may regard it as being un-American, akin to sending U.S. manufacturing jobs to foreign plants. There is also the simple matter of communications. Hard-to-understand accents or cultural differences make it difficult to build a rapport between a foreign telemarketer and a U.S. customer.

According to BuyerZone.com (see Exhibit 14–8), you can reduce some of the risk and still lock in "significant cost savings by choosing providers whose call centers are in the Caribbean, Canada, or other locations where accents are not as strong and English commonly spoken. In places where English is not the first language, products with simple sales cycles and highly structured sales scripts can be easier for telemarketing agents to follow." Tim Searcy, Executive Director of the American Teleservices Association (ATA), stated in 2005 that "India and Canada are the two largest locations where people are doing outsourcing," while he also reaffirmed that he knew of about 60 companies with 87,000 telemarketers in India.

EXHIBIT 14-8

BuyerZone.com Web Page

BuyerZone.com

View all categories | Help

Get FREE Outbound Telemarketing Quotes from Multiple Firms

▷ Describe your needs, get matched with multiple qualified telemarketing companies

▷ Get quotes for telemarketing campaigns targeting businesses, consumers, and/or non-profits

▷ It's FREE and easy to use. Start a request now.

How It Works

1. Complete this simple and FREE quote request form
2. Receive customized price quotes
3. Select the best solutions for your needs - save time and money

Featured Suppliers

TeleContact Resource Services

TeleLeaders

CCS

Create your telemarketing services (outbound) Request for Quotes
[Number of Questions: 11 ~ Average time to complete: 1 min, 20 sec]

1) What are the primary objectives of your telemarketing campaign? [required]
(please check all that apply)

☐ Sell products or services
☐ Generate and qualify leads
☐ Clean and update lists
☐ Schedule appointments
☐ Perform research or surveys
☐ Announce an event
☐ Register people for an event
☐ Fundraise
☐ Other (please specify):
[_____]

Please note: Our telemarketing companies cannot accept requests for solely commission-based or "pay-per performance" telemarketing campaigns.

If you have call center needs not listed here (such as inbound call center services or call center software) please visit our Call Center & Telemarketing Solutions page for more information.

2) Is this request for a one-time campaign or do you plan to run multiple telemarketing campaigns over time? [required]

○ One-time campaign
○ One-time campaign that may lead to further telemarketing efforts
○ Multiple campaigns

3) When do you want to start this telemarketing campaign? [required]

○ ASAP
○ In two weeks
○ In one month
○ More than two months

4) Who are you primarily targeting with this campaign? [required]

○ Small businesses (less than 100 employees)
○ Medium-sized businesses (100 to 1,000 employees)
○ Large businesses (more than 1,000 employees)
○ Non-profit organizations
○ Consumers or private residents
○ Other

5) How many outbound prospects would you like to contact during this telemarketing campaign? [required]

○ Not sure
○ 1 to 1,499
○ 1,500 to 4,999
○ 5,000 to 9,999
○ 10,000 to 49,999
○ 50,000+

6) What is the primary geographic area you are targeting for this telemarketing campaign? [required]

○ Within one town or city
○ Within one state
○ Within a small group of states
○ National
○ Not sure

Buyer's Guide

Read our in-depth telemarketing firms buyer's guide:

- Introduction
- Reasons to outsource
- Preparing your search
- The offshore debate
- Evaluating firms
- Comparing call centers
- Telemarketing success
- Pricing
- Buying tips

All telemarketing advice...

About BuyerZone

BuyerZone is the leading online marketplace for business purchasing.

- Founded in 1992
- 1,000,000+ users
- 50,000+ monthly requests
- 7,000+ active suppliers

In The Headlines

USA TODAY

"BuyerZone is the sort of site that the Internet seems designed for... an amazing service."

USA Today

Featured Suppliers

- TeleContact
- TeleLeaders
- Customer Contact

Related Categories

- Call Center Services
- Promotional Products
- Web Conferencing
- Conference Calling
- Remote Data Backup

Additional Categories

- Alarm Systems
- Conferencing Service
- Copier Leasing
- Electronic Medical Billing
- Employee Leasing Companies
- Employee Time Clocks
- Corporate Event Planning
- Folding Machines
- Multi-line Phone System
- Restaurant POS Systems
- Used Copiers

All of our categories...

Supplier Program

Do you sell **Telemarketing Services** or other business products or services?

CASE STUDY: CMA Ontario Telemarketing Campaigns

Contributed by Greenfield Services, Inc., based in Alexandria, Ontario.

BACKGROUND

The Certified Management Accountants of Ontario (CMA) is a self-governing professional organization that awards the Certified Management Accountant (CMA) designation to qualified candidates in Ontario. Of CMA Canada's 47,000 members across Canada and around the world, 20,000 members call Ontario home.

The first path to become a CMA is to graduate from a CMA–Masters combined program offered in partnership with five Ontario University Business Schools (Ivey, Laurier, Queen's, Rotman, and Waterloo). Candidates undertaking their CMA through this path are deemed University Associate Members.

The second path is for Workforce Members who register for the CMA Executive Program. In this path, university graduates submit their transcript for evaluation, to ensure completion of CMA's requisite topics.

Candidates who do not meet the requirements may choose to pursue missing credits on their own or may enroll in the CMA's seven-month Accelerated Program, which is designed to prepare candidates to write the entrance exam. Upon passing the entrance exam, CMA candidates begin an intense two-year Strategic Leadership Program, and are expected to continue earning practical experience at the same time.

Because of the significant investment in both time and financial resources, the decision to undertake the CMA route is not one that is taken lightly. Workforce candidates often remain registered with the association for a number of years as they go back to school to acquire missing credits, write the entrance exam, and go through the Strategic Leadership Program.

CMA Ontario faces stiff competition from university MBA programs, as well as the other accounting designations such as Chartered Accountant (CA) and Chartered General Accountant (CGA).

CHALLENGE

In the summer of 2003, CMA Ontario was faced with flat Accelerated Program enrollment. While it boasted a sizable database of Workforce Candidates, this database had not been regularly maintained. The Accreditation Department was responsible for updating candidate information but it was fully consumed with the day-to-day demands of information fulfillment, transcript evaluations, as well as exam and course registrations.

While undeliverable records from mailings were removed from the candidate database, the Accreditation Department did not have the manpower to proactively cleanse the database of records for people who were no longer interested in pursuing their CMA. Because they were so busy answering incoming telephone inquiries and processing applications, there was no time to proactively engage candidates and persuade them to take the necessary steps.

Consequently, CMA Ontario enlisted the help of Greenfield Services, Inc., an outbound teleservices and business development firm dedicated to the needs of professional and trade associations.

SOLUTION

Working closely with the CMA Ontario Marketing Department, the outbound teleservices organization devised a calling program with script targeted to each of the following candidate segments:

1. Candidates who had met the educational requirements to write the exam immediately.
2. Candidates lacking just a few credits and thus eligible for the Accelerated Program.
3. Candidates lacking a substantial number of credits that could not be redressed through the Accelerated Program and thus requiring a return to school.

CASE STUDY: CMA Ontario Telemarketing Campaigns *(Continued)*

4. Candidates who had shown an interest in obtaining a CMA in the past, but who never completed a transcript evaluation, and thus whose status was unknown.

CMA's proprietary database system could not provide direct, live access to the outbound teleservices agents without custom programming and additional costs. Timing was also of the essence; CMA needed to proceed with the calls quickly.

The decision was made to export data from the CMA system into MS-Excel and import it into Greenfield's system. The data was sorted according to each candidate segment, matching the different scripts. All data contained the CMA client ID, full contact information, including name, home and/or business address, as well as phone numbers.

Calls were scheduled to take place three weeks after the entrance exam and Accelerated Program registration mailings, and a full four weeks prior to the registration deadlines. This would allow candidates enough time to respond, thus avoiding calls to early registrants.

Before the start of calls, care was taken to remove candidates who had already contacted the Accreditation Department or registered for the exam or Accelerated Program. Each subsequent day during the calling campaign the updated list of registrants was forwarded to Greenfield to minimize the possibility of initiating contact with a candidate who had already responded.

Copies of all mailing materials were shared with telephone agents and intense training took place prior to the start of calls. The objective was to sound professional and knowledgeable, as an extension of the CMA Accreditation Department.

Upon connection, agents ascertained receipt of the mailed information, advised candidates of upcoming deadlines for the entrance exam (for segment 1 above), and Accelerated Program (segment 2) and encouraged them to register. For segment 3, agents explained the need to pursue the required courses, often "smoothing out" the ruffled feathers

of those who had to go back to school to earn the requisites. With segment 4, individuals were encouraged to complete and return their transcript evaluation to initiate the process.

In all cases, agents verified the contact information on file, and added secondary phone numbers (cell phone numbers) and e-mail addresses as required. Agents attempted to contact each candidate up to three times, often at different contact numbers or at different times of the day or evening. If a connection did not occur on the third attempt, a personalized voicemail based on the preapproved script was left with the appropriate call to action.

While calls were being made, agents corrected mailing information and looked up incorrect phone numbers on www.canada411.com, www.411.ca, and/or www.google.com.

Through the calls, the outbound teleservices company's agents proactively answered questions that otherwise could have bogged down the Accreditation Department. Whenever requested, transcript evaluation forms, Accelerated Program and exam registration forms were faxed or e-mailed to candidates directly through the database system interface.

RESULTS

In the first full year of telemarketing, a total of 7,169 CMA candidates were contacted. The total project required almost 900 calling hours, something that never could have been achieved with existing CMA Ontario staff resources.

An MS-Excel file was returned to CMA Ontario with instructions to:

- Delete candidates who were no longer interested in pursuing their CMA.
- Update candidate contact information as required.

This process eliminated close to 32 percent of the original records, thereby lessening the printing and mailing requirements for the next round of

CASE STUDY: CMA Ontario Telemarketing Campaigns *(Continued)*

mailings six months later. There was also a significant decrease in undeliverable mail.

After the first year of calls, transcript evaluations increased by 6 percent, while Accelerated Program enrollment rose by 8 percent and entrance exam registrations by 7 percent. More dramatic improvements were experienced in year two, with a 31 percent increase in transcript evaluations, a 40 percent increase in Accelerated Program enrollment, and a 25.5 percent increase in entrance exam registrations.

By year three, transcript evaluations decreased by 5 percent (though still showing a healthy improvement over the initial year), while Accelerated Program enrollment rose again by 43 percent and entrance exams by 23 percent. In addition to telemarketing, a number of other factors positively influenced the outcome of this CMA Ontario success story, such as the launch of a new advertising campaign. But the integration of direct mail with the follow-up call was an unequivocal, measurable outcome. By implementing a formalized follow-up program through telemarketing, CMA Ontario significantly increased its new intake numbers. In addition, by keeping the database more current through consistent follow-up, overall costs were reduced.

PILOT PROJECT

You are the marketing director of a local suburban bank. You have a customer base of 10,000 people that have checking accounts with the bank, but no ATM cards or other services with the bank. You have their phone numbers as well as other personal information about them.

You have been asked to develop a teleservices campaign to call and offer these customers the convenience of an ATM card as well as a special offer for mortgage refinancing. Develop a test plan for this program.

A. How many people would you call to test this program. Why?

B. What kinds of qualifying questions would you ask and what information might you request from each customer in the process of making your calls?

C. What information that you have about these customers would you use in the call?

D. When would be the best time to call?

E. What range of response rate would you expect for such a program?

Key Points

▶ Lead-generation calls let companies prospect by phone and deploy salespeople in following up on "hot" leads. However, care should be given to manage the lead flow, because a good telephone lead-generation program may produce more leads than the sales force can handle in a timely fashion.

▶ A successful outbound program depends upon four basic elements: list or target audience, offer being communicated, telephone sales representative, and script or message to be communicated. Of these four, the list is the most important.

▶ Outbound business-to-business calling involves account management rather than direct sales. These calls seek to develop a rapport with the decision maker and periodically make calls where no sale is attempted.

▶ Outbound calls generally use a call guide to develop a genuine rapport and initiate a conversation with a prospect. In regulated industries, verbatim scripts are used because creative material has to be approved both by the client's legal staff as well as government offices.

▶ Two sets of numbers are key to estimating telemarketing costs: cost per call for handling *inbound* calls from business firms and consumers, and cost per decision-maker contact in making *outbound* calls to business firms and consumers. Outbound calls are usually of longer duration, and often require more experienced, higher-paid personnel.

▶ Compliance with state and federal "Telephone Sales Rules" is mandatory for all organizations using telemarketing. Regulators don't hesitate to levy large fines for abuses.

▶ All marketers must maintain "Do Not Call" lists of customers who ask not to receive phone calls, while most consumer marketers have the added burden of purging their prospect files against state and federal DNC registries.

INTERNET DIRECT
MARKETING

CHAPTER 15

OVERVIEW OF INTERNET DIRECT MARKETING

The Internet has revolutionized marketing communications both on- and off-line. From e-mail with personalized URLs (PURLs) to search marketing, the Internet has created a trend in which customers have become the center of their own marketing universes.

The Internet's long global reach, real-time immediacy, detailed knowledge sharing, and capacity to enable information-based dialogue with users has helped marketers to achieve much more direct forms of customer marketing. Marketers have discovered the Internet's potential but are still learning its rules of engagement.

The Internet, yet another medium vying for marketing dollars, continues to win a greater share. Arguably, it is responsible for much of the clutter in customer acquisition. Without argument, it has provided new tools for marketers to build and grow customer relationships. These tools enable precise, relevant, and timely communications.

The thoughtful use of the tools and techniques of direct marketing appear to be a key driver of success on the net. Organizations that offer customers convenience, service, selection, solid guarantees, and good customer service—all part of a successful mail-order business—have achieved success. The use of targeted, measurable media allows marketers to compute their return on investment, while learning which tactics work and which do not.

This is important. Chief marketing officers are under increased pressure from management to provide full accountability for campaigns as well as individual programs. Marketing expenditures for Internet direct marketing media— banner ads, e-mail, and search marketing—can be tracked, assessed, and benchmarked against expected performance standards, helping to meet this need.

And, the Internet continues to create new media opportunities for marketers. Blogs, podcasts, RSS, viral marketing, and word of mouth enable marketers to access large consumer and business social networks. These networks and communities attract individuals with like-minded interests, motivations, and demographics.

Unlike more obtrusive media, these media put the user in control, not the marketer. Consumers can research, share information, and learn about products and services without having contact with sales or marketing departments of organizations.

Podcasts, RSS, etc., should be included in recommendations for multi-channel dialogues. However, they may not be as effective as stand-alone media. They don't have the ability to overtly stimulate purchase behavior. They do have the ability to fit within an integrated marketing communications campaign, where direct mail, print, broadcast, search, banner ads, e-mail, and/or other direct response media are included. This section will focus on interactive marketing and media that marketers can control, including search, e-mail, banner ads, and E-commerce.

Internet Applications

Organizations use the Internet as an advertising medium, a sales and marketing channel, even a distribution medium. Virtually every business has the potential to be a multichannel marketer. Theaters sell tickets online for pick-up later that day. Airlines sell tickets online and deliver them electronically, eliminating the need for a paper ticket. While airlines charge a premium for paper tickets or phone reservations, they use technology to alert passengers to delays or schedule changes with wireless and cell phone technology, a real convenience for frequent flyers.

Software companies, resellers, and application service providers can sell and deliver software online. Retailers and mail-order companies alike have made E-commerce an important marketing and sales channel. Auction sites such as eBay earn fees on transactions and have created new communities of buyers and sellers. Traditional newspaper classified sections have found stiff competition for their print editions from general online classifieds such as Craigslist.com, career sites such as Monster.com, real estate and apartment sites such as Realtor.com, and automobile sites such as Cars.com.

E-business applies information and Internet technology to business conducted among buyers, sellers, and other trading partners. It can improve performance, create value, and establish customer relationships. E-business includes three key components:

- *E-communications*, through which organizations deliver messages to prospects and customers, including banners, buttons, e-mail communication, and other forms of online advertising.

- *E-commerce*, which comprises a variety of online commercial enterprises that include selling, logistics, data sharing, etc.

- *E-care*, which includes customer contact, service, and fulfillment, and has become one of the most important areas of E-business.

As this chapter shows, there is a clear application for the acquisition and relationship building tools and techniques of direct marketing to E-business.

Empowered and Engaged Users

The Internet has grown faster than nearly any other medium. It took radio nearly 38 years to reach 50 million users. Television took 13 years. Cable, whose growth came at a point when television was starting to reach saturation levels in households, took ten years to grow to 50 million users. The Internet took just five years to reach an estimated 50 million users. While there are more U.S. households today than there were 20, 30, or 50 years ago, this growth is still remarkable.

According to a report by *eMarketer* (eMarketer.com), the number of online users reached over one billion at the end of 2006. Of these billion people, approximately 845 million use the Internet regularly. The United States has the most Internet users and broadband households, but as digital innovation expands outside North America, that may soon change.

As shown in Exhibit 15–1, Asia-Pacific is the largest broadband center, containing nearly 40 percent of the world's broadband households. Latin America was the fastest-growing broadband region worldwide, achieving 70 percent subscriber growth.

These users are not the customers of yesterday. Buyers recognize that they don't have to play by the rules anymore. In fact, in this environment, they *set* the rules.

Customers can quickly search the Web for products that meet their expectations and find products and services they can customize to fit their needs, wants,

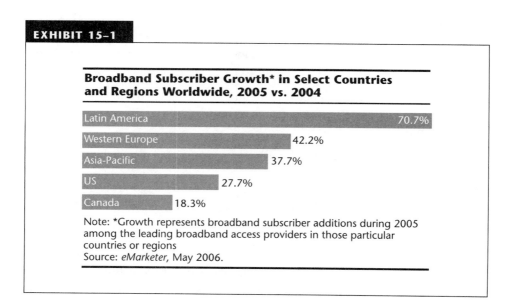

EXHIBIT 15–1

Broadband Subscriber Growth* in Select Countries and Regions Worldwide, 2005 vs. 2004

Latin America	70.7%
Western Europe	42.2%
Asia-Pacific	37.7%
US	27.7%
Canada	18.3%

Note: *Growth represents broadband subscriber additions during 2005 among the leading broadband access providers in those particular countries or regions
Source: *eMarketer*, May 2006.

lifestyles, and how they want to do business. Often buyers, not sellers, set the price paid. And if a buyer doesn't like a product, a price, or customer service, another "store" is a mere click away. A far cry from the old days, when comparing prices or service meant visiting multiple stores!

Researchers who have tracked the behavior of Internet users have discovered that the number one online activity is *not* buying, but shopping. Consumers use the Web to browse, compare, and learn. They are often impatient, and will click from site to site quickly if they encounter hard-to-load graphics or purchasing procedures that are unwieldy and confusing.

Privacy and Security—Important Concerns

The advent of identity theft has given new meaning to the Latin term *caveat emptor*, buyer beware. Users are discovering that e-mail, chat rooms, and bulletin boards are not completely private communications vehicles. Comments posted on the Web may be retrieved years later. Consumers are correct to worry what will happen to personal, health, or financial information volunteered to an organization online. A number of private and public information gaffes have led consumers to question just how safe their data is.

Consumers may trade personal data for online convenience and service, but they want to know how a company will keep it from falling into the wrong hands. Prominently posted privacy policies like the one shown in Exhibit 15–2 can help reassure Web site visitors that their information will be safe. Today's best privacy policies share four traits:

1. *Notice and disclosure.* They explain how information is gathered and how it will be used.

2. *Choice and consent.* They let users decide whether their personal information may be used, or whether they want to receive e-mail solicitations.

3. *Data quality and access.* They explain how data is updated and give users access to make sure captured data is accurate. Some let users update their own information.

4. *Data security.* They explain measures taken to safeguard personal information.

Direct Marketing and the Internet: A Perfect Marriage

The dot-com bust of the 1990s thinned the ranks of E-businesses with highly inflated stock values, great publicity, and no positive cash flow. But marketing on the Web has never been more important to businesses.

EXHIBIT 15–2

CNN Privacy Statement

(a)

(b)

Direct marketers have succeeded because they applied the profitable direct business model to the Web. Instead of seeing what would sell online and then creating a business model around it, they approached the Web like a test. They determined up-front how much to invest, how much sales revenue would be needed, and how much the enterprise would cost. Applying this discipline enabled them to avoid the pitfalls that trapped businesses without direct marketing expertise.

Fulfillment is another reason for their online success. Direct marketers know how to pack, pick, and ship 100 to 10,000 boxes a day with shipping partners who are equal to the challenge. Their fulfillment systems are flexible, ready to gear up for the holiday season and scale back for summer—not true for E-tailers or dot-coms whose systems have disintegrated under holiday demand.

Direct marketers also know how to forecast demand and purchase inventory. They know how to judge the results of online efforts on some kind of a cost-per-metric basis. But most important, they know how to attract prospects and convert them to customers. They know how to capture and use customer information to fine-tune communications, while respecting a customer's wish for privacy.

Converting browsers to buyers requires powerful direct marketing strategies. In this environment, customer-centric strategies are critical. Fortunately, direct marketers have decades of experience fine-tuning strategies that center on the customer.

Cuts Costs and Saves Time

In *The McKinsey Quarterly*, T. Michael Nevens noted that the Internet's single most significant effect is to cut the cost of interaction—the searching, coordinating, and monitoring that people and companies must do when they exchange goods, services, or ideas. The cost of searching for a mortgage, executing a bank transaction, and obtaining customer support, for example, drops significantly when these activities are handled electronically.

Time can be saved in sourcing products. Buyers can be freed to work on tasks with long-term strategic value to the organization. Organizations can see improvements in supply-chain management and procurement. Other benefits and savings include:

- Reduced overall operating costs

- Lower prices paid

- Optimized supply base

- Greater control over spending and inventory

- More efficient use of personnel through instantaneous communications and outsourcing

- Savings in order handling and processing through reduced transaction costs

- Enhanced marketing and customer service

The Automobile Market ... Adapting to the Internet

The automobile marketplace is an example where the shift from traditional mass media approach to a more focused Internet direct marketing approach is evident. Internet direct marketing has helped to empower consumers while lowering the pitch of car sales and reducing the stress of automobile buying. Automobile manufacturers, local dealer groups, and dealers themselves have gravitated to the use of Web sites, Web portals (e.g., Cars.com), and e-mail for consumer education, building brand awareness and generating qualified leads.

According to the "2005 Outlook: The Boom Continues for Online Auto Ads" by market research firm Borrell Associates, many of the 61 million consumers who bought new or used cars in 2004 began their search online. Web sites generated 22 percent of all new car sales. Among Internet users who purchased a used car, 11 percent found it online, while 9 percent found theirs using a classified newspaper ad.

Borrell Associates categorized the automotive Web sites into four categories:

- *Portal sites.* Major traffic sites like AOL, MSN, and Yahoo!, which direct their large traffic pipelines to specific interest, then lease out space in those sites to used-car listings "aggregators" and to sell new-car referrals to franchised dealers.

- *Aggregator sites.* Autobytel, Cars.com, AutoTrader.com, etc., which include Web sites of media companies such as newspapers and TV stations.

- *Reference sites.* Kelleybluebook.com, Edmunds.com, NADA.com, etc.— sites providing rich content for car buyers researching price/feature comparisons.

- *Advertisers.* This includes auto manufacturers, dealer associations, and local dealer sites. Dealer associations are just getting into the game. Note that manufacturers, such as General Motors, are helping their dealer groups to build Web sites to increase their advertising reach.

Auto dealers now see the Internet as one more channel to bring customers into their showrooms. This comes at a time when the Web has clearly become the preferred means for consumers to shop and research during the buying process. Auto dealers often identify specialists within their sales force to nurture these well-qualified, but well-educated (e.g., invoice prices, options, features, etc.) consumers.

Offers Value-Added Products and Services

The Web enables companies to offer value-added products and services. This includes enhancing and delivering old information in new forms or creating new kinds of information delivered when, where, and how customers want it through Internet appliances, portable Web devices, and a host of new gadgets.

Extends a Company's Reach

Because they operate 24 hours a day, 7 days a week, without much supervision, E-commerce sites can extend a company's reach beyond working hours and without regard to location.

Using the Internet to connect offices of the same or different companies is easier to set up, maintain, and manage than an Electronic Data Interchange (EDI) system, a private network that connects far-flung computer networks but requires network interface software, applications software, and dedicated phone lines. The resulting cost savings can be enormous.

An intranet system, a private Web network set up within one organization, enables enterprise-wide collaboration and coordination. Typically, intranets allow authorized users to gain access from inside as well as outside their offices.

A company may set up a password-protected system for customers, often with a Web site that has customized pricing and content. This is called an extranet system. While Internet, intranet, and extranet systems run over the same Internet backbone, they are distinguished by how they are used and accessed.

Online Business Models

On the Internet, businesses are transforming themselves by using inventive new ways to generate revenue and often contravening long-held beliefs. There are advertising-funded sites that lose money on product sales, but hope to make it back on advertising. Content sites like Wall Street Journal Online, New York Times, and others have implemented online subscription models. Some sites charge transaction fees for bringing buyers and sellers together.

Affiliate programs offer commissions to sites that allow links to direct their customers to the affiliate's Web site. Amazon.com has thousands of such affiliates, which has contributed greatly to their success. Some online marketers create Web sites for their customers, extending the reach of their own marketing efforts, while earning commissions and profits on each sale.

In more traditional approaches, sellers offer their products to buyers. The growth of pure Internet businesses, called dot-coms, has been well documented. Traditional "bricks and mortar" businesses have become "clicks and mortar" businesses by combining traditional and Web-based strategies to implement multi-channel E-business strategies.

Currently, the most common E-business strategies are:

1. *Clicks and mortar*: online outposts for traditional "bricks and mortar" companies like Sears or Schwab, set up to move some or all of their business to the Internet.

2. *Clicks and mail order*: Web sites set up by companies that understand direct-to-consumer marketing and are familiar with customer service, fulfillment, and other important back-end activities. Lands' End and Hanna Andersson are good examples of this category of E-commerce.

3. *Clicks, bricks, and mail order*: an emerging trend among companies that see Internet as just another sales channel, this category includes companies that

engage in retail, mail order, and online activities. Eddie Bauer is a good example. Buy an article online or from Eddie Bauer, and you can return it to the retail store—an option not offered by many clicks and mortar enterprises, which do not accept a store return.

Companies that pursue these strategies will grow while reducing costs of sales, distribution, and service due to improvements in customer contact center workload, marketing materials production, inventory management, and order processing.

Clicks and Mail Order: How Direct Marketers Use the Web

A 2004 survey conducted by Primedia Business Market Research found that many businesses used their Web sites for sales leads and marketing applications. As shown in Exhibit 15–3, 54 percent of those companies surveyed used their Web sites to collect e-mail marketing leads and to provide customers with product and company information.

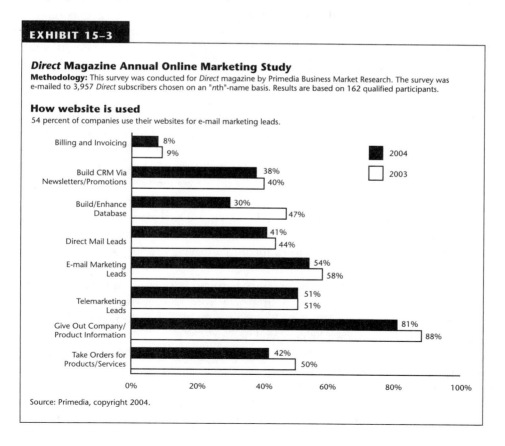

EXHIBIT 15–3

Direct **Magazine Annual Online Marketing Study**
Methodology: This survey was conducted for *Direct* magazine by Primedia Business Market Research. The survey was e-mailed to 3,957 *Direct* subscribers chosen on an "*n*th"-name basis. Results are based on 162 qualified participants.

How website is used
54 percent of companies use their websites for e-mail marketing leads.

Category	2004	2003
Billing and Invoicing	8%	9%
Build CRM Via Newsletters/Promotions	38%	40%
Build/Enhance Database	30%	47%
Direct Mail Leads	41%	44%
E-mail Marketing Leads	54%	58%
Telemarketing Leads	51%	51%
Give Out Company/Product Information	81%	88%
Take Orders for Products/Services	42%	50%

Source: Primedia, copyright 2004.

Social Networking

One of the fastest-growing tools for online direct marketing is social networking. Often called the tools of Web 2.0 (or the Intelligent Web), social networking attempts to harness the collective intelligence of many users to share their specialized knowledge. This promises greater information sharing and richer user experiences. Social networking includes a number of "user-generated" tools, where the initial users invite members of their own business or personal social networks to join.

Social networking tools allows members to view each others' profiles, update address books, create new links, and make other online connections. This process is repeated by new users, sometimes creating vast communities or networks. For example, MySpace reported that they had 116 million members by December 2006 (See Exhibit 15–4).

Another social networking tool with marketing communications application are blogs (derived from "web log"), where journal-style entries are created regarding a topic of interest to the sponsor. Entries are displayed in reverse chronological order, so that a reader can follow the writer's "thread" and others' comments from the most recent back to the beginning. A blog may combine text and images plus links to other blogs, Web pages, and media related to its subject. While many are text-based, some blogs include audio (podcasts) or videos (vlogs).

According to David Sifry, CEO of Technorati (www.technorati.com), a blogging Web site, there were 57 million blogs as of October 2006, with about 55 percent active. Sifry estimates that 100,000 new blogs are created daily.

What should be of interest to marketers is how these tools apply to business. Many companies and brands now have MySpace Web sites with the goal of creating communities of users who will spread positive "word of mouth."

According to Debra Aho Williamson, a senior analyst at *eMarketer*, social networks are becoming more niche-oriented as the popularity of MySpace and Friendsters grows. "The inevitable reaction to when something gets too big? Leave for a smaller, more personal experience," wrote Williamson in an August 2006 *eMarketer* report.

In the report, Williamson cites Fuzzster, a social network for pet lovers; Yub.com, a site for shopaholics; Model Mayhem, a network for models and photographers; and Mog, a network for music lovers, as a few social networking sites for targeted interests.

Social networks can also be organized around business-to-business networks as noted by BusinessWeek.com, in an article from January 29, 2007 ("LinkedIn Reaches Out"). LinkedIn has 9 million members, all focused on career development by growing their own professional networks.

Social networking tools work for direct marketing when they combine engaging content with a focus on something of interest to groups that can be identified by demographics such as age and personal or business interests. This has gotten the attention of marketers, who *Business Week* estimates will spend $1.9 billion on social networks by 2010, up from $280 million in 2006. *Business Week* notes that sites gaining the highest share of budgets are those that can tell marketers something about their audiences' likely spending habits.

RSS Feeds

Another growing online marketing medium are RSS feeds. RSS feeds, short for RDF (Rich) Site Summary, are syndicated Web content, such as news feeds, events, and excerpts from discussion forums, made for distribution on different sites. Wired, USA Today, Wall Street Journal Online, and even the likes of PerezHilton.com all accept advertising in their RSS feeds.

This small, niche market has a promising profile. Demographic studies indicate RSS subscribers are heavy Internet users who use the medium to gather information. They are savvy consumers who are comfortable on the Internet and tend to be the pioneers of technology trends. Also, users must subscribe or sign up to receive RSS feeds, an act that indicates a committed interest in the Web site's content.

Because it is still a newer marketing medium, response rates and best practices are scant. As a general rule, direct response ads should complement the content of the feeds. Instead of the traditional hard-sell "click here, buy now" type ad, marketers might consider prompting an action that allows feed readers to access more information. Other factors to consider are:

- Ad formats are in text or graphics. Feed ads range from a headline-style, text-only ad to something that resembles a traditional banner ad.

- Tailor your message to the audience. As with any other advertising medium, think about how and why the target audience is using the RSS feed, then craft the message to match the user's mind-set.

- To purchase ads, marketers can either work with feed publishers directly or use companies such as FeedBurner, Pheedo, and Kanoodle that aggregate feeds into advertising networks. Google and Yahoo! also test feeds.

- Consider the frequency and duration that the feed is updated. Some are updated several times a day, others feed once per month.

- Feed ads are priced on a cost-per-impression (CPM) or cost-per-click (CPC) basis. Cost will vary according to the feed and target audience.

Search Engine Marketing

Search engine marketing (SEM) has become one of the most important Web tools for marketers. According to the *Economist*, there are 300 million searches completed on the Internet each day. It is no surprise that SEM has become an essential direct marketing medium for nearly any organization with a Web site.

SEM is any form of pay-for-performance or paid inclusion where marketers compensate search engines (e.g., Google, MSN, Yahoo!, Ask.com, etc.) to guarantee that their Web sites have more visible placement within that engine's search results.

SEM has grown as search has become more important to users. According to a study conducted by the Pew Internet and American Life Project, 63 percent of all U.S. Internet users use search and 77 percent of Internet users use e-mail. The same study found that in 2005, 59 million people used search daily, 74 million people used e-mail. These top the list of American's daily online activities (See Exhibit 15–4).

There are a number of factors that have led to the growth of SEM. Broadband adoption in the United States has contributed to the growing use of search. The online population has better and faster access to the Internet, which makes the overall online experience more satisfying.

Marketers are beginning to observe interesting search behavior. Many users seem to rely on search rather than bookmarking Web pages or trying to remember URLs. That may explain why Yahoo! reported that in May 2006 there were nearly one million searches for amazon.com. Instead of typing that well-known URL into browsers, users instead searched for the URL amazon.com, and continued into the Web site from the search.

How Search Engines Work

Most search engines use software programs known as spiders or bots (short for robots) that continuously crawl the Web in search of Web pages. Spiders look

---

EXHIBIT 15–4

Adults' Daily Internet Activities, September 2005

Internet Activity	Percent
E-mail	77%
Search engine	63%
Get news	46%
Do job-related research	29%
Use instant messaging	18%
Do online banking	18%
Take part in chat room	8%
Make a travel reservation	5%
Read blogs	3%
Participate in online auction	3%

Source: Pew Internet & American Life Project, 2005.

for links that lead them to individual Web pages. When they find a Web page, they copy much or all of the text on that page into the search engine's own database. The spiders only copy text written in HTML. Spiders constantly crawl the Web, returning to Web pages every 1–3 months.

Search engines are simply big databases that store the data on billions of Web pages. When a user searches, they are simply doing a database query. Each search engine has created their own unique indexing and ranking system to help provide the most relevant results to those queries. The rankings take into consideration a number of factors, including the number of links to a page, the number and times a keyword appears in a page, and the location of the keyword in the page.

Final search results are based on algorithms, mathematical formulas that are at the heart of all software programs. Each search engine has its own proprietary algorithm. To ensure that marketers or competitors can't gain advantage by guessing the most important variables in the algorithm, search engines change the formulas from time to time.

Yahoo! and a few other search portals work differently. Yahoo! is a Web directory, not a search engine. Web sites that want to be listed using their own keywords must submit a short description of their Web site. Editors from Web directories also review the Web sites and write up their own descriptions. When a user does a search, the keywords are matched only to what is written in the submitted description. A completely different approach to organic listings must be taken with Web directories and search engines. Well-written descriptions and good content are the best answer to Web directories.

Search Engine Optimization

With the growth of the World Wide Web, it is harder and harder to be found. Smart marketers do all they can to get high rankings without the use of paid inclusion. These are called organic or natural search results. Search engine optimiztion (SEO) includes a number of Web design features and processes.

SEO requires an understanding of how search engine spiders crawl the Web. Because spiders look for links, the more links to an individual Web page, the more likely a page is to be found and "crawled."

Search engine spiders don't "see" Web pages. The spider only sees the text-based HTML code that the page is written in. They do not "see" or read flash animations, JavaScript, mouseovers, illustrations, photography, or any typography that is embedded as a graphic (sometimes used by designers in headlines and subheads). The spiders look for keywords in the titles, headlines, subheads, and within the body text of Web pages. It is good to look at some top-ranked pages and review how they are organized, how many words they have, etc.

Search engines look for natural writing, not forced writing or lists of key-words. A good page length is 200–400 words. Many search engines don't rank pages with less than 100 words. While the exact search engine algorithms are proprietary, they all consider the following attributes:

- *Keyword prominence.* Most search engines look for keywords in titles, headlines, subheads, and at the beginning of a page or sentence. However, the crawlers of some search engines also search the bottom of a page.

- *Keyword density.* Also known as weight, this is the number of times a keyword appears within a page. Search engines often penalize Web pages for too many or too few mentions on a page. On average, important keywords should be repeated approximately five times per page.

- *Keyword proximity.* Proximity refers to how close within the text the keywords appear to each other. It is generally accepted that it is better to have them appear close together, while maintaining sentence clarity.

When optimizing pages, avoid repeating lists of "invisible" keywords hidden from users' view. This common technique is considered "spamming" by search engines. At best, the search engine crawlers will ignore those pages; at worst, they will be blacklisted by search engine staff that review pages highlighted by the spiders.

Paid Search

Pay-for-performance is the basic SEM model. In this model, marketers bid on a number of keywords and keyword phrases that are relevant to their brand, the products/services that they offer, and to their Web site. Marketers only pay when users click onto their search ads.

The marketer's liability is limited to only paying per click. This is similar to what is called per inquiry in other media. A click-through does not necessarily lead to a purchase, a qualified lead, or other kinds of information-gathering response. It is simply a click on the ad. Marketers spend a great deal of time ensuring that they test and focus on keywords and search ad copy that leads to the responses that they hope to achieve.

Marketers can further limit their liability by capping their daily, weekly, or monthly spending on keywords. This is very useful in testing, as a marketer can budget what is necessary to learn which keywords, search ads, offers, and landing page copy works best. However, capping the budget is just as useful when marketers choose to balance their marketing spending across a number of media.

Paid inclusion is an SEM model in which Web site owners pay a search engine or Web directory to guarantee that their sites will be indexed, that is, show up in search results. Paid inclusion may also ensure that the search engine's crawler software visits the client's site more frequently. Paid search improves rankings but doesn't guarantee that a Web site will have the greatest visibility. It is a complement to, not a replacement for, pay-per-performance search.

Search Ad Campaigns

Search ad campaigns are media buys. They are becoming more sophisticated as search engines go beyond global keyword buys to offering geographic and local targeting, daypart buys, and behavioral and contextual targeting.

To cover the search marketplace, media buys can be made across a number of search engines and directories. Both searchers and search engine marketers have a number of choices. Nielsen/NetRatings measures results of more than 60 sites in the United States for Searchenginewatch.com (see Exhibit 15–5). While Google maintains the largest share, they account for less than 50 percent of all searches. Yahoo! accounts for 28 percent, MSN 13.2 percent, AOL 7.6 percent, Ask.com 5.9 percent, rounding out the top five, and others 2.6 percent.

Meta-search engines such as DogPile, Ixquick, and HOTBOT display search results from a number of search engines/directories from keywords. For example, DogPile (www.dogpile.com) lists the top-ranked Web pages from 15 search engines/directories separately.

EXHIBIT 15–5

Top Search Engines

This chart shows the percentage of online searches done by U.S. home and work Web surfers in November 2005. The activity at more than 60 search sites makes up the total volume upon which percentages are based—5.1 billion searches during November 2005.

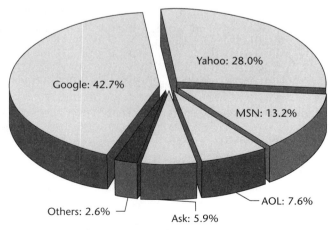

Source: comScore for SearchEngineWatch.com.

Keyword Strategies

Placing keywords is much like a media buy. Like other media buys, having insight into user motivations, needs, and wants is important. It is good to visualize what a user is thinking about as they search for products or services. For instance, the user may type in a phrase or a single search term. For searchers, the context of their search will help them to decide what search terms to use. This makes the search very targeted to their individual needs. For example, a user doesn't need to have selected a specific model to start a search for a car. They can look for used or new cars, certain body styles (e.g., convertibles, SUVs, vans, etc.), manufacturers, or models. A user might look for reviews of different models, specifications, comparisons of models, different price points, etc. Each of these searches would start differently than by simply searching for "cars." Having thought-out search terms for these different kinds of searches would be imperative for attracting different kinds of users or searchers at different stages of their search.

When developing keywords, it is helpful to mine the data from your site's own internal search engine. You can search you own log data as a starting point. Major search engines also publish the most searched terms and phrases. Other Web sites such as keyworddiscovery.com (Trellian) offer paid services to identify keywords. These organizations compile information from up to 200 search engines, cataloging searches over the most recent period of time.

When bidding on keywords, start by matching keywords and phrases to the product or service provided. Create and include phrases as well as single words. Include several permutations to the phrases (different order). This is important because no two searchers think exactly alike. Rewrite phrases in the form of a question. This helps to match with users who ask questions. Include synonyms, substitutes, and related words to selected keywords. Having a good thesaurus or other synonym suggestion tool is invaluable. Include common misspellings and typographical errors (You'd be surprised how many searches include reversed letter orders, typographical errors, or misspelled words). Include brand names of products/services, and model numbers when available.

Exhibit 15–6 is a sample of keywords for food safety training. Note the different phrases, word orders, purposeful typographical error, and misspelling.

When bidding for keywords, the marketer/advertiser chooses:

- Keywords and phrases

- The ad linked to the keyword

- Targeting considerations (geographical, local, site categories, specific sites, etc.)

- The maximum cost per click (CPC) that can be bid

- The maximum daily, weekly, or monthly dollars spent

EXHIBIT 15–6

Keyword Diversity is King

A sample of keywords for the phrase *food safety training*:

food safety, food safety training, food safety training (Typo), food safety education, food safety instruction, food safety certification, food safety compliance, food safety resource, food safety training & alliance, restaurant food safety, restruant food safety (Misspelled), restaurant food safety training, restaurant food safety education, food purity education, food safety standards, safe food handling education, foodservice safety training, food service safety training, foodservice safety education, safe food handling training, safe food handling instruction, safe food handling education, food preparation safety training, restaurant sanitary training, food safety best practices.

(Note: The Typo and Misspelling were chosen purposely).

Most search engine bid processes are similar to that of Google's. Google aggregates the active bids on a specific keyword. Their bid process takes into account the maximum bid amount as well as the click-through rate for an ad in determining its placement within search results. Ads that have a higher click-through rate get greater prominence on the page, even though they may have a higher bid maximum. Users see more ads others have clicked on (a kind of behavioral targeting). This increases the likelihood that an ad will be clicked on, which also results in the search engines earning more revenue.

Local Search

Local search is gaining more interest from marketers and search engines. In local search, results are limited to a specific proximity, city, or region. Results, in tandem with new online mapping products (e.g., Google Maps), can provide store or product information and door-to-door directions. These can be accessed from desktops, laptops, or a myriad of smart cell phones or Personal Digital Assistants, allowing for search and directions on the go.

This brings a host of new users to search marketing, as local retailers, restaurants, and service firms (e.g., carpet cleaners, dry cleaners, exterminators, plumbers, etc.) gravitate to local search. It also increases competition for newspaper classifieds, yellow pages, and directory assistance as users adapt to getting quick, complete local information from their computer or other devices.

Google's share of local search, 43.7 percent, is the largest market share. It also serves the largest share of the Internet population for local search. Web users visit local segments of larger search engines or smaller sites set up to serve a particular city or region. Other Internet users search with "local qualifiers" to return location-targeted results (See Exhibit 15–7).

EXHIBIT 15–7

Local Search Data, November 2005

	Local Searches	Share of Local
Total Internet	447,829,790	100.0%
Google sites	195,790,534	43.7%
Yahoo! sites	126,243,837	28.2%
MSN/Microsoft sites	61,548,838	13.7%
Time Warner Network	33,556,682	7.5%
Ask.com	24,717,632	5.5%
Infospace Network	4,188,728	0.9%
Lycos, Inc.	1,373,255	0.3%

Source: comScore Media Metrix, 2005.

Creating a Landing Page

A landing page is a specialized Web page or group of pages (also called a micro-site) that visitors are directed to once they have clicked onto the link from an e-mail, search result, or banner ad. The page is focused on a product or service, with the objective of getting the user to take an action that will ultimately lead to the desired response, such as a purchase. The goal of the landing page is to convert prospects by having them quickly take an action that may be followed up with later.

Landing page versions are often created for each e-mail, banner, search term, offer, or communication that a marketer sends out. This helps to make the content relevant to prospects and customers. Using personalized URLs, marketers can create on-the-fly dynamic landing pages, which are unique to each respondent. These can be used in direct mail as well as e-mail.

There are a number of questions that must be answered before creating a landing page:

- What is the product/service that you are offering?
- Who is the target prospect that you are appealing to?
- What is the rationale for their interest in the offer?
- What qualifications do they need to meet to respond or purchase?

Because landing pages are an important direct marketing technique, they use all of the tools at the disposal of direct marketers.

Page Length. There is no standard for the length of landing pages or amount of copy within them. The amount of content is a function of the complexity or uniqueness of the product offered, with more complex products needing more content.

Nevertheless, sentences may be short—even bullet points that are easy for the eye to scan. Don't worry about brevity in copy. You can offer additional links for those wanting more information.

Page Design. Landing pages should be image-consistent with communications in the campaign. It is important to have visual cues that the landing page is part of the campaign that brought the reader to the page in the first place. Headlines, type, and colors should echo that consistency. Use white space on the page to encourage readers to explore the entire page. Photos and illustrations pull the reader's eye to the page quickly and are always a good tool to use.

Call to Action. Landing pages need strong calls to action throughout the Web page. The first call to action is usually toward the top of the page and targets impulse responses. However, individual users often have different needs, which come up throughout the sales process, so that calls to action must be scattered throughout the copy. The calls to action should link directly to a response page that allows the reader to purchase, subscribe, or otherwise complete their response.

Offers. Landing pages should make great use of offers. If the user doesn't click onto the main offer link, additional offers can be included that still work to capture the e-mail address or other information about the reader. This is an important "moment of truth," which should not be overlooked because the reader does not choose the marketer's preferred call to action.

Testing Landing Pages

Testing is a key ingredient in successful landing pages. For example, when using landing pages with search marketing, you can test offers, copy, graphics, etc. The best tests are done one step at a time. Test, then adjust. Test, then adjust again. Remember to test only one variable at a time. Testing more than one variable (e.g., copy and offer) makes reading the test impossible.

Landing Page Response Forms

Whether a response form seeks an order, magazine subscription, a lead, or information for a survey, everything possible must be done to get the response. Forgetting online concerns about privacy may encourage some people to give you incorrect e-mail addresses or phony names. Leaving doubt as to how information will be used or whether there is a privacy policy will reduce response.

Here's a short list of do's to get the greatest response from landing pages:

- Ask only for the information that you need to collect

- Explain why you are collecting the information

- Explain how you will use the information
- Promise not to rent or resell the user's e-mail addresses
- Include a link to your privacy policy
- Create a thank-you page
- Use a confirmation page to acknowledge receipt of the user's information

The Last Word on Landing Pages

Landing pages are an important development in Web marketing. The ability to adopt Web pages to complement and provide relevant content for each of a marketer's communications, enables a better environment for engagement and response. Response is, after all, the primary goal of direct marketing.

Search and Landing Page Analytics

A key element in the tools and techniques of direct marketing is to measure results. The more and deeper the results, the better. Marketers are not disappointed when applying such analytics to search engine marketing.

Learning which keywords work best is just the start. A good analysis of a cost-per-click program will reveal overall keyword conversion, the number of conversions from organic search, campaign conversion, the number of users that follow the expected page navigation path, and the bounce rate upon entering the landing page.

Marketers can get reports that track visits, page views, visitor loyalty, performance of various segments, content performance, and a number of keyword user Web parameters (e.g., the user's browser and version, language, connection speed, etc.).

In addition, a navigation analysis will provide information on how users are navigating from the PPC ad through the Web site. Reports provide details of the percentage of users that click through each copy or graphic link. This helps the marketer to decide which content to emphasize, how to best structure copy and Web layout, which pages to make the best landing pages to various ads, and what content within the Web site may need to be enhanced.

Search engine program analysis provides a host of information to make more informed choices. Google analytics, which at this writing is offered free to Google AdSense customers, allows users who are their customers to do most of the analytics that was described above. However, all users of search marketing should do as much analysis as possible. It is one way to help optimize your results and go much deeper than only learning what keywords work best.

A New Frontier: Wireless Internet Applications

An area poised for growth is wireless Internet. This is a yet unproven direct marketing medium. This space has gained a lot of attention, but few users to date. "Companies are using text messages to notify customers of special deals and banner ads to sponsor items, such as ringtone downloads," noted Julie Ask, research director at Jupiter Research.

There are a number of reasons for the continued interest. Cellular phones are becoming more computer-like, with larger screens and greater bandwidth, enabling them to deliver communication messages. Payment systems such as PayPal now allow cell phone users to send payments using SMS (Short Message Service) or e-mail.

Cell phones are popular with many marketers' key demographics, high school and college students. Many college students are relying only on wireless phones, abandoning wired connections completely. As many as 69 percent of U.S. high school age youth own cell phones, according to an American Advertising Federation (AAF) survey. Those in the high school and college market tend to be attracted to products with short lifecycles, such as music and movies, which get concentrated communication spending as new music and movies arrive.

The marketplace for cell phone communications is mixed. A survey by research firm In-Stat found that 80 percent of cell phone users opposed the idea. Consumers supporting it seem to be allowing marketers to subsidize premium services like directory assistance, ringtones, and messaging.

Short Message Service

Short Message Service (SMS) is a service available on most cell phones, Personal Digital Assistants (PDAs), and other mobile devices. It allows the sending of text messages between cell phones, PDAs, and some wired landline telephones.

SMS, or text messaging, is used to deliver premium content such as news alerts, financial data, and ringtones. Cell phone subscribers are charged for receiving premium content. SMS can be used for online payments and bricks-and-mortar services. For example, some vending machines now allow payment by SMS, with the cost of the purchase added to the user's cell phone bill. Other premium content allows users to register and receive free text messages when items they have selected are on sale, or when new items are introduced.

Most "wireless advertising" today is in the form of highly targeted, time-sensitive, text-based ad messages. Consumers use wireless to gain information and complete transactions because they need something specific, and they need it now. While opt-in ads can be used to help build brand awareness, it is not clear if the wireless platform can offer much more than support for such efforts.

One of the strengths of wireless is also its greatest drawback: it can reach users anywhere there is service. Using location-finding technologies that are a required feature of future cell phones, a marketer with a database of consumer preferences and wireless e-mail addresses would be able to alert a consumer in the vicinity of their store about relevant product offerings or discounts. The transaction might not be completed online, but the message would advance consumers toward a purchase decision. Privacy concerns with proximity tracking may be an issue as well.

Text messaging between cell phones is much more common outside of the United States than within. It often takes the place of e-mail. Mobile marketing has started to grow in Europe, Asia, and Latin America where text messaging is more common. Forrester Research recently reported that 43 percent of U.S. marketers are using or planning to use mobile marketing over the next year. Much of this use is for awareness building or sales promotion. As yet, there has not been much successful testing of mobile marketing for commerce or direct marketing. Coca Cola has reported some successful promotional uses in France, Germany, the UK, and Mexico. And, Pearson Prentice Hall embedded 12 codes into their 2007 textbook titled *Marketing: Real People, Real Choices* as a way of creating greater engagement with users of the text. Most of the tests have had as their objective downloads of games, ringtones, or news to cell phones.

Mobile marketing is still in its infancy. While it garners great interest, this has not yet translated into significant budget commitments by clients, especially in the United States. While it is worth testing the use of mobile marketing as a tool and technique of direct marketing, its role is still not certain.

CASE STUDY: Purina Friskies Milkoholics

Adapted from the Direct Marketing Association International Echo Awards 2006.

CHALLENGE

Purina Friskies, once the market leader in the dry cat food category, was losing market share and in need of a campaign to win consumers back to the brand. At the time of this campaign, there had been a lot of activity in the cluttered pet food market: Purina was promoting Purina One and Cat Chow, competing against Whiskas and Chef.

Friskies developed Friskies with Milk Essentials to differentiate itself in the dry cat food arena. Milk Essentials combined the taste of milk that cats love without the lactose that causes digestion problems.

MARKETING GOALS

Purina wanted to retain existing customers and attract a new segment to the brand, which Purina dubbed Indulgent Nutritionists (INs). This segment, typically females 20–49 years old, has a special bond with their cats. The target is not interested in the science of cat food, but believes if the food is good and their cat loves it, they are doing well by their felines.

The five main objectives of the campaign were: boost market penetration from 16.7 percent to 17.7 percent; get 5 percent of all cat-owning households (927,000 households) to try the product; attract new users—not by taking them from other Purina products but by converting them from Whiskas;

and grow the database by an additional 20 percent of Friskies households.

Purina databases were mined to identify the target prospect base. Research was conducted online and it revealed a key insight: cat owners knew their cats loved milk but were unaware that the lactose in milk caused most cats digestion problems. The campaign approach was to educate the audience about this problem and offer Friskies with Milk Essentials as the solution.

MARKETING TACTICS

- *Phase 1*: Drive traffic to the Web by anonymously introducing the idea of milkoholism in cats via multiple billboard, targeted and relevant magazine, and Web banner advertising.
- *Phase 2*: Introduce Purina Friskies with Milk Essentials as a solution to milkoholism, using a combination of channels to drive trial (doorstep drop and Web), and encourage feedback and interaction via the Web (www.milkoholics.co.nz) and radio for data capture efforts.

- *Phase 3*: Drive sales via trial and sampling. Promotion vehicles were radio, public relations, street theater outside supermarkets, point of purchase activity, and magazine advertising. Also, data capture systems were put in place among channels.

CREATIVE STRATEGY

By creating a fictional "holism"—feline milkoholism—a humorous platform was established from which to roll out a campaign that was fun and memorable (See Exhibits 15–8, 15–9).

RESULTS

The campaign was a success on all accounts. Market penetration increased from 16.7 percent to 18.7 percent and the brand achieved 13.8 percent growth. The highest-value sales in the last two years were achieved during the promotional period, while 6.7 percent or 62,348 cat-owning households sampled the product. Friskies acquired 28.5 percent of the core target market, or 19,115 new households, and grew its database by 38 percent.

CASE STUDY: **Purina Friskies Milkoholics** *(continued)*

EXHIBIT 15–8

Purina Friskies Milkoholics Print Ad

CASE STUDY: Purina Friskies Milkoholics (continued)

EXHIBIT 15–9

Purina Friskies Milkoholics Bill Board

PILOT PROJECT Although the Purina Friskies Milkoholics made use of e-mail and the Web, the client wants to create more engagement with customers through the use of "Web 2.0" tactics that incorporate "user-generated" and social networking tools. Blogs, wikis, Fuzzster, U-Tube, and MySpace all come to mind. How could Friskies Milkoholics take advantage of this trend.

  A. Do social networking tools make sense given the passion and interests of pet owners?

  B. What specific social networking tools would you recommend? Answer why you would choose one over the others.

  C. Would these elements stand alone, or is there some way to tie them into ongoing programs?

D. Is it a good idea for leading brands to allow users to generate content that they can't control? Should Friskies be concerned about this or not? Why?

Key Points

- Internet direct marketing has become an important element in marketers' multichannel campaigns.

- Privacy and data security remain among the greatest concerns of consumers who go online.

- Search engine optimization provides a way for marketers to adapt their Web site to the algorithms of the search engines and directories to improve their organic or natural search results.

- Search engine marketing includes a variety of pay-for-performance tools that marketers find to be the most important in helping put consumers in contact with them online.

- E-mail continues to be a growing medium, but it may be more effective for converting, up-selling, cross-selling, and winning back customers than for new customer acquisition.

- While content remains important online, good copy, be it keywords in search marketing or subject lines in e-mail, can still make a big difference.

- Internet direct marketing channels meet the increased demand for program accountability. Marketing expenditures for banner ads, e-mail, and search engines can be tracked, scrutinized, and benchmarked against expected performance standards.

E-COMMUNICATIONS

The Internet may be the ultimate direct marketing message delivery medium. It has a low cost of entry, the ability to pinpoint targeting, and real-time measurement capability. Together, this allows highly tailored messages to be delivered to individual consumers, during the purchase decision, right up to the all-important moment of truth.

Many forms of online communications are being created or evolving. E-mail is getting more use than ever before. Search engines are now a major marketing medium. According to JupiterResearch's report "U.S. Online Advertising Forecast 2005 to 2011," online ad spending will reach $25.9 million by 2011. Search engine marketing spending surpassed display ad spending in 2005 and will continue to dominate online advertising for the next five years.

Webcasts and podcasts are also growing in use. And cellular phones and PDAs, now enabled for streaming video, promise to be the next big direct marketing medium. However, E-communications is not without controversy. E-communications are obtrusive, even when consumers ask them not to be. While consumers like the convenience of online ordering, they have mixed feelings when organizations contact them by e-mail, even though the organizations may have obtained permission from consumers before contacting them—called "opt-in."

This chapter examines how to get the most from two E-communications vehicles: online advertising and e-mail. When carefully adapted, these techniques prove to be successful.

Growth of E-Communications

As an advertising medium, the Internet is still small when compared with television, newspapers, direct mail, and other media. However, it is likely that as online ad spending grows, these ad dollars will likely come from traditional media. This trend is already under way.

E-communications enable individually addressable media channels that can help to build brands, but in a more customized way than traditional awareness-building media. These highly tailored messages can be inexpensively delivered to individual consumers—to acquire them as new customers, inform them, and gain their loyalty. And it does this by getting them to respond in way that can be measured.

Many traditional marketers use Internet media to build one-on-one relationships with prospects and customers on the Web. This is done by targeting their message to individual users based on geography, content, purchasing behaviors, and demographic or firmographic information. While that doesn't necessarily guarantee better communications, it has the potential to make advertising more effective and rewarding for both users and Web marketers.

Internet direct marketing can be used to help build consumer and business-to-business brands like television, radio, print, and out of home. Like direct mail, it can deliver or make available vast amounts of information relevant to prospects and customers. It can be used for traffic building for an online retailer or mall. It can be used to enable transactions like a visit to a retail store, the mail response to a catalog, or a call to a stockbroker.

Using E-Communications to Build Customer Perceptions

Building perceptions of online brands is a challenge. Brands are typically built on awareness, a created desire to be part of a larger group, and emotional decisions. The Internet works with one-to-one, dialogue-enabling activities and rational, considered decisions. That is where the synergy between brand building and direct communications is important.

Traditional brand advertising builds on a common communications platform and consistent messaging across every point of contact. A direct marketer's role is to reinforce the brand message(s) and to turn positive perceptions into actions. Exhibit 16–1 shows the role of direct marketing and brand advertising in the process of building an online brand.

Online brand marketers have many tools at their disposal. Banner linking and affiliate marketing have helped generate thousands of orders from affiliate sites that link to Amazon.com as their bookseller. Sponsorships also play a role in building online brands. They don't always generate direct responses, but they can enhance credibility by sponsoring a Web site, the content area of a portal site, or some category that relates to an organization's target market.

Offline advertising is also important. It may seem paradoxical that with so much communications flexibility, few businesses have been grown online without the help of offline media. The growth of most dot-com businesses has come, in part, from their use of television, radio, print, billboards, and direct mail to help

---

EXHIBIT 16–1

Marketing Flowchart

Mass Communications

Integrated (Digital) Brand Marketing
Help More ⟶ Know More ⟶ Sell More
Collaborative Focus

⇑⇑

Direct Marketing
Know More ⟶ Sell More
Transaction Focus

⇑⇑

Mass Marketing
Communicate More ⟶ Sell More
Image Focus

---

build awareness of their brands. Top online brands such as AOL, Amazon.com, Yahoo!, and TD Ameritrade owe their initial and continued growth, in part, to offline advertising campaigns.

Banner Ads and Other Formats

The Internet is the first medium in history that wasn't created by advertising. Nevertheless, advertising has played a role since 1994, when *Wired* magazine launched HotWired, the first advertising-supported Web site. Banner ads for AT&T, IBM, and Zima asked readers to respond by clicking on the banner.

This was a bold experiment for HotWired and its first advertisers, and no one was certain how "Netizens" would respond. Prodigy, a commercial online service launched in 1990 with advertising support, was the lone example of online advertising. The "gated village" charged subscribers to go online for Prodigy's proprietary content as well as for e-mail privileges. Other online services had not come around to the idea of advertising either. CompuServe was a subscription-only service; even AOL did not consider accepting paid advertising until 1995.

One of the early adopters was Zima, a clear-malt beer brand. Zima wanted to find a way to advertise to its young, college-age target market in a channel that fit the brand's cool image. Zima built a Web site that incorporated the essence of its brand. To build traffic for the brand, Zima paid HotWired for a banner ad it hoped would drive people to its Web site. It worked. With the excitement of being among the first to test-drive the next new thing, users came in droves to try it out. The product never lived up to its smart communications strategy. Although it achieved its goal of gaining trial, repeat purchase and conversion were low. Even with innovative communications strategies, products and services still must meet customer expectations, or they will fail.

Banner ads are one of the most important tools used in Internet direct marketing. Today, 4–5 percent of Internet users click on banner ads. However, click-through rates (CTRs) have been declining as the novelty of banner ads has worn off and the clutter of online promotion increased.

Traditional advertisers hoped that banner ads on the Internet could be used as a branding medium to build awareness or create an image for their products and services. Originally, the small size of banner ads was a significant drawback. Banner ads have since evolved to include multiple-size ads in static, animated, and interactive formats.Sizes currently in use include banners, buttons, skyscrapers, and even an oversized horizontal banner identified as a "leaderboard." Classmates.com uses the interstitial banner, which appears in a separate pop-up browser window. The advantage of interstitial banners is that they can be large (in byte size) while still allowing the main page to load. The Interactive Advertising Bureau (IAB) has devised guidelines for standard and nonstandard banner ads (See Exhibit 16-2).

Standard banner ads come in various sizes, which are determined in pixels. The standard ad banner is 468×60 pixels, equaling a total of 28,080 square pixels (*Pixel* is an abbreviation of "picture element," a single point in a graphic image). The most commonly used default screen size in a monitor is 640×480 pixels, a total of 307,020 square pixels. This means that in most cases, a typical Web page is 91 percent editorial and 9 percent advertising. The advertising-to-editorial ratio of consumer magazines is in the 50/50 range. Local television is closer to 60 percent programming and 40 percent advertising.

Whether or not an advertiser's objectives are direct response or brand-oriented, studies have found that larger ad units simply perform better in most circumstances (See Exhibits 16–3 and 16–4).

Static Banner Ads

Static banners—that is, fixed images on a page—are easy to create and have a small file size. They can easily be downloaded by practically any user, unlike large-file banners, which have significant download times that are too slow for computer users whose modems have dial-in speeds of 56 kbs or less. Impatient users may click away from the banner before it fully loads.

The downside to static banner ads is that they look unexciting and generate significantly lower response rates than animated and interactive banners.

EXHIBIT 16–2

Interactive Advertising Bureau (IAB) Guidelines for Banner Ads

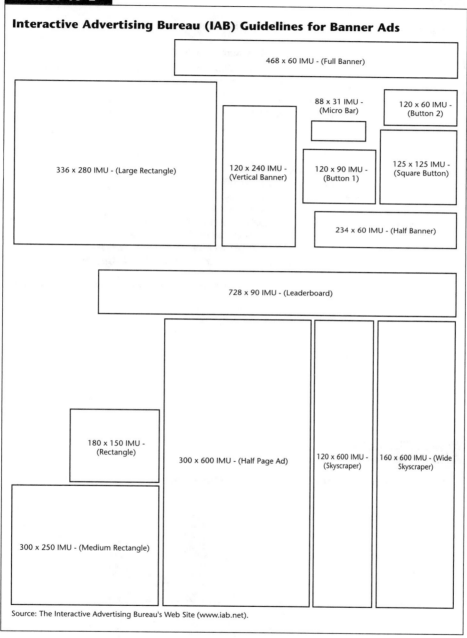

Source: The Interactive Advertising Bureau's Web Site (www.iab.net).

EXHIBIT 16–3

Larger Ad Units Generate Higher Click Rates

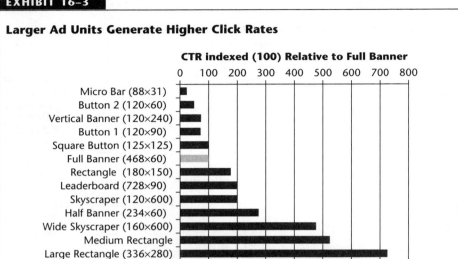

Source: DoubleClick, based on aggregated data from 136 large U.S.-based DART for Advertiser customers, nearly 20 billion impressions, Q1 2006.

EXHIBIT 16–4

Larger Ad Units Better at Raising Purchase Intent

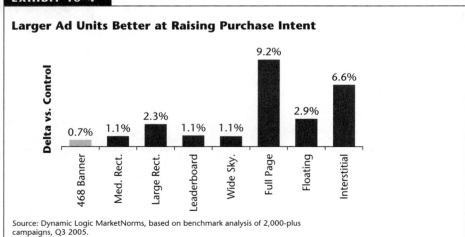

Source: Dynamic Logic MarketNorms, based on benchmark analysis of 2,000-plus campaigns, Q3 2005.

However, static banners are often created for button- and microbutton-size banner ads (125×125 pixels or less), where space is limited and general acceptance by Web sites is important.

Animated Banner Ads

Animated banners use multiple frames to give the impression of movement, deliver graphic impact, and provide more room for copy to deliver the advertiser's message. They nearly always pull a higher CTR than static banners.

Animated banners usually include at least three frames with copy and graphics. The first frame acts like the teaser copy on an outer envelope—to gain attention and interest. The next frame continues the copy or graphic platform. The last frame pays off on the copy and has a call to action (e.g., "Click here"). Additional frames may be used to create the illusion or deliver a longer message.

All animations use additional bandwidth. While many sites allow continuous looping of the banner, large sites often have restrictions (e.g., Yahoo! allows only four seconds of animation). To maximize your efforts, you need to be familiar with the media plan to know where each ad is running.

Most animated banners use small, easy-to-create GIF files, although graphics programs like Flash and sound files are sometimes embedded in banners. Additional programs can make them large and unwieldy. Also, not all Web sites can serve banners with additional programs embedded, nor can all browsers view them. This means that two versions of the banner must be created, adding cost and complexity to the program. However, server software can identify which browser software and plug-in programs a user is running, and then load the compatible version of the ad.

Interactive Banner Ads

Interactive banner ads allow users to fill out forms, answer surveys, play games, or place orders within the banner. This kind of banner has gained acceptance by users, Web sites that accept ads, and banner advertisers. It allows the user to click and act upon the banner without leaving the Web site—an ingenious solution to one of the inherent drawbacks of banner ads.

Simple but effective interactive banners can be created in HTML using a drop-down menu or table. These are relatively small files. They do require some additional work by Web servers but can be easily accessed through slower dial-in connections.

Banners that have a higher level of interactive capability use rich media. These are larger files that require higher bandwidth connections to be activated. However, they can deliver a banner ad that has greater brand building and direct marketing capabilities. For example, using Java script, a games program may be activated with the banner, or an order for a product or service could be executed.

EXHIBIT 16–5

Virgin Atlantic's Interactive Banner Ads Won Best Online Campaign from *Advertising Age* **in 2005**

Source: Virgin Atlantic's Web site (www.virgin-atlantic.com).

Exhibit 16–5 shows an award-winning banner ad campaign from Virgin Atlantic. These ads, created by Crispin Porter & Bogusky, were targeted to the business-class flier. They invite viewer interaction in fun and unexpected ways.

As DSL, cable modems, and other high-bandwidth alternatives grow more common, interactive banner ads will gain greater acceptance. Today, they often require users to have additional plug-in programs on their browsers, such as RealNetworks Inc., Shockwave, Flash, etc. They are accepted by only a handful of ad sites, and require additional technology and programming by banner ad creators and ad servers. This means that such ads might not load while a user is at a Web site, or may not serve properly. It is a must to create a second ad that can be served to users who aren't able to download the interactive ad banner. JupiterResearch reports that by 2009, rich media ad units will account for over half of all spending on online display ads.

Banner Ad Success Borrows from Direct Response

Banners are more like direct response ads than image and awareness ads. Like other direct response ads, they can be tested and measured to determine which ads pull best and which don't pull at all. Testing has demonstrated that some banner ads work better on certain Web sites than on others, and that small adjustments in copy, color, or offer can greatly increase CTRs. Because response—and therefore test results—are almost instantaneous, some marketers test as many as 100 ads a month against the control.

Unlike traditional direct marketing ads, banner ads have a high burnout rate. A carefully targeted banner ad campaign may get stale quickly, as users see the same banner ads many times. Marketers usually create a series of three or more ads which are rotated on a server. Pushing the reload or refresh button on a browser will cause a different ad to be served. Unlike the long lead times in print advertising (ad materials must be submitted well in advance of publication), banner ads that don't get optimal CTRs or that have worn out can be replaced the same day. This greatly reduces the time for testing; banner campaigns make such tests virtually real-time.

Creating Responsive Banner Ads

Creating responsive banner ads, like creating effective television, print, or direct mail ads, follows good direct marketing creative practice. Testing has confirmed that the following guidelines lead to banner ads that get the highest number of clicks:

- Keep it simple. Too much text, too many graphics, too many colors overload users and discourage them from clicking through.

- Show people. Banner ads that depict people that users can identify with get higher CTRs.

- Use clear qualifying language. The better the copy describes what a site is about, the better qualified the person clicking through will be.

- Use a strong call to action. The call-to-click should define the main action(s) prospects are expected to take.

- Create a sense of urgency. Ask users to click now; no one can click on a banner once it's gone.

- Use the words "Click here" on the banner. Simple as this sounds, banner ads with "Click here" consistently pull better than banner ads without.

- Use color carefully. Look at the sites where the banner ad will run and choose colors that will complement the campaign objective on those sites.

- Use movement. It draws attention to the ad on an otherwise static page.

- Think of a banner ad as teaser copy for a Web site. Create a meta-page or a unique "splash page" for transition.

- Use high production values. The cleaner and more professional a banner ad looks, the more credibility it conveys, and the higher the CTR will be.

- Test, test, test. Test new banner ads, new offers, new calls to action, new approaches, and rich media.

Planning Banner Ad Campaign Objectives

Planning banner ad campaigns follows good direct marketing practice. Before developing the campaign, it is imperative to determine the end goal of the campaign. Quantify the goal by specifying how many sales, leads, members, subscribers, downloads, completed surveys, etc., are expected for the program. How the campaign is executed, measured, targeted, and created will all depend on these factors.

Start with a quantified objective such as a certain number of CTRs. Banner ad campaigns are often likened to traffic building. One goal of the banner ad is to drive the highest number of qualified CTRs. However, banner campaigns will ultimately be judged on how well they reach a marketer's final goal.

Changes in copy, call to action, animation, interactivity, color, the offer, banner size, and media placement can all impact how many people click through and how qualified they are. Banner ad media weight (e.g., total impressions) will impact the number of CTRs, as will technology issues (e.g., too many hits for the site server or Internet Service Provider to manage).

While many marketers may also have a branding goal as a direct response objective, one of these objectives must take precedence. Most campaigns are judged on a cost-per-action basis. The accountability offered by the Web lends itself perfectly to this objective.

Media Planning and Testing

To target banner ads, seek affinities between the ad's message and a Web site's audience. Do your best to match site demographics/psychographics with those of your target audience. Geography, content, and brand are also issues to consider when planning a campaign. Geography may seem like a surprising criterion for a medium that spans the globe, but a local restaurant chain, a regional auto dealer, and other companies seeking to promote a particular location will want to select sites with regional appeal.

An organization's Web log files are a good starting point for determining where to test banner ads. Log files maintain records of every "hit" on a Web site and may be accessed through your own server. Use them to discover the domains and sites where visitors came from and how long they stayed. They show domains and sites where existing traffic is already coming. It makes sense that the best of these would be good sites to place an organization's banner ads.

Choosing sites may not be easy. Start by testing sites that best reach the target audience and offer a lower CPM. After learning which sites perform the best, the test can be expanded to include the winners as well as additional sites from categories that performed well. If some additional budget is available, testing new or even broader categories may be appropriate. This allows for a continued effort to accomplish quantified goals, while continuing to reveal what works and what doesn't.

Web Ad Networks

Web ad networks offer a number of advantages to marketers. They simplify Web media planning and buying by aggregating small, medium, or large Web sites. They offer advertisers a way to gain a reasonable amount of unduplicated reach from visitors to many different Web sites with the convenience of a single media buy.

While aggregation offers a benefit for people too busy to track down and review media kits for hundreds or thousands of small Web sites, it also has its downside. Although it is possible to specify or exclude certain broad categories of sites, it is difficult to request specific sites. Aggregators will try to place your ad on sites with compatible demographics and regionality, but buys are run-of-network or run-of-category. Most networks do not distribute impressions equally throughout all of the Web sites within their network. Many sell "remnant inventory" from sites that may not have been able to sell their inventory individually.

Ad networks do offer the ability to test categories of sites at a significantly lower cost than testing just one or two sites. This allows advertisers to get their message in front of a lot of individuals, in different environments, with minimal financial exposure.

Upon completion of an ad network test, the results can show which sites or categories of sites performed best against the objective. The planner or buyer can then work with the network and negotiate a new buy that is more targeted, based on the actual test results. Networks also allow a banner ad campaign to be adjusted while the program is still in test. On short notice—even the same day—the schedule can be adjusted to replace banner ads in underperforming Web sites or categories.

Not all ad networks are the same. Atlas Solutions, DoubleClick, 24/7 Real Media, TACODA Audience Networks, BehaviorLink, and Advertising.com may be better choices for banner campaigns whose goals are brand building or awareness. BurstMedia, a network that aggregates medium and smaller sites, is best used where the greater reach using different categories and channels is a benefit. The same thing happens in other markets in the same industry. Time Inc. Business and Finance Network (www.businessandfinancenetwork.com) has spread its products and services across various categories, including banner ads, integrated opportunities, channels, targeting, roadblocks, podcasting, webinars, and digital magazines through its group of premium Web sites (e.g., CNN).

These programs link various banner ad campaigns to sponsorships, co-branded landing pages and jump pages, content integration, rich media, sweepstakes, and other promotional tools. Such programs are likely better where branding matters more than response.

Thus, networks play an important role. They allow marketers to increase their reach across many different Web sites and categories. They have become an essential ingredient in online media planning. Their ability to aggregate Web sites and to test and implement changes means that they should be considered in any Internet direct marketing banner ad campaign.

Banner Ad Analytics

There are a variety of online measurement standards. Online advertising expenditures and audiences may be measured by number of ads served (e.g., impressions), number of ads clicked through (banner ads actually clicked on by a user), and dollar volume (a traditional ad spending metric).

Some organizations measure usage at the ad server, while others sign up consumer panels that agree to have their behavior monitored. Forrester online research firm (www.forrester.com), Internet Advertising Bureau (www.iab.net), Nielsen NetRatings (www.netratings.com), among many others, offer slightly different views of demographics, session time, or other metrics.

A Web site's server also captures valuable information on its log files about every visitor to the site. Information to be harvested from the Web site's server includes:

- Time and date of each request
- What pages, files, etc., were requested
- The Internet Protocol (IP) address of the requesting computer
- The browser and version used by the visitor (e.g., Netscape 4.7, Explorer 5.0, etc.)
- Computer operating system used by the visitor (PC, Macintosh, etc.)
- The referring URL, e.g., where a visitor has clicked onto a link

No matter which method of measurement is used, the Internet's real-time immediacy means that results are reported quickly. The response curve to banner ads is so steep that it is possible to gauge the performance of a banner ad an hour or two after it appears.

Using E-Mail in Internet Direct Marketing

E-mail is one of the most effective tools in the Internet direct marketing arsenal. Airlines, online travel agents, E-commerce sites, and a host of others have successfully implemented e-mail programs that generate significant results. E-mail is the natural evolution from direct mail. E-mail can be the highest ROI form of direct marketing currently available. A complete e-mail campaign (list rental, creative development, fulfillment, etc.) can be conducted for pennies per contact and generate high response rates—CTRs of 10 to 20 percent.

E-mail allows a level of sophistication not achievable by direct mail. Marketers can determine the best days of the week to mail, the best hours of the day to mail (it is different for B2B vs. B2C), and test dozens, even hundreds of variables in a short period of time, something not possible in traditional direct mail.

Today, best practice calls for the use of e-mail as part of a multichannel marketer campaign. According to a 2006 study by JupiterResearch, 71 percent of e-mail marketers reported that they used offline direct marketing, including print and catalog marketing, in addition to e-mail. Nearly half (47 percent) reported using banner ads and 34 percent reported using search engine marketing. According to David Daniels, author of the report and Research Director at JupiterResearch, this indicates that e-mail marketing has become an important part of the overall marketing mix.

There are two ways to get lists for e-mail programs. You can rent "opt-in" lists of users who have given permission to use their names in this way, or you can create a unique database of visitors to a Web site. Using a Web site's own database is the safest and most responsive way to do online e-mail programs.

The Benefits of Internet Direct Mail

- Reaches its target in seconds, not days or weeks.
- Begins to get responses seconds after it is sent. With 90 percent of the responses in just four days later, results can be tabulated and analyzed faster.
- Can reach customers and prospects in 160 countries irrespective of political borders, time zones, currencies, or postal systems.
- Is simple to produce. There's no need to involve designer, Web developers, or programmers unless the campaign will incorporate sophisticated graphics.
- Costs less and can be more profitable. Printing and mailing 100,000 pieces can cost $60,000 to $80,000. Internet direct mail costs pennies per prospect—and can yield a profit even with a 1 percent response rate.
- Works as well or better than regular direct mail. Targeted e-mail results in a sale 5 to 15 percent of the time, compared to 0.5 to 2 percent for banner ads. Response rates are higher, not lower, than conventional direct mail.

Source: Internet Direct Mail: The Complete Guide to Successful E-Mail Marketing Campaigns by Stevan Roberts, Michelle Feit, and Robert Bly.

Rented Opt-In Lists

Many firms offer lists that have been compiled from places within the Internet. However, before you use such lists, gain a good understanding of how the names were compiled. Virtually every online list claims to be opt-in, but it is easy for companies to use software that sifts the Internet, compiling names without users' knowledge. Mailing such names will create an avalanche of response by users who are offended.

The best protection is to work with a reputable online list broker or permission list marketers that use opt-in lists—no bulk Unsolicited Commercial E-mail (UCE), or spam. Companies such as PostMaster Direct, Listrak (from listrak.com), and YesMail all have lists where users have voluntarily signed up ("opted in") to receive commercial e-mail about topics and products that interest them (see Exhibit 16–6).

The precise definition of "opt-in e-mail" is unclear and has been a matter of intense debate. According to the Web site MarketingTerms.com, single opt-in simply means that actions were taken to sign up for the e-mail in question. The term "double opt-in" means that the subscriber has actively confirmed a subscription, typically by responding to an automatically generated message sent to the e-mail address. Proponents of double opt-in may not actually use that term, as they feel any e-mail labeled "opt-in" must be verified.

Recent litigation has forced companies such as YesMail to agree that the only true opt-in is double opt-in, in which a user gives permission and then confirms that permission by responding to an e-mail from the Web site that says, in effect, "Unless you respond to this e-mail, you are not opted in."

Creating an Online Database

Creating an online database is the best way to ensure that the names mailed have indeed given their permission. Database names will also be the most responsive.

To build an online list, clearly inform customers or visitors to a Web site how you intend to use their submitted e-mail address. Many companies default any e-mail addresses they receive at their site into their outbound marketing lists. It remains imperative to give users a way to turn off this default. Better yet, leave the default *off* and provide the user a valuable reason to turn it on when they sign up. The list will be smaller, but better qualified.

If you have already collected e-mail addresses but aren't certain that you have gained users' permission, send a short, simple e-mail of your intentions. Ask users to reply or follow a Web link if they wish to receive your white papers, newsletters, promotions, or even opt out at this point.

Seth Godin, author of *Permission Marketing: Turning Strangers into Friends, and Friends into Customers*, notes that users and customers don't give permission forever.

EXHIBIT 16–6

Category Registration at Forrester Online Research Firm (www.Forrester.com)

This site allows users to register to receive permission e-mails by category or Web site and to specify the volume, frequency, and format of e-mails received.

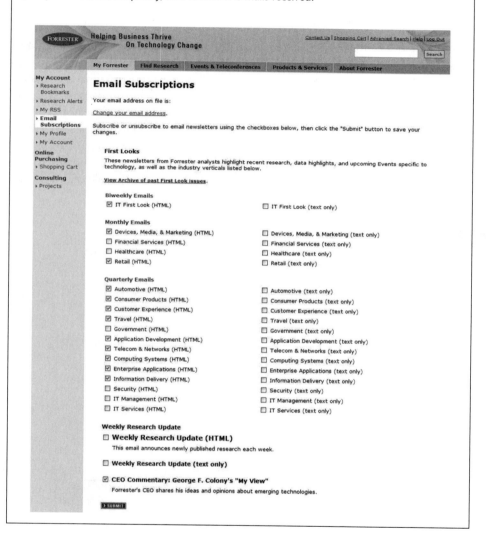

Godin recommends that marketers regularly communicate with the names on their permission databases to renew that permission and continue to build a long-term relationship.

According to EmailLabs.com, there are many factors to build and maintain an online database of subscribers. How you present your opt-in pages and forms determines the rate of list growth, the quality of your list, and establishes subscriber expectations that drive e-mail performance.

EmailLabs has developed a list of best practices to help marketers optimize their e-mail marketing (See Exhibit 16–7).

Creating E-Mail Campaigns

Like other direct marketing mail, e-mail has the goal of generating the greatest ROI. Deliverability (e.g., getting through to recipients), readership, click-through, and conversion are key issues in analyzing e-mail programs. E-mail has a very steep response curve. Whereas in traditional direct marketing customers may respond over a number of weeks, online customers respond very quickly—or not at all.

Creating e-mails that generate response takes skill and experience. There are many variables that affect response, including the format (text, HTML, etc.); from line; subject line; introductory or lead copy; length of body copy and content; calls to action; the offer; deadlines; links within the e-mail; even the unsubscribe message.

EXHIBIT 16–7

EmailLabs' Chart

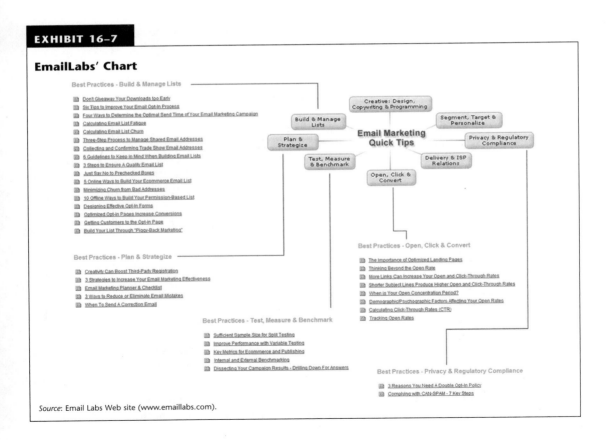

Source: Email Labs Web site (www.emaillabs.com).

E-mail has proven to be a useful medium on its own, and a durable and useful part of multichannel marketing campaigns. While it may not be the perfect customer acquisition tool, its use in back-end programs and customer marketing is secure. For example, E-commerce sites can reduce abandoned shopping carts by using e-mail to remind customers that there are still products in their cart. An automated *e-mail based on a previous purchase* (EBOPP) can be sent to buyers to generate additional sales from recent buyers. *E-mails based on special interests* (EBOSIs) can be sent to customers offering cross-sell opportunities based on knowledge of past purchases.

Tools and Techniques of Direct Marketing Apply to E-Mail

Marketers need to start with an identified target market and the e-mail lists and addresses to reach them. Next, they need to create e-mails that have engaging creative, actionable copy, a clear message and image, and brand- and message-consistent graphics. The higher the production values in e-mails, the better the response.

In addition, e-mails should include appropriate offers to the target audience, multiple calls to action, and ways to respond that the target group has indicated a willingness to use. Remember that e-mails don't close the sale or the conversion; usually a Web site does. That means that you need to measure, track, and analyze results to both the e-mail and conversion. And, in e-mail, testing is key.

Writing Effective E-Mails

Good e-mails have messages tailored to the audience. The copy should be relevant, short, and concise. The tone should be casual, as if it came from a real person, not written as if it were from a corporate brochure. There can be a touch of informality, familiarity, warmth, and sincerity in e-mail copy. Nevertheless, its tone should be consistent with your brand, products/services, customers, prospects, customer experience, and objectives.

The subject and lead (e.g., the first three lines of the message) are most important. Often, this is the only copy a prospect or customer will read. Don't start with "There are," "We," "Important," or the organization name. Try something like "Sorry to interrupt. I realize it's hard to pull yourself away from those great videos on YouTube. But, I've got news that will interest you." Create excitement, and let people know what action you want them to take.

The call to action is critical if you expect recipients to respond. Calls to action should be specific, telling the reader what you want them to do, and what they will get when they do it. Including a deadline for action often improves results. Links, which are important to conversion, should be used liberally in e-mail. Marketers should not be afraid to use two, three, even four linked calls to action within e-mail copy.

And, while "unsubscribe" messages may be required, put them at the bottom of the page, not at the top of the message. The bottom position provides more positive response and fewer "unsubscribe" returns.

Writing Effective Subject Lines

E-mail subject lines should be short—as few words as possible. Most e-mail browsers limit subject lines to 50 characters. Use five to ten words to be most effective. The use of ALL CAPS doesn't improve response. Readers think that you are shouting at them. Avoid words like Limited Time, Free, Offer, Wow, Only. Also, exclamation points and words that are obviously spam are not only a turnoff to readers, they are among the top words filtered by spam software.

Targeting and Personalization Can Triple E-Mail Results

E-mail marketers have learned that personalized e-mails have higher deliverability than nonpersonalized e-mails. As a result, customer response rates nearly double when three to six data elements are personalized in e-mail communications. Results can triple when seven or more elements are used.

Key data attributes for personalization include:

- Name
- Interests
- Gender
- Age
- Purchase history
- Message frequency preference

Source: Yesmail Data and Analytics Group.

E-Mail Frequency

Because of its low cost, there is a temptation to over e-mail prospects and customers. Marketers must balance continuity against annoyance. Ask what frequency your customers are used to. Many campaigns are run over six weeks, with four drops on days 1, 15, 30, and 45. However, every marketer must develop a frequency ratio for each campaign, each segment based on experience and the objectives of the campaign. Best practice is to plan campaigns as part of an overall integrated marketing communication plan. Multichannel campaigns provide a synergy that seems to generate additional response across all media.

Testing is much less expensive in e-mail than in direct mail. Amy Africa, of Web consulting firm Eight by Eight, recommends that marketers test a number of things in e-mail:

- Time of day that the e-mail is sent (different in B2B vs. B2C)

- Day of week (both TOD and DAW change over time)

- Format (Test, HTML, Rich Media, etc.)

- From address (best to make it from a person, not a department or organization)

- Subject line (spam filters affect this)

- Size of e-mail (don't assume everyone wants short e-mails)

- Offer and length of offer (don't be afraid to explain fully or repeat the offer)

- Placement and number of visuals (attractive visuals pull the eye in)

E-Mail Newsletters

E-mail newsletters, in addition to communicating with customers, are a good method for building e-mail databases. They integrate perfectly as part of CRM programs that marketers may be implementing. Newsletters should provide relevant content, news, and other items of interest to subscribers. They can be highly personalized for each recipient using dynamic content. They can be sent on a schedule (e.g., monthly) or be event-triggered when a user completes some action with a Web site (e.g., subscribe, purchase, or request information). Newsletters can include customizable surveys, forms, and other profile pages to capture information from customers on an ongoing basis.

Marketers that use newsletters track the history of recipients and get detailed reporting of their Web activity. The ongoing reporting provides important feedback as to the status of the customer. When there is no customer activity, an occasional e-mail offering an unsubscribe option may be a way to cull prospects that have lost interest or reactivate customers that have not been heard from over a period of time.

E-Mail Analytics

Measuring results from e-mail is made more difficult because users must complete a number of actions, then respond to different channels, such as a Web site or landing page. Web analytics software can help measure response and conversion at the back end and what happens to the e-mails.

E-mail software helps to calculate the open rate—how many people actually looked at the e-mail—and it can tell how many people deleted the e-mail. Click-through rates can be monitored by both the e-mail software and Web analytics.

And, e-mail software can measure how many users are repeats, that is, responded to the same e-mail more than once.

E-mail browsing software is constantly updated, for example adding viewing panes where users can preview their e-mail without opening, deleting, or clicking on it. While new features are added to browsing software, e-mail service bureaus continue to update their software as well. This helps to keep the e-mail marketing space one of the most interesting for marketers and users.

Managing Unsolicited Commercial E-Mail

The postal direct marketing world operates on the principle of opt-out. Opt-out means that the marketer can target anyone they wish and the person must contact the mailer to "opt out" of future mailings. Opt-out works in postal marketing because the economics dictate that marketers will target and limit their outbound mail. It is simply unprofitable to mass-mail untargeted, low-response names.

However, in e-mail the economics dictate the opposite. With virtually no incremental variable cost, mass e-mailing 10,000 names costs nearly the same as e-mailing 10 million. Such untargeted, unwanted e-mail is known as Unsolicited Commercial E-mail or UCE (aka spam). UCE first surfaced in 1994, when an immigration law firm called Canter & Siegel used e-mail to offer foreign nationals help in acquiring green cards necessary to gain employment in the United States. UCE has become one of the most difficult issues for marketers.

The barrage of e-mail has led consumers to label any e-mail communication that is not relevant or looks suspicious as spam. Many consumers have two, three, or more e-mail boxes, hoping to have one e-mail box that is relatively free of UCEs. To avoid having e-mail filtered, marketers need to consider the nature of the recipient's consent, the content and presentation of the message, and the quality of the preexisting or current business relationship.

The Can Spam Act of 2003

Despite efforts by marketers to self-police, the amount of UCEs has increased. As a result, the U.S. Congress passed the Controlling the Assault of Non-Solicited Pornography and Marketing Act, also called the Can Spam Act of 2003. This legislation took effect in January 2004.

Can Spam applies to all commercial e-mail originating in the United States and containing an advertisement or promotion of a commercial product or service. The legislation requires that e-mail messages stand out as legitimate and valuable. The national law preempts all state spam laws. Under Can Spam, all commercial e-mail must "clearly and conspicuously" include the following:

- *Identification* that the message is a solicitation, except where the recipient has given prior *affirmative consent* (opt-in).

- *Notice* of opportunity to opt out, including a return e-mail address or other Internet-based mechanism by which the recipient may opt out.

- A valid physical postal address (e.g., a street address) of the sender.

In addition, senders may not use fraudulent header information or deceptive subject lines (e.g., fw or re). Also, they cannot harvest e-mail messages automatically or purchase harvested e-mail addresses. And, senders must allow for opt-out of future commercial e-mail messages for up to 30 days after the transmission of the message, and all opt-outs must be honored within ten business days. The sale or transfer of e-mail addresses for which there has been an opt-out is prohibited.

Excluded from the law are e-mails that are transactional or relationship-based, such as those that show an account status, subscription, or other communication with existing customers. Existing customers are defined as those with a prior relationship going back up to 18 months.

Beyond Can Spam

Despite the enactment of Can Spam, consumers' e-mail boxes are fuller than ever. The Direct Marketing Association (DMA) and the Interactive Advertising Bureau (IAB) recognize the issues that consumers, government, and industry have with e-mail. These groups are working on a way to ensure that consumers trust the organizations they receive e-mail from. The IAB has identified the following as critical elements for building positive e-mail reputation:

- *ISP whitelists and automated feedback loops*: ISP-level tools help identify "good" senders and facilitate e-mail delivery—reputation at the local level.

- *Authentication*: technology protocols that establish the true identities of senders and allow for the development of a sender's e-mail reputation.

- *Accreditation services*: third-party programs that certify sender policies and practices and contribute to a sender's e-mail reputation.

- *Reputation services*: monitors that gather all available data intelligence on senders and aggregate a global reputation score.

The Last Word on E-Mail

Despite its proliferation and overuse, e-mail remains a powerful tool. When personalized and targeted, its low cost and relatively high response make it especially powerful as a customer marketing tool. While its use will continue to cause some controversy, it remains an important element in the tools and techniques of direct marketing.

CASE STUDY: DealerADvantage e-Newsletter from Cars.com

Written by Jacobs & Clevenger with approval of its client, Cars.com.

BACKGROUND

Within the last decade, the world of car shopping has changed dramatically. So have the communications streams that auto dealers use to entice customers into their dealerships.

In the past, the primary marketing force was newspaper advertising. However, newspapers are taking on a far less dominant role in promoting auto sales today. Online searches have become an essential conduit in connecting auto dealers and prospects. In fact, statistics indicate that the closer a shopper is to a purchase decision, the more inclined they are to search for a vehicle online.

In the world of automotive sales, Cars.com is one of the fastest-growing online resources for buying and selling new and used vehicles. Cars.com reaches more than 8 million car shoppers, and connects a buyer and seller every 7 seconds.

Dealers Are the Driving Force

The foundation for the success of Cars.com is its nationwide network of auto dealers. They advertise with Cars.com by posting their dealership's inventory in an online marketplace.

Considering the overall profile of auto dealers, some powerful similarities come to light. As a rule, dealers focus sharply on bottom-line sales. They are also extremely busy, skeptical, visually oriented, and always results-focused.

However, when examining the dealer profile more closely, key differences begin to take shape. Individual car dealers have varying degrees of Internet expertise, adding to the challenge of selling and sustaining the value of an online product. In addition, decision makers vary greatly. Some are general managers of independent dealerships, who constantly juggle responsibilities. Others are Internet sales managers, who must prove the viability and performance of online listing services. Dealerships also vary greatly in overall size and in their adoption of the Internet as a sales tool.

CHALLENGES

The primary challenges facing Cars.com dealer communications were:
- Retaining existing dealers.
- Driving engagement among a group that is highly action-oriented.
- Providing current dealers with tools and information to ensure they are optimizing Cars.com as an effective promotional resource.
- Positioning Cars.com as a market leader and support system for prospective dealerships, including those that are just getting into online listing services.

SOLUTION

In order to answer these diverse challenges, marketing initiatives focused on acquiring and retaining auto dealerships as advertisers.

From the onset, one extremely valuable asset was evident. As a Web-based company, Cars.com has e-mail addresses for their dealerships, allowing the communication flow to be both instant and ongoing.

Two vital insights helped drive the marketing efforts.
- Engagement tends to be key with Web-based companies.
- Dealers tend to be skeptical about sales-oriented communications.

Clearly, ongoing communications would be essential. However, it is almost impossible to "sell a salesperson," so every touchpoint would require a highly interactive format and a truly informative perspective.

Marketing Makes Headlines for Cars.com

To help Cars.com connect with current dealers and prospects, Jacobs & Clevenger developed an e-newsletter. Each month, the Dealer**ADvantage** e-newsletter delivered interactive tools, fresh articles, expert opinions, and industry insight. Even the title was targeted to engage dealers immediately (See Exhibit 16–8).

Knowing that the customer mindset of dealers is bottom-line focused, the agency was careful to ensure that the e-newsletter content was actionable and sales-oriented. The content of Dealer**ADvantage** was based upon proven tips and techniques that showed dealers how to optimize their Internet presence on Cars.com, including many valuable learnings from the Cars.com training team.

To maintain an unbiased and informative tone, Dealer**ADvantage** provided nonpartisan, objective content. This helped to establish Cars.com as a trusted industry resource. The editorial was also timely and relevant, because hot-button issues could be revised from month to month based on industry trends.

The design of Dealer**ADvantage** was guided by e-mail best practices, which included keeping most relevant content within the preview pane, allowing essential text to be readable with images turned off. In addition, content was provided in a short, scannable, and concise format. To build additional intrigue, Dealer**ADvantage** leveraged an interactive engagement device such as the Cars.com "CarsStars Report," which let Cars.com dealers find the hottest-selling cars in their market.

Because many independent dealers do not have corporate e-mail addresses and instead rely upon a service provider such as AOL, Hotmail, or Gmail, it was important to utilize an e-mail delivery tool that ensured white listing with major Internet service providers. This ensured an acceptable e-mail delivery rate.

RESULTS

The Dealer**ADvantage** e-newsletter has proven to be a low-cost, highly tailored, and truly informative electronic communications vehicle for Cars.com and its dealers.

- The inaugural and follow-up editions continue to be a success.
- The open and click-through rates are consistent with industry averages, which exceeded expectations considering the increasingly cluttered marketplace and challenging target audience.
- Dealer engagement is strong, as the interactive component and request for reports exceeded forecasts and planned capacity.
- Low opt-out rates signify that dealers see genuine value in receiving the Dealer**ADvantage** e-newsletter from Cars.com.

EXHIBIT 16–8

DealerADvantage e-Newsletter from Cars.com

From: News from Cars.com [mailto:newsupdates@cars.com]
Subject: Cars.com Newsletter: Competitive Pricing

Can't view? Click here

DealerADvantage
News and tips to drive online success
In partnership with *chicagotribune.com*

Volume 19 • August 2007   Forward this Edition • Subscribe • Past Issues

Dealer Poll

How does your dealership plan to leverage video in online advertising?

- We are using inventory based video to showcase used vehicles on our website and on third party sites
- We are posting our existing commercials to online sites
- We are creating custom videos for the online environment
- We are not currently using video, but plan to explore it in 2008
- We have no plans to use video in our online advertising

Click here to respond

DealerADvantage

So Now You're an Internet Sales Manager
Delivering Online Results
Friday, Sept. 14, Noon ET
Are you new to the Internet sales department? Want to get ahead? Join us for a free webinar where you'll get tips of the trade from top ISMs and find out what they wish they knew when they started as an ISM.

Enroll Now

Did you miss
Jump Starting New Car Sales?
Click here to view recording.

Fast Facts

83% of dealers say clicks to their website from 3rd party auto internet sites are equally or more valuable than clicks from search engines.

Source: Cars.com Research – 2007

Tips & Techniques

Running on Automatic

When you're away from your desk helping another customer or the dealership is closed, an email auto responder may be just the ticket to connect with leadsenders in a timely fashion. While this first point of contact can be a powerful first step on the road to a sale, it can also send buyers running to your competition if it's not used properly. Are your auto responses on track to make a deal? Read more to find out.

Learn more

Not Just for Online Shoppers
Expedite Sales with Online Pricing Tools

When customers want to research the price of a vehicle, the internet is often the first place they turn. A wide variety of pricing tools help them understand what they'll have to pay to drive off your lot in a new set of wheels. While these tools are certainly great for consumers, have you thought about how you can actually help you increase your bottom line? Yes, online pricing tools can use them to enhance your bottom line? Yes, online pricing tools can use them to enhance your bottom line? Read more to find out how you can put online pricing tools to work for your dealership to set competitive prices, level-set customer expectations and build trust for a faster sale.

Learn more

Follow the Trail
Vehicle Sales Reports Help Measure Online Advertising Effectiveness, Stock Your Store for Success

By Ralph Ebersole
Cars.com

What's in a sale? If you work with an automotive shopping site such as Cars.com that tracks the number and type of car-buyer contacts your listings receive until they sell, the answer extends beyond a healthy profit for the store and a solid commission for you. Not only do these reports allow you to identify the source of the sale (e.g., email, phone call, walk-in visit or click to your website), they also ensure you have the cars that car buyers want. Properly utilizing this data, in turn, improves the effectiveness of your online advertising and increases the profit on each vehicle you sell.

Learn more

How to Sell Cars to YouTube Generation
By Wards Staff, *Ward's Dealer Business*

The MySpace/iPod/Text/Blackberry/YouTube generation gets information from a myriad of sources, all originating from the Internet.

Learn more

Has the Internet outgrown the Internet Department?
By David Kain, *Kain Automotive*

Ten years ago when a dealer wished to sell cars online it was actually quite a simple model; Assign a salesperson to the job, buy a computer, buy some leads, make some appointments and sell some cars. This model persisted for the next several years at most dealerships and the marketing actions necessary to compete online in your local market were actually manageable within an Internet department. When the first dealer and third party websites came along that allowed dealers to post "live inventory" it changed the dynamic completely.

Learn more

6.5 Tips to Make E-mail Work at Your Dealership
By Cory Mosley, *Mosley Automotive Group*

Has the internet really changed the used-car business? Yes and no.

Learn more

Best of DealerADvantage

Save the Sale
When Questions Arise, Helping Car Buyers Find Peace of Mind Keeps the Shopping Process Moving

Concerns? You've probably heard a few, from "Why don't you know if you have the vehicle in stock?" and "Why do you need my phone number?" and "How much do you think my current vehicle is worth?" How you address these questions and guide the prospect back to the business at hand — buying a car — will do more than help control the conversation. It could help you earn the sale.

Learn more

Become a Cars.com Dealer   DealerCenter

PILOT PROJECT

The Cars.com Dealer**ADvantage** e-newsletter is sent to dealers on a monthly basis. Achieving the optimal mailing frequency is always an issue for marketers.

Develop a plan to help Cars.com learn the most efficient frequency for its e-newsletter (e.g., daily, weekly, monthly, quarterly, twice a year, etc.).

A. Should it be sent more frequently? Less frequently? Why?

B. If they increase frequency, would they necessarily increase readership?

C. What variables can Cars.com use to measure this?

D. Are there issues other than frequency that Cars.com should be concerned with?

Key Points

▶ Keep banner ads simple. Show people, use clear qualifying language, create a sense of urgency, and include a strong call to action. Ads with "Click here" consistently pull better than banner ads without.

▶ Test banner ads to learn which pull best and which don't pull at all. Some sites work better than others and small adjustments in copy, color, or offer can greatly increase CTRs. Test results will be almost instantaneous.

▶ Establish a goal for a banner ad campaign by specifying how many sales, leads, members, subscribers, downloads, completed surveys, etc., are expected for the program. One goal is to drive the highest number of qualified CTRs. Banner ad media weight (e.g., total impressions) will impact the number of CTRs, as will technology issues (e.g., too many hits for the site server or Internet Service Provider (ISP) to manage).

▶ Target banner ads by seeking affinities between the ad's message and a Web site's audience. Match site demographics/psychographics with those of the target audience.

▶ E-mail promotions have virtually no postage or printing costs and development time can be lightning fast. A complete e-mail campaign (list rental, creative development, fulfillment, etc.) can be conducted for pennies per contact and generate high response rates, CTRs of 10–20 percent.

▶ In e-mails, the subject and lead (e.g., the first three lines of the message) are the most important. However, include and repeat a strong call to action if you want readers to respond.

▶ There are two sources of lists for e-mail programs: "opt-in" lists of users who have given permission to use their names in this way, and a Web site's own database—the safest and most responsive way to do online e-mail programs.

E-COMMERCE

Electronic commerce (E-commerce) is the electronic link from businesses to suppliers, distributors, manufacturers, and customers that facilitates, creates, or supports transactions and interactions.

E-commerce is more than selling online. Business activities, enabled by technology, link organizations to prospects and customers for communication and collaboration. This enhances an organization's ability to gain instant feedback and improve its business processes in real time.

E-commerce also extends to end-users, channel partners, vendors, and other intermediaries. It enables a free exchange of information, services, and interactions among individuals and organizations that are a part of a company's value chain. Because the Internet is not constrained by borders or boundaries, it enables organizations to become part of, or create, a global marketplace for their products and services.

E-commerce works, but only when it customizes the experience for users. Customer-centric E-commerce Web sites can help build customer relationships by allowing customers to personalize and individualize their association. They recognize an organization's customers who previously purchased online as well as from other channels. They offer choices for customer services, such as real-time keyboard chat or online voice operators. Such sites actually learn user preferences using collaborative filtering and rule-based software. Amazon.com is an example of an E-commerce Web site that takes full advantage of customer data to recognize customers, keep track of purchases, and make product recommendations based on customers' behavior and purchase preferences.

Consumer E-Commerce Growth

Consumer marketing online is starting to take root. In a *USA Today* article written in May 2006, Scott Silverman, executive director of Shop.org, attributed this to consumer comfort with the Internet. "... people are used to the Internet now, for e-mail and doing research. If retailers aren't in that [online] game, they're at a huge disadvantage," he said.

According to figures from Shop.org, the online arm of the National Retail Federation and Forrester Research (Exhibit 17–1), online retail sales (including travel) are slated to jump 20 percent in 2006 to $211.4 billion, compared to $176.4 billion in 2005. By comparison, in-store retail sales are growing at 3 percent. It is clear that consumers are starting to buy into the convenience of Internet shopping.

Jeffrey Grau, *eMarketer* senior analyst, said not only are online shoppers making more purchases online, they are buying more types of products. "Today, consumers are purchasing big-ticket items on the Internet like refrigerators and treadmills, and even high-priced luxury items such as designer apparel and jewelry."

According to research from the U.S. Census Bureau (Exhibit 17–2), the total retail sales for the first quarter of 2005 were estimated at $916.9 billion, an increase of 1.5 percent (± 0.2 percent) from the fourth quarter of 2004. The first quarter 2005 E-commerce estimate increased 23.8 percent (± 3.3 percent) from the first quarter of 2004 while total retail sales increased 7.3 percent (± 0.5 percent) in the same period. E-commerce sales in the first quarter accounted for 2.2 percent of total sales.

E-commerce will continue to grow in financial services, insurance, travel, entertainment, and sports. Even groceries are a growing online category.

EXHIBIT 17–1

Retail E-Commerce Sales in the United States, 2005 and 2006 (billions)

Retail E-commerce (excluding travel)
- $113.6
- $138.0

Retail E-commerce (including travel)
- $176.4
- $211.4

■ 2005   ■ 2006

Note: Includes computer hardware and software, autos and auto parts, apparel, accessories and footwear, home furnishings, consumer electronics, music and video, food, beverage and grocery, appliances and tools, toys and video games, gift cards and gift certificates, sporting goods and apparel, office supplies, books, event and movie tickets, jewelry, flowers and cards, baby products, computer peripherals, over-the-counter medicines and personal care, cosmetics and fragrances, and pet supplies.

Source: Shop.org and Forrester Research, May 2006.

EXHIBIT 17–2

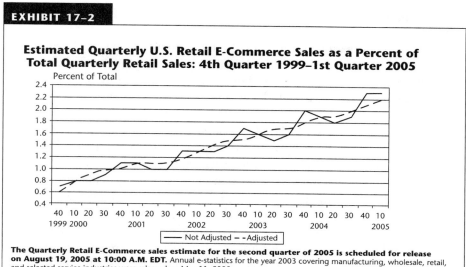

Estimated Quarterly U.S. Retail E-Commerce Sales as a Percent of Total Quarterly Retail Sales: 4th Quarter 1999–1st Quarter 2005

The Quarterly Retail E-Commerce sales estimate for the second quarter of 2005 is scheduled for release on August 19, 2005 at 10:00 A.M. EDT. Annual e-statistics for the year 2003 covering manufacturing, wholesale, retail, and selected service industries were released on May 11, 2005.

Source: U.S. Census Bureau

Infomediaries

Infomediaries are aggregators of information for consumers and businesses. They act as information exchanges and marketplaces for specific categories of products and services, bringing buyers and sellers together. Most infomediaries provide a means for a sale to be completed online. The infomediary earns a percentage or transaction fee on each sale. Buyers may request proposals on products or services. Sellers then provide price quotes based on the specifications provided by the buyer. The benefit to the buyer is that they may be able to quickly get quotes from a number of qualified sellers. The benefit to sellers is that it puts them in touch with buyers ready to make purchases, many of whom they might not be in contact with any other way. eBay, an online auction site, brings together buyers and sellers of a variety of goods and services. For example, consumers can bid on or buy heirlooms or designer reproductions, toy die-cast cars, or nearly any make or model of used car. Business buyers can bid on computers, copiers, or capital goods costing over $100,000 (e.g., catering equipment, MRI machines, etc.). In 2006, eBay's gross merchandise volume is estimated to be $12.5 billion.

Infomediaries vary as much as the Internet. W.W. Grainger created Grainger.com for industrial supplies. IMXExchange.com was created as a place for mortgage brokers to find loans for their customers. LendingTree is a consumer lending and realty services exchange where users get competitive loan offers from major, national, regional, and local lenders and search a network of Realtors® from major franchises and independents nationwide. InsWeb.com is an insurance marketplace that allows consumers to shop online for competitive quotes on automobile, term life, homeowners', renters', and individual health insurance.

Procurement

Procurement is an area where the savings from E-commerce can easily be seen. More than 60 percent of office products, janitorial supplies, shipping materials, and other frequently repurchased products are bought without long-term contracts or preferred customer pricing in small-dollar purchases averaging $50 to $100 or less per order.

Traditionally, orders are placed by a purchasing agent who creates a purchase order that is called in or faxed to a sales rep at the vendor company. The sales person inputs the order and sends it to a warehouse, where the order is picked, packed for shipping, and put into an area for deliveries. Many maintenance, repair, and operating (MRO) supplies vendor organizations have their own delivery fleets, and the order will typically be delivered the next day. Labor costs can account for as much as $125 per transaction, while the average order total often is much less. The same order entered by a user into an E-commerce system will have a comparable labor cost as low as $1.50. Rather than using a freight company, the order will be shipped out via UPS at additional savings.

Channel Conflicts Exist

Channel conflicts can and do exist as the result of implementing an E-commerce strategy. Business-to-business marketers often find their Web presence a challenge to their sales force, distributors, or other channel partners. Channel conflicts exist in consumer categories as well.

Jeans manufacturer Levi's bowed to pressure and stopped selling direct to consumers when retailers threatened to stop carrying their brands. Home Depot, the leading home improvement products chain, has a policy of not carrying the products of manufacturers that sell direct.

Yet, many marketers find that selling across multiple channels is imperative in today's customer-centric marketplace. Some buyers will only buy products through retail channels. Others prefer catalogs. As home computer penetration continues to grow, and more products and services are offered online, more consumers are becoming comfortable purchasing this way. What is most important for an organization to learn is how their customers like to buy from them, then meet that need.

Redesigning Customer Business Processes for E-Commerce

How does an organization choose the right online business model? To make the most of this or any opportunity, an organization must pinpoint its core strengths. Then, it must turn on the creative juices to come up with new revenue streams, utilizing those core strengths.

Most organizations developing E-commerce initiatives have a carefully crafted objectives statement that promises that the investment in E-business will improve customer satisfaction, improve customer loyalty, and help them to gain a greater share of market/customers. These are fine objectives for any organization in today's highly competitive marketplace. But this is only a start at developing a successful online business model.

To achieve these goals requires translating an organization's business approach into processes that are Web-centric. Web-centric processes are fast, easy to use, and stripped down. Revenues may come, but profits may not be so forthcoming. To understand these processes, organizations need to look at every aspect of these processes from a customer's point of view.

Customers don't endlessly search for information. They go online for a purpose. They want quick access to information, fast answers to their questions, and a purchase process that is easy and thorough. Many E-commerce sites fall flat in these areas. Some even fail at the ordering stage.

Shopping cart abandonment is one of the greatest challenges of E-commerce. According to a 2006 report from Forrester Research, the average abandoned-cart rate was just about 50 percent, while some 88 percent of online shoppers abandoned shopping carts in 2005. The report found that an estimated $33 billion was lost due to abandoned carts. The Forrester study results, shown in Exhibit 17–3, indicate the major cause of abandonment is sticker shock over shipping charges. Studies have shown that by moving the shipping and handling costs to a screen with the completed order, they cut their shopping cart abandonment rate in half.

EXHIBIT 17–3

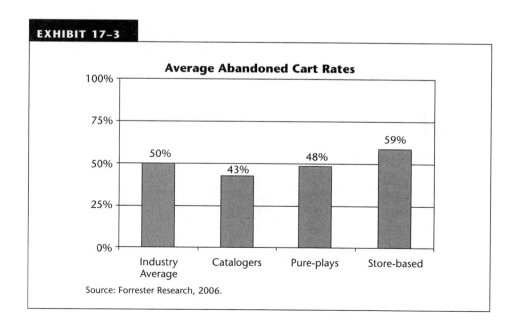

Source: Forrester Research, 2006.

The Perfect Shopping Cart

MarketLive has created a list of guidelines for creating the perfect shopping cart (See Exhibit 17–4). Keep in mind that the shopping cart is the first page of the checkout process—and therefore the most important.

Many organizations find that they must change their existing thinking to streamline their systems for E-commerce. Before processes can be streamlined, E-commerce teams must learn how target markets and purchasing behavior work for others as well as from within their organization.

To accomplish this, entrepreneurs need to gain an understanding of how interactions are triggered within their organization. Determine your organization's E-business processes as you believe they work. Identify the gaps in these processes and the work-arounds. Learn about the routine adjustments to the standard processes that ensure that orders are filled, billing problems solved, and delivery expedited. Then map out the new E-business processes and how they will work together (See Exhibit 17–5).

In many ways an E-business launch resembles a catalog launch. To learn more about the tools and techniques of catalog marketing, see Chapter 19.

EXHIBIT 17–4

The Perfect Shopping Cart Principles

1. The shopping cart must be present and accessible throughout the entire shopping experience.
2. The shopping cart must enhance and build trust with the customer.
3. The shopping cart must be easy to use and reduce known purchase barriers.
4. The shopping cart must preserve the relevant shopping experience and not interfere with the path to purchase.
5. The shopping cart should be used to increase the average order size by informing, merchandising, and making clear that your products are unique, special, and different.

Source: MarketLive 2006 report "The Perfect Shopping Cart."

EXHIBIT 17–5

Map Out New Closed Loop E-Business Processes

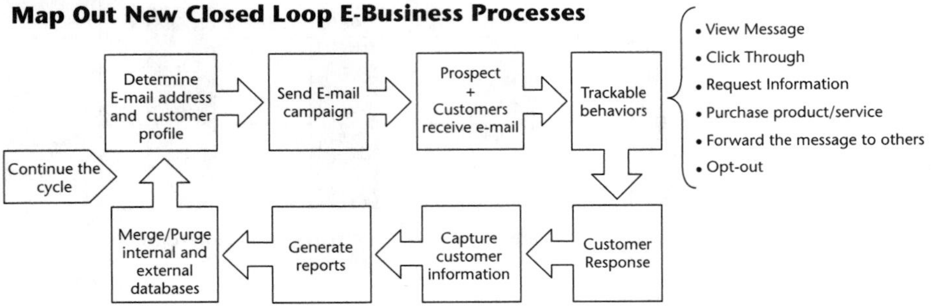

Explore Online Customer Relationship Management

Start by considering the customer relationship management (CRM) elements within your organization. Determine if you will be able to link your customer profile data to online responses and transactions. Identify actionable pieces of information that can be used to launch applications within your systems to make the process more rewarding for your customers. This will require linking your online database with data gathered in sales, customer service, and marketing departments.

Example: American Airlines (AA.com) captures profile information through its online users and feeds it to its AAdvantage Frequent Flyer database. Using this profile, AA e-mails special offers based on a customer's home airport, where they like to travel, etc. Customers can purchase electronic tickets or electronic upgrade certificates at the Web site, which go into American Airline's general reservations system and can be accessed by a telephone sales rep or an agent at the airport. No matter how the customer chooses to communicate with the company, American Airlines staff can access the records and manage the B2B and/or B2C type of relationship.

Generate a Set of Business Rules

Every organization has a set of business rules to guide their interactions with customers. Some of these rules of engagement are implicit while others are explicit. They cover a myriad of areas. Combined with customer profiles, you can target the right information, offers, products, and pricing to the right customers.

Identify the business rules your company follows. Look at discount policies (if customer X, then discount prices 15 percent); credit terms (do not ship until credit card is approved, or ship net 30 to D&B rated firms); customer options (customer requests hold order until complete to reduce shipping costs); and special promotions (waive freight charges on orders until June 30).

Identify Business Events

Business events are the necessary steps in dealing with customer processes. Common business events include placing an order, checking credit, checking inventory, shipping products, invoicing customers, collecting payment, etc. Each event will trigger interaction among your customers and the software applications within your E-commerce site. You need to ensure that information and tasks flow smoothly from one system to another for each event.

For example, what happens when customers order a product that is out of stock? Do you want customers to see the current inventory status when they go to the site, or will you advise them after they have ordered that it is out of stock? Will you charge customers for out of stock products when they are ordered or when they ship? Will customers get an order confirmation and will the confirmation tell them when the product will be in stock? Will you contact them and/or offer them an opportunity to cancel the order after X days? What is required by government regulations and are you in compliance or better than compliance?

Build a Business Object Dictionary

Every organization has a language unto itself. "Customer," "account," "order," and "product" often mean different things to different organizations. In order to design electronic applications for customers to interact with, technical staff must have agreed-upon descriptions of these words or business objects. For example, a "customer" can be someone who purchased a product or service within a week, a month, or a year; inquiries, prospects, or people who have visited a store or Web site as customers; or end-users or the purchasing agents who place the orders.

Business objects are elements that have an agreed-upon definition and create a common language within the organization. It would be difficult to design an E-commerce strategy without knowing those definitions up front.

The Buyer/Seller Model

To implement E-commerce, an organization's business processes must be transformed to accommodate E-business. Even direct marketing organizations have found it necessary to rethink their processes to fit this real-time form of marketing.

Walid Mougayar, president of CYBERManagement, developed the buyer/seller model shown in Exhibit 17–6. The exhibit outlines the selling process through traditional or electronic channels. And, it relates the sell-side processes with the customer-buying processes, to help close the loop.

The balance of this section follows Mougayar's outline and discusses the seller processes that should be considered as an organization implements an E-commerce strategy.

Distribution

Before you launch an E-commerce site, consider the steps your customers navigate in the purchase decision. Focusing on your customers will yield insights that may help you clarify the kinds and amount of content on your Web site.

If you learn that customers have a void in their information not filled by other marketers, you may wish to fill that void with content on your site. If they gain significant information through word of mouth or from information shared with

EXHIBIT 17-6

The Buyer/Seller Model

This model shows corresponding steps during the presale, order, and postsale E-commerce purchase processes.

	Sellers	**Buyers**
Presale	• Distribution • Promotion • Display • Pricing policy	• Search/Inquire for product • Discover products • Compare products • Negotiate terms
Order	• Receive order • Authorize payment • Schedule order • Build or retrieve from inventory	• Place order • Receive acknowledgment • Initiate payment • Receive product
Postsale	• Ship product • Receive payment • Support products • Marketing research	• Track purchase • Debit account • Request support • Give feedback

others in their field, you may consider creating a community area to facilitate dialogue among peers.

If your customers purchase your products through established intermediaries such as distributors, as is common in the B2B marketplace, you may wish to create private intranets for them. These Web sites can be transparent, so customers purchasing products on the distributor's Web site will see the distributor's logo, pricing, and order process instead of your company's.

The same thing can be done for an organization's largest customers, if their purchases are great enough. Such personalized Web sites are common for procurement products—office supplies, maintenance, repair, and operating (MRO) supplies—where the average order is less than $150. Computer products firms like Cisco and Dell have thousands of customer Web sites.

Another aspect to consider: the peaks and valleys of your business. Many times an E-commerce site can help open up new markets to fill in these peaks and valleys, or migrate customers to a more cost- and time-efficient method of buying and selling. Many E-tailers find that a large portion of their business occurs over the annual holiday period. Every system in your E-commerce business must be prepared for the inevitable peaks caused by this shopping period. Businesses without robust, scalable systems may find themselves with dissatisfied customers or no customers at all.

Promotion

Getting users to a Web site, keeping them there as long as possible, and getting them to come back—these are the goals for most marketers.

E-commerce sites use banner ads, e-mail programs, search engines, portals, and many other strategies to help customers and prospects discover them online. Chapter 16 discusses many of these tactics.

Affiliate programs allow companies to expand their online presence by placing links for Web sites and even individual products on affiliated Web sites across the Web. Affiliate programs offer credibility and status to fledgling Web sites and can generate revenue for a Web site that is not fully enabled for E-commerce. A commission on each sale is paid to the affiliate, so there is little up-front cost for either organization. Commissions vary, but range from 5 to 20 percent of sales. Amazon.com pays 5 percent for a purchase linked to its general Web site, and 15 percent for specific product page links, such as from an affiliated author's Web site to his book page at Amazon.com.

Word of mouth or viral marketing programs create a "buzz" for a product or service by urging customers or prospects to e-mail friends about an organization or offering incentives for users to talk about the Web site in chat rooms or other places where potential users lurk. More like public relations than targeted marketing, viral marketing programs are effective, but giving users incentives to share information via e-mail is controversial because it may be perceived as "spam."

Promotion has been one of the greatest factors in the growth of Web businesses. Some companies have spent huge sums building their brands both online and offline. Online marketers will likely continue to use a mix of media in the future. Offline media will be used to create awareness, and build and promote brands. A mix of online and offline media, applying the tools and techniques of direct marketing, will be used to drive traffic to their Web sites.

Display

The online user interface—the E-commerce Web site itself—is a key element in the mix. Other chapters describe optimum characteristics for the site such as frequent updates and design changes, graphics that are fast and easy to load, layout that allows fast click-throughs, and similar customer-friendly design.

Extensive use of graphics slows the processes of accessing, loading, and ordering from Web pages. Online users want choices, the option to view even more models than might normally be in stock, so that they can compare features, benefits, and prices against those on other sites. Many online customers report that their online shopping experiences are often unsatisfying. They can't find what they want because of poor layout, they can't purchase the product because the site isn't commerce-enabled or the product is out of stock. The process of buying is too long and painful on too many sites. The self-service nature of the Internet means that customers are only willing to spend so much time searching. They are empowered online, and know that competitors are only a click away.

Jakob Neilsen, the Web's leading usability expert, believes that basic principles of good design are simple. If pages don't load quickly, customers won't wait. If customers can't find what they want, they won't buy. If pages are confusing or hard to read, customers will look elsewhere. Exhibit 17–7 lists Nielsen's Top Ten Design Web Mistakes, a list direct marketers should take to heart.

Managing the customer experience has become important for E-commerce marketers. The customer experience benefits more from usability than from design. Testing for usability is one way to learn how well customers can move around your Web site. Such testing is often done in rooms with an observer watching the user's keystrokes. If a user makes two or three keystroke errors while trying to navigate a task on a Web site, it is considered an error in design, not typing.

Some of the most visited sites on the Web are the most simple ones. Yahoo!, Netscape, Dell, and Cisco all see millions of dollars in revenue a day pass through their Web sites. Yet all of their sites are devoid of fancy splash pages, flash intros, and heavy graphics. A rich user experience is built around the right content and the ability to access it quickly and easily. There seems to be a lesson there for E-commerce marketers.

Online Shopping

In the past, a well-conceived pricing strategy was based on a combination of factors that considered cost, competition, and demand. Today, pricing is tempered with the reality that customers have many sources for a lower price.

EXHIBIT 17–7

Nielsen's Top Ten Mistakes in Web Design

1. Use of frame
2. Gratuitous use of bleeding edge technology
3. Scrolling text, marquees, and constantly running animations
4. Complex URLs
5. Orphan pages
6. Long scrolling pages
7. Lack of navigation support
8. Nonstandard link colors
9. Outdated information
10. Overly long download times

The Internet has become a center for shopping, if not buying. It is the first place that consumers go to look for information on products and services, and to research costs as well as prices. On the Internet, it is easy to find some company willing to offer a product at a lower cost.

Shopping agents or shopping bots make this easier. These programs search the Internet, scouring Web sites for the lowest price.

There are now almost as many shopping bots as there are E-commerce sites: Bizrate.com, MySimon.com, Pricegrabber.com, Shopping.com, and Froogle (www.froogle.google.com) are just a few of the more recognizable shopping bots (See Exhibit 17–8). However, there are no unbiased comparison shopping sites. Many have arrangements with merchants to display those retailers' goods in a search. Some profit from these activities. To learn more about agent technology, go to www.botspot.com, a Web site devoted to intelligent agent technology.

Receive the Order

The online ordering process requires some type of shopping cart application. Many firms offer such software. The marketer still has a number of decisions to

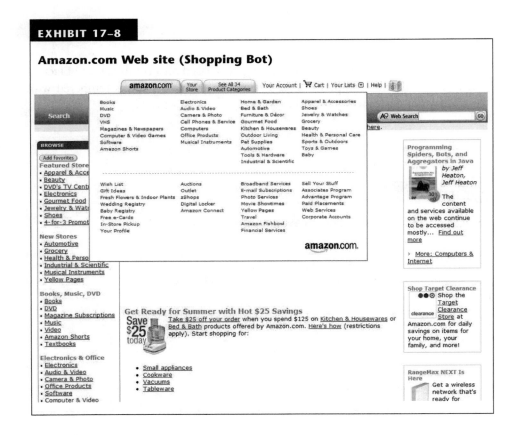

EXHIBIT 17–8

Amazon.com Web site (Shopping Bot)

make regarding how to present information to customers. By and large, all the customer wants to do is to complete their order as simply and quickly as possible. With over 50 percent of shopping carts abandoned, customers may not be finding this part of the experience as they would like it.

To ensure that information all fits on a standard screen, some marketers have broken up their order forms into pieces. Most capture a customer's name, address, phone information, and e-mail address on the first form. A second form captures purchased products in the shopping cart or lists products on a wish list, allowing for deletions or changes. A third form captures credit information. Then all the information is shown with a tally of the order. Some firms only tally shipping and handling costs at the end of a transaction, not when subtotaling product purchases. These and many other reasons may have to do with the order abandonment rates.

Authorize Payment

Many of the largest Web sites handle ordering and payment authorization in real time. Other sites do this as an offline process. Sites that have heavy traffic often use an outside firm for credit card clearing. Because these firms manage this process for many Web sites, they often can save money by offering lower merchant discount rates (the 1 to 4 percent of each transaction paid by the merchants to the credit card firm). This process is usually transparent to the customer.

Once the credit card is cleared, the customer can have their order acknowledged. Order acknowledgments are usually sent as e-mail, confirming the order number, products purchased, total debited to their credit card, and a shipping date. Firms that handle credit-processing offline, or that do not have their inventory systems online, may take hours or days to acknowledge an order. Best practice in this category is for this acknowledgment to be sent moments after the order is confirmed in the shopping cart. This affords customers a feeling of confidence about the company behind the Web site.

Schedule Order

Fulfillment of the order is no different for E-commerce companies than for other direct marketing companies. Some organizations handle this process automatically while others must manually send the completed order to the fulfillment center. Scheduling when the order will be picked is based on inventory and shipping times.

Large firms may have more than one warehouse or fulfillment center, due to geographical or timing considerations, such as when trucks going to different locations leave. This is often a far more complex task than is apparent to the consumer.

In the early days, start-ups such as Amazon.com may have taken orders without having inventory. They only kept best-sellers in stock, and ordered other books from a wholesaler each day. This is no longer true. This version of the "built on demand" meant a delay while Amazon.com waited for a book wholesaler to deliver ordered books to them. A virtual business may seem like a good idea, but it is not sustainable when selling products. Amazon.com has eight warehouses around the United States to get deliveries to their customers quicker.

Build or Retrieve from Inventory

This part of the fulfillment process is key. Building the product specified or picking/packing the right products are not easy tasks. Imagine having to coordinate this for 25,000 orders a day! Many products do not lend themselves to totally automated systems. Most firms still have people involved in many stages of the operation. Computer printouts tell where in the warehouse everything on an order is located so that the order can be assembled efficiently.

Often, picked products are put directly into shipping boxes. Computer software usually dictates the size of box based on the products to be shipped. Once all the products are picked and the box is at the end of the line, it is checked one more time, packing materials are put into the box, it is sealed and labeled for shipment, then forwarded to the staging area.

Staging areas, where product ready for shipment is held, are sections of a warehouse or loading platform designated by geography and the method of shipping chosen. For instance, products going to the East Coast by overnight air express may be in a red section while those going within the state by motor freight or ground transport may be in a green section. Shipments going by U.S. mail may all be assembled in a blue area. Color coding helps workers be more accurate in assembling shipments.

Many firms use fulfillment centers managed by others to complete the fulfillment process. Large shippers such as UPS and FedEx have entered this business. These firms fulfill thousands of orders in their centers. They can achieve greater efficiency than companies unaccustomed to customer expectations of real-time fulfillment. They are an option to be considered for both start-ups and growing firms.

Ship Product

There are many choices for shipping products. UPS and FedEx have the lion's share of E-commerce shipping business. Speed and the capability for a consumer to track orders are the chief reasons these organizations are a favorite of E-businesses and consumers alike. However, there are many firms that offer similar services to E-commerce companies. The USPS offers tracking with proof of delivery for Express Mail and tracking for Priority Mail, but not for standard shipments. The USPS reputation is not one of delivery reliability, which is an issue for consumers.

Companies with customers outside of the United States may also want to consider shippers that can accommodate domestic as well as foreign deliveries. Late order pick-up is another need for some businesses. Outpost.com, a computer product seller, promises next-day shipping on orders placed before midnight EST on weekdays. They were able to accomplish this through a special arrangement negotiated with their key shipper. However, many buyers have shipper preferences. It is best to offer a variety of shipping options to complement these preferences.

Receive Payment

Offer a variety of options for payment, and line up a reliable partner to verify and clear credit card payments. Take care to institute a system that can detect fraud. Credit card companies are holding E-commerce companies responsible for some of the bad debt created by online fraud. Take all steps necessary to avoid being a victim.

Micropayment systems or "electronic wallets" that handle small dollar amount payments have not yet gained acceptance among consumers, but are worth watching. According to Wikipedia, the online English Encyclopedia, the definition of micropayments is a means for transferring money, in situations where collecting money with the usual payment systems is impractical, or very expensive, in terms of the amount of money being collected.

Market Research

Customer feedback is essential to gaining good customer insight, and the Internet is the perfect channel for companies to learn more about their customers. Online surveys, targeted e-mail surveys, and questions at Web sites can help companies gain knowledge about customers as well as prospects.

Some firms rate customer experiences. At the end of an order, a screen comes up asking if the customer is willing to share answers about his or her experience. Such instant feedback is a terrific way to gain real-time insight into customer concerns. Firms such as Nielsen/NetRatings can provide the timely, actionable Internet audience information and analysis required for strategic decision-making.

Feedback from customers and prospects can help an organization to gain a greater share of customers, as well as learn about issues that they might not have known existed. It enables an E-business to quickly recognize and adapt to changing conditions and develop online business strategies based on deep customer insights. Even fledgling E-commerce firms can afford this kind of feedback. The truth is, companies can't afford not to.

E-Care: The Care and Feeding of Online Customers

E-care is Internet direct marketing used for customer service, helping users to learn order status, get additional instructions, and improve customer satisfaction.

An integral part of E-commerce, E-care brings companies closer to their customers by serving them the way they want to be served. The field has evolved quickly from the days when companies felt that posting a list of frequently asked questions (FAQs) was sufficient to handle customer concerns. Today, the key is to offer real-time communications that give customers instant information about products and services, inventory levels, shipments, and returns.

E-care seeks to make these tasks as simple as possible for customers. To simplify the task of contacting the company, it may offer a variety of communications channels—voice, e-mail, or instant chat. To make it easy for customers to get the information they need, it seeks to develop clear policies, strong guarantees, and easy-to-follow online instructions at every step of the ordering and return process. Even some of the best E-commerce companies still can't seem to clearly explain how to return products!

On the Internet, customers, not content, are king. Effective E-commerce sites are created with the idea of how they improve the customer relationship in mind. Repurposed content from catalogs, brochures, or annual reports seldom communicates information in a way that online customers are looking for. Customers don't care that a company's retail, catalog, and E-commerce may be separate divisions, they want an integrated customer experience. Anything that becomes a barrier to finding products and information—heavy graphics, poor site layout, incomplete content, etc.—acts as a deterrent to customers. Because the Internet is so collaborative, creating confidence and trust is a must with customers.

All of these functions are part of E-care, one of the fastest-growing costs to E-commerce companies, and an area that has changed tremendously since the debut of the Internet.

In the early days of E-commerce, the focus was on enabling transactions. E-commerce sites often looked like electronic catalogs, with grand designs, large product pictures, and short product descriptions. Customer service consisted of frequently asked questions (FAQs) section. Usually buried in the FAQ was the telephone number for the customer service department, along with a notice that its hours were 9–5 weekdays.

However, customers began to get fed up with the apparent lack of concern that E-commerce sites had regarding customer service and many firms began to offer customer service via real-time chat. The firms learned that one customer service agent could help six or more customers at once due to the lag in typing.

Firms like Lands' End went a step further, offering live operator voice support while a user was online. Nowadays, with all these factors in consideration, companies such as Accudata and InfoUSA have filled that gap in human touch in their sales performance in their individual online setting (See Exhibit 17–9). InfoUSA tries to provide sales and marketing support listing for products for all types of businesses. They have been able to fill that online gap of performance toward customer service and their outcome delivery with "live help."

EXHIBIT 17-9

InfoUSA Web site

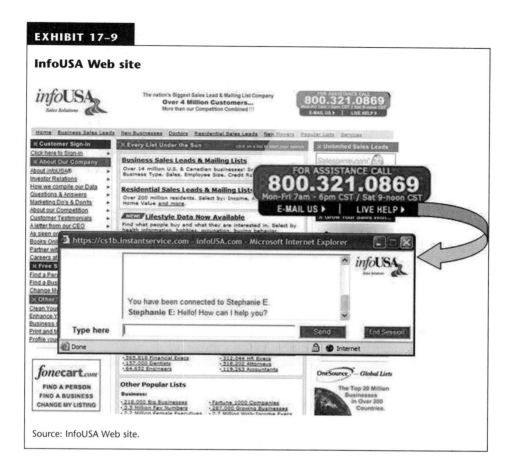

Source: InfoUSA Web site.

Internet consultant Kelly Mooney, of Resource Marketing, Inc., has created a best practice shopping audit of what makes customers click. Here is Mooney's E-care checklist:

Customer Service

Pre-buying help: Assist customers with live operators if necessary
Post-buying acknowledgment: Most customers wait for an e-mail
Guarantee: Customer expects this in all forms of direct marketing
Privacy disclosure: Nothing is more important in building trust

Personalization

Customized pages: From home pages to the whole experience
Wish lists: Customers see this as a value-added service
One-click ordering: Speeds up the ordering experience
Shipping and handling information stored: Convenience is key

Gift Giving

Offer ideas and save dates: This becomes a value-added benefit
Gift-wrapping alternatives: Choice is key for customers
Personalized gift cards: Personalization technology simplifies this

Browsing and Buying

Navigation: Customers want things to be two or three clicks away
Visual merchandising: Balance access with design
Product availability: Customers want to know before they order

Promotions

Purchase incentives: Rebates and points programs are all the rage
Contest/sweeps: As popular online as offline
Loyalty programs: Most customers want to come back, honest!

Community

Access to unique brand content: Community is more than chat
Games/interactivity: Customers look for involvement
Sneak previews: Customers want something they can't get elsewhere

Delivery of a variety of E-care services is essential for customer conversion and retention. One of the things the Internet does well is to connect people with information. Organizations that can offer a combination of automated technology and human intelligence have the best chance for success in the future. E-commerce companies that fail to provide a more personal, relevant E-care experience for their online customers risk losing those customers to companies that do. Companies that offer customers requesting support a variety of E-care services will see the investments in these services translated into a combination of higher conversion rates, lower support costs, valuable customer intelligence, and increased customer loyalty.

CASE STUDY: **Netflix.com: There's a Movie Waiting for You**

Adapted from the New York American Marketing Association EFFIE Awards 2006.

BACKGROUND

Netflix.com, an online movie rental service, had created a new service category and dominated it initially. Between 2000 and 2004, it grew steadily from 292,000 to 2.6 million subscribers. While the mail-in DVD rental category grew, the in-store movie rental sector shrank by 20 percent.

In late 2004, other players entered the category. Amazon.com launched a DVD rental service in the United Kingdom at a low price point. And in early 2005, Blockbuster debuted its own online store, Blockbuster.com. Once the only company in the category, Netflix was now fighting its main competitor in two channels: Blockbuster and Blockbuster.com. Netflix developed a marketing campaign to grow its base, differentiate itself, and outrun Blockbuster.

CASE STUDY: **Netflix.com: There's a Movie Waiting for You** *(continued)*

OBJECTIVES

The campaign goals were to increase brand awareness by 8 percent and subscriptions by 50 percent against the 2004 base of 2.2 million subscribers. Subscriptions—those not linked to multichannel direct marketing, but only to Netflix's mass offline advertising—were targeted for 17 percent growth. The goal was to decrease churn rates (cancellations) by at least 0.75 points and decrease subscriber acquisition costs to less than $35 per subscriber.

TARGET AUDIENCE

Netflix had originally been popular within a boutique audience of younger, techno-savvy males comfortable with the Internet and a love of film. However, quantitative and qualitative research in 2004 revealed that the mainstream audience for Netflix wasn't just film buffs but time-starved 35–45-year-old suburban moms and dads who used Netflix to get caught up on their movie watching.

CREATIVE STRATEGY

Research showed that while Blockbuster was a routine for people, Netflix had an advantage: it was perceived as having the best elements of renting a movie without the hassles of due dates, late fees, and standing in line. With this in mind, Netflix was positioned as movie enjoyment made easy. The creative solution was a TV and radio campaign in which a movie genre ("Foreign Drama," "WWII," "Sci-Fi," "Children's," "Costume Drama") came to life.

Media Mix

Netflix's media strategy had always been governed by a need to keep total subscriber acquisition costs in check. In 2005, the media mix was expanded to grow the subscription base. National cable continued to be the main driving force for trials while spot TV in select markets provided additional reach. Network radio was added, as it provided another low-cost efficient means of reaching an extended audience while still delivering on the "cost per incremental trial." Online advertising, an original part of Netflix's messaging from the start, was kept in place throughout the TV campaign.

RESULTS

Within weeks of the campaign's debut in July 2005, results indicated that people both noticed the campaign and responded. Both trial and membership subscriptions were at record levels.

In spring 2005, brand awareness was at 40 percent; by September it had increased to 51.6 percent. By fall 2005, total subscriber numbers grew 61 percent to 3.6 million compared to 2.2 million in 2004. Overall, trial numbers were positive, but those trials not attributable to any other source than offline advertising improved by 23 percent over the same period in 2004.

The campaign helped create additional brand momentum, which greatly reduced the number of subscription cancellations. Churn rate was 4.3 percent compared to 5.6 percent in 2004. Subscriber acquisition costs in 2005 dropped to $35 per new subscriber from $38 per new subscriber in 2004.

PILOT PROJECT   Crutchfield.com is one of the top online retail sites. With over 3 million visits per month, Crutchfield.com offers users extensive product knowledge and unfaltering customer service.

Crutchfield.com recently introduced two new applications. Digital Drive-Thru combines their information base and customer service by allowing iPod users to learn how to best connect to their car's sound system. Users type their iPod model as well as the make and model of their vehicle into a digital tool, which provides product recommendations and installation instructions.

A second new application is "TV Fit Finder." This application allows buyers to find TVs that will fit their current home entertainment furniture or furniture to fit their existing TV.

However, not even the best E-commerce retailers can stay ahead of the curve forever. Review the Crutchfield.com Web site. Look through the extensive applications for ideas that they may have missed.

A.   Does Crutchfield.com have any social networking application? If not, which would you recommend? If they do have any, which additional applications would you recommend? Why?

B.   How frequently does Crutchfield.com include with the Web site their customer service number for phone calls? Do they have a click-to-talk-to-agent button?

C.   Identify three additional E-commerce applications that Crutchfield could employ to improve their Web site. Explain how each would benefit Crutchfield.com and their customers.

Key Points

▶ E-commerce has become an important distribution channel, although there is still more *shopping* than *buying* online.

▶ While a Web presence may trigger channel conflict among sales forces, distributors, and other channel partners, it is imperative to sell through channels their customers would like to buy from.

▶ To achieve its business goals online, an organization must translate its business processes into fast, easy-to-use processes that are Web-centric. To do so, it should examine every aspect of these processes from a customer's point of view, and understand how interactions are triggered within the organization.

▶ Identify the business rules your company follows, and the business events common to your business: placing an order, checking credit, checking inventory, shipping products, invoicing customers, collecting payment, etc. Each event will trigger interaction among your customers and the software applications within your E-commerce site. You need to ensure that information and tasks flow smoothly from one system to another for each event.

▶ Know exactly what "customer," "account," "order," and "product" mean to your organization. These business objects have an agreed-upon definition and create a common language within the organization. It is difficult to design an E-commerce strategy without agreeing upon those definitions up front.

MANAGING THE CREATIVE PROCESS

CHAPTER 18

CREATING DIRECT
MAIL PACKAGES

Direct mail is one of the main media of direct marketing. It includes a variety of different formats such as postcards, self-mailers, catalogs, and the traditional direct mail package (See Exhibit 18–1). With the advent of the Internet, many had relegated direct mail to a minor role. That prediction seems to be wrong. Direct mail is as strong, or stronger, than ever.

According to the United States Postal Service (USPS), the average U.S. consumer receives 25 pieces of standard mail per week (e.g., promotional mail). While consumers in other countries receive much less postal mail, advertising and promotional mail is growing in both developing nations and mature countries. In the United States, the Winterberry Group pegs real year-over-year growth at 7.5 percent annually over the next few years. Some factors contributing to this growth include:

- Increased use of direct mail for customer acquisition

- Greater use of Customer Relationship Marketing (CRM), which utilizes targeted direct mail campaigns

- More use of direct mail in multichannel campaigns

- More direct mail usage in cross-channel promotions, which offer multiple ways for recipients to respond (e.g., mail, phone, and Web response options)

- Improvements in digital printing technology (also known as printing on demand) have enabled cost-efficient, short-run promotions

Consumer Perceptions of Direct Mail

Do consumers like getting mail and do they read it? The USPS answered that question in "The Mail Moment," a 2005 research study that confirmed many behaviors marketers had previously hypothesized.

EXHIBIT 18-1

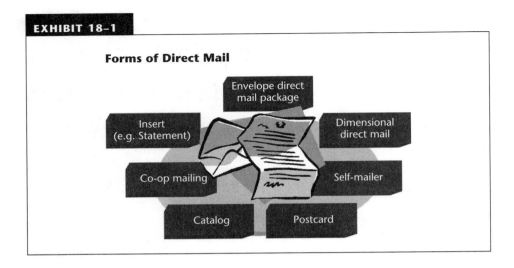

Forms of Direct Mail

The study showed that consumers look forward to receiving mail promotions. Consumers sort through the mail and organize it immediately. Consumers make sure that the right decision maker has an opportunity to look at the mail. And, while they review direct mail, they give it their undivided attention. The USPS calls this highly interactive ritual "The Mail Moment."

The USPS "Mail Moment" study shows that mail is welcomed into people's homes. It fills a special need in their private lives. Direct mail provides marketers an opportunity to communicate with consumers about things that are important to consumers, and to interact with them directly.

Mail stirs positive emotions, engaging readers in a highly personal marketing experience. And, given the time pressures of consumers, they spend a considerable amount of time with their mail. Below are key insights from the study:

Consumers like receiving mail
56 percent of respondents say receiving mail is a "real pleasure"
55 percent "look forward" to discovering the mail they receive
67 percent feel mail is more personal than the Internet

Mail gets the message into waiting hands
98 percent of consumers bring in their mail the day it is delivered
72 percent of whom bring it in as soon as possible
77 percent sort through their mail immediately

Mail is sorted, then given to the right person of the household
90 percent determine which mail is kept for review
81 percent review financial documents
84 percent are the principal grocery shoppers

Consumers spend more time with their mail than was previously imagined

Consumers spend *an average of 30 minutes* reading mail on any given occasion

Consumers spend 45 minutes with magazines, 30 minutes with catalogs, and 25 minutes with direct mail

Commercial messages in mail perform distinct tasks

Browsing for new consumption

Managing the home

Overseeing finances

Postage

Postage is one of the most expensive components in budgeting for a mailing. USPS offers standard rates when mailings meet certain minimum quantities. Large mailers can take advantage of different discounts based on how the mailing is sorted for the post office. To take advantage of the greatest discounts, mailing lists must be sent to service bureaus that have licensed software from USPS. This postal software is used to standardize addresses, to update and change addresses using the National Change of Address (NCOA), and to utilize the Coding Accuracy Support System (CASS) to certify the mailing. The software calculates the postage based on rates each mailing qualifies for.

USPS rates change often. New rate cases, the process where new rates are set, occur every few years. Standard rates are lower for nonprofit organizations. They are significantly less than first-class rates, which at the time of this writing is 39 cents per piece. Standard rates for letters weighing 3.3 ounces or less range from a low of 18 cents per piece to 28.2 cents per piece. Rates are published on USPS.com.

Often criticized unfairly, the USPS is an amazing organization which delivers 212 billion pieces of mail annually. It has programs that promote the use of direct mail for businesses as a marketing tool and programs that promote consumer education and usage of mail order.

Elements of the Direct Mail Package

Creating successful direct mail packages requires significant planning and consideration. From the placement of the teaser copy on the envelope, to ensuring that the paper folds between lines of type and not through the lines, developing a direct mail package is a carefully orchestrated process.

Direct mail packages can come in different formats and sizes and with a varying number of elements. Different formats are used to break through the clutter of a reader's mailbox. Formats can signal something about the mailing to the reader, which helps the reader to decide how to prioritize the mailing for reading.

Not all of these elements are included in every mailing. Testing helps the marketer learn which of the elements improve response enough to be cost-efficient, and which elements can be eliminated. Program objectives can impact this as well (e.g., generate the greatest number of responses vs. generate the lowest cost per response).

Over time, the authors have learned that letters and other devices do improve response, even when the communication seems straightforward or most of the response comes from channels other than mail. A reply envelope, where postage is prepaid by the mailer, reminds recipients to respond. Including one increases response, *although recipients don't use it*. Instead, they respond by phone, the Web, or a follow-up contact. The following section outlines the key elements of a direct mail package.

The Outer Envelope

The purpose of the outer envelope (OE) is to carry the other elements of the direct mail package and invite receivers to see what is inside the envelope. A consumer may only glance at the envelope for a few seconds. It must capture the underlying concept of the mailing, while remaining consistent with the mailing's objective, message, category, product/service, and offer.

The OE should reflect what the marketer thinks will drive the reader's decision to respond to their offer. It may graphically announce that it is advertising mail: oversized and printed on coated stock, with bold graphics, four-color photography, and strong teaser copy. Or, it can be a standard white business envelope, with no teaser copy, meant to look like personal business mail.

The envelope comes in many formats and sizes. It may be a #10, the standard business-size envelope. It can be an odd size (9 inches × 12 inches, 6 inches × 9 inches, Monarch); opaque, see-through, poly bag, or a box; it can have a plain window, pistol-grip window, or multiple windows; and it can come in plain white or bold colors.

The envelope has three areas of importance:

- *The corner card.* The upper left-hand corner indicates who sent the mail. The corner card is much more than just a place for the reply address. It can be left blank, creating a mystery. It can use a personal name and/or title, indicating that the mail was sent from an individual. It can be used as part of the teaser copy, with a sense of urgency or other message incorporated.

- *The teaser copy.* Copy that teases the reader into opening the envelope. There are different kinds of teaser copy, and often more than one type of teaser is combined to create even more interest. *Benefit teaser* copy makes a promise or offers a benefit to the reader if they open the envelope: "Revealed Inside: Three money saving facts your life insurance company does not want you to know." *Offer teasers* focus on the offer, such as "Take advantage of o percent percent interest, guaranteed for your first six months." The *curiosity teaser* makes an appeal that is relevant to the target audience. One such teaser was written by the late Bill Jayme for *Psychology Today* "Do you close the bathroom door when no one else is home?"

- *The postage*. Postage can be Priority Mail, First Class, or Standard Mail (used for bulk mailings). Any class of postage can be displayed on the envelope using a printed indicia, postage meter (common in B2B mailings), or postage stamps (to mimic the look of a personal mailing).

There are many considerations related to the outer envelope. For example, the lack of teaser copy *is* teaser copy itself. That approach is not a preference of the authors. The authors believe that the outer envelope should capture attention, engage the recipient, and inspire response, even before they open the envelope.

In Exhibit 18–2, Washington Mutual Credit Card OE, is a #10 envelope with a double window. Note the sender's name showing through the top window in the "corner card" area at the top left corner, the Standard Mail indicia at the top right corner, and the teaser copy outlining benefits.

The Letter

A direct mail letter is not a personal correspondence. Nevertheless, it borrows elements such as the salutation, personal signature, and a postscript. The letter is a

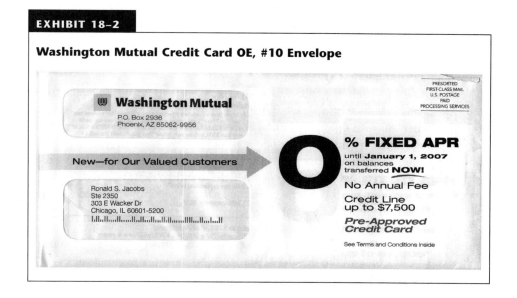

EXHIBIT 18–2

Washington Mutual Credit Card OE, #10 Envelope

salesman in an envelope. Its goal is to *connect* with the reader, to tell a story, and to provide a rationale for why the mailing was sent. The letter is not meant to inform the reader. It is meant to persuade the reader to act. It should be as long as necessary to get that job done.

Letters are not about the writer, the company, or its product/service. Consumers and business people care about themselves. The letter must address *their* needs, solve *their* problems, and explain how *their* lives will be improved by acting upon the products and services that are being offered. Direct mail letters liberally use a "you" and "your" copy approach, describing the benefits of action to the reader, and explaining what the reader will get when they respond. This approach helps to connect with the reader and keep the focus off the writer.

The first paragraphs of the letter initiates the Direct Mail Kit's (DMK) relationship with the reader. Sale copy within the letter may make a promise or allude to a key benefit, refer in some way to the offer, and explain the offer that the letter asks the reader to eventually act upon. Bullet points make the letter easier to read than long blocks of text.

The call to action at the end of the letter is usually punctuated with the signature, a printed copy of a real signature whenever possible. In literature, movies, and theatre, the concept of a "willing suspension of disbelief" is well known. The reader or audience surrenders reality, logic, and plausibility for the sake of enjoyment. You watch an actor, know it is an actor, yet you root for them as if they are their character. Seeming incongruities, holes in the plot, and deviations from physical laws are reconciled through that *willing suspension of disbelief*.

Direct mail may work in much the same way. Recipients know that a direct mail package is not a personal letter addressed to them, but personalization generally improves response. They know that a direct mail letter wasn't personally signed, but a printed blue signature often improves response. Recipients reconcile the slim chance that they may be the winner of sweepstakes and believe that it could happen to them.

The direct marketing process works year after year because it seems to tap into that *willing suspension of disbelief*. This may be why these tools and techniques, no matter what our own opinion of them is, continue to improve results regardless of how sophisticated we think our audience is.

After the headline and first sentence, the P.S. commands the highest readership in the letter. It is used to repeat a key benefit, or add a twist or another idea to something that has already been written in the letter. Frequently it is used to repeat the call to action in slightly different words.

Exhibit 18–3, Washington Mutual letter with attached response device, illustrates many of the elements discussed above. Note the calls to action in subheads, the personalized P.S., and the deadline date. Despite having a response device, the letter provides multiple channels for response (mail, Web, and phone).

EXHIBIT 18–3

Washington Mutual Letter with Attached Response Device

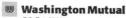

Washington Mutual
P.O. Box 2936
Phoenix, AZ 85062-9956

You're Pre-Approved* for a Washington Mutual MasterCard®

Now—for our valued customers!

Ronald S. Jacobs
Ste 2350
303 E Wacker Dr
Chicago, IL 60601-5200

0% FIXED APR
until **September 1, 2007**
on balances
transferred **NOW!***

No Annual Fee
Credit Line
up to $7,500*

Dear Ronald Jacobs,

As a valued customer, you're pre-approved* for a new Washington Mutual MasterCard credit card with no annual fee and all the other great benefits you expect from Washington Mutual.

Reply now to get 0% FIXED APR
until September 1, 2007 on balances transferred now*

You'll receive a low 0% FIXED APR until September 1, 2007 on balances transferred now (not on purchases or cash advances). Keep in mind that your 0% APR may increase if you default on any account with us or are reported as past due with another creditor. Payments are applied to balances with lower APRs before those with higher APRs, and a fee of 3% ($5 minimum/$75 maximum) per transfer will apply. Please see the back of the letter for Terms and Conditions.

Start with a credit line up to $7,500*

You can use this credit line to make purchases at millions of locations that accept MasterCard credit cards. You'll get all the travel and shopping benefits you'd expect from MasterCard, plus you'll enjoy added benefits like free online access to your credit score,* money-saving discounts to popular restaurants and retailers,* automatic credit line reviews, and $0 liability for unauthorized charges. Plus, this card has no annual fee.

Respond to this pre-approved offer now

Use your reservation number **24L-79049-0797-E** and visit **www.getmastercardnow.com**, complete and mail the Reply Form below, or call toll-free **1-800-206-2277**.

Sincerely,

Craig Schmeizer

Craig Schmeizer
Senior Vice President

P.S. Ronald Jacobs: Transfer a balance now to get the lowest rate—0% APR—on balance transfers until September 1, 2007.

Respond before 08/21/06
Visit www.getmastercardnow.com,
mail back your form, or
call ☎ 1-800-206-2277

*Please see the Terms and Conditions on reverse for important information about this pre-approved offer, rates and applicable balance transfer fees. The median credit line received in 2005 was $2,000.

WR89_MB_GAAR_0_0907_12

049401*00260*S6

You can choose to stop receiving "prescreened" offers of credit from this and other companies by calling toll-free 1-888-567-8688. See PRESCREEN & OPT-OUT NOTICE on other side for more information about prescreened offers.

PRE-APPROVED REPLY FORM

Washington Mutual

☑ **YES!**
Send my no-annual-fee MasterCard® now

If you do not check a box, you will receive the Seal Platinum MasterCard.

Choose your card design:

386 ☐	Rainy Day	389 ☐	Water Lilies
387 ☐	Tahitian Landscape	390 ☐	Irises
388 ☐	Sunflowers	396 ☐	Seal Platinum

Please correct information below if necessary.

Ronald S. Jacobs
Ste 2350
303 E Wacker Dr
Chicago, IL 60601-5200

Product #: 224L2F

This offer expires:
August 21, 2006

Social Security Number
( ) -
U.S. Home Phone
( ) -
Work/Second Phone
$
*Annual Household Income
*You do not need to include income from alimony, child support, or separate maintenance unless you would like us to consider it.

Please send a second card for this account at no extra cost for:

First Name   M.I.   Last Name

Your E-mail Address (optional)

Do you have a checking account? ☐ Yes ☐ No

Employment: ☐ Self-Employed ☐ Employed
☐ Retired ☐ Other

Your Date of Birth *(Mo/Day/Yr)*

YES!
(Initial here) I want to protect my Washington Mutual credit card account history by enrolling in OPTIONAL Credit Protection (CP). I understand enrollment is not required to obtain credit. I have read and agree to the enclosed CP Terms and Conditions and authorize the membership fee indicated to be billed to my account monthly.

X
Signature
This form is non-transferable and must be signed by the person to whom it is addressed. I certify that I am at least 18 years of age. I have read and agree to the Terms and Conditions on the back of the letter and the enclosed Initial Disclosures.

Optional Balance Transfer Request

YES! I want to transfer the following balance(s) from my higher-rate accounts to the MasterCard.
I want to start the balance transfer process; therefore, I agree to review your Privacy Policy later along with other account information.

	Account Number	Name of Credit Card Lender	Amount to Be Paid and Transferred (minimum $100 per transfer)
1			$
2			$
3			$
4			$

MASTERCARD

WR89-MB-GAAR-0-0907-RF

Direct mail is the single greatest tool used in fund-raising. While cause-related groups may use many other methods, nonprofit organizations report that they acquire the majority of first-time members and donors through the use of successful direct mail campaigns. The direct mail letter is often cited by fund-raisers as the single most important element in convincing donors or members to respond. In fund-raising, the offer, appeal, and messaging may be different, but many of the tools and techniques discussed in this book are relevant.

Below is an example of how these tools and techniques were used to create an extremely successful fund-raising direct mail campaign.

CASE STUDY: The Use of Direct Mail in Fund-raising

Contributed by Goodman Marketing Partners, San Rafael, CA.

CHALLENGE

KCSM-TV is an independent television station that relies primarily on membership revenue to run its operations. Based in San Mateo, approx. 10 miles south of San Francisco, its main competitor is KQED, a popular PBS affiliate in San Francisco. Both stations tap into the same consumer pocketbooks for revenue. However, since KQED has a much larger budget and falls within the single-digit line-up on the dial (Channel 9 versus KCSM at Cable 17), it is a

stronger brand. With KCSM membership declining and brand awareness low, the station sought to grow its membership base, increase brand visibility, and retain existing members.

STRATEGY

Programming was the key point of difference between KQED and KCSM. KCSM operates independently: it purchases its own programming and is able to air programs on its own schedule.

A direct mail campaign focused on the station's independent status. At the heart of the campaign was KCSM programming director Steve Opson, and

CASE STUDY: The Use of Direct Mail in Fund-raising *(continued)*

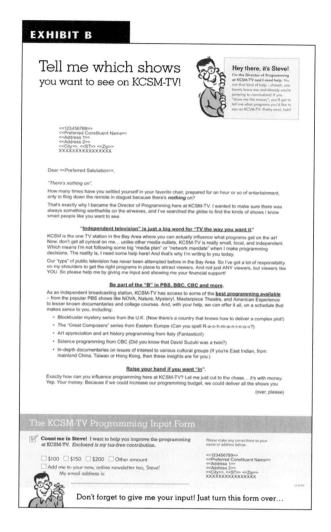

his quirky programming style. By utilizing a caricature of Steve and giving him a distinct voice, Steve became the spokesperson for the benefits of independent television programming.

In letters to current and lapsed members, Steve asked for programming ideas and input on specific shows. In the first mailing, a #10 package was mailed with a letter of introduction from Steve (See Exhibits A and B). The letter had a personalized, attached response device. Recipients were asked to send a gift of $100 to "help him deliver better television." Several weeks later, a second #10 package was directed to members due for renewal and to lapsed members. The latter group was

CASE STUDY: The Use of Direct Mail in Fund-raising *(continued)*

EXHIBIT C

KCSM-TV 3182 Campus Drive, PMB 506
San Mateo, CA 94403-3123

NON- PROFIT ORG.
U.S. POSTAGE
PAID
SAN MATEO
COMMUNITY COLLEGE

'allo mate!"

I'm here taking a gander at BBC programming for your favorite independent TV station, KCSM, and the choices are simply smashing! — mysteries, comedies, dramas, biographies and Bob's your uncle! (Personally, I don't have an uncle named Bob, but these Brits sure think I do!)

But to make sure our programming stays tickety boo, we need the financial support of people like you. So, renew your membership today. Call 1-888-883-5276 or go online to www.kcsm.org/helpsteve.htm. And then reward yourself with a cuppa!

Cheerio,
Steve Opson

P.S. With your help, KCSM-TV can continue to be "blooming great!", so renew your membership now!

The British are coming!
The British are coming!

ASCDE
John Q. Sample
Any Street
City, State 12345

classified as renewals that had expired in the previous six months. Follow-up postcards, sent to nonresponders, originated from Steve's travels "around the globe in search of new programming" (See Exhibit C).

Multiple response channels were created for recipients, including a Steve Internet landing page. This served to keep the "Steve" brand top of mind and integrated well with the other campaign elements. It also allowed KCSM to track online gifts as a result of direct mail efforts. In addition to a toll-free number, a postage-paid envelope was included so that consumers could fill out the back of the reply device with their programming input while providing a check or credit card information.

The campaign was supported on air as a "Steve" bumper slide appeared before a new show aired (positioning the new show as one of Steve's picks). Steve's caricature was included on the front of the KCSM monthly TV guide and continues to be leveraged through a number of on-air promotional vehicles.

RESULTS

Direct mail response rates exceeded 35 percent. Membership renewals increased over 250 percent compared to the same period last year, and the average gift amount has more than doubled. The online channel has received triple the volume of responses from the prior year.

Do consumers read the letter? According to research conducted by Dan Hill, and described in his book *Body of Truth*, as few as 10 percent of people do a thorough and in-depth reading of advertising copy. Therefore, headlines, subheads, and the P.S. must tell the whole story, detail benefits, explain the offer, and include a strong call to action.

Direct mail letters are written by professionals; they are rarely written by the individual who signs the letter. A fund-raising effort for the Republican National Committee signed by U.S. Vice President Dick Cheney was not written by Mr. Cheney. However, his signature adds to the credibility. The promotion was sent in a Priority Look envelope, which created urgency that contributed to the effort's success.

We often see large direct mail packages—especially multidimensional ones—mailed without a letter. The authors believe that the letter is one of the most important elements within a direct mail package, and should always be included. Testing letter copy is a far better use of resources than testing whether to include a letter or not. In our experience, a letter always improves response.

The Brochure

Most mailing packages require a good brochure in addition to a letter. The brochure can be a small, two-color element or an elaborate broadside as large as a poster. The brochure acts as a reference, to help the reader visualize the product or service and make it tangible so that the reader can respond.

In consumer mailings, the brochure embodies the emotional concept of the mailing. It illustrates the world the reader will be projected into when they respond. In business mailings, the brochure contains information too detailed or lengthy to include in the letter. But the job it has to do is the same, and it deserves the best creative effort.

Graphically, the cover of the brochure should invite the reader in. Every panel of the brochure should stand alone to encourage immediate response, but the sales message should not be panelized. Headlines and graphics should run across panels to broaden the visual field. When the brochure is open, the reader should see the whole brand, product, or service story.

Copy in the brochure explains product benefits (and features) graphically with photos, illustrations, tables, and graphs. The whole selling story should be in headlines and subheads, with text supported by bulleted copy.

Response information (e.g., phone number, URL, return address, etc.) should also be included in the brochure, in the event that the brochure is separated from the rest of the mailing. There can even be a second response device within the brochure for pass-along readers.

The brochure in Exhibit 18–4, from International Trucks DMK, is printed in four colors, and includes references to the benefits, calls to action, and the offer.

EXHIBIT 18–4

International Trucks DMK

The creative is image-consistent with other communications for the International Trucks brand.

Response Devices

Results hinge on the response device. Often, it is the first element that a reader reviews in a direct mail package. It needs to give explicit instructions on what the recipient must do to complete the purchase of the product/service or to respond. It should stand out and be easy to find.

Within the written copy of the direct mail package, it is never called a "response device." It is called an application, order form, enrollment form, subscription form, savings certificate, or donor card. It should be made to sound both more important and less threatening than the words *response device*.

Whatever it is called, it should be clear, convenient, and easy to complete. Whenever possible, it should arrive with the prospect's response information pre-addressed. It should use check boxes to simplify response. It usually repeats the offer and a call to action. It describes payment terms (cash, check, credit cards, installments, deferred payment); shows price, tax, shipping charges, and the total if possible; provides multiple channels for response; includes the complete address and phone number for response; contains an unobtrusive key code so that response can be tracked; and repeats the mailing instructions.

The cluttered look of a response device doesn't seem to take away from response, but actually improves it. Often, there is so much information that the terms and conditions must go on the back or on separate pages, as is common with most sweepstakes offers. This is also common with insurance and credit card mailers, the heaviest users of direct mail. These locations are clear and conspicuous to consumers.

Consumers are accustomed to the idea that offers have additional terms and conditions not included on the response device, letters, or brochure within a DMK. These terms and conditions clarify, explain, and illuminate offers in direct mail.

Despite the length and location of terms and conditions, marketers have an expectation that they will be reviewed and accepted by readers. A consumer's signature and response provides the acceptance. It is a fair exchange.

A well-designed response device often includes more than one way for the recipient to respond. With the proliferation of non-mail response channels (e-mail, Web, phone, etc.), it is fair to wonder if including a response device is still necessary today. The truth is that few people respond by mail. Nevertheless, the response device is more than symbolic. It focuses the recipient's thoughts on the call to action and the act of responding. It often sets response in motion, although it isn't returned by mail. The authors think that including a response device in direct mail is a good idea. However, it is testable, and marketers can learn how important the response device is for them.

The response device in Exhibit 18–5, World Classics Wine Club, is pre-addressed and oversized to not get lost in the DMK. It has a stub that will be removed so that the response device will fit in a smaller outer envelope.

Involvement Devices

Direct mail is a tactile medium. While marketers attempt to involve the prospect or customer's mind with compelling copy and inviting graphics, they also want to

EXHIBIT 18–5

World Classics Wine Club

get the person's body, especially their hands, involved. Good direct mail packages combine paper stocks with different weights of paper and different finishes (e.g., coated vs. uncoated), to provide a different feeling for each element. Some mailings include elements that are mentally or physically involving. Sweepstakes mailing often seem a challenge. The reader first finds the products or magazines that they want and puts the stamps onto the card. Then, they put the prize numbers on the card and insert the card into the reply envelope. It is action that makes the involvement device work.

Die-cut tokens or self-adhesive stickers are popular involvement devices. They work best when they are affixed to the response device, and punched out or peeled off from another element such as the letter. Scratch-offs are another popular involvement device that gets the hand moving. The response device is the "moment of truth" for the reader. Using an involvement device helps lead the reader through the direct mail package to the response device, and the goal of taking action.

Exhibit 18–6, a self-mailer with rub-off, illustrates how involvement devices can be used. This one is on the outside, creating involvement before the reader gets inside to learn about the offer.

Buckslip

The buckslip was named because it was originally the size and shape of a United States one dollar bill (approximately 6¼ inches × 3¼ inches). It serves to add information or

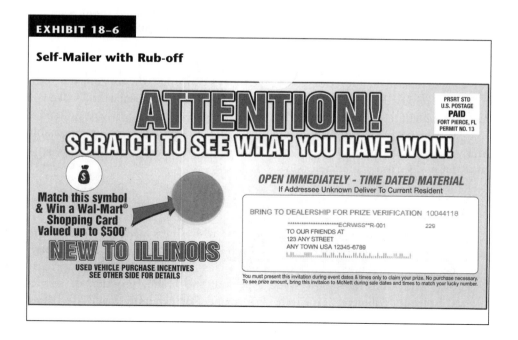

EXHIBIT 18–6

Self-Mailer with Rub-off

draw attention to some aspect of the offer, with the goal of lifting response. It may focus on a call to action, a free gift, early response, an extra giveaway or incentive, a phone number or a way to respond (e.g. "Sign up on the Web today!").

Whatever a buckslip communicates, it does in a kind of visual shorthand. They are typically printed on one side only, using a cheap-looking colored paper that screams "Urgent" or "What's printed on this is a deal." They include a headline, a short copy block, a summary of one aspect of the offer, and often a visual or graphic (e.g., a photo, illustration, etc.). The overall look is intended to make the buckslip appear as a mini-flyer, intended to break through and stand out from the other elements in a direct mail package.

Exhibit 18–7, Capital One buckslip, illustrates a buckslip with multiple purposes. One side restates the benefits of the offer and has a call to action. On the reverse side it illustrates a variety of card designs that the respondent can choose from.

Lift Letter

The objective of a lift letter is to provide one more opportunity, in addition to the main letter, to close the sales. A lift letter restates the offer and key benefits, but in a different way than the letter. Copy in the lift letter includes a guarantee, testimonials, or other sweeteners to reduce the reader's skepticism, and to have them believe the claims about the product or service offered. It should be written from the personal point of view of a publisher, president, or other influential individual. It is usually signed by someone other than the signer of the main letter.

It is typically designed as a folded note, with a headline on the outside that encourages the reader to look at this element if they are undecided about responding. The inside should be organized like a letter, with a headline, short paragraph or two, subhead(s), highlighted copy, and a P.S. Lift letters have their roots in the publishing business but have become a staple in many direct marketing programs. It is easy to misuse the lift letter. To engage today's consumer, the tone must be positive, not condescending (i.e., "Here are five more reasons that smart folks like you have responded to this offer," not, "I can't believe you haven't already responded").

Exhibit 18–8, Taste of California lift letter, is the lift letter for a membership in a wine club. It exhorts the reader to "trial-join" with no obligation. It restates the offer and mentions multiple ways to respond.

Case Studies and Testimonials

Case studies have become important in business-to-business mailings. Testimonials play the same role in consumer mailings. Both build credibility and infer authority that seems to be unbiased. They often use a classic problem/solution approach. The case study illustrates how some aspect of the brand, product, or service offered, solved a problem, improved performance, or generally made life better, easier, or more satisfied.

EXHIBIT 18-7

Capital One Buckslip

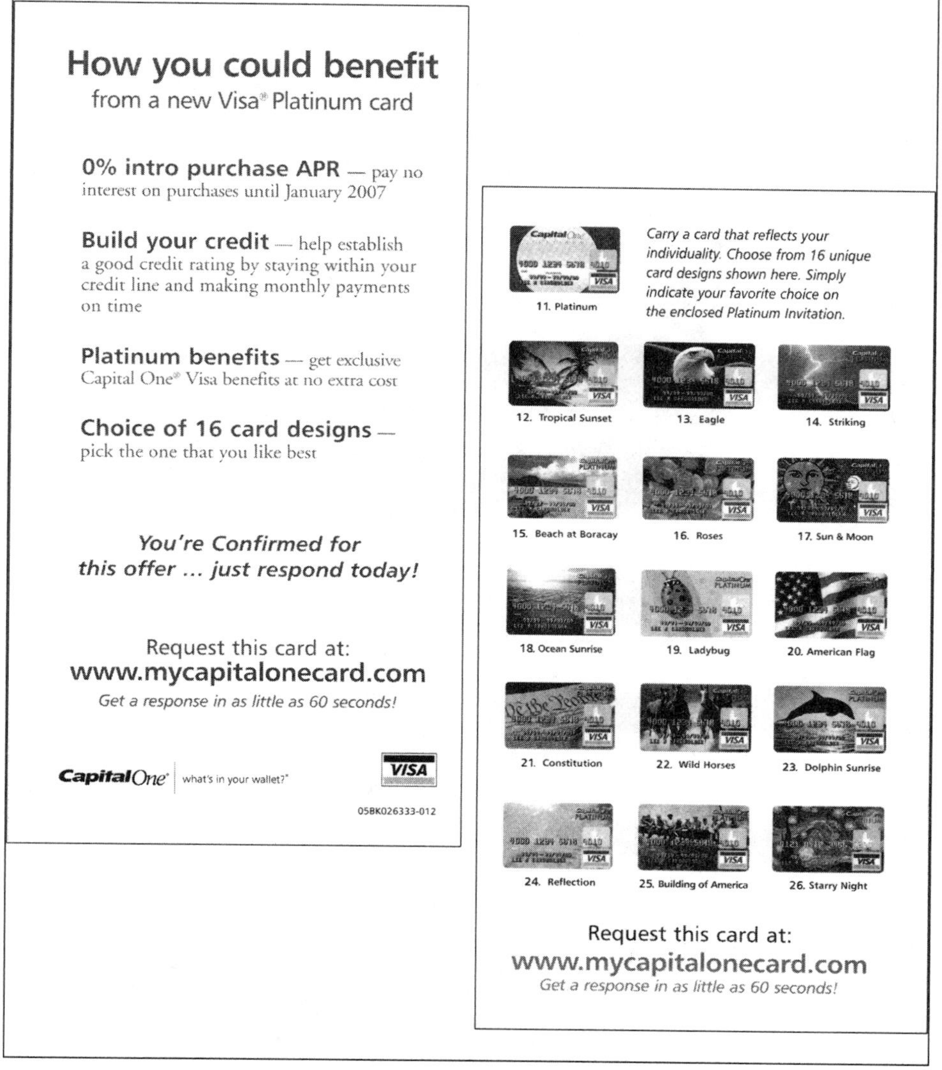

How you could benefit
from a new Visa® Platinum card

0% intro purchase APR — pay no interest on purchases until January 2007

Build your credit — help establish a good credit rating by staying within your credit line and making monthly payments on time

Platinum benefits — get exclusive Capital One® Visa benefits at no extra cost

Choice of 16 card designs — pick the one that you like best

You're Confirmed for this offer ... just respond today!

Request this card at:
www.mycapitalonecard.com
Get a response in as little as 60 seconds!

CapitalOne® | what's in your wallet?®   **VISA**

05BK026333-012

Carry a card that reflects your individuality. Choose from 16 unique card designs shown here. Simply indicate your favorite choice on the enclosed Platinum Invitation.

11. Platinum

12. Tropical Sunset   13. Eagle   14. Striking

15. Beach at Boracay   16. Roses   17. Sun & Moon

18. Ocean Sunrise   19. Ladybug   20. American Flag

21. Constitution   22. Wild Horses   23. Dolphin Sunrise

24. Reflection   25. Building of America   26. Starry Night

Request this card at:
www.mycapitalonecard.com
Get a response in as little as 60 seconds!

Case studies and testimonials need to sound authentic. Those featured in the case study or testimonials should be identified by individual name, title, and company name. Well-known companies help more than well-known names. And, cases customized by business category or decision-maker title (e.g., feature a CMO in mailing to CMOs) create relevancy and show how benefits specifically apply.

EXHIBIT 18-8

Taste of California Lift Letter

To: Anyone hesitating, even just a little.
From: John D. Davis
Subject: Delicious Proposition

Our World Classics Wine Club is a bargain to begin with, but now you'll get free delivery on your first wine shipment– **a savings of $8.95**– and that's extraordinary!

So even if you're not ready to join, why not trial-join? Give the club a "taste," and see what it's like to receive two classic wines from the world's favorite grapes, regions and winemakers. Remember, unlike most wine clubs, there is no membership fee and you may cancel at any time.

You see, there is nothing to lose. But you stand to gain bargain-priced, cellar-worthy wines that are entirely and irresistibly delicious.

Cheers,

John D. Davis

John D. Davis, Founder

P.S. Don't miss this time-limited opportunity. Please mail or fax the enclosed Free Shipping Certificate, or call 800-615-7304 toll-free today!

PO Box 683, Holmes, PA 19043-9974
toll-free: 1-800-615-7304, www.atasteofcalifornia.com

WCLL 1/06

Case studies and testimonials are typically printed on one page folded in half with a headline on the outer panel. Copy blocks should tell the story in a logical fashion. Include as many details as possible; including results adds credibility. Remember to keep the case on strategy with the objectives of the direct mail package. It is often easy to find a case study that doesn't quite fit the goals of the mailing. Resist that temptation, as that may depress results, not help response.

Self-Mailers

Self-mailers are stand-alone, one-piece mailings. They are most often used for single product offers, seminars, and lead generation. They are favored in the B2B marketplace.

Self-mailers combine the teaser copy of an envelope, the persuasive power of a letter, the information value of a brochure, and the call to action of a response device—often on the cover! They are more cost-efficient than a direct mail package, but with separate elements. However, they seldom generate the response of a direct mail package.

Self-mailers deliver more visual appeal and sales copy faster than a traditional direct mail package. Copy in a self-mailer should be easy to read and graphics should make it easy to skip through easily to the end. Self-mailers use lots of bulleted copy and checklists. Highlight the offer, the guarantee, benefits, and reply. Include a letter with a border to give the self-mailer a more personal feel. It's worth testing to find out if a self-mailer will work for you.

Exhibit 18–9 is a self-mailer for International Trucks. Note that the address area of the self-mailer includes contact information and the recipient's local dealer, as well as teaser copy and reference to the special lease offer.

Postcards

Postcards are one of the low-cost direct mail tools. They are the ultimate self-mailer, with just enough room for a very short message. They are often used as a teaser or a follow-up for a multi-part campaign. And, they are a very cost-efficient way to drive traffic to a Web site.

Postcards say to the reader that this will be an easy decision and won't take much time. They can be used for low-risk, soft offers in prospecting and reminders to customers. They can be personalized, but not usually with any private information, as they are generally just delivered through the mail as is. Publishers often use a double postcard, with one side being the reply card.

Exhibit 18–10, MB Tele Aid reminder card, is sent to people who have subscribed to Tele Aid Service but not yet activated the service. Tele Aid offers in-car or toll-free voice security and convenience services (e.g., remote unlocking when keys are left inside, trip routing, retail/restaurant locater service, etc.).

EXHIBIT 18–9

International Trucks Self-Mailer

Dimensional Mailings

Dimensional direct mail packages, often called box mailings, are mainly used in B2B mailings to reach decision makers. They are also good for high-revenue offers and for lead generation because they break through the clutter of flat-envelope direct mail, and often get past screeners into the prospect's hands. Dimensional pieces have a high cost, sometimes costing $100 per contact. Nevertheless, marketers use them as often as it takes only one or two sales to offset the costs of an entire mailing.

Dimensional mailings work best when the focus of the creative is on the key element or incentive within the dimensional mailing. The incentive should be

EXHIBIT 18-10

Tele Aid Reminder Card

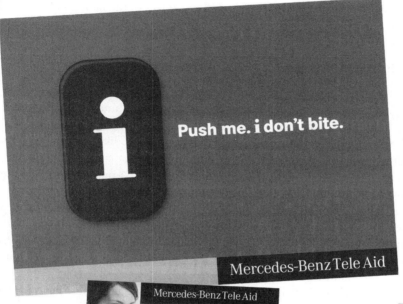

Push me. i don't bite.

Mercedes-Benz Tele Aid

Mercedes-Benz Tele Aid

You have subscribed to Tele Aid, a security and luxury service, but you have not yet completed your acquaintance call.

Why is the Acquaintance Call important?

1. It will confirm that your Tele Aid System is working properly.
2. It will allow us to confirm your personal contact information (address, phone number, etc.).
3. It will allow you to review the many security and luxury features of Tele Aid.

All you need to do is press the i-button and tell us you've received this reminder.

Please take this important step now, it only takes a few minutes.

Mercedes-Benz Tele Aid
Customer Services
P.O. Box 167985
Irving, TX 75016-7985
800-756-9018
mbusa@teleaid.com
MBUSA.com

M-501-AC

Your Vehicle Information
ID: 0.0.0.1-282237783
2006, E 320 SEDAN

PRSRT FIRST CLASS
US POSTAGE PAID
DALLAS TX
PERMIT NO. 407

ADDRESS SERVICE REQUESTED

RON JACOBS
JACOBS & CLEVENGER
303 E WACKER DR
CHICAGO IL   60601-5212

skillfully used to demonstrate the superiority of a brand, product, or service. The dimensional element can act as the brochure, but you still need a letter and response device. While the incentive device is always important, the objective of the mailing is to gain a response. When designed to work with the objectives of the campaign and to be consistent with the overall objectives of the marketer's communications program, dimensionals can be a very effective tool.

Co-op Mailings

Co-op mailings are where multiple offers, often from different mailers, are included in a single envelope. The cost of mailing is shared among a number of companies based on a predetermined formula. Often, co-op mailings are scheduled on a monthly timetable, with mailing dates fixed. They are more like a media purchase than a mailing program. ValPak and ADVO are large co-op mailing programs.

Because costs are shared across a number of brands, co-ops can cost less than 25 percent of solo mailings. However, response rates are often less than 25 percent of a solo mailing. Consumer co-op mailers can usually be targeted by small geographic areas (e.g., ZIP codes). There is a lot of clutter in consumer co-ops. They carry promotional coupons, retail traffic builders, and direct mail promotions. Purchases from co-ops are usually impulse products such as collectibles, mailing labels, and replacement checks.

Business co-ops are usually sent to subscribers to magazines or newspapers, where the interests of those on the mailing list are well known. Business co-ops are usually used for lead generation in office products, services, and other general business offers.

Inserts in a co-op must stand on their own. They are like self-mailers, or small ads. They are usually one page, just smaller than the size of the envelope. The offers, benefits, call to action, and response are on one side; photos or graphics on the other side. They don't usually include a response envelope.

Co-ops are a low-cost method for testing direct mail. While retailers use them as stand-alone media, most marketers in the consumer and business marketplace see them as part of an overall campaign.

Copy and design need to work together. They play off of each other to propel the reader to action. When you see the same direct mail package in your mailbox more than once a year, it is likely a control, a direct mail package that has beaten other creative executions in tests. Creating the direct mail package requires careful thought and planning. Marketers need to see the brand, product, or service through a customer's eyes. Customer insights gained through research and analysis help. The writer and designer need to submerge themselves in the audience. Successful direct mail needs to stay within your customer's comfort zone, expand on product benefits, and boost your results. Don't include things that don't work for you or make the cost of the direct mail package too high to meet its goals.

Evaluating Direct Response Advertising Copy

A successful direct mail package combines great graphics with even greater copy. Copy in a direct mail package is content, and content has been king since the ninth century, when the Chinese first hand-printed Buddhist writings on scrolls, using wooden blocks (Gutenberg, who was unaware of Chinese techniques, printed 180 copies of his Bible in 1454).

In direct mail, there are a number of kinds of copy. Benefit copy is the most important copy in a direct mail package. A benefit is not a feature. Features are selling points, attributes that belong to a product or service. Benefits are what make the attributes useful to the reader. Great direct marketing copy is benefit-oriented. It tells the reader what they will get when they respond. This helps the reader to project themselves into the brand, product, or service story woven into the copy. And, that helps them to act and respond.

Descriptive copy is also included in a direct package. Descriptive copy replaces personal examination, the ability to touch and feel a product before making a purchase decision. The copy needs to describe the benefits in ways that capture and engage the reader's attention.

Support copy answers readers' objections. It offers a rationale behind claims made. This may include data, statistics, research, cases, testimonials, and other information from credible sources. It provides a reason for why the reader should believe the claims made in the copy.

Sweetener copy provides yet more reasons the reader should accept the offer. It may include additional aspects of the offer, incentives, and choices. However, in direct mail too many choices can depress response, as readers struggle to make a decision. Copy should always make it easier for the reader to respond, requiring a delicate balance.

Facilitating copy is copy that relieves anxiety (e.g., offers guarantees); makes responding easier (e.g., provides a toll-free phone number); and offers easy payment terms (bill me later, send no money, etc.).

No matter what kind of copy is written, it must connect with the prospects or customers targeted. It must address their needs and maintain their attention; the longer you can keep their attention, the greater the probability of a response, which is the goal of all direct mail.

Focus on Benefits

Brands, products, and services have different attributes. These attributes are usually referred to as features, advantages, motives, and benefits. Each one is important, but benefits are the most important because they resonate with readers and trigger a response across the direct marketing spectrum. People simply like to know what's in it for them.

These attributes are often misunderstood. Ask for benefits, and you are often given features. One way to keep them straight is to think of them as different layers of the onion. Starting with the features, you peel back the onion layer by layer. This gets you to the inner layer, the benefits.

- *Features—the outer layer.* A feature is a factual attribute of a brand, product, or service. Example: "We offer 24/7 customer service availability."

- *Advantages—the second layer.* Advantages are descriptive attributes of what features do. Example: "Representatives are ready to take your calls, or answer your Web mails or e-mails 24 hours a day, 7 days a week."

- *Motives—the third layer.* Motives are the purposes that features satisfy. Example: "Puts consumers in control, by providing information when, where, and how they want it."

- *Benefits—the inner last layer.* Benefits are what features mean in consumer terms. Example: "While branches are available during business hours ... Web, e-mail, and phone representatives are ready to instantly provide answers to your questions, send you information, or help you fill out forms whenever your need."

When marketing communications focus on features, it makes the customer do the job of deciding why the feature should be important to them. It is in the marketer's best interest to make the benefit connection for their customers. When consumers can quickly answer "What's in it for me?," they are more likely to respond than when they have questions about a brand, product, or service's benefits. Benefits become a key response trigger and smart marketers take full advantage of that knowledge.

Copy Appeals and Basic Human Wants

Once the benefits are identified, a marketer must decide upon on the appeals that will do the best selling job. This is referred to in different ways. Some talk about how you "position" the product in the prospect's mind. Others refer to "coming up with the big idea" behind the copy. What is it about your offer and benefit story that is most appealing? When you stop to think about it, people respond to any given proposition for one of two reasons: to gain something they do not have or to avoid losing something they now possess.

Exhibit 18–11 shows how basic human wants can be divided into these two categories. Professional copywriters carefully sift and weigh the list of basic human wants to determine the main appeal of their proposition.

Eleven Guidelines to Good Copy

Does your proposition help people feel important? People like to keep up with "the Joneses." People like to be made to feel that they are a part of a select group.

EXHIBIT 18–11

Two Categories of Human Wants

The Desire to Gain	The Desire to Avoid Loss
To make money	To avoid criticism
To save time	To keep possessions
To avoid effort	To avoid physical pain
To achieve comfort	To avoid loss of reputation
To have health	To avoid loss of money
To be popular	To avoid trouble
To experience pleasure	
To be clean	
To be praised	
To be in style	
To gratify curiosity	
To satisfy an appetite	
To have beautiful possessions	
To attract romantic partners	
To be an individual	
To emulate others	
To take advantage of opportunities	

A tremendous number of people are susceptible to snob appeal. Perhaps you can offer a terrific bargain by mail and capitalize on the appeal of saving money. The desire to "get it wholesale" is very strong.

We have updated these guidelines for writing copy that gets results. They were originally penned by Don Kanter, a long-time vice president with Stone & Adler.

1. Does the writer know the brand, product, or service? Have they done their homework and covered the main selling points and benefits?

2. Does the writer know the marketplace, the target group, or segments? Is the copy targeted and relevant to the most likely prospects or customers?

3. Is the writer talking to the prospect in a language that the prospect will understand (i.e., addressing consumers differently than business people, etc.)?

4. Does the writer make a promise to the prospect, prove that they can deliver it, and support it with rationale that can be acted upon?

5. Does the writer get to the point at once? Does he or she make that all-important promise right away?

6. Is the copy, especially the headlines and lead paragraphs, relevant and specific to the selling proposition?

7. Is the copy simple, direct, and concise? (There is a great temptation to overwrite, especially in direct mail)

8. Is the copy logical and clear? Does it flow from one idea to the next?

9. Is the copy enthusiastic? Convincing? Does it sound as if the writer believes in what they are asking the prospect or customer to act upon?

10. Is the copy complete? Are questions that a reader will want answered and are key selling points and benefits clear?

11. Is the copy designed to generate response? Or, is it designed to impress the reader with the writer's ability? While creating award-winning promotions is good for the ego, results are what count in direct marketing.

Writing Letters to Formula

These guidelines establish a major point: no one should just "sit down to write a letter." Notes, even random notes, are essential. Appeals. Benefits. Selling points. Market facts. Offers. Free gifts, if any. Possible leads. Testimonials. Guarantees. Problems to overcome. From this mix of notes and random ideas, a persuasive letter must emerge. The question is: "How do you do that?" One way is to follow a formula.

The AIDA formula is among the best known:

Attract	ATTENTION
Develop	INTEREST
Create	DESIRE
Get	ACTION

This is a good route to follow, but some explanations are in order. "Attract attention" refers to the lead and/or the first paragraph of the letter. Passive attention won't cut it; instead, an instant desire to learn more must occur. Example: *The lowest price on a computer this year . . . and no interest payments for 24 months!*

A lead of this type predictably will grab attention and heighten the interest in learning more.   Another method for attracting attention is to use a "Johnson box" right at the top of the letterhead and before the salutation, which tells the whole story in capsulized form.

The rest of the AIDA formula follows quite logically (See Exhibit 18–12 for a letter that applies the AIDA formula). Attracting attention leads to a heightened interest to learn more about the product or service. Interest leads to a desire to possess. The final step—getting action—is the moment of truth.

The copywriter's mission is to overcome human inertia, to get positive action *now*. This may be accomplished by setting a deadline date, offering a free gift for prompt action, or offering free shipping and handling charges if an order is received before a certain date.

Many years ago Bob Stone came up with a letter-writing formula that he believed was a few steps beyond the AIDA formula because it follows a more detailed route. Used wisely, Stone believes, it should not stifle creativity. All seven steps are illustrated in the Kiplinger Letter shown in Exhibit 18–13. The Kiplinger letter is a long-running control, which says something about the staying power of good copy.

Bob Stone's Seven-Step Formula for Winning Letters

1. *Promise your most important benefit in your headline or first paragraph.* You need to grab the reader's attention with something relevant at the beginning of a letter. Leading with the most important benefit is a good start. Some writers use the "Johnson Box": short, terse copy that summarizes the main benefits, positioned with or without a box, above the headline.

2. *Immediately enlarge on your most important benefit.* This step is crucial. Many writers come up with a great lead, and then fail to follow through. Or they catch attention with their heading, but then take two or three paragraphs to warm up to their subject. The reader's attention is gone! Try hard to elaborate on your most important benefit right away, and you'll build up interest fast.

3. *Tell readers specifically what they are going to get.* It's amazing how many letters lack details on basic benefits, features, terms, and conditions. Perhaps the writer is so close to the proposition that he or she assumes the readers know all about it. A dangerous assumption! When you tell the reader what they are going to get, don't overlook the intangibles that go along with your product or service. For example, they are getting smart appearance in addition to a pair of slacks, knowledge in addition to a 340-page book.

4. *Back up your statements with proof and endorsements.* Most prospects are somewhat skeptical about advertising. They know it sometimes gets a little overly enthusiastic about a product. So they accept it with a grain of salt. If you can back up your own statements with third-party testimonials or a list of satisfied users, everything you say becomes more believable.

5. *Tell readers what they might lose if they don't act.* As noted, people respond affirmatively either to gain something they do not possess or to avoid losing something they already have. Here's a good spot in your letter to overcome human inertia—imply what could be lost if action is postponed. People don't like to be left out. A skillful writer can use this human trait as a powerful influence in his or her message.

6. *Rephrase your prominent benefits in your closing offer.* As a good salesperson does, sum up the benefits to the prospect in your closing offer. This is the proper prelude to asking for action. This is where you can intensify the prospect's desire to have the product. The stronger the benefits you can persuade the reader to recall, the easier it will be for him or her to justify an affirmative decision.

7. *Incite action.* Now. This is the spot where you win or lose the battle with inertia. Once a letter is put aside or sorted into the wrong pile, they're out of luck. So wind up with a call for action, and a logical reason for acting now. Too many letters close with a statement like "supplies are limited." That argument lacks credibility. Make the reason a believable one. For example, "It could be many months before we go back to press on this book." Or "Orders are shipped on a first-come basis. The sooner yours is received, the sooner you can be enjoying your new widget."

EXHIBIT 18–12

Application of AIDA Formula

Shown here is the front of the teaser envelope and letter. Brochure cover and reservation certificate appear on the next page.

KCDMA
KANSAS CITY DIRECT MARKETING ASSOCIATION

P.O. Box 419264 / Kansas City, MO 64141-6264
816-561-5323 / Fax: 816-561-1991 / www.kcdma.org

Monday

********************AUTO**MIXED AADC 640
Mr Bob Stone
Bob Stone Inc
3029 Iroquois Rd
Wilmette IL 60091-1106

Dear Bob,

Chemistry was fun when we were kids … mixing and stirring up potentially explosive combinations of various elements.

Today, it may not be all that different. If you're like me, you're working with marketing elements to boost response rates, get the message out and change behavior. In other words, getting the formula just right.

But just because yesterday's campaign was successful doesn't guarantee that tomorrow's will get the same response. You have to know what media works best for you, and what you can do to create the energy that gets your customers to buy. Every element in your media mix must work together if you're going to keep your customers satisfied and coming back for more.

And that's what KCDMA's Direct Marketing Conference 1999 is all about. On October 6 and 7, find out how to combine and integrate your media to fuel record-breaking results.

On Wednesday, start with **The Basic Institute** and discover beyond-the-basics formulas and more. Even if you've been in direct marketing for years, you'll find the day a refreshing way to recharge and reenergize your marketing efforts. Then, on Thursday, join the innovators in our industry for **DM Day**. You'll hear five powerhouse presentations about how integrating your efforts can send your responses into orbit.

Take a few minutes to review the enclosed brochure, then send in your Reservation Certificate to enroll today. Make sure you can create the right chemistry to get the results you deserve.

Sincerely,

Pam Linwood, PDM, President
Kansas City Direct Marketing Association

P.S.   You can't afford to experiment with your customers. Plan now to attend KCDMA's Direct Marketing Conference '99, and learn to apply the formulas that will generate record-breaking results. Register before September 17, and you'll get Ernan Roman's classic book *Integrated Direct Marketing*. Don't wait, because this offer will dissolve soon!

EXHIBIT 18-13

The Kiplinger Letter

STANLEY R. MAYES *ASSISTANT TO THE PRESIDENT*

THE KIPLINGER WASHINGTON EDITORS, INC.

1729 H STREET, NORTHWEST, WASHINGTON, D. C. 20006   TELEPHONE: 887-6400

THE KIPLINGER WASHINGTON LETTER   THE KIPLINGER TAX LETTER
THE KIPLINGER AGRICULTURAL LETTER   THE KIPLINGER FLORIDA LETTER
THE KIPLINGER CALIFORNIA LETTER   THE KIPLINGER TEXAS LETTER
CHANGING TIMES MAGAZINE

<u>More Growth and Inflation Ahead...</u>
<u>and what YOU can do about it.</u>

The next few years will see business climb to the highest
level this country has ever known. And with it...inflation.

This combination may be hard for you to accept under today's
conditions. But the fact remains that those who do prepare for both
inflation AND growth ahead will reap big dividends for their foresight,
and avoid the blunders others will make.

You'll get the information you need for this type
of planning in the Kiplinger Washington Letter...
and the enclosed form will bring you the next 26
issues of this helpful service on a "Try-out" basis.
The fee: Less than 81¢ per week...<u>only $21 for the
6 months just ahead</u>...and tax deductible for business
or investment purposes.

During the depression, in 1935, the Kiplinger Letter warned
of inflation and told what to do about it. Those who heeded its advice
were ready when prices began to rise.

Again, in January of 1946, the Letter renounced the widely-
held view that a severe post-war depression was inevitable. Instead
it predicted shortages, rising wages and prices, a high level of
business. And again, those who heeded its advice were able to avoid
losses, to cash in on the surging economy of the late '40s, early '50s
and mid '60s. It then kept its clients prepared for the swings of the
'70s, keeping them a step ahead each time.

Now Kiplinger not only foresees expansion ahead, but also
continuing inflation, and in his weekly Letter to clients he points
out profit opportunities in the future...and also dangers.

The Kiplinger Letter not only keeps you informed of present
trends and developments, but also gives you advance notice on the
short & long-range business outlook...inflation forecasts...energy
predictions...housing...federal legislative prospects...politics...
investment trends & pointers...tax outlook & advice...labor, wage
settlement prospects...upcoming gov't rules & regulations...ANYTHING
that will have an effect on you, your business, your personal finances,
your family.

To take advantage of this opportunity to try the Letter and
benefit from its keen judgments and helpful advice during the fast-

(Over, please)

EXHIBIT 18–13

The Kiplinger Letter (*Continued*)

changing months ahead...fill in and return the enclosed form along with your $21 payment. And do it with this guarantee: That you may cancel the service and get a prompt refund of the unused part of your payment any time you feel it is not worth far more to you than it costs.

I'll start your service as soon as I hear from you, and you'll have each weekly issue on your desk every Monday morning thereafter.

Sincerely,

Stanley Mayes

Stanley Mayes
Assistant to the President

SAM:kga

P. S.   More than half of all new subscribers sign up for a full year at $42. In appreciation, we'll send you FREE five special Kiplinger Reports on receipt of your payment when you take a full year's service, too. Details are spelled out on the enclosed slip. Same money-back guarantee and tax deductibility apply.

Not everyone writes to formulas. A somewhat different approach to take is to employ a problem/solution strategic approach. Under this approach, the creative people review the problems to be faced and then come up with strategic solutions for each of the problems. Much like writing case studies, this approach helps the reader to see how responding will help them in their business or personal lives. Should you write to formula or break the rules? Perhaps the best answer is this: if you are just starting out writing copy, write to formula. It will keep you on track. Let the seasoned professionals set their own rules. They've earned the right! Below is an outline of a direct mail creative strategy brief.

Letter Length, Appearance, and P.S.

Question: do people read long copy? Answer: yes! People will read something for as long as it interests them. An uninteresting one-page letter can be too long. A skillfully woven four-pager can hold the reader until the end. Thus, a letter should be long enough to cover the subject adequately and short enough to retain interest. Don't be afraid of long copy. If you have something to say and can say it well, it will probably do better than short copy. After all, the longer you hold a reader's interest, the more sales points you can get across and the more likely you are to generate a response.

Can this be true, even in this age of online interactivity? And, can long copy work in e-mail as well? Yes, notes Nick Usborne, freelance copywriter, author, and speaker. Usborne notes that "If you can hold someone's attention with your writing, a long page gives you the space to deliver all the benefits, cover all the features, and address a myriad of reader questions and concerns. So long as the letter carries momentum and holds the reader's attention, people will keep scrolling."

Regardless of letter length, it should always look attractive and be easy to read. Keep paragraphs down to six or seven lines. Use subheads and indented paragraphs to break up long copy. Emphasize pertinent thoughts, knowing that many readers will scan indented paragraphs before they decide whether to read a letter clear through. Use underscoring, CAPITAL LETTERS, and a second ink color to make key words and sentences stand out. And, use ellipses . . . and dashes—to break up long sentences.

Finally, it usually pays to include a postscript. The P.S. is one of the most effective parts of any letter. Many prospects will glance through a letter. The eye will pick up an indented paragraph here, stop on an underlined statement there, and finally come to rest on the P.S. If you can express an important idea in the P.S., the reader *might* go back and read the whole letter. This makes the P.S. worthy of your best efforts. Use it to restate a key benefit, or to offer an added inducement, like a free gift. Even when somebody has read the rest of the letter, the P.S. can make the difference between whether or not the prospect places an order. Use the P.S. to finish on a strong note, sign off with the strongest appeal you have.

Versioned and Personalized Copy

One of the strengths of direct mail is that mailings can be personalized with individual information, or versioned across market segments. Rather than talking about the general advantages and benefits of the product, you can zero in on those that fit each market segment. Test it for yourself. If your product story is substantially different for certain audience segments—and you can identify and select them on the lists you're using—develop special versions of your regular copy and give the technique a try.

Versioned copy can have the objective of reselling buyers of a brand, product, service, or category. It can be versioned to upsell them a better or improved product. It can cross-sell them a different product. Or, it can be slanted to previous buyers. Customers like to think a firm remembers them and will give them special treatment. In going back to your satisfied buyers, there's less need to resell your company. You can concentrate on the product or the service being offered.

Personalized letters usually outpull nonpersonalized ones, but not always. When you use personalization, use all the information you can. But don't overuse the person's name throughout the letter. A good rule to follow: write a personalized letter as you would write a letter to any person you know fairly well.

Exhibit 18–14. Capital One Platinum Card DMK, is an example of a personalized mailing with many bells and whistles. The letter, while attached to the application, still uses bolding and bullet points. And the outer envelope has a "Pull" tab on the right, allowing it to be opened from the side. The tipped-on plastic card is a common way of making the concept of "credit" tangible within the mailing.

Direct Mail Production

Direct mail packages are designed around production specifications to be as efficient as possible. Mailings are produced around standard sizes that are easy to print, personalize, insert into envelopes automatically, and mail efficiently. The 8½ × 11 inch letter

EXHIBIT 18-14

Capital One Platinum Card DMK

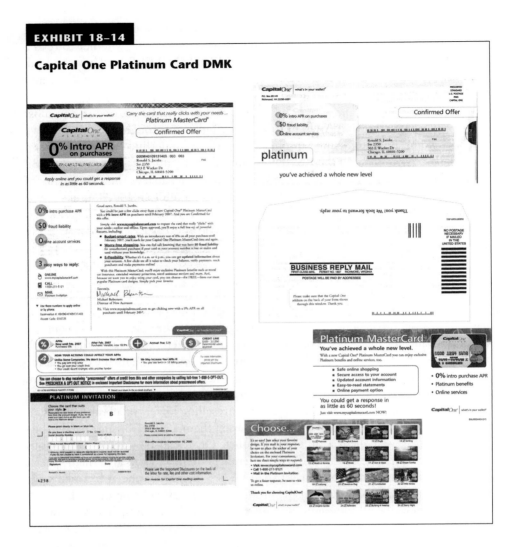

illustrates this. It can be folded twice and automatically inserted in a #10 envelope. Fold it in half, to 5½ × 8½ inches, and it can be efficiently inserted into a 6 × 9 inch envelope. Leave it flat, and it fits into a 9 × 12 inch. This size letter can be preprinted on one or two sides, or efficiently run through digital printers to be personalized.

Need a longer letter? Print it as an 11 × 17 inch, four-page letter. Fold the larger size once, and it is now 8½ × 11 inches, which can continue to be folded to fit standard envelope sizes. Brochures often follow the same sizes.

When used in a #10 envelope package, lift letters are often printed on 5½ × 8½ inches and folded once (note that 5½ × 8½ inches is exactly half the size of 8½ × 11 inches). To save money, and simplify production, response devices and buckslips are often printed approximately 8½ inches × 3½ inches, where three are cut out of an 8¼ inch × 11 inch form. This size fits flat into a #10 OE and a #9 BRE (Business Reply Envelope). Larger outside envelops simply allow for larger sizes, but they are still based on this concept (Note: Sizes are approximate. Paper stock and printing press sizes vary widely. There are differences between Standard American Equivalent and metric sizes as well as among manufacturers working within one of the two standards).

Printing on demand (POD) uses the same sizes and is an alternative for complicated, personalized, short-run mailing. This is common where mailings are versioned for different segments of customers or prospect files.

The main advantage is that the mailing is printed as needed. Set-up or "make ready" costs are minimized, but printing on demand is more expensive than traditional printing, and it must be estimated for each mailing to maximize its efficiency.

Exhibit 18–15, Hewlett-Packard POD DMK, illustrates how printing on demand is often used. It is mailed in a clear envelope and the prospect's name and address show through on one side, while the prospect's first name is used in copy, and shows through on the back side.

The Deceptive Mail Prevention and Enforcement Act of 1999

Although the Deceptive Mail Prevention and Enforcement Act of 1999 was enacted to cover "sweepstakes mailings, skill contests, facsimile checks, and mailings made to resemble government documents," it has far-reaching implications for all mailers. The law is very specific about what a marketer can and cannot do. Just wanting to do the right thing may not be enough to meet the standards. Marketers using direct mail must acquaint themselves with all federal and state laws that apply.

The law restricts mailings with misleading references to the United States Government in a way that a reasonable person might think that the mailing came from or was endorsed by a government agency. Mailings should not refer to the Postmaster General, Postmaster, a federal agency, department, commission, or federal program in a manner that gives the impression that the mailing or offer is endorsed or sent by the federal government.

In general, a mailing that attempts to sell a product or service that the federal government offers to all at no charge must clearly disclose that fact. Disclosure is not necessary if the government only offers the product or service free to some persons, but not all.

Fund-raising mailings should not pretend to come from the government or falsely state or imply that someone's government benefits will be reduced unless a product or service is purchased. A "facsimile check," defined as one that is not negotiable yet is made to look like something that is, must disclose on the check

EXHIBIT 18–15

Hewlett-Packard POD DMK

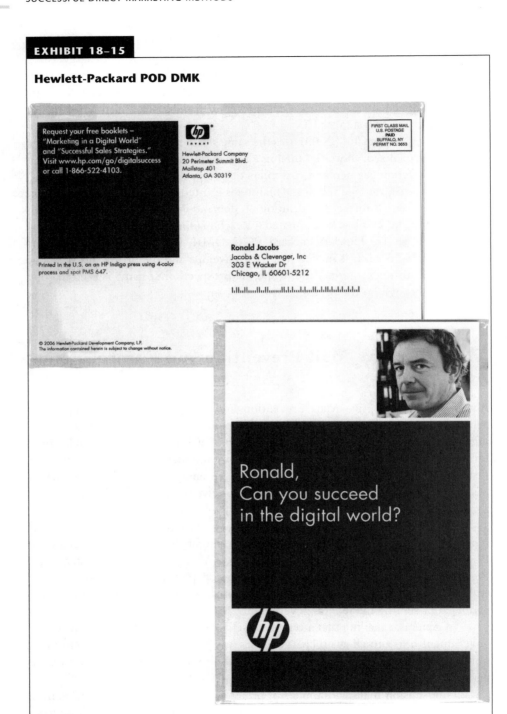

that it is not negotiable and has no cash value. A key provision notes that required disclosures, such as sweepstakes rules, terms, and conditions, must be "clearly and conspicuously displayed," that is, "readily noticeable, readable and understandable" by an "average" member of the target audience.

In addition, mailings for sweepstakes mailings must disclose:

1. That a purchase is not necessary to enter, and will not improve the chances of winning. These disclosures must appear in the mailing, in the rules, and on the entry form and be very easy to find, read, and understand.

2. A name and business address where the sponsor can be contacted.

3. The estimated odds of winning each prize. If the odds depend upon the number of entries, the stated odds should be based on an estimate of the number of entries.

4. The quantity, estimated retail value, and nature of every prize.

5. A clear statement of the payment schedule of any prize. For example, if a $1 million prize is to be awarded in equal payments over 20 years, the disclosure should indicate that the $1 million shall be paid in equal amounts of $50,000 per year for 20 years starting in 2000.

Under this law, a sweepstakes mailer must also include an address or toll-free phone number where a recipient or caregiver may request to have his or her name removed from the mailing list. This restriction is true even when the person is a "customer" or has previously responded to sweepstakes promotions from the organization.

The law has enforcement capabilities built in. It requires the U.S. Postal Service not to deliver and to dispose of mailings found to be deceptive. The USPS may intercept sweepstakes and skill contest entries mailed back to a company in violation of the law, and return them to the senders. And, the legislation provided for fines by offenders up to $1 million.

The federal law does not preempt any state laws, which allows for states to enact more restrictive laws if they choose.

The Last Word on Direct Mail Creative

It is difficult to find the right balance of time to give to copy and layout in direct marketing. Too often, marketers spend time obsessing over a few words, buried deeply in copy, which don't seem to make a difference. Research shows that readers just skim mail anyway. Yet, when marketers are careless and a mailing goes out with a typographic error, a misprinted offer, or an inconsistent illustration, consumers let the marketer know in a hurry. It becomes clear why marketers need to take so much care, concern, and time in creating and executing direct mail.

Case Study: BlueCross BlueShield "Shades of Blue" Direct Mailing

Adapted from the Direct Marketing Association International Echo Awards 2006.

BACKGROUND

BlueCross BlueShield of South Carolina's typical new customer acquisition strategy is to use special enrollment periods. In primary enrollment periods, prospects were offered special incentives to apply (i.e., all application fees are waived and applicants need not answer any health questions; additionally, the waiting period for preexisting conditions is waived).

CHALLENGE

This campaign, which ran in spring, lacked the customary special incentives used during the primary enrollment period. Therefore, the challenge was to convince the target to respond minus the usual incentives.

STRATEGY

BlueCross BlueShield of South Carolina sought to leverage its strong presence in the community to reinforce the company's trustworthiness. A prominent mention of the value-added discounts (within the product) was used to pique consumer interest. Also, a free gift of flowering seeds was included to capture the target's attention.

MARKETING TACTICS

In order to manage leads, mailings of this piece were split into three groups. The piece was mailed to approximately 130,800 targets—approximately 43,600 at each of the three drops.

The free gift was a custom blend of seeds for BlueCross BlueShield of South Carolina. The seed mix included three types of blue flowers designed

EXHIBIT 18–16

"Shades of Blue" DM

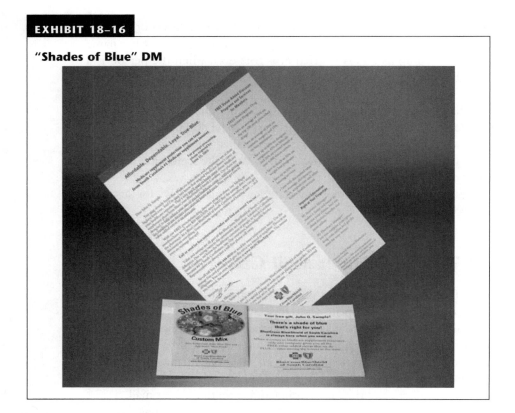

Case Study: BlueCross BlueShield "Shades of Blue" Direct Mailing *(Continued)*

---

to blossom in a southern climate from summer to winter. The seeds and packaging were dubbed "Shades of Blue." The brand-heavy message in the package complemented the free gift with phrases: "Our roots are in your community," "We're the seasoned experts," "You're covered all year long," and "There's a shade of blue that's right for you" (See Exhibit 18–16).

RESULTS

"Shades of Blue" generated a 2.3 percent response rate and over 16,000 leads with a CPI (cost per impression) of just over $5.00. This response was better than the combined results of two direct mail packages from the previous spring. Collectively, the two efforts net 2,761 leads, a 1.84 percent response rate, and a CPI of $21.74.

PILOT PROJECT

According to the Direct Marketing Association, in 2006, 17 percent of all direct marketing advertising dollars were spent by the financial services industry. And, direct mail was chosen as the primary channel by 43 percent of those marketers. Bank of America and Capital One were the number one and number two customers of the U.S. Postal Service in 2006.

Monitor your mailbox over one week, and determine how many direct mail packages offering credit cards you receive. Compare credit card mailers versus other direct mail packages for other categories. Dissect each direct mail package for similarities and differences.

A. What size envelope or format was used?

B. How many colors is it printed in?

C. How many elements were in each direct mail package?

D. What percentage of the copy is promotional versus terms, conditions, and other disclosures?

E. Identify the main copy points, offer, and calls to action.

Key Points

▶ Direct mail comes in a variety of formats, sizes, and shapes depending upon the target group, objectives, and budget.

▶ The most effective mailing package consists of outside envelope, letter, brochure, response form, and business reply envelope.

▶ Response devices are another important element in direct mail and should be included, even when mail is not the main way of responding.

▶ Details that make a mailing seem more relevant, such as personalization and blue signatures on letters, improve response.

▶ Copy should emphasize benefits to the reader, and support the benefits with features, advantages, and motives.

CREATING
AND MANAGING
CATALOGS

Catalogs play an important role in the lives of consumers and business buyers. Nevertheless, few catalogs today stand on their own. They are part of multichannel marketing strategies that, in addition to paper catalogs, may include Web catalogs, E-commerce sites, and retail and other direct-to-consumer channels.

E-commerce sites, such as Amazon.com, mail catalogs. Home Depot, Target, Wal-Mart, and Pier 1 all launched catalogs within the last 12 to 18 months because companies realize that direct marketing must be one of the core competencies. And, the business-to-business segment hasn't been left out. Retailers such as Best Buy use the catalog as a tool to drive traffic to stores and boost Internet sales.

According to the DMA, direct mail companies in the United States mailed over 18 billion catalogs in 2004. For the foreseeable future, the two media can be expected to grow and prosper together, primarily because of their different, yet complementary, uses. This chapter describes and explains the catalog process and the strategies used to build and manage a successful catalog company. The catalog process chart in Exhibit 19-1, from J. Schmid* & Associates, identifies the eight core competencies of a winning catalog. They are: niche/positioning/branding; offer proposition; creative execution; new customer acquisition; customer list communication; fulfillment; database; and postanalysis. Refer to this chart as you read the rest of this chapter.

---

*Jack Schmid, of Kansas City, Kansas, heads J. Schmid & Associates, Inc. He has served such consumer and business-to-business clients as Hershey Foods, Xerox Corporation, Fingerhut, Anheuser-Busch, RadioShack, New Pig Corporation, Sara Lee, and Hallmark Cards. He is author of *Starting and Growing a Catalog Business.*

EXHIBIT 19–1

The Catalog Process

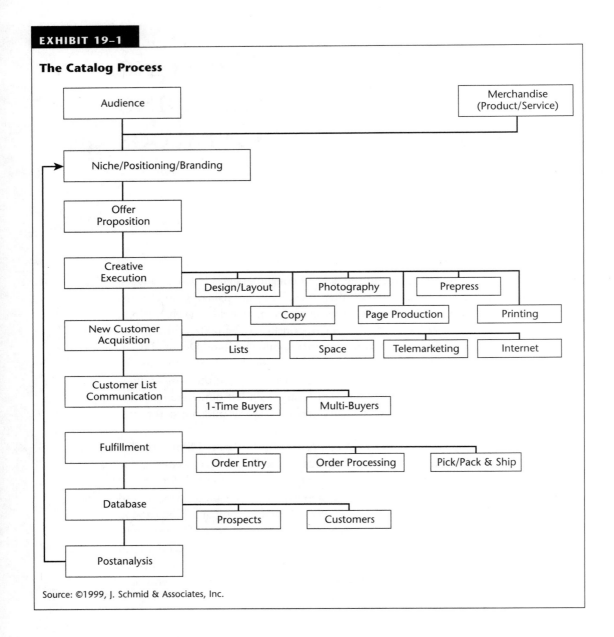

Source: ©1999, J. Schmid & Associates, Inc.

Core Competency #1: Merchandising

Catalogs are a blend of merchandise and audience. Most catalogs are merchandise-driven, that is, they start from a merchandise point of view and address the purchaser of the product. Many of the pioneers in cataloging—people like Roger Horchow of the Horchow Collection, Chuck Williams of Williams Sonoma,

Manny Fingerhut of Fingerhut—were merchandisers who started with a solid product concept and from there built a growing business.

Even if a catalog is market- or audience-driven (that is, it starts with an audience which determines what products can be sold), merchandising is of vital importance. The familiar adage "Nothing comes before the product" means that if catalogers desire to build repeat buyers—a prime goal for profitability—they must start with and build a strong merchandising program that will continue to attract customers over time. Merchandising has been likened to the foundation of a building. Without a strong foundation, it is difficult to build a solid building or business.

Understanding the psychology of the catalog buyer is essential to catalog merchandising (See Exhibit 19–2). If the goal is to build repeat buyers, then understanding who those customers are and why they come back is paramount. Exhibit 19–2 also differentiates between frequent mail-order buyers and

EXHIBIT 19–2

The Psychology of the Catalog Buyer

Frequent Buyers	Infrequent Buyers
Convenience	
A quick and easy way to shop	Hassles in dealing with the PO
A comfortable alternative to retail shopping	Waiting for an order
A way to avoid crowds	Returning merchandise
Merchandise	
Unusual merchandise	Cannot see or feel merchandise
New products and styles	Hard to judge quality
Found merchandise that fits	Problems with fit, color, etc.
Consumer's Outlook	
Confident	Skeptical
In control	Afraid of losing control
Excited, anticipation	Fear of "rip-offs"
Dream fulfillment	
Value	
Lower prices on special promotions	Can shop around at retail
Added value from not having to drive to store	More sales at retail
Can comparison shop by using multiple catalogs	Can control bills
Brand	
Expertise in dealing with companies in direct mail selling uncommon brand names	Lack of expertise in buying unknown needs
Trust direct mail companies	Uncertain about the reputation of direct mail companies
Need	
Can wait for a number of products	Want immediate gratification at time of purchase
Order well in advance of special need	Waiting time is frustrating

"touch-and-feel shoppers," those who prefer retail stores and who distrust catalog shopping. Internet shoppers can be equated to "frequent buyers," but they are even more driven by convenience and a confident outlook.

Know Thy Customer

"Know thy customer" is the first rule of catalog merchandising. A catalog product buyer must understand why and how people use the catalog. A classic mistake made by those who select products for catalogs is putting their own tastes and preferences first and paying little heed to what they know about the ultimate consumers.

How do you get to know your customers? Here are some tactics used by successful catalogs:

- A customer survey that rides along in the box shipment to first-time customers

- Annual surveys to repeat buyers—by mail, phone, and even the Internet—that seek information on customers and what additional products they might like to see in the catalog

- Phone contact with customers through telemarketing representatives

- Regular dialogue between key people in the company and customers regarding how various aspects of the catalog might be improved, usually by taking phone call orders

- Customer focus groups

- Customer advisory boards

The key is to listen to what customers are saying in research surveys and phone conversations.

Build on Your Winners

Successful catalogers watch what their customers buy and listen to what they say. From a merchandise/sales standpoint, the worst catalog is the first catalog. With each succeeding mailing, a catalog should build on the merchandise categories and the price points that the customer is buying. Postanalysis of catalog sales results is essential.

Eddie Bauer listened to its customers. The successful cataloger, inventor of the down parka, made his name synonymous with high-quality outdoor clothing and sporting goods. From its growth years during World War II, the company listened and watched as its customers' lifestyles evolved and began expanding its product line through a mail-order catalog in 1945. From its merchandise mix of men's and women's clothing, footwear, and luggage, Eddie Bauer's thrust is Internet buying, and it promotes its Web site on its cover and inside the catalog with sales and promotions in both mediums (See Exhibits 19–3A, 19–3B, and 19–3C).

EXHIBIT 19–3A

Eddie Bauer Early Summer 2007 Front Cover

EXHIBIT 19-3B

Eddie Bauer Early Summer 2007 Back Cover

Convertible cargos…the secret to summertime cool.

Ripstop Convertible Cargo Pants
• sit below waist
• relaxed through seat and thigh
Pants zip off into shorts for quick
adaptation to changing temperatures.
Side back elastic for increased
comfort. Slanted front pockets, two
side zip pockets, back flap pockets
with self-fastening closures. Cotton.
Machine wash. Imported. Expedition
Green, Putty (shown on model).
Sizes: Regular 30, 32-36, 38-44 even;
Long Rise 34-44 even. Shorts inseam:
Reg. 9"; Long Rise 10". Specify pants
inseam and we'll finish to 36";
Long Rise to 37". Or unfinished.
B03 253 4338 Regular $59.50
B03 253 4339 Long Rise $65

expedition green
putty

Polo, B33 253 6462, $34.50.
Sandals, A19 253 1296, $80.
Both also available online.

Eddie Bauer®
EST. 1920

Send catalog orders to:
PO Box 7001
Groveport, OH 43125

For store locations and catalog orders, call 800.426.8020
Shop online at eddiebauer.com
Early Summer 2007 • Prices expire 6/22/07

I.D. #

Application Code

Media Code

Printed in USA

EXHIBIT 19–3C

Eddie Bauer Early Summer 2007 Catalog Spread

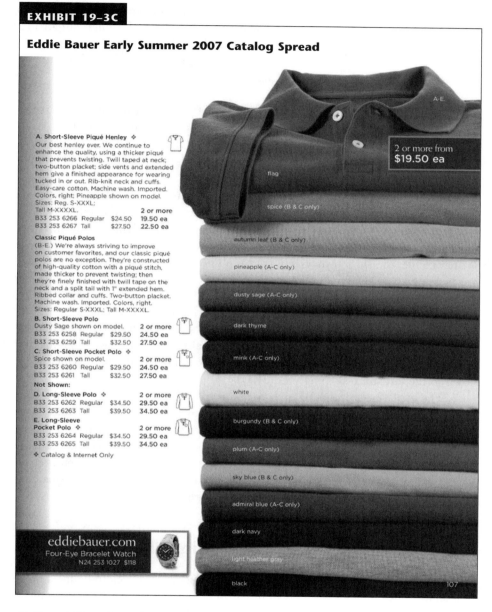

A. Short-Sleeve Piqué Henley ❖
Our best henley ever. We continue to enhance the quality, using a thicker piqué that prevents twisting. Twill taped at neck; two-button placket; side vents and extended hem give a finished appearance for wearing tucked in or out. Rib-knit neck and cuffs. Easy-care cotton. Machine wash. Imported. Colors, right; Pineapple shown on model. Sizes: Reg. S-XXXL; Tall M-XXXXL.

		2 or more
B33 253 6266 Regular	$24.50	19.50 ea
B33 253 6267 Tall	$27.50	22.50 ea

Classic Piqué Polos
(B-E.) We're always striving to improve on customer favorites, and our classic piqué polos are no exception. They're constructed of high-quality cotton with a piqué stitch, made thicker to prevent twisting; then they're finely finished with twill tape on the neck and a split tail with 1" extended hem. Ribbed collar and cuffs. Two-button placket. Machine wash. Imported. Colors, right. Sizes: Regular S-XXXL; Tall M-XXXXL.

B. Short-Sleeve Polo
Dusty Sage shown on model.

		2 or more
B33 253 6258 Regular	$29.50	24.50 ea
B33 253 6259 Tall	$32.50	27.50 ea

C. Short-Sleeve Pocket Polo ❖
Spice shown on model.

		2 or more
B33 253 6260 Regular	$29.50	24.50 ea
B33 253 6261 Tall	$32.50	27.50 ea

Not Shown:

D. Long-Sleeve Polo ❖

		2 or more
B33 253 6262 Regular	$34.50	29.50 ea
B33 253 6263 Tall	$39.50	34.50 ea

E. Long-Sleeve Pocket Polo ❖

		2 or more
B33 253 6264 Regular	$34.50	29.50 ea
B33 253 6265 Tall	$39.50	34.50 ea

❖ Catalog & Internet Only

2 or more from $19.50 ea

flag
spice (B & C only)
autumn leaf (B & C only)
pineapple (A-C only)
dusty sage (A-C only)
dark thyme
mink (A-C only)
white
burgundy (B & C only)
plum (A-C only)
sky blue (B & C only)
admiral blue (A-C only)
dark navy
light heather gray
black

eddiebauer.com
Four-Eye Bracelet Watch
N24 253 1027 $118

107

Other Merchandise Strategies

What other merchandise strategies are smart catalogers using? Here are several that have proved successful.

Improve Product Quality While Reducing Cost. Customers are concerned about the value of products they buy through a catalog or the Internet.

Value is a perceived price/quality relationship. Smart catalogers constantly try to improve product quality while improving their margins. Through importing, buying in larger quantities, and improving vendor relationships, a catalog's challenge is to buy better and at the same time give customers more for their money. Surely that will keep them coming back.

Strengthen New-Product Development Efforts. During periods of recession, it is common for companies to cut back or discontinue new product development. New product development, however, is the lifeblood of the catalog. Winning catalogers keep it at the forefront of their minds and budgets at all times.

Strengthen Inventory Control Systems. One major difference between retailing and cataloging is exemplified by the statement, "Retailers sell what they buy and catalogers buy what they sell." Retailers buy merchandise for an entire season. If a woman comes into a shop to buy an advertised dress and finds her size is unavailable, the shop owners will try to sell her another dress in her size. They are "selling what they bought." A catalog, however, normally will commit for only 40–50 percent of its anticipated needs for a season. Then it will read the selling results early in the season and reorder ("buying what they are selling").

It is vital for catalogs to have reliable vendors who can back them up in merchandise and turn around reorders quickly. It is also crucial to have a buying and re-buying staff, as well as computer systems, that can help forecast product needs down to the last stock-keeping unit (SKU).

The final aspect of catalog inventory control is disposing of leftover merchandise at the end of a season. Items can be repeated in a future catalog or featured on special sales pages, in package inserts of remainder products, in a telephone special, or on the Internet. Outlet stores, annual warehouse sales, and special sales at large events like state fairs are also useful. Remainder merchants can also dispose of unsold merchandise. Most successful catalogs have fine-tuned their remainder systems so they minimize the markdown expense that haunts retail stores.

Core Competency #2: Positioning the Catalog

To set themselves apart from the competition, most catalogs seek to define a niche or a unique position and develop a brand for their catalog. A niche is both a unique identity and a special place in the market where there is a void that is not being met by the competition. A catalog can differentiate itself from competition by merchandise selection, creative style or format, offers, and customer service.

"Brand development" is a relatively new term for catalogers. Branding has been the purview of manufacturers such as Procter & Gamble but seldom is given consideration by catalogers. Branding is having "top of mind" recognition when a customer thinks about a product. L.L. Bean has brand awareness and brand equity in the outdoor market. Dell and Gateway have brand strength in computers.

Branding and positioning are very complementary creative components. A strong brand defines a need and differentiates itself.

THE ULTIMATE BRAND IS:	THE ULTIMATE BRAND ELIMINATES:	THE ULTIMATE BRAND ENSURES:
• The definer	• Wasted efforts	• Long-term growth
• The differentiator	• Duplication	• Instant recognition
• The replicator	• Wrong directions	• Consistency
• The multiplier	• Confusion	• Singularity of effort
• The expander	• Inconsistency	• Focus
• The door-opener	• Fragmentation	• Adherence to standards
• The Ultimate Salesperson		

Source: Manhattan Creative Strategies.

Defining the Catalog's Niche and Brand

What does a cataloger need to think about before beginning creative execution? Often catalogers, particularly first-timers, jump right into the creative process without first thinking through some very basic issues. Here are some key questions that must be answered:

1. Who is the company, the catalog? What product or service does it sell? Is there any brand awareness or strength?

2. To whom does it sell? Who are its primary customers, secondary customers, and even tertiary customers?

3. How is the catalog unique? What sets it apart from its competitors? Its products? Its service? Its offers? Its pricing?

4. Who is the competition? What are their niches? What are their strengths? Weaknesses? Do they have brand recognition? Do they have a serious void or weakness that can be exploited?

Differentiating the Catalog from the Competition

There are innumerable ways to set a catalog apart, but here are five variables to consider:

1. *Merchandise.* This is a vital area in which to be different. Perhaps it is acceptable to be No. 2 in the auto rental area, as Avis has shown, but to be No. 2 in a catalog niche, and not have a defined difference in product, can be financially disastrous.

2. *Pricing or use of credit.* A pricing method can help set a catalog apart. Current Inc.'s catalog uses a three-part pricing strategy that basically says to the customer: "The more items you buy, the better the price." Discounters such as

Damark or Viking are also good at using pricing to help build a unique identity. Fingerhut sells only on credit (its own), and establishes a niche in doing so.

3. *Catalog format and creative presentation.* Besides merchandising, the catalog's creative format, design, and copy can make a tremendous difference in establishing its niche. Think of Patagonia and its unique in-use photography (all supplied by readers and customers); Gooseberry Patch's unique catalog size and illustrative art; and L.L. Bean's square shape, cover art, and catalog layout. Exhibit 19–4 shows how good creative can transform a brand.

4. *Offer.* An offer, or proposition, is what the cataloger is willing to give to customers in return for their response. What catalog has a unique offer that sets it apart? Hammacher Schlemmer consistently offers a special in its catalog: "Buy two items and get a third free." Nordstrom's offers free pickup on any return. Murad will send a catalog and free product samples in exchange for prospects' skin care information.

5. *Customer service/fulfillment.* Here is an ideal way to set a catalog apart: service so good that it is the envy of every competitor. It starts with the ability to accept orders by mail, phone, fax, or the Internet with well-trained people and a database system that allows real-time access to customers' records. Next is online inventory so customers know before finishing the order whether the size and color of the item is in stock, and can make a decision about alternatives. Then it's the delivery time of the product. Finally comes the handling of returns and inquiries. Without a doubt, customer service can set a catalog apart.

EXHIBIT 19–4

Manhattan Creative Strategies

Before and Afters

Manhattan Creative Strategies
(MCS) transformed one of its
clients' catalogs from a product-
oriented flip-thru to a lifestyle-
enhancing experience.

Core Competencies #3 and #4: New Customer Acquisition and Customer List Communication

It is critical for a catalog to build a buyer list—a group of people or companies that will keep coming back again and again to order.

When a new catalog starts, it has no buyers and probably no affinity names—names of potential buyers who have some relationship to the company or catalog. About 1.8 million people visit Hershey Chocolate World every year. Some sign up to receive a Hershey Chocolate catalog during the holiday season. Although these are not proven catalog buyers, they represent a list of prospects with which the company has had some relationship. There is a good chance that these prospects will be pleased to receive and order from a chocolate catalog.

If a company has no affinity names, it must rely on building its customer list from list brokers (e.g., InfoUSA, Accudata, Edith Roman, among others) and other alternative media that can be targeted to its audience. It is not unusual for the buyer list to outperform an outside list or nonaffinity names many times over. This is why it usually takes a new catalog three years to break even and about five years to recapture its initial investment.

Front-End/Back-End Marketing

A concept well understood by veteran catalogers is front-end and back-end marketing (See Exhibit 19–5). Front-end marketing refers to prospecting or new customer acquisition. Few catalogers make money on prospecting; it is a cost-related activity. The objectives of front-end marketing are to acquire new first-time customers, or to acquire leads and inquiries that can be converted into first-time buyers, and to acquire the most names at the least cost. Smart catalogers measure precisely what it costs to acquire a new, first-time buyer and are tenacious about tracking where the name came from.

Back-end marketing refers to working the customer list. This is where the profitability of the catalog comes from. The objectives of back-end marketing are to convert first-time buyers into second-time buyers, to maximize the number of profitable mailings to this list each year, and to determine where the best long-term customers come from so that the catalog can change or modify its front-end media. A winning catalog carefully observes the growth of its buyer file, watching especially for buyers who have purchased more than twice. Large catalogers often divide the marketing functions by front end and back end. The small cataloger must understand and play both roles within the company.

The Customer Hierarchy

The cataloger has to understand the hierarchy of a customer (See Exhibit 19–6). Because the primary goal of a catalog is to get repeat orders from its customer list,

EXHIBIT 19–5

Front-End/Back-End Concept of Marketing

| Prospects = Costs |

| Customers = Profits |

Objective   **How Results Are Measured**

| Front-End Marketing |

Acquire New, First-Time Customers   Cost per Customer
Acquire New Leads   Cost per Lead
Acquire New Inquiries   Cost per Name
Convert Leads and Inquiries to Customers   Cost of Conversion
Minimize Cost of Building the Customer File

| Back-End Marketing |

Convert First-Time Buyers into   Growth of Multibuyer File
   Second-Time Buyers
Maximize Number of Mailings to   Number of Customer Mailings
   Customer List Each Year
Make a Profit   Return on Investment
                                                           Return on Sales
                                                           Value of a Customer Over
                                                              Three Years

EXHIBIT 19–6

The Customer Hierarchy

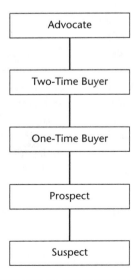

a successful catalog must build trust, credibility, and confidence. In this process, there are three distinct hurdles to be surmounted. The first is converting prospects to first-time buyers. Perhaps these first-time buyers should be called "tryers." They are cautious, have a low response rate, have a lower average order size, and expect the catalog to prove itself worthy before ordering again.

What message do buyers give when they purchase a second time? Generally, it is this: "You're okay. I like your products and your service is acceptable." Average order value goes up. A higher response rate is the norm.

A further step is building the multi-buyers into advocates who will recommend the catalog to others. They will peruse the catalog carefully and they usually respond at many times the rate of first-time buyers. This phenomenon is what makes a successful, profitable catalog.

New Customer Acquisition Strategies

Historically, catalogs have relied heavily on rented lists to develop their customer base. But this isn't the only method. Because of rising postal and mailing costs, catalogers are seeking alternative ways to obtain new buyers. Innovation is the name of the prospecting game. Here are 16 options, other than list rentals, that catalogs are using today:

1. *The Internet.* As a minimum, every catalog should have a Web site from which a potential customer can request a catalog. While the verdict is still out on lifetime value of Internet catalog requesters, this is an important medium for every cataloger.

2. *Customer referrals.* These are very good quality names. Ask "advocate" customers for names of friends, relatives, co-workers, and the like.

3. *Space advertising.* Many of today's large catalogs built their buyer lists through space advertising. There are many options: small space ads (one-sixth page) versus large-space ads (full page) and the direct sales of a product versus generating a lead or inquiry.

4. *Magazine catalog sections.* Many consumers and some business magazines publish an annual or a biannual catalog lead-generation section.

5. *Free-standing newspaper inserts (FSIs).* These are usually applicable to more "down-scale" marketers.

6. *Package inserts.* These ride along in the box shipment of another mailer, and can promote a catalog request or sell a winning product.

7. *Co-op mailings.* Carol Wright is an example.

8. *Trade shows.* These are especially effective for business catalogs.

9. *Television.*

10. *Catalog of catalogs.* Today there are several lead-generation publications, such as *Shop-at-Home Directory* and *The Best Catalogs in the World*, which exclusively promote catalogs.

11. *Card decks.*

12. *Credit card or billing inserts.*

13. *Doctor's or dentist's office "take-ones."*

14. *Back panels of cereal boxes.*

15. *Public relations.*

16. *Gift recipients.*

Winning catalogs use a variety of innovative strategies to acquire new customers. Consider the following list:

1. Source-coding every new customer acquisition effort, tracking results, and capturing original source codes on the customer database.

2. Seeking as much publicity as possible by creating events (e.g., marathon races sponsored by marketers of health-related products).

3. Measuring the cost of acquiring names by each type of medium and determining what the catalog can afford to spend for a new customer.

4. Developing customer referral programs such as those used by book clubs.

5. Carefully watching the seasonality of mailings and concentrating prospecting in the prime season.

6. Targeting, targeting, targeting mailings, especially when using list rentals.

7. Telephoning to pre-qualify names before mailing a business-to-business catalog or sending a postcard before the catalog mails to pre-qualify the name.

8. Keeping names of old buyers and inquiries that are no longer mailed, putting them into merge/purge in order, and matching them against outside rental names (de-dupe).

9. Establishing and maintaining a detailed prospect database of inquiries, gift recipients, people who paid for a catalog and the like, and capturing original source codes and dates of inquiry.

10. Getting the catalog to the prospect who requests it as fast as possible and letting the prospect know that "this is the catalog you requested" (Maximum turnaround time should be no more than a week).

11. Correlating back-end customer name value with front-end name source to maximize quality of names over quantity of names.

12. Watching the aging of buyers, inquiries, and catalog requests (People who have not purchased in more than 12 months need a special message or incentive to remind them that they asked for the catalogs they receive).

The Customer List: A Catalog's Most Important Asset

Though few catalogs identify customer lists on the company's balance sheet, it is their most important asset. The buyers are their major source of revenue through sales of merchandise or list rentals. To maximize the use of this asset, however, the list must be maintained and mailed.

List Maintenance. The use of the Postal Service's National Change of Address program (NCOA) during the merge/purge of the customer list with outside lists is well worth the cost and effort in ensuring better delivery. In addition, most catalogers will include a "return service" request for address correction by the USPS in at least one or two mailings a year. In this way they can update the names of people or companies that have moved and eliminate catalogs being discarded for insufficient address.

Mailing the Customer List. Mailing catalogs is expensive. Also, too often companies tend to under-mail their best customers. During the mid-1970s, for example, Fingerhut was mailing its customer list 20 times a year. By using simple segmentation techniques such as recency, frequency, monetary, and product category, the company was able to test and ultimately increase its mailings to 30 times a year. Most catalogers probably under-utilize or under-mail their customer list. One reason is that they tend to treat all customers alike.

Using the Customer List More Effectively. To more effectively and efficiently use the customer list, track buyers by source. A catalog fulfillment database system will let you track, measure, and segment the customer list and track its growth on a weekly or monthly basis.

Know who the best customers are. Survey them. Ask them for help. Research them. Talk to them on the phone. And when you discover your best customers, mail them more often, and treat them like good friends.

Build a simple segmentation system to prioritize the buyer file. All customers are not created equal. Keep track of when and what customers buy, how they respond (phone/fax/mail/e-mail), how they pay (check/cash/credit card/purchase order), and how and why they return merchandise. Maintain the list and keep it updated. Remember that 20 percent of the list changes each year. Rent the list for extra income.

Reactivate former-year buyers. It is easier and less expensive to approach a past customer than it is to obtain a new, first-time buyer. After all, once you have a relationship with your customer, why give up on it!

Circulation Planning

Circulation, a familiar word to magazine publishers, is starting to mean more to catalogers. It means: When are you mailing which catalog, and to whom? At a recent catalog conference, a forum of small catalogers identified circulation as the most important marketing skill for profitable growth.

Core Competency #5: Creative Execution

The challenge in catalog creative execution is in differentiating the catalog from its competition. There are six aspects of the creative process:

- Pagination
- Design and layout
- Color as a design element
- Typography as a design element
- Copy
- Photography or illustrative art

Pagination

Many catalog experts think pagination, or planning the overall scheme of the catalog, is the most important aspect of the creative process. Pagination determines the catalog's organization (e.g., by product category, mixing product, product function, theme, color, or price). Pagination determines exactly what product goes where in the catalog and how much space each product will be given. It is the master plan for the catalog.

The most important thing to keep in mind in pagination is knowing who the customers are and how they will use the catalog. Sound pagination puts the best-selling products in the "hot spots" of the catalog, and thereby maximizes sales. Another consideration of pagination is the niche, or positioning, of the catalog. A catalog must provide the ambience that its audience expects. Pagination ensures that there is "flow" from page to page, and from product category to product category.

Design and Layout

If pagination is the master plan, then design and layout form the blueprint that will guide the creative construction process. The catalog is design-driven. Two critical areas of design are covers and page or spread layouts.

Catalog Covers. The front and back covers have the following roles:

- Attracting customers' attention

- Telling what the catalog is selling

- Reinforcing the catalog's niche

- Getting readers inside the catalog

- Offering a benefit

- Selling products

- Getting the catalog mailed

- Offering service information such as the telephone/fax/Web site, guarantee, and credibility information

Preliminary design of a new catalog concentrates a lot of effort on getting the right "feel" on the cover. A great example would be Ross-Simons, who mailed a catalog in 2006 that featured a collection of jewelry and gifts from around the world. Its catalog covers convey a sense of the rare finds contained within.

Page or Spread Layouts. The second critical area of catalog design is page or spread layout (Most professionals advocate spreads because the eyes tend to scan two facing pages). Layout options break into five categories:

1. Grid layout

2. Free form (asymmetrical)

3. Single item per page

4. Art and copy separation

5. Product grouping

Because the layouts provide the blueprint for copy and photography, it is important that they reinforce the image of the company selling the products. Successful catalogers:

- Make the product the hero. The product is what is being sold, not the models, the props, or the backgrounds.

- Use "hot spots" (front and back covers, inside front cover, and inside back cover spreads, the center of a saddle-stitched catalog, the order form, additional spreads in the front of the catalog (e.g., pages 4–5, 6–7) effectively in promoting winning products—those with the best margins.

- Remember their customers and how they will use the catalog.

- Use a logical eye flow within a spread from the right-hand page to the left-hand page, and back again to the right-hand page.

- Use the telephone/fax number/Web site address and other information such as testimonials, technical specifications, and the like as part of the design of the catalog.

- Strive for consistency in layout from catalog to catalog so the customer will not be confused.

Color as a Design Element

People react differently to the use of color in catalogs. Red and yellow are strong colors that attract attention. Blue is seldom used with food. Research shows that people prefer the use of white, beige, or gray for backgrounds. Catalog readers like contrast between the product and the background. White space is clearly a design element. Too much of it and layouts appear to have gaping holes; too little, and readers are confused. Care in the use of color in cataloging is especially important in page backgrounds, photo backgrounds, headlines, and screens for special sections.

Typography as a Design Element

Everyone learns to read black on white, left to right, left-justified columns, top to bottom, with short column length, reasonably sized type, and a serif typeface. Varying from these patterns affects readability and customer response. Attractive type helps readability and ease of catalog use. Unattractive type can actually turn off the reader, and result in lost sales. Catalogers must remember their catalog's positioning and target audience in selecting the appropriate type. Art directors should be careful not to overuse reverse type, overprint type on a busy photo, or use all capital letters, extended line length and type, or calligraphy that is difficult to read.

Catalog Copy: Your Salesperson

Saying that a catalog tends to be layout-driven does not imply that copy is unimportant! While the layout helps to attract and direct the reader's attention, it is the copy that closes the sale. Catalog copy must perform the following functions. It must reinforce the catalog's niche or positioning, "grab" readers with headlines, inform, educate, entertain, and reassure the reader while building credibility and confidence. Of course, it must also describe the product and close the sale.

It is not unusual to have a number of writers working on catalog copy. It is therefore important for all of the writers to understand the positioning of the catalog, to know precisely who the target customer is, and to have agreed on a copy style or voice. Many catalogs have even developed style manuals to achieve consistency. There are many copy styles from which to choose. The right one is selected with the customer in mind.

Photography or Illustrative Art

Photography, a key design element, helps attract readers' attention to the product. It also shows product features and color differences. Photography or artwork builds credibility for the product and romances the product. But, most importantly, the photo or illustrative art makes the product the hero.

The photographer, art director, and photo stylist together can make products come alive with effective use of propping, accessorizing, lighting, and level of contrast. Whatever the photo style or type of camera, and whether or not models are used, photography is a vital part of the catalog creative process. Illustrative art is also used in catalogs to promote greater understanding of hard-to-shoot subjects, to be different from other catalogs, or, sometimes, to effect a cost savings.

Core Competency #6: Catalog Fulfillment

Fulfillment, an essential element of a profitable catalog, closes the loop with the customer and is a "must have" function for catalogers. Order entry by phone, mail, Internet, and fax as well as data entry and fulfillment systems; warehousing and pick, pack, and shipping; credit handling; return handling; customer communications—all have become essential to the fulfillment function. Today's customers demand quality service in every aspect of the catalog operation.

Core Competency #7: Catalog Database Strategies

The fulfillment function provides information about prospects and customers. Catalogers relish having information about their customers that will help them improve the response percentage, obtain a larger average order, and get customers to buy more frequently.

With today's improved computer hardware and software, the arduous task of maintaining critical customer purchase information and demographic data has become very manageable. There are fairly good generic Windows-based software packages available and they are affordable! At the upper end of the catalog management systems are a number of expensive systems that can handle all of a cataloger's needs, including Internet connectivity. There is no excuse for a catalog not to have a state-of-the-art fulfillment and database system to track customer activity.

Core Competency #8: Analysis— the Numbers Side of Cataloging

Closing the loop. Ensuring that every catalog is better than the last one. Making sure that catalog promotions are measurable. This is what analysis is all about. Analysis helps critique each mailing and therefore makes the next one better.

Most prosperous catalogs devote a lot of effort and staff time to the numbers side of the business. Here is a checklist of the typical analyses that catalogers perform:

1. List/source/media analysis

2. Merchandise analyses:

   - Price points analysis

   - Square-inch analysis

   - Product category analysis

   - Sales by catalog item, page, and spread

3. Inventory analyses:

   - Product returns

   - Cancellations

   - Back orders

   - Remainders/markdowns of merchandise

4. Analyses of tests such as offers, covers, seasonality, and lists

5. Mailing plan: actual results versus projection

6. Profit and loss: actual results versus plan

7. Lifetime value of customers

Cataloging and the Internet

The impact of the Internet on cataloging of every kind—business, consumer, and retail—has already been felt. Most smart direct marketers feel that the surface has barely been scratched.

The rush to the Internet is understandable, considering that statistics show that between 30–100 percent of online revenues are coming from new customers. Web sites are a boon for new and growing catalogers who place a high priority on building customer lists as well as for established catalogers seeking new business.

The huge top-level Web sites, of course, are building their brand and the accompanying share of mind, and they are investing millions of dollars in developing their sites and links to get potential customers to visit. Hardly a television commercial, radio spot, or even billboard is without a Web address today.

But the Internet levels the playing field among companies of all sizes. Smaller and new start-up companies can have a Web site by building and maintaining it themselves. They have much lower costs of sustaining a Web presence than their big-company counterparts.

Paper and digital cataloging should be pursued hand in hand. If planned correctly, catalog photography can be used online. The printed catalog can promote the E-catalog, and the E-catalog can be used for intermediate communications with customers, and so on. For business, consumer, and retail catalogs, the Internet *must* be part of the marketing mix. Business-to-business Internet selling is maturing quite nicely, but consumer and retail-oriented catalogs need to ensure that the Internet is not delayed or forgotten.

The growth of Internet sales will come at the expense of traditional (offline) marketing. Companies that espouse the Internet as a complementary selling tool for the printed word are going to steal market share from those who remain traditional catalog (printed word) purists.

Being Passive Aggressive

To establish an online offering, catalogers must overcome the passive nature of the Internet as a communication medium. Where traditional catalogers are accustomed to mailing to prospects and customers based on targeted selections, E-catalogers are generally at the mercy of the surfer. In other words, your customers, or prospective customers, have to find you. Web sites have been likened to retail stores. Unless you are in a high-traffic mall or advertise your store, there is little chance that prospective customers will ever find you.

Herein lies the primary difference between paper catalogs and online catalogs: paper catalogs are intrusive by nature, online catalogs are passive by nature. Once businesses understand this fundamental limitation of E-cataloging, they can become creative in the ways that generate more traffic and, most importantly, more sales through the Web.

Three Factors of Online Success

Success in online cataloging is a result of the marriage of technical elements (programming), graphics (creative), and marketing (direct marketing principles).

Each one plays a role in the success or failure of an online venture. For instance, a site that is too graphically intense may load slowly and discourage participation. Likewise, a site with too few graphics may be unappealing to visitors or fail to show products in a positive light. Finally, a beautifully crafted, highly engaging site is wasted if the ordering process is cumbersome and confusing.

Technical Skills

From a technical standpoint, companies must consider the target market's "lowest common denominator" with regard to browser version, monitor settings, plug-ins, and connection speeds. Using the newest available technologies makes for very exciting Web pages. However, you may alienate more people than you impress if your fancy technology exceeds the capabilities of your audience. While modems are getting faster, more than half of all users connect at 56 kbs—too slow for many of the new bells and whistles.

On the server side, two technical issues must be considered:

1. Are the customer and product databases updated in real time or must orders be batch processed?

2. Are customers given the ability to track orders throughout the order and shipping process?

Questions like these help determine whether or not your E-catalog is making online ordering easier and more beneficial for your customers. Much-heralded Dell Computers (www.dell.com) lets customers track orders from the time the order is placed to the time it ships, and follows up each shipment with a confirmation e-mail that tells the customer his or her computer has left the building (See Exhibit 19–7).

Graphics Skills

Graphically, E-catalogers must again consider the technical capabilities of the customer's computer. Making sure that GIF images are optimized and reduced to a limited color palette vastly improves download times by making image files smaller. Large images can be saved in segments to improve download times, and no image needs to be displayed at a higher resolution than 72 pixels per inch, unless you intend for it to be printed from the Internet for reuse.

With advances in monitors and scanners, image presentation is better than ever. However, presenting too many images or images that are very large in size makes downloading almost unbearably slow. Sluggish downloads increase the likelihood that no one will stay at your site long enough to make a purchase. J.Crew.com is a good example of a site that is quite good from a graphic standpoint. J. Crew picks up photography from the printed catalog, but also keeps images manageable in size.

Marketing Skills

Marketing the online catalog may be the most difficult task of all. The million-dollar question always seems to be: How do we get more traffic to our site?

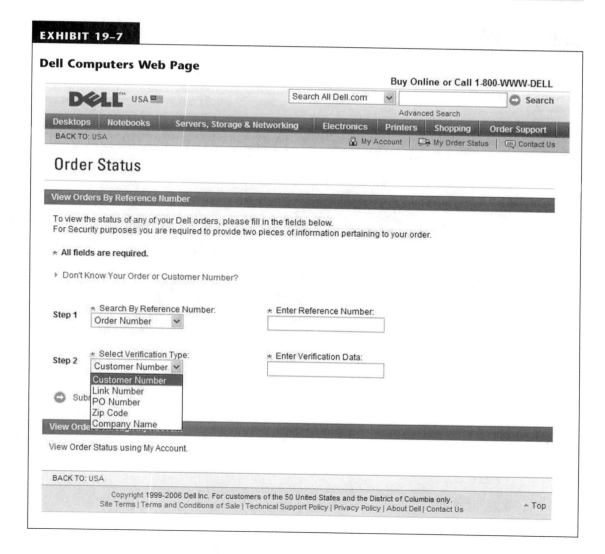

EXHIBIT 19-7

Dell Computers Web Page

The half-million-dollar question is: How do we get traffic to come back? A number of strategies exist to answer both questions.

Generating first-time traffic to a site is crucial and not always easy. One way is to participate in online catalog portals such as Shop.com, Catalogs.Google.com, Catalogs.com, or CatalogLink.com. These portals offer links to the E-catalog's site and, in some cases, product sales (See Exhibit 19–8). It is also a good idea to develop online alliances with vendors and clients where you reciprocate placement of links on each other's site. You should also register your site with the most applicable search engines and directories (there are literally hundreds to choose from).

Send targeted e-mail to available online mailing lists—making sure, of course, that the recipients on the list have opted in to the list; opt-out e-mail is not a part of the DMA's Privacy Promise guidelines.

EXHIBIT 19–8

Shop.com

Include your Web site on every piece of marketing material that goes out the door—particularly to prospects. Paper catalogs should show the Web site address and toll-free telephone number on every page if they expect people to use it for ordering directly.

The ease with which shoppers can leave your site to go to another one makes customer retention an integral part of building an online revenue stream. There are several key elements to keeping customers coming back, many of them common to traditional cataloging.

Get permission to communicate. Getting customers to opt in to an e-mail marketing program makes follow-up communication much easier. J. Crew, Victoria's Secret, and Cabella's do an excellent job of keeping the lines of communication open with customers through all seasons. Omaha Steaks (omahasteaks.com) even puts out an electronic version of the Omaha Steaks catalog via e-mail, shown in Exhibit 19–9. The message itself is a self-sufficient online ordering device.

Drive repeat purchases with special e-mailed offers or offers made in the paper catalog to encourage online sales. IWA (International Wine Accessories), used a special cover to drive customers to their Web site www.iwawine.com stating 100 new products (See Exhibit 19–10). When customers request a catalog from the Internet and opt in, promptly send out the paper catalog and follow it up with a welcoming e-mail. In other words, reach these customers in the same manner they reached you.

Provide helpful customer service. Without a customer service representative to walk customers through the ordering process, your site needs to provide everything needed to order with comfort and ease. Remember the crucial element—a shopper/prospect should never be more than one click away from ordering.

Make purchasing easy by designing an order form that captures the necessary information succinctly. Don't forget to capture a source code if you're driving sales to the Web from the paper catalog.

Keep the site fresh. Some E-catalogs update their sites daily with online specials. Just as with paper catalogs, existing customers want to see what's new. Use icons and special bursts to point out those items. If you lack the staff for more frequent updates, be sure to refresh your content at least once a quarter.

The beauty of the Internet is that an organization can secure multiple addresses and operate transparently as two distinct organizations, not unlike catalogers that publish multiple titles. This chameleon quality means that catalogers can use the Web, among other things, as an avenue to liquidate inventory. A good example of this type of operation would be the company Overstock (www.overstock.com), an online outlet that sells a variety of name-brand overproduced and discontinued items (See Exhibit 19–11).

The Future of Cataloging

Today, the most successful online catalogers are taking advantage of the economies that come from integrating the traditional catalog with the E-catalog. Whether sharing photography and copy elements or using one medium to generate sales and traffic for the other, it is undeniable that the two formats go hand in hand. Exhibit 19–12 shows Bloomingdale's online catalog, which uses two different formats, broadband (using some type of Flash player functionality) and HTML (which uses JPEG images), with an immediate pop-up window for both styles giving a lot more detailed

EXHIBIT 19-9

Omaha Steaks Online Catalog

OMAHA STEAKS
PREMIUM HEARTLAND QUALITY · SINCE 1917

1.800.960.8400
100% SATISFACTION GUARANTEED

HOME | MEMBER BENEFITS | GIFT CENTER | CUSTOMER SERVICE | ORDER FROM MAILING | FIND A STORE | FOODSERVICE | BUSINESS INCENTIVES | COMPANY INFO | JOBS

Best Sellers · Overstocks · Recipes · Shipping · Win Free Steaks · Order Status · Contact Us · Login

SEARCH

[ ] [GO]

SHOPPING CATEGORIES
▶ Premium Beef
  Filet Mignons
  Boneless Strip Steaks
  Filet of Prime Rib
  Top Sirloin Steaks
  T-Bone & Porterhouse
  Private Reserve®
  Specialty Steaks
  Traditional Beef Entrees
  Steak Combos
  Burgers
  Beef Roasts
▶ Seafood Selections
▶ Veal, Pork & Lamb
▶ Poultry Selections
▶ Classic Pastas
▶ Delectable Desserts
▶ Appetizers
▶ Side Dishes
▶ Specialty Selections
▶ Sauces & Seasonings
▶ Gift Plans & Ideas
▶ Cookbooks
▶ Pet Treats

Give the gift of
Omaha Steaks! Order a
Gift Certificate

Personalize Your Gift
with a **Greeting Card**.

Site Problems?
Request A Catalog
Buy The Right Steak
Good Life Cookbook
Become An Affiliate
Safe Shopping Guarantee

NEW...
Regional Favorites
from Omaha Steaks!

Savor the favorite
tastes enjoyed in
different parts of the
United States.
Start Shopping

When Only the Best Will Do...Omaha Steaks!

Pages: 1 | 2

Bringing families together since 1917, Omaha Steaks offers a wide selection of legendary steaks and gourmet selections that our guaranteed to make your next family gathering one to remember. You'll find exclusive savings on every page.

Filet Mignons

4 (6 oz.) Filet Mignons
Regular $71.99, Save $22.00 Your Special Price $49.99
8 (5 oz.) Filet Mignons
Regular $100.00, Save $30.01 Your Special Price $69.99

Bacon-Wrapped Specialties

A Tantalizing Taste Combination!

6 (5 oz.) Bacon-Wrapped Filets
Regular $76.00, Save $21.01
Your Special Price $54.99

6 (6 oz.) Bacon-Wrapped Filet of Top Sirloin
Regular $58.00, Save $18.01
Your Special Price $39.99

Save on Top Sirloins!

Lean, Firm and Full of Flavor!

6 (8 oz.) Top Sirloins
Regular $83.00, Save $33.01
Your Special Price $49.99

6 (6 oz.) Top Sirloins
Regular $65.00, Save $25.01
Your Special Price $39.99

Save up to 62%...Complete Dinner Value Packs

Dinners should always be this easy and delicious! From a truly unforgettable main course, to a delicious selection of sides to the perfect sweet ending, your family and friends will be asking for seconds (and maybe thirds!) with Omaha Steaks Complete Dinner Menus!

The Casual Affair
4 (7 oz.) Flat Iron Steaks
8 (3 oz.) Pepper Jack Risotto Cakes
2 (6.5 oz.) Green Beans With Red Peppers
1 (6 in.) Chocolate Lover's Cake
Regular $116.00, Save $66.01
Your Special Price $49.99

The Patio Party Pack
8 (5 oz.) Gourmet Burgers
8 (2 oz.) Onion Poppyseed Buns
1 (20 oz.) Tray BBQ Baked Beans w/ Beef Brisket
18 (1 oz.) Cream Puffs
Regular $80.00, Save $46.00
Your Special Price $34.00

The Sensational Seafood Supper
4 (6 oz.) Lemon Peppered Tilapia Fillets
2 (5 oz.) Trays Broccoli & Cauliflower
1 (6 in.) New York Cheesecake
Regular $68.00, Save $38.01
Your Special Price $29.99

Just Like Home
1 (2 lb.) Fully Cooked Pot Roast
2 (12 oz.) Roasted Garlic Mashed Potatoes
2 (8 oz.) Sweet Corn Medley
6 (3.8 oz.) Chocolate Molten Lava Cakes
Regular $96.00, Save $60.00
Your Special Price $36.00

Pages: 1 | 2

Home | Member Benefits | Gift Center | Customer Service | Company Info | Privacy Policy | Our Guarantee | Business Partners

Prefer to order by phone? CALL OMAHASTEAKS.COM 1.800.960.8400
Fax your order for FREE to 1.877.329.6328 (click here for details)

Powered by
e-ONECOMMERCE

Sizzling
4th of July SALE
going on now!
Click Here

New to Omaha Steaks?
Click Here to learn about our company and our products.

Today's Special
Fourth of July
Hot Deal
The Weekender Combo
8 (4 oz.) Top Sirloins
8 (4 oz.) Gourmet Burgers
8 (3 oz.) Gourmet Franks
Now Only $39.99!

Overstocks
6 (6 oz.) Filet Mignons
Now Only $69.99!
see more Overstocks

Best Sellers
The Best Seller
2 (6 oz.) Filet Mignons
2 (11 oz.) Boneless Strips
2 (8 oz.) Top Sirloins
2 (8 oz.) Rib Eyes
Now Only $79.99!
see more Best Sellers

Quick & Easy
4 (8 oz.) Prime Rib Slices
Now Only $39.99!
see more Quick & Easy Items

What's New?
Jumbo Cooked Shrimp & Sweet & Tangy Cocktail Sauce
1 (1.5 lb.) Bag Jumbo Cooked Shrimp
1 (7 oz.) Sweet & Tangy Cocktail Sauce
Now Only $34.99!
see more New Items

FREE STEAKS

WIN $1,000
Worth Of **FREE STEAKS!**
Click Here

NEWSLetter
Subscribe to our newsletter and receive exclusive offers specially selected for you!

What's For Dinner?

à la ZING

A La Zing offers gourmet meals, ready in minutes!

EXHIBIT 19-10

IWA Inc.

IWA's cover burst helps direct customers from a paper catalog to its online version.

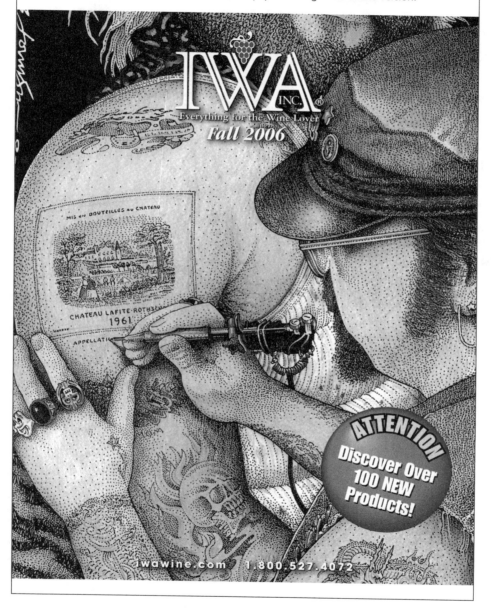

EXHIBIT 19–11

Overstock.com's Web site

information about each item when browsing and rolling the mouse over them. In Exhibit 19–12, you can see the functionalities of the broadband: from going to the 1 main page; 2 selecting which catalog to look for; 3 choosing from the menu options of the catalog itself, which go from: 4 Normal View; 5 Thumbnail View; 6 Zoom View; and 7 Magnifier, which all makes the experience of being in touch with the products more convenient for the customer (wherever he or she is viewing them online).

Other retailers, such as Hallmark (see Exhibit 19–13), have kept it more simple. Hallmark.com uses HTML with JPEG images embedded in it and a PDF document that can be downloaded, is readable and is printed through the Adobe

EXHIBIT 19–12

Bloomingdale's Online Catalog

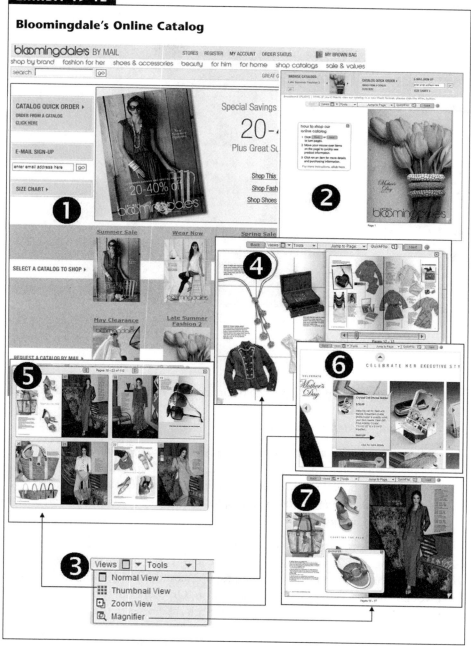

EXHIBIT 19-13

Hallmark's PDF Catalog

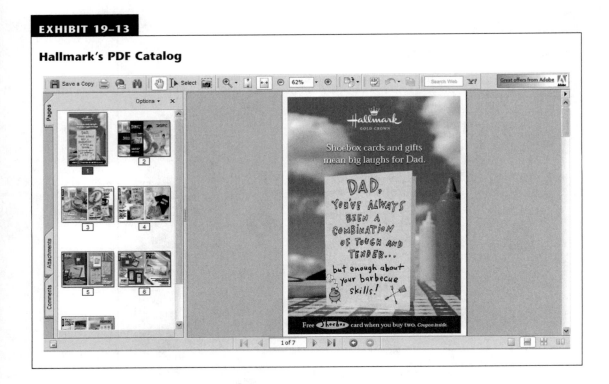

Reader software that is usually provided for free at Web sites such as Adobe.com, CNet.com, etc.

According to *Multichannel Merchant*,

> *More than 96% of catalogers sell products in both print and online and selling through other channels such as retail, direct sales and outbound telemarketing is commonplace. Direct-to-consumer marketing and product fulfillment extends the reach of retailers, wholesalers and manufacturers to better serve their customers.*

Even search engines such as Google have entered the online catalog industry. Google Catalogs allows consumers to browse and search merchant-provided catalogs right on their computer. The online catalogs are designed so that the user can flip through any catalog just like a paper version. Or, users can type in a product or category and search within the catalog or through categories in the Google Catalog library (See Exhibits 19–14A, 19–14B, and 19–14C).

The catalog process presented in this chapter will continue to be important. To survive and prosper, catalogs cannot do some of the tasks mentioned in the catalog process and leave others to chance. Winning catalogs—paper or electronic—must be able to perform every task well. That is the challenge and the opportunity.

EXHIBIT 19–14A

Google Catalog Beta Web Search Engine

Catalogs ^{BETA}

Search Catalogs	Advanced Catalog Search
	Google Catalogs Help

Discover and browse catalogs online.

Browse catalogs by category:

Apparel & Accessories	Computers	Home & Garden
Arts & Crafts	Consumer Electronics	Lifestyle & Gift
Arts & Entertainment	Education	Sports & Outdoors
Automotive	Food & Gourmet	Toys & Hobbies
Books, Music & Film	Health & Personal Care	
Business To Business	Home	

EXHIBIT 19–14B

Sample of Online Catalogs Found Under Google's "Food & Gourmet" Category

EXHIBIT 19–14C

Online Catalog for Fairytale Brownies Found in Food & Gourmet Category on Google Catalogs

CASE STUDY: J. Jill: Insights into a Multichannel Retailer

Written by J. Steven Kelly, Francey Smith, and Regine Vanheems for the Chicago Association of Direct Marketing Education Foundation Case Writers' Workshop.

BACKGROUND

J. Jill promotes high-quality apparel fit for the woman whose lifestyle requires versatility in her wardrobe. J. Jill had developed from an operation that was catalog-only to a multichannel retailer involving the Internet (www.jjill.com), J. Jill catalog, and J. Jill retail stores. The retailer's marketing programs targeted affluent women aged 35–55 years old, who wear what J. Jill describes as "sophisticated casual lifestyle clothing with a unique, artistic expression."

Originally a direct marketer via catalogs, J. Jill had been mailing 26 different catalog editions per year since 1996. A recent total of annual mailings numbered over 77 million sent to customers in domestic markets. J. Jill opened its first store in the fall of 1999 and currently has over 85 stores in over 30 states. With its stores, Internet presence, catalogs, and phone center, J. Jill had opened all possible touch points to their customers and was truly a multichannel operator.

Recognizing the value of retail stores in its revenue generation, J. Jill had taken on a dramatic policy of growing stores at the rate of about 35 per year. It was expected that the major growth would come from stores and there became a clear need for an evolution in merchandising and in the way J. Jill sources and flows products. This would require shifts in merchandising and execution from new core competencies and expertise.

CHALLENGES

J. Jill's goals to transform the customer experience and build business as a multichannel retailer would be severely tested by a number of significant challenges.

A primary challenge was the highly competitive marketplace. Other women's apparel retailers had already made significant inroads toward securing the target of affluent women. J. Jill would have to compete with Chico, Coldwater Creek, and Christopher & Banks for this prized market share.

Another challenge existed in the implementation of the multichannel process. J. Jill needed to determine whether the direct (online and catalog) and store operations should be merged or run separately. Moreover, delivering consistency to customers across channels while shopping would not be easy. This would require resources and investment in appropriate technology. The end goal was a "hassle-free multichannel retailing" experience for the customer. This would include participating in the same loyalty program across channels, ordering online for payment and store pick-up, and returning online purchases to physical stores. However, implementation would require organizational learning and time.

Removing the Wall to CRM

A fundamental question became how to remove the "wall" that existed between J. Jill marketing and operating divisions so that it could enhance long-term customer loyalty. There was also concern regarding the cost involved in bringing channels together compared to the payoff in revenue from the enhanced customer satisfaction the experience would deliver.

Finally, there were unresolved questions about whether retail stores would steal or "cannibalize" sales from the catalog channel, and whether cross-channel promotions would be possible without a combined system.

SOLUTION

For J. Jill, synchronizing the diverse channels could be a competitive edge and a tangible way to improve the management of relationships with current customers.

CASE STUDY: J. Jill: Insights into a Multichannel Retailer *(Continued)*

Creating a link between the touch points (store, Web, catalog, and phone center) could allow the firm to understand its customers better, which would translate into products and services that meet customer needs more accurately. This multichannel approach would also be an opportunity to interact more often with customers and would allow for a higher contact quality.

Linking channels could also potentially help the firm increase the share of wallet of its present customers. Developing strong relationships with the customers and enhancing their trust in the company through multiple touch points could certainly be an efficient means to develop cross-selling and up-selling opportunities. Consequently, this would be one of the most important components of an innovative new approach of doing business.

Furthermore the merge of the touch points could be an efficient strategy for retaining customers who value the resulting purchasing convenience. Creating some added value or new services outputs could give them fewer reasons or opportunities to switch to competitors and be more loyal.

Multichannel integration could also provide opportunities to personalize the offer and to customize the services. This could lead to a "one-to-one" approach, and provide the foundation for competitive differentiation. This integration could create "lock-in effects" as well, helping to maintain and manage customers over their lifecycle.

A Single View for Clear Vision

Management envisioned that J. Jill needed to develop a customer-centric organization that would create a single view of the J. Jill customer.

For J. Jill, this meant better data capture. Presently, the retail customer information was not available to the catalog side and vice versa. Customers could be regular catalog buyers and also shop in the stores, but retail would not be aware of this tendency. Conversely, retail customers could receive catalogs, but the frequency of their receipt (periodically or monthly or more) was not related to their *total* J. Jill experience. Clearly, synchronicity in customer data was essential in order to achieve the single view of the current customer experience and preferences and leverage it to establish stronger CRM practices.

Another interesting aspect about developing the single view is that this approach would allow the analysis of customers to move between channels in a dynamic way. If J. Jill decided to keep customers free of choosing whatever channel or combination of channels they preferred, the retailer would be able to follow those customers' moves and evaluate their impact on share of wallet.

Toward this end, building a common database offered the possibility to measure the profitability of customer flow across channels. The purpose is to foster the most profitable flows and to implement an efficient customer flow strategy.

In the end, a single view of J. Jill customers would allow a number of important advantages. Once J. Jill established a single view of their customers across all channels they would be able to apply the data for catalog circulation, prospect for both retail and catalog customers, and apply customers' ZIP codes for retail site selection.

Like most modern catalog marketers, J. Jill has become a multichannel marketer, with catalogs, retail stores, and a Web site. How can this marketer integrate these different channels, and make them work together? Develop a multichannel promotional brief for J. Jill and describe:

A.   Will the effort be focused on prospects, customers, or both?

B.   When it will be launched?

C.   What mix of channels will you use (e-mail, catalog, etc.)?

D.   Will this effort have as its objective a drive to Web or retail traffic building?

Explain why you chose this goal.

Key Points

▶ Paper and digital catalogs should be pursued hand in hand. The printed catalog can promote the E-catalog, and the E-catalog can be used for intermediate communications with customers.

▶ Develop a distinct niche and a brand for the catalog—a place in the market where there is a void not met by the competition. Set your catalog apart from its competition by merchandise, creative style or format, offers, and customer service. Understanding your competition, its niches, and its strengths and weaknesses will also facilitate positioning.

▶ Front-end marketing seeks to acquire new first-time customers, leads, and inquiries that can be converted into first-time buyers, and the most names at the least cost. Back-end marketing seeks to convert first-time buyers into second-time buyers, to maximize the number of profitable mailings to the list each year, and to determine where the best long-term customers come from so that the catalog can change or modify its front-end media. Front-end marketing costs money; back-end marketing yields profits—but both are essential functions.

▶ Maximize the value of your customer list by maintaining it and mailing it frequently. Don't under-utilize or under-mail! Track, measure, and segment the customer list to prioritize the buyer file. Test to find out how frequently you can mail.

▶ Sound pagination puts the best-selling products in the "hot spots" of the catalog and thereby maximizes sales. Pagination ensures that there is "flow" from page to page and from product category to product category.

▶ Reinforce the catalog's positioning and target market through design, use of color and photography, type, and copy. Catalog copy should "grab" readers with headlines, inform, educate, entertain, and reassure the reader while building credibility and confidence—plus describe the product and close the sale.

▶ The effective use of a database can provide customer information that helps catalogers improve the response percentage, obtain a larger average order, and get customers to buy more frequently.

▶ Analyses of list, source, media, merchandise, tests and offers, mailing plans, response, and profit help critique each mailing and therefore improve each subsequent issue.

▶ When developing an online catalog, consider the target market's "lowest common denominator" with regard to things like browser version, monitor settings, plug-ins, and connection speeds. Avoid large images that download slowly.

▶ Generate first-time traffic to a site by participating in online catalog portals that offer links to the E-catalog's site and product sales. Place links on the sites of vendors and clients. Register the site with the most applicable search engines and directories. Send targeted e-mail to available "opt in" online mailing lists, and include your Web site on every piece of marketing material.

▶ Retain customers by enrolling them in an e-mail marketing program that sends follow-up communications. Drive repeat purchases with special e-mailed offers or offers made in the paper catalog to encourage online sales.

CREATING PRINT ADVERTISING

Knowing the "mechanics" of print advertising is essential to success, but no more so than knowing how to create winning ads. You may be running the "right" size ads at the "right" time in the "right" publication but still have advertising that is *least noted*. If that is the case, it is likely that the trouble lies in creative.

The competition your ad faces is every other ad in a given issue of a publication. It is not unusual to be one of 100 or more advertisers in a given magazine or newspaper. So you are competing for reading time with every reader of the magazine, not counting concurrent competition from TV, radio, E-commerce, and now podcasts. The job of the ad writer, put simply, is to stop the reader and engage his or her attention and interest.

Visualizing the Prospect

Every good magazine ad should attract the most attention from the likeliest prospects. Capable creators of direct response advertising visualize their prospects with varying degrees of precision when they sit down at the computer or drawing board.

Good direct response advertising makes its strongest appeal to its best prospects and then gathers in as many additional prospects as possible. And who are the prospects? They are the ones with the strongest desire for what you are selling. You must look for the common denominators. For instance, let us say you are selling a book on the American Revolution. Here are some of the relevant common denominators that would be shared by many people in your total audience:

1. An interest in the American Revolution in particular

2. An interest in American history in general

3. A patriotic interest in America

4. An interest in history

5. An interest in big, beautiful coffee-table books

6. An interest in impressing friends with historical lore

7. A love of bargains

8. An interest in seeing children in the family become adults with high achievement

Now, out of a total audience of 1,000, some readers would possess all eight denominators, some would possess some combination of six, some a different combination of six, some just one of the eight, and so on.

If you could know the secret hearts of all 1,000 individuals and rank them by their desire to buy, you would place at the very top of the list those who possessed all eight denominators, followed by those who possessed just seven, and so on down to the bottom of the scale, where you would place those who possessed none.

Obviously, you should make as many sales as possible among your hottest prospects first, for that is where your sales will be easiest. Then you want to reach down the scale to sell as many of the others as you can. By the time you get down to the people possessing only one of the denominators, you will probably find interest so faint that it would be almost impossible to make your sales effort pay unless it were fantastically appealing.

Obvious? Yes, to mail-order professionals who learned the hard way. But to the novice it is not so obvious. In an eagerness to sell to everybody, he or she might muff the easiest sales by using a curiosity-only appeal that conceals what is really being offered.

On the other hand, the veteran but uninspired pro might gather up all the easy sales lying on the surface but, through lack of creative imagination, fail to reach deeper into the market. For instance, let us say that of 1,000 readers, 50 possess all eight denominators. A crude omnibus appeal that could scoop up many of them would be something like: "At last! For every liberty-loving American family, especially those with children whose friends are amazed by their understanding of American history, here is a big, beautiful book about the American Revolution that you will display with pride. Yours for only one-fifth of what you'd expect to pay!" A terrible headline, but at least one that those possessing the denominators of interest would stop to look at and consider. You might get only 5 percent readership, but it will be the right 5 percent.

On the other hand, suppose you want to do something terribly creative to reach a wider market. So, you do a beautiful advertising message headed: "The Impossible Dream," in which you somehow work your way from that starting point to what it is you are selling. Again, you might get only 5 percent readership, but these readers will be scattered along the entire length of your scale of interest. Of the 50 people who stopped to read your message, only two or three will be prime prospects possessing all eight denominators. Many people really interested in books on the American Revolution, in inspiring their children with patriotic sentiments, and in acquiring big impressive books at big savings will have hurried past, unaware.

The point: don't let prime prospects get away. In mail order you can't afford to. Some people out there don't have to be sold; they already want what you have, and if you tell them that you have it, they will buy it. Alone they will not constitute enough of a market to make your selling effort pay, but without them you haven't got a chance. So, through your clarity and directness, you gather in these prime prospects; then through your creative imagination, you reach beyond them to awaken and excite mild prospects as well.

The half-page print ad for Liberty Medical (Exhibit 20–1) is an example of a direct marketing print ad created with an appeal to specific prospects in mind — seniors that suffer from the illness diabetes. Note how the headline, copy, large response coupon area, photograph and choice of a spokesperson are all target audience specific.

EXHIBIT 20–1

Liberty Medical Print Ad

Writing the Headline

Once the prospect is clearly visualized, a good headline almost writes itself. For example, here is an effective and successful headline from an ad by Quadrangle/New York Times Book Company. It defines the prospect so simply and accurately that the interested reader feels an instant tug:

> *"For people who are almost (but not quite) satisfied with their house plants . . . and can't figure out what they're doing wrong . . ."*

A very successful ad for the Washington School of Art, offering a correspondence course, resulted from bringing the psychographic profile of the prime prospect into sharp focus. The prospect was someone who had been drawing pictures better than the rest of us since the first grade. Such people are filled with a rare combination of pride in their talent and shame at their lack of perfection. And their goal is not necessarily fame or fortune, but simply to become a "real artist," a phrase that has different meanings for different people. The winning headline simply reached out to the right people and offered them the right benefit:

> *"If you can draw fairly well (but still not good enough), we'll turn you into a real artist."*

Of course, a good headline does not necessarily present an explicit definition of the prospect, but it is always implied. Here are some classic headlines and the prospects the writer undoubtedly visualized.

> *"Can a man or woman my age become a hotel executive?"*

The prospect is, probably, a middle-aged man or woman who needs, for whatever reason, an interesting, pleasant, not too technically demanding occupational skill such as hotel management and is eager for reassurance that you can teach an old dog new tricks. Note, however, how wide the net is cast. No one is excluded. Even people who worry they are too young to be a hotel executive can theoretically read themselves into this headline.

> *"Don't envy the plumber—be one"*

The prospect is a poorly paid worker, probably blue-collar, who is looking for a way to improve his lot, and who has looked with both indignation and envy at the plumber, who appears not much more skilled but earns several times as much per hour.

> *"How to stumble upon a fortune in gems"*

The prospect is everybody, all of us, who all our lives have daydreamed of gaining sudden wealth without extreme sacrifice.

> *"Is your home picture-poor?"*

The prospect is someone, probably a woman, with a home who has a number of bare or inadequately decorated walls, and who feels not only a personal lack but also, perhaps more importantly, a vague underlying sense of social shame at this conspicuous cultural "poverty." Whether she appreciates it or not, she recognizes that art, books, and music are regarded as part of the "good life" and are supposed to add a certain richness to life.

"Become a 'non-degree' engineer"

This is really a modern version of "Don't envy the plumber." The prospect is an unskilled or semi-skilled factory worker who looks with a mixture of resentment and grudging envy on the aristocracy in his midst, the college grads who earn much more, dress better, and enjoy special privileges because they are credentialed engineers. The prospect would like to enjoy at least some of their job status but is unwilling or unable to go to college and get an engineering degree.

"Are you tired of cooking with odds and ends?"

The prospect is that Everywoman or Everyman who has accumulated over the years an enameled pan here, an aluminum pot there, an iron skillet elsewhere, and to whom a matched set of anything represents neatness, order, and elegance.

"Can you call someone a failure at 30?"

The prospect is a young, white-collar worker, 25–32 years old, who is deeply concerned that life isn't turning out the way he or she dreamed and that he or she is on the verge of failing to "make it"—permanently.

The small-space (2 × 2¼ inches), catalog request ad in Exhibit 20–2 for Hitchcock Shoes is typical of "hand-raiser" ads, which are used to get prospects to self-select and qualify for interest in a product or service. The headline is designed to quickly get the attention of people in the market for extra-wide shoes.

EXHIBIT 20–2

Hitchcock Shoe Company Catalog Ad

Selecting Advantages and Benefits

Advantages belong to the product. Benefits belong to the consumer. If the product or service is unique or unfamiliar to the prospect, stressing benefits is important. But if it is simply a new, improved model in a highly competitive field where there already exists an established demand, the product advantage or advantages become important.

When laptop computers were first introduced, such benefits as weight and screen size and resolution were important attributes. But, as the market became flooded with competing types and brands and professionals began to use laptops instead of—rather than in addition to—a desktop computer, product advantages such as power and memory became more important.

There are two kinds of benefits: the immediate or obvious benefit and the not-so-obvious ultimate benefit—the real potential meaning for the customer's life, or the product or service being sold. The ultimate benefit often proves to have a greater effect, for it reaches deeper into the prospect's feelings.

The Rosetta Stone Language Learning print ad (see Exhibit 20–3) uses a non-traditional layout, without a headline. The copy describes the not-so-obvious benefits of learning a foreign language. The ad offers a choice of response methods, directing readers to a Web site or phone number for more information.

EXHIBIT 20-3

Rosetta Stone Print Ad

Victor Schwab, one of the great mail-order pioneers, was fond of quoting Dr. Samuel Johnson's approach to auctioning off the contents of a brewery: "We are not here to sell boilers and vats, but the potentiality of growing rich beyond the dreams of avarice."

It pays to ask yourself over and over again: "What am I selling? Yes, I know it's a book or a steak knife, or a home-study course in upholstering—but what am I really selling? What human values are at stake?"

For example, suppose you have the job of selling a correspondence course in advertising. Here is a list of ultimate benefits and the way they can be expressed in headlines for the course. Some of the headlines are patently absurd, but they illustrate the mind-stretching process involved in looking for the ultimate benefit in your product or service:

- *Health:* Successful ad people are healthier and happier than you think—and now you can be one of them.

- *Money:* What's your best chance of earning $150,000 a year by the time you are 30?

- *Security:* You are always in demand when you can write advertising that sells.

- *Pride:* Imagine your pride when you can coin a slogan repeated by 50 million people.

- *Approval:* Did you write that ad? Why, I've seen it everywhere.

- *Enjoyment:* Get more fun out of your daily job. Become a successful ad writer!

- *Excitement:* Imagine working until 4:00 A.M.—and loving every minute of it!

- *Power:* The heads of giant corporations will listen to your advice when you've mastered the secrets of advertising that works (Just a wee bit of exaggeration there, perhaps).

- *Fulfillment:* Are you wasting a natural talent for advertising?

- *Freedom:* People who can get million-dollar advertising ideas don't have to worry about punching a time clock.

- *Identity:* Join the top advertising professionals who keep the wheels of our economy turning.

- *Relaxation:* How some people succeed in advertising without getting ulcers.

- *Escape:* Hate going to work in the morning? Get a job you'll love—in advertising!

- *Curiosity:* Now go behind the scenes of America's top advertising agencies and find out how multimillion-dollar campaigns are born!

- *Possessions:* I took your course five years ago—today I own two homes, two cars, and a Chris-Craft.

- *Hunger:* A really good ad person always knows where his or her next meal is coming from.

Classic Copy Structure

In a classic mail-order copy argument, a good lead should be visualized as the first step in a straight path of feeling and logic from the headline or display theme to the concluding call for action. In that all-important first step, the readers should be able to see clearly where the path is taking them. Otherwise they might not want to go. (This is the huge error of ads that seek to pique your curiosity with something irrelevant and then make a tie-in to the real point. Who's got time for satisfying that much curiosity these days?)

The sections of a classic copy argument can be labeled *problem, promise of solution, explanation of promise, proof,* and *call to action.* However, if you are going to start with the problem, it seems like a good idea at least to hint right away at the forthcoming solution. Then the readers won't mind if you don't get to the point right away, as long as they know where you are going. A generation ago, when the pace of life was slower, a brilliant copywriter could get away with spending the first third of his copy leisurely outlining the problem before finally getting around to the solution. But in these hectic times, it's riskier.

Here is an ad seeking Duraclean dealers in which the problem lead contains the promise of solution:

- I found the easy way to escape from being a "wage slave."

- I kept my job while my customer list grew . . . then found myself in a high-profit business. Five years ago, I wouldn't have believed that I could be where I am today.

- I was deeply in debt. My self-confidence had been shaken by a disastrous business setback. Having nobody behind me, I had floundered and failed for lack of experience, help, and guidance.

The copy could have started out simply, "Five years ago, I was deeply in debt," and so on. But the promise of happier days to come provides a carrot on a stick, drawing us down the garden path. You could argue that the headline had already announced the promise. But in most cases, good copy should be able to stand alone and make a complete argument even if all the display type were removed.

Here, from an ad for isometric exercises, is an example of the flashback technique.

[*Starts with the promise*]

- Imagine a 6-second exercise that helps you keep fit better than 24 push-ups.

- Or another that's capable of doubling muscular strength in 3 weeks!

Both of these "quickie" exercises are part of a fantastically simple body-building method developed by Donald J. Salls, Alabama Doctor of Education, fitness expert, and coach. His own trim physique, his family's vigorous health, and the nail-hard brawn of his teams are dramatic proof of the results he gets—not to mention the steady stream of reports from housewives, athletes, even schoolchildren, who have discovered Dr. Salls' remarkable exercises.

[*Flashback to problem*]

Most Americans find exercise a tedious chore. Yet, we all recognize the urgent personal and social needs for keeping our bodies strong, shapely, and healthy. What man wouldn't take secret pride in displaying a more muscular figure?

What woman doesn't long for a slimmer, more attractive figure? The endless time and trouble required to get such results has been a major, if not impossible, hurdle for so many of us. But now [*return to the promise*] doctors, trainers, and physical educators are beginning to recommend the easy, new approach to body fitness and contour control that Dr. Salls has distilled down to his wonderfully simple set of 10 exercises.

Of course, a really strong, exciting promise doesn't necessarily need a statement of the problem at all. If you're selling a "New Tree That Grows a Foot a Month," it could be argued that you don't actually have to spell out how frustrating it is to spend years waiting for ordinary trees to grow; this is well known and implied.

Other Ways to Structure Copy

There are as many different ways to structure a piece of advertising copy as there are to build a house. But response advertising, whether in magazines or newspapers, has special requirements. The general advertiser is satisfied with making an impression, but the response advertiser must stimulate immediate action. Your copy must pile in your readers' minds argument after argument, sales point after sales point, until their resistance collapses under the sheer weight of your persuasiveness, and they do what you ask.

One of the greatest faults in the copy of writers who are not wise in the ways of response is failure to apply this steadily increasing pressure. This may sound like old-fashioned "hard sell," but, ideally, the impression your copy makes should be just the opposite. The best copy, like the best salesperson, does not appear to be selling at all, but simply to be sharing information or proposals of mutual benefit to the buyer and seller.

The full-page Oreck XL Ultra print ad (Exhibit 20–4) uses a traditional direct response ad layout. The headline promises a benefit to respondents, although the benefit is tied into the offer. The long-copy approach highlights many sales points. It repeats the guarantee and offer more than once, helping to convince the reader to respond.

Of course, in selling certain kinds of staple merchandise, copy structuring is not important. There, the advertising can be compared to a painting in that the aim is to convey as much as possible at first glance and then convey more and more with each repeated look. You wouldn't sell a 35-piece electric drill set with a 1,000-word essay, but rather you would sell it by spreading out the set in glowing full-color illustrations richly studded with feature "call-outs." But where you are engaged in selling intangibles, an idea or ideas instead of familiar merchandise, the way you structure your copy can be vitally important.

In addition to the classic form mentioned above, here are some other ways to structure copy. With the "cluster of diamonds" technique, you assemble a great many precious details of what you are selling and present them to the reader in an appropriate setting. A good example is the "67 Reasons Why" subscription advertising of *U.S. News and World Report*, listing 67 capsule descriptions of typical recent news articles in the magazine. The "setting"—the surrounding copy containing general information and argumentation—is as important as the specific jewels in the cluster. Neither would be sufficiently attractive without the other.

The "string of pearls" technique is similar but not quite the same. Each "pearl" is a complete little gem of selling, and a number of them are simply strung together in almost any sequence to make a chain. The late David Ogilvy's "Surprising Amsterdam" series of ads was like this. Each surprising fact about Amsterdam was like a small-space ad for the city, but only when all these little ads are strung together do you feel compelled to get up from your easy chair and send for those KLM brochures. This technique is especially useful, by the way, when you have a vast subject like an encyclopedia to discuss. You have not one but many stories to tell. If you simply ramble on and on, most readers won't stay with you. So make a little list of stories you want to tell, write a tight little one-paragraph essay on each point, announce the subject of each essay in a boldface subhead, and then string them all together like pearls, with an appropriate beginning and ending.

The "fan dancers" technique is like a line of chorus girls equipped with Sally Rand fans. The dancers are always about to reveal their secret charms, but they never quite do. You've seen this kind of copy many times. One of the best examples is the circular received in answer to an irresistible classified ad in *Popular Mechanics*.

EXHIBIT 20–4

Oreck XL Ultra Print Ad

Just for trying my Oreck XL® Ultra, I'll give you a $150 Verilux Reading Lamp Free!

Free Shipping.
(A $29.95 Savings!)

You may never need your reading glasses again.

Free $169 Housekeeper® Compact Canister.

Hi, I'm David Oreck, let's shed some light on the subject of vacuum cleaners.

First, most vacuums sold today spew dust that can carry germs back into your home. And you and your family get to breathe it in. But not the Hypo-Allergenic Oreck XL Ultra with its eight-filter system. Second, most vacuums sold today are overweight, hard to use and a chore to lug up and down stairs. But not the Oreck XL Ultra. At only 8 lbs. light, it's a fraction of the weight of most vacuums (but has the suction power equivalent of 102 mph!) and a pleasure to use. And finally, most vacuums sold today are so poorly made their guarantees are embarrassing. But not the Oreck XL Ultra. It has a 10-year guarantee, and to keep it running like new, we give you ten free annual tune ups (a $300 value). Nobody does this but Oreck!

I'M SO CONVINCED MY 8-LB ORECK XL ULTRA IS SUPERIOR TO ANY OTHER VACUUM that I'll give you this Verilux Lamp just for trying my vacuum for 30 days – risk free.* This $150 Verilux Lamp increases the contrast between black and white to make reading easier. Since 1956 Verilux has specialized in naturally-balanced, visually-efficient lighting solutions. Even fine print will be crisp, clear and easy to see. You'll be able to read without squinting or straining.

FREE WITH PURCHASE OF THE ORECK XL ULTRA IS MY ORECK HOUSEKEEPER® COMPACT CANISTER. It's the one you've seen on TV pick up a 16-lb. bowling ball. Hand-held or shoulder-worn, it's the perfect above-the-floor vacuum.

TRY THE HYPO-ALLERGENIC 8-LB. XL ULTRA RISK FREE FOR 30 DAYS. Then decide. If you don't love it, you don't keep it.* But keep the lamp as a gift. *There's no obligation.* What do you have to lose except the hidden dirt your present vacuum leaves behind?

1-888-215-5136 ext. DD412

Risk Free 30-Day Home Trial. Free Shipping. DD412

☐ Please call me to arrange a risk free 30-day trial of the Oreck XL® Ultra and send me a $150 Verilux® Reading Lamp just for trying the Oreck XL Ultra. I understand I'll receive the Housekeeper® Canister free with purchase and that shipping is free.

☐ Yes, I would like more information on the amazing 8 pound Oreck XL Ultra and include details of Oreck's 15-month Interest-Free Payment Plan.

* Mail in voucher enclosed with the vacuum to receive your free Lamp.

Name _____

Address _____

City _____ State _____ Zip _____

Tel (___) _____ e-mail _____
optional   Call 1-888-215-5136 or visit oreck.com/arp

ORECK

Nothing gets by an Oreck.®
Oreck Direct, LLC. 100 Plantation Road, New Orleans, LA 70123

PBY2R

The ad simply said "505 odd, successful enterprises. Expect something odd." The circular described the entire contents of a book of money-making ideas in maddening fashion. Something like: "No. 24. Here's an idea that requires nothing but old coat hangers. A retired couple on a Kansas farm nets $240 weekly with this one."

With the "machine gun" technique, you simply spray facts and arguments in the general direction of the reader, in the hope that at least some of them will hit. This is called the no-structure structure, and it is the first refuge of the amateur. If you have a great product and manage to convey your enthusiasm for it through the sheer exuberance of your copy, you will succeed, not because of your technique, but despite it. And the higher the levels of taste and education of your readers, the less chance you will have.

Establishing the Uniqueness of Your Product or Service

What is the unique claim to fame of the product or service you are selling? This could be one of your strongest selling points. The word "only" is a great advertising word. If what you offer is "better" or "best," this is merely a claim in support of your argument that the reader should come to you for the product or services offered. But if what you are offering is the "only" one of its kind, then readers must come to you if they want the benefits that only you can offer.

Here are some ways in which you might be able to stake out a unique position in the marketplace for the product or service you are selling: "We're the largest." People respect bigness in a company or a sales total. They reason that if a product leads the others in its field, it must be good. Thus, the "No. 1 Best-Seller" is always a potent phrase, for it is not just an airy claim but a hard fact that proves some kind of merit.

But what if you're not the largest? Perhaps you can still establish a unique position, as in "We're the largest of our kind." By simply defining your identity more sharply, you might still be able to claim some kind of size superiority. For example, there was the Trenton merchant who used to boast that he had "the largest clothing store in the world in a garage!"

Like many business-to-business print ads, the ServSafe ad (see Exhibit 20–5) is a transactional branding ad. Its goal is to build awareness of the ServSafe responsible alcohol training program, while generating leads. The ad highlights the ServSafe brand, respected among decision makers for food safety training, and positions the program as a more credible option than training alcohol servers in-house.

A mail-order photo finisher decided that one benefit it had to sell was the sheer bigness of its operation. It wasn't the biggest—that distinction belonged, of course, to Eastman Kodak. But it was second. And Eastman Kodak was involved in selling a lot of other things, too, such as film and cameras and chemicals.

EXHIBIT 20–5

ServSafe Ad

Its photo-finishing service was only one of many divisions. So the advertiser was able to fashion a unique claim: "America's Largest Independent Photo Finisher."

"We're the fastest-growing." If you're on the way to becoming the largest, that's about as impressive a proof of merit as being the largest. In fact, it can be even more impressive, because it adds the excitement of the underdog coming up fast. *U.S. News & World Report* used this to good effect during the 1950s while its circulation was growing from approximately 400,000 to about three times that figure as "America's Fastest-Growing Newsmagazine."

"We offer a unique combination of advantages." It could be that no one claim you can make is unique, but that none of your competitors is able to equal your claim that you have all of a certain number of advantages.

In the early 1960s, the Literary Guild began to compete in earnest with the Book-of-the-Month Club (BOMC). The Literary Guild started offering books that compared very favorably with those offered by BOMC. But the latter had a couple of unique claims that the Guild couldn't match—BOMC's distinguished board of judges, and its book-dividend system, with a history of having distributed $375 million worth of books to members.

How to compete? The Guild couldn't claim the greatest savings; one of Doubleday's other clubs actually saved the subscriber more off the publisher's price. It couldn't claim that it had books offered by no other club; some of Doubleday's other clubs were offering some of the same books, and even BOMC would sometimes make special arrangements to offer a book being featured by the Guild.

But the Guild was able to feature a unique set of advantages that undoubtedly played a part in the success it has enjoyed: "Only the Literary Guild saves you 40–60 percent on books like these as soon as they are published." Other clubs could make either of these two claims, but only the Guild could claim both.

"We have a uniquely advantageous location." A classic of this was James Webb Young's great ad for "Old Jim Young's Mountain Grown Apples—Every Bite Crackles, and the Juice Runs Down Your Lips." In it Jim Young, trader, tells how the natives snickered when his pappy bought himself an abandoned homestead in a little valley high up in the Jemes Mountains. But "Pappy" Young, one of the slickest farmers ever to come out of Madison Avenue, knew that "this little mountain valley is just a natural apple spot—as they say some hillsides are in France for certain wine grapes. The summer sun beats down into this valley all day, to color and ripen apples perfectly; but the cold mountain air drains down through it at night to make them crisp and firm. Then it turns out that the soil there is full of volcanic ash, and for some reason that seems to produce apples with a flavor that is really something."

Haband Ties used to make a big thing out of being located in Paterson, New Jersey, the silk center of the nation. Even though most of the company's ties and other apparel were made of synthetic fibers, somehow the idea of buying ties from the silk center made the reader feel that he was buying ties at the very source. In the same way, maple syrup from Vermont should be a lot easier to sell than maple syrup from Arizona.

Finally, suppose you believe that you have something unique to sell, but you hesitate to start an argument with your competitors by making a flat claim that they might challenge. In that case, you can imply your uniqueness by the way in which you word the claim. "Here's one mouthwash that keeps your mouth sweet and fresh all day long" doesn't flatly claim that it's the only one. It simply says, "At least we've got this desirable quality, whether any other product does or not." *Newsweek* identified itself as "the newsmagazine that separates fact from opinion"—a powerful use of that innocent word *the* that devastates the competition.

| CASE STUDY: | The British American Drama Academy Lead/Prospect Campaign |

Submitted by Susan Kryl, Kryl & Company Inc., Chicago, IL.

BACKGROUND

The British American Drama Academy (BADA) is headquartered in London, at Regent's Park. The Academy was founded in 1983 to enable students from around the world to study classical theater with leading actors and directors of the British stage. BADA runs two semester-long courses for college students—the London Theater Program and the Shakespeare Program—and two month-long summer programs open to all applicants, Midsummer in Oxford and the Midsummer Conservatory Program.

Midsummer in Oxford, based at Balliol—one of Oxford's oldest colleges—offers a total immersion program in classical acting. It is accredited by the University of California at Los Angeles (UCLA) and is run in association with UCLA and The Yale School of Drama. The program regularly features Britain's leading actors and directors as members of its faculty. Recent participants have included Sir Ben Kingsley, Alan Rickman, Fiona Shaw, Brian Cox, and Henry Goodman. Many of the students from the Midsummer in Oxford program have gone on to achieve great success in the acting profession, including David Schwimmer, Oliver Platt, Paul Rudd, and Orlando Bloom. The number of students accepted into the Midsummer in Oxford program is limited; no class is larger than 16 students.

OBJECTIVES

The objective of the direct response ad campaign was to drive traffic to the BADA Web site and generate inquiries from prospects for the Midsummer in Oxford program.

TARGET AUDIENCE

Serious acting students at all levels—undergraduate to professional—and influencers, including drama teachers and academic mentors, friends, classmates, parents, and grandparents.

MARKETING STRATEGY

The strategy of the print advertising campaign was to generate inquiries as part of a two-step lead/conversion program. Ad responders can call a phone number in the print ad for a brochure, or visit the BADA Web site to obtain a brochure and an application (See Exhibits 20–6, 20–7 and 20–8).

CHALLENGE

A key challenge for this campaign is to convey the benefits and unique features of the Midsummer in Oxford program within the constraints of a small budget, and to motivate the prospect to call or visit the Web site for more information.

SOLUTION

Small-space black-and-white ads were created in several sizes to maximize the budget, facilitate frequency, and to accommodate a variety of media specifications. The borders around the ads, composite photographs of students and teachers, featured recognizable actors in the process of teaching. The aim was to illustrate the breadth and variety of the learning experience, thereby creating excitement and encouraging response.

The print media mix ranged from glossy monthly magazines to weekly newsprint and included theater trade publications, general newspapers, and, occasionally, college newspapers. Although the focus of the media strategy was vertical, drama-oriented publications, the ads in the *New York Times* accomplished two goals: (1) they enable BADA to reach influencers (and perhaps "funders") such as parents and grandparents of potential students; and (2) BADA benefits from the prestige associated with the publication.

EXHIBIT 20–6

BADA Print Ad

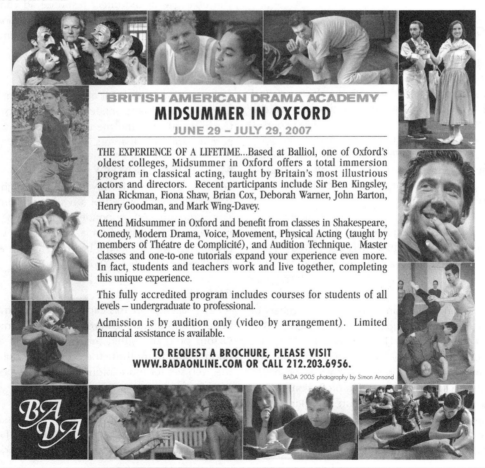

EXHIBIT 20–7

BADA Brochure

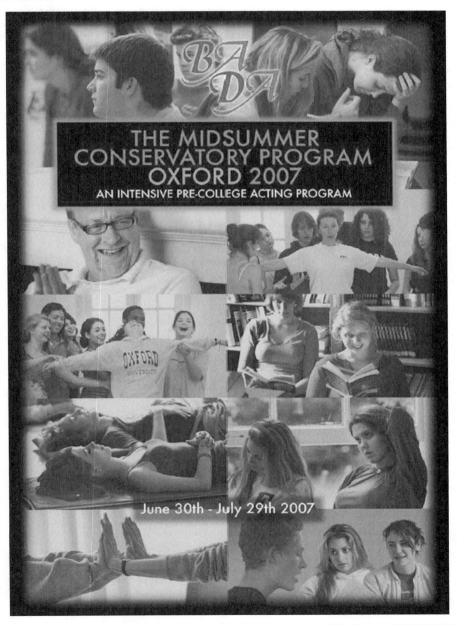

CASE STUDY: **The British American Drama Academy Lead/Prospect Campaign** *(continued)*

EXHIBIT 20–8

BADA Print Ad

THE MIDSUMMER CONSERVATORY PROGRAM   APPLICATION FORM

Name _____

Date of Birth _____

Gender _____

Permanent Home Address *(this address will be used for all correspondence)*

_____

_____

_____

_____

Home Telephone _____

Parent/Guardian Name (1) *(address if different from above)*

_____

_____

Parent/Guardian Name (2) *(address if different from above)*

_____

_____

_____

Name of School

_____

Preferred Audition Location

    New York ☐
    Los Angeles ☐
    Washington DC ☐
    Video ☐

Admission to the program is by audition. Most auditions are conducted by BADA staff who travel to the United States specifically to audition prospective students. The anticipated audition schedule is published in the fulfillment brochure and on the Web site, although applicants are notified about auditions when their completed applications have been received. Auditions are also conducted by U.S.-based Midsummer in Oxford instructors. In special circumstances, and by arrangement, BADA will accept an audition on video.

During the auditions, applicants for the program are required to present two three-minute contrasting monologues, one of which must be from Shakespeare, the other a "cold" (sight unseen) reading of prose or poetry.

MEDIA SCHEDULE

The media schedule runs in the first quarter of the year, and is heaviest in January with some early February insertions. The schedule includes one-third page and one-quarter page ads in vertical publications: *American Theatre, Dramatics, Backstage, Backstage West,* and *PerformInk,* and small ads in the Arts & Leisure section of the *New York Times.*

Vertical publications are more efficient than mass media, with *Backstage/Backstage West* outperforming all other publications. While the *New York Times* has been retained on the media schedule, tests of the *Los Angeles Times*, the *Toronto Globe & Mail,* and the *Chicago Reader* have not been effective. And a recent test of the new *Time Out New York* was disappointing.

RESULTS

For more than a decade, the print campaign has generated quality leads to enable BADA to operate the Midsummer in Oxford program at full capacity. Each season, BADA receives about 600 inquiries for brochures, the majority of them via telephone. However, during this campaign nearly two-thirds of the applications were generated from the Web site.

As a copywriter at a multichannel direct marketing advertising agency, one of your jobs is to create print ads that generate response. The headline of a print ad is critical in gaining attention. Typically, headlines promise a benefit to the target group that compels them to read further into the ad.

The agency has been appointed by a home study school offering a course in computer game development. The creative direction asks you to come up designs to generate inquiries for the program.

Develop one headline for each of these ultimate benefits:

- Health
- Money
- Security
- Pride
- Approval
- Excitement
- Gratification
- Fulfillment
- Freedom
- Identity
- Escape
- Curiosity
- Possessions
- Enjoyment
- Creativity

Key Points

- ▶ Print ads must stop the reader and engage his or her attention and interest in order to stand out among the advertisers in a magazine or newspaper. While the general ad may rest after making an impression, the response ad must stimulate immediate action.

- ▶ Make your strongest appeal to your best prospects—people with the strongest desire for what you are selling. Use clarity and directness to gather in prime prospects; then use creative imagination to reach beyond them to awaken and excite mild prospects as well.

- ▶ If the product or service is unique or unfamiliar, stress benefits. If it is simply a new, improved model in a highly competitive field with established demand, stress product advantages.

- ▶ A good lead is the first step in a straight path of feeling and logic from the headline or display theme to the concluding call for action. Readers should be able to see clearly where the path is taking them.

- ▶ The sections of a classic copy argument can be labeled *problem, promise of solution, explanation of promise, proof,* and *call to action.* If you start with the problem, hint right away at the forthcoming solution.

- ▶ Other ways to structure copy include the "cluster of diamonds" technique, which assembles and presents details in an appropriate setting; the "string of pearls" technique, which strings together complete little gems of selling in a sequence; and the "fan dancers" technique, which teases readers with short product facts. Avoid the "machine gun" technique—simply spraying facts and arguments in the general direction of the reader, in the hope that at least some of them will hit.

- ▶ Establish the unique claim to fame of the product or service. Is it better? Best? Largest? Newest? Fastest growing? Use it to stake out a unique position in the marketplace for the product or service you are selling.

MARKETING
INTELLIGENCE

MODELING FOR BUSINESS DECISION SUPPORT

W hile no one can predict the future, marketers can reduce the risk of failure by using technology to combine product, market, and customer knowledge drawn from an organization's database. The outcome—expressed in a model—can help marketers support business strategy decisions.

"Modeling" means simplifying a complex situation and observing key components or relationships. The Wright brothers built model airplanes before they tested a full-scale one. Architects build models of proposed buildings. In a similar way, marketers build models to simplify and see clearly what is going on in their customer campaigns.

Different kinds of models provide different results. Marketers use profile, predictive, or segmentation models. Specific models are created based on business goals and the results the marketer is hoping to achieve. For example, marketers can use models to help to acquire look-alikes of their existing customers. Models can identify customers for up-selling or cross-selling additional products or services. Other objectives of modeling include increasing product usage, converting leads to orders, predicting future customer behavior, determining the size and success of a campaign, and segmenting populations for campaign management and marketing strategies.

Modeling is a critical tool that helps marketers who have more data than they know what to do with. Using modeling, marketers can identify "best" customers from a 10-million-name database and present conclusions in visual, easy to understand graphs or charts. Of course, *best* has many definitions. For some organizations, *best* means customers who have purchased the most recently, frequently, or spent the most money. Others define *best* as customers with the greatest propensity to buy, or those likely to produce the greatest profit. The definition depends on where an organization is in its growth phase, and whether it is trying to maximize profits or sales.

Modeling doesn't actually sift through all the names on a database. A statistically reliable sample of 10,000 names is enough to gain important knowledge about huge data sets. Modeling also doesn't automatically yield visual reports.

Most models generate tabular information that can be challenging to read, and a statistician is still best qualified to interpret the complex mathematical relationships between variables. But a simple spreadsheet program can turn the information into a graph that marketing, finance, and other nontechnical management can understand.

Modeling is not the same as testing or data mining. Like traditional testing, modeling isolates causal variables to determine their impact. The essential elements are a controlled offer to a known selection of customers coupled with the capability of tracking the results. However, with traditional in-the-mail testing, a marketer must correctly anticipate the variable that has the greatest impact, and a relatively small number of variables can be tested at one time. In contrast, modeling permits marketers to test a large number of variables and discover, in the process, which has the greatest impact.

Modeling is directed. Before it begins, you need to define the variables that will be modeled and predetermine what you are looking for. Data mining is an open-ended exploratory process, which gives marketers (the miners) access to data with dynamic, easy-to-use, graphical query tools. Skilled data miners can often find surprises in their data, which lead to marketing breakthroughs, changes in the offer, product, or customer profile. Data mining is less directed, so considerable time can be spent without drawing significant conclusions.

The modeling process is not so much data mining as data *sluicing*. Sluicing is the process of washing river gravel through a machine that finds the gold. It is far more efficient and automated than the traditional panning for gold. Large amounts of data may be sifted through quickly until all that is left are shiny nuggets of information: the customers you've described as the precise ones you want to reach.

Because it allows marketers to define and pinpoint their "best" customers and prospects, modeling is an important first step in designing contact strategies that enhance the lifetime value of a customer.

The Purpose of Modeling: Looking Back in Order to Look Ahead

The starting point of all modeling is looking at past campaigns and the results. The clearest examples of modeling are analyzing who was contacted, who responded, and who didn't. Comparing characteristics between the two groups gives a marketer insight into what made the difference between responding and not responding—insight that can be applied to the next campaign.

To look back in time, modeling begins by making customers or prospects look like they did when mailed, then compares who responded, purchased, and so forth. By comparing the difference between responders and nonresponders, it is possible to identify the correlation between independent variables and the dependent variable. This ability to look into the past at many more variables makes modeling much more powerful than traditional segmentation methods.

While tomorrow may not be exactly like yesterday—seasonality, changes in the economy, politics, and events can all affect future response—generally, modeling suggests that similar things can be expected to work again. Look-alikes for the best customers today will likely work in the future. Modeling will never exactly predict the future, but it will give a clearer picture of the recent past, which, all things being equal, is the best that most marketers can hope for.

Customer and Prospect Modeling

Marketers most frequently use customer and prospect models. Customer models use purchase history, credit usage, and other behavior data to sort the customers from best to worst so that it is clear who most qualifies for a specific offer. If all customers are included in a mailing, then the order in which you rank them makes little difference. When a very specific model for a single offering is built, only a small percentage of customers will be viable, and modeling can generate a tremendous payback.

While modeling began as a segmenting tool, it plays an increasingly important role in communications. Knowledge gained about certain customers can help marketers identify compelling reasons for the segment to buy—reasons that can be prominently featured in creative executions. A credit card company that discovered that its optimal customers used the card five times a month might develop a program to prompt customers who use the card three times a month to use it twice more. Modeling demonstrated to a membership organization the relationship between usage of key benefits and customer retention. Discovering that members who did not use benefits did not renew, it designed programs to stimulate usage of the benefits. Renewal rates rose because members who used the benefits were better able to understand the value proposition.

Unlike customer models, prospect models have no behavior variables. Prospect models are designed to find the worst neighborhoods and avoid mailing into them. There are several popular dependent variables. Most common are response rate per postal code, and revenue per piece per postal code. Presumably, the best mailing lists have already been identified. They would normally be mailed in their entirety. Middle performing lists might be reduced by 30 to 50 percent, and poor lists could be reduced by 50 to 90 percent. This elimination of the marginal ZIP codes allows many more lists to be used, dramatically improving the number of names available while maintaining overall performance.

Defining the Variables

The key to successful modeling is carefully defining the variables. Variables are characteristics linked to customers. Key types of characteristics might include neighborhood factors (median income, age, dwelling value, or high school graduation rate), household factors (mortgage amount, income, type of car, presence of children, education level), behavior (how recently, frequently, and how much people have purchased, types of merchandise purchased), and contact (subject and frequency of offers sent).

Modeling uses two kinds of variables: independent and dependent. A model compares one *dependent variable* against any number of *independent variables*. The use of multiple variables is known as multivariate analysis.

The independent variables—what you already know about the customer, or what you can observe—are used to build a predictive model. The list of independent variables pretty much stays the same through all models.

The dependent variable is the key ingredient in the modeling process—really the defining characteristic of the model. It is the behavior being analyzed, the difference between two groups of customers. In other words, it is the factor that you want to be able to predict or forecast.

Calculating the dependent variable can be very simple or complex. With a single price offer, there are two variables—response vs. no response. But some customers may buy more than others, some may return items, or cancel their service permanently. Some will be heavy users of customer service, others will not. All these events will affect individual customer profitability. Since as few as 10 percent of your customers generate 90 percent of your profits, it would be foolish to reduce their behavior to the simple response/nonresponse level. Instead, the dependent variable should be calculated as carefully as possible for each person contacted. It should certainly include sales minus costs (order entry cost, cost of goods sold, and contact cost).

For example, geography is a variable that is often important in consumer marketing. Using a geodemographic mapping program, customer counts can be overlaid with median household income. If the customers appear concentrated in areas of high (or low) income, it would suggest a connection that could be further explored (and illustrated) by summing (and graphing) the total population vs. customers in high-, medium-, and low-income geographies.

Income could be the dependent variable for a marketer trying to determine a certain segment's propensity to buy. All other characteristics—age, number of children, home ownership, and so forth—would be independent. Successive models would run through these variables, testing income against different independent variables until it arrived at a result of statistical importance.

When it comes to variables, more is almost always better. Using modeling, marketers can refine model after model until they can pinpoint the exact set of characteristics or variables that have the greatest impact on the decision to buy. Modelers go through the process multiple times until they have a result they feel comfortable with.

Observation alone may not reveal why a variable is important—but if that variable is left out of the analysis, a key ingredient is missed. For example, AT&T observed that phone color was an important variable when assessing which businesses stayed with them after the breakup. No one knew why, but companies with black phones were the most likely to stay with AT&T.

Three behavior variables are consistently most important and form the foundation for customer segmentation, especially in combination with each other: RFM (Recency, Frequency, Monetary). But while RFM clearly and consistently identifies the best customers, it cannot break out people who have only ordered once, didn't spend much, and haven't been heard from in quite a while. By adding purchase and activity, product category, or individual, neighborhood, and spending variables, modeling can move beyond simple RFM to find good in the bad and bad in the good. Descriptive categorical variables such as state of residence, sex, occupation, or even number and kind of pets are also useful, and can be analyzed using cross-tabulation, frequency distributions, or CHAID.

It is important to define the dependent variable carefully. A specific model will have far greater force than a general one. Asking the question, "Who is most likely to buy something?" will generate a weak model with recency likely at the top. All things being equal, people who have bought recently are most likely to buy next. If, however, you ask, "Who is most likely to buy from the fishing catalog?" (as opposed to hunting, camping, or boating), you will generate a very interesting model where recency may not even be found. The second model will have about ten times the power of the first. Gain—the difference between the top performing decile and the bottom—is important in modeling, which can be very expensive.

Logic, not modeling, tells marketers that customers who have bought most recently or spent the biggest dollar amounts are likely to buy again and spend more. But adding categorical data will reveal which customers are more likely to buy more of which product. The resulting gains chart doesn't just say "These people will buy more"; it says "These people are going to be X percent more likely to buy than those people."

Exhibit 21–1 is a picture of customers scored on frequency. Five is given to the customers who accumulate 20 percent of the purchases—perhaps only 1 to 4 percent of all customers. Response percentage can be improved simply by eliminating the ones. Instead of simply eliminating the low frequency customers as shown in Exhibit 21–2, a spending variable could be added. The big spenders (5 on the horizontal scale) would be mailed, and the high-frequency low spenders would not be.

Collecting Variables

There are two basic techniques for connecting customer characteristics to those contacted: recording relevant behavior and dynamically generating variables.

The simplest way to collect variables is to just keep a record of the relevant behavior scores for each customer at the time they were mailed. This snapshot records RFM, product scores, demographic values, and anything else on hand at the time of the mailing. It can be somewhat cumbersome to keep precise track of

EXHIBIT 21–1

Frequency Distribution

Part A uses a histogram, and Part B uses a bar graph to represent customers scored using a Frequency Distribution.

Part A

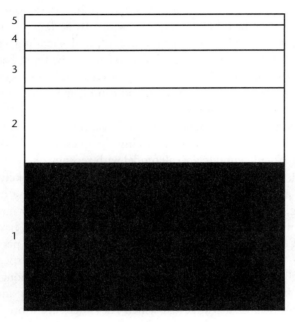

Part B

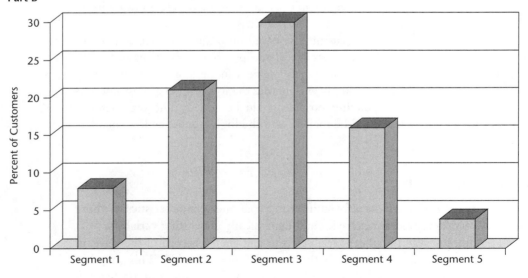

EXHIBIT 21–2

Modeling Chart Showing Dozens of Variables

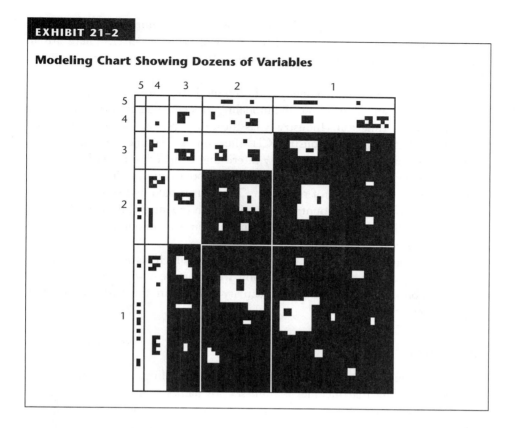

all these snapshots for each customer, and it takes time. Suppose, for example, that other companies are successfully using the "werewolf" variable. Named for the werewolf that changes from man to beast only at the full moon, this variable notes the phase of the moon for specific events. You can't wait to try it. Alas, it's not one of the variables in your database. You won't be able to include it in your models until it gets into your snapshots several months to a year later.

The alternative method is to dynamically create all your behavior variables. Rarely will the variables coming off the order processing system be completely accurate, so it is in your best interest to recalculate them. Since the marketing database should be calculating variables, it is relatively simple to specify the date ranges for your recalculation. The data preparation would include building a sample database and recalculating all the behavior variable scores to what they would have been at the mail date. This technique effectively rolls the customer file back in time. Now you cannot only make your customers look like they did at the mail date, but you can also calculate the werewolf variable for your entire customer file . . . and use it immediately.

The key to regularly improving models is regularly improving the variables. As more creative data types are used, models will become better. There are an infinite number of variables for any event or object. Do not settle for two or three. Play the "what if" game.

A high-end menswear company had been modeling for several years and was concerned that it was wearing out the modeling process. The company had never used the North American Industry Classification System (NAICS) (formerly known as the U.S. Standard Industrial Classification (SIC) numeric codes for types of businesses), but couldn't think of any interesting connection between business-to-business data and their customer base. "How about country clubs per capita?" came a voice from the back of the room. The census data had postal code area, population, and number of country clubs so CC/km (country clubs per kilometer) could also be built. It took a few days to generate, but sure enough, it turned up in the next sportswear model.

Neither sample size (as long as it's huge) nor which statistical technique is applied (as long as you are careful, and know what you are doing) are as important as the variables. Behind it all, the creativity will be in the variable creation. The variables drive the model.

Validation

Validation is one of the most important elements of modeling. To validate a model, construct a mailing that includes a "null set" of names that were not modeled. If they are drawn from the same universe but haven't been modeled, their response rate can be expected to be lower. Lower response rates from this segment validate the model. Equal or higher response rates indicate problems.

Validation reports look exactly like traditional list reports. Each model cell or decile has a name count; in addition, the number of orders, response rate, average order size, etc., can be generated. The best cells in the model should perform the best in the validation—if not, there will be an opportunity to retune the model before mailing. There are additional, more complex, methods of validation, but regardless of statistical technique, validation must be part of the modeling process.

Useful Modeling Techniques

Marketers can model many things. Response modeling is very common. Modeling response involves determining which characteristics of a product or service need to be highlighted to make a prospect or customer buy. The cost of direct mail or an Internet marketing campaign is directly proportional to the number of prospects being targeted: each contact, whether by e-mail, direct mail, or telephone, increases costs.

Only prospects or customers that purchase the offered product or service contribute to revenue. The goal of most modeling is reducing the number of contacted while at the same time increasing response rates. This reduces promotion costs while increasing profits. Two useful techniques for response modeling are regression and Chi-squared Automatic Interactive Detector (CHAID).

Regression

Regression modeling, the most commonly used analytical technique, comes in a number of flavors: simple, multiple, multivariate, logit, logistic, and stepwise, to name a few. Regression models compare individual variables to the dependent variable. The one that best correlates is given the highest statistical weight in the model, the next best correlation a lower weight, etc. Because regression models tend to isolate a small number of really significant variables and eliminate or ignore less important variables, they are more easily understood by nonstatisticians. Their relatively simple output also makes it is easy to generate a scoring equation to apply the model to current customers.

A disadvantage is that this simplification can also eliminate important variables whose impact is more complex. Regression then requires relatively skilled people to prepare the data correctly. If you know what you are doing, regression will perform comparably to any other technique.

A cable television company developed a regression model that could help isolate the point in time when customers have a propensity to reduce or disconnect service. The company was able to segment by service level (e.g., basic, plus, premium) and pay-per-view usage. Direct mail and phone retention efforts were directed at subscribers weeks before this point in time. Customers with a higher propensity to disconnect were offered free movies and additional premium channels. Customers with a low propensity to disconnect were sent "love mailings" that reminded users of program benefits but without an incentive. This program significantly improved retention percentages, extending the lifetime value of each subscriber.

CHAID

CHAID is another well-proven modeling technique. Instead of looking for correlations, CHAID estimates the probability of independence. The lower the probability, the more important the variable. As the name implies, the process is highly automatic. CHAID also evaluates all variables—as many as 1,000—and builds a tree with the most important variable at the top, less important variables under each cell. It is very easy to understand.

CHAID reports let nonstatistical users almost instantly gain considerable insight into important data relationships, which in turn triggers creative inspiration for creating new variables. A CHAID model evaluates complex interactions among predictive variables and the results in an easy-to-understand tree diagram.

The trunk of the tree represents the total database universe. The model automatically determines how to group the values of this predictor into a manageable number of categories.

Let us say that to build a model to identify your most profitable customers, you begin by analyzing 12 age categories. The CHAID model could collapse that to six or even four statistically significant groups. Within each age group, household size might be the next most important variable. The model could identify what household size generated the greatest profit. For example, single-person households might not generate as much profit as households with two to four people.

You could then learn that within two-to four-person households, homes that owned sports utility vehicles had a higher profitability. At the next level, you could discover that households with two to four persons and a sports utility vehicle return an average profit three times that of similar-sized households with a luxury import car. However, the model might show that within the sports utility segment, a white-collar head of household would be twice as profitable as a blue-collar household. These facts are revealed in the tree diagram.

Modeling: Expensive, Essential, and Not for Statisticians Only

Modeling is expensive, but essential. To be effective, a model must beat what a manager could have done with a little thought.

Exhibit 21–3 illustrates a substantial catalog test in which 1.2 million pieces were tested using two mailing methods: RFM and CHAID modeling. Both techniques selected most of the good names, and both eliminated most of the poorer names. However, the exact results differed substantially. Unique names were key-coded separately; common names were randomly allocated back into each sample. This yielded an easy-to-understand comparison between the old and new method. The modeled panel generated $454,000 more profit from the same mailing quantity—well worth the investment.

It is surprising how few companies invest in statistical modeling despite its demonstrated effectiveness. One reason may be that many companies, especially business-to-business marketers, mail universes that appear to be too small to justify the cost of modeling. Smaller universes make the cost of modeling appear to be a higher percentage of creating the list.

Yet modeling is worth every dollar of its cost. It helps correct the leading problem in direct marketing: mailing people who don't want your mail and calling people who don't want your calls. Modeling brings an organization closer to the people who *do* want to receive your mail and calls. The high cost of modeling should not keep an organization from investing in a technique that will improve its profitability more than any other tool.

EXHIBIT 21-3

RFM versus CHAID
This graph shows catalog test between customers selected by RFM and by CHAID.

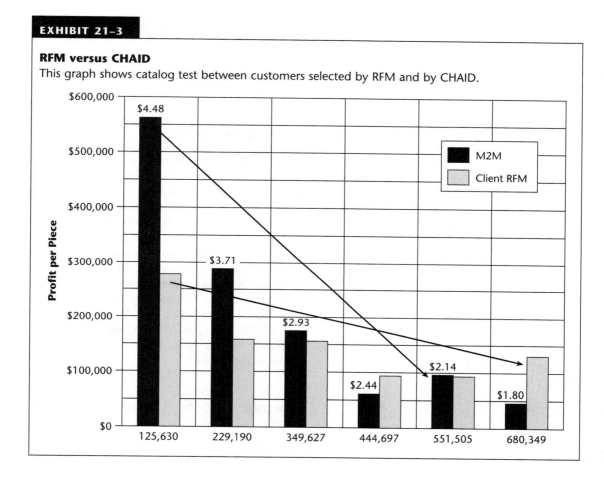

Another reason marketers avoid modeling is its perceived complexity. Marketers (and even more, senior managers) get nervous when faced with abstract neural algorithms. If they can't understand it, how can they tell if there is something wrong with it? Graphs and charts can make outcomes comprehensible by making the abstract more tangible.

While experts are important, effective modeling cannot be completely assigned to the "statistician." It takes more than one person to develop a modeling capability. Careful, methodical people are needed to load data, update the database, and to pull names. Creative people are needed to build, validate, and analyze the results of the model and create new variables. These skills are not combined in one single person.

Finally, modeling must be accountable to business people who clearly understand the customers. It is not enough to just produce better mailings or campaigns; insight must be gained and communicated.

Modeling is neither as easy as flying by the seat of the pants nor as hard as self-administered brain surgery. Somewhere in between lies the art of turning data into money. Understand this if nothing else: careful analysis of marketing campaigns will certainly improve contact accuracy. Modeling is the direct marketing technology of the future. Ignore it at your peril!

CASE STUDY: Benefiting from Predictive Modeling with Databases

BACKGROUND

A travel company that offers package tours through mail order to older persons desires to increase its marketing effectiveness by segmenting its marketplace within the state of Florida.

CHALLENGE

The firm has developed, from census and proprietary data sources, a total of 103 demographic variables describing each of 35,000 geographic ZIP code areas. Test variables are expressed as either averages or frequency distributions. Using these demographic independent variables in addition to age, the travel company wants to segment its marketplace in Florida.

SOLUTION

Several of these variables have been normalized. That is, they have been indexed to some larger area such as a Sectional Center (the first three digits of a five-digit code) or a state (such as Mississippi versus New York) in order to achieve environmental, as opposed to absolute, measurement. This means that the relative income level in a rural Mississippi ZIP code area is compared with the relative income level of an urban area in New York City rather than in absolute dollars. A "high" dollar income level in the rural Mississippi area could be relatively "low" in New York City.

Variables have also been subjected to factor analysis in order to discover the typical lifestyle factors and the associated independent variables. The dependent variable is market penetration, defined in this instance as the response rate (total responses divided by the total number of pieces mailed) to the travel company's direct mail offer of tours to the older residents of Florida.

To maximize the number of observations and assure statistical validity of both measurement and prediction, the response rate is calculated within clusters of ZIP code areas with common characteristics produced using cluster analysis. Ultimately, these clusters will be described as market segments in which penetration levels can be correlated with their characteristics. At this stage, both environmental (indexed) measurement and interaction among the variables defining clusters are important considerations.

Calculation of penetration is simple. Within each cluster of ZIP code areas, the response rate is calculated as shown here:

ZIP CODE AREA CLUSTERS	TOTAL NO. OF PIECES MAILED	TOTAL NO. OF RESPONSES	PERCENTAGE OF RESPONSES
A	5,793	60	1.04%
B	2,735	33	1.21
C	6,731	136	2.02
D	4,341	118	2.74

From this table, it is readily apparent that there is an increasing rate of response from A to B, from B to C, and from C to D. These differences can be explained by evaluating the independent variables entering in, and deemed significant through regression analysis shown in Exhibit 21–4. Regression analysis enables the transfer of these findings from a sample to the total population without first having mailed that total population. The linear regression equation (of the form: $Y = a + bX$) becomes a formula for predicting estimated response rates from ZIP code area clusters not yet solicited but having similar characteristics to those sampled.

CASE STUDY: Benefiting from Predictive Modeling with Databases *(continued)*

EXHIBIT 21–4

Stepwise Multivariate Regression Analysis

STEP #1
  VARIABLE ENTERING   X-5
R = 0.583959   R SQ. = 0.341008
  F LEVEL =   23.8036
  STANDARD ERROR OF Y =   0.06341
  CONSTANT TERM =   0.27470726

VARIABLE NO.	COEFFICIENT	STD ERR OF COEFF
X-5	-0.28683022E-01	0.00594

STEP #2
  VARIABLE ENTERING   X-2
R = 0.717396   R SQ. = 0.514658
  F LEVEL =   16.1004
  STANDARD ERROR OF Y =   0.05504
  CONSTANT TERM =   0.25037676

VARIABLE NO.	COEFFICIENT	STD ERR OF COEFF
X-2	0.11710477	0.02951
X-5	-0.25006641E-01	0.00524

STEP #3
  VARIABLE ENTERING   X-16
R = 0.814453   R SQ. = 0.663334
  F LEVEL =   19.4310
  STANDARD ERROR OF Y =   0.04637
  CONSTANT TERM =   0.17120540

VARIABLE NO.	COEFFICIENT	STD ERR OF COEFF
X-2	0.12946498	0.02503
X-5	-0.21160301E-01	0.00450
X-16	0.10500204E-01	0.00241

STEP #4
  VARIABLE ENTERING   X-14
R = 0.831825   R SQ. = 0.691934
  F LEVEL =   3.9919
  STANDARD ERROR OF Y =   0.04488
  CONSTANT TERM =   0.11676645

VARIABLE NO.	COEFFICIENT	STD ERR OF COEFF
X-2	0.12659431	0.02427
X-5	-0.18140811E-01	0.00462
X-14	0.27103789E-01	0.01373
X-16	0.99606328E-02	0.00235

STEP #10
  VARIABLE ENTERING   X-22
R = 0.896520   R SQ. = 0.803748
  F LEVEL =   2.8542
  STANDARD ERROR OF Y =   0.03766
  CONSTANT TERM =   0.39812356

VARIABLE NO.	COEFFICIENT	STD ERR OF COEFF
X-2	0.13928533	0.02095
X-9	-0.20301903E-02	0.00064
X-10	-0.87198131E-02	0.00257
X-14	0.69082797E-01	0.01875
X-15	0.13623666E-01	0.00421
X-16	0.22368859E-01	0.00380
X-22	-0.15226589E-02	0.00091
X-23	-0.21373443E-02	0.00081

CASE STUDY: **Benefiting from Predictive Modeling with Databases**   *(continued)*

Correlation analysis by the travel company identifies the strength of the relationship between cluster response rates (the dependent variable), and each of the 103 selected demographics (independent variables). Exhibit 21–4 reproduces a condensed printout of the stepwise multivariate regression analysis that follows the correlation analysis. From 27 available independent variables, each a surrogate of a demographic characteristic of ZIP code areas, ten steps are taken. Eight variables remain at the conclusion of step 10. The reference numbers of these eight variables, together with their simple correlation coefficients, are shown at the bottom of Exhibit 21–4.

The resulting R^2 value of 0.803748 (the multiple coefficient of determination) indicates that 80 percent of the variance in response is explained by the presence or absence of these eight variables. The derived regression equation enables a rank ordering of predicted response rates attributable to each five-digit ZIP code area within each cluster.

Exhibit 21–5 shows the highest to the lowest, as well as the cumulative, predicted penetration percentages (response rates). It also shows both individual and cumulative base mailing list counts for each ZIP code area within each cluster. Note the variance of the actual response rate, shown for each ZIP code area in the third column, attributable to the small number mailed in each area. Exhibit 21–5 reveals that, from a total mailing quantity of 1,277,262 pieces, the overall average response rate is predicted to be 1.95 percent. The response rate from the top cluster (#39) is predicted at 4.49 percent; that from the bottom cluster (#30) is predicted at 0.76 percent. The ratio, top versus bottom, is very nearly 1:6. Note, too, that the response rate from the top cluster is 2.3 times the overall average of 1.95 percent; that from the bottom is 39 percent.

To attain an average response of 2.55 percent (31 percent better than average), the company should stop after cluster #10, with marginal response of 2.06 percent, mailing 511,276 pieces. Limiting mailing quantity to 242,935 pieces, about 20 percent of the list availability, average response would be 2.87 percent, an improvement of 47 percent over the 1.95 percent overall average.

From this analysis, the company decides how big a market segment is needed, then predicts what overall response rate will be. It sets its minimum response rate requirement (average or marginal), then determines how many pieces it can mail. At this point, of primary importance to the travel company is a description of the profiles that exist in Florida. Just what influence might each of these exert on the response rate to a travel tour offer directed to older persons? Factor analysis produces these three explanatory lifestyle profiles, which are present in clusters with high response rates.

Rural Residers. Variables positively associated with this factor include rural farm and rural non-farm types of areas; farm manager and farm laborer occupations; housing in mobile homes and trailers; housing equipped with food freezers, lacking formal kitchens; East European ancestry. Negatively associated variables are access to public water and sewers; finance industry; multi-family dwelling units.

Social Class. "Lower half" variables positively associated with this factor include occupation as laborers, operatives, service workers, unemployed; poverty levels; divorced, separated, and widowed marital status; older housing; longer tenure of residence. "Upper half" variables, negatively associated, are high housing value; housing equipped with amenities such as air conditioning and dishwashers; two or more autos; high income; high education levels; occupations in management, sales, professional, technical; finance industry.

Ancestry/Heritage. Variables with positive association are native-born with English as mother tongue; foreign-born with countries of origin including the United Kingdom, Canada, Ireland, Austria, and Germany; housing in owner-occupied single-family units. Negatively associated variables include foreign-born; emigrated from Cuba; Spanish as mother tongue; multiple-family rental housing.

CASE STUDY: **Benefiting from Predictive Modeling with Databases** (continued)

Rank Ordering of Zip Code Clusters According to Response Rate Predicted by Regression Analysis

Cluster	Zip #	Penetration Actual	Percentages Pred	Cum Pred	****Base Counts**** Zip Only	Cumulative
39	32009	.00	.0449	.0449	89	89
	32265	.00	.0449	.0449	4	93
	32560	.1070	.0449	.0449	93	186
	32563	.00	.0449	.0449	6	192
	32710	.00	.0449	.0449	37	229
	32732	.00	.0449	.0449	200	429
	32740	.00	.0449	.0449	42	471
	32766	.1500	.0449	.0449	200	671
	33070	.0460	.0449	.0449	651	1322
	33470	.00	.0449	.0449	132	1454
	33527	.00	.0449	.0449	716+	2170
	33534	.0590	.0449	.0449	505	2675
	33550	.00	.0449	.0449	194	2869
	33556	.0750	.0449	.0449	528	3397
	33569	.0480	.0449	.0449	1637	5034
	33584	.0390	.0449	.0449	1001	6035
	33586	.00	.0449	.0449	62	6097
	33592	.0770	.0449	.0449	518	6615
	33600	.0750	.0449	.0449	398	7013
	33943	.00	.0449	.0449	139	7152
3	32600	.0420	.0342	.0363	28855	36007
11	32301	.0560	.0327	.0360	3533	39540
	32304	.0230	.0327	.0358	2532	42072
	32500	.0360	.0327	.0355	4873	46945
	32570	.0120	.0327	.0354	2312	49257
	32601	.0330	.0327	.0350	7826	57083
	33030	.0120	.0327	.0348	5564	62647
13	32211	.0240	.0246	.0291	6134	222185
	32303	.0160	.0246	.0290	4243	226428
	32561	.0330	.0246	.0289	1203	227631
	32701	.0140	.0246	.0289	2038	229669
	32751	.0140	.0246	.0288	3379	233048
	32786	.00	.0246	.0288	229	233277
	32789	.0170	.0246	.0287	7543	240820
	33511	.0370	.0246	.0287	2115	242935
10	33900	.0210	.0206	.0255	53503	511276
37	33062	.0170	.0111	.0198	6834	1234153
	33140	.00	.0111	.0198	56	1234209
	33154	.0060	.0111	.0198	3120	1237329
	33160	.0130	.0111	.0197	16354	1253683
	33306	.0100	.0111	.0197	986	1254669
30	33064	.0210	.0076	.0196	8210	1262870
	33516	.00	.0076	.1095	11202	1274072
	33570	.0090	.0076	.0195	3190	1277262

CASE STUDY: Benefiting from Predictive Modeling with Databases *(continued)*

RESULTS

Because the overall response to this offer is double the break-even requirement for the acquisition of new customers, the travel company decides to validate its research. Six months after the first offer, the entire list is remailed, rank-ordered in quintiles of response as predicted from regression analysis. As expected, the overall response drops to about half that of the first effort. What is important, however, is that the relationship (response rate indices) of the quintiles are virtually the same for both efforts, as detailed in Exhibit 21–6.

EXHIBIT 21–6

Response Rate Indices for Each Quintile

Rank Ordered Quintile	No. of Pieces Mailed	First Effort Response (%)	First Effort Index	Second Effort Response (%)	Secomd Effort Index
1	242,935	2.87%	147	1.36%	143
2	268,341	2.26	116	1.08	111
3	230,592	1.94	99	0.96	99
4	290,001	1.54	79	0.81	84
5	245,393	1.19	61	0.67	67

PILOT PROJECT   An important modeling application is predicting attrition or churn. Credit card companies need to identify customers least likely to renew before the annual fee cycle. Long-distance and wireless phone companies want to identify customers who are most likely to switch, and to determine when they will switch.

You have been asked to help a wireless company develop an attrition model. This company has enjoyed a net customer growth rate of 40 percent annually. Its net revenue is $200 million annually and it has approximately 400,000 customers. The customer attrition (churn) rate is 2.5 percent per month or 30 percent annually; however, only 60 percent of total attrition is voluntary.

How much net revenue does this company lose annually to total churn? How much is each reversible churn point worth to them? How many customers does it lose through voluntary churn? If the company was able to reduce total churn by 5 points per year (from 30 percent to 25 percent), how much additional revenue would it generate? What additional information would you need to create an attrition model for this company?

Key Points

▶ Modeling enables marketers to simplify and see clearly what is going on in its customer campaigns. Using modeling, marketers can identify "best" customers from a 10-million-name database and present their conclusions in visual, easy-to-understand graphs or charts. Comparing customer characteristics provides insight into what made the difference between responding and not responding—an important first step in designing contact strategies that enhance the lifetime value of a customer.

▶ Modeling permits marketers to test a large number of variables and discover which has the greatest impact. Modeling compares one *dependent variable* (the behavior being analyzed—the factor you want to be able to predict or forecast) against any number of *independent variables* (what you know about the customer, or what you can observe). The use of multiple variables is known as multivariate analysis. The key to regularly improving models is regularly improving the variables.

▶ Because modeling can reduce the number of those contacted and increase response rates, it is worth every dollar of its cost. It helps correct the leading problem in direct marketing: mailing people who don't want your mail and calling people who don't want your calls. Modeling brings an organization closer to the people who *do* want to receive your mail and calls. Do not let the high cost of modeling keep you from investing in a technique that will improve your organization's profitability more than any other tool.

MATHEMATICS OF
DIRECT MARKETING

We are indebted to the late Bob Kestnbaum, founder of Kestnbaum & Company, and to Pamela Ames, his vice president of many years, for this chapter. For many years the Kestnbaum organization serviced all the major general mail-order houses, leading specialty firms like L.L. Bean and Bear Creek, and telephone companies, banks and insurance companies, automotive manufacturers, and major airlines.

The mathematics of direct marketing is a high-tension web of interacting revenues and costs supported by three strands: sales, marketing cost, and contribution to marketing cost and profit. There is no single balance of the strands that is right for all direct marketing businesses, but similar threads exist in all direct marketing programs. Marketers need to learn the elements in general, quantify them for their specific situation, and then determine which can be tuned to create a stronger business (See Exhibit 22–1).

The unique ability to track and measure results of specific marketing decisions supports a high level of analysis. The belief that the future will be somewhat similar to the past supports reasonable forecasting of the probable results from marketing decisions. The availability of individual specific databases, computers, and statistics supports differential marketing investment at the customer level.

The challenge for marketers is to identify, evaluate, and respond to the vast amount of available marketing information without drowning in the flow. The decision to spend marketing money is applied at the individual customer level, but in actuality, the marketer usually keeps the number of decisions within reason by identifying groups of customers with similar propensities to buy. The marketer never bets on an individual's buying behavior, but willingly bets on the combined buying behavior of sets of people, usually thousands at a time.

EXHIBIT 22-1

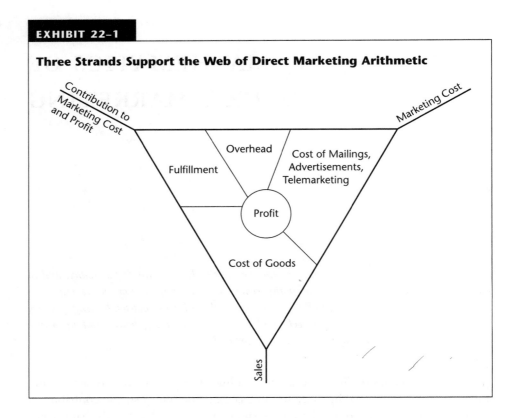

Three Strands Support the Web of Direct Marketing Arithmetic

Single Transaction Costs and Contribution to Marketing Costs and Profit

A convenient starting point for understanding any direct marketing activity is to determine the amount of money from a single transaction that is available for marketing cost and profit after direct costs associated with the transaction are subtracted. This entails working with averages, cost allocations, and the cost structure of the full business. These direct costs are known before marketing decisions and are often relatively stable over long periods. If different marketing programs have different average transaction sizes and cost structures associated with them, then each must be analyzed separately.

At a very high level, the direct costs can be classified into three categories: merchandise or service, fulfillment, and direct overhead. The merchandise or service costs should include all expenses and staffing related to purchasing, making, transporting, and storing the product(s) or service(s) being sold. Fulfillment costs should include all costs and people related to processing, filling, and delivering an order. Such diverse items as customer service, bad debt, costs of returns and exchanges, and charges for payment by credit card are usually included in fulfillment. Direct overhead can include costs associated with computer services, finance/accounting, office space, and a charge for some management staff.

Exhibit 22–2 shows a very simple example of this idea. This company has two quite different offers with average transaction sizes of $50 and $80. We chose to treat shipping and handling (S&H) charges paid by the customer as an offset to fulfillment costs. Some companies list shipping and handling revenues as other income that would increase both the average order and the fulfillment costs but not change the contribution to marketing costs and profit. However, all of the percentages would change. Notice in Exhibit 22–2 that the fulfillment cost of $6 is the same for both orders. If the nature of transactions in a given business is reasonably similar, fulfillment tends to be a constant cost per transaction.

As a reminder that this is a very high-level view, Exhibit 22–3 shows a possible breakdown of this $6 fulfillment cost. Even this list is simplified, but it shows that considerable analysis can be applied to determine reasonable values for each of the direct cost elements. Usually companies perform these analyses over a long time, as much as a year. If there is strong seasonality to the business, calculate separately for seasons.

It might seem strange to exclude all marketing costs from these calculations, but the goal is to understand the share of revenue committed to "fulfilling the promise" if a customer makes a purchase. These costs are relatively fixed, predictable, and stable. The revenue remaining after covering these direct costs can be applied to paying marketing costs and obtaining some profit. Exhibit 22–4 shows how this approach divides revenue into these direct costs and the contribution to marketing cost and profit.

Marketing Costs

In direct marketing, the costs of placing advertisements, making mailings, or selling by telephone are really selling expenses rather than advertising. The messages,

---

EXHIBIT 22–2

Contribution to Marketing Cost and Profit

	Offer A	Offer B
Average transaction (goods only, no S&H)	$50.00	$80.00
Cost of goods	20.00 (40.0%)	36.00 (45.0%)
Fulfillment (after S&H revenue offset)	6.00 (12.0%)	6.00 (7.5%)
Overhead	5.00 (10.0%)	8.00 (10.0%)
Contribution to marketing cost and profit	$19.00 (38.0%)	$30.00 (37.5%)

EXHIBIT 22–3

Cost Detail for Fulfillment of Transaction During Fall Season

Cost Center	Assumptions	Cost per Transaction
Transaction processing	All transactions	$3.53
Inbound phone	70% of transactions at $3.50/call	2.45
Credit card discount	75% of transactions at 2.5%/transaction	1.65
Customer service	6% of transactions at $8/case	0.48
Returns and exchanges	3% of transactions at $15/case	0.45
Collections and bad debt	0.5% of transactions at $88/case	0.44
Pick and pack	All transactions	1.75
Postage	All transactions	2.91
Management	All transactions	0.09
S&H revenue	All transactions	– 7.75
Net cost per transaction		$6.00

EXHIBIT 22–4

Where the Dollars Go

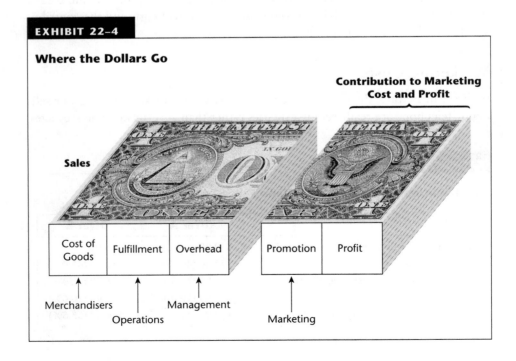

delivered by the chosen media, are the salespeople of direct marketing. Referred to as marketing costs, they are highly controllable. Very importantly, they are committed to a given program before any sales are obtained.

When catalogs or other mailed materials are used, it is customary to express costs on the basis of each thousand pieces mailed (CPM) or otherwise distributed. When an advertisement is placed in a magazine or electronic medium, the cost of each advertising appearance or group of appearances is used. Telemarketers usually work with cost per completed call.

Often it is advisable to test variations in advertisements and/or mailing packages. Because variations are tested in small quantities, extra costs are incurred for printing and additional creative efforts. It would be misleading to include these one-time extra costs as part of the regular profitability calculation. It is generally preferable to include the added costs of creative and small printing quantities associated with testing as a budgeted part of overhead expense.

Evaluation of potential profitability of a total direct marketing effort should be computed on the basis of marketing costs one expects to encounter in an ongoing larger-scale program of the size normally conducted in the business.

Exhibit 22–5 provides a simplified marketing cost worksheet for a multi-channel marketer showing how traditional direct marketers think in costs per thousand people contacted as well as total costs of the program. Some traditional direct marketers choose to think in terms of $0.55 per name contacted instead of $550 per thousand contacts, but many prefer thinking in "units" of one thousand.

EXHIBIT 22–5

Marketing Cost Worksheet

	Quantity	Cost	Cost per 1,000
Catalog	500	$110,000	$220
Transaction form	500	16,000	32
List unduplication	600	4,200	7
Address/mail	500	12,000	24
Postage	500	115,000	230
Creative/testing/overhead		16,000	32
		$273,200	$545
House list preparation	150	750	5
Rented names	450	45,000	100
		$318,950	

Total cost per thousand house names, $550; rented names, $645

Several items are interesting to note: 600,000 names were processed to obtain 500,000 contacts; creative, testing, and the cost of the marketing department staff are carried as a lump sum, possibly a budget line item. Two sharply different promotion costs are computed to account for whether the name was owned or rented.

Response Rate

Once you know the promotion costs and the contribution to marketing costs and profit associated with each transaction, you can calculate the response rate required to achieve a given level of profitability. Think of the promotion costs as the money invested at the beginning of the program, and the contribution per transaction multiplied by the number of transactions as the return on that investment.

Using the current examples, one question for Offer B from Exhibit 22–6 might be how many net transactions contributing $30 each are needed to recover marketing costs of $550 per thousand? The answer, shown in Exhibit 22–6, is 550/30 or 18.33, a 1.83 percent net response with product sales of $1,467 per thousand contacted (18.33 × 80). For Offer A, how many completed transactions contributing $19 each are needed to recover marketing costs of $550 per thousand? The answer is 550/19 or 28.95, a 2.90 percent net response with product sales of $1,447 per thousand contacted (28.95 × 50).

However, these calculations merely break even, the sales needed to cover selling costs but make zero profit. If the goal were 10 percent pretax profit, we must

---

EXHIBIT 22–6

Break-Even to a Goal

	Offer A (Zero Profit)	Offer A (10% Profit)	Offer B (Zero Profit)	Offer B (10% Profit)
House transactions				
Response percentage	2.90%	3.93%	1.83%	2.50%
Average transaction	$50	$50	$80	$80
Sales per 1,000	1,447	1,964	1,467	2,000
Contribution per 1,000				
(38%, 37.5%)	550	746	550	750
Promotion cost per 1,000	550	550	550	550
Profit		196		200
Rental transactions				
Response percentage	3.39%	4.61%	2.15%	2.93%
Average transaction	$50	$50	$80	$80
Sales per 1,000	1,697	2,304	1,720	2,345
Contribution per 1,000				
(38 %, 37.5%)	645	875	645	880
Promotion cost per 1,000	645	645	645	645
Profit		230		235

set aside the target profit, and use the remainder of contribution to cover marketing cost. For the $80 transaction, a 10 percent profit target of $8 must be deducted from contribution. The questions would become how many transactions contributing $22 ($30 − $8) or $14 ($19 − $5) each are needed to recover marketing costs of $550 per thousand.

Note that these calculations are based on completed transactions or net revenue. If returns are 5 percent of gross orders, each of the preceding answers would need to be divided by 1 − (5/95), or 0.947. Also, these sales per thousand are product revenues, which are less than the total revenue received when shipping and handling are included.

Key Performance Indicators

There are two types of numbers: measures of heft, and measures of rate. Measures of heft use a single measure such as contacts, orders, revenue, direct costs, marketing costs, or profit. Measures of rate are the quotient of two measures, often two heft measures: response percent means orders per hundred contacts or orders divided by contacts times 100, while average order size means dollars per order or total revenue divided by total orders.

Hefts provide the size of the endeavor and are treasured by finance, but rates provide comparisons to other marketing efforts and are treasured by marketers. However, Return on Marketing Investment, ROMI, which is profit divided by marketing costs, is highly valued by all.

Unfortunately, there is no standardized list of direct marketing measures, and most players pride themselves on creating acronyms. One company has a "dictionary" of more than 75 measures, such as CPO, CPM, OPM, that it provides to new employees. The way to understand the key performance indicators of any business is to translate to words you understand; and remember that "per" means divide.

Setting the Marketing Investment

Long-Term or Lifetime Value of a Customer

In a typical direct marketing business, 40 to 60 percent of customers who buy once will purchase again. Some two-time buyers will buy a third time and so on. The first transaction should be the beginning of a long-term, repeat buying relationship for many customers. The greater the average value of new customers acquired, the more a company should be willing to spend to acquire those customers so as to reap future revenues and profits from the repurchases. This concept is known as the long-term or lifetime value of a customer (LTV).

The LTV of a new customer is the net present value of all future revenues minus all attributable costs that are associated with an average customer. Note that it is based on profits, not revenue. A discount factor is used to recognize that money earned in the future is worth less than money earned today. Some offspring of the LTV idea are the remaining value of an established customer and the value of a reactivated dormant customer. Also, some businesses are trying to estimate different LTVs for groups of customers such as inquirers or rented names or buyers with high-dollar first orders.

If profit or loss earned on the first purchase is excluded from the long-term value calculation, the net of the first transaction can be thought of as the acquisition investment. Future purchases begin to offset that investment and contribute to the long-term value.

Marketing contacts have the single greatest impact on LTV: too few contacts will lower LTV, but too many will lower it even faster.

LTV can be estimated by extrapolating current customer performance under "business as usual" assumptions. There are numerous approaches to estimating LTV, which probably suggests that there is no one "right" way. Most approaches eventually derive a table like the one shown in Exhibit 22–7. Notice how the same principles that have already been developed are used, except now the numbers represent multiple contacts over multiple years.

The LTV calculation is based on all activity from a group of new customers subsequent to their acquisition. Because fewer and fewer customers buy in each

EXHIBIT 22–7

Six-Year Value of 1,000 New Buyers

	Year 1	Year 2	Year 3	Year 4	Year 5	Year 6
Purchase transactions	279	233	168	132	100	79
Average transaction size	$51.22	$51.35	$51.60	$51.75	$52.01	$52.06
Gross product sales	$14,296	$11,940	$8,659	$6,834	$5,200	$4,101
Returns	572	478	346	273	208	164
Net sales	13,724	11,462	8,313	6,561	4,992	3,937
Merchandise costs	6,213	5,189	3,763	2,970	2,260	1,783
Operating costs	1,381	1,153	836	660	502	396
Overhead	2,041	1,704	1,236	975	742	586
Contribution	4,089	3,416	2,477	1,956	1,488	1,172
Selling cost	2,687	2,608	1,799	1,495	1,146	911
List rental income	311	111	84	65	50	39
Cash flow	1,713	919	762	526	392	300
Discounted at 15 percent	1,490	695	501	301	195	130
Cumulative present value	1,490	2,184	2,685	2,986	3,181	3,311
Discounted at 25 percent	1,370	588	390	215	128	79
Cumulative present value	1,370	1,959	2,349	2,564	2,693	2,771

succeeding year, sales decline each year, even if remaining customers increase their purchases. In this example, the LTV is $8.73 per new customer if profits are discounted at 15 percent, or $7.05 if a 25 percent discount factor is used. If another year were added, the LTV would increase by less than $0.50. The combination of customer attrition and the effect of discounting make it meaningless in most businesses to carry out the calculation for more than 5–7 years. That is why some prefer the description *long-term value* over *lifetime value*.

If a business can develop an estimated LTV for new customers, this can be used to establish how much to spend on acquiring them. Given the uncertainty of the future, and the ability to do "business as usual," many companies prefer to invest only 30 to 40 percent of the expected LTV in acquisition, or to apply a 25 to 30 percent hurdle rate as a discount. Either way, LTV is primarily used to help set an allowable cost or loss for acquiring customers and quantify the return on that investment. It also can be used to estimate the value of a current house file and to set an appropriate level of ongoing marketing expense.

Customer Groups and Targeting Within Customer Groups

One key to successful contact planning is divide and conquer. That is, potential buyers should be separated into large groups with similar marketing potential. Each of these groups would be evaluated separately. For example, past buyers can be separated into one-time and multi-buyers, and rental lists can be grouped by list categories. This supports marketing contact decisions at a finer level.

Buying potential within each group can be further differentiated using RFM or statistical models that estimate likelihood of purchase from a given contact. Based on historic buying rates and patterns, these estimates need to be adjusted for changes in the offer, the competition, or the economy.

The goal is to forecast buying levels and resulting profitability in order to identify which customers or potential customers to contact, given specific marketing goals. The aim is to create a hierarchy of expectations, establish profitability at each level, and find the "margin," the weakest set of people who should be contacted. Exhibits 22–8 and 22–9 provide examples of estimated performance for representative groups, but they do NOT make the contact decision.

Contact Goals

The contact decision must be made relative to established business goals. These should vary by group and should provide not only desired performance on average, but also desired performance at the margin. The most difficult and most important goals are those that state profitability of the weakest cells you elect to contact. If the worst cell contacted breaks even, the whole program will be profitable.

EXHIBIT 22–8

Historic Performance for Onetime Buyers

Recency of Last Purchase	Response Percentage	Sales per 1,000	Profit per Buyer at Promotion Costs of		
			$450/K	$500/K	$550/K
Less than 6 months	4.2%	$2,520	$9.09	$7.90	$6.70
6–12 months	3.5	1,995	5.95	4.52	3.10
12–24 months	2.4	1,248	– 1.59	3.67	– 5.76
24–36 months	1.8	900	– 8.50	– 11.28	– 14.06
36–48 months	1.2	564	– 21.99	– 26.16	– 30.32
48+ months	0.9	405	– 35.15	– 40.71	– 46.26

However, even if the poorest cell contacted shows a loss, the whole program still could be highly profitable.

Depending on overall business needs, it is reasonable to set different marginal goals at different times. When near-term profit is crucial, the goals can be set very high. When volume, expansion, and growth are important, the marginal goals can be lowered as the business elects to invest in the future. This could entail acquiring new customers as well as reactivating stagnant customers, both at a short-term loss.

Exhibit 22–10 provides a simplified mail plan that uses the three key strands of promotion cost, purchase size, and single-order contribution to marketing cost and profit, plus marginal profit-per-buyer goals to establish minimal performance

EXHIBIT 22–9

Historic Performance for Rental List 506

Select	Response Percentage	Sales per 1,000	Profit per Buyer at Promotion Costs of		
			$550/K	$600/K	$650/K
Buyers in the last 3 months	2.8%	$1,596	– $0.83	– $2.62	– $4.40
4–12-month multibuyers	3.5	1,995	3.10	1.67	0.24
12–24-month multibuyers	2.1	1,092	– 9.03	– 11.41	– 13.79
4–12-month single buyers	2.6	1,482	– 2.34	– 4.27	– 6.19
12–24-month single buyers	1.7	884	– 15.19	– 18.13	– 21.08

EXHIBIT 22–10

Sample Mail Plan

	Promotion Cost/K	Average Transaction	Contribution Percentage	Goals for Marginal Profit/Buyer	Required to Reach Marginal Goal	
					Sales/K	Response
House file						
Big spenders	$400	$100	33%	– $5	$1,052	1.05%
Middlers	400	75	33	– 2	1,121	1.50
Pikers	400	50	33	0	1,212	2.42
Inquirers	400	60	33	– 3	1,053	1.75
External lists						
MO rental	525	75	33	– 5	1,324	1.76
Subscribers	475	60	33	– 4	1,197	2.00
Compiled	450	50	33	– 3	1,154	2.31

to meet the goals. Considering the interactions of these multiple elements, the required purchase rate from the "last" or marginal cells varies from barely 1 percent to more than 2.4 percent, while the sales per thousand varies within a much tighter band. Can you imagine some of the thinking that went into establishing these groups, and setting such varied goals? Can you believe that each group has been differentiated so that only those customers and prospects who might be expected to meet the minimal standards could be chosen for contact?

Continuous Revenue Relationships

All of the discussion so far assumes you have a good estimate of the revenue from an initial response. However, the fastest-growing area within database marketing involves companies who establish an ongoing revenue stream from the first response. When someone chooses a long-distance phone service provider, the revenue or "transaction size" will be the sum of a continuous revenue stream that extends over an unknown time frame. Insurance and investment companies, Internet access providers, banks, utilities, credit card companies, cable TV providers, and music or books or coffee continuities all have continuous revenue relationships rather than single-order relationships: the initial join or enrollment creates a multiple-payment revenue stream without the necessity of further marketing contacts.

Continuous revenue programs can be quantified using the principles established in this chapter, but estimating the average revenue and the contribution to marketing cost and profit becomes much more difficult. Retention and level of spending combine to set the revenue, with the unfortunate fact that often those who spend the most leave the soonest. Direct costs often are hard to quantify at the individual customer level and that makes contribution to marketing cost and profit a soft number.

The dynamics of continuous revenue relationships are such that, while each payment may be small, on average the total revenue from one customer is high. This usually justifies spending much larger amounts to acquire the customer, including sweeteners and signing bonuses. This marketing investment is spent up-front, but the revenue comes in over many months. If retention and/or revenue are overestimated, it is easy to make poor marketing judgements—but greater reward is definitely associated with the greater risk.

Inquiry Conversion Programs

Previous examples in this chapter have assumed that the first transaction is a purchase triggered by advertisements or direct contacts. Sometimes the difficulty in targeting possible buyers makes it more profitable to generate inquiries using various low-cost methods and then convert those inquiries into buyers by using one or more mailings, telephone calls, and/or sales visits. This usually is advantageous when selling high-ticket items, when prospects need pre-qualification or cultivation, when personal contact is needed to close the sale, or when the same inquirers become good prospects for multiple additional offers.

Inquiries can be generated through any channel available to a marketer. For example, if an advertisement costing $5,000 placed in a magazine produces 1,000 inquiries, the cost per inquiry would be $5. In addition, there will be a cost of perhaps $75 per thousand to process inquiries into a computer file. This processing should be done promptly, and the promotion activity taken immediately, because all studies have shown that the sooner the response to an inquiry is received, the higher is the likelihood of response.

Varying the media, kinds of advertisements, appeals, and offers will affect the cost of generating inquiries and possibly the rate at which they convert to buyers. Typically, the more highly qualified an inquiry, the more costly it will be to generate, but the higher the conversion rate will be. The thoughtful marketer will experiment continuously with various ways of producing inquiries and various means of converting them to fine-tune a program and to maximize profits.

The marketer has the right to repromote inquiries, and most companies find that an inquiry list will support repeated conversion contacts. There will be a fall-off in response to each successive effort, but it is profitable to continue making conversion contacts until the incremental cost of the last one is greater than the contribution it generates.

Exhibit 22–11 shows a typical set of inquiry conversion results when multiple contacts are used. The costs of acquiring the inquiry and making repeated

EXHIBIT 22–11

Inquiry Conversion with Multiple Follow-up Contracts

	Inquiry Acquisition Cost	Contact #1	Contact #2	Contact #3	Contact #4	Total Program
Quantity mailed		$1,000	940	912	898	3,750
Response percentage		6.0%	3.0%	1.5%	0.6%	2.9%
Net transactions		60	28	14	5	107
Net sales		$9,000	$4,200	$2,100	$750	$16,050
Contribution		3,600	1,680	840	300	6,420
Selling cost	$5,075	400	376	365	359	6,575
Profit	– 5,075	3,200	1,304	475	– 59	– 155
Cumulative profit	– 5,075	– 1,875	– 571	– 96	– 155	
Cumulative profit per buyer		– 31.25	– 6.49	– 0.94	– 1.45	

conversion efforts are the marketing investment. As inquirers are converted to buyers, the quantity available for subsequent contacts goes down. The likelihood of response goes down very quickly as the best prospects are captured and removed from the group. The true measure of performance is the cumulative cost and profit associated with the series of contacts including acquisition costs. Did they go one contact too far here, should they go one more, or did they do it just right?

Engineering a Direct Marketing Business

Spreadsheet-based computer models can be used to simulate a direct marketing business quite accurately. Usually these use monthly time frames and spread both response and costs so that the final model provides a reasonable set of expectations for cash flow. Many companies have found these extremely useful for long-term planning and identifying the profit sensitivity to key parameters.

In addition, these models can be used to assess the consequences of changes in strategy or policy. Exhibit 22–12 illustrates the impact on return on investment of the pursuit of three different strategies to build a catalog mail-order business. The model assumes the same amount of money is invested in each strategy. The strategies are to:

1. Mail more catalogs to rented lists to acquire more customers.

2. Expand the catalogs by adding more products and increasing the number of pages.

3. Create an extra catalog to be mailed to better customers during the fall season.

EXHIBIT 22–12

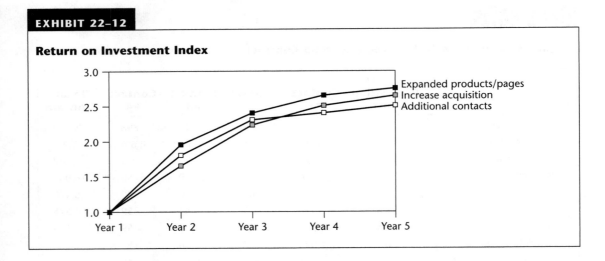

Return on Investment Index

Over the five-year horizon for which results are simulated, the company in question would invest most advantageously in expanding its product line. Notice, however, that the customer acquisition strategy appears to be closing the gap quickly at the end of the period and might be expected to outperform the product line expansion strategy in the sixth or seventh year. Further study might indicate that this particular company could blend the two approaches by expanding the size of some of its catalogs and also increasing its customer acquisition.

This example underscores the fact that direct marketing is accountable marketing where the impact of specific marketing actions can be estimated, tested, and evaluated. If the marketer is willing, able, and persistent, the potential exists to understand the impact of decisions and make significant, measurable contributions to the profitability of the business. The web of interacting costs and profit drivers is remarkably resilient, rebounding and adjusting to small pressures. Sharp blows or inordinate forces can cause great damage, but the web glistens in the morning dew and has singular attractive powers.

CASE STUDY: The Dressing Under Duress Society or DUDS

BACKGROUND
A space ad program with a circulation of 90,000 offered a Funky Furzy shirt for $17.95 plus $5.95 shipping and handling. The ad cost $8,000; a total of 1,412 shirts were sold. Each order was for one shirt and no shirts were returned. The company uses shipping and handling as an offset to fulfillment and as a contribution to marketing cost and a profit of 34 percent.

CHALLENGE
Prepare a presentation for upper management that fully quantifies the results, explains what was learned by the effort, and suggests the future opportunities supported by your analysis.

SOLUTION
Many numbers can and should be calculated: total product sales, total revenue, and total profit. Others

are quite uninformative, such as sales per thousand circulated or ad cost per thousand circulated.

The most important numbers are the acquisition of space ad buyer names at a profit of 44 cents each, and a ROMI of 7.7 percent over a very short time frame. You are challenged to derive these two numbers.

DUDS is able to acquire new buyers at a profit, at least in this one publication using this particular product. This is unusual in today's world when new buyers are usually acquired at a loss. Any time it can be repeated with similar results, there are no reasons not to do so.

As for future opportunities, the results suggest a series of tests to expand this small program. The small circulation suggests a specialty media; so,

there may be opportunities to seek new buyers at a profit in similar specialty media using the same product. Given natural wear-out of a product, it is important to test other products within the same publication to establish a group of profitable space ad products if possible. These other products should test the boundaries of price point as well as product type.

Finally, there is a need to promote these space ad buyers with other direct programs to see if they will become profitable repurchasers from other programs. This single, small, but successful program can serve as a springboard to a host of spin-offs where results may not be quite so rosy but the sheer quantity of programs will begin to create some business heft.

PILOT PROJECT

1. A test mailing of 15,000 pieces with a total promotion cost of $4,500 generated $13,500 net sales. The average order size was $50, and each order contributed $20 to promotion costs and profit after paying for the cost of goods, fulfillment, and an overhead allocation. Compute the following:

- Total orders
- Total contribution
- Total profit
- Profit as percentage of net sales
- Response percentage

- Orders/thousand
- Promotion cost/thousand
- Contribution/thousand
- Profit/thousand

2. A company has the following cost profile:

Cost of goods	40.0 percent of net sales
Operating expenses	11.6 percent of net sales
Overhead expenses	14.4 percent of net sales

- What is the contribution to promotion costs and profit?
- Find the sales/thousand break-even if:

(a) Promotion cost is $425/thousand

(b) Promotion cost is $425/thousand and there is a targeted profit of 9 percent

3. A firm has two different methods by which it can generate average orders of $80 with a contribution to promotion costs and profit of $32. Complete the break-even analysis.

	MAGAZINE SPACE AD	SMALL CATALOG
Promotion cost/thousand		
Break-even:		
Orders/thousand		
Response percentage		
Sales/thousand		
Break-even given a 15 percent profit target:		
Orders/thousand		
Response percentage		
Sales/thousand		

Answers to Pilot Project

1a.	270	1g.	$300
1b.	$5,400	1h.	$360
1c.	$900	1i.	$60
1d.	6.67%	2a.	34% of net sales
1e.	1.80%	2b.	(1) $1,250
1f.	18	2c.	(2) $1,700

	MAGAZINE SPACE AD	SMALL CATALOG
Promotion cost/thousand	$12	$360
Break-even:		
Orders/thousand	0.375	11.25
Response percentage	0.0375%	1.125%
Sales/thousand	$30	$900
Break-even given a 15 percent profit target:		
Orders/thousand	0.6	18
Response percentage	0.06%	1.8%
Sales/thousand	48	$1,440

Key Point

▶ Direct marketing is accountable. The impact of specific marketing actions can be estimated, tested, and evaluated. By mastering the mathematical concepts in this chapter, a marketer can understand the impact of decisions and make significant, measurable contributions to the profitability of the business.

INNOVATION THROUGH CREATIVITY AND TESTING

"The more you test, the more profitable your direct mail will become . . ."

■ *David Ogilvy*

Traditional direct marketers are often able to create, validate, and improve on their ideas using two very different processes. One process is subjective and relies upon a number of techniques designed to inspire ideation. The other technique is objective and used to validate these ideas. Applying these two processes—*creativity* and *testing*—over and over again, marketers are able to achieve refinement and success in their campaigns.

Talking about creativity and testing together may seem odd. One relies upon right-brain thinking and the other left-brain thinking. Both are necessary to successfully apply the tools and techniques of direct marketing.

Creativity focuses on generating novel and useful ideas that are the solutions to problems, opportunities, and challenges. It relies upon divergent thinking, the ability to imagine original, diverse, and elaborate ideas. Creativity also relies upon convergent thinking. This has to do with appropriateness, the ability to evaluate, critique, and choose the best idea from a selection of ideas.

Testing can be thought of as extension of convergent thinking. Testing is a basis for developing real-world performance measures of creative ideas. It is a way to learn how the market votes regarding a new idea. This direct linkage is one of the things that make the practice of direct marketing unique. Using the tools and techniques of direct marketing, creative ideas that might not otherwise be considered can be tested and proven in the marketplace. Testing is still the best way to find true breakthroughs.

The never-ending quest for a breakthrough is motivated by fantastic payoff potential. When it was introduced in the 1930s, "Book-of-the-Month Club" was a breakthrough concept leading to billions of dollars in book sales. Amazon.com chose to go where no bookseller had gone before . . . to the Internet. Its success is well documented. There are many, many more.

Creativity and Being Creative

Anyone can be creative. What hinders most people from coming up with creative ideas is a belief that they are not creative. There is no empirical evidence that people are born creative. It is more a state of being than a gift. "Being creative" means overcoming the obstacles to creativity that are within each of us.

Obstacles to creative thinking include a fear of criticism, lack of confidence, and stress. Sometimes we may be too busy or have to deal with other issues. We may not allow enough time to relax and renew our mind and spirit. Or, we may have conflicting goals and objectives that keep us from focusing on creative solutions. Exercises and tools to stimulate creativity can help, but ultimately creativity stems from a point of view about an individual's self and abilities. The iconoclastic behavior of people cited as creative is likely a reflection on how they focus on solutions to problems, release pressure, and have the confidence to be "themselves."

Any organization can also be creative, but many choose not to be. There are two reasons that organizations fail to generate new ideas: (1) the tendency to "play it safe" to protect the bottom line, and (2) not enough way-out testing to lead to creative new breakthroughs.

But how does one develop breakthrough ideas? Are there specific techniques that can be applied? Yes.

Brainstorming

Brainstorming, first popularized in the 1950s by Alex Osborne of BBD&O, continues to be an effective method of finding new creative solutions to difficult problems. Brainstorming is part of a three-phase process:

1. Before starting, create an agenda and carefully define problem(s) in writing.

2. Set quotas for ideas and a time limit for each section of the agenda.

3. Review the house rules with participants before each brainstorming session.

Let us look at some rules for brainstorming, and then consider a few examples of breakthroughs that have emerged from the process.

Selecting a Leader

Select a leader and have him or her take all responsibility for contact with reality. Everyone else in the brainstorming meeting is to "think wild." In a brainstorming meeting, the leader plays a low-key role. It is important to avoid influencing the participants. The duties of the leader are as follows:

- To see that detailed notes are taken on all ideas expressed

- To see that the agenda and time schedule are followed

- To admonish any critical thinkers in the group—no negative thinking is allowed during the brainstorming session

- To see that the group takes time to "build up" each idea

- To keep all participants involved and contributing

House Rules During Brainstorming

1. Suspend all critical judgment of your own—or other people's—ideas. Don't ask yourself if this is a good idea or a bad idea. Accept it and rack your brain for ways to improve the concept.

2. Welcome freewheeling, off-the-wall thinking. Wild, crazy, funny, far-out ideas are important. Why? Ideas that are the most way out often shock us into a totally new viewpoint of the problem.

3. Quantity, not quality, is the objective during the brainstorm session. This sounds contradictory—it's not. Remember that every member of the group has been briefed on the problem in advance. You have a carefully planned agenda of material to cover. Consequently, your group is well directed toward the right problem. Therefore go for quantity in the idea session.

4. Build up each idea. Here's where most brainstorming sessions fail. They just collect ideas as fast as they come and let it go at that. The leaders should carefully slow the group down so they stop with each idea and help build it up. Enhance each idea, no matter how crazy or offbeat it seems.

It is the leader's responsibility to see that these four guidelines are adhered to in every meeting; but he or she should do this in a very low-key, informal manner. It is important that the leader not become a dominant authority figure in meetings.

When the session is over, then—and only then—use your normal, everyday judgment to logically select ideas with the most potential from all of the available alternatives.

Brainstorming Examples

Example 1. *The problem:* Insurance companies are not allowed to give free gifts as incentives for applying for an insurance policy. How can we offer a free gift and stay within the law? Sounds like an impossible problem, right? Wrong. Brainstorming participants broke through with a positive solution, a blockbuster.

The breakthrough: The brainstorming idea that hit pay dirt was to offer the free gift to everyone, whether they apply for the policy or not.

The result: A 38 percent increase in applications.

Example 2. *The problem*: How can we avoid paying postage for sending prizes to "no" entrants in an "everybody wins" sweepstakes? (Possible savings in postage to the marketer if the problem could be solved was about $250,000)

The breakthrough: We asked "no" entrants to provide a stamped, self-addressed envelope. We included a prize in the shipping carton for those who said "yes" (The USPS approved the requirement at the time).

The result: This was the most successful sweepstakes contest the sponsor ever conducted. The sponsor also enjoyed savings of $250,000 in postage.

Example 3. *The problem*: We have 36 competitors selling to schools. They all promise "prompt shipment" of their pompoms. How can we dramatize the fact that we ship our pompoms in 24 hours and thus capture the bulk of the market?

The breakthrough: We inserted a Jiffy Order Card in the catalog, in addition to the regular order form, featuring guaranteed shipment within 24 hours.

The result: Pompom sales increased 40 percent!

Example 4. *The problem*: As a leading agricultural chemical company, we manufacture both a corn herbicide and a corn insecticide. Each product has its own positioning in the farm market and each product has a different share of market in various geographic areas across the nation. How can new users for each product be won over from the competition?

The breakthrough: We created a combination rebate program. Because the ratio of herbicide to insecticide remains relatively constant regardless of order size, we offered a rebate on both products when purchased at the same time.

The result: A significant number of farmers who had planned to purchase the two products from different manufacturers took advantage of the rebate offer and purchased both products from the sponsor, with an average order of $25,000.

Creative Stimulators

The degree of truly creative output is directly related to two factors: (1) clear and specific definitions of problems to be solved, and (2) the right "atmosphere" for developing creative solutions. There are many tools and tricks used to stimulate creative thought in addition to brainstorming.

SCAMPER is one such method. It was designed for finding creative solutions for new products, consumer advertising, and many other general uses. SCAMPER is an acronym which stands for questions relating to the following:

Substitute
Combine
Add or **Ad**apt
Modify
Put to other uses
Eliminate
Reverse or **R**earrange

Frank Daniels, a former creative director with Stone & Adler, used a version of SCAMPER as an effective system for stimulating creative people to think about solutions for marketing products/services direct. This version uses many of the same points as SCAMPER, but adds points that recognize the need to balance creative solutions with the need to stimulate an immediate response.

The examples that follow were applied to Lanier Worldwide, Inc., a major provider of office equipment including copiers, fax machines, and dictating equipment. Creativity was being stimulated for promoting a mini-recorder, Lanier's Pocket Secretary. A key thought accompanies each of the stimulators as well as a series of questions designed to promote creative solutions.

S—Can We **Substitute**?

The major product benefit for a product is often so similar to major product benefits of competitive products that it is difficult for the consumer to perceive the difference. Substituting another theme, such as Avis did when the company changed its theme to "We Try Harder," can often establish a point of difference. These questions inspire participants to think in terms of substitution.

Key Thought. Substitute the familiar for another familiar theme for emphasis; substitute the unfamiliar for the familiar for emphasis.

- Can a well-known theme for another product be substituted for our theme, or can a well-known benefit for another product be substituted for our benefit?

- Can an incongruous situation be used to focus emphasis on our theme or benefits?

- Can a series of incongruous situations be found for every benefit we have? Can they be used in one ad? Can they form a continuity series of ads?

- What can be substituted for our product appeal that will emphasize the difference between us and our competitors?

- Can an obviously dissimilar object be substituted for the image of our product?

- Can a physical object be used to give more concrete representation of a product intangible?

- Is our product replacing a process rapidly becoming dated? Can we substitute the past for the present, or the future for the past or the present?

- Can we visualize our product where the competitor's product is normally expected to be?

- Can we visualize our product as the only one of its kind in the world, as if there were no substitutes for our product?

C—Can We **Combine**?

Combining two or more elements often results in new thought processes. The following questions are designed to encourage brainstorming participants to think in terms of combinations.

Key Thought. Combine appropriate parts of well-known things to emphasize the benefits of our product. "Think of owning a Rolls-Royce the size of a Volkswagen" (Lanier Pocket Secretary).

- What can be combined physically or conceptually to emphasize product benefits?

- Can the product be combined with another so that both benefit?

- Where in the product offer would a combination of thoughts be of most help?

- What opposites can be combined to show a difference from competitive products?

- What can we combine with our product to make it more fun to own, use, and look at?

- Can part of one of our benefits be combined with part of another to enhance both?

- Can newness be combined with tradition?

- Can a product benefit be combined with a specific audience need through visual devices? Copy devices?

- What can we combine from the advertising and sales program to the benefit of both? Can salespersons' efforts be combined into advertising?

- Can we demonstrate product advantages by using "misfit" combination demonstrations?

- Can we combine manufacturing information performance tests with advertising to demonstrate advantages?

A—Can We <u>Add</u> or <u>Adapt</u>

An axiom of selling is that the customer often unconsciously compares the added benefits of a competitor's product with those of your product. The product with the most added benefits traditionally sells better. These questions are designed to ferret out added benefits and adapt them for a particular product.

Key Thought. Look for ways to change the way that benefits are expressed by relating functional advantages of unrelated products or things. "We've taken all the best cassette recorder features and added one from the toaster" (pop-out delivery).

- What has been added to our product that is missing from others?

- Do we have a deficiency due to excess that can be turned into advantage?

- Is our product usable in many different ways aside from the intended use?

- Is our product instantly noticeable? Is it unusual in terms of size, shape, and color? What unrelated symbols can we use to emphasize this unique characteristic?

- Does our product make something easier? What have we added by taking this something away?

- Does our product make order out of chaos or meaningful chaos out of total chaos? What have we added by taking this something away?

- What does the purchase of our product add to the buyer's physical condition, mental condition, subconscious condition, present condition, and future condition?

- Where will the buyer be if he or she does not purchase? What will be missing from the buyer's life?

- Does our product give its full benefit to the buyer immediately, or does the buyer build up (add to) his or her well-being through continued possession?

M—Can We <u>Modify</u>: Are There Time Elements That Can Be Emphasized?

Saving time and having extra time are conventional human wants. This series of questions is designed to expand one's thinking toward making time a plus factor in the product offer.

Key Thought. Modify time factor(s) in present offer, present schedules, and present product positioning to motivate action.

- Does seasonal timing have an effect on individual benefits?
- Can present seasonal timing be reversed for special effect?
- Can limited offers be effective?
- Can early buyers be given special consideration?
- Can off-season offers be made?
- Are there better days, weeks, or months for our offers?
- Can we compress or extend present promotional sequencing?
- Can our price be keyed to selected times of the week, month, and year?
- Can we feature no-time-limit offers?
- Can we feature limited-time offers?
- Can we feature fast delivery or follow-up?

P—Can We <u>Put</u> to Other Uses?

Favorable associations are one way to show how products can be used in other ways. They are often the most effective way to emphasize product benefits. "Like sterling on silver," a classic example of a favorable association, is a comment that accrues to the benefit of the product being compared with other products.

Key Thought. Associate benefits with product usage and features, or lack thereof, to surprise and delight. Show and tell comfort and success as part of the product features and benefits.

- Form a link with unrelated things or situations to emphasize benefits.
- Can we link our product to another, already successful product to emphasize benefits?
- Can we appeal to popular history, literature, poetry, or art to emphasize benefits?

- What does the potential buyer associate with our product? How can we use this association to advantage?

- When does the potential buyer associate our product with potential use?

- Can associations be drawn with present or future events?

- Can associations be made with abstractions that can be expressed visually, musically, with words, and so forth?

- Can funny, corny, challenging associations be made?

- Can associations be made with suppliers of component parts?

- Is our product so unique that it needs no associations?

- Can our product be associated with many different situations?

E—Can We <u>Eliminate</u> or Simplify?

Taking away can often be as appealing as adding to. Less weight, less complexity, less fuss, less bother are fundamental appeals. These questions steer brainstorming participants in that direction.

Key Thought. Subtract from the obvious to focus attention on the benefits of our product or service. "We've weighed all the mini-recorders and made ours lighter."

- What deficiencies does our product have competitively?

- What advantages do we have?

- What features are the newest? The most unusual?

- How can our product use/cost be minimized over time?

- Can a buyer use less of another product if he or she buys ours?

- Can the evidence of total lack of desire for our product be used to illustrate its benefits?

- Can the limitations of our benefits be used as an appeal?

- What does lack of our product in the buyer's living habits do to him or her?

- Does our product offer a chance to eliminate any common element in all competitive products?

- Does our product reduce or eliminate (subtract) anything in the process of performing its work?

- Will our product deflate (subtract from) a problem for the buyers?

Can the product be simplified? What is the simple way to describe and illustrate our major product benefit? As sophisticated as our world is today, the truism persists that people relate best to simple things. These questions urge participants to state benefits with dramatic simplicity.

Key Thought. Dramatize benefits individually or collectively with childishly simple examples, symbols, images.

- Which of our appeals is strongest over our competition? How can we simplify to illustrate?

- Is there a way to simplify all benefits for emphasis?

- Where is most of the confusion about our product in the buyer's mind?

- Can we illustrate by simplification?

- Is our appeal abstract? Can we substitute simple, real visualizations to emphasize?

- Could a familiar quotation or picture be used to make our appeal more understandable?

- Is our product complex? Can we break it up (literally) into more understandable pieces to emphasize benefits?

- Can we overlap one benefit with another to make product utility more understandable?

- Can we contrast an old way of doing something with the confusing part of our product to create understanding?

- Is product appeal rigidly directed at too small a segment of the market? Too broad a segment?

- Can we emphasize benefits by having an unskilled person or child make good use of the product in a completely out-of-context situation?

R—Can We Make a <u>Reversal</u>?

The ordinary can become extraordinary as usual situations are reversed. A man wearing a tennis skirt. A woman wearing a football helmet. A trained bear pushing a power mower. These questions are designed to motivate participants to think in terms of reversing usual situations.

Key Thought. Emphasize a benefit by completely reversing the usual situation.

- What are the diametrically opposed situations for each of our product benefits?

- For each copy point already established, make a complete reverse statement.

- How would a totally uninformed person describe our product?

- Can male- and female-oriented roles be reversed?

- Can art and copy be totally reversed to emphasize a point?

- How many incongruous product situations can be shown graphically? Verbally?

- Can we find humor in the complete reversal of anticipated product uses or benefits?

Test the Big Things

Testing is one of the most important direct marketing techniques. The notion that creative, media, mailing lists, offers, etc., can all be tested to reduce marketers' risk is one of the greatest attractions of direct marketing. With the growth of online marketing and the ability to do real-time testing, the need to understand when and what to test has never been greater.

Whether testable ideas come out of pure research, brainstorming, or self-developed creativity, the same picture applies: test the big things. Trivia testing (e.g., the tilt of a postage stamp, the effects of various colors, one graphic versus another, etc.) is passé. Breakthroughs are possible only when you test the big things. Following are six big areas from which breakthroughs emerge:

1. The products or services you offer

2. The media you use (lists, print, broadcast, the Internet)

3. The propositions you make

4. The copy platforms you use

5. The formats you use

6. The timing you choose

Five of the areas for testing appear on most published lists these days. But testing new products and new product features is rarely recommended. Yet everything starts with the product or service you offer.

Many direct marketers religiously test new ads, new mailing packages, new media, new copy approaches, new formats, and new timing schedules season after season with never a thought to testing new product features. Finally, the most imaginative of creative approaches fails to overcome the waning appeal of the same old product, so still another product bites the dust.

This need not happen. For example, consider the most commonplace of mail order items, the address label. Scores of firms offer them in black ink on standard white stock. Competition is keen. Prices all run about the same. From this variety of competitive styles, however, a few emerge with new product features: gold stock, colored ink, seasonal borders, and so forth. Tests are made to determine appeal. The new product features appeal to a bigger audience.

As we consider our products, we should all ask ourselves these questions:

- Do we have products or services that have become obsolete?

- Is there a way to improve upon them?

- Is there a way to combine two ideas that already exist into something that hasn't already been thought of? (Gutenberg combined a die punch with a wine press, and ended up with the printing press).

Projectable Mailing Sample Sizes

Some direct marketers live by probability tables that tell the mailer what the sample size must be at various response levels within a specified error limit, such as 5 or 10 percent. No one argues the statistical validity of probability tables. Although probability tables can't be relied on too heavily because it is impossible to construct a truly scientific sample, such tables, within limits, can be helpful. Exhibit 23–1 is based on a 95 percent confidence level at various limits of error.

Testing Components vs. Testing Mailing Packages

In the endless search for breakthroughs, the question continually arises: in direct mail, should we test components or mailing packages? There are two schools of thought on this. The prevailing one is that the big breakthroughs come about through the testing of completely different mailing packages as opposed to testing individual components within a mailing package. Something can be learned from each procedure, of course. However, the more logical procedure is to first find the big difference in mailing packages and then follow with tests of individual components in the losing packages, which can often make the winning packages even better.

In package testing, one starts with a complete concept, and builds all components to fit the image of the concept. Consider the differences between two package concepts.

CONTENTS	PACKAGE ONE	PACKAGE TWO
Envelope	9 × 12 inches	No. 10
Letter	8 single-side pages, stapled, not personalized	4 double-side pages, personalized
Circular	None	4-page, illustrated
Order Form	8½ × 11 inches, perforated stub	8½ × 3½ inches

EXHIBIT 23–1

Test Sample Sizes Required for 95 percent Confidence Level for Mailing Response Levels from 0.1 Percent to 4.0 Percent

R (Response)	Limits of Error (Expressed as Percentage Points)														
	.02	.04	.06	.08	.10	.12	.14	.16	.18	.20	.30	.40	.50	.60	.70
.1	95,929	23,982	10,659	5,995	3,837	2,665	1,957	1,499	1,184	959	426	240	153	106	78
.2	191,666	47,916	21,296	11,979	7,667	5,324	3,911	2,994	2,366	1,917	852	479	307	213	156
.3	287,211	71,803	31,912	17,951	11,488	7,978	5,861	4,487	3,546	2,872	1,276	718	459	319	234
.4	382,564	95,641	42,507	23,910	15,303	10,627	7,807	5,977	4,723	3,826	1,700	956	612	425	312
.5	477,724	119,431	53,080	29,858	19,109	13,270	9,749	7,464	5,987	4,777	2,123	1,194	764	530	390
.6	572,693	143,173	63,632	35,793	22,908	15,908	11,687	8,948	7,070	5,727	2,545	1,432	916	636	467
.7	667,470	166,867	74,163	41,717	26,699	18,541	13,622	10,429	8,240	6,675	2,966	1,669	1,068	741	545
.8	762,054	190,514	84,673	47,628	30,482	21,168	15,552	11,907	9,408	7,621	3,387	1,905	1,219	847	622
.9	856,447	214,112	95,160	53,528	34,258	23,790	17,478	13,382	10,573	8,564	3,806	2,141	1,370	951	699
1.0	950,648	237,662	105,628	59,415	38,026	26,407	19,401	14,854	11,736	9,506	4,225	2,376	1,521	1,056	776
1.1	1,044,656	261,164	116,072	65,291	41,786	29,018	21,319	16,322	12,897	10,446	4,643	2,611	1,671	1,160	853
1.2	1,138,472	284,618	126,496	71,155	45,539	31,624	23,234	17,788	14,055	11,385	5,060	2,846	1,821	1,265	929
1.3	1,232,097	308,024	136,899	77,006	49,284	34,225	25,145	19,254	15,211	12,321	5,476	3,080	1,971	1,369	1,006
1.4	1,325,529	331,382	147,280	82,845	53,021	36,820	27,051	20,711	16,364	13,255	5,891	3,314	2,121	1,473	1,082
1.5	1,418,769	354,692	157,640	88,673	56,751	39,410	28,954	22,168	17,515	14,188	6,305	3,547	2,270	1,576	1,158
1.6	1,511,818	377,954	167,980	94,489	60,473	41,995	30,853	23,622	18,664	15,118	6,719	3,780	2,419	1,680	1,234
1.7	1,604,674	401,168	178,297	100,292	64,187	44,574	32,748	25,073	19,811	16,047	7,132	4,012	2,567	1,783	1,310
1.8	1,697,338	424,334	188,592	106,083	67,894	47,148	34,639	26,521	20,955	16,973	7,543	4,243	2,716	1,886	1,385
1.9	1,789,810	447,452	198,868	111,863	71,592	49,717	36,526	27,966	22,096	17,898	7,955	4,474	2,863	1,988	1,461
2.0	1,882,090	470,523	209,121	117,631	75,284	52,280	38,410	29,407	23,235	18,821	8,365	4,705	3,011	2,091	1,536

EXHIBIT 23–1

Test Sample Sizes Required for 95 percent Confidence Level for Mailing Response Levels from 0.1 Percent to 4.0 Percent *(continued)*

R (Response)	.02	.04	.06	.08	.10	.12	.14	.16	.18	.20	.30	.40	.50	.60	.70
					Limits of Error (Expressed as Percentage Points)										
2.1	1,974,178	493,544	219,352	123,386	78,967	54,838	40,289	30,846	24,372	19,742	8,774	4,935	3,158	2,193	1,611
2.2	2,066,074	516,518	229,564	129,129	82,643	57,391	42,165	32,282	25,507	20,661	9,182	5,165	3,306	2,295	1,686
2.3	2,157,778	539,444	239,753	134,861	86,311	59,938	44,036	33,715	26,638	21,578	9,590	5,394	3,452	2,397	1,761
2.4	2,249,290	562,322	249,920	140,581	89,972	62,480	45,903	35,145	27,769	22,493	9,997	5,623	3,599	2,499	1,836
2.5	2,340,609	585,152	260,068	146,288	93,624	65,017	47,767	36,572	28,896	23,406	10,403	5,851	3,745	2,600	1,911
2.6	2,431,737	607,934	270,192	151,983	97,269	67,547	49,627	37,996	30,021	24,317	10,807	6,079	3,891	2,702	1,985
2.7	2,522,673	630,668	280,296	157,667	100,907	70,074	51,483	39,416	31,144	25,227	11,211	6,307	4,036	2,803	2,059
2.8	2,613,416	653,354	290,380	163,339	104,537	72,595	53,335	40,834	32,264	26,134	11,615	6,534	4,181	2,904	2,133
2.9	2,703,968	675,922	300,440	168,998	108,159	75,110	55,183	42,249	33,382	27,039	12,017	6,760	4,326	3,004	2,207
3.0	2,794,328	698,582	310,480	174,645	111,773	77,620	57,026	43,661	34,497	27,943	12,419	6,986	4,471	3,105	2,281
3.1	2,884,495	721,124	320,499	180,281	115,380	80,125	58,867	45,070	35,611	28,845	12,820	7,211	4,615	3,205	2,355
3.2	2,974,470	743,618	330,496	185,904	118,979	82,623	60,702	46,476	36,721	29,745	13,220	7,436	4,759	3,305	2,428
3.3	3,064,254	766,063	340,471	191,516	122,570	85,118	62,535	47,878	37,830	30,642	13,619	7,660	4,903	3,404	2,501
3.4	3,153,845	788,461	350,427	197,115	126,154	87,607	64,364	49,278	38,936	31,538	14,017	7,884	5,046	3,504	2,574
3.5	3,243,244	810,811	360,360	202,703	129,730	90,089	66,188	50,675	40,040	32,432	14,414	8,108	5,189	3,603	2,647
3.6	3,332,452	833,113	370,271	208,278	133,298	92,568	68,009	52,069	41,141	33,325	14,811	8,331	5,332	3,702	2,720
3.7	3,421,467	855,367	380,163	213,842	136,859	95,041	69,825	53,460	42,240	34,214	15,207	8,554	5,474	3,801	2,793
3.8	3,510,290	877,572	390,031	219,393	140,412	97,507	71,638	54,848	43,336	35,103	15,601	8,776	5,616	3,900	2,865
3.9	3,598,921	899,730	399,878	224,932	143,957	99,969	73,446	56,233	44,430	35,989	15,995	8,997	5,758	3,988	2,938
4.0	3,687,360	921,840	409,706	230,460	147,494	102,426	75,252	57,615	45,522	36,874	16,388	9,218	5,900	4,097	3,010

The differences between these two package concepts are considerable. Chances are great that there will be a substantial difference in response. Once the winning package evolves, component tests make excellent sense. Let us say the 9 × 12 inch package is the winner. A logical subsequent test would be to fold the same inserts into a 6 × 9 inch envelope. A reply envelope could be considered as an additional test. Personalizing the first page of the eight-page letter could be still another test.

As described by many marketers, testing is a progressive art and science. With very precise tools and a good tracking management group and methods, it can help make the difference with marginal efforts more successful and with solid campaigns more profitable.

How to Test Print Advertising

For direct marketing practitioners who are multimedia users, testing print advertising is just as important as testing direct mail; and, as with direct mail, it is important that the tests be designed to produce valid results.

The split helps determine the relative strengths of different ads. For example, run two ads, A and B, in a specific issue or edition of a publication so that two portions of the total run are equally divided and identical in circulation. The only difference is that ad A will run in half of the issue and ad B will run in the other half.

For measuring the strength of the ads, a split includes an offer requiring the reader to act by writing or sending in a coupon. Then you simply compare the responses with the individual ads. If done properly, this A/B split method can be accurate to two decimal points. There is also the advantage of real-world testing to find out what people actually do, not just what they say they do. And, because all factors are held equal, the difference in results can be attributed directly to your advertising (See Exhibit 23–2). Although the A/B split can't tell you why individuals respond to your ad, the technique can tell you what they responded to.

EXHIBIT 23–2

Variations in the Uses of Splits

A/B Split	Clump Split	Flip-Flop Split
A	A	A
B	A	B
A	A	B
B	B	A
	B	
	B	

A real bonus is that when you have completed your tests, you'll have a list of solid prospects.

A/B Splits. In an ideal situation, an issue of a split-run publication will carry ad A in every other copy and ad B in the alternate copies.

Clump Splits. Most often, however, publications cannot produce an exact A/B split. They will promise a clump. That is, every lift of 50 copies, for instance, will be evenly split, or even every lift of 25 or 10. The clump can be very accurate when the test is done in large circulations.

Flip-Flops. For publications that offer no split at all, you can create your own. Take two comparable publications, X and Y. Run ad A in X and ad B in Y for the first phase. Then for the second phase, reverse the insertions: ad B in X and ad A in Y. Total the respective results for A and B and compare.

The Split That Is Not

We recently asked one magazine publisher if he ran splits. The production manager told us, "Oh, yes, we run a perfect split. Our circulation divides exactly—one-half east of the Mississippi and one-half west." Look out. That is not a valid split.

In the A/B split, how can you compare one run against another run of the same ad? Following are ideas for keying coupons or response copy:

- Dating. On your coupons, try JA320NA for January 3, 2006, in *Newsweek* for ad A and JA320NB for the same insertion of ad B.

- Department numbers. Use Dept. A for Ad A and Dept. B for Ad B in your company's address.

- Color of coupon. One color for ad A, another for ad B.

- Color of ink.

- Names. In ad A, ask readers to send correspondence to Mr. Anderson; for ad B, have them write to Mr. Brown.

- Telephone numbers

- Shape of coupon

- The obvious. Right on the coupon, use "For Readers of Glamour" in ad A and "For Glamour Readers" in ad B.

- Abbreviations. In your address, New York for ad A, N.Y. for ad B.

- Typeface. In coupon A, all caps for NAME and so forth, and in coupon B, upper and lowercase for Name and so on.

The possibilities are virtually unlimited. All you need is a code that is in keeping with your ad and the publication, one you find easy to understand and use.

Insert Cards

Testing the use of insert cards with print ads can also yield important results. Sometimes the card can be turned into a full-page card insert. This is another way to simultaneously test multiple ads in magazines. Scores of magazines now accept such inserts. This allows for many different ways to test offers and creative.

Testing Hypotheses in Print Ads

When testing ads in publications, marketers look for breakthroughs, not small differences. As Tom Collins, a pioneer in print ad testing, puts it, "We are not merely testing ads, we are testing hypotheses. Then, when a hypothesis appears to have been proved by the results, it is often possible to construct other, even more successful ads, on the same hypothesis."

Test hypotheses tend to fall into four main categories:

1. What is the best price and offer?

2. Who is the best prospect?

3. What is the most appealing product advantage?

4. What is the most important ultimate benefit? (e.g., pride, admiration, safety, wealth, peace of mind)

Testing Online

The growth of marketing online has added unique dimensions to testing. One of those dimensions is time. Marketers testing three banner ads, served in rotation, on high-volume Web sites can sometimes learn within a day how well each ad is doing. They can track which ad had the greatest click-through rate (CTR), what site the ad was clicked on, and what action the user took as a result of clicking. This can be compared to ad server logs, allowing for volumes of response data to be created for broad online campaigns.

Marketers can learn if one ad pulls better against the others on one Web site, one category of Web sites (e.g., portals, search sites, etc.), or across the board. They can modify or change an ad or ads and test new ads on the fly. The low production costs for online promotion allows for significant variations in testing and real-time adjustments of programs to improve results.

Marketers using direct mail might have to wait weeks for results. For print mail, the wait might be months. Television direct response marketers get fast feedback, similar to online methods. However, the high cost of TV production makes it unlikely that a marketer would revise two or three spots that didn't do well, and retest them without further research into why they didn't work (e.g., is it the creative, offer, spokesperson, product, etc.?).

Online testing is maturing well beyond the banner ad. Organizations are testing customer migration strategies to move established customers from expensive traditional marketing processes to online processes. National Semiconductor saved millions of dollars by moving product sell sheets to its E-commerce site rather than mailing out printed copies. More than 11,000 product sheets are downloaded every day on their Web site. With the potential savings of such magnitude, marketers will continue to test these methods.

According to MarketingExperiments.com, a marketer can use A/B split testing in an online environment to:

- Better understand visitor behaviors and priorities when visiting your site.

- Solve specific problems you have with your site pages. In other words, use it as a diagnostic tool to find out what is going wrong and how to fix it.

- Dramatically challenge assumptions you may have about the "best" way to design or write a page (Test not only changes in minor elements, but also complete and dramatic redesigns of an entire page).

Multivariable Testing

Over the past few years, technology, math, and science have combined to create a way of testing that is quicker, stealthier, cheaper, and more accurate. Multivariable testing matches with the realities of Web, e-mail, and multichannel marketing campaigns. It allows marketers to test dozens of new concepts and discrete value propositions concurrently. It is a technique important for traditional direct marketers to be aware of.

Multivariable testing, DOE, and the Taguchi Method are all based on the statistical field of "experimental design." It allows marketers to go beyond the traditional scientific method, which relies on controlled testing of one variable at a time. For example, an E-commerce marketer can use multivariable testing to determine how changing the mix of products, prices, placement, offers, headlines, body copy, banner ads, etc., on a landing page can improve the outcomes. An e-mail marketer or direct mailer can test different creative packages, copy, layout, elements within the mailing, incentives, prices, mailing lists, customer segments, etc.

Multivariable (experimental design) testing saves both time and money by using a mathematical shortcut that allows marketers to execute a few tests, and get much more information than they would get had they tested all possible combinations of variables. Those experienced with multivariable testing say that in general, results show that about 25 percent of variables tested help improve their marketing campaigns, 55 percent make no difference, and about 20 percent make things worse.

Multivariable tests can achieve the same results as split-run test, but with a larger number of variables, smaller sample sizes, and greater depth of insight.

In multivariable testing, marketers can view results of 2 to 35 variables in a single test, providing a dizzying array of results. In split-run tests, each variable must be tested with a single sample. In multivariable testing, the sample size remains the same, while a number of variables can be analyzed (hence multivariable). In multivariable tests, results describe the main effects of the test, comparative effects of variables, and interactions among variables. So, a marketer not only learns the discrete relationship of one variable to another, they can see the interactions among the many variables in the test.

Multivariable testing is an alternative to traditional single variable testing. It is not a one-size-fits-all solution. It is an advanced statistical concept, with many choices of test designs, statistical techniques, and strategies. It is a direct marketing technique well worth trying, but one that requires the help of people experienced in advanced statistical techniques.

Notes Gordon H. Bell, of LucidView,

Multivariable testing looks easy when done well. The key is developing skills with a variety of techniques, gaining experience in the unique challenges of every new application, and combining scientific expertise with marketing experience in order to maximize the return on every multivariable test.

Creativity and Testing, Not Creativity Versus Testing

For all of its strengths, testing answers only one part of the equation. It tells a marketer "what" works, not "why" it works. To learn "why" different techniques work requires the use of research. This will be discussed in Chapter 24 on research.

Idea development and testing are soulmates. When thought of together, the options are endless. These options are applicable when marketing to consumers, businesses, across product/service categories, and across media. The two things to keep uppermost in mind are: (1) strive for breakthrough ideas, and (2) test the big things.

| **CASE STUDY:** | **Direct Mail Subscriptions Tests** |

Contributed by Gordon H. Bell, President of LucidView based in Oak Ridge, TN.

BACKGROUND

Magazine publishers depend on direct mail to grow their subscriber base. But tight budgets and unresponsive consumers create a serious challenge:

how can one grow sales while mailing less? One marketer, with a limited budget, discovered a way to improve marketing ROI, but with greater speed, efficiency, and pinpoint accuracy. The key to the solution was testing using experimental design. This case study covers the six-step process that put subscriptions and marketing ROI to the ultimate test.

STEP 1: CREATIVE FREEDOM

After finding a direct mail program to focus on, a brainstorming session was scheduled. Starting with their control mail package—the mailing that had a high and consistent response rate over the years—the team brainstormed 63 changes that might increase response and profitability. Ideas included changes to the outer envelope, order form, letter, inserts, price, and offer.

STEP 2: SCIENTIFIC DISCIPLINE

The team narrowed the list to 11 direct mail elements, focusing on bold, independent, and actionable changes. They chose two levels to test for each. The "minus" level was usually the control. The "plus" level was a change that someone thought would increase response rate or reduce costs (See Exhibit 23–3).

A: Envelope color scheme. The creative group came up with new, brighter colors to use for the fonts and graphics. This new color palette was tested against the standard color scheme on the envelope.

B: Background graphic on envelope. The team wanted to add a product-related picture to catch the attention of their target readers. They decided to test a background graphic in a light shade on the right side of the main address window.

C: Second window. To provide a stronger enticement to open the envelope, they wanted to test a second window on the left side, showing the full-color magazine cover on the order form inside.

D: Expiration date display. As a way to encourage people to respond immediately, the team wanted the expiration date to stand out more clearly, so they created a larger envelope window that shows the expiration date above the recipient's name.

E: Teaser on envelope. The teaser—a short phrase on the outside of the envelope—currently focused on the low cost of the subscription. One copywriter thought that a benefits-focused message would be a stronger incentive to subscribe.

F: Starburst on envelope back. The back of the control envelope was fairly plain. The team

---

EXHIBIT 23–3

Test Elements, Control, and New Idea

Test Elements	(–) Control	(+) New Idea
A: Envelope color scheme	Control	New color palette
B: Background graphic on envelope	No	Yes
C: Second window	No	Yes, showing magazine cover
D: Expiration date display	Control	Show through envelope window
E: Teaser on envelope	Value message	Benefits message
F: Starburst on envelope back	No	Yes
G: Free gift buckslip	Yes	No
H: Lift note	Yes	No
I: Order form layout	Control	New layout
J: Letter length	Long	Short
K: Letter copy style	Control	New copy

decided to test a bright starburst with a brief call-to-action message, supporting the main message and graphics on the front and inside.

G: Free gift buckslip. The offer included a free gift with each paid subscription. The gift was mentioned in the letter and on the order form and described in detail on a full-color separate sheet of paper in the mailing (a "buckslip"). One marketing manager thought that eliminating the buckslip would have little impact on response and reduce printing costs.

H: Lift note. Control mailings included a small note from the editor explaining the special benefits of the magazine. This "lift note" did not cost as much as the buckslip, but the team wanted to know if it really helped response. They considered testing a different version of the lift note, but decided instead to test eliminating it.

I: Order form layout. The creative team often rearranged the information, words, and graphics on the order form in each mailing. With no solid data showing which layout was best, they selected two different versions to test.

J: Letter length. Most mailings were sent with a separate letter explaining the magazine and the offer. The team believed that a long letter gave prospects more information, but they wondered if a short letter might help speed the decision process.

K: Letter copy style. Along with length (J), the team wanted to test a new message and positioning. With two different lengths, the copywriter created a long and short version with the new copy style, plus a short version of the control letter.

STEP 3: STATISTICAL POWER

Using multivariable testing techniques, a 12-recipe test design was developed to simultaneously test all 11 elements in one mail drop. Each of the 12 versions included a unique combination of plus and minus levels of all 11 elements. Whereas each split-run test cell gives one data point on one variable,

each scientific test recipe provides a new piece of information about every variable in the test.

With the same number of versions as the team would need for split-run testing (11 test cells + control), the scientific test design, below, offers important advantages (Exhibit 23–4):

- **Sample size** can be the same as for a simple one-variable test (an 86 percent reduction vs. A/B splits).
- **Main effects** are more accurate and robust (clearly quantify the impact of each element).
- **Interactions** between elements can be analyzed (showing how effects change in combination).
- **Optimal mail package** can be created by implementing the new ideas that help, avoiding changes that hurt, and selecting the cheaper alternative for elements that have no impact.

The key metric for the test was response rate—the percentage of recipients who mailed in the subscription order form. Overall sample size for the test was 201,000 names, divided equally among all 12 test recipes (16,750 per recipe). With a 4.0 percent average response rate for the control, this sample size meant that the test had a good chance of uncovering elements that shifted response by about 6 percent (from 4.0 percent to 4.24 percent) and a 50/50 chance of uncovering effects as small as 4.3 percent.

The creative team was given "recipe sheets" listing the combination of elements in each version, based on the above matrix. The test elements were clearly defined before the creative group got to work on the recipes, so all 12 versions of the mailing added just three days to the creative schedule. Each recipe was labeled with a different keycode and randomly assigned 16,750 names.

Eleven new outer envelopes were created (for elements A–F), one new order form (I), and three new letters (J, K). Recipe #12 is simply the control package.

EXHIBIT 23–4

Split-Run Testing

Recipes	Envelope color scheme A	Background graphic on envelope B	Second window C	Expiration date display D	Teaser on envelope E	Starburst on envelope back F	Free gift buckslip G	Lift note H	Order form layout I	Letter length J	Letter copy style K	Response
1	+	–	+	–	–	–	+	+	+	–	+	4.79%
2	–	+	–	–	–	+	+	+	–	+	+	3.64%
3	+	+	–	+	–	–	–	+	+	+	–	3.84%
4	+	–	–	–	+	+	+	–	+	+	–	4.32%
5	–	+	+	–	+	–	–	–	+	+	+	5.56%
6	–	–	–	+	+	+	–	+	+	–	+	4.61%
7	+	–	+	+	–	+	–	–	–	+	+	5.65%
8	–	–	+	+	+	–	+	+	–	+	–	5.53%
9	+	+	–	+	+	–	+	–	–	–	+	4.50%
10	–	+	+	+	–	+	+	–	+	–	–	5.31%
11	+	+	+	–	+	+	–	+	–	–	–	5.85%
12	–	–	–	–	–	–	–	–	–	–	–	4.01%

Each other recipe had about half the elements set at the control (–) level and half set at the new (+) level.

For example, recipe #1 required:

- An envelope with the new color scheme (A+), no background graphic (B–), a second window (C+), the control address window (D–), the control teaser (E–), and no starburst on back (F–)
- No buckslip (G+) or lift note (H+)
- New order form (I+)
- Long letter (J–) with the new copy style (K+)

STEP 4: MARKETING INSIGHTS

All 12 recipes were produced, double-checked, and mailed on the same day. Following the team's standard response curves, results were analyzed after four weeks. Six elements were statistically significant, *increasing response more than 50 percent*. The 11 effects are summarized in the bar chart, below (See Exhibit 23–5).

The chart showed the size of each main effect, the optimal level of each, and which effects were

CASE STUDY: **Direct Mail Subscriptions Tests** *(continued)*

EXHIBIT 23–5

Test Result: 11 Main Effects

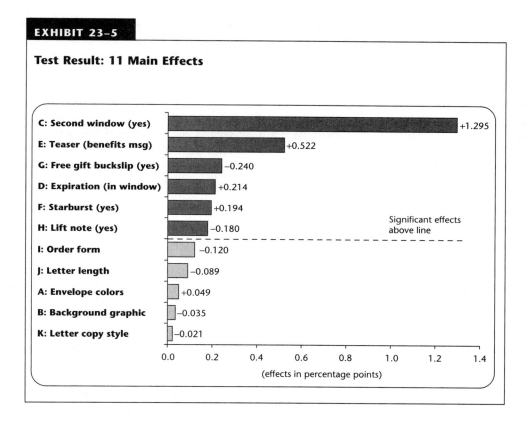

C: Second window (yes) — +1.295
E: Teaser (benefits msg) — +0.522
G: Free gift buckslip (yes) — −0.240
D: Expiration (in window) — +0.214
F: Starburst (yes) — +0.194
H: Lift note (yes) — −0.180

Significant effects above line

I: Order form — −0.120
J: Letter length — −0.089
A: Envelope colors — +0.049
B: Background graphic — −0.035
K: Letter copy style — −0.021

0.0   0.2   0.4   0.6   0.8   1.0   1.2   1.4

(effects in percentage points)

---

statistically significant. In the chart, effects are ordered from largest (at top) to smallest (at bottom). The element name is on the left (with the optimal level in parentheses) and the effect is shown on the right as the length of each bar and the number at the end. The sign of each effect shows which level is better: with a positive effect, the "+" level will increase response and with a negative effect, the "−" level will increase response.

For example, the largest effect was the second window (C), with an effect of +1.295. Adding the second window on the envelope to show the magazine cover increases response 1.295 percentage points, from 4.0 percent to about 5.3 percent (a 32.4 percent increase in the number of responses).

Also, with 9,649 total orders, overall response rate for the test was about 4.8 percent versus 4.0 percent for the control (recipe #12).

Significant Effects

This summary allowed analysis of various combinations and the profitability of each. Adding the four positive effects (C, E, D, and F) to the control response rate gives a predicted response rate of 6.225 percent, a 55.6 percent jump in response over the control. The six significant effects include:

C+: Second window. The team was surprised at the large impact of this fairly simple change. The second window added little cost and gave an impressive 32.4 percent jump in response. They also realized the power of a full-color magazine cover and the importance of building interest before people even open the envelope. This change made so much sense after the fact, but the team had never thought to test it before.

E+: New teaser (benefits message). The teaser with a message about the benefits of the magazine increased response 0.522 percentage points (13 percent) over the control teaser focusing on the offer.

G–: Free gift buckslip. Removing the buckslip reduced response by 0.240 percentage points (6 percent). With this data, they could calculate a break-even point for the full-color buckslip. For their best prospects the buckslip was profitable. Some less responsive segments were more profitable without it.

D+: Expiration date display (show through window). In addition to the second window (C+ above), a larger name/address window also helped. The offer expiration message, "Return this form within 10 days," was kept the same on the order form, but the envelope window was enlarged so that the message showed through the window, above the recipient's name and address. This change increased response by 0.214 percentage points (5.35 percent).

F+: Starburst on envelope back. Adding the bright starburst with a "look inside . . ." message increased response by 0.194 percentage points (4.85 percent). In addition to the benefit of the starburst itself, the team realized that the back of the envelope can have a large impact on response and should not be ignored.

H–: Lift note. Eliminating the lift note was almost as harmful as removing the buckslip. Average response dropped 0.180 percentage points (4.5 percent) across the six mailings with no lift note. This made the copywriter happy and justified the minimal cost of the note.

STEP 5: PROFIT

Implementing the optimal combination of all 11 elements, response rate jumped over 50 percent,

from 4.0 percent to 6.1 percent, and remained between 5.8 percent and 6.4 percent for subsequent mail drops. The test paid for itself the next drop when results were implemented.

In addition to the six significant elements, there were important insights from the five others. Changes to the letter (J and K) had no impact so their control letters remained the same. The new order form, envelope colors, and background graphic also had no significant impact, so they kept these at the control.

STEP 6: CONTINUE TESTING—A PRICE AND OFFER TEST

The marketer learned more in one 11-element test than they had learned over the last two years of testing. Not only did they pinpoint how to increase response over 50 percent, but they also avoided making changes that had a negative impact on results.

With price such an important element in every subscription offer, testing continued to focus on price-related variables. They could do more creative tests in the future, but the next test included the five elements below. It was decided that two bold levels for each element would be tested (See Exhibit 23–6).

A: Subscription price (annual). The current subscription price was $19.97 for 12 monthly issues. Since increasing the number of subscribers was so important, they selected a lower $12.99 annual subscription price to test.

B: Subscription period. With one-year subscriptions, they sent out numerous renewal notices every year to keep customers coming back. They thought that a longer subscription period—18 months instead of 12—might not hurt response and could reduce marketing costs and increase the overall subscriber base. However, they wanted the per-issue price to remain the same whether offering a 12- or 18-month subscription. So for the test, the price (A) was adjusted depending on the subscription period (B):

CASE STUDY: **Direct Mail Subscriptions Tests** *(continued)*

EXHIBIT 23–6

Continuing Testing—a Price and Offer Test

Test Elements	(–) Control	(+) New idea
A: Subscription price (annual)	$19.97	$12.99
B: Subscription period	1 year	18 months
C: Show cover price	No	Yes
D: Include 2- and 3-year subscription options	No	Yes, checkboxes
E: Expiration date format	Number of days	Specific date (6/19/03)

- The current subscription price (A–) would be $19.97 for one year or $29.95 for 18 months
- The lower subscription price (A+) would be $12.99 for one year or $19.49 for 18 months

C: Show cover price. Sometimes they would show the annual cover price and sometimes not. They wanted to test whether it was useful information or got in the way of the offer.

D: Include 2-year and 3-year subscription options. Since subscription renewals required additional mailings and customer commitment, the marketing team wanted to add checkboxes offering customers the option to select a 2- or 3-year subscription at a lower per-issue price.

E: Expiration date format. The last test showed that the expiration date increased response when it shows through the envelope window. In this next test, the team wanted to know if a specific date would be a stronger call to action, for example, "Return this form by 6/19/03," versus ". . . within 10 days."

TEST DESIGN

Focusing on five price and offer elements, interactions were more likely, so they used a different type of test design that would more accurately identify and quantify potential interactions. Though larger test designs (i.e., more test recipes) permit the analysis of numerous interactions, the consultant suggested the 8-recipe test design, below. This test design allowed analysis of the most likely interactions while limiting the number of test recipes (See Exhibit 23–7).

Like the first 12-recipe test, this test design included the control (all minus) recipe as the last row. The additional seven recipes were unique combinations of all five elements, providing the greatest amount of information in a small number of versions.

The team wanted to use a smaller sample size for this test, since price changes had a risk of hurting profitability. Sixty thousand names were split evenly among the eight recipes (7,500 names per recipe). In total, 3,630 people responded, with response rates for each recipe listed in the matrix. Response rate for the control was 5.80 percent. Results are shown below (See Exhibit 23–8).

TEST RESULTS

With this test design, the five main effects and two interaction columns were independent. Three of the five main effects and one interaction were significant.

A+: Subscription price (low). The $12.99 annual subscription price increased average response 1.333 percentage points over the higher $19.97 price (23 percent lift).

B–: Subscription period (1 year). The longer, 18-month subscription reduced response, on average, 0.693 percentage points (12 percent).

E+: Expiration date format (specific date). Changing the wording of the offer expiration from

EXHIBIT 23–7

Test Design

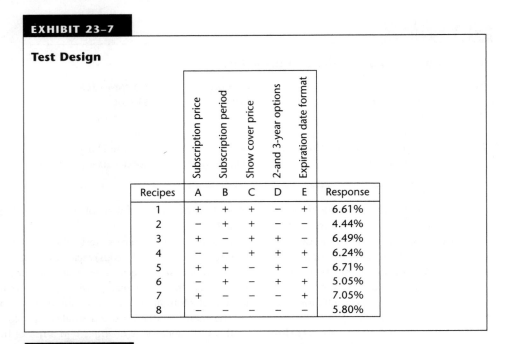

Recipes	A	B	C	D	E	Response
1	+	+	+	−	+	6.61%
2	−	+	+	−	−	4.44%
3	+	−	+	+	−	6.49%
4	−	−	+	+	+	6.24%
5	+	+	−	+	−	6.71%
6	−	+	−	+	+	5.05%
7	+	−	−	−	+	7.05%
8	−	−	−	−	−	5.80%

Column headers (A–E): A: Subscription price, B: Subscription period, C: Show cover price, D: 2-and 3-year options, E: Expiration date format

EXHIBIT 23–8

Test Result: Main Effects and Interactions

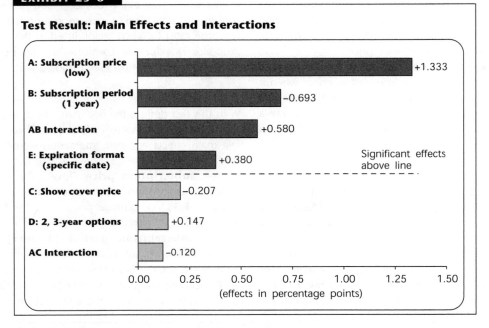

A: Subscription price (low) — +1.333
B: Subscription period (1 year) — −0.693
AB Interaction — +0.580
E: Expiration format (specific date) — +0.380

Significant effects above line

C: Show cover price — −0.207
D: 2, 3-year options — +0.147
AC Interaction — −0.120

0.00   0.25   0.50   0.75   1.00   1.25   1.50
(effects in percentage points)

"10 days" to a specific date increased response 0.380 percentage points (6.55 percent).

AB Interaction

Interaction effects are often difficult to interpret. Is a positive effect good or bad? Since both A–B– and A+B+ give a positive AB interaction, which combination is best? As is often true, a simple picture can often elucidate the answers. The significant AB interaction is pictured below (See Exhibit 23–9).

First of all, this AB interaction supports both main effects. The lower subscription price (both A+ points on the right) always has a higher response rate than the higher price (A– on the left). Also, the one-year subscription period (B– : 1 year subscription) and (B+: 18 months) respectively. However, an interaction occurs when these lines are not parallel.

This plot shows that the very worst combination is A–B+: an 18-month subscription offer at the higher price ($29.95) is much worse than the main effects would predict. But look at the two points on the right. . . .

When the subscription price is low, there is little difference in response rate between the 1-year and

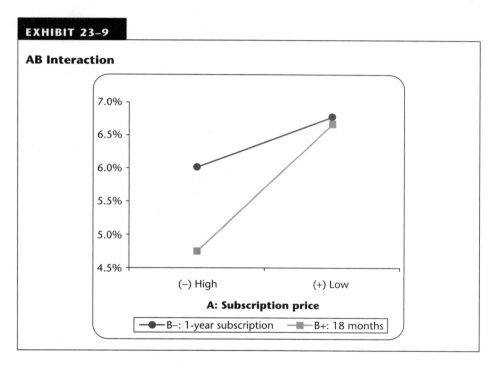

EXHIBIT 23–9

AB Interaction

CASE STUDY: **Direct Mail Subscriptions Tests** *(continued)*

18-month subscriptions. In fact, the low-priced 18-month subscription ($19.49) has a higher response rate than the high-priced 1-year subscription ($19.97).

In contrast to the results from both main effects, the AB interaction gives the marketing team a way to maintain per-subscription revenue while extending the subscription period to 18-months. This surprising result offers a new opportunity for growth, letting them:

- *Increase response rate 18 percent* by changing the expiration date format, lowering the per-issue subscription price, yet extending the subscription period to 18 months
- Maintain revenue per order
- In the long term, increase the subscriber base and reduce marketing costs by delaying renewals
- More accurately calculate profitability, combining data from the main effects and interaction

In addition, the nonsignificant effects were important. The 2- and 3-year options (D) did not hurt response and led to a few long-term subscribers, so the team decided the checkboxes could only help in the long run. Showing the cover price (C) had no impact, so the team decided to leave it off to avoid unnecessary clutter.

RESULTS

In only two direct mail tests, the client learned more than they had in years of split-run testing. More importantly, they zeroed in on a few key, low-cost changes that together led to a 70 percent jump in response:

- **One test of 11 creative elements**—6 envelope, plus insert, letter, and order form changes—pinpointed 6 significant elements for a 55 percent jump in response (using 1/7th the usual sample size)
- **One test of 5 price and offer elements** showed how to increase response *and* profitability through a surprising two-way interaction (that split-run tests would never uncover)

These two scientific tests quantified the impact of 16 direct mail elements and led to a 70 percent increase in response rate.

With growing profits and deeper insights, the team could see the marketplace more clearly and speed ahead in the right direction. Testing didn't solve all of their challenges, but it gave them the freedom to leverage their ideas, rapidly prove what sells, and stay on the leading edge of a highly competitive marketplace.

PILOT PROJECT   This case demonstrates how creative ideas must constantly be tested as market conditions change or new opportunities arise. Do your own brainstorming and think of ways for publications to test new ways of building subscriptions. Should it test promotion techniques, creative ideas, media, offers, etc.? Think of as many different big things to test as possible. Then, apply the concept of convergent thinking to evaluate, critique, and select the most appropriate test ideas.

Key Points

▶ Direct marketers use the subjective process of creativity to generate novel and useful ideas and the objective technique of testing to validate those ideas.

Thus, creative ideas that might not otherwise be considered can be tested and proven in the marketplace.

▸ Creativity can be developed in all people and organizations using brainstorming and other creative stimulators. The degree of truly creative output is directly related to two factors: (1) clear and specific definitions of problems to be solved, and (2) the right "atmosphere" for developing creative solutions. Brainstorming addresses these factors.

▸ Avoid trivia testing (e.g., the tilt of a postage stamp, the effects of various colors, one graphic versus another, etc.) and test the big things: products or services, media, propositions, copy platforms, formats, timing, and new products.

▸ Online testing provides results within a day—even hours. Marketers can learn if one ad pulls better against the others on one Web site, one category of Web sites (e.g., portals, search sites, etc.), or across the board. The low production costs for online promotion means they can modify or change ads and test new ads on the fly.

▸ Multivariable testing can achieve the same results as split-run tests, but with a larger number of variables, smaller sample sizes, and greater depth of insight. However, it requires working with practitioners skilled in advance statistical design.

RESEARCH FOR DIRECT MARKETERS

Over the years, the use of research in direct marketing has evolved as traditional and nontraditional direct marketing have converged, integrated marketing communications have grown, and marketers have sought to get closer to their customers. Research helps marketers gain customer insights. These insights aid decision making and reduce the uncertainty of actions taken by marketers. There is no better way to hear the voice of the customer than to listen to it. Together, with data analysis, customer insight can be a powerful tool.

Marketers use a variety of quantitative and qualitative research techniques to gain the information that they are looking for. These include focus groups, surveys, personal interviews, and ethnographic, anthropological, and observational research. The type of research used is based on the goals or specific customer insights that the marketer wants to obtain. Frequently, these methods are combined to provide results with the outcomes that marketers are trying to achieve.

Research provides marketers with a better understanding of the needs, wants, and motivations of prospects, customers, and segments, and helps to target them more discretely and relevantly. And, it can help marketers to develop new offers and refine their visual and message elements. This can lead to dramatic increases in response rates and enhance the marketer's image while making the sale.

Research can help marketers develop more effective prospecting programs by gaining an in-depth understanding of the types and numbers of "high-propensity prospects" available and translating these consumer segments into targetable groups that can be directly accessed. This could help reduce quantities mailed as well as mailing costs.

Customer insights help to provide the strategic direction for growing traditional direct marketing businesses in terms of identifying new products and service categories with high growth potential, assessing the most dynamic segments within each category, and screening for the most viable products and services within each segment.

Insights gained from research can help nontraditional direct marketers such as consumer goods manufacturers, retailers, telecom providers, and airlines identify the issues around direct distribution systems such as barriers to entry (channel conflicts, shopping habits, etc.) and key opportunities for success.

Nontraditional marketers can use direct mail to identify and test new positions for a brand economically and discretely, without telling the media or competitors, and without disturbing their current franchise. They can develop targeted promotions to selected prospects and customers who provide specific measurable results. And, customer insights can help marketers develop mass-customized communications that deliver discrete, measurable messages targeted to specific customers or prospect profiles.

Online Research

With the growth of the Internet, a variety of online research techniques have become available that are lower cost, quickly administered, and provide good results. Online research has quickly moved from supplementing traditional telephone and mail surveys to become the method of choice for many marketers. Marketers are doing original primary research and participating in ongoing panel research to provide continually updated results. *Advertising Age* estimates that spending for online market research reached $1.35 billion in 2006.

Online surveys can be targeted at customers or focused on prospects. Typically, surveys are e-mailed to respondents, with links to the actual survey at the Web site. Often, they include entry into a contest or some other incentive to respond. Mail surveys have used incentives for years.

Survey software generally performs real-time cross-tabulations. Because e-mail has a very short response curve, marketers can see the results by segments very quickly. This technique helps make market research affordable for nearly any marketer. It is easy to see why online marketing research is growing, and why it is becoming a method of choice for ad hoc quantitative research.

Research and Testing: A Complementary Process

Since the inception of direct marketing, the primary method for assessing programs has been the "in-market" or "in-mail" test. The results produced by these tests are measurable, quantifiable, and predictable. They provide a quantified measurement of overt response in terms of "making the sale," "producing a qualified sales lead," or "stimulating someone to request further information."

By overlaying this overt behavior with geodemographic data, it has been possible to build statistical models that can define high-propensity response groups, providing far more precise methods for marketing and prospecting.

Frequently, research and testing are viewed as an either/or proposition. There are financial trade-offs in choosing whether to test or to use marketing research.

Such reasoning, however, overlooks the fact that testing is an integral part of the total marketing research process and that marketing research and testing are, therefore, not separate issues.

The most important question concerning marketing research is: "When should I spend money on marketing research?" The answer is easy: spend money on marketing research before testing "the big things."

Direct marketers who complain that research has not worked frequently use it to evaluate subtactical issues. For example, they employ focus groups to respond to various offers or laundry lists of product attributes. As Exhibit 24–1 shows, this lower, subtactical level is where the test plan should be implemented, not researched. Overlay selections and specific offers should not be considered before a new target audience is defined and selected. Headlines and product attributes should not be evaluated without first developing a strong, relevant product positioning for the new target segment. Many research dollars are wasted on researching such subtactical issues.

Marketing research dollars are most effectively spent on evaluating strategic issues—evaluating the big things to be sure they are worth spending the time and money for testing. The use of marketing research in testing the big things serves two functions. First, it provides the basis for the financial go/no-go testing decision. That is, the cost estimate of the research can be compared with the projected revenue and profits obtained if the test is successful.

Second, marketing research can serve as a valuable insurance policy against possible test failure if the strategic marketing variables to be tested turn out not to be "the big things." Thus, the estimated cost of the research can be compared with the projected profit and time losses if the test is a failure.

EXHIBIT 24–1

Stages in the Research Process

Formulate Problem
⇩
Determine Research Design
⇩
Determine Data Collection Method
⇩
Design Data Collection Forms
⇩
Design sample and collect data
⇩
Analyze and Interpret the data
⇩
Prepare the Research Report

The rest of this chapter demonstrates how marketing research has been, and can be, used to help in developing and refining research to focus on things that can have the greatest impact and most important outcomes on marketing results and ROI.

Testing and the Total Marketing Research Process

The testing process consists of four phases: (1) exploratory research, (2) pretesting, (3) testing, and (4) post-testing assessment. All phases of testing must be included in the marketing research process to achieve valid directions for the most effective utilization of resources (See Exhibit 24–2).

Phase 1: Exploratory Research

The exploratory phase of the testing process deals with defining and understanding the target audience as well as the marketplace in which you compete. The focal point of the exploratory phase is situation analysis, which deals with understanding the geodemographic characteristics of the target audience as well as its attitudes,

EXHIBIT 24–2

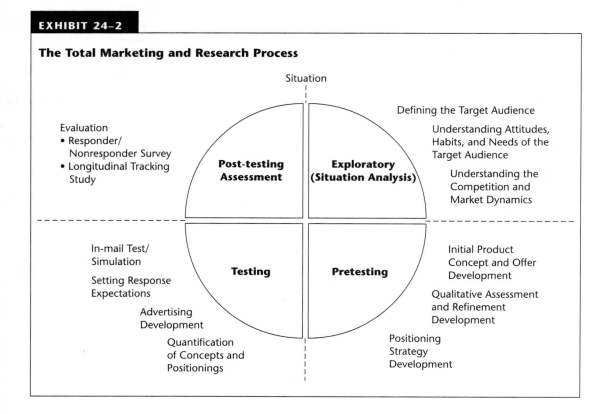

The Total Marketing and Research Process

habits, and needs—particularly those characteristics that are most influential on heavy, regular usage of your product or service.

The situation analysis should also cover the competition and market dynamics in terms of what attributes and benefits each competitive product or service brings to the market, and why consumers are attracted to them. The end result of this situation analysis should be points of maximum leverage on which a direct marketing program can be developed. Such leverage points usually center on special ways of segmenting a target audience, methods for reaching each specified target audience segment, and special ways of segmenting products or services.

Phase 2: Pretesting

The pretesting phase consists of developing, assessing, and refining the marketing and creative products before in-market testing. Several issues should be addressed in this phase.

- Determine that your product or service is offering an attribute or benefit that the consumer really wants—that is, something that is preemptive, setting it apart from the competition.

- Develop and refine the creative and the offer. In this area, qualitative research such as focus groups or in-depth individual interviews can help determine whether the creative approach is communicating information about the product or service, and the offer, in a manner that is clear, believable, and relevant to consumers in the target audience.

- Research usually referred to as copy testing can be used to assess alternative creative executions, and offers. This research is usually quantitative in nature; that is, a survey is used to develop comparative profiles of the creative, and the offer. Such research is useful in two ways.

   First, it helps to provide objective criteria for improving the creative or the offer, rather than giving them some subjective grade. Second, and even of greater importance, however, is that this research can reduce the number of alternatives to be tested, thus greatly reducing test costs and increasing the accuracy of reading back-end results. Research done in the pretest phase can often help to uncover variables or clarify issues that should be addressed in the testing phase.

Phase 3: Testing

One question asked by businesses new to direct marketing is: "When can we stop testing?" and the answer, of course, is "never." The testing process is dynamic and continuous (which is why the diagram in Exhibit 24–2 is a circle). The main objective in all testing is to learn, modify, and improve.

The testing phase brings together five key variables for assessment in the market, later called five testing.

1. The product or service

2. The medium or method of accessing the defined target audience

3. The time or season

4. The advertising/communication

5. The offer or promotion

The test plan consists of the combinations in which these variables will be tested as well as the determination of response expectations and financial objectives.

Although all of the elements of the test plan are crucial, the most important single variable in direct marketing is the medium, or the access to the consumer, because this access provides the strongest point of leverage for all other test variables. In fact, if the medium cannot provide access to qualified consumers in sufficient quantities, the rest of the elements in the direct marketing mix become almost irrelevant by comparison. That is why testing is so critical to finding the lists that will access high-propensity prospects in sufficient quantities.

An alternative method of testing is simulation, which can be used in conjunction with five testing. Simulation systems such as STAR (Simulator Testing Advertising Response—a system developed by Direct Marketing Research Associates and Erard Moore Associates) predict response without running actual space advertising, package/statement inserts, or direct mail packages. Simulation can save time and costs by reducing the number of variables to be tested in-market, and often by eliminating the need to address variables or issues that are of little importance to the direct marketing mix.

Simulation uses a close facsimile of an actual ad or direct mail package mailed to a sample of consumers with a questionnaire and letter. Separate packages are mailed to test and control cells. Data from the questionnaires are combined with actual responses to the simulated mailing to develop a prediction of relative response performance.

Phase 4: Post-testing Assessment

Post-testing assessment is potentially the area of greatest strength for direct marketing research. Assessment attempts both the analysis of test response and the development of diagnostic information in order to determine why the response rate was achieved and what can be done to achieve higher response rates.

The analysis of response rates is a measurement of overt behavior in terms of making a sale, a request for more information, or qualifying a sales lead. Marketing research can also provide diagnostic insights that can help to measure the quality of the response. For example, responder/nonresponder surveys can help pinpoint issues:

- Incremental sales: the degree to which new consumers were attracted to the offer versus the sales' merely subsidizing current customers, particularly heavy or frequent buyers

- Competitive conquest: the degree to which competitive customers tried your product or service and were converted to regular customers

- Attitudinal shifts: the degree to which the brand image of your product or service was enhanced by direct advertising.

In addition, questionnaires, which can help provide much added value to both the consumer and the marketer, can be included as an integral part of the mailing package.

The response to relevant questions about the product or service helps to establish a vital two-way communication, or dialogue, between the marketer and the consumer. The dialogue can help establish a relationship with the consumer that can give the product or service a preemptive position in the mind of the consumer.

The information provided by consumers can be used to qualify or segment them, giving the marketer valuable insights into subsequent positioning of products or services, and more precisely targeting the appropriate message to the appropriate segment.

Primary and Secondary Research

Much of this chapter deals with the use of primary data, that is, research collected for a specific purpose. It is expensive to do primary research, but it is the only way to gain insight into the attitudes, behaviors, and drivers of an organization's own customers. Because it is so expensive, it is important to learn all you can about a market, a product category, customer groups, etc., before you attempt to do primary research. You can often do this with secondary data.

Marketers use a significant amount of secondary data, which is published, purchased, or syndicated research collected for some other purpose but that is relevant and can be applied to the needs of others. Secondary data is available from sources including federal, state, and local governments; trade associations; private research organizations; media providers; foundations; universities; and financial institutions. Much information can be found in the research section of a business or university library. Today, the Internet provides a key source for locating such data.

Many of the sources of secondary data are available on the World Wide Web. There are many search engines and directories that can lead you to the information that you are looking for. Some have specialized libraries of data that can help in your searches. Search engines such as Alta Vista (www.altavista.com), Google (www.google.com), Ask.com, and LexisNexis are important tools in beginning a search for information.

Learning good online search techniques is important to your success. Most search engines have a FAQ section and tutorials that help you learn the peculiarities of their systems. It is well worth spending the time and effort to learn to use the tools of the search engine that best fits your needs.

Organizations such as the Direct Marketing Association and the American Association of Advertising Agencies offer research services to members. Working with skilled researchers at such groups can be a real benefit to smaller organizations that can't afford full-time research staff.

While doing your own online searches may allow you to broaden and customize your search, it is still time-consuming. Having a professional do your research can yield more information and allow you more time to develop strategy, tactics, and your other responsibilities.

Direct Marketing Research for Consumer Products

In the past, direct marketers centered their research activities on analyzing consumers' geodemographic characteristics and purchase behaviors. Direct marketers used these approaches because these two variables are most readily linked with list and prospect selection. Attitudinal, psychographic, and lifestyle data have been much underutilized by direct marketers because these factors are not readily translated to list or prospect selection.

To realistically define, understand, reach, and communicate with target audiences, however, it is imperative that research deal with consumers on all four relevant levels:

1. Demographics

2. Psychographics and lifestyles

3. Attitudes

4. Purchase behavior

All four factors must be integrated to form pictures of "real" consumers: who they are and where they live (geodemographics); what their basic attitudes and values toward life are, and how these attitudes are translated into the way these persons live (psychographics and lifestyles); their perceptions, attitudes, and values with respect to various product and service categories (attitudes); and how these perceptions, attitudes, and values translate into selection making in the marketplace (purchase behavior).

Positive Attribute Group

The Stone & Adler Study of Consumer Behavior and Attitudes Toward Direct Marketing was the first attempt to perform such an interdisciplinary synthesis. The study was designed, fielded, and analyzed with the help of Goldring & Company Inc. and the Home Testing Institute. Once the data were collected within each of the four levels, they were integrated through a software program called PAG (Positive Attribute Group).

PAG is a comprehensive analytical technique for determining the combination of purchase activities, demographics, psychographics and lifestyles, and attitudes toward direct marketing at work in the direct marketing environment. PAG enabled us to segment the direct marketing environment, and identify the four variables and their combinations that were active in each segment.

The PAG program subsequently produced six consumer clusters arrayed in an order (of importance) that breathed life into each of the clusters.

Cluster 1: Mailbox Gourmets. Mailbox Gourmets are the magical 26 percent of the population targeted by almost all direct marketers. In terms of psychographics and lifestyles, Mailbox Gourmets perceive themselves to be sophisticated. They want more of everything, especially travel. They are extremely active and involved, and perceive themselves as not having enough leisure time.

Mailbox Gourmets are affluent. Their demographics show them to be above average in education and income, and to be engaged in white-collar occupations. This cluster is also female-intensive. Although three-fourths are married, this percentage is slightly below marriage averages. The family structure is less traditional with more two-paycheck families or single professionals, particularly women.

It is not surprising that their attitudes toward direct marketing are extremely positive. They enjoy it, are comfortable with it, and perceive themselves to be experts when transacting by mail, phone, or Internet.

All of this information translates into direct marketing purchasing behavior that earns this cluster its name: They spend a lot (significantly more than any other cluster) and they buy often.

Cluster 2: Young Turks. In terms of psychographics and lifestyles, the Young Turks are very trendy, as one would expect. They also consider themselves to be—whether they are, in fact, or not—sophisticated and worldly. Demographically, this group accounts for 10 percent of the households, and forms a perfect Yuppie profile: they are single, male-intensive, well educated, and economically aspiring.

Although Young Turks are also very positive toward direct marketing, they tend to be cautious because they are emerging consumers. This makes them very "presentation sensitive." Because they are so active, they are more likely to order via an 800 number or the Internet than any other cluster group. The Young Turks are the second-highest group in terms of dollars spent and purchase frequency, but their expenditures are significantly less than those of the Mailbox Gourmets.

Cluster 3: Life Begins at 50. The Life-Begins-at-50 cluster comprises 7 percent of households and is completely middle-of-the-road in terms of psychographics and lifestyle. Demographics indicate that these older consumers are "empty nesters": their children are grown, away at college, or married. As a group they are engaged in a mixture of blue- and white-collar occupations.

Like the Young Turks, the Life-Begins-at-50 cluster is also quite positive but cautious toward direct marketing. The cautiousness, in this case, is due to the fact that these people are the experienced "old pros" who have been shopping direct for 20–30 years. This experience has been transformed into a demanding attitude. They know what they want and the marketer had better give it to them.

These data translate into direct marketing dollar expenditures and purchase frequencies just below those of the Young Turks, but the products this cluster is likely to buy are vastly different. The Life-Begins-at-50 cluster is more likely to buy higher-ticket items such as home furnishings or housewares. They are also more likely to buy vitamins and minerals and to belong to a book club. Young Turks, on the other hand, are more likely to purchase products related to self-indulgence such as electronic toys and sports equipment.

Cluster 4: Dear Occupant. Now we come to the great faceless, nameless masses that account for 14 percent of households—"Dear Occupant." Actually, they are the leftovers in the clustering process, and therefore represent those who were:

- Neither too positive nor too negative in their attitudes

- Neither affluent nor destitute

- Neither the lightest nor the heaviest buyers

As such, they are truly the mundane, the moderate, and the middle.

Cluster 5: Kitchen Patriots. When members of these households (23 percent of the total) are not out shopping at their favorite shopping mall or mass merchandiser, they are likely to be home reading the daily newspaper, a magazine, or their mail at the kitchen table.

In terms of lifestyles and psychographics, this cluster is the backbone of traditional American morality and values:

- They are extremely patriotic.

- Home, family, and community are extremely important to them.

- They have sufficient leisure time, which is one reason they shop so much; in fact, many of them have more time than money.

- Demographically, this group is blue-collar intensive, average in income and education, and indexes highest among those 55 years old and older.

Although the Kitchen Patriots' attitudes toward direct marketing are basically negative, they like to browse through their mail, including direct mail pieces, and catalogs. But because of their negative attitudes toward direct marketing, coupled with their propensity toward retail shopping, Kitchen Patriots tend to be non-direct-marketing buyers or light, selective buyers at best.

Cluster 6: Above-It-Alls. Finally, we have the most negative, the pro-retail cluster, the "Above-It-Alls" that account for 20 percent of all households. They are nearly a carbon copy of the Mailbox Gourmet, with a major difference: they are anti-mailbox. In terms of lifestyles and psychographics, this cluster is career-oriented, active, and involved in fads and causes. It perceives itself as taking a leadership position and it is athletic.

Demographically, Above-It-Alls are somewhat more affluent than Mailbox Gourmets. They tend to be more traditional in household compositions. Wives are, more often than not, full-time homemakers—which, of course, gives them more time for retail shopping. This cluster also tends toward strictly suburban, unlike the Mailbox Gourmets, who are split between suburbs and cities. The Above-It-Alls' attitude toward direct marketing is basically negative. In fact, not only do Above-It-Alls like mail, in general, much less than any other group, but they also don't like to browse. In particular, they don't see direct marketing as a convenience. Not surprisingly, this cluster rates as non-direct-marketing buyers or light, selective buyers at best. They want to see and touch the merchandise first, try it on, and obtain instant gratification both in purchasing and returning merchandise.

Using Attitudinal Research to Profile Target Audiences and Product Categories

Attitudinal research can be helpful in profiling target audiences and product categories. Such profiling is essential in two situations: new business development, and expanding an established business.

For new business development, it is important to know who are the users within a category. Not only is it important to know who they are geodemographically for the purpose of list selection, but it is also important to know who they are attitudinally. Attitudinal understanding leads to meaningful positioning to the target audience. Thus the target audience can be communicated with in the most relevant, believable, and understandable manner.

For expanding an established business, profiling can provide an important perspective to the direct marketers by showing how high is up. Unfortunately, too many direct marketers are trapped by their house files; they don't have the necessary information to make the best strategic use of media when prospecting.

Profiling can provide these insights by allowing direct marketers to compare customers on their files against category users on a national basis. Thus, direct marketers can judge whether they are obtaining their fair share of the target audience pie. If they are not, they can fine-tune their demographics for media selection. Even more importantly, they can fine-tune their creative approach and offer so that they have a better chance of being seen and read by their target audience prospect.

A marketer's first step in profiling and segmentation is to perform a buyer concentration analysis from its customer file, as shown in Exhibit 24–3. Such a buyer concentration study will segment the file into groups of heavy or frequent buyers, medium buyers, and light or infrequent buyers.

The second step consists of overlaying the buyer segments with attitudinal and lifestyle data, and then developing a second level of segmentation, as shown in Exhibit 24–4. This segmentation is accomplished by selecting a sample of names from the house file and administering a survey questionnaire containing attitudinal and lifestyle questions. By combining the answers to these questions with the geodemographic and purchase behavior data already on file, PAG clusters can then be developed. At this stage, two analyses are critical: (1) the percentage of the customer file that comprises each of the six clusters, and (2) the percentage of light, medium, and heavy buyers that comprises each of the six clusters.

The third step consists of developing a profile comparing your customer file and a nationally representative sample of consumers (i.e., a consumer database). This comparison allows you to determine whether you are getting your fair share of the following consumer segments:

- Affluent/upscale consumers

EXHIBIT 24–3

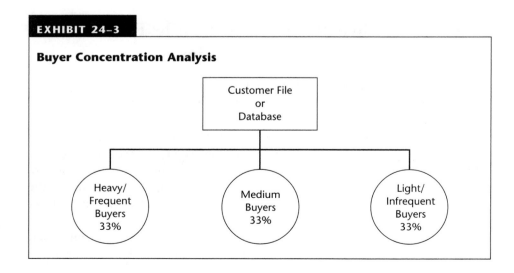

Buyer Concentration Analysis

EXHIBIT 24–4

Attitudinal and Lifestyle Overlay

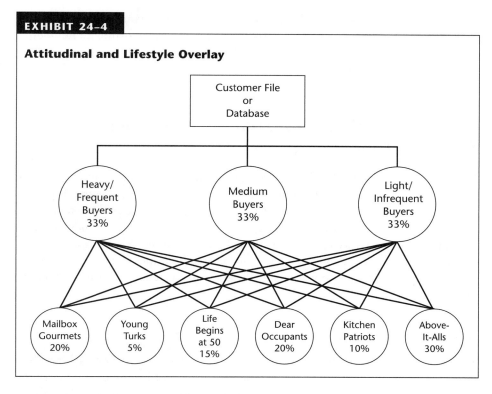

- Younger or emerging consumers entering the marketplace

- Transitional consumers who are changing their lifestyles and their purchasing habits.

For example, the comparative profile shown in Exhibit 24–5 points to a possible problem with the highest-propensity direct marketing consumers who are

EXHIBIT 24–5

Comparative Consumer Profile

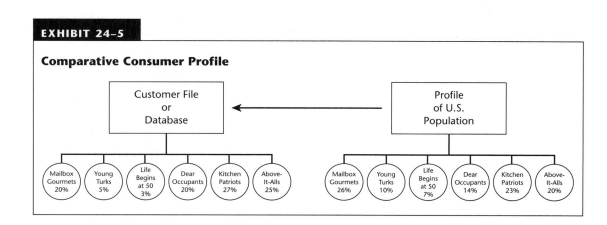

significantly underrepresented in the customer file. There could be similar problems if the buyer concentration analysis shows that a disproportionate number of Mailbox Gourmets, Young Turks, and Life-Begins-at-50 consumers are merely medium and light buyers.

Using Attitudinal Research for Customer Segmentation

Attitudinal research also facilitates the segmentation of customers for precise file selection and developing highly targeted products, services, and creative appeals.

The use of national consumer databases can bring additional strategic marketing insights to your business when applied across a variety of product and service categories as well as segments within these categories (See Chapter 3 for a discussion on databases, and Chapter 21 for more about modeling). Let us review some examples of such applications in three diverse categories: insurance, credit cards, and clothing catalogs.

Insurance Profiles

The Stone & Adler Study of Behavior and Attitudes Toward Direct Marketing examined both the incidences of insurance inquiries and insurance purchases (by mail or phone) during a preceding 12-month period. The total incidences of inquiries were higher than expected at 26 percent. When the incidences of inquiries were analyzed by individual consumer clusters, it was observed that inquiries were relatively flat across all six clusters (See Exhibit 24–6).

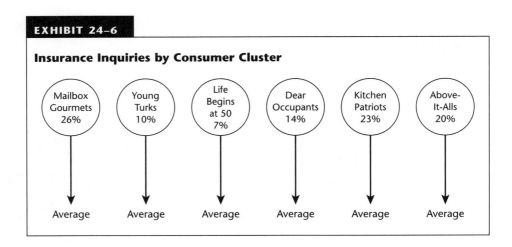

EXHIBIT 24–6

Insurance Inquiries by Consumer Cluster

Mailbox Gourmets 26%	Young Turks 10%	Life Begins at 50 7%	Dear Occupants 14%	Kitchen Patriots 23%	Above-It-Alls 20%
Average	Average	Average	Average	Average	Average

Thus, inquiries were not skewed toward those clusters that were direct mail responsive. In other words, of the total inquiries, the extremely direct-marketing-positive Mailbox Gourmets accounted for 26 percent of the inquiries, while the extremely direct-marketing-negative Above-It-Alls accounted for 20 percent of the inquiries, which is directly proportional to their representation in the general population. If the inquiries were indexed by cluster, therefore, each cluster would index at 100.

The incidence of insurance conversions by mail or phone totaled approximately 44 percent of the conversions, or 11 percent of the total sample (Exhibit 24–7). When the incidences of conversions were analyzed by individual consumer clusters, the same pattern emerged for conversions as for inquiries.

Conversions were also relatively flat across all six clusters. That is, conversions were not skewed toward those clusters that were the most direct mail responsive in other categories. Again, conversions were proportionate to each cluster's representation in the total U.S. population. All clusters would therefore index at or near 100.

The conclusion drawn was that insurance was one of the least direct marketing responsive of all the 26 product and service categories surveyed in the Stone & Adler study. However, the potential direct marketing audience for insurance is much larger than many other categories, because it has a less negative bias toward direct marketing.

But to take advantage of such an opportunity, direct marketers must strategically use research data of the type shown above to:

- Define the highest-propensity consumer segments for each type of insurance product

- Understand the needs for each type of insurance product from the perspective of each consumer segment

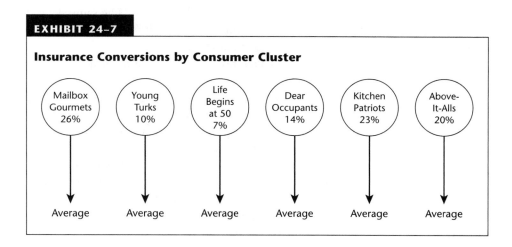

EXHIBIT 24–7

Insurance Conversions by Consumer Cluster

Mailbox Gourmets 26%	Young Turks 10%	Life Begins at 50 7%	Dear Occupants 14%	Kitchen Patriots 23%	Above-It-Alls 20%
Average	Average	Average	Average	Average	Average

- Communicate the positioning, offer, and benefits of each insurance product in a manner that is understandable, relevant, and believable to the targeted consumer segments

Credit Card Acquisition Profiles

Credit card acquisition in the Stone & Adler study included only new credit cards from new credit card sources that were obtained within the past 12 months. Acquisition did not include any credit cards that had expired, and for which the company sent a new one. Acquisitions were based on either a solicitation received in the mail or a coupon sent in from a newspaper or magazine ad.

Acquisition profiles were developed for the four major categories of cards:

1. Bank cards such as Visa and MasterCard

2. Travel and entertainment cards such as American Express or Diners Club

3. Department store cards such as those from Sears, J.C. Penney, Wards, Neiman-Marcus, Saks Fifth Avenue, and local department stores

4. Gasoline cards such as Amoco, Shell, and Texaco

The total incidence of bank card acquisition was 20 percent. As you can see in Exhibit 24–8, the incidence by cluster was heavily skewed toward the clusters that are the most positive toward direct marketing.

The total incidence of travel and entertainment card acquisition was 5 percent, which was the lowest of all four credit card market segments, and a good indication of the maturity that this segment is displaying. Again, acquisition of travel and entertainment cards, for the most part, is skewed toward the most direct-marketing-positive clusters (See Exhibit 24–9).

The total incidence of department store card acquisition was 23 percent. This percentage was the highest of all four credit card segments. The same skewed pattern that we observed in bank and travel and entertainment cards persists, except that it is even more accentuated (See Exhibit 24–10).

The gasoline credit card segment also showed a degree of maturity similar to that of travel and entertainment cards, with an incidence of acquisition at 12 percent. The skewing of acquisition toward positive direct marketing clusters is the least pronounced in this market segment (See Exhibit 24–11).

In summary, when above-average acquisition patterns are observed across all four credit card segments, clearly the most positive direct marketing clusters demonstrate the highest propensity to obtain credit cards (See Exhibit 24–12).

What are the implications of credit card acquisition being so heavily skewed toward positive direct marketing consumers? First, there is a general need for credit. Clearly, there is a new need for total credit in the form of multiple cards, not merely one card. But who are these high-propensity credit card acquirers?

EXHIBIT 24–8

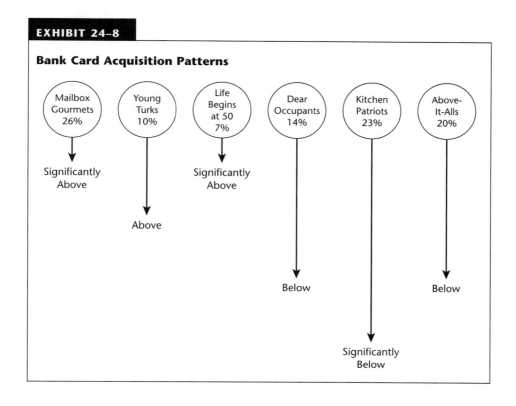

Bank Card Acquisition Patterns

Supplementary work in this area shows that there are identifiable, targetable groups such as emerging and transitional consumers.

Emerging consumers can be found in the Young Turks cluster and among the younger Mailbox Gourmets. Demographically, these are recent college or technical school graduates, young aspiring professionals, newlyweds, and new parents (Full Nest I). Transitional consumers can be most readily found in the Life-Begins-at-50 cluster and among the older Mailbox Gourmets. These people are undergoing major lifestyle changes such as divorce, remarriage, or a midlife career change, all of which affect credit needs.

Catalog Clothing Buyer Profiles

Respondents to the Stone & Adler study were asked whether they had purchased any clothing within the past three months either at retail outlets or through mail order (where "you sent in a mail order form or phoned in your order, and the item was delivered to your home, office, or elsewhere"). At 74 percent, the total incidence of purchasing clothing from all sources, both retail and direct, was the highest of all 26 categories measured in the Stone & Adler study.

EXHIBIT 24–9

Travel and Entertainment Card Acquisition Patterns

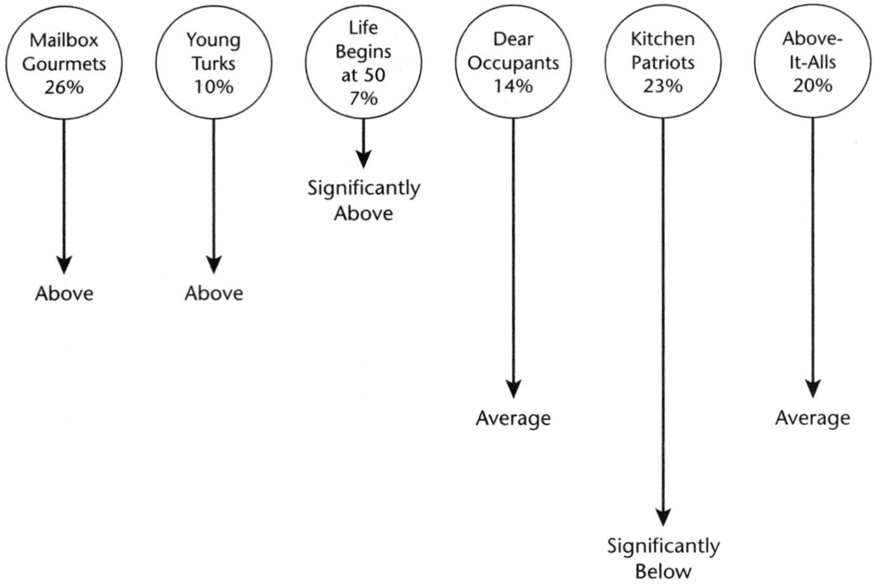

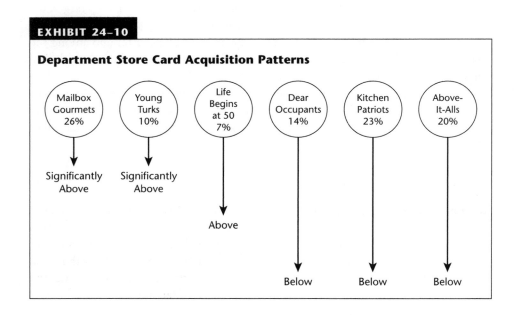

EXHIBIT 24–10

Department Store Card Acquisition Patterns

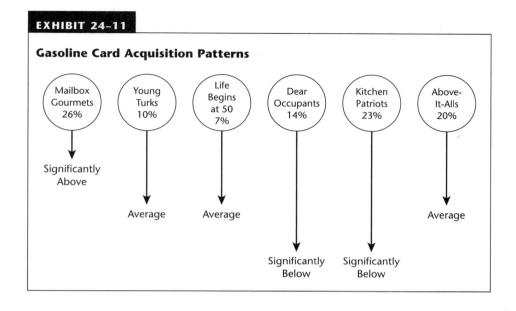

EXHIBIT 24-11

Gasoline Card Acquisition Patterns

As shown in Exhibit 24–13, the Mailbox Gourmets and Young Turks, the two most positive direct marketing clusters, demonstrated the highest incidence; the Kitchen Patriots and Above-It-Alls, the most negative direct marketing groups, showed the lowest incidence.

When we isolate catalog clothing purchases, a somewhat different pattern emerges (Exhibit 24–14). The incidence of purchase among Mailbox Gourmets registers significantly above average at 52 percent on an index of 200. Conversely, the

EXHIBIT 24-12

Above-Average Acquisition Patterns

	Mailbox Gourmets 26%	Young Turks 10%	Life Begins at 50 7%	Dear Occupants 14%	Kitchen Patriots 23%	Above-It-Alls 20%
Bank cards	X	X	X			
T-and-E cards	X	X	X			
Department store cards	X	X	X			
Gasoline cards	X					

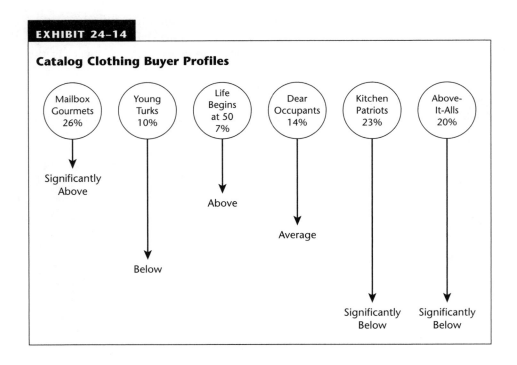

EXHIBIT 24–13

Clothing Buyer Profile—Retail and Direct

Mailbox Gourmets 26%	Young Turks 10%	Life Begins at 50 7%	Dear Occupants 14%	Kitchen Patriots 23%	Above-It-Alls 20%
Above	Above	Average	Average	Below	Below

EXHIBIT 24–14

Catalog Clothing Buyer Profiles

Mailbox Gourmets 26%	Young Turks 10%	Life Begins at 50 7%	Dear Occupants 14%	Kitchen Patriots 23%	Above-It-Alls 20%
Significantly Above	Below	Above	Average	Significantly Below	Significantly Below

incidence among Young Turks slips below average at 8 percent; the incidence among Kitchen Patriots slips to under one-half of their representation in the sample of 11 percent; while purchase incidence of Above-It-Alls registers a mere 5 percent, or one-quarter of their representation in the sample. Several strategic implications can be drawn from these data.

- Mailbox Gourmets are conspicuous consumers in the clothing category. They buy more at both retail and catalog. Unfortunately, the growing mailbox clutter is also centering on this group because Mailbox Gourmets are on everyone's mailing list. Research should be used, therefore, to develop intrusive catalogs and mass media advertising to break through the clutter, and to develop unique types or lines of merchandise that will continue to attract the loyalty of Mailbox Gourmets.

- Although the Life-Begins-at-50 cluster exhibited the second-highest propensity to buy clothing from catalogs, their purchases tend to be concentrated on a much narrower range of merchandise than the Mailbox Gourmets. Research should be used, therefore, to develop creative messages that motivate this cluster to try products they have not purchased by mail before, and to select the merchandise with the highest propensity to generate trial.

- The underperformance by the Young Turks represents a major lost opportunity to clothing catalog marketers, particularly in terms of an extremely high net present value. Research could help by directing catalog marketers on the best ways of communicating with the Young Turks, and reassuring them about the key issues of styling and fit.

- Although the Kitchen Patriots and Above-It-Alls do not represent a major opportunity for direct mail clothing sales, they should not be summarily dismissed by direct marketers. Since direct mail, particularly catalogs, is used by both of these groups as reference materials for retail shopping, direct marketing can be used effectively among both groups as a targeted advertising vehicle to increase retail traffic.

Research for Business-to-Business Applications

Many people ask whether the principles of marketing and research are the same for business-to-business products and services as they are for consumer products and services. After all, this line of reasoning goes, the people making purchases for businesses are the same consumers who buy television sets, automobiles, and toothpaste, aren't they? Not exactly.

When John Q. Consumer begins buying products for a business, the situation becomes much more complicated than it is for consumer products. In a business environment, he is part of a much larger, more complex institutional hierarchy. Thus, responsibility for the purchase decision, as well as the ultimate consumption of the products or services, is a much more involved process.

For example, regardless of the organization of the business, the target audience within a business will normally have at least three hierarchical levels (See Exhibit 24–15). The purchaser is the person responsible for recommending and making the purchase, whether he or she is the purchasing agent, office manager, or director of human resources. The gatekeeper is a CEO or chief financial officer from whom the purchaser must often obtain approval. The end-user is often a department manager in the production, accounting, or marketing department whose department will actually be using the products or services purchased. In fact, either the gatekeeper or end-user can originate the purchasing process as well as influence it.

Finding Qualified Prospects

To make matters even more difficult, there are problems with finding qualified prospects on each of these three levels. First, not everyone contacted is in the market for your products or services. At one extreme are prospects who are simply not interested in your product or service category or in the particular brand you are selling. Others who are interested in the category might have recently purchased and made long-term commitments, and will not be available for an extended time.

At the other extreme are a group of prospects called active considerers. Not even all of these prospects are available, because they must first be converted from prospects to serious shoppers.

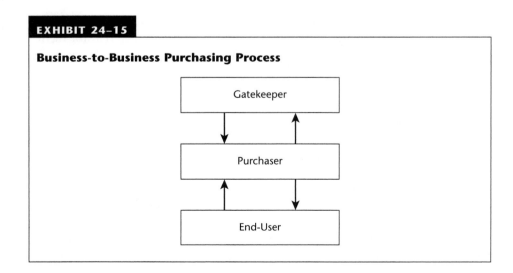

EXHIBIT 24–15

Business-to-Business Purchasing Process

Thus, direct marketers often approach business-to-business marketing problems by merely testing and retesting rather than carefully defining and thoroughly understanding each level of prospect audience being targeted. You can readily see why the odds of success are so often slight. Profiling, covered in Chapter 4, fills the gap.

Primary Research for Marketing and Creative Development

Sometimes there is insufficient information available for profiling, particularly when a new market or segment is being entered. Such situations call for the marketer to obtain primary information directly from prospects in the form of qualitative information (focus groups or in-depth personal interviews) and/or quantitative data (surveys).

The need for research relating to a new marketing venture arose when a large computer manufacturer asked Jacobs & Clevenger to develop qualified leads for marketing data warehouse software. This software only ran on this company's mini-computers. While the company was a leader in the field and had a large installed user base, not all of the users were for prospects for this product. A software partner of the computer manufacturer that would be responsible for servicing and maintaining the software had created the software.

Because this was a new marketing venture for the company, research was needed to provide a basic understanding of the attitudes toward, and the decision-making process involved in, selecting this software solution.

- How is the need for data warehousing software arrived at? How is the purchase process initiated?

- Who is involved in the decision-making process?

- What criteria are used in the decision-making process?

- What information sources are used in the decision-making process?

- Research was also needed to understand what the effect of the computer manufacturer as an entrant in this market would have on key prospects.

Because the proposed target audience for this system were the Fortune 1,000 companies, the research process began with focus groups consisting of key decision makers for software systems selected from a sample of the manufacturer's installed base. A wide variety of industry groups were included.

To begin with, the exercise of finding the real key decision makers in the sample corporations became a survey unto itself. Often, three to five contacts had to be made before a decision maker was reached.

Because data warehouses are enterprise-level software applications, this decision was made at a very high level within the corporation. Jacobs & Clevenger quickly learned that there were multiple decision makers and influencers in every company.

This knowledge had major implications for the ultimate targeting, because the actual titles of the decision makers varied. In many large corporations, the Chief Executive Officer (CEO) was involved in the decision process. Because financial data would be stored on the data warehouse, the Chief Financial Officer (CFO) of the organization was involved. And because this was a software product, the Chief Information Officer (CIO) was involved in the decision.

Research showed that traditional titles such as president, controller, or manager of information technology did little to reveal who the final decision maker was. In many firms, titles were unique, causing even more difficulty in identifying the decision makers and influencers. This was consistent with other projects that the agency had worked on.

Decision-Making Process

Regardless of the decision maker's title, however, he or she formed one level within a three-level purchase process decision matrix (See Exhibit 24-16).

The purchase process centered on the manager/director of information technology (IT) as the functional leader, the technical expert. Research showed that data warehouse software was considered a major purchase because it affected nearly every department within a firm. It was clear that the final decision would change in each organization. Research revealed that there was no way to predict if the CEO, CFO, or CIO was the originator of the purchasing process.

However, each decision maker or influencer came at the process from a different perspective. The CIO wondered how the new software would integrate with the organization's other software, as well as how much time it would take to

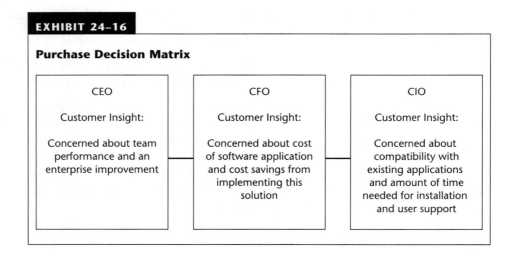

EXHIBIT 24-16

Purchase Decision Matrix

CEO	CFO	CIO
Customer Insight:	Customer Insight:	Customer Insight:
Concerned about team performance and an enterprise improvement	Concerned about cost of software application and cost savings from implementing this solution	Concerned about compatibility with existing applications and amount of time needed for installation and user support

support and maintain the new software. The CEO's or president's involvement in the decision-making process tended to revolve around the issues of teamwork and process improvement in the operating efficiencies of the whole organization. The CFO was interested in cost savings provided by the data warehouse, as well as the initial cost of the software, installation, and maintenance.

The Marketing Environment

The introduction of this new software came at the beginning of the data warehouse evolution. The category was not well known. Demand had not been created for this new product category.

Prospects were uncertain of their need for this type of software. They needed to understand what a data warehouse could do to solve the problems that they might be having. Therefore, for most target prospects, the emphasis was on educating them to the concept as much as it was in solving a problem that they were not certain they had.

The procedures for purchasing software appeared to be ritualized and formal. Many corporations have ongoing software investigation committees. Purchases are often made based on an "approved vendor list" consisting of large, well-known companies such as IBM or Microsoft (This company was on the approved vendor lists of most companies, but thought of as a computer hardware company, not a software solutions provider). These decisions are of such high visibility that key decision makers tend to be relatively conservative in terms of not looking to be "the first" to try a new product or software application. One decision maker put it simply: "I have no desire to be on the bleeding edge."

Major Criteria for Software Selection

A major requirement when purchasing new software is system compatibility. Companies have invested a significant amount of money on their hardware and software; new products must be able to integrate with a minimum of conflict. This was true of the new data warehouse software.

New software systems often require faster processing, more memory, and additional storage. This is one reason computer hardware manufacturers began offering software solutions; but it does conflict with a concern of prospects. It is a discussion point that must be addressed as part of the overall decision-making process. Decision makers expect to factor it in to their final decision. It can often be a deal breaker when the costs are too high.

Most software applications have user interfaces. They are purchased to be used by managers and support workers rather than for data-processing staff. New software must require a minimum of training and support; data from the new software must be compatible with standard word-processing, spreadsheet, and presentation software.

Sources of Information in Decision Making

When looking for information on new software solutions, key decision makers tended to rely on the following sources:

- Word of mouth from peers in the field and other technical people at work, which are viewed as the most important source of information

- Marketing representatives and their companies' literature

- Seminars

- Trade publications

- The Internet

- Direct mail

A variety of other information was developed from the study:

- Reactions to concept statements describing the proposed software application and its features

- A gap analysis of buyer expectations versus what the product delivered

- Key user benefits as described by prospects

- A competitive analysis to determine features offered by competitive products

- A propensity-to-buy analysis based on this company versus competitors offering such software

Conclusions and Implications

The conclusions and implications on which the subsequent campaign strategy was developed revolved around five issues:

- Educating users on a new category of products (data warehouses)

- Credibility, or the ability to convince prospects that the computer hardware manufacturer understood their business category and had the high level of experience and technical expertise to offer sophisticated software solutions

- Complexity of the decision-making process with multiple levels of target audiences, each having its own needs and points of view

- Conservatism on the part of key decision makers because of the high visibility of the decision and the concomitant need for risk reduction through vendor approval lists

- Compatibility with current systems in terms of both hardware and software

The Future of Research in Direct Marketing

The future of research will be dictated by the problems that it is asked to address. For example, as traditional marketing categories continue to mature and competitors face increasing clutter, the problem of identifying, understanding, and reaching the highest-propensity prospects looms larger and larger.

Hence the major problem common to both traditional and nontraditional direct marketers is identifying and understanding key target audience segments. This is particularly true in terms of focusing on points of greatest strategic leverage and developing techniques to gain direct access to these segments. The problem is shared and must be jointly solved by research and media working in tandem.

As long as the disciplines of research and media are treated as separate functions, they will not be able to participate in the consumer insights and delivery process that is needed to address the problems of both traditional and nontraditional direct marketers.

As you can see by the integrated process shown in Exhibit 24–17, the process begins with research defining who the target audience is and why it behaves the way it does.

The primary purpose of this chapter has been to show the value of research and the types of research that can identify target markets and lead to well-executed

EXHIBIT 24–17

Consumer Insights and Delivery Process

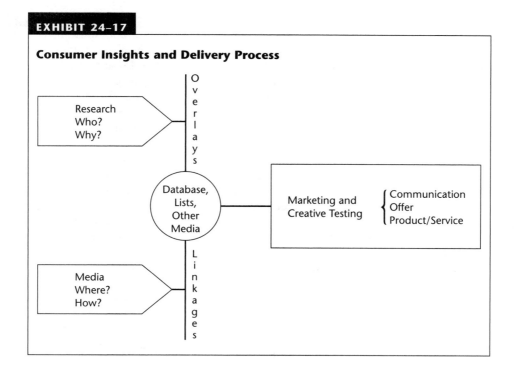

direct response advertising. Conducting the actual research is best left to professional researchers. Knowing what should be researched is imperative.

Research does not yield solutions to marketing problems. It provides answers to questions, reduces uncertainty, and helps marketers to reduce the risk around marketing decisions. It can lead to a number of alternatives that may require further exploration. Research and customer insights are aids to good judgment, but not a substitute for it. Marketers still need vision, imagination, and courage to be successful.

CASE STUDY:	Sensory Logic

Contributed by Andrew Langdell, Communications Director of Sensory Logic Inc., Minneapolis, MN.

BACKGROUND

As one of the most popular forms of marketing, direct mail is valued for its ability to be closely monitored, precisely targeted, and constantly tracked. Clearly, the most important factors in direct mail success are list accuracy and relevance, but other aspects such as design, copy, and visual choices drive and affect market response. But even the best-planned direct mail achieves an average response rate of 2.61 percent (www.directmag.com).

As we all know from our own experience, it is probably fair to assume that people sort their mail into three piles: bills, interesting items, and immediate trash. Therefore, finding ways to get the audience to keep your mailer in hand instead of tossing it in the can is extremely important. After all, the difference between 2 percent and 3 percent could be thousands of customers and hundreds of thousands of dollars.

One of the largest problems that direct mailers face is the difficulty of obtaining accurate market research on different strategic efforts prior to real-world use and real-world expense. While list accuracy can be assessed prior to distribution, it is difficult to test the initial, emotional responses that recipients have to the mailings themselves. As the entire process of receiving a direct mail offer and reading it or trashing it can happen in only a few seconds, discovering the primary reaction of consumers is imperative. Though questions concerning front-end design like color scheme, amount of text, layout, and physical size are undoubtedly addressed

by consumer response, it makes sense to determine what design attributes truly create an emotional connection in order to increase the efficiency and effectiveness of offers.

METHOD

To determine which direct mail designs would increase consumer response, a major financial services company hired Sensory Logic, a consumer insights firm, to test different credit card application mailings.

Sensory Logic uses the process of facial coding to determine true consumer emotional affect. As recent developments in neuroscience demonstrated, emotions are the driving force behind action. While people do rationalize decisions, it is usually done after the choice to purchase, use, or acknowledge has been made emotionally. Furthermore, due to the orientation and connectivity of the brain, emotional and rational thought are often not directly related to one another. Using the Facial Action Coding System, a scientifically valid method that correlates facial expression to emotional reaction, Sensory Logic accesses the gut feelings of customers even if they aren't able to, or don't want to, verbalize them. By translating these responses into appeal (likeability) and impact (motivation) scores, it is possible to compare stimuli for emotional effectiveness.

GOALS

The goals of the financial services company were threefold:
- Determine which designs persuade the target market to apply for a Company X credit card

- Determine which elements of the direct mail envelopes the target market likes
- Determine ways to improve on current copy and design

Eighty participants took part in the study. The group demographics consisted of:
- A 50/50 split between male and female respondents
- Aged 21–60 years of age with half being under 40 and half over the age of 40
- Two-thirds Caucasian with the other third a representative mix of other ethnicities
- Balanced mix of marital status
- Primary or joint decision makers for household finances
- Holder of a credit card from a major issuer (Visa, MasterCard, etc.)

Nineteen different envelope designs were evaluated for market effectiveness and affect. There were a variety of visual and textual concepts used. The two main conceptual themes involved a "hope" or a "fear" approach.

The "hope" approach centered on clean visuals reinforced with uplifting messages like "You're pre-approved for a Visa," or "Confirmed: $2,500 limit" (See Exhibit 24–18). The message/envelope combos were intended to appeal to consumers' desire to be happy and worry-free. By leading with a message of low risk and high reward, the financial services firm hoped that recipients would consider the envelope almost as a prize instead of throwing it in the garbage.

The "fear" strategy adopted scare tactics in an attempt to keep the direct mailing in the hands of consumers (See Exhibit 24–19). By pairing ominous copy, such as "Expiration notice," "Signature required. Open immediately," and "Urgent," along with visually engaging envelopes designed to emphasize the negative message or resemble "official" documents, the financial services firm hoped to frighten people into taking notice of and opening the mail in order to convert them with good rates and financing inside.

TEST PROCEDURE

Each participant went through a process designed to gauge their true emotional response to mailer designs and gain insight into their attitudes on the company. The direct mail designs were shown to participants via a laptop with a webcam mounted on it. To account for order bias, half of the group saw the envelopes in one order and the other half saw them in the reverse order.

Three questions were asked for each of the designs:
- What are your impressions of this package?
- How well does this package grab your attention?
- How likely would you be to open it?

During each question, the participant was recorded via webcam. This provided the video needed to facially code reactions to the questions and compare emotional response levels, as well as create transcripts of their verbal responses for comparison to emotional data.

RESULTS

"Hope" strategy elements that stood out and appealed to consumers were clean designs and simple copy that clearly defines the WIIFM (what's in it for me) for the consumer. Including the company name in the sender address area was received well. As one would expect, the best offers in terms of APR and credit limit had the best emotional response.

For the "fear" strategy, visually arresting designs that stand out from regular mail (courier documents, "registered" text, etc.) succeeded in drawing attention. Also, the more threatening the text, the better the response was. A line like "expiration notice" will get more attention than "attention required." When done correctly, the "fear" strategy creates an aversion to killing the messenger—meaning that the recipient will open the mail in order to ensure that the contents are not significantly important or possibly detrimental. The upper "fear" envelope shown earlier used these elements to achieve

CASE STUDY: **Sensory Logic** *(continued)*

EXHIBIT 24–18

Hope Letters

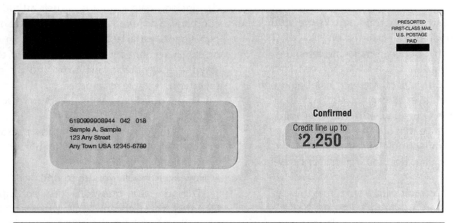

CASE STUDY: **Sensory Logic** *(continued)*

EXHIBIT 24–19

Fear Letters

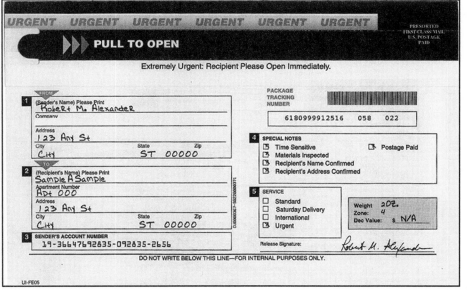

CASE STUDY: **Sensory Logic** *(continued)*

the best market response out of all designs (more than 20 percent higher than the closest competitor).

For both tactics, size difference inherently made envelopes stand out. This is especially true for "hope" as a larger envelope provides more room to place information on, thereby reducing the anxiety associated with cluttered design.

But the real story emerges when the various envelopes were used in the real world. The financial services company graciously provided Sensory Logic with the results of the direct mail campaign's implementation. The results were clear. As the two graphs show, the emotional responses to the envelope strategies and market response were directly correlated for both "hope" and "fear."

For the hope strategy, the more positive the response, the higher the market response was (Exhibit 24–20). One piece received over 20 percent more positive emotional response than the others and had a response rate 30 percent over the group average. This piece was almost not allowed to run due to its marginal lead based on rational data.

Conversely, the fear strategy saw that higher negative emotional reaction led to higher market response (Exhibit 24–21). In summary, the goal was to avoid purgatory. Pieces that weren't on-emotion in terms of generating the intended emotional effect registered low in market response rate. On the other hand, pieces that pushed the right button (hope or fear) usually performed well. And the single biggest take-away: "fear" tactics generated a higher percentage of successful entries.

Hope Strategy
82 percent of hope-based direct mail offers demonstrated strong correlation between increasing positive emotional response and market response. The more positive the emotional response, the higher the market response.

Fear Strategy
88 percent of fear-based direct mail offers demonstrated strong correlation between increasing negative emotional response and market response. The more negative the emotional response, the higher the market response.

EXHIBIT 24–20

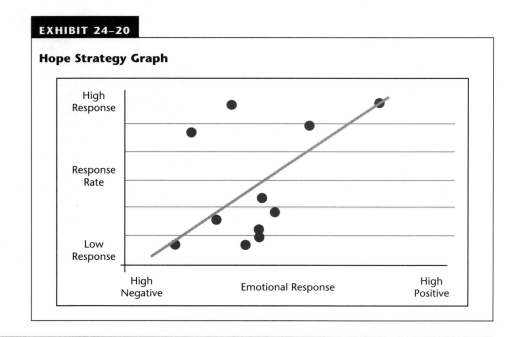

Hope Strategy Graph

EXHIBIT 24–21

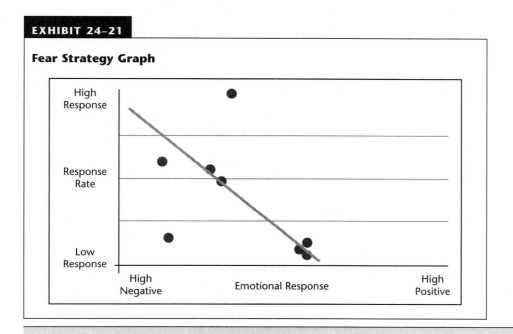

Fear Strategy Graph

PILOT PROJECT   Multichannel direct marketing is a way to provide convenience to customers by offering them more than one way for them to buy. Depending on their need, customers may shop from more than one outlet. A main benefit to companies is that multichannel shoppers are not only more loyal, but they also spend more.

The ideal multichannel marketing formula is to have an integrated message and a consistent customer experience while using the different channels of catalogs, retail stores, and Web sites. Given the general commerce landscape and competitive threats, companies need to understand their customers and their experience.

Prepare a research plan to gather basic information for a multichannel marketer of men's clothing. They have a database of 250,000 current customers (i.e., they have purchased within the last 12 months), with an average order size of $120.00. You will want to address customers, competitive customers, and customers that use individual as well as multiple channels for their purchases. This plan should include a statement of research objectives for each project item, and the specific type of research technique best suited to meet the objectives.

Key Points

▶ Research and testing are not an either/or proposition. Testing is an integral part of the total marketing research process.

▶ Marketing research dollars are most effectively spent on evaluating strategic issues—evaluating the big things to be sure they are worth spending the time and money for testing. Doing so provides the basis for the financial go/no-go testing decision, and serves as a valuable insurance policy against possible test failure if the strategic marketing variables to be tested turn out not to be "the big things."

▶ Online research has become the method of choice for many marketers because of its low cost, speed to administer, and good results.

▶ The four phases of testing process must be included in the marketing research process to achieve valid directions for the most effective utilization of resources: (1) exploratory research, (2) pretesting, (3) testing, and (4) post-testing assessment.

▶ Secondary data can be obtained from federal, state, and local governments; trade associations; private research organizations; media providers; foundations, universities, and financial institutions; and the World Wide Web. However, online searches are time-consuming. Having a professional do your research can yield more information and allow you more time to develop strategy, tactics, and your other responsibilities.

▶ To realistically define, understand, reach, and communicate with target audiences, research must deal with consumers on all four relevant levels: geo-demographics, psychographics and lifestyles, attitudes, and purchase behavior.

▶ Attitudinal research can be helpful in profiling target audiences and product categories, especially in new business development and when expanding an established business. Attitudinal research also facilitates the segmentation of customers for precise file selection and developing highly targeted products, services, and creative appeals.

▶ Direct marketers should approach business-to-business marketing problems by carefully defining and thoroughly understanding each level of prospect audience being targeted, not by merely testing and retesting.

▶ In a new business-to-business marketing venture, research can provide a basic understanding of the attitudes toward, and the decision-making process involved in, selecting a particular product or solution.

GLOSSARY

ABC 'Audit Bureau of Circulations' Audits and certifies magazine circulation.

Action devices Items and techniques used in direct mail to encourage positive response (e.g., tokens, scent strips).

Active buyer Customers whose latest purchase was made within the last 12 months. *See also* **Buyer** and **Actives**.

Active member Customer who is fulfilling the original commitment or who has fulfilled that commitment and has made one or more purchases in the last 12 months.

Active subscriber Customer who has committed for regular delivery of magazines, books, or goods or services for a period of time still in effect.

Actives Customers who have made purchases within a prescribed time, usually one year; subscribers whose subscriptions have not expired.

Acquisition cost The cost of creating or acquiring a new customer. The maximum allowable cost of a customer is usually based on their lifetime value, less the organization's profit goal.

Additions New names, either of individuals or companies, added to a mailing list.

Address Correction Requested Endorsement printed in the upper left-hand corner of the address portion of the mailing piece (below the return address), which authorizes the U.S. Postal Service, for a fee, to provide the known new address of a person no longer at the address on the mailing piece.

ad hoc report A summary of computer information conceived after the master files have been created, usually produced by an after-the-fact reporting system designed for the purpose.

ADI (Area of Dominant Influence) Geographic division of markets by Arbitron, based on preponderance of television viewing.

Advertising schedule List of advertisements booked by media showing details of sizes, timing, and costs.

Affinity Relationships among customers and their purchases, lifestyles, etc. (e.g., people who travel internationally are often prospects for fine dining, wine, or luxury goods).

Against the grain Folding paper at right angles to the grain of the paper; a sheet of paper will fold easily along the grain but will possibly crack when folded against the grain.

AIDA Most popular formula for the preparation of direct mail copy. The letters stand for (get) Attention, (arouse) Interest, (stimulate) Desire, (ask for) Action.

Airbrush Small pressure gun shaped like a pencil that sprays paint by means of compressed air. Used to obtain tone or graduated tonal effects in artwork.

Airtime Jargon term denoting the amount of actual transmission time available for an advertisement on television and radio.

Algorithm A sequence of instructions that describes how to solve a particular problem.

American Standard Code of Information Interchange (ASCII) Widely used code adopted by the American Standards Association for transmission of information.

ANOVA (Analysis of Variance) In research, the results of testing the impact of a variable upon the desired response. If more than one independent variable is tested, the approach is called a "two-way ANOVA."

Art paper Paper coated with a mineral substance to produce a glossy surface.

Artwork Finished layout consisting of drawings, photographs, lettering, and copy.

Assigned mailing dates Dates by which the list user has to mail a specific list; no other date is acceptable without approval of the list owner.

Assumptive close Closing technique in which the salesperson offers the product or service with the assumption that the target has made the decision to buy.

Asterisk bills State laws that require telephone companies to advise subscribers that they can have an asterisk placed in front of their names if they do not want to receive telemarketing calls.

Attrition model A model that predicts which customers are most likely to leave. Usually expressed as a percentage of likelihood.

Attrition rate The percentage of customers who are no longer active from one purchase period to the next.

Audience Total number of individuals reached by a promotion or advertisement.

Audit Printed report of the counts involved in a particular list or file.

Automatic call distributor (ACD) Equipment that automatically manages and controls incoming calls, sends calls to the telephone representative who has been idle the longest, answers and queues calls during busy periods, and plays recorded messages for waiting callers. It automatically sends overflow calls to a second group and provides management reports on the call activity. It can stand alone or be integrated with a PBX.

Automatic dialing recorded message player (ADRMP) Machine that dials preprogrammed telephone numbers, automatically plays a prerecorded message (normally a sales pitch), then records responses.

Automatic interaction detection (AID) Program for segmenting a list from a heterogeneous to a homogeneous market.

Automatic redial Telephone feature that permits the last number dialed to be automatically dialed again at the push of one button.

Automatic route selection (ARS) Switching system that chooses the least costly path from available owned or leased circuits.

Backbone Back of a bound book connecting the two covers; also known as the *spine*.

Back-end Activities necessary to complete a mail-order transaction once an order has been received; measurements of buyers' performance after they have ordered the first item in a series offering.

Bangtail Promotional envelope with a second flap that is perforated and designed for use as an order blank.

Banker envelope Envelope with the flap on the long edge.

Banner A graphic image, usually 469 by 60 pixels, displaying an ad with a clickable link.

Batch Grouping of orders.

Batch processing Technique of executing a set of orders/selections in batches as opposed to executing each order/selection as it is received; batches can be created by computer programming or manually by date.

Benefits Features of a product or service. Benefits are what sell the product or services.

Bill enclosure Promotional piece or notice enclosed with a bill, invoice, or statement.

Bindery Place where final trimming, stitching/stapling, order-form insertion, and any necessary off-press folding is done.

Binding Finishing process that glues, staples, or stitches the pages of a catalog to the cover.

Bingo cards Reply card inserted in a publication and used by readers to request literature and samples from companies whose products and services are either advertised in the publication or mentioned in its editorial columns and feature articles.

Bleed Extension of the printed image to the trim edge of a sheet or page.

Block A subset of a block group that includes about 14 households.

Block group A subset of a census tract, usually no smaller than 600 people. In rural areas, it is called an "enumeration district."

Body type Types used for the main body of the text as distinct from its headings.

Boiler room/bucket shop Term to describe outbound phone rooms where facilities are less than ideal for the telephone sales representative and sometimes for the activity itself. High turnover of representatives and low overhead for the owners are trademarks of this kind of operation.

Boldface type Type that is heavier than standard text type, often used for headlines and paragraph lead-ins, and to emphasize letters, words, or sentences.

Bond paper Grade of writing or printing paper used when strength, durability, and permanence are essential.

Book Catalog.

Booklet Usually, a small flyer-type promotional piece.

Boom In broadcasting, a semirigid tubelike apparatus that extends from the headset and positions the microphone close to the user's mouth.

Bounce-back Offer enclosed with a mailing sent to a customer in fulfillment of an order.

Brand A name, term, design, symbol, or other feature that identifies one seller's good or service from others. A brand may identify one item, a family of items, or all items of a seller.

Brand image A group of characteristics or associated relationships that a consumer attributes to or identifies with a specific brand.

BRC or BRE Business Reply Card or Business Reply Envelopes are pre-addressed and have postage paid by the advertiser.

Bringing up the color Color correcting; intensifying color on press or in separations.

Broadcast media Direct response source that includes radio, television, and cable television.

Broadside Single sheet of paper, printed on one or two sides, folded for mailing or direct distribution, and opening into a single, large advertisement.

Brochure Strictly defined, a high-quality pamphlet, with specially planned layout, typography, and illustrations; also used loosely to describe any promotional pamphlet or booklet.

Broker Agent authorized to buy or sell for an organization or another individual.

Bromide Photographic print made from a negative, or a positive used as a proof.

Bulk Thickness of paper.

Bulk mail *See* **Standard Mail**

Burnout Exhaustion and lack of motivation often experienced by telephone sales representatives working long shifts without proper training or compensation.

Burst To separate continuous-form paper into discrete sheets.

Business list Any compilation of individuals or companies based on a business-associated interest, inquiry, membership, subscription, or purchase.

Business-to-business Any business activities directed toward corporate or industrial decision makers, decision influencers, or buyers.

Business-to-business telemarketing Telemarketing to industry.

Buyer One who orders merchandise, books, records, information, or services.

C/A Change of address.

Call In telemarketing, this term encompasses uncompleted and completed connections, busys, temporarily disconnected, disconnected–no referral, disconnected but referred, and no-answers; does not include status of results such as sale/no-sale/follow-up.

Call-back Any contact required to follow-up an activity.

Call center An organization's inbound telephone center.

Call forcing Call distribution feature that automatically directs a waiting call to an available agent. The agent receives an audible tone burst that signals the call coming through. A button need not be pressed to receive this call.

Call guide Informal roster of points to be covered during a telephone sales presentation that allows for personalization.

Call management Process of selecting and managing the optimum mix of equipment, network services, and labor to achieve maximum productivity from a teleservices center.

Call management system Equipment that gives detailed information on telephone activity and cost.

Call objective Clear reason for the call; the best calls are those that tend to have only one objective.

Call objective guideline Worksheet that allows preparation for the specific objective; often used in training and for new product introductions.

Call queuing Placing incoming calls in a waiting line for access to an operator station.

Case Complete and measurable telephone sales cycle from beginning to end (e.g., 100 names on a list equals 100 cases).

Cash buyer Buyer who encloses payment with order.

Cash on delivery (COD) Expression meaning that a customer pays for an order when it is received.

Cash with order Requirement made by some list owners for full payment at the time an order is placed for the list.

CASS (Coding Accuracy Support System) Offered by the Postal Service to mailers, service bureaus, and software vendors to improve the accuracy of delivery points codes, ZIP +4 codes, 5-digit ZIP codes, and carrier route information on mail pieces.

Catalog A promotional book or booklet offering a variety of merchandise displaying photos of merchandise, with descriptive details and prices.

Catalog buyer Person who has bought products or services from a catalog.

Catalog request Order for the catalog itself. The catalog might be free, there could be a nominal charge for postage and handling, or there could be a more substantial charge that is often refunded or credited on the first order.

Cell size Smallest unit or segment quantity of an individual variant within a test program.

Census tract Area within a ZIP code group denoting households with uniform social and economic characteristics.

CHAD Change of address; also called C/A.

Charge buyer Person who has charged merchandise ordered by mail; or a person who has paid for merchandise only after it has been delivered.

Cheshire label Specially prepared paper (rolls, fanfold, or accordion fold) used to reproduce names and addresses to be mechanically affixed to mailing pieces.

Chromalins One method of proofing a color separation. Four separate, extremely thin plastic sheets (one for each color) are overlaid, producing a color reproduction of the separations.

Churning The practice of customers switching to another supplier based on special discount offers. Cellular telephone and credit card customers often have high *churn rates*.

Circulars General term for printed advertising in any form, including printed matter sent out by direct mail.

Cleaning lists *See* **List Hygiene**

Click The action of a user pressing the mouse button.

Click-through The action of a user clicking on an ad banner or HTML link which results in a new Web page being loaded.

Clustering Grouping households on a list according to geographic, demographic, or psychographic characteristics. A number of clustering systems are available from companies such as Claritas, Donnelly Marketing, CACI, etc.

Cluster selection Selection routine based on taking a group of names in a series (e.g., a cluster selection on an nth name basis might be the first 10 out of every 100 or the first 125 out of 175; a cluster selection using limited ZIP codes might be the first 200 names in each of the specified ZIP codes).

COAM Customer owned and maintained equipment.

Coding (1) System for ascertaining from replies the mailing list or other source from which an address was obtained; (2) structure of letters and numbers used to classify characteristics of an address on a list.

Cold calls Sales calls to an audience unfamiliar to the caller.

Cold lists Lists that have no actual or arranged affinity with the advertiser (i.e., they have not bought from, belonged to, or inquired of the advertiser itself or of any particular affinity group).

Collate (1) To assemble individual elements of a mailing in sequence for inserting into a mailing envelope; (2) program that combines two or more ordered files to produce a single ordered file; also the act of combining such files. *See also* **Merge/purge**.

Collation Orderly assembly of sheets or signatures during the bindery process.

Color print Printed reproduction of a transparency or negative, inexpensive but not of top quality; also called a *"C" print*.

Commercial envelope Oblong envelope with a top flap.

Communicator call report (CCR) List identifying for each telephone sales representative what calls were handled during a shift, the date, the contact name, and all information pertaining to the details of each call made.

Compiled list Names and addresses derived from directories, newspapers, public records, retail sales slips, trade show registrations, and the like, to identify groups of people with something in common.

Compiler Organization that develops lists of names and addresses from directories, newspapers, public records, registrations, and other sources, identifying groups of people, companies, or institutions with something in common.

Completed cancel Person who has completed a specific commitment to buy products or services before canceling.

Completed contact Any contact that finalizes a preplanned portion of a sales cycle.

Comprehensive Complete and detailed layout for a printed piece; also called *comp* or *compare*.

Computer letter Computer-printed message providing personalized, fill-in information from a source file in predesignated positions; full-printed letter with personalized insertions.

Computer personalization Printing of letters or other promotional pieces by a computer using names, addresses, special phrases, or other information based on data appearing in one or more computer records;

the objective is to use the information in the computer record to tailor the promotional message to a specific individual.

Computer record All of the information about an individual, a company, or a transaction stored on a specific magnetic tape or disk.

Computer service bureau Facility providing general or specific data-processing.

Consultative selling Personalized method of sales that identifies a customer's needs and then sells a product or service to meet those needs.

Consumer list List of names (usually with home address) compiled or resulting from a common inquiry or buying activity indicating a general buying interest.

Consumer location system Market identification system containing information derived from Target Group Index and ACORN.

Contact Any conversation with a decision maker or any communication that advances a case toward completion.

Contact-to-closed-case ratio Number of completed contacts required to complete a case (e.g., contact mail contact would be a two-contact-to-closed-case ratio).

Continuity program Products or services bought as a series of small purchases, rather than all at one time, generally based on a common theme and shipped at regular or specific time intervals.

Contributor list Names and addresses of persons who have given to a specific funding effort. *See also* **Donor list**.

Control Last successful mailing package without any changes that allows

a true measurement of the performance of each of the variants on test; generally used to test against new variants.

Controlled circulation Distribution at no charge of a publication to individuals or companies on the basis of their titles or occupations; typically, recipients are asked from time to time to verify the information that qualifies them to receive the publication.

Controlled duplication Method by which names and addresses from two or more lists are matched (usually by computer) in order to eliminate or limit extra mailings to the same name and address.

Conversion (1) Process of reformatting, or changing from one data-processing system to another; (2) securing specific action such as a purchase or contribution from a name on a mailing list or as a result of an inquiry.

Conversion rate Percentage of potential customers who, through a direct mail solicitation, become buyers.

Co-op mailing Mailing of two or more offers included in the same envelope or other carrier, with each participating mailer sharing the mailing cost based on some predetermined formula.

Copy Written material intended for inclusion in the various components of a mailing package or advertisement.

Copy date Date by which advertising material ready for printing must reach a publishing house for inclusion in a particular issue.

Cost per inquiry (CPI) Simple arithmetical formula derived by dividing the total cost of a mailing or an advertisement by the number of inquiries received.

Cost per order (CPO) Similar to cost per inquiry but based on actual orders rather than inquiries.

Cost per thousand (CPM) Common rate for list rentals when fee is based on every 1,000 names rented to telemarketers.

Coupon Part of an advertising promotion piece intended to be filled in by the inquirer or customer and returned to the advertiser; it often entitles the bearer to a discount on an item at time of purchase.

Coupon clipper Person who has given evidence of responding to free or nominal-cost offers out of curiosity, with little or no serious interest or buying intent.

Creative Preprinting aspects of catalog preparation: design, layout, copy writing, and photography; used as a noun in the catalog business.

Crop To trim part of a photo or copy.

Cross-selling Encouraging existing customers to purchase products or services from other categories, departments, or divisions.

CTO Contribution to overhead (profit).

Customer bonding Process in which a particular company relates with their base customers entailing trust toward their business activities. For most companies this particular term conveys with Customer Relationship Management (CRM) issues.

Cyberspace This is a coined word from the novel *Neuromancer* by William Gibson. The word referred to a computer network that people plugged their brains into. Today the word is used to refer to the Internet or BBS services such as CompuServe.

Databank Information resources of an organization or business.

Database Collection of data to support the requirements and requests for information of a specific group of users.

Database definition The clear understanding between telemarketing management and database management about what will be captured and displayed from the database.

Data capture/entry Any method of collecting and recording information.

Data processing Organization of data for the purpose of producing desired information; involves recording, classifying, sorting, summarizing, calculating, disseminating, and storing data.

Data sheet Leaflet containing factual information about a product or service.

Deadbeat Person who has ordered a product or service and, without just cause, hasn't paid for it.

Decile The portion of a frequency distribution that contains one-tenth of the total sample.

Decoy Unique name especially inserted in a mailing list for verifying list usage.

De-dupe *See* **Duplication elimination.**

Delinquent Person who has fallen behind or has stopped scheduled payment for a product or service.

Delivery Method of oral presentation used (e.g., businesslike, informal, formal).

Delivery date Date a list user or designated representative of the list user receives a specific list order from the list owner.

Demographics Description of the vital statistics of an audience or population; includes personal characteristics, name, title, occupation, address, phone number, etc.

Direct mail Printed matter usually carrying a sales message or announcement designed to elicit a response from a carefully selected consumer or business market.

Direct mail advertising Any promotional effort using the Postal Service, or other direct delivery service, for distribution of the advertising message.

Direct Mail Kit (DMK) An acronym long used to mean direct mail package.

Direct Marketing Association (DMA) Organization representing special interests of those in the business of direct marketing.

Direct response Advertising through any medium inviting direct response by any measurable means (mail, telephone, walk-in, etc.).

DRTV or direct response television The selling of anything directly over television, generally bypassing retail stores. DRTV has three primary marketing subgroups: short form, long form (infomercials) and live home shopping.

DMA Mail Preference Service Service provided by the Direct Marketing Association that allows consumers to request that their names be added to or deleted from mailing lists.

Donor list List of persons who have given money to one or more charitable organizations. *See also* **Contributor list**.

Doubling day Point in time established by previous experience by which 50 percent of all returns to a mailing will normally have been received.

Drop closing Process of completing a sale by initially offering top-of-the-line items or services and then adjusting the offer to a lower range of prices.

Drop date *See* **Final date**.

Drop out Deletion of type from all four colors, resulting in "white" type.

Drop ship Fulfillment function whereby the manufacturer of the product does the actual shipping of the item to the customer.

Dummy (1) Mock-up giving a preview of a printed piece, showing placement of the material to be printed; (2) fictitious name with a mailable address inserted into a mailing list to verify usage of that list.

Dummy name Fictitious name and address inserted into a mailing list to verify usage of that list; also known as a *sleeper*.

Duplicate Two or more identical name-and-address records.

Duplication elimination Specific kind of controlled duplication providing that no matter how many times a name and address is on a list or how many lists contain that name and address, it will be accepted for mailing only once by that mailer; also known as dupe elimination or de-duping.

800 service Inbound long-distance service that is free to the caller and paid for by the recipient.

E-mail Short for *electronic mail*, the transmission of messages over computer networks. The messages can be entered from a keyboard, PDA, mobile telephone, or be electronic files stored on a disk.

Enamel Coated paper that has a glossy finish.

Enhancement Using compiled and proprietary data to upgrade information contained in a list or database. Often referred to as "appending" data.

Envelope stuffer Any advertising or promotional material enclosed with business letters, statements, or invoices.

Ergonomics Study of the problems of people adjusting to their environment, especially seeking to adapt work or working conditions to suit the workers.

Exchange Arrangement whereby two mailers exchange equal numbers of mailing list names.

Exhibition list List of people who have registered as attendees at trade or consumer exhibitions.

Expiration Subscription that is not renewed.

Expiration date Date on which a subscription expires.

Expire Former customer who is no longer an active buyer.

File maintenance Activity of keeping a file up to date by adding, changing, or deleting data. *See also* **List maintenance** and **Update**.

Fill-in Name, address, or words added to a preprinted letter.

Film positive Photographic print on transparent film taken from artwork for use by the printer.

Final date Targeted date for mail to be in the hands of those to whom it is addressed.

Finished size Overall dimensions of a piece of printed matter after folding and other procedures have been completed.

First-class letter contract Post office service for mailers that consist of at least 5,000 identical items, can sort into towns, and require first-class service; offers discounts of up to 12 percent.

First-time buyer Person who buys a product or service from a specific company for the first time.

Fixed field Way of laying out, or formatting, list information in a computer file that puts every piece of data in a specific position relative to every other piece of data. If a piece of data is missing from an individual record, or if its assigned space is not completely used, that space is not filled. Any piece of data exceeding its assigned space limitation must be abbreviated or contracted.

Fixed lists Cost per sale including all other costs except promotions.

Flag Computerized means of identifying data added to a file; usage of a list segment by a given mailer.

Flat Paper industry's term for unprinted paper adopted by the direct mail industry to refer either to unprinted paper or, more particularly, to printed paper prior to folding.

Flat charge Fixed cost for the sum total of a rental list; usually applies to smaller lists.

Flat file A computer-readable file that contains no information in any field about the order in which to read records. Also known as a *sequential file*.

Flight A given mailing, particularly when multiple drops are to be made on different days to reduce the number arriving at one company at one time.

Focus group A moderated session, where a group of prospects or customers are assembled to discuss a product or service. The results are qualitative, but useful in learning what consumers think about a product, a company, or an advertising message.

Folio Page number as it appears on a printed page.

Follow-up contact Any contact required to finalize a previous commitment or to close a transaction.

Follow-up system Part of an automated telemarketing system that keeps track of calls that should be recycled into the outgoing program and rescheduled at a later time; its purpose is to trap information and release it to communicators at the appropriate time.

Foreign mail Lists of householders and businesses outside the United States.

Format Size, style, type page, margins, printing requirements, and the like that are characteristic of a publication.

Former buyer Person who has bought one or more times from a company but has made no purchase in the last 12 months.

Fortune 300 *Fortune* magazine's selection of the 50 largest companies in 6 classifications: banking, retailing, wholesaling, insurance, construction, and utilities.

Fortune 1,000 Thousand largest industrial companies in the United States, as published by *Fortune* magazine; almost all have sales volumes per year of over $1 billion.

Four-line address Typical individual-name list with at-business addresses requires a minimum of four lines: name of individual; name of company; local address; and city, state, and ZIP code.

Four-up, three-up, two-up Number of similar items printed on one sheet of paper (e.g., four-up indicates the sheet will be guillotined to print four finished articles). Also called four-to-view, three-to-view, etc.

Freelancer Independent artist, writer, or photographer who is not on staff but works on a per-project or hourly rate as the need arises.

Free-ride *See* **Envelope stuffer** and **Piggy-back**.

Free-standing insert (FSI) Promotional piece loosely inserted or nested in a newspaper or magazine.

Frequency Number of times an individual has ordered within a specific period of time. *See also* **Monetary value** and **Recency**.

Friend of a friend Name of someone thought to be interested in a specific advertiser's product or service, submitted by a third party.

Front-end Activities necessary, or the measurement of direct marketing activities, to obtain an order.

Fulfillment Process of supplying goods after an order has been received.

Fund-raising list List of individuals or companies based on a known contribution to one or more fund-raising appeals.

Galley listing or sheet list Printout of list data on sheets, usually in ZIP or alphabetic order.

Galleys Proofs of typesetting in column width taken before page make-up.

Gathering Assembly of folded signatures into correct sequence.

Genderization Program run to add gender to mailing lists (based on first names where available).

Geocoding The process of assigning geographic designations to name and address records.

Geodemographics Census data appended to a household file once it has been geocoded. This includes variables such as income, education, home type, etc. Derived from census data reported for the neighborhood of the household.

Geographics Any method of subdividing a list based on geographic or political subdivisions (ZIP codes, sectional centers, cities, counties, states, regions).

Gift buyer One who buys a product or service for another.

Giftees List of individuals sent gifts or magazines by mail, by friends, donors, or business firms. Giftees are not truly mail-order buyers; rather they are mail-order recipients and beneficiaries.

Gimmick Attention-getting device, usually dimensional, attached to a direct mail printed piece.

Governments Often-overlooked source of lists (e.g., lists of cars, homes, dogs, bankers, hairdressers, plumbers, veterinarians, buyers, subscribers, inquirers, TV stations, ham operators, and CBs).

Grid test Means of testing more than one variable at the same time; a useful method for testing different offers by different packages over a group of prospect lists.

Groundwood pulp Paper that contains wood pulp.

Groups Number of individuals having a unifying relationship (e.g., club, association, membership, church, fraternal order, political group, sporting group, collector group, travel group, singing group).

Guarantee Pledge of satisfaction made by the seller to the buyer and specifying the terms by which the seller will make good his pledge.

Gummed label *See* **Label, gummed**.

Half-life Formula for estimating the total response to be expected from a direct response effort shortly after the first responses are received; makes valid continuation decisions possible based on statistically valid partial data.

Halftone Photograph or other tonal illustration reproduced by lines of small dots.

Handling charge Fixed charge added per segment for special list requests; also shows up as part of shipping and handling charges for transportation of labels, cards, sheets, or tape.

Hard copy Printout on a sheet list or galley of all data available on a magnetic source such as a tape, hard disk, or floppy disk.

Headline Primary wording utilized to induce a direct marketing recipient to read and react.

Head of family From telephone or car data, the name and sex of the individual on the registration file.

Heat transfer Form of label that transfers reverse carbon images on the back of a sheet of mailing pieces by means of heat and pressure.

High-potential/immediate-need Any case that requires immediate contact by the outside sales force.

High school student list Several compilers provide lists of high school juniors and seniors with their home addresses; original data, usually printed phone rosters, are not available for all schools or localities.

High-ticket buyer Buyer who has purchased expensive items by mail.

Hit Name appearing on two or more mailing lists.

Home office For major businesses, the executive or home office location as differentiated from the location of branch offices or plants.

Home Shopping TV Live, 24-hour per day home shopping offered on cable or broadcast television through networks such as HSN, QVC, and Value Vision.

Homogenization Unfortunate and misleading combination of responses from various sources; often the use of a single "average" response for a mailing made to customers and prospects alike.

Hot line Most recent buyers on a list that undergoes periodic updating (Those who have just purchased by mail are the most likely buyers of other products and services by mail).

Hot-line list The most recent names available on a specific list, but no older than three months; use of the term *hot line* should be modified by weekly, monthly, etc.

Household penetration The percentage of households within a specific geography that have purchased, subscribed or used a product or service.

Households (HH) Homes selectable on a demographic basis; householders (consumers) can be selectable on a psychographic basis.

House list Any list of names owned by a company as a result of compilation, inquiry or buyer action, or acquisition, that is used to promote that company's products or services.

House list duplicate Duplication of name-and-address records between the list user's own lists and any list being mailed by the list user on a one-time use arrangement.

HTML (Hypertext Markup Language) The standard set of formatting codes that are inserted into a text file to be published on the World Wide Web. These codes affect how the text in the file will be displayed when viewed.

Hypertext Text that includes hotlinks to other text or files, which allows the reader to easily access information by merely moving to and selecting the hotlinked word, phrase, or image.

Inactive buyer Buyer who has not placed an order or responded during a specified period.

Inbound calls Calls that come into a telemarketing center.

Inbound telesales A department within a telemarketing operation devoted to the handling of incoming calls.

Income Perhaps the most important demographic selection factor on consumer files. Major compiled files provide surprisingly accurate individual family incomes up to about $40,000. Incomes can be selected in $1,000 increments; counts are available by income ranges for every ZIP code.

Incoming specialist Trained professional telephone specialist skilled at handling incoming order requests and cross-selling or up-selling to close a sale.

Indexing Creation of a standard, say, 100 percent of recovery of promotion cost, to allow comparison between mailings of different sizes.

Indicia The required indication in the area usually reserved for the postage stamp designating the type of mailing.

Individual Most mailings are made to individuals, although all occupant or resident mail is, in effect, to an address only. A portion of business mail is addressed to the establishment (by name and address) only, or to a title and not to an individual.

Influentials In business mail order, those executives who have decision-making power on what and when to buy; those who exercise clout in their business classification or community; in consumer mail, those individuals (executive, professionals, educators, clergy, etc.) who make a difference in their localities or workplaces.

Infomercial A 30-miniute TV program the object of which is to motivate the viewer to respond directly by purchasing the featured product or service. Also known as a long-form TV commercial.

In-house Related to services or products that can be furnished by the advertiser himself (e.g., in-house lists, in-house print).

In-house telemarketing Telemarketing done within a company as a primary or supplementary method of marketing and selling that company's own products.

Initial/original source code Code for the source that brought the name to the customer file for the first time.

Ink-jet Computer-generated ink droplets that apply ink through a small orifice to form characters; often used for purposes of personalization.

Input data Original data, usually in hard copy form, to be converted and added to a given file. Also, taped lists made ready for a merge/purge, or for a databank.

Inquiry (1) Request for literature or other information about a product or service; (2) response in the form of an inquiry for more information or for a copy of a catalog.

Inset Leaflet or other printed material bound in with the pages of a publication rather than inserted loose.

Insert Leaflet or other printed material inserted loose in a publication or mailing package.

Installment buyer Person who orders goods or services and pays for them in two or more periodic payments after their delivery.

Insurance lists Lists of people who have inquired about or purchased various forms of insurance; lists of insurance agents, brokers, adjusters, executives.

Intelpost Royal Mail electronic transmission service for copy, artwork, and other urgent documents.

International 800 service Telephone service allowing toll-free calls to another country.

Internet A large network of networks and computers, all of which use the Internet protocol. The Internet was first developed by the U.S. Department of Defense in the 1960s and 1970s.

Intralist duplication Duplication of name and address records within a given list.

Italic Sloping version of a typeface, usually used for emphasis.

Item In the selection process for a mail-order list, term denoting the type of goods or service purchased;

in input terms, it is a part of a record to be converted.

JPEG "Joint Photographic Experts Group" An image file format commonly used for ad banners.

Julian dating Three-digit numerical system for date-stamping a transaction by day: January 1 is 001, December 31 is 365.

Key code Means of identifying a given promotional effort so that responses can be identified and tracked.

Key code (generic) Form of hierarchical coding by which promotional vehicles can be analyzed within type of media—newspapers, magazines, Sunday supplements, freestanding stuffers, mailing lists, radio promotion, TV promotion, takeovers, and so on.

Key code (key) Group of letters and/or numbers, colors, or other markings, used to measure the specific effectiveness of media, lists, advertisements, offers, etc., or any parts thereof.

Keystroke Means of converting hard copy to machine-readable form through a keyboard or similar means.

Key verifying For 100 percent accuracy, having two operators at the data-entry stage enter the same data.

Kill To delete a record from a file.

Label Slip of paper containing the name and address of the recipient that is applied to a mailing for delivery.

Label, gummed Perforated label form on paper stock that must be individually separated and moistened before being applied with hand pressure to the mailing piece.

Label, one-up Conventional pressure-sensitive labels for computer addressing are four-across horizontal; one-up labels are in a vertical strip with center holes for machine affixing.

Label, peel off (pressure-sensitive) Self-adhesive label form that can be peeled off its backing form and pressed onto a mailing piece.

Laid paper Paper having parallel lines watermarked at equal distances, giving a ribbed effect.

Lapsed subscribers Subscribers that have allowed their subscriptions to expire without renewing. When remarketed to, they often respond at a higher rate than prospects.

Laser letters Letters printed by a high-speed computerized imaging method. Lasers can print two letters side by side, each of 35 or 40 lines, in one second.

Late charge Charge imposed by some list owners for list rental fees not paid within a specific period.

Layout (1) Artist's sketch showing relative positioning of illustrations, headlines, and copy; (2) positioning of subject matter on a press sheet for most efficient production.

Lead generation Mailing used to invite inquiries for sales follow-up.

Lead qualification Determination, by telemarketing, of customer's level of interest in and willingness and ability to buy a product or service.

Length of line The computer, which has the capacity to print 132 characters across a 14½-inch sheet, has forced discipline in the choice of line length. In four-across cheshiring, the longest line cannot be more than 30 characters; for five-across this limit is 23 characters. Capable data processors, utilizing all 8 lines available on a 1-inch-deep label, can provide two full lines, if need be, for the title line.

Length of residence Major compilers who utilize telephone or car registration data maintain the number of years (up to 16) a given family has been at the same address, thereby providing another selection factor available from these stratified lists.

Letterhead Printing on a letter that identifies the sender.

Lettershop Business organization that handles the mechanical details of mailings such as addressing, imprinting, and collating; most offer some printing facilities, and many offer some degree of creative direct mail services.

Lifestyle selectivity Selectivity based on the lifestyle habits of segments of the population as revealed through lists indicating what people need, what they buy, what they own, what they join, and what they support; major lists based on consumer surveys provide data on hobbies, ownership, and interests.

Lifetime value (LTV) In direct mail and marketing, the total profit or loss estimated or realized from a customer over the active life of that customer's record.

Lift letter Separate piece added to conventional solo mailings asking the reader to consider the offer just once more.

List acquisition (1) Lease or purchase of lists from external services; (2) use of internal corporate lists.

List affinity Correlation of a mailing offer to selected mailing list availabilities.

List bank Names held in inventory for future use.

List broker Specialist who makes all necessary arrangements for one company to use the list(s) of another company. A broker's services include research, selection, recommendation, and subsequent evaluation.

List building Process of collecting and utilizing list data and transaction data for list purposes.

List bulletin Announcement of a new list or of a change in a list previously announced.

List buyer Technically, one who actually buys mailing lists; in practice, one who orders mailing lists for one-time use. *See* **List user** and **Mailer.**

List card Conventional 5 × 8 inch card used to provide essential data about a given list.

List catalog Directory of lists with counts prepared and distributed, usually free, by list managers and list compilers.

List cleaning List updating or the process of correcting a mailing list.

List compilation Business of creating lists from printed records.

List compiler One who develops lists of names and addresses from directories, newspapers, public records, sales slips, trade show registrations, and other sources for identifying groups of people or companies having something in common.

List count Number of names and addresses on a given segment of a mailing list; a count provided before printing tapes or labels; the universe of names available by segment or classification.

List criteria Factors on a mailing list that differentiate one segment from another; can be demographic, psychographic, or physical in nature.

List, customer-compiled In prior years, list typed and prepared to customer order. Today, virtually all lists are precompiled on tape for any selection the user orders.

List databank *See* **Databank**.

List enhancement Addition of data pertaining to each individual record that increases the value of a list.

List exchange Barter arrangement between two companies for the use of a mailing list; may be list for list, list for space, or list for comparable value other than money.

List hygiene Correcting names, addresses, and ZIP codes on house or rented mailing lists. This also reduces duplicates and corrects spelling, punctuation, and other addressing errors.

List key *See* **Key code**.

List, mailing Names and addresses of individuals and/or companies having in common a specific interest, characteristic, or activity.

List maintenance Any manual, mechanical, or electronic system for keeping name-and-address records (with or without other data) up to date at any specific point(s) in time.

List management system Database system that manages customer and prospect lists, used to merge and purge duplicates between in-house lists and those obtained from outside sources and to select names for direct mail promotions and outgoing telemarketing programs.

List manager Person who, as an employee of a list owner or as an outside agent, is responsible for the use, by others, of a specific mailing list(s), and who oversees list maintenance, list promotion and marketing, list clearance and record keeping, and collecting for use of the list by others.

List manager, in-house Independent manager serving multiple lists. Some large list owners opt to manage the list rental activity through full-time in-house employees.

List monitoring *See* **Monitoring**.

List owner Person who, by promotional activity or compilation, has developed a list of names having something in common; or one who has purchased (as opposed to rented, reproduced, or used on a one-time basis) such a list from the list developer.

List performance Response logged to a mailed list or list segment.

List protection Safeguarding of a list through review of mailing and mailer, insertion of list seeds, and obtaining of a guarantee of one-time use only.

List ranking Arranging list items in descending order on the basis of logged response and/or logged dollars of sales.

List rental Arrangement whereby a list owner furnishes names to a mailer and receives a royalty from the mailer.

List rental history Report showing tests and continuations by users of a given list.

List royalty Payment to a list owner for use of a list on a one-time basis.

List sample Group of names selected from a list in order to evaluate the responsiveness of that list.

List selection Process of segregating smaller groups within a list, i.e., creating a list within a list. Also called *list segmentation*.

List sequence Order in which names and addresses appear in a list: by ZIP code, alphabetically, chronologically, etc.

List sort Process of putting a list in a specific sequence.

List source Original source used to generate names on a mailing list.

List test Part of a list selected to try to determine the effectiveness of the entire list. *See* **List sample**.

List user Company that uses names and addresses on someone else's lists as prospects for its product or service.

Load up Process of offering a buyer the opportunity of buying an entire series at one time after the customer has purchased the first item in that series.

Logotype (logo) Symbol or statement used consistently to identify a company or product.

Look-up service Service organization that adds telephone numbers to lists.

Machine-coated paper Paper coated on one or both sides during manufacture.

Machine-readable data Imprinted alphanumeric data, including name and address, that can be read and converted to magnetic form by an optical character reader.

Magalog Mail-order catalog that includes paid advertisements and, in some cases, brief editorials, making it similar to a magazine in format.

Magnetic tape Film for storing electronically recorded data, often in list format to allow computerized matching with other lists for purposes of appending phone numbers or eliminating duplications.

Magnetic tape charge Charge made for the tape reel on which a list is furnished and which usually is not returnable for credit.

Mail count Amount of mail deposited with the Postal Service on a given date as reported on the certification form.

Mail date Drop date planned for a mailing, usually as agreed upon by the mailing list owner and the list user.

Mailer (1) Direct mail advertiser who promotes a product or service using outside lists or house lists or both; (2) printed direct mail advertising piece; (3) folding carton, wrapper, or tube used to protect materials in the mails.

Mailgram Combination telegram-letter, with the telegram transmitted to a postal facility close to the addressee and then delivered as first-class mail.

Mailing house Direct mail service establishment that affixes labels, sorts, bags, and ties the mail, and delivers it in qualified ZIP code strings to the Postal Service for certification.

Mailing List/Users and Suppliers Association Association founded in 1983, specifically targeted to mailing list uses and abuses.

Mailing machine Machine that attaches labels to mailing pieces and otherwise prepares such pieces for deposit in the postal system.

Mailing package The complete direct mail unit as it arrives in the consumer's mailbox.

Mail monitoring Means of determining length of time required for individual pieces of mail to reach their destinations; also utilized to verify content and ascertain any unauthorized use.

Mail order Method of conducting business wherein merchandise or services are promoted directly to the user, orders are received by mail or telephone, and merchandise is mailed to the purchaser.

Mail order buyer Person who orders and pays for a product or service through the mail.

Mail Preference Service (MPS) Service of the Direct Marketing Association for consumers who wish to have their names removed from national commercial mailing lists.

Make-ready In letterpress, the building up of the press form so that heavy and light areas print with the correct impression.

Make-up Positioning of type and illustrations to conform to a layout; in lithography usually called a paste-up.

Management information system (MIS) System, automated or manual, that provides sales support information for both the sales representative to enhance sales activity and management to evaluate sales performance.

Manual telephone sales center Completely paper-driven telephone sales center.

Marginal list test Test that almost, but not quite, qualifies for a continuation.

Market Total of all individuals or organizations that represent potential buyers.

Market identification Establishment of criteria to predetermine specific markets that will be primary targets of a telemarketing project.

Marketing mix Various marketing elements and strategies that must be used together to achieve maximum effectiveness.

Market penetration Proportion of buyers on a list to the total list or to the total area. For business lists, penetration is usually analyzed by two-digit or four-digit Standard Industrial Classification codes.

Markup Details of the size and style of type to be used; also known as type specification.

Marriage mail Form of co-op in which the offers of two or more disparate mailers are combined in one folder or envelope for delivery to the same address.

Master file File that is of a permanent nature, or regarded in a particular job as authoritative, or one that contains all sub files.

Match To cause the typing of addresses, salutations, or inserts into letters to agree with other copy that is already imprinted.

Match code Code determined by either the creator or the user of a file for matching records contained in another file.

Matched city pairs For testing purposes when individual markets must be utilized, a means to do A in City Y but not B, doing both A and B in City X with the premise that the two cities are reasonably matched as to size, income spread, and lifestyles.

Matte finish Dull paper finish that has no gloss.

Maximum cost per order Lifetime value of each major cell of customers on a customer file; helps set a limit on the price to pay for a new customer.

Mean The sum of the values of the items divided by the number of items. Also known as *arithmetic average*. Frequently used as a measure of location for a frequency or probability distribution.

Mechanical Finished artwork ready for printing production; generally includes matter pasted in position.

Mechanical addressing systems System in which small lists are filed on cards or plates and addressing is done by mechanical means.

Media Plural of *medium*, the means of transmitting information or an advertising message (direct mail package, inserts, magazines, posters, television, etc.).

Media data form Established format for presenting comparative data on publications.

Media insert Insert, either loose or bound, generally in business and consumer publications.

Median The value of the middle item when all the items are arranged in either ascending or descending order of magnitude. Frequently used as a measure of location for a frequency or probability distribution.

Median demographic data Data based on medians rather than on individuals (e.g., a census age is the median for a group of householders).

Medium Channel or system of communication (e.g., specific magazine, newspaper, TV station, or mailing list).

Member get member A promotion where existing members are offered a gift for enrolling new members.

Merge To combine two or more lists into a single list using the same sequential order, and then to sort them together, usually by ZIP code.

Merge/purge To combine two or more lists for list enhancement, suppression, or duplication elimination by a computerized matching process.

Military lists Lists of persons in military service.

Minicatalog New prospecting device consisting of a fanfolded set of mini-pages 3 × 5 inches, used as cardvertisers, billing stuffers, and package inserts; also utilized by some mailers as a bounce-back.

Minimum (1) Minimum billing applied to list rentals involving a small number of names; (2) minimum billing for given mailing and/or computerized sources.

Minimum order requirement Stipulation, irrespective of the quantity ordered, that payment of a given number of dollars will be expected.

Mobility rate Annual rate at which families move or businesses fail, change names, or are absorbed each year.

Mode The mode is the score in a population that occurs most frequently. The mode is not the frequency of the most numerous score. It is the value of that score itself.

Model A symbolic representation of reality. In quantitative forecasting methods, a specific model is used to represent the basic pattern contained in the data. This may be a regression model, which is causal in nature, or a time-series model.

Modeling Process involving the use of spreadsheets via a computer that provides reasonable answers to "what-if" scenarios.

Modem The hardware that translates between digital and analog enabling a digital computer to talk through an analog phone line.

Monetary value Total expenditures by a customer during a specific time, generally 12 months.

Monitoring Listening in on telephone conversation from extensions, usually for training of telephone sales representatives; also known as service observing.

Mono In printing, printed in a single color.

MPS *See* **Mail Preference Service**.

MSA (Metropolitan Statistical Area) Areas that contain a city of 50,000+ population or an area of 50,000 people within a larger city.

Multibuyers Identification through a merge/purge of all records found on two or more lists.

Multichannel communications Broadcast message distributed to customers through more than one channel at a time, blending and integrating the message through all of them.

Multichannel marketing Using two or more message delivery methods (e.g., direct mail, catalog, e-mail, Web, print, TV, etc.) for a product or service, while offering the choice of two or more channels for response or purchase (e.g., direct mail, phone, e-mail, Web, retail, etc.).

Multifamily *See* **Multiple dwelling**.

Multimedia The presentation of text, graphical images, moving images (animation, video clips), and sound in a single package, to create an effect greater than the sum of the parts.

Multiple buyer Person who has bought two or more times (not one who has bought two or more items at one time only); also known as *multibuyer* or *repeat buyer*.

Multiple contact case Situation in which more than one contact with a prospect or customer is needed to complete or close a sale.

Multiple dwelling Housing unit for three or more families at the same address.

Multiple regression Statistical technique that measures the relationship between responses to a mailing with census demographics and list characteristics of one or more selected mailing lists; used to determine the best types of people/areas to mail to, and to analyze customers or subscribers.

Multiple regression analysis Statistical procedure that studies multiple independent variables simultaneously to identify a pattern or patterns that can lead to an increase in response.

Multiple SICs On major files of large businesses, the augmentation of the primary Standard Industrial Classification with up to three or more four-digit SICs. Business merge/purges often disclose multiple SIC alignments unavailable on any single list source.

Name Single entry on a mailing list.

Name acquisition Technique of soliciting a response to obtain names and addresses for a mailing list.

Name drain Loss, mainly by large businesses, of the names and addresses of prospective customers who write to them or visit their stores.

National Change of Address (NCOA) Service of the U.S. Postal Service that provides national data on changes of address.

Negative Photographic image on film in which black values in the original subject are transparent, white values are opaque, light grays are dark, and dark grays are light.

Negative option Buying plan in which a customer or club member agrees to accept and pay for products or services announced in advance at regular intervals unless the individual notifies the company, within a reasonable time after announcement, not to ship the merchandise.

Nesting Placing one enclosure within another before insertion into a mailing envelope.

Net name arrangement Agreement, at the time of ordering or before, whereby a list owner agrees to accept adjusted payment for less than the total names shipped to the list user. Such arrangements can be for a percentage of names shipped or names actually mailed or for only those names actually mailed.

Net names Actual number of names on a given list mailed after a merge/purge; the concept of paying only for such names.

Net-net names Agreement made by a renter with a list owner to pay only for names that survive such screens as income, credit, house list duplicates, prior-list suppress names, and ZIP suppress programs; the surviving portion can be quite small.

Net Promoter Score (NPS) A metric allowing an organization to measure customer experience and the opportunity for profitable growth by asking customers *"Would you recommend us to friend?"* It is calculated as follows: NPS = P–D, where P are Promoters (loyal enthusiasts) and D are Detractors (unhappy customers).

Net unique name file Resultant one-per-record unique unduplicated list, one of the chief outputs of a merge/purge operation.

Neural network An information processing model that emulates the densely interconnected, parallel structure of the human brain processes. Good for pattern recognition and classification, able to make generalized decisions regarding imprecise input data and capable of learning. Used to solve problems too complex for traditional methodologies.

New case Telephone contact yet to be made.

New connects New names added to the connected lines of telephone, gas, and electric utilities.

New households New connects by local phone companies; data on new names from one telephone book to another are over one year old.

Newspaper lists List data on engagements, births, deaths, and news-making items and changes published in newspapers.

Nine-digit ZIP code Postal Service system designed to provide an automated means of utilizing an extended ZIP code to sort mail down to small contiguous areas within a carrier route.

Nixie Mailing piece returned to a mailer (under proper authorization) by the Postal Service because of an incorrect, or undeliverable, name and address.

Nonprofit rate Preferential Postal Service rate extended to organizations that are not maintained for profit.

No-pay Person who has not paid for goods or services ordered. Also known as an *uncollectable*, a *deadbeat*, or a *delinquent*.

North American Industry Classification System (NAICS) A set of industry categories standardized between the United States and Canada. In the United States, it will eventually replace the Standard Industrial Classification (SIC) code system.

North/south labels Mailing labels that read from top to bottom and that can be affixed with Cheshire equipment.

Novelty format Attention-getting direct mail format.

nth name or interval Statistical means of a given number of names equally selected over the full universe of the list segment being sampled. The nth number interval is derived by dividing the total names in the list by the sample number desired.

nth name selection Method of selecting a portion of a mailing list for test mailings (e.g., every fifth, tenth, twentieth name).

Objective case Each telemarketing project has a specific objective for each case (e.g., make a sale, reactivate an account, arrange for an appointment).

Occupant list Mailing list that contains only addresses (no names of individuals and/or companies).

OCR *See* **Optical Character Reader**.

Offer The terms promoting a specific product or service.

Offices Compilations of businesses with telephones providing offices of professionals and of multiple professionals per office, where desired, brought together by their common telephone number.

Offset litho Method of transferring the printing image from flat plate to paper via a covered cylinder.

One-off *See* **One-time use of a list.**

One-shot mailing Offer designed to make the sale in a single transaction.

One-stage mailing Mailing designed to take orders directly without any follow-up process.

One-time buyer Buyer who has not ordered a second time from a given company.

One-time use of a list Intrinsic part of the normal list usage, list reproduction, or list exchange agreement in which it is understood that the mailer will not use the names on the list more than once without specific prior approval of the list owner.

One-to-one marketing Specific strategy taken by marketers to develop personalized messages in order to interact with current customers with the promise to have a much better customer loyalty and a better return on their marketing investment.

One-year contract Form of lease in which the renter is granted unlimited use for one year of a given set of compiled records; usually treated as a "sale for one year."

Online availability Linkup system in which an operator at a remote terminal can obtain list information from a data bank or database at another location.

Opacity Property of a sheet of paper that minimizes the show-through of printing from the reverse side or from the next sheet.

Open account Customer record that at a specific time reflects an unpaid balance for goods and services ordered without delinquency.

Operations review Annual or semiannual review of the entire telephone sales center and strategic plan of a company.

Opportunity seeker Class of mail-order buyer or prospect that seeks a new and different way to make an income; ranges from people who look for ways to work at home to expensive franchises.

Optical character reader (OCR) Electronic scanning device that can read characters, either typed with a special OCR font or computer created, and convert these characters to magnetic form.

Optical scanner Input device that optically reads a line of printed characters and converts each character to its electronic equivalent for processing.

"Or Current Resident" Line added by computer to a three-line consumer list in an attempt to obtain greater deliverability and readership in case of a change in residential occupants.

Order blank envelope Order form printed on one side of a sheet, with a mailing address on the reverse; the recipient simply fills in the order and folds and seals the form like an envelope.

Order card Reply card used to initiate an order by mail.

Order entry procedure Process of capturing the name, address, item, dollars, and key for a transaction, and connecting it to electronic data, which then trigger creation of a picking document, a billing document, and usually the effect of that transaction upon inventory and inventory control.

Order form Printed form on which a customer can provide information to initiate an order by mail.

Order margin Sum represented by the difference between all costs (except promotion) and the selling price (after returns).

Origination All the work needed to prepare a promotional package (e.g., copy, design, photography, typesetting, color separation).

Outbound calls Calls that are placed by the telemarketing center. *See also* **Inbound calls.**

Outbound telesales Proactive approach to a given market by a planned program to develop leads and/or sales.

Outside list manager *See* **List manager.**

Overlay In artwork, a transparent or translucent covering over the copy where color breaks, instructions, or corrections are marked.

Overprinting Double printing; printing over an area that already has been printed.

Owners Owners of mail-order response lists and operators of mail response companies who "own" the customer and inquiry lists that they offer on the list rental market. All such proprietary lists must be "cleared" by such owners or their agents to be rented for one-time mailing by others.

Package insert Any promotional piece included in merchandise packages that advertises goods or services available from the same or different sellers.

Package test Test of part or all of the elements of one mailing piece against another.

Page proofs Proofs taken after make-up into pages, prior to printing.

Paid cancel Person who completes a basic buying commitment before canceling that commitment. *See also* **Completed cancel**.

Paid circulation Distribution of a publication to individuals or organizations that have paid for a subscription.

Paid during service Method of paying for magazine subscriptions in installments, usually weekly or monthly, and usually collected personally by the original salesperson or a representative of the publisher.

Panel Group of people having similar interests that is used for research purposes.

Para sales force Sales team that works as a supplement to another sales team either on the telephone or in the field.

Pareto's rule/law Also known as the 80/20 rule. It was named after Vilfredo Pareto, an Italian economist and sociologist. In the late 19th century, he studied the distribution of wealth in Europe and found that 80 percent was held by 20 percent of the population.

Pass (1) One run of the paper through the printing press; (2) to clear a page for a subscription.

Pass-along effect Additional readership acquired as executives forward particularly interesting mail to their associates. Business catalog makers seek to harness this effect by printing a group of germane titles on the cover as a suggested routing for such pass-along readership.

Passing a file Process of reading a file sequentially by computer to select and/or copy specific data.

Past buyer *See* **Former buyer**.

Paste-up Process by which an artist puts together type copy and photographs into final artwork ready for photographic reproduction.

Payment, method of Record or tag showing how a customer paid for a purchase (by check or credit card or money order); available as a selection factor on a number of response lists.

Payment rate Percentage of respondents who buy on credit or take a trial on credit and who then pay.

Peel-off label Self-adhesive label attached to a backing sheet that is attached to a mailing piece. The label is intended to be removed from the mailing piece and attached to an order blank or card.

Peg count Tally of the number of calls made or received over a set period.

Pending case Case in which an initial contact has been made and the communicator is waiting for a response or additional information.

Penetration Relationship of the number of individuals or families on a particular list (by state, ZIP code, SIC code, etc.) compared to the total number possible.

Penetration analysis Study made of the "share of market" held by a given mailer within various universes by classification or other demographic characteristics; for business mailers, the chief means to ascertain which markets by SIC and number of employees are most successfully penetrated in order to prospect more efficiently.

Perceptual mapping A research technique which uses graph coordinates to analyze the relationships among a group of products, positioning, etc., to identify market gaps and opportunities.

Performance evaluation Weekly or monthly review of a salesperson's performance by first-line supervision.

Periodical Publication issued at specific intervals.

Peripheral listing Creation of a variant kind of audience from that specified (e.g., addressing to the parents of College Student or High School Student X, titling to Mrs. X from a list of doctors by name and address at home, addressing a child by name to attract the eye of the parent, or inviting the new neighbors to view a new car at a given address).

Personalization Adding the name of the recipient to a mailing piece, or the use of a computer to input data about the psychographics of the customer being addressed.

Phone list Mailing list compiled from names listed in telephone directories.

Photosetting Production of type matter in positive form on bromide or film by the use of electromechanical equipment that is usually computer-assisted.

Pick-up and delivery charges Charges relating to collection or delivery of outside lists or components involved in the mailing process.

Piece rate Third-class mail breaks into two main rate categories—third-class bulk rate (for discounts) and third-class piece rate. For the price of a first-class stamp, a piece weighing up to 3 ½ ounces may be placed in the mail stream without any prior sortation, a charge that is currently over 40 percent greater than the unit charge for third-class bulk mail.

Piggy-back Offer that hitches a free ride with another offer.

Pigment Powdered substance used to give color, body, or opacity to printing inks.

Pilot Trial program designed to test the feasibility of a possible telemarketing program.

Platemaking Process by which artwork is converted into letterpress or offset plates for printing.

Pocket envelope Envelope with the flap on its short side.

Point Measure used to describe type sizes.

Political lists Mailing lists that break into two main categories: voter registration files mailed primarily during political campaigns and fund-raising files of donors to various political causes.

Poly bag Transparent polyethylene bag used as envelopes for mailings.

Pop-up Printed piece containing a paper construction pasted inside a fold that, when the fold is opened, "pops up" to form a three-dimensional illustration.

Positive Photographic image on film that corresponds to the original copy; the reverse of a negative.

Positive option Method of distributing products and services incorporating the same advance notice techniques as a negative option but requiring a specific order each time from the member or subscriber, generally more costly and less predictable than negative option.

Postage refund Sum returned to a mailer by an owner or manager for nondeliverables exceeding a stipulated guarantee.

Postcard Single sheet self-mailer on card stock.

Postcard mailers Booklet containing business reply cards that are individually perforated for selective return to order products or obtain information.

Post-paid impression (PPI) *See* **Printed postage impression**.

Precall planning Preparation before a sales call to promote maximum effectiveness.

Preclearance Act of getting clearance on a rental before sending in the order.

Predictive modeling A statistical process that estimates the value of a dependent variable, given data values of predictor variables. Used to predetermine response rates of mail offers based on historical response data.

Premium Item offered to a potential buyer, free or at a nominal price, as an inducement to purchase or obtain for trial a product or service offered via mail order.

Premium buyer Person who buys a product or service in order to get another product or service (usually free or at a special price), or person who responds to an offer of a special premium on the package or label (or sometimes in the advertising) of another product.

Preprint Advertising insert printed in advance for a newspaper or magazine.

Prerecorded message Taped message often recorded by a celebrity or authority figure that is played to inbound callers or included in an outbound call.

Presort To prepare mail for direct delivery to post offices or to carriers at post offices. Over half of all for-profit third-class bulk mail is now mailed at carrier-route presort discount rates.

Press date Date on which a publication goes to print.

Prestructured marketing Marketing using computer software that provides a highly efficient system for annual fund-raising and capital drives, special events, and membership development by providing detailed information on specific target groups.

Price lining Setting of prices by a seller in accordance with certain price points believed to be attractive to buyers.

Printed postage impression (PPI) System enabling producers of bulk mailings to preprint "Postage Paid" on their envelopes; a wide range of designs is available allowing compatibility of style with other print detail on the envelope.

Printer's error Error in printed copy that is the fault of the typesetter and corrected at the printer's expense.

Printout Copy on a sheet of a list, or of some selected data on a list such as matched pairs indicating duplication from a merge/purge, or an array of largest buyers or donors.

Priority For a continuation, method of arranging the tested lists and list segments in descending order on the basis of number of responses or number of dollars of sales per thousand pieces mailed; for political mail, a special next-day delivery service offered by the Postal Service.

Prior list suppress Utilization of prior data to remove matching data from a new run and thus reduce the payment for the list data as used.

Private mail Mail handled by special arrangement outside the Postal Service.

Proactive telemarketing Seller-initiated or outbound calling.

Probability The degree of plausibility, based on available data, of a given event to occur. Expressed as a number from 0 through 1 (impossible = 0; certain = 1).

Process colors Black and three primary colors—magenta (red), cyan (blue), and yellow—into which full-color artwork is separated before printing.

Product information cards Business reply cards bound in a booklet for selective return to order products or obtain information; also sometimes mailed loose in the form of a pack of cards.

Professional lists Direct marketing lists that break down into some 30 categories, from architects to veterinarians. For example, a new list on the market based on a classified list of doctors (MDs) with phones has verified addresses and phone numbers of over 100,000 of some 190,000 physicians in private practice.

Profiling To build a picture of a target customer by utilizing information from various sources.

Projected roll-out response Based on test results, the response anticipated from a large continuation or program.

Prompt Form of sales presentation by a professional telesalesperson that is composed of predetermined but unscripted steps in the telephone call that will be presented in every closed case.

Proof Impression taken from types, blocks, or plates for checking for errors and making amendments prior to printing.

Prospect Name on a mailing list considered to be that of a potential buyer for a given product or service who has not previously made such a purchase.

Prospecting Using mailings to get leads for further sales contacts rather than to make direct sales.

Protected mailing period Period of time, usually one or two weeks prior to and one or two weeks after the mail date for a large quantity of names, in which the list owner guarantees no competitor will be given access to the list.

Pseudocarrier routes The Postal Service Carrier Route (CRIS) tape lists millions of bits of data delineating 160,000 individual carrier routes. Major consumer compilers break up the areas not serviced by individual carriers into 240,000 extra pseudocarrier routes for marketing penetration selection or omission.

Psychographics Characteristics or qualities used to denote the lifestyle or attitude of customers and prospective customers.

Publisher's letter Letter enclosed in a mailing package to stress a specific selling point.

Pull Proportion of response by mail or phone to a given promotional activity.

Purge Process of eliminating duplicates and/or unwanted names and addresses from one or more lists.

Pyramiding Method of testing mailing lists that starts with small numbers and, based on positive indications, follows with increasingly large numbers of the balance of the list until the entire list is mailed.

Qualification sortation Third-class bulk mail sorted to meet Postal Service qualifications for three different mail streams.

Qualified lead Potential customers that have been determined to need, want, and be able to purchase a specific product or service.

Qualitative In research, relates to or involves quality or kind. Considered not projectable.

Quantitative In research, relates to or involves the measurement of quantity or amount. Often used to describe projectable data.

Quantity pricing Pricing, usually by compilers, offering price breaks for varying list quantities rented over a period of a year.

Questionnaire Printed form presented to a specific audience to solicit answers to specific questions.

Query A question structured in a database language to sort, group, or select records from a table or multiple tables.

Queue A function of an automatic call distributor that holds all (incoming) calls in the order in which they arrive until the next available agent takes the first in line, moving the next call up in sequence.

Quintile The portion of a frequency distribution containing one fifth of the total sample.

Quotation Price presented to a prospective mailer before running a list order requiring special processing.

Random access Access mode in which records are obtained from or placed into a mass storage file in a nonsequential manner so that any record can be rapidly accessed.

Random sampling A statistical sampling method involving selection, in such a way that every unit within that population has the same probability of being selected as any other unit.

Rate card Issued by the publishers of magazines, journals, and newspapers detailing advertising costs, advertisement sizes, and the mechanical details of production.

Rating points Method of measurement of TV or radio audience size.

Reactive telemarketing Customer-initiated buying by telephone (inbound calling).

Readership Number of people who read a publication as opposed to the number of people who receive it.

Rebate *See* **Bulk rebate**.

Recency Latest purchase or other activity recorded for an individual or company on a specific customer list. *See also* **Frequency** and **Monetary value**.

Record Data elements that are grouped together and treated as one unit, typically stored in a table.

Each element is identified by a unique field name.

Record layout Description covering the entire record length to denote where on a tape each part (or field) of the record appears, such as name, local address, city, state, ZIP code, and other relevant data.

Record length Number of characters occupied by each record on a file.

Referral name *See* **Friend of a friend**.

Reformatting Changing a magnetic tape format from one arrangement to another, more usable format; also called *conversion*.

Refund (1) For a list, return of part of payment due to shortage in count or excessive nondeliverables (over the guarantee); (2) for a product sold by mail, a return of the purchase price if an item is returned in good condition.

Registration list List constructed from state or local political-division registration data.

Regression analysis Statistical means to improve the predictability of response based on an analysis of multiple stratified relationships within a file.

Relational database A storage format in which data items can be stored in separate files but linked together to form different relations, thus giving great flexibility.

Relationship marketing Form of marketing being developed by direct marketers with emphasis on building longer-term relationship with a company's customers rather than on individual transactions.

Renewal Subscription that has been renewed prior to or at expiration time or within six months thereafter.

Rental *See* **List rental**.

Repeat buyer *See* **Multiple buyer**.

Repeat mailing Mailing of the same or very similar packages to the addresses on a list for the second time.

Reply card Sender-addressed card included in a mailing on which the recipient can indicate a response to the offer.

Reply-O-Letter One of a number of patented direct mail formats for facilitating replies from prospects, featuring a die-cut opening on the face of the letter and a pocket on the reverse; an addressed reply card is inserted in the pocket and the name and address shows through the die-cut opening.

Reprint Special repeat printing of an individual article or advertisement from a publication.

Repro High-quality reproduction proof, usually intended to be used as artwork for printing.

Reproduction right Authorization by a list owner for a specific mailer to use that list on a one-time basis.

Request for proposal (RFP) Pro-forma device for outlining specific purchasing requirements that can be responded to in kind by vendors.

Response Incoming telephone contacts generated by media.

Response curve Anticipated incoming contact volume charting its peak and its decline, based on hours, days, weeks, or months.

Response rate Gross or net response received as a percentage of total promotions mailed or contacts made.

Return envelopes Addressed reply envelopes, either stamped or unstamped—as distinguished from business reply envelopes that carry a postage payment guarantee—included with a mailing.

Return postage guaranteed Legend imprinted on the address face of envelopes or other mailing pieces when the mailer wishes the Postal Service to return undeliverable third-class bulk mail. A charge equivalent to the single-piece, third-class rate is made for each piece returned. *See also* **List cleaning.**

Returns Responses to a direct mail program.

Reverse To change printing areas so that the parts usually black or shaded are reversed and appear white or gray.

RFM Acronym for recency-frequency-monetary value ratio, a formula used to evaluate the sales potential of names on a mailing list.

ROP *See* **Run of paper.**

Roll-out Main or largest mailing in a direct mail campaign sent to the remaining names on the list after tests to sample portions of the list have shown positive results.

Rough Rough sketch or preliminary outline of a leaflet or advertisement; also known as a *comp*.

Royalty Sum paid per unit mailed or sold for the use of a list, an imprimatur, a patent, or the like.

RSS feed RSS, short for RDF (Rich) Site Summary, is a family of file formats used for Web syndication by news Web sites and weblogs, which provides a short description of content along with a link to the full version of the content that is delivered as an XML file called an RSS feed, webfeed, RSS stream, or RSS channel.

Running charge Price a list owner charges for names run or passed but not used by a specific mailer.

Run of paper (ROP) (1) Term applied to color printing on regular paper and presses, as distinct from separate sections printed on special color presses; also called run of press. (2) Term sometimes used to describe an advertisement positioned by publisher's choice—in other than a preferred position—for which a special charge is made.

Run-on price Price from a supplier for continuing to produce (generally print or envelopes) once an initial run is in process; includes only materials and ongoing charges, and not origination or machine makeready.

Saddle stitching Stapling a publication from the back to the center.

Sale Formal agreement to buy, make an appointment, or any other definition of a sale as determined by the objective of a specific case.

Sales conversion rate Number of sales in relation to number of calls initiated or received.

Sales message Description of the features and benefits of a product or service.

Sales presentation Structured anatomy of an offer describing how the product or service works.

Salting Deliberate placing of decoy or dummy names in a list for the purpose of tracing list usage and delivery. *See also* **Decoy** and **Dummy.**

Salting via seeds, dummies, or decoys Adding names with special characteristics to a list for protection and identification purposes.

Sample package (mailing piece) Example of the package to be mailed by the list user to a particular list. Such a mailing piece is submitted to the list owner for approval prior to commitment for one-time use of that list.

Scented ink Printing ink to which a fragrance has been added.

Score Impressing of an indent or a mark in the paper to make folding easier.

Scoring The process of using the correlation derived from a model to project and forecast the potential propensity of lifestyles and penetrations.

Scratch and sniff *See* **Scented ink.**

Screen (1) Use of an outside list (based on credit, income, deliverability, ZIP code selection) to suppress records on a list to be mailed; (2) halftone process in plate-making that reduces the density of color in an illustration.

Screen printing Method of printing from stencils placed on a fine mesh tightly stretched on a frame, through which ink or paint is forced.

Script Prepared text presentation used by sales personnel as a tool to convey a sales message in its entirety.

Seasonality Selection of time of year; the influence of seasonal timing on response rates.

Second class Second-class mail in the postal rate system; covers periodicals.

Sectional center (SCF or SCF center) Postal Service distribution unit comprising different post offices whose ZIP codes start with the same first three digits.

Sectional center facility (SCF) Geographic area designated by the first three digits of a ZIP code.

Seed Dummy or decoy name inserted into a mailing list.

Seeding Planting of dummy names in a mailing list to check usage, delivery, or unauthorized reuse.

Segment Portion of a list or file selected on the basis of a special set of characteristics.

Segmentation Process of separating characteristic groups within a list for target marketing.

Selection Process of segregating or selecting specific records from a list according to specific criteria.

Selection charge Fee above the basic cost of a list for a given selection.

Selection criteria Characteristics that identify segments or subgroups within a list.

Self-cover Cover printed on the same paper as the test pages.

Self-mailer Direct mail piece mailed without an envelope.

Self-standing stuffers Promotional printed pieces delivered as part of a daily or Sunday newspaper.

Senior citizen lists Lists of older individuals past a specific age, available for over age 50, 55, 60, or 65.

Separations Color separations either prepared by an artist using separate overlays for each color or achieved photographically by use of filters.

Sequence Arrangement of items according to a specified set of rules or instructions.

Series rate Special rate offered by publications and other media for a series of advertisements as opposed to a single insertion.

Set-up charge Flat charge assessed on some lists in addition to the cost per thousand.

Sheet fed Relating to a printing technique whereby paper is fed into the printing press in single sheets, as opposed to paper on a roll.

Short-form TV A direct response TV format which, in the United States, uses 30-second, 60-second or 120-second TV commercials.

Signature In book, magazine, and catalog production, name given to a large printed sheet after it has been folded to the required size; a number of signatures make up a publication.

Significant difference In mathematical terms, difference between tests of two or more variables, which is similar differentiation. The significant difference varies with the confidence level desired. Most direct mail penetration utilizes a 95 percent confidence level, wherein 95 times out of 100 the results found in the test will come close to duplicating on a retest or combination.

Single-family household Private home, housing only one household, as distinct from multiple-family residences.

Singles (1) One- or single-person household; (2) list of unmarried adults, usually for social linking.

Single-step *See* **One-stage mailing.**

Social network A group of individuals or organizations that are linked together by family, friendship, business, or other interests.

Social networking site A Web site, usually with a membership requirement, that provides a virtual community for individuals with like interests to share information, knowledge, or videos, and enables them to communicate by voice, chat, instant messaging, videoconference, or blogs.

Solo mailing Mailing promoting a single product or a limited group of related products, and usually consisting of a letter, brochure, and reply device enclosed in an envelope.

Sorting (1) Computerized process of changing the given sequence of a list to a different sequence; (2) interfilling two or more lists.

Source count Number of names and addresses, in any given list, for the media (or list sources) from which the names and addresses were derived.

Space ads Mail-order ads in newspapers, magazines, and self-standing stuffers; one of the major media utilized for prospecting for new customers.

Space buyer Media buyer (usually in an advertising agency) who places print mail-order advertising.

Space-sold record Any record on a house file (customers, inquirers, catalog requests) that has been generated through advertising space placed in publications.

Special position Designated location in a publication ordered by the advertiser for his advertisement, usually at extra cost.

Specific list source Original source material for a compiled file.

Specific order decoy Seed or dummy inserted in the output of a list order for that order only. The specific seed, which identifies the order, is usually in addition to list protection decoys in the same list.

Specifier Individual who can specify or purchase a product or service, particularly at larger businesses; in many cases, this is not the individual who enters the order.

Spine *See* **Backbone.**

Split run Printing of two or more variants of a promotional ad run on an nth or A/B split through the entire printing: use of geographic segments of a publication for testing of variants.

Split test Two or more samples from the same list, each considered to be representative of the entire list and used for package tests or to test the homogeneity of the list.

Spot color Use of one additional color in printing.

SRDS Standard Rate & Data Service, which prints a rates and data book covering basic information on over 20,000 mailing lists.

Standard deviation The standard deviation is one of several indices of variability that statisticians use to characterize the dispersion among the measures in a given population. Numerically, the standard deviation is the square root of the variance.

Standard Industrial Classification (SIC) Classification of businesses as defined by the U.S. Department of Commerce, used to segment telephone calling lists and direct marketing mailing lists.

Standard Mail Standard Mail, formerly known as Bulk Mail, is the most economical method of sending printed material through the postal system. Standard Mail is only for domestic addresses. Each mailing must be identical in size, weight, envelope, and content. It may not contain subject matter considered to be First-Class Mail content. Each mailing must contain a minimum of 200 pieces. The mailer receives increased discounts for greater levels of presorting.

State count Number of names and addresses, in a given list, for each state.

Statement stuffer Small printed piece designed to be inserted in an envelope carrying a customer's statement of account.

Step up Use of special premiums to get mail-order buyers to increase their unit of purchase.

Stock art Art sold for use by a number of advertisers.

Stock cut Printing engravings kept in stock by the printer or publisher.

Stock format Direct mail format with preprinted illustrations and/or headings to which an advertiser adds its own copy.

Stopper Advertising slang for a striking headline or illustration intended to attract immediate attention.

Storage Data-processing term indicating the volume of name-and-address and attached data that can be stored for future use on a given computer system.

Student lists Lists of college or high school students. For college students, both home and school addresses are available; for high school students, home addresses for junior and seniors are available.

Stuffers Printed advertising enclosures placed in other media (e.g., newspapers, merchandise packages, and mailings for other products).

Subblock Along with enumeration districts, the smallest geographic segment of the country for which the U.S. Census Bureau provides demographic data.

Subscriber Individual who has paid to receive a periodical.

Success model Set of logical steps followed by successful salespeople to sell a product or service and used as a training example for new salespeople.

Suppression Utilization of data on one or more files to remove any duplication of specific names before a mailing.

Suppression of previous usage Utilization of the previous usage or match codes of the records used as a suppress file. Unduplication can also be assured through fifth-digit pulls, first-digit-of-name pulls, or actual tagging of each prior record used.

Suppression of subscribers Utilization of the subscriber file to suppress a publication's current readers from rental lists prior to mailing.

Surname selection Ethnic selection based on surnames; a method for selection of such easily identifiable groups as Irish, Italian (and hence Catholic), Jewish, and Spanish. Specialists have extended this type of coding to groups such as German, English, Scots, and Scandinavian.

Suspect (1) Prospect somewhat more likely to order than a cold prospect; (2) in some two-step operations, a name given the initial inquirer when only one in X can be expected to convert.

Swatching Attaching samples of material to a printed piece.

Sweepstakes list (sweeps) List of responders, most of them nonbuyers, to a sweepstakes offer.

Syndicated mailing Mailing prepared for distribution by firms other than the manufacturer or syndicator.

Syndication (1) Selling or distributing mailing lists; (2) offering for sale the findings of a research company.

Syndicator Operation that makes available prepared direct mail promotions for specific products or services to a list owner for mailing to its own list; most syndicators also offer product fulfillment services.

Tabloid Preprinted advertising insert of four or more pages, usually about half the size of a regular newspaper page, designed for insertion into a newspaper.

Tagging (1) Process of adding information to a list; (2) transfer of data or control information for usage and unduplication.

Take-one Leaflet displayed at point of sale or in areas where potential consumers congregate (e.g., credit card recruitment leaflets, display and dispenser units at hotels and restaurants).

Tape Magnetic tape, the principal means of recording, storing, and retrieving data for computerized mailing list operations.

Tape conversion Conversion of hardcopy data to magnetic tape.

Tape format (layout) Location of each field, character by character, of each record on a list on tape.

Tape record All the information about an individual or company contained on a specific magnetic tape.

Tape reel Medium on which data for computer addressing or merge/purge are handled.

Target Person to whom a sales call is directed.

Target group index (TGI) Analysis of purchasing habits among consumers covering 4,500 brands/services in over 500 product fields.

Target market Most likely group determined to have the highest potential for buying a product or service.

Tear sheet Printed page cut from a publication; sometimes used in place of a complete voucher copy as evidence of publication. *See also* **Voucher copy.**

Teaser Advertisement or promotion planned to excite curiosity about a later advertisement or promotion.

Telco Telephone-operating company.

Telecommunication Any electrical transmission of voice or data from sender to receiver(s), including telegraphy, telephony, data transmission, and video-telephony.

Telecommuting Practice of employees working in their homes while linked to their office by telephone and, in most cases, a computer, sometimes referred to as telework.

Telecomputer Nontechnical term for an Automatic Dialing Recorded Message Player (ADRMP), a machine that automatically dials, plays a prerecorded message, and records responses.

Telemarketing Use of the telephone as an interactive medium for promotion or promotion response; the contemporary term is teleservices.

Telemarketing-insensitive medium Any medium used to advertise a product or service that does not properly highlight a telephone number.

Telemarketing service bureau One who sells the service of conducting telemarketing calls; also called telemarketing agency.

Telephone household Household with a listed phone number. (Random access calling can ring unlisted and nonpublished numbers).

Telephone list List of consumers or establishments compiled with phone numbers from published phone directories.

Telephone list appending Adding of telephone numbers to mailing lists.

Telephone marketing Any activity in direct marketing involving the telephone (e.g., list building or telephone follow-up to a lead-generation program).

Telephone Preference Service (TPS) Program of the Direct Marketing Association that allows consumers who do not want telemarketing calls to have their names removed from most telemarketers' lists with only one request.

Telephone sales Implementation of the telemarketing plan.

Telephone sales representative (TSR) Person who markets and sells by telephone; also known as a *telemarketer* or *agent.*

Telephone sales supervisor (TSS) Person who oversees the performance of TSRs.

Telephone sales techniques Formalized methods that structure the entire sales process.

Telephone service center *See* **TSC.**

Teleprospecting Cold canvassing of telephone households or telephone nonhouseholds by personal phone calls (not to be confused with telemarketing, which pertains to calls made to customers or inquirers).

Teleprospecting list List of prospects with phones used for telephonic (cold calling) prospecting.

Telesales Function dedicated to receiving or making outgoing contact by telephone.

Test Period of time in which a minimum of 100 cases are completed for analysis and management decisions about whether a particular project or program is viable.

Test campaign Mailings of test pieces to a number of outside lists to establish a bank for continuation mailings; must not be to only one list, which is a "continuous series of one experiment."

Testing Preliminary mailing or distribution intended as a preview or pilot before a major campaign. Test mailings are used to determine probable acceptance of a product or service and are usually made to specially selected lists.

Test market Trial market for a new product or service offer.

Test panel List of the parts or samples in a split test.

Test quantity Test mailing to a sufficiently large number of names from a list to enable the mailer to evaluate the responsiveness of the list.

Test tape Selection of representative records within a mailing list that enables a list user or service bureau to prepare for reformatting or converting the list to a more efficient form for the user.

Text Body matter of a page or book as distinguished from the headings.

TGI *See* **Target group index**.

Third-class mail Bulk mail. The U.S. Postal Service delivery of direct mail promotions weighing less than one pound.

Third-party endorsement In a mailing made for the joint benefit of an outside mailer and a company over the company's customer file, the imprimatur of the company (e.g., *Britannica* mailing the *Farm Journal* list with an offer ostensibly from the publication to its subscribers).

Third-party unit Service bureau that makes calls for hire; also known as a contract unit.

Three-digit ZIP First three digits of a five-digit ZIP code denoting a given sectional center facility of the Postal Service.

Three-line address For consumer mail, a conventional home or household address of an individual; for business mail, the name and address of an establishment without the name of an individual.

Three-up *See* **Four-up**.

Throwaway Advertisement or promotional piece intended for widespread free distribution. Generally printed on inexpensive paper stock, it is most often distributed by hand to passersby or house to house.

Tie-in Cooperative mailing effort involving two or more advertisers.

Till forbid Order for service that is to continue until specifically canceled by the buyer; also known as TF.

Time Media buyer (usually at a specialized agency for direct response electronic) who "buys" time periods and spots for direct response radio or TV promotion.

Time zone sequencing Preparation of national telemarketing lists according to time zones so that calls can be made at the most productive times.

Tint Light color, usually used for backgrounds.

Tip-on Item glued to a printed piece.

Title Designation before (prefix) or after (suffix) a name to accurately identify an individual (prefixes: Mr., Mrs., Dr., Sister, etc.; suffixes: M.D., Jr., President, Sales, etc.).

Title addressing Utilizing the title or function at a business; adding a title to a business address rather than addressing to a specific person by name.

Token Involvement device, often consisting of a perforated portion of an order card designed to be removed from its original position and placed in another designated area on the order card, to signify a desire to purchase the product or service offered.

Town marker Symbol used to identify the end of a mailing list's geographic unit; originated for towns but now used for ZIP codes and sectional centers.

Track record Accounting of what a given list or list segment has done for given mailers in the past.

Trademark The legal term for a brand. If used for the firm as a whole, the preferred term is trade name.

Trade show registrants (1) Persons who stopped at a given trade show booth and signed up to receive additional information or a sales call; (2) persons assigned by their companies to operate a trade show booth or booths.

Traffic Number of calls made or received per hour, day, or month on a single line or trunk of a telephone system.

Traffic builder Direct mail piece intended primarily to attract recipients to the mailer's place of business.

Transit advertising Out of home promotions that appears on or around public transportation such as taxi cabs, buses, metros, train stations, waiting areas and shelters.

Transparency Positive color film such as a slide.

Trial buyer Person who buys a short-term supply of a product, or who buys the product with the understanding that it may be examined, used, or tested for a specified time before they need to decide whether to pay for it or return it.

Trials Individuals who ordered a short-term subscription to a magazine, newsletter, or continuity program. In list rental, trials are not equal to those who convert to customer status.

Trial subscriber Person who orders a service or publication on a conditional basis, which may relate to delaying payment, the right to cancel, a shorter than normal term, or a special introductory price.

Truncation Dropping the end of words or names to fit an address line into 30 characters for four-across Cheshire addressing.

TSC Telephone sales center, the department that is responsible for making and receiving telemarketing sales contacts.

Turnover rate Number of times within a year that a list is or can be rented.

Two-stage sell Process that involves two mailings or approaches—the first inviting an inquiry and the second converting the inquiry to a sale.

Typeface All printing type of a specific design.

Type specification *See* **Markup**.

Uncollectible One who hasn't paid for goods and services at the end of a normal series of collection efforts.

Undeliverable Mailing piece returned as not being deliverable; also known as a nixie.

Unique ZIP code Five-digit ZIP code assigned by the Postal Service to a company or organization to expedite delivery of its large volume of incoming letter mail. With the advent of ZIP+4, a large number of businesses and institutions now have their own unique ZIP code.

Unit of sale Average dollar amount spent by customers on a mailing list.

Universe Total numbers of individuals that might be included on a mailing list; all of those fitting a single set of specifications.

Update Addition of recent transactions and current information to the master (main) list to reflect the current status of each record on the list.

Upfront Securing payment for a product offered by mail order before the product is sent.

UPS United Parcel Service, a major supplier of small-package delivery.

Up-scale list Generic description of a list of affluents; can be mail-responsive or compiled.

Up-selling Promotion of more expensive products or services over the product originally discussed.

URL (Universal Resource Locator) The unique address for each page on the Web. It points to the IP address and domain where the resource is located.

Usage history Record of the utilization of a given list by mailers, managers, or brokers.

U.S. Business Universe Database containing the names and addresses of virtually every business, institution, and office of a professional in the United States.

Usenet Usenet forums, called "newsgroups," are bulletin-board-like forums centered around every conceivable topic of human interest and endeavor. They are always open to the public (except for the few commercial newsgroups), enabling anyone to read or post.

User Firm that uses telemarketing in its overall marketing program, whether it is executed in-house or by a telemarketing service vendor.

Utilities One of the major groupings of business lists, public service industries (such as water, power, light), often included with mining, contracting, manufacturing, and transportation as part of the industrial complex.

Validation mailing Second modest mailing to confirm initial test results prior to making a large continuation or rollout.

Variable field Way of laying out list information for formatting that assigns a specific sequence to the data, but not specific positions.

Variable-length record Means of packing characters on a name and address record so as to eliminate blank spaces. For most rental work such lists must then be reformatted to fixed fields in which each field, whether filled or unfilled, occupies the same numerical positions on a tape.

Variables (criteria) Identifiable and selectable characteristics that can be tested for mailing purposes.

Variance A summary statistic (parameter) for a sample population that is the average of squared deviations from the mean.

Vendor Supplier of any facet of direct response advertising: lists, creative, printing, marketing, computerization, merge/purge, fulfillment.

Verification Process of determining the validity of an order by sending a questionnaire to the customer.

Volume discount Scheduled discount for volume buyers of a given compiled list.

Voters registration list List utilized to add multiple family members as well as age data to compiled consumer files.

Voucher copy Free copy of a publication sent to an advertiser or organization as evidence that an advertisement has been published.

Wallet flap envelope Special business reply envelope that utilizes the inside of a large flap to serve as the order form.

Warranty list List of buyers who mail in warranty cards identifying the particular product and its type, with or without additional demographic data.

Web browsers Graphical interface to content on the World Wide Web (e.g., Netscape, Mosaic).

Weighting (1) For evaluation of customer lists, a means of applying values to the RFUISM data for each cell (for larger lists this is better done by a computer regression analysis); (2) for merge/purge, a means of applying a form of mathematical analysis to each component for unduplicating.

White mail Incoming mail that is not on a form sent out by the advertiser; all mail other than orders and payments.

Wholesaler (reseller) Merchandiser of lists compiled or owned by others, usually working with compiled lists mainly covering a local area; differentiated from a broker by type of list and coverage.

Window envelope Envelope with a die-cut portion on the front that permits viewing the address printed on an enclosure; the die-cut window may or may not be covered with a transparent material.

Wing mailer Label-affixing device that uses strips of paper on which addresses have been printed.

With the grain When folding paper, parallel to the grain.

Word processor Computer software utilized to produce individualized letters; also useful in updating and expanding smaller mailing lists.

Working women In direct mail, a relatively new selection factor. Lists may be either compiled (e.g., women executives of S&P major companies) or mail order responsive (e.g., paid subscribers to *Working Woman* magazine).

Workstation (1) Area where telephone reps perform their jobs; (2) integrated voice/data terminal.

Yield (1) Count anticipated from a computer inquiry; (2) responses received from a promotional effort; (3) mailable totals from a merge/purge.

Yuppies Young, upwardly mobile professional people.

ZIP Code (Zone Improvement Plan) Registered trademark of the Postal

Service; a five- or nine-digit code identifying regions in the United States.

ZIP code count In a list, the number of names and addresses within each ZIP code.

Zip code omission Loss of a ZIP code on a given mailing list.

ZIP code sequence Arrangement of names and addresses on a list according to the numeric progression of the ZIP code in each record. This form of list formatting is mandatory for mailing at bulk third-class mail

rates, based on the Postal Service sorting requirement.

Zip code string Merging of multiple selections into one ZIP code string to avoid minimums.

ZIP +4 Designation by the Postal Service for the nine-digit ZIP-coding structure.

Z score Also called a *standard score*. The z score for an item indicates how far, and in what direction, that item deviates from its distribution's mean, expressed in units of its distribution's standard deviation.

Index

Page numbers for exhibits have suffix **e**